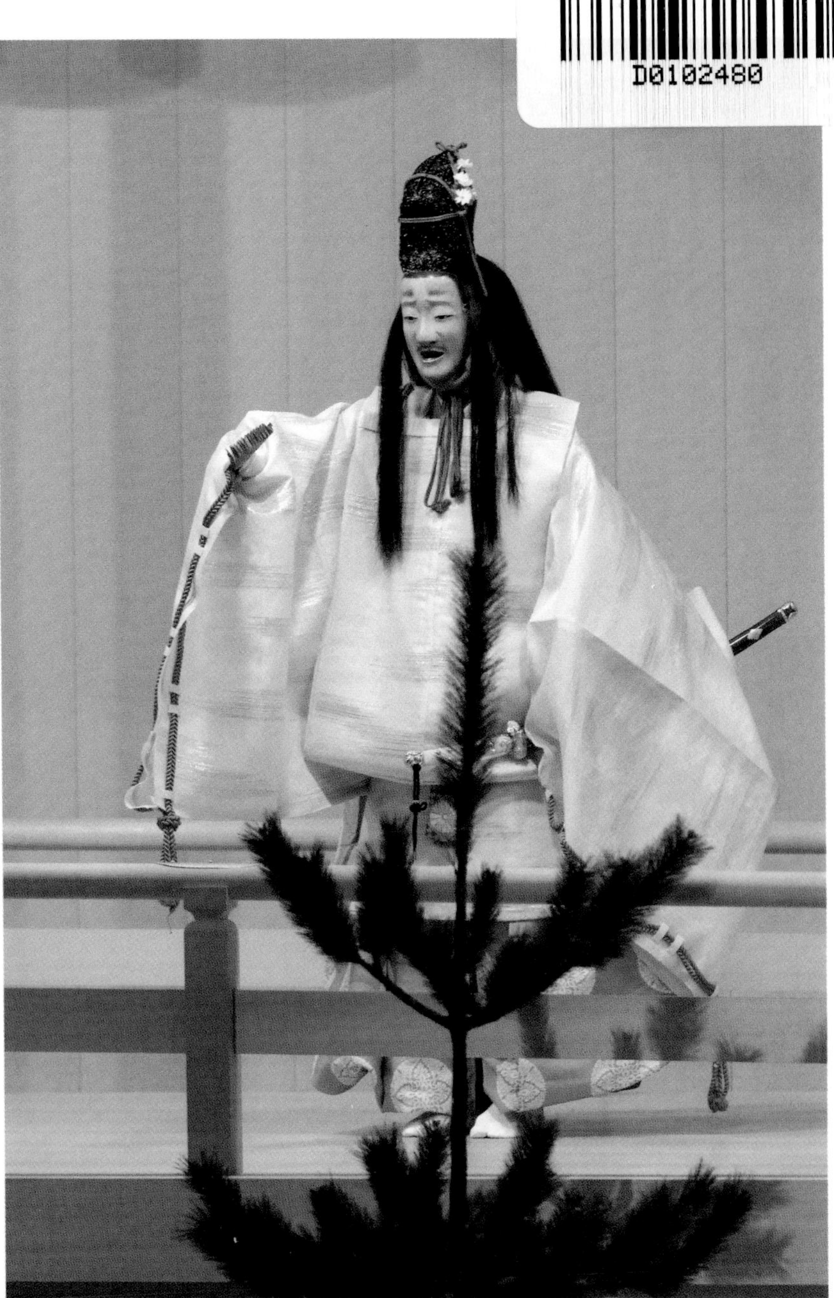

The *shite* from the second act of *Tōru*, a play that Zeami quotes repeatedly in *Performance Notes*. The figure shows nō master Nomura Shirō in the role of the ghost of Minister Tōru, standing on the *hashigakari* in one variety of *eboshi* court cap and a *kariginu* outer robe. (Photograph courtesy of Suzuki Kaoru)

ZEAMI

Performance Notes

Translated by **TOM HARE**

Columbia University Press *New York*

Columbia University Press wishes to express its appreciation for assistance given by the Pushkin Fund toward the cost of publishing this book.

Columbia University Press wishes to express its appreciation for assistance given by the University Committee on Research in the Humanities and Social Sciences at Princeton University toward the cost of publishing this book.

Columbia University Press
Publishers Since 1893
New York Chichester, West Sussex

Library of Congress Cataloging-in-Publication Data
Zeami, 1363–1443.
Zeami, performance notes / translated by Tom Hare.
p. cm.—(Translations from the Asian classics)
Includes bibliographical references and index.
ISBN 978-0-231-13958-8 (cloth : alk. paper)
ISBN 978-0-231-51141-4 (electronic)
1. Zeami, 1363–1443—Translations into English. 2. No. I. Hare, Tom, 1952– II. Title.
PL792.S4A2 2008
895.68'2409—dc22
2007037034

Columbia University Press books are printed
on permanent and durable acid-free paper.
Printed in the United States of America
c 10 9 8 7 6 5 4 3 2 1

To three wonderful teachers,

Kathryn Kawakami, Oriya Ritsuko, and Toshiko Takaezu

CONTENTS

ACKNOWLEDGMENTS

In translating these texts, I had help from many friends, teachers, colleagues, and other generous individuals at libraries, universities, and research institutions in Japan and the United States. I would like to thank them here and acknowledge their invaluable contributions. Monica Bethe, Susan Matisoff, and Reiko Yamanaka shared their deep knowledge of nō with me at several stages of the enterprise. Former students Paul Atkins, Reginald Jackson, and Takeyoshi Nishiuchi brought valuable insights, as did fellow scholars Karen Brazell, Bernard Faure, Steven Nelson, Nishino Haruo, Shelley Fenno Quinn, Mae Smethurst, Sharon Takeda, and Michael Watson.

I profited from the assistance of Kanze Kiyokazu, Makino Yasuko, Nitta Ichirō, Suzuki Kaoru, Takahashi Yūsuke, Tsukube Shōzō, and Yanai Taeko in acquiring research materials, illustrations, and copyright permissions. This work was begun at Stanford University with support from the Center for East Asian Studies there and was completed at Princeton University with the support of David Dobkin, dean of the faculty, and Sandra Bermann, chair of the Department of Comparative Literature.

My nō teacher, Nomura Shirō, has been a generous mentor and friend for many years, and without his patient instruction in performance, many of Zeami's discussions would have been entirely opaque to me. Similarly, Fujita Daigorō, Sugi Ichikazu, Maekawa Mitsunaga, and Yasufuku Tatsuo taught me about the instrumental music of nō and gave me an entrée into the complex but intoxicating world of nō music. Yokomichi Mario and, more recently, Omote Akira, helped me with technical details in these texts and related material and also provided exemplary models for scholarship. Earl Miner, my first teacher of Japanese poetry, passed away while I was working on this translation. Like Professors Omote and Yokomichi, he offered me a wonderful model for scholarship on Japanese literature. He is much missed.

I am grateful to Jennifer Crewe, Afua Adusei, Irene Pavitt, and Margaret B. Yamashita for their editorial assistance and other help with publication. Their sharp eyes and clear heads identified rough spots in my work and helped me improve them. Any mistakes that remain are entirely my own responsibility.

I would also like to thank Melinda Takeuchi for her commiseration during the process and express my gratitude to my family for their patience and forbearance during my work on this translation.

ABBREVIATIONS

Abbreviations are used in the footnotes and endnotes for the following works:

KKS — *Kokin wakashū*, ed. Katagiri Yōichi (Tokyo: Sōeisha, 1980).

NKBT — Takagi Ichinosuke et al., eds., Nihon koten bungaku taikei, 102 vols. (Tokyo: Iwanami shoten, 1957–1968).

SKKS — *Shin kokin wakashū*, ed. Kubota Jun, 2 vols. (Tokyo: Shinchōsha, 1979).

ZS — Thomas Blenman Hare, *Zeami's Style: The Noh Plays of Zeami Motokiyo* (Stanford, Calif.: Stanford University Press, 1986).

ZZ — *Zeami, Zenchiku*, ed. Omote Akira and Katō Shūichi, Nihon shisō taikei, vol. 24 (Tokyo: Iwanami shoten, 1974).

ZEAMI

Introduction

Performance is of a kind with life itself in its immediacy, impermanence, and grounding in experience and might be indistinguishable from life but for the interposition of a special bent of awareness. Subjects in performance, being subject to a concern for how they are perceived by other subjects, their audience, enjoy or suffer a more extensive, and yet more circumscribed, field of consciousness than most of the subjects of life.

Zeami (Hada no Motokiyo, 1363–1443) was an actor, a troupe leader, and a poet of unique capabilities and ambitions at the height of Japan's "middle ages." He is widely credited with the transformation of *sarugaku no nō*, "the performance of *sarugaku*," into nō drama proper, the "classic" theater of Japan. The idea that such a transformation took place within a single generation is an exaggeration and distortion; rather, nō took centuries to become the performing art so designated today. But if we load too much of the transformation of *sarugaku* onto Zeami's shoulders and overestimate his role in doing so, we also may be inclined to underestimate his intellectual and cultural importance by limiting his agency to the creation of a dramatic genre. His role in Japanese culture is far greater than that, and the reasons are apparent not only in the thirty or forty masterpieces he wrote for the stage but also in a remarkable body of texts in which he focuses explicitly on performance.

These *Performance Notes*, as I call them, were written down over more than thirty years. Throughout, Zeami drew frequent attention to their written-ness. In important ways this written-ness overtook his project, even though what he intended to convey was perpetually at odds with writing. Emblematic of this paradox is the title of the final book in the first text translated here, the "Separate Pages of Oral Instructions," from *Transmitting the Flower Through Effects and Attitudes*. The obtrusively self-deconstructive title points to a double supplementarity: these "separate pages" comprise an elaboration on remarks made earlier in this body of notes, even as they are also a stand-in for something that is held to be unwritten, or even unwritable, because it entails a physical excess that cannot be contained in writing and should not be submitted to the promiscuity of texts.

In this self-conscious and self-referential way, the *Performance Notes* differ from the many plays that Zeami created and from the rest of the large repertory that eventually became nō drama. Even though the plays were written down at some point, they had far less stake in being written than the *Notes* did because their essence was performance. The play texts are more matter-of-fact and instrumental than the *Notes*. Although they are more than simply lines to be spoken on stage—since they also include such technical specifications as constraints on pronunciation, vocal notations, stage directions, and formal discriminations—they are, nonetheless, an afterthought to the performance itself. Even those play texts of Zeami's extant in autograph manuscripts appear to have been written as licenses for performance, or certifications of transmission in the tradition, rather than as scripts for the members of Zeami's own troupe (many of whom may have been illiterate).[1]

In addition, the *Notes* reveal various kinds of anxiety vis-à-vis their very existence as texts. It is true that some of this anxiety stems from the familiar pathologies of writing: its "différance" (as Derrida has it), its inexactitude, and the incommensurability of text with performance, but a different sort of anxiety is evident as well, at times explicitly so, in the texts. That anxiety stems from the fear that the *Notes* might be too precise, too revealing, and too close to performance and thus might prove to be a commercial liability, releasing performance from the immediate control of Zeami and his artistic descendants. This latter aspect of the *Notes*' written-ness delineates the socioeconomic context in which nō came into existence, a context of rivalry and suspense over patronage, whose popularity crossing class boundaries had the potential for either success or humiliation.

This second variety of anxiety had a domineering influence on the life of Zeami's *Performance Notes*. With only a few exceptions, they were unavailable to a general readership until the twentieth century. Parts of the most famous *Notes*, misnamed *Kadensho*,[2] were redacted and reshaped for inclusion with other information about nō performance in a late-sixteenth-century printed book entitled *Hachijō Kadensho*, and one of the texts (*Learning the Profession*) in the *Notes* was, from the beginning, intended for broader circulation than all the rest. A latter-day troupe leader, Kanze Motoakira (1722–1774), even had it printed in a 1772 woodblock edition.

In 1909 the first substantial body of the *Performance Notes* was made accessible to general readers in Yoshida Tōgō's edition of sixteen of the most prominent texts. Further substantial additions came later in the twentieth century, as late as 1955, and since these texts have come to light, Zeami's status as a representative intellectual of the so-called middle ages has soared in Japan.[3]

The *Performance Notes* were written in hard, confused, violent, and garish times. A long simmering succession dispute in the royal line was definitively settled only in 1392. In 1399 a powerful clan in western Honshū, the Ōuchi, rebelled against the central authority of the shogun. Insurrections broke out in eastern Japan in 1415 and continued for two years. Shortly thereafter, a Korean fleet attacked Tsushima Island off the western Japanese coast. In 1420, central Japan suffered a drought, followed from 1422 to 1423 by famine and wars in the north. In 1427, the young shogun died, and his father, the real power in the country, reassumed the formal role of military dictator. But he himself died the next year, leaving the succession to a lottery, which pulled his brother out of a high clerical position and into shogunal supremacy for a vicious and bloody twelve-year reign, ending in his assassination (at a dramatic performance!). Meanwhile, new uprisings had spilled into Kyoto, followed by famine and, in 1435, further military campaigns. Moreover, during this time, pirates plagued Japan's commerce with Ming China. Even so, when regarded from later in the century, these times would come to seem like a respite of peace, prosperity, and cultural brilliance as civil war, disorder, and misery clamped down on the country for decades.

The last years of the fourteenth century and the first half of the fifteenth century were a time of extraordinarily rich cultural interaction. Poetry was reconceived, and the subtle and sophisticated critical tradition of several hundred years was invigorated with more social diversity and more ambitious formalism in *renga* (linked verse). Zen institutions reached unprecedented size and influence; written and oral traditions pushed back and forth in martial narrative; and painting and poetic composition in Chinese furnished the capital with salons of wondrous imagination and grand cosmopolitanism.

Zeami's place in this mix is unique. He was the son of an entertainer whom we know today as Kannami (1333–1384), a man with family and tradition in the countryside southeast of the ancient capital of Nara. Even though its political centrality was remote in history and hardly remembered, Nara was an important ecclesiastical site. It was no Vatican but a plain dotted with sacred places of a tattered antiquity as well as venerable Buddhist and Shinto–Buddhist institutions of continuing intellectual and socioeconomic importance. Kannami and his troupe were based in Nara but traveled elsewhere in central Japan, and in fact Kannami eventually died in Suruga Province some 150 miles to the east.

Zeami was rooted in Nara, as are many of the stories told in his plays, but he turned north to the city of Kyoto for patronage, a city itself animated by vast Buddhist institutions, by the impuissant but prestigious royal court newly brought to heel by Ashikaga strongmen. The strongman most instrumental to Zeami's success, the shogun Ashikaga Yoshimitsu (1358–1408), was only a few years older but socially remote. In bestowing his favor on Zeami, Yoshimitsu promised generous patronage but also exacted sexual and, to some extent, artistic submission.

Yoshimitsu proved to be a good patron, but his successor, Yoshimochi, a painter and connoisseur as well as the shogun, favored another actor. By this time, however, Zeami was probably a prosperous and celebrated figure and had other venues and supporters. The change, though, seems to have precipitated various reconsiderations in Zeami's aesthetics. It certainly made him aware of his rival's accomplishments, as he openly acknowledged in his memoir, *Conversations on Sarugaku*.[4]

Life in the city under Ashikaga patronage put Zeami in contact with the Ivy League of Buddhist education and offered encounters with the intelligentsia, magnates, and statesmen of fifteenth-century Japan, and he took advantage of the opportunities. Literate—but perhaps uncharacteristically so, given his background—Zeami acquired a practical facility with "knowledge" as his society constructed it: *waka* poetics and arcana, Buddhist philosophical speculation, aesthetics, Pure Land devotionalism, myths and legends, Chinese anecdotes, a modicum of Confucian philosophy, views of the material world formed by Chinese rationalism, and so forth. This was a bounteous culture for the growth of his dramatic genius.

When he began to write the *Notes*, Zeami's father already had been dead for fourteen or fifteen years. Nonetheless, Zeami had maintained the troupe, produced heirs, and made a material living for himself and the troupe. When he composed his first play is unknown, though he often attached dates to the *Notes*. They are "notes" in many senses and not insignificantly in a recursive and accretive sense: with revision, collation, conflation and reuse; at the end, touchingly, as sharp and enigmatic, grieving yet persistently inquisitive memorials.

In modern Japanese, the *Notes* are called *nōgakuron*, which, badly translated, means "nō drama theory." This term is not right because it is both too specific and too general. The *Notes* are undoubtedly important to understanding nō drama in its historical development and the way it is performed and regarded today. At the same time, the *Notes* are important in a far more capacious way than "nō drama theory" would purport to be. And to be prickly, if it's "theory of nō" you are after, then actually, the *Notes* are not precisely that but "*sarugaku* theory," *sarugaku* being the antecedent of nō and the term that Zeami uses to refer to his performing art.[5] (Zeami uses the word *nō* as well, but usually to refer to either "performance" in a general sense or to a specific play text.)

The *Notes* are diverse. The most famous and the first to be written, as I mentioned earlier, is *Fūshi kwaden* (*Transmitting the Flower Through Effects and Attitudes*). This shows most clearly the evolution in Zeami's thinking from the days of his early successes through the more tempered, albeit more ambitious, views of his later years. Dramatic imitation is a conspicuous concern in the text's earliest books, as this was Zeami's home ground, the familiar style of the four related troupes among which he was raised. He calls that ground *Yamato sarugaku*, after the region around Nara. "In Yamato, it's dramatic imitation we emphasize, maintaining as broad a repertory as possible," and accordingly, Zeami tells us how the actor should imitate such and such a character on stage. These notes on dramatic imitation are preceded in *Transmitting the Flower* by notes on training, whose emphasis on dramatic imitation is at odds with the priority given to singing and dance. "You should not instruct the child to do things apart from singing or Sparring or Dance," says Zeami. "Even if he is capable of dramatic imitation, you should not teach him [that] in any detail." One reason for this is that children possess, simply by virtue of being children, a quality called *yūgen*, which should serve as the basis for any serious career in performance. In itself, this quality is sufficient to create interest in children's performances. *Yūgen* is not, however, recognized as characteristic of Yamato *sarugaku* but of rival troupes of the sister art of *dengaku* and Ōmi *sarugaku* (named for its place of origin, closer to Kyoto).

Here I must digress: in this introduction I use a number of terms, which I will describe briefly. Some of these terms are Japanese words that cannot be translated satisfactorily and so are best romanized and treated as if they were English. Others can be, I think, adequately translated by English words but still have a particular prominence in the *Notes* and thus merit an introductory discussion. In the category of no satisfactory translation is the word *yūgen*, in the translatable category, "flower."

Yūgen is a word with an imposing reputation. It has a past in both poetics and, more remotely, Buddhism. In the latter context, it seems to have entailed mystery, darkness, and depth, but in an inviting way. An important poet of the turn of the thirteenth century claimed he got confused just hearing the word,[6] but it nonetheless shaped the aesthetic canon of *waka* poetry in the remarkable renaissance associated with the eighth imperially commissioned anthology of *waka*, the *Shin kokin wakashū*, in 1205. From that time to the present, poems expressing *yūgen* came to occupy a central place in the canon. Generally these poems treat natural scenes with no conspicuous or predictably beautiful focus of attention but with the promise of emotional depth and far-reaching associations and allusions.

In Zeami's usage of *yūgen*, such a foundation remains, but he adds a surface romance or even eroticism. In nō, *yūgen* is sometimes said to evoke the flawless elegance of a beautiful and high-ranking woman in the days of Hikaru Genji, the "Shining Prince" of Japan's most celebrated romance of the eleventh century. Curiously, though, Zeami does not write many plays on thematic material from *The Tale of Genji*, and his references to *yūgen* embrace a broader range of attractions than can be accounted for thematically. Indeed, the virtues of *yūgen* in *sarugaku* are less concerned with theme than with the abstract and formal beauty of singing and dance, neither of which is particularly mimetic in *sarugaku* and nō.[7]

In the later books of *Transmitting the Flower*, a compromise between imitation and *yūgen* is apprehended in the figure of the flower. The term "flower" (*hana* or, in Sinicized compounds, *kwa*, modern Japanese *ka*) is ubiquitous in the *Notes*. It always pertains to something attractive that catches the audience's attention.[8] In early occurrences, "flower" seems to imply visual interest, as one might expect, given the metaphor, but increasingly in the middle and later books of the *Notes*, it implies other kinds of attractions, aural, intellectual, emotional, or spiritual.

The botanic element of the metaphor is often germane. Zeami's flower comes into bloom as the high point of a performance, and it wilts afterward. It bears fruit in professional experience and technical mastery but does not leave a tangible residue. In later texts from the *Notes*, it can be construed in an abstract way that sublates the experience of the senses into a mental or intellectual excitement. Beyond that, the flower fades, or sublimates, into Buddhist emptiness, which, though still plausibly manifest empirically, is typically characterized in the negative by means of the prefix *mu*-, which means "not to exist."[9]

Much of what we come to see later in the *Notes* already is present in nascent form in the diversity of *Transmitting the Flower Through Effects and Attitudes*. It usually is possible to see a thread there, later to be woven into more extensive characterizations of performance, but the later texts tend to be more concentrated and have a somewhat different orientation. By the time Zeami wrote, say, *Three Courses* (1423) or *A Mirror to the Flower* (1424), he had absorbed the influence of his rivals and had streamlined his earlier orientation toward dramatic imitation into three general modes of performance that he then applied individually to create a wide variety of roles. By the time Zeami conceived the later texts, he also had acquired more Chinese learning and thus wrote more self-consciously Sinicized discourses, sometimes merely pedantically but other times adding to the contextual enrichment of his theories. Buddhism is present throughout the *Notes*, but it is better integrated and more philosophically oriented in later texts in the *Notes* than in *Transmitting the Flower.*

Zeami's respect for Chinese learning and Buddhist philosophy, so apparent in his later *Notes*, is matched by a penetrating engagement with Japan's own literary and intellectual traditions. *Waka* poetics and criticism of *The Tale of Genji*, *The Tales of Ise*, and the *Kokin wakashū* find a place in Zeami's later plays, as do strains of Buddhist devotionalism and East Asian syncretism, combining Confucian, Buddhist, and Shinto elements. If Zeami acquired a taste for esoteric Buddhism (perhaps from a connection with the Shingon temple Daigoji, southeast of the capital) in his early life,[10] he became even more familiar with and interested in Zen in his mid- and later life.

Both Zeami's plays and his *Notes* are motivated by a kind of neoclassicism inspired by aesthetic and religious milestones in the past. In discussing singing, for instance, he harks back to the Chinese theory underpinning *gagaku*. It is difficult, however, to see the practical relevance of much of this theory to modern nō performance. It may be that the singing in *sarugaku* proper (as distinct from nō) had closer performative links to the pitch systems of *gagaku*, but in any case, the evocation of this ancient musicology does not serve exclusively practical ends. Instead, the systems are part of a broader, all-embracing system of elements or phases that strained toward intellectual reciprocity in fields as diverse as sound, color, the physical substance of the world, seasonal change, smell, political organization, and the like.[11] When he was young, Zeami seems to have taken for granted such consistency and reciprocity in the world. In his middle years, he took a more conscious interest in these systems and based some of the principles of *sarugaku* on them. For example, *jo-ha-kyū*, his principle of temporal organization (from *Pick Up a Jewel and Take the Flower in Hand*), is taken to condition all things that exist in time:

> Upon careful consideration, it becomes apparent that all phenomena in the universe, positive and negative, great and small, sentient and insentient, are each equipped for *jo-ha-kyū*. Even the chirping of birds and the crying of insects—the way each cries with its own particular sense—is *jo-ha-kyū*.

Although *jo-ha-kyū* has great explanatory power for understanding the structure of plays and their modular components, and even for understanding the unfolding of a day-long or several day-long events,[12] it can seem arbitrary and unpersuasive when taken out of performance and applied to quotidian events. For all that, Zeami maintains his commitment to the principle throughout the *Notes*, although this is not, apparently, the case for some of the other comprehensive systems that inform his earlier thought.

Zeami's theories about music or, more specifically, singing come from Chinese philosophy and poetics. From time to time, Zeami refers to this scheme, citing the Mao preface to the *Classic of Songs*. According to the theory, a sovereign should be able to diagnose the nation's health by careful attention to its songs. If the songs express pleasure, the government is in accord with the people; if the music is irate, it is because the government has alienated the people; and if the singing shows despondency, the government is about to fall.[13]

Zeami coordinates the long Japanese tradition of celebratory song with the sociopolitical implications of this view of music to create a category of performance called *shiugen* (modern Japanese *shūgen*). *Shiugen* is, as he says, straightforward and auspicious. It should not exhibit much melodic embellishment; it should not be difficult to understand; and it should celebrate the world, the realm, the reign, conventional social relationships, and so forth.

For a time, *shiugen* was thought to be the foundation of all singing and to underlie any artistic success in performance. It is strange, though, that so many of the plays in Zeami's repertory are about pain, sadness, loneliness, longing, and grief. We find, moreover, that *shiugen* in itself is not particularly interesting and that the best of the *shiugen* plays, *Takasago*, is notable partly because it departs from its own conventions.[14]

By 1419, Zeami had found a complementary aesthetic in singing which he identified as *bauwoku*. The term is still not clearly understood apart from the fact that it entails a more nuanced and melancholy emotional texture.[15] As the number of texts in the *Notes* proliferated, the range of aesthetic categories for singing also increased, eventually encompassing five purportedly distinct classes or sorts of singing. A detailed discussion of them is not necessary here because they are mentioned frequently in the *Notes* (indeed, two of the texts in the *Notes* are devoted precisely to these five classes),[16] but I shall briefly describe them for our immediate purposes. *Shiugen* remained the first category. *Bauwoku*, however, apparently was replaced by four other categories.[17] *Yūkyoku*, "elegant expressiveness," is more intricately detailed and sensitive than *shiugen*. In the plays categorized as *yūkyoku*, it has varying degrees of depth, as Zeami says, but apparently these plays' elegance and beauty are more prominent than any other classifying feature. *Renbo*, "love and longing," features romantic love, infatuation, and tenderness, and *aishyau* (modern Japanese *aishō*), "grief and suffering," seems to deepen the emotional tenor of *renbo* to include dejection or even tragedy. The fifth category is not defined by where it lies on an emotional register, at some remove from the auspiciousness of *shiugen*, but by the virtuosity with which it is performed. This category is called *rangyoku*, and its conceptual underpinning has a longer genealogy in the *Notes* than does either *renbo* or *aishyau*. Although the word *rangyoku* itself does not appear until the *Article on the Five Sorts of Singing*, just before 1430, the first graph in the compound, *ran*, is evident in Zeami's earlier technical vocabulary, whether in the compound *ran'i*[18] or in the native Japanese pronunciation, *take(taru)*, "virtuosic."

The change from a thematic register, based on the emotional intensity of the play (apparent in *yūkyoku*, *renbo*, and *aishyau*), to the rank of the performers' artistic attainment in *rangyoku)* is symptomatic of Zeami's altered understanding of the values of performance and the subjective position of the actor. On the one hand, the category *rangyoku* is at once comprehensive of all the other categories, but on the other hand, it also transgresses some of their most salient features. By the time Zeami created this category, he had largely revised his ethical poetics of sound, shifting from generic and thematic difference to a scale based on the individual performers' skill and attainment.

This shift is closely related to a concern for the actors' personal artistic attainments which, though already strong in the first of the *Notes*, becomes more dominant and more carefully articulated throughout Zeami's career.

Readers may find the frequent mention of rank in the *Notes* somewhat alienating and obscure, but it links Zeami's thought to the strictly hierarchical social theory of traditional Japan. The term in Japanese is *kurawi* (modern Japanese *kurai*), with a long-standing application to the system of court ranks established very early in the development of the Japanese state. But Zeami's usage is not bureaucratic in that respect, and it changed as his thought developed. Already in *Transmitting the Flower*, he discusses *kurawi* in comparison with the synonyms *take* (my "stature") and *kasa* (my "grandeur"):

> Q: How is one to understand the distinctions of rank in performance?
>
> A: This is readily apparent to the eyes of connoisseurs. Although rises in rank are generally a matter of layer upon layer of experience in performance, surprisingly there are actors about ten years old who already show a naturally high rank in their manner of expression. But without training, such natural rank is wasted. Typically, the acquisition of rank comes as a result of experience and training. Innate rank is, in contrast, a matter of "stature."[19] What we refer to as "grandeur" is yet something else. Most people assume that "stature" and "grandeur" are the same. What I mean by "grandeur" is the appearance of both gravity and vitality. One might alternatively say that "grandeur" has a broad and general meaning. "Rank" and "stature" are somewhat different. There is, for example, a thing such as innate *yūgen*. This entails "rank." But some actors with "stature" do not have the slightest *yūgen*. This is "stature" without *yūgen*.

All three terms—"rank," "stature," and "grandeur"—relate to the performer's artistic identity. They all express positive values in performance and relate to one another within a semiotic network of prominence, visibility, eminence, and taste. Unlike "stature" and "grandeur," however, "rank" exists on a scale. Zeami's references to it are typically positive, but a "low rank" in performance is possible,[20] whereas a "low stature" or "low grandeur" is a contradiction in terms. Rank can, apparently, be acquired through training, but not by everyone. The "naturally high rank" inherent in the performance of some child actors would seem to be related to what we might call talent, and like talent, it needs experience and development in order to mature into the rank of an adult actor. All the same, rank is not the conscious object of one's training, and it cannot be effectively imitated:

> It is not effective to strive for rank in your training. Not only will you fail to secure a higher rank, but what you have already secured in training may decline. In the end, rank and stature are matters of innate capacity, and if you do not have them, there is probably nothing you can do about that.

The importance of rank in Zeami's conception of artistic integrity is fascinating to trace (it has an important afterlife in modern nō performance, in which individual plays are ranked),[21] but its significance for us here lies not in its genealogy but in the fracture it reveals in Zeami's ethics of performance.

Although the biographical circumstances in which Zeami acted and wrote are known only sketchily, it is not difficult to imagine that he felt extraordinary pressures in achieving fame and patronage in the capital. His position was perennially contingent on success in performance, and as the *Notes* abundantly testify, some elements in performance are beyond the control of any performer, no matter how gifted. In 1384, when Zeami was just over twenty, his father Kannami died, and the material support of the troupe became primarily his responsibility. He was torn between the aesthetic standards of his native tradition in rural Yamato and the expectations of elegance and sophistication held by patrons and viewers in the city. In addition, he was well aware that rival *sarugaku* troupes had long been situated closer to the capital and were more familiar with the tastes of the elite. Kannami had cautioned him that the art of *sarugaku* was "dependent on the affection and respect of the masses," but of the two most important virtues of his father's Yamato acting tradition, the portrayal of demons and mad women, Zeami counted the former to be of dubious aesthetic value in the decorous and sophisticated world of the capital.

Brilliantly—and, some might say, opportunistically—Zeami incorporated his rivals' virtues into Yamato acting under the rubric of *yūgen*. In imitation of the poetic and critical theory to which elite patronage gave him access, he articulated a theory of rank and musical genre and bought into the hierarchical and decorum-centered aesthetic structures of the Kyoto elites. These ranked structures were highly influential in the early articulation of a canon of nō performance, by which I am referring to the minutely prescriptive performance practices of the art. In *sarugaku* under Zeami's hand, these canons were still in their infancy, but they are readily discernible in his categorizations of character types, his identification of modes of singing and enunciation, and his detailed instructions on how to write plays. (*Sarugaku* was so malleable that it adjusted quickly and with little resistance, but for nō, especially in the sixteenth and seventeenth centuries, the process of canonization continued to grow more prescriptive and detailed.)

Within Zeami's own experience of performance, however, there were powerful contradictions in this institutionalization and standardization. His father was a clear instantiation of these contradictions in that, for instance, he could overcome material reality to great success on stage. Even though he was a large man, he could make himself small and fragile in the role of a woman or turn himself into a twelve-year-old boy in the role of Lay Priest Jinen.[22] More tellingly, Kannami was able to transgress the boundaries of orthodox performance: he could use hitherto unacceptable performance techniques without ill effect. As Zeami put it, he had arrived in the realm of *kauko kyakurai*, "facing about and doubling back."[23]

Despite his recognition of hierarchies of rank and performance conventions, Zeami was deeply committed to subjectivity. Whether in his most celebrated plays, works such as *Izutsu*, *Atsumori*, and *Kinuta*, or more unusual, even quirky, ones like *Nue*, *Koi no omoni*, and *Aritohoshi*, Zeami maintains a penetrating interest in his subjects' inner worlds. But these inner worlds do not submit entirely to conventionalization and hierarchy. Rather, they are unique and subtly articulated engagements with conflicted motivation, fraught with paradox and ambivalence. Moreover, the exclusive purpose of rank, canon, and convention in his ethics of performance is the most eloquent and convincing portrayal of these subjects.

The subjectivity of a character on stage is inextricable from the subjectivity of the individual actor, so the intricacy and depth of a character's mind must have analogies in the actor's mind. In the end, the actor, like the character, cannot be fully subject to either convention or canon. This recognition is certainly relevant to the creation of the category of singing called *rangyoku*, and it also may account for the uncertainty or conjecture that runs through the *Notes*. "I wonder," says Zeami in *Transmitting the Flower*, "perhaps," "might it not be . . . ," "or is it rather . . . ," "I remain puzzled by this." Of *yūgen*, he admits, "Having pondered this problem for some time, I have come to wonder whether *yūgen* is not a matter of innate ability. Is a rank of great virtuosity a matter of long experience? This is worth thinking over time and time again."

Despite the extensive conventions and standards to which the art is subject, Zeami never becomes simply doctrinaire in his approach, and in his acceptance of ambiguity and paradox, he expresses perhaps better than anyone else in his tradition the fascination with and suspicion of mind that are characteristic of medieval Japanese thought.

Consider, for example, the following: In the catalog of character types comprising the second book of *Transmitting the Flower*, Zeami mentions "Chinese Roles":

> Now these roles are unusual, and there are really no models to train from. The characters' attire, though, is of crucial importance. And also the mask you wear, even though it is of a human being like anyone else, should convey something out of the ordinary and have something peculiar about it. The role is a good one for a seasoned actor. There is no particular plan for it apart from getting yourself up in the Chinese style. Above all, in both song and movement on stage, the Chinese style is not likely to be very interesting if it actually resembles Chinese practice, so you should only go as far as to give it a certain Chinesey flavor.

> Despite its being a small matter in its own right, what I just said about "something peculiar" is related to more far-reaching problems. How, you might ask, is it acceptable to portray something as peculiar when there is nothing at hand to imitate in order to create a Chinese style? One way or another, therefore, you must make something look Chinesey to other eyes by using a manner of expression that is different from commonplace behavior.

This passage deals with a broader problem of difference in dramatic imitation. The suggestion that the peculiar is what imparts a sense of appropriateness to this role entangles Zeami in the problem of fiction taken for fact. In *Transmitting the Flower*, he is perfectly aware that although the main point of dramatic imitation is to resemble the object imitated in every regard, sometimes what does not actually resemble reality still gives the illusion of reality. It is this dimensionality of Zeami's awareness that makes his articulations of subjectivity so enticing. But there is a dilemma here relating to the actor's autonomy. The difference between a stage performance and simply being must have become a preoccupation for Zeami (as indeed it might be for any philosophically inclined actor). Perhaps any such philosophical inclination would be intensified by the political subjugation of anyone of Zeami's class in the fifteenth century.

The problem may be most apparent with regard to imitation. When Zeami points to the importance and difficulty of imitating an old man, he tries to reduce "imitation" to a minimum and effect an identification of the actor with the object of his art:

> In dramatic imitation, surely there is a rank of no imitation. Once you have brought dramatic imitation to its limits and have truly entered into the object of imitation, you have no intention to imitate. . . . If, for example, it is a matter of imitating an old man, an accomplished actor will approach the role with the same intent as that of an ordinary old man who has gotten himself up in fancy dress to dance. . . . Being an old man to begin with, the actor has no need to imitate an old man. No, instead he concentrates all his efforts on the role he performs in dramatic imitation suiting the occasion.[24]

Imitation as imitation preserves the artificiality or duplicity that it aims most ambitiously to eliminate, so it somehow must be refined into nonexistence. This task is extraordinarily difficult. It may be partly for this reason that imitation proper gradually gives way to an interest in singing and dancing in performance in the *Notes*. *Yūgen* also provides one kind of escape from the dualism of imitation. In its expressive foundation, it may reduce imitation to a minimum while maintaining enough interest to hold the audience's attention.

Other strategies of engagement with the audience's perception also try to remove the artificiality of imitation. Zeami's so-called vision apart (J. *riken*), for instance, purports to endow the actor with a pervasive awareness of his appearance in order to eliminate any awkwardness in posture or demeanor. But on a more sophisticated level, this transcends subjective barriers of all sorts, over extended periods of time as well as space, to effect a spontaneous excitement or wonder in the audience (and perhaps in the performer as well).

If a proficiency in "facing about and doubling back" provides such a technique, then when the actor needs to transcend the bounds of decorum and hierarchy to descend to a level of performance that would normally be uninteresting or even vulgar, he will have a concomitant proficiency, or level of attainment in performance, that both engenders and resides in his perfect freedom. This proficiency is *yūgaku* (遊楽), and like many of Zeami's favorite technical terms, it changes its meaning over the course of his thought. This term, *yūgaku*, has given me a lot of trouble as a translator, and I will address it from that particular perspective in appendix 3. In any case, with some reluctance, I have settled on the translation "fine play in performance" for *yūgaku*.

At first, *yūgaku* seems to be merely a synonym for *sarugaku*. In the 1420 text *A Course to Attain the Flower*, Zeami starts by noting, "As you gain long experience in [this art characterized by *yūgaku*]," various things will happen that attest to your proficiency in producing a beautiful display. The content of this passage indicates a new understanding of "this art characterized by *yūgaku*" that entails spontaneity, freedom, and the transcendence of normal experience in performance:

> As you gain long experience in the fine play in performance, if you find that Instance has produced Substance anew, then there surely will be a wonderful visual display. Once you have created visual display in which the expressive attraction attains the greatest achievement, then there will be no distinction between Substance and Instance. When this happens, and the performance rank of long experience is such that instantiated expression of all manner becomes none other than the Substance of performance, that, I believe, must be the wondrous style.

Substance and Instance are two aspects of performance, perhaps reflections of each other or cause and effect, but under normal circumstances, they are distinct and the substitution of one for the other in, for example, a student's inappropriate imitation of certain aspects of his master's performance, is a fault in performance. In the preceding quotation, though, the normal generation of Instance from Substance is achieved with such fidelity that the Instance on stage is a complete instantiation of the Substance in the actor's mind, with exquisite visual consequences. If we follow Zeami's characterization of Substance as what is perceived by the mind and Instance as what is perceived by our vision, then the chain he describes here amounts to the actor's creation on stage of a scene from within the mind, which is then reinternalized as Substance in order to allow subsequent Instances on stage. Lacking experience with the type of virtuoso performance in which this occurs, we are left with puzzling abstractions disconnected from real experience. But even in that disadvantaged position, we can recognize the enormous ambition of Zeami's conception. In transgressing or erasing the normal boundaries between Substance and Instance, the actor has created something wondrous, something of great excitement that precedes the intellectual or rational contextualization for that excitement.

The issue is elucidated further in the 1428 *Pick Up a Jewel and Take the Flower in Hand*. Here Zeami alludes to the locus classicus of "interest" in Japanese mythology, the occasion when the Sun Goddess, who had secluded herself in a cave in a fit of pique, is enticed back into the world of perception (thus supposedly ending a solar eclipse):

> This designation "interesting" derives from the happy occasion when the Great Goddess, captivated by the fine play in performance of *kagura* at Ama-no-kaguyama, deigned to push aside the boulder before her cave. She then could see the radiance of each and every one of the other gods' faces, and she was given to name this as white-in-the-face [i.e., "interesting"]. It cannot have been at that very instant that someone said, "Interesting." Rather, "interesting" was the name given to mark the experience as distinct. Before such a distinction had been made, what might one have possibly said?
>
> In this connection, if we examine the issue with regard to performance strategies in our vocation, the spontaneous perception in which something is regarded as interesting by means of the fine play in performance is excitement without intent. . . .
>
> Now, once the Great Goddess had closed off the heavenly cave with a boulder, earth and sea reverted to a state of timeless obscurity and were utterly dark; when, in absence of any intent, it then became light, in that instant of awareness, was there not simply the perception of joy? This would be felicity in vision.[25] This would be the occasion of a spontaneous smile. When she deigned to close off the cave with a boulder and it was utterly dark and language was cut off, that was "the wondrous"; when it had become light, that was "the flower"; and when a distinction was made through conscious awareness, that was "the interesting." Is it there-

> fore the case that excitement without intent, that is, spontaneous perception, is simply felicity in vision? On the occasion of a spontaneous smile, language is cut off and there is truly nothing. Such a situation as this is called "wondrous." The mind's apprehension of this as wondrous is "the wondrous flower." That, then, is why we have made the wondrous flower the foremost of the Nine Ranks and defined it as the flower of golden essence. There is a realm in which an excitation from the scene within the intent, startling the mind's ear through the attractions of dancing and singing, spontaneously arouses excitement in the audience—that is the wondrous flower. That is interest. That is excitement without intent.

The psychological insight here—that the spontaneous perception of joy, preceding any conceptualization of its cause, creates "wonder"—lies at the heart of Zeami's idea of *yūgaku* and exemplifies the ideal of an actor's freedom in his ethics of performance. The actor's meticulously trained and cultivated mind can be given free rein to create a preconscious and spontaneous expression of beauty or bliss on stage, an insight with broad philosophical connections in East Asian thought.

The Chinese graph *yū* (orth. *iu*, 遊) of *yūgaku* has settled into a rather restrictive context of "play" in modern Japanese. Read as *asobu*, it is the word for child's play or adult relaxation or erotic dalliance. In early Chinese, however, it had, among others, a sense of untrammeled wandering,[26] of travel for the purpose of learning, of release from official entanglements. These senses of the word were active, too, in early Japanese readings of *asobu*, as well as an apparently exclusively Japanese use meaning "play music."

If the word implies release from conscious labor, in Zeami's writing it nonetheless implies a consummate degree of skill before such a release is effected. It expresses a kind of ecstasis in performative freedom that draws on the legacy of the Daoist sages and Zen practitioners of "no-mind," as well as more proximate masters and teachers of *sarugaku* performance itself.

Asobu also suggests a lack of artifice, as we see in the following explication of a famous *waka* poem from *Effective Vision of Learning the Vocation of Fine Play in Performance* (undated but probably written around 1430):

> Koma tomete sode uchiharahu kage mo nashi
> Sano no watari no yuki no yuhugure[27]
>
> No hint of shelter
> to rest my pony
> or brush off my sleeves:
> The Sano Ford,
> where dusk descends over snow-filled skies.

I'm not sure what is so interesting about this poem, famous though it is—and it certainly is interesting to listen to. It sounds simply like the experience of someone at the roadside on a journey, with snow falling and no place to seek shelter. But since I am not an initiate in the Way of Poetry, I thought that perhaps there was some other reason for excitement that I was missing, so I asked a poet by vocation. All he told me, though, was that the poem should be taken at face value.

So what I got out of that was that there was no particular frame of mind in which the snow became the focus of appreciation. It was simply an expression of what it is like to be on the road at the riverside with no good place to take shelter from the storm and no perspective by which one might get one's bearings, so the poet just gave voice to what was staring him in the face. Perhaps then the task of a real master is this: to create an excitement that is not to be explained in such and such a manner. *The Tendai Interpretation of "Wondrous"* states, "There where the path of language is of no avail, where one cannot fathom the principle, and the operations of the mind founder; that is wondrous." This must be the sort of attitude we have before us. In this art of ours, when one has attained the rank of a real master and such, then just as with this poem, "No hint of shelter," there isn't the slightest bit of artificiality and grasping in the mind for a particular manner of expression. Instead, an excitement that transcends excitement[28] becomes apparent in the vantage from vision apart, and the fame of one's house spreads far and wide; this is what is meant by a truly accomplished master of the wondrous expressive capacity of the fine play of performance.

It would be redundant and obtuse for me to go on about what Zeami says when his own explanation is itself so much more detailed and persuasive. But before I conclude this introduction, there are a few items that I should mention, about the typical configurations of nō plays and the conventions I have used in this translation.

Today nō is roughly divided into "plays about ghosts and supernatural beings" (*mugen nō*) and "plays in which the characters on stage are alive in the dramatic present" (*genzai nō*). Neither term is Zeami's, but the underlying division is apparent in his plays and in nō plays ever since. *Genzai* nō have many different configurations and cannot be usefully described here, but the majority of the repertory, as it exists both today and historically, is composed of *mugen* plays. Although Zeami did not use the term *mugen* to describe them, he was central to the creation of this staple of the nō stage.[29]

Zeami's *mugen* plays most characteristically treat the interior life of a ghost. Why a ghost? Perhaps because there is much to be gained dramatically in the perspective afforded on a life that is over but not complete. The main characters of these plays, called *shite*, literally "doer" or "agent," remain in the world because of some deep attachment to a past love, anger, pride, or some other strong emotional tie or obsession. As ghosts they return to the world not to terrorize or haunt the living but to reenact important and unfinished episodes in their lives. Their presence is usually mediated by a secondary actor, in modern terms, the *waki* (the one at the side).[30] Sometimes various sorts of subsidiary characters join them. Usually they are the companions (*waki-tsure*) of the *waki* and mirror his role in the play. The *shite* may have a companion (*tsure*) as well, but if he does, it is usually because of a somewhat more complicated dramatic structure. (*Tsure* are more typical of *genzai* nō than of *mugen* nō.) Another actor, called the *ai-kyōgen* (from the sister art, kyōgen) takes part in most plays, most prominently during an interlude called the *ai*. In performance today, a chorus of eight voices and a musical ensemble, including one flute player and two or three drummers, fills out the cast. The typical play, as Zeami explains in detail in *Three Courses*, consists of five sections. In the first section the *waki* appears and introduces himself. In the second section the *shite* appears, usually disguised as a villager or commoner of some sort, and delivers a soliloquy. The *waki* overhears this, the *shite* being unaware of his presence. In the third section, the *waki* may ask the *shite* about the soliloquy or about other circumstances underlying the *shite*'s presence in the setting of the drama. During the fourth section, the *shite* delivers a narrative explaining (and usually raising further questions about) those circumstances. Often the *shite* reveals or gives important clues to his or her identity in this narrative, only to then disappear into thin air.

Once the *shite* has "disappeared"—that is, stomped on the stage in a prescribed way and walked off stage—the *ai-kyōgen* comes on stage to deliver a simplified account of the narrative that the *shite* delivered in the fourth section. Once the *ai-kyōgen* has finished, he leaves the stage to make way for the final section of the play. In this section, the *shite* again appears, this time in his or her "true" form. The *shite* performs a dance or series of dances (one of which is usually accompanied by purely instrumental music) and brings the play to a close.

There are as many variations on this overall pattern as there are plays in the repertory, some only tiny and some very substantial, but overall the pattern holds, and the play's formal instantiation of the pattern is an important part of why it is a nō play rather than some other kind of performance. This is one reason that the nō is considered a "classic" dramatic form.

As will be apparent in the *Performance Notes*, many conventions of performance were being introduced even as Zeami was writing the *Notes*. Over two hundred or three hundred years, these conventions were fixed into canons of performance, giving nō its unique gravity and abstract formalism. When these canons of performance are apparent in the *Performance Notes*, I have pointed that out. I have also noted various features of fifteenth-century performance described in the *Notes* that did not become part of the canon.

Conventions

The *Performance Notes* are full of information about performance, training, history, and subjectivity, and one of the primary purposes of this translation is to convey this in English. In bringing Zeami into English, my goal has also been to pay attention to his idiosyncrasies, his idiolect, his introduction of new topics, his pretensions to Chinese, his turns of phrase, his penchant for metaphor, his occasional run-on sentences, and his repetitiveness. I have not made it my business to try to improve his style but instead have tried to reflect the uniqueness of not only what he says but also how he says it. When I have noticed idiosyncrasies and expressive habits in the text, I have tried to preserve them in English whenever possible.

Much of what the *Performance Notes* contains was written and rewritten over many years, presumably to reflect greater experience, to recognize exceptions to the rule, and to supplement earlier practice with later refinements and alterations. This seems to be reflected in both the content and the format of the *Notes*. For example, Zeami frequently uses the term *mata* at the beginning of a new section of text, and in some texts, he signals the insertion of a new paragraph with the Chinese graph for the number one (printed as • here). We usually cannot tell from material features of the manuscripts themselves when these additions were made, but their content often reflects some change or addition to advice given previously, sometimes even quoting the earlier text to set the new comment in context. There occasionally are verbal clues not only to the supplementary nature of some of these comments but also to the degree of Zeami's hesitation, informality, or spontaneity when he makes them. He is rarely dogmatic or sententious and frequently makes us aware of the contingent nature of his comments, saying, in effect, "Also, it occurs to me, . . ." or "Now that I think of it. . . ."

In many cases, I have not found it possible to establish a one-to-one match between Zeami's technical terminology and my English renderings. Wherever possible I have tried to translate consistently the most technical words (when I could not, I simply romanized them out of despair that any translation could suffice). In some cases, though, a word clearly has a technical meaning to Zeami and also has popular connotations that depart somewhat from that technical meaning. One example is *jyauzu* (modern Japanese *jōzu*). At times Zeami uses this term to refer to technical accomplishment, in which case one might translate it as "expert(ise)," "skillful(ness)," "proficiency," or the like.[31] At other times, though, it seems to suggest another kind of success in performance, which relates only partly to acquired technical skill and at least as much to inherent ability, talent.[32]

A notorious example is the word *kokoro*, a common word used to designate the locus of human cognitive, perceptual, and emotional capacity, usually translated as "heart" or "mind." This word is also, however, the most frequently used term for "meaning" or for a particularly important meaning, say, "essence." Although other, more precise words denote "intentionality" or the discursive content of the mind, *kokoro* is the one often found in Zeami's text. Because this word deserves extended treatment in its own right, I discuss it further in appendix 3, where it is found in the company of other important and slippery terms of art.

In this volume, Zeami's texts are arranged in roughly chronological order. (I follow Omote Akira in this as in so many other matters in this enterprise.)[33] In some cases, we do not know the date of composition for a given text, so I placed it where it seems to best reflect its place vis-à-vis other, dated texts in the collection. In other cases, even when a particular text is dated, we cannot be sure that the entire text was written close to the date recorded. That is, the date may be merely an adjunct to Zeami's signature on the manuscript. In one case, that of *A Mirror to the Flower*, the given date seems to reflect a final collation of relatively disparate materials, so Omote situates the text not by this date but by its overall stature and the place it seems to hold conceptually relative to other texts, some of which bear earlier dates than *A Mirror to the Flower*. I have followed Omote in this.

Following the translated texts are three appendixes, a glossary, a bibliography, and an index. The appendixes describe the music and dance of *sarugaku* in Zeami's time, the physical and editorial details regarding each of the translated texts, and Zeami's languages (and my translations of them).

Appendix 1 examines the occasionally daunting level of detail in Zeami's discussions of music. He was familiar with the terminology of other types of music and dance of his time and borrowed freely from this terminology as well as from the music theory of the time, whether or not it really matched what he was talking about in *sarugaku*. It would have been overly repetitive to account for all these technical terms each time one of them occurred, so I describe their most important aspects here. This is also the place where I discuss general issues of historical performance.

Appendix 2 examines the problems in the textual tradition, details of provenance, and, in some cases, salient material features of the text relevant to this translation. Finally, appendix 3 looks at Zeami's rhetoric and voice in detail and explains more fully some of my choices in translating problematic terms or groups of terms. It is followed by a glossary of frequently used technical terms.

In general, I have romanized technical terms relating to costuming, masks, and musical performance, for example, *kanmuri* and *nōshi*, *eboshi* and *kariginu*, *kuse*, *shōdan*. Such terms are included in the glossary when they occur frequently or throughout Zeami's career; otherwise, they are discussed in the footnotes. The names of individuals are treated similarly.

The gender of pronouns in the translation is usually male because of the exclusive nature of the guilds responsible for *sarugaku* performance in the fifteenth century. That is, when a third-person singular pronoun is needed in the translation, I use the male pronoun unless it is clear that a female is intended.

Zeami's text is written using medieval orthography, and my policy is to reflect such spelling in romanization when quoting his text or the texts to which he refers or alludes. I use romanizations from modern Japanese for modern words, place-names, and personal names. Although sometimes this introduces inconsistencies,[34] I think it generally is better philological practice, even in romanizations, to reflect as much as possible the way in which the original texts were written. In some cases, moreover, modern romanizations obscure the meanings that are apparent in historical romanizations. For instance, the name of the nō play *Aritohoshi* plays on the words *ari* (be) and *hoshi* (star), but the second word is obscured in the modern romanization, *Aridōshi*. Even given this general policy, some readers may find inconsistencies. Sometimes, for instance, Zeami's spellings do not conform to orthodox historical orthography (*rekishiteki kanazukai*). For example, he writes *Aritohoshi* as *Aritowoshi*, and that too obscures the pun, but perhaps less so than the modern version. Moreover, the important term *yūgen* appears in these texts in *kana* as both *yu-u-ge-n* and *yu-fu-ge-n*, whereas technically it should be spelled *i-u-ge-n*.

I made certain compromises in this context. In general, when I thought that a given word might be known to some readers in a romanization from modern Japanese, I generally used it (e.g., *jo-ha-kyū* for the more correct *jo-ha-kiu*). When I thought that the word was less familiar than that, I used historical romanization (*bauwoku* rather than *bōoku*). Often, particularly from the mid-1420s onward, Zeami used Chinese graphs for a word or an expression, without any phonetic gloss. When I found it necessary to refer to such texts in romanization, I used orthodox historical orthography (as reflected in, for example, Kindaichi Haruhiko's *Shinmeikai kogo jiten*). When the traditional orthography is substantially different from the modern (Hepburn) romanization, I include the modern version in parentheses, identified as "mod. J." (modern Japanese). Likewise, when it seemed to me advisable to include a historical romanization for words that, according to my general rule, appear in modern versions, I supplied the historical version in parentheses preceded by the abbreviation "orth." (orthographically). In the few cases in which a Chinese word is romanized, it is preceded by the abbreviation "Ch.," the word "Mandarin," or the like.

When Zeami quotes song texts or nō plays, they are both transliterated and translated. In such cases, certain other technical details may intrude on my general romanization practice. When those texts are clearly written in *kana*, I tried to reflect that in the romanization. When there is ambiguity, I follow the general principles used in Yokomichi Mario and Omote Akira's *Yōkyokushū*.[35] Song texts are sometimes quoted with technical specifications regarding the specific type of song being quoted.[36] When such specifications are included in the translation, they are written in superscript small caps. In the case of *Five Sorts of Singing*, I did not use romanizations for the many quotations from *sarugaku* songs found there but presented them in Japanese, on facing pages, for reasons explained in the introduction to that text.

Notes

1. Omote Akira and Getsuyōkai, eds., *Zeami jihitsu nōhon shū* (Tokyo: Iwanami shoten, 1997), vol. 2 (*kōtei hen*), p. 1.

2. The title of *Transmitting the Flower* is discussed further in appendix 2.

3. More information about the textual history of the *Notes* can be found in appendix 2 and in the introductions to each of the texts translated here.

4. This has been translated by Erika de Poorter, *Zeami's Talks on Sarugaku: An Annotated Translation of the Sarugaku Dangi, with an Introduction on Zeami Motokiyo* (Amsterdam: Gieben, 1986).

5. *Sarugaku* is generally written with the Chinese graphs meaning "monkey music," but Zeami insisted that instead the word is related to the religious music of Japan's indigenous pantheism (so-called Shinto), pointing to the graphic form of the words in question.

6. Kamo no Chōmei, *Mumyōshō*, in *Kamo no Chōmei zenshū*, ed. Yanase Kazuo (Tokyo: Kazama shobō, 1980), p. 88 (separately paginated).

7. Certain terms of widespread usage in the *Notes* are discussed in the introduction or in the appendixes.

8. In addition to *Fūshikwaden* (*Transmitting the Flower Through Effects and Attitudes*), we could list the titles *Kwashiu* (An Extract from *Learning the Flower*, 1418), *Shikwadau* (*A Course to Attain the Flower*, 1420), *Kwakyau* (*A Mirror to the Flower*, 1424), *Shiugyoku tokkwa* (*Pick Up a Jewel and Take the Flower in Hand*, 1428), and *Kyauraikwa* (*The Flower in . . . Yet Doubling Back*, 1433).

9. The term is found in such compounds as *mukyoku*, *mushin*, and *mumon*.

10. For details, see *ZS*, pp. 16, 23.

11. A helpful account of the phases can be found in "The Five Phases," in Wm. Theodore de Bary and Irene Bloom, eds., *Sources of Chinese Tradition*, 2d ed. (New York: Columbia University Press, 1999), vol. 1, p. 348.

12. See the discussion in *A Mirror to the Flower*.

13. Zeami quotes the Mao preface most extensively in *Articles on the Five Sorts of Singing*, but he also refers to it at several points in the *Notes*.

14. *Takasago* celebrates the longevity of the pine, the benevolence of the ruler, the felicity of conjugal fidelity, and so on, and has always been one of the most popular plays in the repertory. But Zeami himself admits that it is in some ways eccentric in *Conversations on Sarugaku*, in *ZZ*, p. 286. I have treated this in detail, in a long discussion and a translation of the play, in *ZS*, pp. 69–70, 77–78.

15. *Bauwoku* is generally written in *kana* in the manuscripts of the *Performance Notes*, but in one text, the graphs 亡臆 (a devastated heart) appear. Scholars have used 望憶 (longing thoughts) and 亡憶 (devastated thoughts) as well, and some versions of the original text write 茅屋 alongside the original *kana*. This means a sedge-thatched hut and is to be taken as a metaphor for the life of lonely poverty that gives birth to the emotion in question. None of these graphs really makes very good sense, and it has been suggested that Zeami actually meant 亡国之音 (*baukoku no on*, the music of a land about to fall) but did not say what he meant because the phrase was bad luck. See *ZS*, pp. 265–66n.30.

An article by Ueki Tomoko in *Zeami* makes a cautious but interesting case for 茅屋 but still leaves the question open to some doubt ("Bauwoku shōkō, Zeami no ongyokuron wo megutte," *Zeami, Chūsei no geijutsu to bunka*, January 2002, pp. 112–27).

16. *Articles on the Five Sorts of Singing* and *The Five Sorts of Singing*. Further comments can be followed through the *Notes*.

17. Zeami seems ambivalent about the categorizations. In *Five Sorts of Singing*, he complains that "no one understands the basic difference between *kusemahi* and *tadautai* singing voice, much less the distinction between *shiugen* and *bauwoku* vocal styles" and claims that he has provisionally divided the art of singing into five different classes: *shiugen*, *yūkyoku*, *renbo*, *aishyau*, and *rangyoku*. There is no precise date for the composition of *Five Sorts of Singing*. The only other mention of *bauwoku* (in this case, actually spelled *bauoku*) from late in Zeami's life is in *Learning the Profession* (1430), where it appears with *shiugen*, *renbo*, *aishyau*, and the heterogeneous categories of *urami* and *ikari* (here, hatred and anger) as well as Dance and Sparring.

18. "On the Rank of Great Virtuosity," in *A Course to Attain the Flower*.

19. *Take* (i.e., 長) is translated as stature, and *kasa* (i.e., 嵩), as grandeur, in contradistinction to *kurai* (位). Zeami seems to be inconsistent in his explanation.

20. Thus in the most immediately relevant of the texts in the *Notes*, the one entitled *Nine Ranks*, in which the bottom three "ranks" have no aesthetic utility apart from one exceptional case (discussed later).

21. For example, the Kanze school divides the entire repertory into eight levels: at the top are twenty-two plays or songs termed "profound instructions" (*omonarai*, internally differentiated into four groups), below these are nine plays called "instructions in the nine" (*kyūban narai*) and then nine more described as "instructions in the quasi nine" (*jun-kyūban narai*). The rest of the repertory is placed into five classes (*kyū*) below these. See the table at the beginning of the Taiseiban edition of *Kanze yōkyoku hyakubanshū*.

22. *Conversations on Sarugaku*, in *ZZ*, p. 268. In *Transmitting the Flower*, he says a sixteen- or seventeen-year-old boy rather than a twelve- or thirteen-year-old boy, but in either case, it is worth remembering that according to traditional Japanese ways of reckoning age, a child is a year or two younger than what we mean when we say a sixteen- or seventeen-year-old, and so on.

23. The term is ultimately traceable to Chinese Chan (Zen) texts and seems most likely to refer to a bodhisattva's ability to attain the full enlightenment of a buddha but to remain in the sensible world to assist others. It instantiates a perhaps more trenchant epistemological paradox in more recent Zen contexts and, of course, in the *Notes*. A shortened form of the term appears in the title of the late text *Kyakuraikwa* (*The Flower in . . . Yet Doubling Back*), and an intriguing reference to this state of experience appears in the text of the song "Rokudai no utai" quoted at the end of *Five Sorts of Singing*.

24. Compare Teika on Narihira: "When composing a love poem, abandon your ordinary self and, imagining how Narihira would have behaved, compose your poem as if you *were* Narihira" ("Kyōgoku chūnagon sōgobun," in Hisamatsu Sen'ichi and Nishio Minoru, eds., *Karonshū nōgakuronshū*, vol. 1, *Chūsei no bungaku*, NKBT, vol. 65 [Tokyo: Iwanami shoten, 1965], p. 333, trans. David Bialock, "Voice, Text, and Poetic Borrowing," *Harvard Journal of Asiatic Studies* 54, no. 1 [1994]: 212–13).

25. The annotation glosses the native Japanese うれしき心, with the Chinese compound 観喜, but Omote (*ZZ*, p. 188), Konishi Jin'ichi (*Zeami shū*, Nihon no shisō, vol. 8 [Tokyo: Chikuma shobō, 1970], p. 312), and Yamazaki Masakazu (*Zeami*, Nihon no meicho, vol. 10 [Tokyo: Chūō kōronsha, 1969]) all regard this as a miswriting of the homonym 歓喜, a word redolent with Buddhist associations (as in the name of the divinity 歓喜天, Chinese for Ganeśa). Might it not be overhasty, though, to assume that Zeami (or whoever made the annotation) misnotated his intent? The compound makes good sense in the context of this discussion as the joy of seeing or, by extension, the joy of perception, and Zeami has a distinct penchant for neologisms.

26. For example, 逍遥遊, the name of one of the books of the classic *Zhuangzi*.

27. Fujiwara no Teika (1162–1241), *SKKS* 671.

28. *Mukan no kan.* Earlier, Zeami spoke of *mushin no kan* (a kind of excitement that transcends the mind), and his assertions about an "excitement that transcends excitement" seem to be related. The various concepts prefixed with negatives such as *mushin* and *mukan* (*mu* being 無) are impossible to translate, as they entail the Zen dialectic that insists on their ineffability. Whatever translations are used for them should be understood as heuristic and "sous rature." See "On Depth," in *A Mirror to the Flower.*

29. One hesitates to say that Zeami invented the form by himself because he ambiguously credits the authorship of one of the most celebrated of all *mugen* plays, *Matsukaze,* to both his father, Kannami, and himself. For a detailed discussion of *mugen* plays, see *ZS.*

30. Both the *shite* and the *waki* have somewhat different meanings in Zeami's usage, which are noted in the appropriate places in the translation.

31. For example, in "On an Expert's Grasp of Excitement," in *A Mirror to the Flower*: "When his Singing, Dance, and Sparring are complete, we call an actor expert."

32. For example, *Transmitting the Flower,* "A pretty little boy with a good voice who is talented besides can hardly go wrong."

33. Omote's epoch-making work (which continues even as I write) has created a new standard for understanding the *Notes.* It is contained in numerous volumes, several of which are listed in the bibliography. Most important of all these is his critical edition *Zeami Zenchiku* (*ZZ*) in the series Nihon shisō taikei.

34. Even when using historical orthography, I have romanized *o-u* as *ō* and *u-u* as *ū*, and analogously, *ko-u* as *kō*, and so on. I romanize the *h-* column of the syllabary as *ha-hi-fu-he-ho.*

35. These discrepancies occur because there are some characteristic differences between orthodox historical orthography and the way these texts have been delivered on stage. The most common example is the formal verbal ending known in modern Japanese as *-sōrō.* On stage, this appears in sentence final form as *-sōro.* Orthodox historical orthography romanizes this as *-safurafu,* but in modern nō performance, it is typically pronounced *-sōro.* When the word is written exclusively with a Chinese graph, I have adopted the expedient *-safuro.*

36. These technical specifications stem from Zeami's own usages, but in later centuries, they were supplemented and revised, for consistency, by Yokomichi Mario. (He calls these units *shōdan.*)

Transmitting the Flower Through Effects and Attitudes
風姿花伝, 1400–1418

Transmitting the Flower as we have it today consists of seven different books or chapters. The first three seem to comprise a unit in themselves and are the earliest statements we have regarding *sarugaku* performance. They discuss training throughout the actor's life, the roles the actor should have at his command, and questions about how to prevail in competitive performance. In the third section Zeami begins to talk in more detail about the aesthetic ideals of *sarugaku*, setting the tone for extensive comments throughout the *Performance Notes*, but he remains closely attuned to the practical deployment of aesthetic strategies for advantage in performance. A note at the end of the third book dates these three texts as a single manuscript to 1400.

Book 4, "Divine Purport," seems to have been compiled separately because of its divergent thematic material. Whereas the first three books are closely concerned with training and performing, this fourth book collects various types of lore about the origins of *sarugaku* in the remote past, relating it to Japan's indigenous mythology and religion as well as to Buddhist legend. At the end of the book is an account of contemporary *sarugaku* troupes and some of their primary responsibilities.

The fifth book, "Ultimate Achievement," returns to performance but at the same time discusses the different aesthetic aims of rival *sarugaku* troupes as well as some other closely related performing arts such as *dengaku*. Book 6, "Written Preparations for the Flower," is Zeami's first discussion of writing plays, and book 7, "Separate Pages of Oral Instructions," contains the most extensive account of the "flower" and its relation to the actor's training and innate ability.

Because of its variety and the relatively long period over which it was compiled, *Transmitting the Flower* gives an instructive picture of the history of Yamato *sarugaku* in the early fifteenth century. If, as Zeami claims, the first three books represent not his own thinking on the subject so much as his father's (in Zeami's words, "what I have done here is to record the general meaning of the things that my late father told me"), we can better understand his adulation of Kannami throughout the *Performance Notes*. All the same, we should be somewhat skeptical about accepting this assertion uncritically. It was not unusual for medieval Japanese thinkers to attribute the points they made to the tradition to which they belonged rather than to their own innovation. In any case, the material in books 5 through 7 is, as Zeami himself admits, more an account of what he learned over the middle decades of his career regarding performance and training than of his inheritance. These books also trace some of the changes that took place in *sarugaku* performance at the time.

As Omote suggests, the emphasis in book 5 on respect for the tastes of the masses and the mastery of diverse performance styles may reveal the keen competition Zeami faced in the early fifteenth century from rivals in *dengaku* and Ōmi *sarugaku*. Book 6, on composing for the *sarugaku* stage, reveals certain textual and rhetorical changes from the earlier books, particularly the use of honorific language at certain points. This suggests that this part of the text was intended for transmission to a different person than were the earlier parts of *Transmitting the Flower.*

If there is some sense of discontinuity in the transmission, there is also a strong sense of continuity in the development of the theory of the "flower" between books 3 and 7, as Omote points out.[1] In addition, there are suggestions that the seventh book may have existed in some sort of draft form even while the third was being written, despite the gap of more than eighteen years between the dates recorded at the ends of the two books. This means that the composition of at least the last book, but probably the last three books, of *Transmitting the Flower* took place over a number of years and thus is a cumulative gathering of notes on performance rather than a discrete treatise about performance written in a period of reflection and production.

Transmitting the Flower is the best known of the *Performance Notes* and is sometimes referred to as *Kadensho*, but for reasons discussed in appendix 2, this title is misleading.

❁

Now if you inquire into the practices and origins of *sarugaku*, with its promotion of long life,[1] some will tell you it arose in the time of Buddha, and others will say it was passed down from the age of the gods; but that time has gone, and in either case, the age is so remote that it is beyond our power to imitate the effects they created. Ever since Prince Shōtoku, during the reign of Empress Suiko, commanded Hada no Kōkatsu[2] to make sixty-six entertainments

1. See Omote's introduction to the excerpts from *Transmitting the Flower*, in *Rengaronshū, nōgakuronshū, haironshū* (Tokyo: Shōgakukan, 1973), p. 214.

2. Shōtoku Taishi (574–622), second son of the sovereign Yōmei, was a central figure in the development of the early Japanese state, responsible for the promotion of Buddhism and the erection of several important architectural monuments. He served as regent for his aunt, the sovereign Suiko (r. 593–628), until his death.

Hada no Kōkatsu (orth. Kaukatsu, fl. early seventh century; the surname is generally read Hata today) was an influential supporter of Prince Shōtoku and his aunt. His importance to Zeami and the legendary accounts of his relation to the origins of *sarugaku* are part of a broader medieval interest in the legendary Shōtoku, connected to the development of a religious cult

and to call them "*sarugaku*" (for both the peace of the realm and the enjoyment of the people), it has persisted generation after generation, taking the beauties of the landscape as an impetus to performance. This is what has caught so many people's attention in recent years. Since that distant time, descendants of that Kōkatsu have transmitted the art in their position as priests at the Kasuga and Hie shrines. And so it is that the performance of groups from Yamato and Ōmi flourishes even today, in service of the gods at these two shrines.[3]

Study the old, then, and make certain that you do not neglect tradition even while appreciating the new. Within his heritage, the accomplished master is, after all, someone who shows no vulgarity in speech and exhibits *yūgen*[4] in his attitude.

Whoever aspires to this vocation should, I think, avoid other arts. He should engage in the vocation of poetry, though, because it is an ornament to graceful performance and an inducement to long life.

It is here, then, that I have set down various notes of general bearing on what I have seen and heard since my youth under the discipline of this art.

• Promiscuity, gambling, and excessive drinking: three major prohibitions against these have been set down by our predecessors.

• Be resolute in training, don't be contentious.

Notes on Training Through the Years

At Seven

• A beginning in this art comes at about the age of seven.[5] In training at this age, there is always something a child does on his own that shows where his talents lie. He should be allowed to follow such natural inclinations, whether

---

focusing on him. Zeami's origins in the Yamato basin also gave him a geographical connection to Shōtoku, whose power base in Ikaruga had been close by.

Zeami mentions Shōtoku several times in the *Notes* and quotes extensively from a song about him in "Five Sounds."

3. Kasuga is the tutelary shrine of the Fujiwara, now in central Nara and thus in the old province of Yamato. The four troupes of Yamato *sarugaku* all had hereditary commissions for performance there. The Hie Shrine is a complex of important shrines on the western shore of Lake Biwa in the old province of Ōmi. It was, similarly, an important venue for performance by the rival Ōmi troupes.

4. For a discussion of *yūgen*, which is romanized and left untranslated, see the introduction. The appearance of this fundamental value of nō performance so early in the *Notes* is a signal of its importance. The social context of *yūgen* is clear here and seems to have significance both on and off stage.

5. According to the traditional way of counting age in East Asia (*kazoedoshi*), this refers to the number of calendar years in which a person has lived and is thus one to two years younger than the corresponding Western count.

they be toward Dancing, Sparring, singing, or just the raw display of energy.[6] You should not be too quick to say what is good and what is bad because if you demand too much, the child will lose interest in performance and weary of it, making no progress.

You should not, though, instruct the child to do things apart from singing or Sparring or Dance. Even if he is capable of dramatic imitation, you should not teach him such techniques in any detail, nor should he be allowed to perform in the first piece of a formal production. You should let him display his talents in the third or fourth piece, as seems appropriate.

At Twelve or Thirteen

About this time, the child will begin to be able to carry a tune, and he will start to understand something about performance, so he should he taught various sorts of roles.

First of all, since he is a child, anything he does will entail *yūgen*. Furthermore, his childhood voice will be at its peak during this period. With these two advantages, his bad points will fade and his good ones blossom. Now, for the most part, you should not have children do too much dramatic imitation.[2] It neither looks good nor increases the child's ability. But as he comes to show real mastery, a child may be permitted to perform almost anything. A pretty little boy with a good voice who is talented besides can hardly go wrong. All the same, such a flower[7] is not the true flower. It is merely the flower of the moment. Training at this time, therefore, should always be gentle. To that extent, it is unlikely to be definitive with regard to the child's lifetime potential.

At this stage, those things the child can do easily should be made the flower of his performance, and the main emphasis should be on his technique. His movements should be exact and his singing understandable

6. *Hataraki*, *mai*, and *ongyoku*—the terms translated as "Sparring," "Dance," and "singing"—are fundamental tools for the actor and are translated into these English words, which will be understood in a more technical sense than would the same words in lowercase. "Sparring" and "Dance" are capitalized as proper nouns for specific kinds of stage activity. I usually, however, leave "singing" in lowercase because by *ongyoku*, Zeami intends at least two (perhaps more) distinctive types of vocalization.

"Singing" refers to the full range of vocal delivery in *sarugaku*, from the heightened speech (*kotoba*) used in dialogues and self-introductions to the various species of singing proper, whether rhythmically "congruent" or "noncongruent." "Sparring" refers usually to the often relatively mimetic movements characteristic of young gods and demons, or warriors in battle. "Dance" refers to the abstract and formal, usually instrumental, dances most typical of women and goddesses. For further discussion, see appendix 1.

7. *Hana* is the common Japanese word for "flower" or "blossom," but Zeami uses it throughout his *Notes* as a symbol for what is most basically attractive in a performance. For more extensive discussion, see the introduction.

syllable by syllable; his basic gestures in the dance should be instilled precisely; and great care should be given to his training.

At Seventeen to Eighteen

This period is of such great importance that you had better not practice too much. First, since your voice will be changing, you will lose one of your dramatic charms. As your legs grow disproportionately long, you will lose your physical charm; the time will have passed when, given your pretty voice, you could perform with effortless flair, and with such alterations, you will outgrow your performance strategy and be left at a loss. This will, moreover, put you in positions that the audience finds comical, and you may be embarrassed; with one thing and another, all this can be disheartening.

In training at this time, even if people point and laugh, pay them no heed. Practice instead in private, at a pitch your voice will allow, and train hard, using your voice as appropriate to evening or morning;[8] be resolute in your awareness that this is the turning point; commit yourself to performance for life with complete devotion; no other means of training exists. If you give up at this point, your performance is sure to cease then and there.

Although it's true that a pitch is relative to the particular voice in question, you should probably sing at *ōshiki* or *banshiki*.[9] If you are too particular about pitch, it is likely to hurt your posture, or it may lead to problems in the voice once you are older.

At Twenty-four to Twenty-five

A man's artistic potential for his entire life begins to be fixed about this time. Consequently, this is a critical threshold in training. Your voice will already have changed, and your body will have reached maturity. This provides two advantages, a voice and a posture; both reach maturity at this time. Performances worthy of a man in his prime are born of these.

About this time, people will begin to take notice and say, "Look how good he's become!" On occasion you may even win in competitions against famous actors because of the freshness of your dramatic achievement at this particular time. People may be excessive with praise, and you might mistake yourself for a fully accomplished actor. This is very dangerous. Your achieve-

8. Further details on the type of voice appropriate to a time of day is found in *Oral Instructions on Singing.*

9. *Ōshiki* and *banshiki* are pitches in the traditional tonal system imported from China. *Ōshiki* corresponds generally to A and *banshiki* to B, but given the lack of standards of absolute pitch in modern nō performance, the significance of these pitch terms provokes some uncertainty. For further discussion, see appendix 1.

ment at this time is not the true flower. It is a flower born of youth and the freshness that spectators see in you. Someone with a discriminating eye will recognize this fact.

The flower at this time is a beginner's achievement, and it will be a great shame if you mistake it for real expertise and then, thinking yourself a great actor, give free rein to your personal eccentricities on stage to make a virtuoso display. Even though you are highly praised and win in competitions with famous actors, you should realize that this is merely a temporary flower born of novelty. You should work at mastering the traditional forms of dramatic imitation and train all the more diligently, inquiring very carefully of truly accomplished actors concerning the fine points. Should you mistake this temporary flower for the true flower, you will fall even further from that real flower. Nearly everyone becomes enthralled with this transitory flower and fails to realize that it will soon fade. We recognize this as a period of "initial intent."[10]

• Ponder this problem[3] long and hard. If you really have a grasp of your level of achievement at this stage, that flower will not disappear throughout your life. If you overestimate your level of achievement, even the flower once attained will wilt away. Take care to understand this well.

At Thirty-four to Thirty-five

Your ability to perform is at its highest peak at about this time. At this point, if you come to a full realization of the various points in these notes and master them in performance, you will most certainly gain the recognition of the powerful and secure your fame. By this time, if you should fail to gain the recognition of the powerful and remain unsatisfied with your portion of fame, then no matter how expert you may be, you should realize that you have not yet reached the fullest flowering of your art. If you do not do this, your performance will decline after the age of forty. The proof of this will be apparent later. You would, then, rise until about age thirty-four or thirty-five, and decline from forty on. Unless you have attained the recognition of the powerful, do not imagine that you have brought your performance to its fullest.

I will alert you to one more thing here. This is the time for you to take account of what you have learned in the past and to set some guidelines for your direction in the future. Unless you attain expertise by this time, it likely will be very difficult for you to attain the recognition of the powerful hereafter.

10. The word *shoshin* (初心) is important to Zeami, but it unfortunately cannot be rendered by a single and consistent English word or phrase. In many cases it means "beginner," or, as at the beginning of this paragraph, "beginner's achievement," but it also stands for an important type of awareness in the performer, to be drawn on throughout his career. In that case, it is translated as "initial intent."

At Forty-four to Forty-five

From this time on, your performance strategy should change fundamentally. Even if you have achieved the recognition of the powerful and become enlightened[11] to a serious understanding of the art, all the same you had better find yourself a good *waki.*[12] Your skill may not deteriorate, but you will unavoidably grow older and lose both the flower of physical strength and the flower of appearance. I don't know about the exceptionally handsome, but for the basically attractive person, it becomes quite unacceptable to perform without a mask when you're old. You'll have to do without advantages of this sort, then.

From about this time, you probably should not attempt any sort of intricate dramatic imitation. Make the most of what is attractive in your performance, but with a light touch—don't break your neck—and let the *waki* show off the flower of his performance, holding back your own so as to support and harmonize with his. Even when you don't have a *waki*, you should probably avoid intricate and physically demanding performances. No matter how you do them, they won't appeal to a spectator's eye.

Whatever flower you haven't lost by this point must be the authentic flower of your talent. Any actor who hasn't lost this flower by the time he is about fifty must surely have gained fame throughout the realm before he was forty. No matter what degree of recognition from the powerful an actor may have acquired, he must be the sort of person who thoroughly understands his own capabilities; he will, consequently, take great care to find a good *waki*, and he won't exhaust himself performing in a play where his faults are sure to be exposed. The mind of someone who understands his own capabilities is the mind of a master.

At Fifty and Beyond

There's probably no better principle at this age than to do nothing. From time to time, somebody says how once old age has taken its toll, a splendid steed is no better than a nag. All the same, an actor of genuine attainment will still have his flower at command even when his repertory has dwindled away and, for better or for worse, he has nothing to show off.

My late father passed away on the nineteenth day of the fifth month when he was fifty-two years old, but on the fourth of that month he offered a perfor-

11. The term used here, *tokuhō* ("get the Dharma" or "achieve enlightenment"), has a specifically Buddhist flavor and is repeated in texts from late in Zeami's career. See *The Flower in . . . Yet Doubling Back.*

12. The *waki* in modern nō performance is a secondary role, usually that of a traveling priest, which introduces most plays and sometimes can be regarded as a kind of surrogate for the audience as a whole. The counterpart to the waki in modern nō is the *shite*, the primary role in a play. In Zeami's usage, *shite* is usually more generally conceived to mean merely "actor," but he generally uses the term *waki* more in the modern sense.

mance to the god of Sengen in the province of Suruga.[13] His performance that day was particularly beautiful and was appreciated by high and low alike. Now by that time, I gather, he had already relinquished most roles to the juniors, and he himself would add just a little something here or there where it was unobtrusive, yet his flower seemed to blossom more and more. Because he had attained the authentic flower, it held fast in his performance without scattering, even until the tree was old and the branches few. To my eyes, this is proof that the flower remains in old bones.

Here above, Notes on Training Through the Years.

Notes on Dramatic Imitation

It is impossible to write about all the types of dramatic imitation. All the same, since it is of utmost importance to this vocation, you should take great care in this regard. Now, the main point is to present a comprehensive likeness of the object portrayed. But be clear on this: the degree to which imitation is appropriate depends on the object of imitation.

A dramatic imitation of the figure of His August Majesty, the king,[4] his ministers and his courtiers, or the comportment of members of the military houses is very difficult because these persons are out of our ken. We should, nevertheless, make every effort to research their language and inquire into their demeanor and to seek their criticisms after they have seen our performances. In addition, we may feel free to imitate precisely various high officials and their accomplishment and refinements. But it's not good to imitate too closely the vulgar habits of bumpkins and louts. Woodcutters, reapers, charcoal makers, and salt makers are probably suitable for detailed imitation, inasmuch as they suggest attractive, eye-catching action on stage. But don't imitate every last detail of even lower occupations. It would be unseemly to bring them before the eyes of high-ranking spectators. Presenting them with such a sight would be too vulgar and would offer nothing to draw their interest. Make sure you give this due consideration.

The Woman

Now the way a woman looks is well matched to the endeavor of a young actor. All the same, it is of the greatest difficulty.

Right from the start, there won't be anything worth watching if the clothes and accessories don't look right. Empresses and consorts are difficult to

13. Suruga Province was the area corresponding more or less to modern-day Shizuoka Prefecture. The Sengen Shrine is the most important shrine in the area and was very popular in the middle ages as a site of the cult of Mount Fuji.

impersonate, since we have no opportunity to observe their movements, so you have to make careful inquiries. The way they wear their robes and broad trousers is not open to your individual interpretation.[5] You must find out how to do it correctly. The way that women of ordinary circumstance look should actually be easy, since you can observe them at any time. A general approximation of the way such a woman wears her robes and short-sleeved gowns should do. As for the look of a dancer or *shirabyōshi*[14] or, again, a "madwoman," she should hold a fan or a branch of leaves or flowers ever so gently. She is to wear her robe and trousers very long, even stepping on them, and her bearing should be gentle. Moreover, her face won't look good if she directs her gaze upward, but if she looks down, that will detract from her appearance from the back. If she holds her head up straight, it is unfeminine. In any case, she should wear something with long sleeves and should not show her hands. Her sash should be loosely tied.

All told, then, you have to be careful about dress so that you can get the look right. It's true that you can't do any sort of dramatic imitation well if the dress is bad, but this is even more true for the look of a woman, so the way she's dressed is essential.

The Old Man

The imitation of an old man is one of the ultimate achievements in our vocation. Since this is a role in which your level of accomplishment is immediately apparent to the viewer, it is of the utmost importance.

Now, this is an attitude that many relatively expert actors have never mastered. It thus is a mistake in critical judgment to assume that someone is accomplished just because he can mimic the frame of an old man involved in some sort of work like woodcutting or making salt. It is the attitude of an old man in *kanmuri* and *nōshi*, or *eboshi* and *kariginu*,[15] that can be represented

14. Shirabyōshi (orth. Shirabyaushi) was an independent performing art of the late Heian and Kamakura periods. It was performed by women (also called *shirabyōshi*) who often doubled as prostitutes and danced wearing male clothing and sometimes carrying swords. A couple of *shirabyōshi* performers gained the patronage of the Heike strongman Kiyomori, according to the *Heike monogatari*, and more broadly, they played a conspicuous role as performers in the early middle ages. By Zeami's time, however, most of them seem to have disappeared, their legend remaining in nō plays and related performing arts. The term *shirabyōshi* appears to have come from the simple rhythmic accompaniment characteristic of their performances, borrowing the technical term *shakubyōshi* from *gagaku*, where it meant abbreviated performance accompanied only by the beating of fans or *shaku* clappers instead of proper drums.

15. *Kanmuri* and *eboshi* are lacquered court hats, the former a formal one, the latter more informal. *Nōshi* (orth. *nahoshi*) and *kariginu* are, similarly, formal and informal robes originally worn by aristocrats and adopted for use as stage dress. *Nōshi* and *kariginu* are tailored in a similar fashion and have overlapping uses in modern nō costuming. For detailed discussions of the robes, see Sharon Takeda, in collaboration with Monica Bethe, *Miracles and Mischief: Noh and Kyōgen*

appropriately only by an accomplished actor. Without years of practice and high rank, one cannot perform the role suitably.

Furthermore, without the flower, there will hardly be anything interesting to watch. In general, the presentation of an old man bent over at the waist and lame in the knees loses the flower and looks decrepit. And there's little of interest in that. Above all, don't fidget and fuss; comport yourself with grace.

Most important of all is the dance of an old man. Your problem is how to look old and yet retain the flower—it's just as if blossoms were to come into bloom on an ancient tree.

The Role Without a Mask

This, too, is very important. Such a character is, by definition, of ordinary station and ought to be easy to portray, but surprisingly, unless the actor has attained high rank, the role without a mask is not worth watching.

It goes without saying that you should perform such roles in accordance with the play's specific requirements. There's hardly reason to expect that you should physically resemble every such character, but nonetheless some people try to do a facial impression of the character, altering their own features to that end. This is not at all worth watching. You should imitate the general movements and carriage of the character in question. You should make no attempt to imitate the facial expression of that character but to maintain your own expression.

The Deranged

These characters afford the most consistently interesting performances in our vocation. Since there are many types of derangement, anyone who aims to master the vocation should exhibit versatility. This problem demands long and hard consideration.

On the one hand is that derangement caused by possession resulting from offense to a god, a buddha, or a demon, living or dead; if you look at the physical disposition of the possessing spirit, you should find indications of how to proceed. Of greatest difficulty are those whose derangement has been caused by separation from a parent or because of the search for a lost child, by being abandoned by a husband or left behind as a widower. If a good actor fails to distinguish the mental state of one from another but simply reacts with a uniform derangement, he will not create excitement among the spectators. If it's a question of derangement on account of anxiety, then that anxiety should

---

Theater in Japan (Los Angeles: Los Angeles County Museum of Art and Agency for Cultural Affairs, Government of Japan, 2002), pp. 228–30.

be the primary aim of your portrayal, and you should think of the derangement as the flower; when you then throw yourself into the derangement, it will be sure to create excitement in the audience and much interest in the performance. With such a technique, if you can provoke tears in your audience at certain points, you should recognize this as unsurpassed skill. You should make careful distinctions regarding this in the depths of your heart.

There is, of course, no question that you should dress appropriately for the performance of a deranged role. But since the role is, after all, of someone with deranged sensibilities, you may demonstrate this conspicuously in your dress, in accordance with the time.[16] You should carry a branch of whatever might be in bloom in the season.

There is something else you should be aware of, even when performing the role of a deranged person. When the derangement is caused by demonic possession, you of course should make the agent of that possession the primary focus of your portrayal, but there's nothing worse than a deranged woman possessed by a warring spirit from the realm of *asuras* or by demonic gods.[17] If you exhibit a demonic rage when portraying a woman because you've made the possessing agent the focus of your performance, it is visually incongruous. But if, on the other hand, you make the portrayal of a woman the aim of your performance, then the logic for the possession won't hold. Something similar will happen if you portray a deranged male possessed by a woman. In short, the secret is not to take such roles in your performances. They show a lack of competence by the writer of the play. An accomplished writer in this vocation is unlikely to use such unpromising material as the focus of his play.[18] The secret here is to keep this in mind in such circumstances.

Also,[19] you are unlikely to be successful in deranged roles in which a mask is not used unless you have attained complete expertise in performance. Unless you reflect the derangement in your facial expression, it won't be persuasive. But if you contort your face without the skill of a master performer, certain parts of the performance will be unsightly. Indeed, you could say that this is one of the ultimate achievements of dramatic imitation. Beginners

16. Zeami doesn't make clear whether he is referring to the dramatic present or the occasion of performance.

17. In Sanskrit, *asura* refers to supernatural beings of a warlike character such as Indra, but for Zeami, the term indicates primarily the ghosts of dead warriors who appear in plays of a particular configuration in the *sarugaku* (and nō) repertory.

18. There is, all the same, a play in the repertory that seems to fulfill these conditions, *Kanawa* (*The Iron Ring*), of unknown authorship.

19. Zeami frequently begins "paragraphs" in his *Notes* with the word *mata* (also). This may suggest that the paragraphs in question are later additions (by Zeami) to a note composed earlier. In any event, the *Notes* were not the result of a single long dissertation on *sarugaku* performance but a compilation of articles over a long period of time. (*Transmitting the Flower*, for instance, was composed over almost two decades, between around 1400 and 1418.)

should refrain from this in an important performance. Roles without masks are very difficult, and deranged roles are very difficult; how difficult then is the attempt to comprehend both within a single intent and to produce a flower in the interesting spots! This requires great discipline in training.

The Priest

Although this role does have a place in our vocation, it does not call for extensive training because it is not common. In the case of a splendidly attired bishop or a high cleric, you should probably take his dignity as foundation and make his solemnity the aim of your portrayal. When it comes to lower-ranking clerics, recluses, and ascetics, their self-abnegation is the foundation, so the depth of their devotion must be palpable. Depending on the thematic material,[20] you may find it necessary to use unexpected techniques.

The Shura

This,[21] too, is one of the objects of dramatic imitation. You may perform the role well, yet there is little of interest in it. It should not be performed often. But if you take a famous character from among the Genji or the Heike[22] and bring out the connection between him and poetry and music, then—as long as the play itself is well written—it will be more interesting than anything else. It's best if there are some particularly flashy places.

Among the energetic movements of *shura* like this are some that verge on the movements of demons. Others contain elements of dance. If the piece reflects the style of the *kusemai*,[23] then some dance-like movement is appropriate. The character should hold a bow, wear a quiver, and carry a blade to give the role some weight. Inquire carefully into the way to hold and brandish the blade, and do it correctly. Be very careful to distinguish which places are appropriate for Sparring and which for the figures of Dance.

20. The term *fushimono* (thematic material) is used only rarely in the *Notes* but is common in the poetics of *renga*.

21. *Shura* is an abbreviated Japanese version of the Sanskrit *asura* discussed earlier.

22. The Genji (or Minamoto) and the Heike (or Taira) were two factions based on partially fictional links of kinship who came into conflict in the latter half of the twelfth century. The conflict between them is popularly understood to have been the central cause of the fall of the Heian governmental structure. The conflict also was the source of a long narrative tradition of texts and oral performances known collectively as the *Heike monogatari* (*The Tales of the Heike*), which served as a rich source of stories for treatment in nō and other performing arts.

23. *Kusemai* (orth. *kusemahi*) originated as an offshoot of the performing art of *shirabyōshi* but put more emphasis on rhythm, especially syncopation. It became particularly popular in the mid-fourteenth century and was adopted for *sarugaku* by Zeami's father, Kannami. Examples of *kusemai* are quoted by Zeami in *Five Sounds*. See also appendix 1.

The God

Now this role has the look of the demonic. And if an element of wrath is in some way apparent in the portrayal, then depending on the god in question, there should be nothing wrong with that sense of the demonic. There is, however, something very different at the heart of this role. Gods are well suited to the graces of Dance. But demons have no impetus at all to Dance.

Without fail, gods must be dressed appropriately to the style of gods and be dignified, and since there's probably no such thing as a god outside a dramatic role, you should pay close attention to costume and to dress the character with great care.

The Demon

This role is a specialty of Yamato *sarugaku*. It is very difficult.

Now then, because there are interesting ways to portray demons such as angry ghosts and people possessed by spirits, they are easy. If you keep your eye on your dramatic opponent and move your feet and hands precisely, moving in accord with the *monogashira*,[24] you will find ways to create interest.

As for a true demon from hell, the better you portray it, the more terrifying it will appear, so there's no opportunity to create interest. Or is it instead that the portrayal is so difficult that it's rarely accomplished with interest?

First of all, the role should be, fundamentally, strong and fearsome. But what creates interest in the mind is different from what creates fear or the impression of strength. So then, the dramatic imitation of a demon really is a matter of very great difficulty. If you truly perform it well, it only stands to reason that it shouldn't be interesting. Its essence is, after all, fear. Fear and interest are as different as black and white. So, shouldn't we say that an actor who can create interest in portraying a demon is a truly expert master? But the actor who does only demons well can hardly be one who understands the flower. That being the case, the demon portrayed by a young actor may appear to be well done, but it isn't interesting at all. Isn't it logical, then, that the demons of one who does only demons well are uninteresting? You should study this in detail. The consideration needed to create an interesting demon is like a flower blooming out of a boulder.

24. It is not entirely certain what Zeami means by *monogashira*. It could refer to the emblem of a demon or a lower-ranking god, which often tops the headgear in such roles, or it could refer to the *kashira* pattern in the drums, which often marks cadences in the music.

Chinese Roles

Now these roles are unusual, and there are really no models to train from. The character's attire, though, is of crucial importance. And also the mask you wear, even though it is of a human being like anyone else, should convey something out of the ordinary and have something peculiar about it. The role is a good one for a seasoned actor. There is no particular plan for it apart from getting yourself up in the Chinese style. Above all, in both song and movement on stage, the Chinese style is not likely to be very interesting if it actually resembles Chinese practice, so you should only go as far as to give it a certain Chinesey flavor.

Despite its being a small matter in its own right, what I just said about "something peculiar" is related to more far-reaching problems. How, you might ask, is it acceptable to portray something as peculiar when there is nothing at hand to imitate in order to create a Chinese style? One way or another, therefore, you must make something look Chinesey to other eyes by using a manner of expression that is different from commonplace behavior; and there you are: it turns into that very thing.

My notes on dramatic imitation are, by and large, as I have presented them above. It is not possible to write at a greater level of detail. All the same, someone who has a good mastery of the notes here will probably be able to figure out the specifics on his own.

Notes in Question-and-Answer Form

Q: Now then, what is involved in looking out on the house before the *sarugaku* begins on the day of a given performance to predict the outcome of a performance, favorable or not?

A: This is a matter of considerable difficulty. One is unlikely to understand unless he is expert in the business of prediction.

When you look at the venue of a day's performance, there should probably be some indication as to whether or not your performance is likely to succeed. Just what that might be is hard to tell. I would venture to say, though, having given it some thought, that for a shrine or temple performance[25] or a performance for the elite, the audience assembles but the house doesn't settle down for a while. Then everything gets very quiet as the audience waits for the performance to begin, and

25. Performances were sometimes held in connection with shrine or temple rituals, often as an offering to the deity in question, either on commission by a patron of the troupe or by the troupe itself.

everyone, with the same intent, looks toward the green room,[26] thinking you're late; just then, having captured the moment, you make an entrance and sing your *issei*,[27] whereupon the house will be pulled right into the mode appropriate to the moment,[28] and the minds of all present will harmonize with and settle into the actor's movements, and no matter what, that day's *sarugaku* is already off on the right foot.

Sarugaku, though, depends on the attendance of the elite, so if they arrive early, you must begin right away. On such an occasion, the house will not yet have settled down; latecomers will be jostling their way in and people will still be in a commotion; and not everyone's mind will be ready for the performance. It thus will be no small matter to capture their attention. On such an occasion, even though you are all made up for the first play of the day, you should exaggerate your movements, sing in a louder voice than normal, stomp your feet a bit higher than usual, and perform with such vitality that you seize the audience's attention. You should do this in order to get the audience settled down. Furthermore, you should perform in such a way as to appeal particularly to the minds of the elite. When this is the case, a *waki* play[29] is unlikely to be entirely successful. All the same, it is crucially important because, above all, you have to appeal to the expectations of the most important members of the audience.

Nonetheless, if your audience has already settled down and has by itself created an expectant silence, you can hardly go wrong. Even so, it's no small matter to diagnose the audience's readiness for the performance unless you are well experienced in the business of prediction.[6]

Also, things can be quite different in an evening performance. In the evening, you begin later, so of course, the audience will be more settled. That being the case, a play that would work well in second place on a daytime program should be put first on the evening program. But if the first piece of the evening gets bogged down, the performance won't get back on track, and you will need a finely honed performance of a high-quality play. In the evening, if your audience

26. A room immediately adjacent to the *hashigakari*. Actors wait there for their cues to go onstage and, today, may do some last-minute costuming there.

27. The *issei* is a particular song form in a noncongruent rhythm with the metrical pattern 5–7–5/7–5 (sometimes with an additional 5–7/5–7). See the glossary.

28. In Zeami's view, a particular occasion calls for a particular musical mode or set of notes and pitch conventions. These vary according to the time of day and season of the year and other considerations. See a further consideration of this in *A Mirror to the Flower*.

29. When Zeami speaks of a "*waki* play," he means a play that is appropriate to perform directly after (lit., "alongside") the ritual opening of a performance, which would normally occur with *Shikisanban* or, as it is called today, *Okina*. In modern parlance, the term *waki nō* is somewhat stricter than this, but there is a significant overlap between Zeami's usage and modern usage.

seems unsettled, they will quiet down right away with the *issei*. For this reason, it's the latter part of a performance that is most advantageous during the day, but the beginning of the performance that is best during the evening. If it's too quiet at the beginning of such a performance, you'll have trouble finding the right time to recover.

A secret principle[7] states that in all things you should know that consummation comes where yin and yang meet in balance. The essence of daytime is yang. Therefore, your strategy is yin, in that you aim to perform with restraint. To give birth to yin in a time of yang is what it means to balance yin and yang. This is how to begin a performance that will eventually lead to a successful consummation. This is the frame of mind that enables the audience to see the interest in a performance. But since evening is yin, when you translate your vitality directly into a good performance and bring the flower into blossom in people's minds, that is yang. This creates a consummation in which yang is matched to the yin of evening. Using the same rationale, if you try to put yang with yang, or yin with yin, you won't achieve a balance, and you are unlikely to bring the performance to consummation. What is interesting without this consummation? Sometimes from time to time even during the day, the audience may, for whatever reason, grow too settled and somber; then you should realize that yin has come into its time, and you should put your mind to work to keep the performance from bogging down. Although the day may sometimes be overtaken by yin, it is quite unlikely that the night will be overtaken by yang. This, I suppose, must be what it means to predict the outcome of a performance.

Q: How is one to judge *jo-ha-kyū*[30] in performance?

A: This is easy to judge. There is *jo-ha-kyū* in all things; so, too, in *sarugaku*. You should judge it according to the expressive nature of the play in question.

First of all, at the beginning of a day of *sarugaku*, you should choose for the *waki* play something dignified and strictly faithful to its source that is not too detailed, in which the song and movement are in a familiar mode of expression; and you should perform it confidently. It should, first of all, exemplify *shiugen*[31] and thus be auspicious. No matter how fine the *waki* play is, if it does not show *shiugen*, it is not likely to succeed. Even if the play is not quite first rate, as long as it entails

30. *Jo-ha-kyū* provides the overall structure for nō and is later discussed extensively by Zeami. See also *ZS*, esp. pp. 50–51, 83–84, 273, 274.

31. This is first instance of Zeami's use of the word *shiugen* (mod. J. *shūgen*), an important class of *sarugaku* performance that has formal as well as thematic and philosophical consequences. See the introduction.

shiugen, there should be no problem. This is because it is for the *jo*. For the second or third piece of the day, you should do a good play in a mode of expression you have mastered. In particular, since the finale[8] must be fast, you should pack it with a variety of stage business.

Also, for the first play on a subsequent day, you should do something whose mode of expression is different from that of the first play on the previous day. You should think about the best place for a tragic play somewhere in the middle of the performance on a subsequent day and perform it then.[32]

Q: What about a winning strategy in competitive *sarugaku*?

A: This is of great importance. First, in order to create a contrast, you must have a diverse repertory and perform plays whose mode of expression is different from your rivals'. When I said in the preface that you should gain some familiarity with poetry, this is what I meant. A play won't turn out just as you intend when someone else performs it, no matter how expert he may be. When the play is one you composed yourself, then the language and the stage business are all part of the plan. Accordingly, if one of the performers has a facility with language, it should be easy for him to compose a play. This is the very life of our vocation.

No matter how expert an actor may be, if he doesn't have any plays of his own, he's like a soldier who has gone to war without his weapons, even if in his own right he could match the force of a thousand. The test of an actor's skill, then, is readily apparent in competitive performance. When your rival performs a colorful play, you should perform a different sort of piece, quietly, with clear points of concentrated interest. In this way, if you do something different from your rival, then no matter how good his performance is, you won't lose to him by much. And if your performance turns out well, then you are certain to win.

Nonetheless, with regard to the actual performance, you should distinguish among first-rate, second-rate, and third-rate plays. We can call those plays good that are faithful to their source, have something fresh about them, and, on top of that, display *yūgen* and have points of particular interest. When a good play is well performed and, moreover, succeeds, that should be accounted the best outcome. When a not particularly special play, faithful to its source and without any obvious faults, is well performed and succeeds, that is second best. When a hack piece is none-

32. Zeami is referring here to a festival performance lasting several days. His term, *naki sarugaku* (tragic play), doesn't necessarily mean tragic in the classical sense. Literally it might be translated as "a crying play"—that is, one intended to draw the tears of the spectators. Such a play might well have a "happy ending," although it should have provoked sadness earlier.

theless well performed with great effort so that its weaknesses vis-à-vis its source are turned to your advantage, that is third best.

Q: There is something I don't understand in this regard. Sometimes an inexperienced young actor wins in competitive performance against an actor with long experience, even a famous actor. I don't understand this.

A: This is none other than the transitory flower of those under thirty that I talked about earlier. Once the flower of an old actor is gone and he has become old-fashioned, then sometimes the younger actor may prevail through the flower of novelty. A real connoisseur will discern that this is so. I suppose what it comes down to in a case like this is a competition in judgment between a connoisseur and an amateur.

There is, though, something worth noting here. It's unlikely that the flower of a young actor, no matter who he may be, will prevail over an actor who has not lost his flower, even after the age of fifty. But sometimes a fairly good actor will be defeated because he has lost his flower. Take a look at a tree, no matter how celebrated a tree, out of its flowering season. Then look at a mongrel cherry with a single layer of petals when it's just begun to blossom here and there. When you think of this example, you can see why the flower of a single morning might win in competition.

What is important is that the flower is the very life of performance in our vocation, and it is a serious mistake for an old actor simply to depend on his past celebrity, completely unaware that his flower is gone. Someone who doesn't understand how the flower works, even though he can play lots of different roles, is like someone who gathers all sorts of plants to put on display out of season. In form and color, each flower among a vast number of trees and plants is unique; what's the same for all is that it's their flowers that our minds regard as interesting. The actor who has brought a particular kind of flower to its fullest will be famous a long time for that particular flower, even though he is unable to play a variety of roles. So unless he has found a solution to the problem of how he appears to his audience, someone who thinks he has a great many flowers in his own sensibility will be like a tree in bloom out in the hinterlands or a wild plum hidden in a thicket.

Also, even "the experts" offer many different levels of skill. No matter how expert and celebrated an actor may be, if he hasn't grasped the problem of the flower, then even though he may get by as "an expert," he is unlikely to hold on to his flower later. But an actor who has a good grasp of the problem of the flower will keep that flower even when his facility in performance declines. As long as the flower is still there, he will be able to do something interesting throughout his life. And so it is that no matter who the young actor might be, he is unlikely to beat an actor for whom this true flower persists.

Q: In performance, surprisingly mediocre actors are nonetheless recognized as really very good at one thing or another. When expert actors don't do this particular thing, is it because they can't do it or because they shouldn't do it?

A: In all matters, some people have a certain kind of proficiency and are recognized for it. Sometimes others, even though they have attained a superior artistic rank, are unable to manage this particular thing. But this applies only to relatively expert actors. But how could a truly great actor, one who is both expert in the techniques of performance and has made the fullest use of his creativity, fail in any of his aims? Of course, not one actor in ten thousand is both expert in the techniques of performance and has also made the fullest use of his creativity, that is because of complacency and a failure to use that creativity.

Now even the expert have their faults, and even the mediocre have their strengths. Nobody really sees this. Even the person in question doesn't know it. The talented actor depends on his name and conceals himself in his accomplishment; he doesn't know his weak points. Since the mediocre actor doesn't have creativity in the first place and doesn't recognize his weaknesses, he also will fail to discern whatever strengths he may command. So both expert and mediocre actors should seek out the opinions of others, each for his own part. But of course, someone who has already mastered performance and made the fullest use of his creativity already knows this.

No matter how laughable an actor may be, if an expert sees some good point in his performance, he should learn it. This is a strategy of the first order. If, on the other hand, the expert actor recognizes a good point in the poor actor's performance but out of a sense of arrogance refuses to imitate someone less skilled than himself, he will be hampered in his own mind and will probably be unable to discern the faults in his own performance. This must be because he has faltered in his perseverance. Also, if the poor actor can discern the weak points in a talented actor's performance, he may say to himself, "If even an expert performer like that has such weak points, then my own performance must have all the more, novice that I am"; if then, with a healthy respect for this, he talks to others and puts his creativity to work, committing himself seriously to training, he is likely to make rapid progress. But if this actor just thinks to himself complacently, "I wouldn't do something awkward like that," he isn't likely to have a clear grasp of his own strengths. Not knowing his strengths, he may think that his weak points are good, too. In this way, he will grow older, but his performance will not improve. This is how a poor actor thinks.

Therefore, if a talented actor grows complacent, his performance will decline. Isn't this even more the case for the complacency of a not particularly effective actor? Think about this problem carefully. Put your creativity to work on this: the talented actor is the model for the mediocre actor; the mediocre is the model for the talented. That the talented actor should incorporate the strong points of the mediocre actor in his repertory makes eminently good sense. By recognizing even the weak points of someone else, you make him your model, how much more so by recognizing his strong points! That's what I mean when I say, be resolute in training, don't be contentious.

Q: How is one to understand the distinctions of rank in performance?

A: This is readily apparent to the eyes of connoisseurs. Although rises in rank are generally a matter of layer upon layer of experience in performance, surprisingly there are actors about ten years old who already show a naturally high rank in their manner of expression. But without training, such natural rank is wasted. Typically, the acquisition of rank comes as a result of experience and training. Innate rank is, in contrast, a matter of "stature."[9] What we refer to as "grandeur" is yet something else. Most people assume that "stature" and "grandeur" are the same. What I mean by "grandeur" is the appearance of both gravity and vitality. One might alternatively say that "grandeur" has a broad and general meaning. "Rank" and "stature" are somewhat different. There is, for example, a thing such as innate *yūgen*. This entails "rank." But some actors with "stature" do not have the slightest *yūgen*. This is "stature" without *yūgen*.

There is something else a novice should think about. It is not effective to strive for rank in your training. Not only will you fail to secure a higher rank, but what you have already secured in training may decline. In the end, rank and stature are matters of innate capacity, and if you do not have them, there is probably nothing you can do about that. Again, sometimes once you have put in adequate time and cleaned off the grime, rank will come by itself. What I mean by training are the models on which skills such as singing, Dance, Sparring, and dramatic imitation are developed to their greatest capacity.

Having pondered this problem for some time, I have come to wonder whether *yūgen* is not a matter of innate ability. Is a rank of great virtuosity a matter of long experience? This is worth thinking about over and over again.

Q: What does it mean to speak of the stage business matching up with the text?

A: This is a detail in training. It's a matter of the stage actions used in performance. It's also a matter of posture and the movement of the body.

You should, for example, direct your mind to accord with the chanted text. When the text says look, you should look; when it says reach out or draw back your arm, you should reach out or draw your arm back accordingly; and when it says "listen" or "a sound is heard," you should lend your ear; if you use your body thus in accordance with each action as specified, you will perform the stage actions as a matter of course. First, move your body; second, move your arms; and third, move your legs. You should plan your movements in accordance with the melody and their visual appeal. It is difficult to make this clear in writing. You should learn in accord with what you see when the time comes.

Once you have made the most of your training in this matter of matching the movements and the text, the singing and the actions of performance will reflect a single understanding. In short, when I say that the singing and the actions of the performance reflect a single understanding, I mean that you understand the idea. If it's a question of mastery, then this must be it. This is a secret. Although the text and the movements occupy separate concerns in the actor's mind, an actor who can make them reflect a single understanding should be considered an unsurpassed master. This makes for a truly strong performance.

Many people also confuse strength and weakness. It's odd that people should understand a performance lacking elegance to be a strong performance or judge that a weak performance exhibits *yūgen*. There must be actors who don't lose their attractiveness, no matter how often one sees them. This is strength. The actor who appears to be in flower no matter how often one sees him has *yūgen*. The actor, then, who has made the most of matching the text with the action reflects the singing and actions in a single understanding; he is an actor who has naturally made the most of both strength and *yūgen*.

Q: It is common in criticism to hear one refer to *shiore*.[10] What does this refer to?

A: It is not possible to express this in words. The sense of it just doesn't come across. All the same, there certainly is a mode of expression called *shiore*. The sense of it, too, is entirely dependent on the flower. Think about it carefully and you'll see that it is not something you can attain through training or with stage business. Is it, then, something you come to know once you have brought the flower to its fullest expression? If it is, then someone who has brought the flower to its fullest expression in one regard should have the experience of knowing *shiore* even if he hasn't done so with every sort of dramatic imitation.

Therefore, what we have referred to as *shiore* should be ranked even higher than the flower. Without the flower, there would be no point to *shiore*. It would simply be sogginess. What is interesting is for the flower to be *shiore*. What interest would there be in a plant or tree subject to *shiore* when it has never been in bloom? Now, since giving expression to the flower is itself very difficult and since this matter of "*shiore*" is considered above that, then it must be something even more demanding. That being the case, it is hard to explain, even with a metaphor.

There is an old poem that reads,

Usugiri no magaki no hana no asajimeri
Aki ha yufube to tare ka ihiken[33]

Bedewed by morning,
a flower in a faint autumnal mist
upon a plaited fence:
who said
the best of autumn's in the dusk?

Another reads,

Iro miede utsurofu mono ha yo no naka no
Hito no kokoro no hana ni zo arikeru[34]

What alters in this world,
without betraying itself to sight
is—now I understand—
the flower
of a person's mind.

I suppose the tone of *shiore* must be something like this. This is a problem to ponder in your mind.

Q: It is clear from reading these notes that the first and foremost concern in performance is to know the flower. It is of crucial importance. It also is open to question. How is one to comprehend this?

33. Fujiwara no Kiyosuke (1104–1177), *SKKS* 340.
34. Ono no Komachi (fl. ca. 850), *KKS* 797, also quoted in the *Kana* preface.

A: This is the most significant of the ultimate accomplishments in our vocation. Every matter of great difficulty, every secret, has its rationale in this.

I believe most of this matter is treated in detail in the previous notes on training and dramatic imitation. The temporary flower, the flower of the voice, the flower of *yūgen*—these are apparent to people's view, but since they are flowers specific to particular techniques of performance, in time they will scatter, just as real blossoms do. Since they are short-lived, as blossoms are, cases of renown throughout the realm are few indeed. But by both coming into bloom and scattering, the authentic flower should be in the control of the mind. In such a case it is long lasting. What should one do to understand this? I believe this is treated in the separate account of oral instructions.

You should not fret too much over this. If, from the age of seven, you have carefully thought about and understood with discrimination the notes on training through the years and the varieties of dramatic imitation, have given your all to performance, and made the fullest use of your creativity, then you will know the kind of flower that doesn't fade. The mind's mastery of the roles of performance is none other than the seed for the flower. So if you are to know the flower, you must first know the seed. The flower must be the mind, and the seed, the techniques of performance.

Someone of old[35] said,

The ground of mind holds many seeds;
each of them sprouts in rains far and wide.
In suddenly awakening to the sense of the flower,
the fruit of *bodhi* will ripen and abide.

Now what I have done here is to record the general meaning of the things that my late father told me, things I subsequently held in my mind for perpetuating our house and revering the art; it is not in order to rival the erudition of others that I have done this but out of

35. The sixth patriarch of Zen (or Chan) Buddhism, Huineng (638–713). The poem that follows is a *ge* (hymn) by him from the Platform Sutra 49, where it appears after the quotation of five hymns by past worthies. (It also is quoted in *Wujia zhengzong zan* [五家正宗宗] and *Jingde zhuandeng lu* [景徳伝燈録].) The *Konparu-bon* and *Sōsetsu-bon* texts of *Transmitting the Flower* provide Japanese glosses in *kana*, but they are not thought to be contemporary with Zeami's quotation of the poem. There are variations in the third verse, and its meaning is not entirely clear. One version reads 自吾[*sic*, for 悟] 花情種, translated by Philip Yampolsky, from a Dunhuang manuscript as "When yourself you have awakened to the living seed of the flower" (*The Platform Sutra of the Sixth Patriarch* [New York: Columbia University Press, 1967], p. 178).

concern for the decline of our vocation, in its forgetfulness of the censure of the world at large. It is only to leave behind precepts for my descendants.[11]

Here above, the various notes of Transmitting the Flower Through Effects and Attitudes.
Ōei 7 [1400]:4:13 signed, Junior Fifth Rank, Subordinate, Saemon Dayū, Hada no Motokiyo[36]

Divine Purport

• *Sarugaku* had its beginning in the age of the gods, when the Great Goddess Amateru secluded herself behind the boulder door in the heavens;[37] she cast the whole world into darkness, so the eight hundred myriad gods, gathering together on Mount Ama-no-kaguyama, performed *kagura* music and for the first time ever used a comic performance[12] in order to catch her august attention. Ama no Uzume no Mikoto came forth from among the group and sang and danced with a consecrated branch from the *sakaki* tree in her hand, her voice raised high, prancing and stomping in the light of bonfires, in order to provoke a divine possession. Secretly listening to her voice, the Great Goddess opened the boulder door a little. The land grew light once again. The faces of the many gods shone white.[13] The festivities on this occasion were, so they say, the beginning of *sarugaku*. A detailed account is to be transmitted orally.

• In the land where Buddha lived, on the occasion of the consecration of the Jetavāna Monastery built by the rich man Sudatta, the Buddha Śākyamuni was preaching a sermon. Devadatta,[38] in the company of ten thousand heathens,

36. In addition to a date (including its zodiacal identification), the signature lists a court rank, Junior Fifth Rank, Subordinate, and post, Saemon Dayū (orth. Dayufu). These were not actually awarded by the royal court but by the priests of Kōfukuji or Tōnomine Temple, as was the practice for celebrated *sarugaku* performers. The name Hada no Motokiyo is mentioned here only in the *Notes*, although there is one mention of the given name Motokiyo by itself in *Conversations on Sarugaku*, Zeami's artistic memoir, as well. On Zeami's names, see the note at the end of appendix 3.

The formality of this list signals that these three books of *Transmitting the Flower* were collected as a single unit at this point in Zeami's career, only later augmented by "Divine Purport," "Ultimate Achievement," "Written Preparations for the Flower," and "Separate Pages of Oral Instructions." For more detail on the formation of *Transmitting the Flower*, see appendix 2.

37. The story is famously recounted in *Kojiki* 1:17, but Zeami would not have been familiar with it there, drawing instead on the *Nihon shoki* or texts derived from it.

38. This paragraph mentions a couple of the Buddha's foremost disciples and a supporter as well as a contemporary troublemaker: Sudatta was Buddha's benefactor and patron. He purchased a prince's garden for him and built a monastery there. Devadatta was Śākyamuni's jealous cousin and caused him various troubles, eventually inciting the assassination of his father. Ānanda was a beloved and devoted disciple who is credited with collecting Buddha's sermons to

made such a great commotion dancing with festooned branches and sheaves of bamboo grass that it became difficult to continue the consecration. Buddha cast his gaze toward Śāriputra who, thus fortified by the Buddha's strength, prepared a performance with drums and songs at the back entrance to the temple, and there, through the ingenuity of Ānanda, the wisdom of Śāriputra, and the eloquence of Pūrṇa, they performed sixty-six acts of dramatic imitation so that the heathens, hearing the sound of the drums and flute, gathered at the back door and settled down to watch. Given this respite, the Buddha continued with the consecration. Our vocation found its Indian origins in this.

• In the land of Japan during the reign of Emperor Kinmei,[39] there was a great flood along the Hatsuse River in Yamato, and a large jar came floating down the river. A courtier caught hold of the jar near the cedar *torii* at Miwa Shrine. There was a baby inside. He was gentle and quiet and a perfect jewel. Since this child had fallen from heaven, the event was announced at court. That night, in His Majesty's dream, the baby spoke, saying, "I am the reincarnation of Qin Shihuang of the Great Realm of China.[40] I have a certain affinity with the realm of the sun and am manifest here now." His Majesty took this for a miracle and summoned him to court. As the baby grew older, his intelligence surpassed that of other people, so at age fifteen, he was made a minister and the surname Shin was bestowed upon him. The graph for Shin is also pronounced Hada;[41] indeed, Hada no Kōkatsu was this very child.[42]

When there were troubles abroad in the land, Prince Shōtoku, in accordance with precedent from the Age of the Gods and from the Land of Buddha, called upon this Kōkatsu to perform sixty-six acts of dramatic imitation and

create the Buddhist canon. Śāriputra was reputed to be among the most intelligent of Buddha's great disciples. Pūrṇa was renowned for his eloquence.

Neither Zeami's immediate source for this account nor his basis for tying it to the origins of *sarugaku* is clear, but the story is told in "Sudatsu shōja wo okosu" (How Sudatta Erected the Monastery), in *Gengū in'en gyō* (*The Sutra of Stories About the Wise and Foolish*), and mentioned in *Taiheiki* 24.

It is likely that Zeami was familiar with the exquisite wooden statues of Ānanda, Śāriputra, and Pūrṇa at Kōfukuji in Nara.

39. Emperor Kinmei is the legendary twenty-ninth Heavenly Sovereign of Japan, reputed to have lived from 510 to 570. Reference to his high regard for Hada no Ōtsuchi is made in the *Nihon shoki*, "Kinmei tennō sokui zenki." Presumably Ōtsuchi's qualities have been transferred here to Kōkatsu.

40. Qin Shihuang was the (in)famous first emperor of the short-lived Qin dynasty (221–206 B.C.E.), associated with unifying China but also considered a cruel ruler and a burner of books.

41. The graph 秦 is pronounced *shin* in Sino-Japanese. The native Japanese reading for the graph is *hada* or *hata*.

42. Hada no Kōkatsu (orth. Kaukatsu or Kawakatsu) was a legendary figure reputed to have served the sovereign Suiko and to have founded Hōryūji temple around a statue entrusted to him by Prince Regent Shōtoku.

likewise had sixty-six masks made, which he gave to Kōkatsu. These acts were performed in the Great Shishinden Hall of the Tachibana Palace. The realm came to order and the country became peaceful. These were *kagura*[43] performances, so with a view toward posterity, Prince Shōtoku took the graph *shin* from the word *kagura* and removed the radical, leaving only the phonetic element.[44] Read in the context of the calendar, this element is pronounced "*saru*," so Shōtoku named the performance *sarugaku* because it "gives voice to" (申) "enjoyment" (楽). This is also because it derives from *kagura*.

This Kōkatsu served the sovereigns Kinmei, Bidatsu, Yōmei, Shushun, and Suiko as well as Prince Shōtoku.[45] He transmitted his artistry to his descendants, and because changelings like Kōkatsu do not leave behind physical remains, he set off in a dugout canoe from the Naniwa coast in the province of Settsu and drifted onto the Western Sea wherever the wind might take him. He arrived at the coast of Shakushi in the province of Harima. When the people on the coast pulled his boat from the water and looked inside, what they found was different in shape from a human being. He possessed various people and made wonders manifest. The people therefore held him in reverence as a god, and the province was prosperous. They called him Great Luminous Deity Taikō, writing 大荒 (greatly vigorous) for Taikō. The potency of his divine power is apparent even in the present age. He is an avatar of the deva Bishamon.[46] When it became necessary for Prince Shōtoku to subdue the traitorous minister Mononobe no Moriya, it was through the miraculous skill in means[47] of this Kōkatsu that Moriya was brought to defeat, so they say.[48]

---

43. *Kagura* is a diverse body of ancient performance in Japan aimed at placating or summoning the *kami* (gods). By the "middle ages," it had reached into the remote countryside with various kinds of religious performances and was closely linked to early *sarugaku*. Several varieties of *kagura* persist in modern Japan, and of the music performed in one of these (at least), is a sort that is closely related to the *kagura mai* performed in contemporary nō.

44. This lore regarding the name *sarugaku* is dependent on the visual structure of the graphs used to write *kagura*, 神楽. The first graph should be split, and the right half, 申, read in accord with its zodiacal significance as *saru*. This is then combined with the other graph from the word *kagura*, and the result is 申楽, pronounced *sarugaku*. Zeami reinterprets the word *sarugaku*, which had normally been written 猿楽—that is, "monkey music"—for the more favorable reading of "music that gives humble voice." Although 申 is popularly understood to mean "monkey" in the context of the East Asian zodiac, it also is used for the humilific or formal verb "to speak" (*mōsu*, orth. *mausu*).

45. Sovereigns Kinmei (510–570), Bidatsu (538–585), Yōmei (d. 587), and Shushun (usually read Sushun, d. 592).

46. The deva Bishamon (Tamonten; Skt. Vaiśravaṇa) is one of the guardians of the four directions, specifically responsible for the northern sphere.

47. Zeami uses the explicitly Buddhist word *hōben* (Skt. *upāya* [skill in means]) here.

48. Mononobe no Moriya (d. 587) was a powerful member of the entourage of the sovereign Yōmei and opposed the introduction of Buddhism to Japan. He was defeated by the pro-Buddhist camp of Soga no Umako and died in battle.

• During the reign of Emperor Murakami in Heian, the Capital of Peace and Tranquillity, *The Records of Sarugaku and Ennen*, written by Prince Shōtoku, came to His Majesty's august attention;[49] they arose, first, in the Age of the Gods and the Land of Buddha and, using the crazy phrases and ornamented diction, were transmitted from Yuezhi[50] and Shindan[51] to Japan, the Realm of the Sun, all the while preserving a karmic affinity with the praise of Buddha and the turning of the Dharma Wheel, quelling demonic connections and attracting happiness and divine succor. When the dances of *sarugaku* were performed, the nation was at peace, the people tranquil, and lives long; since this was revealed truth in Prince Shōtoku's very hand, Emperor Murakami determined that *sarugaku* be used as prayer throughout the realm. The descendant to whom this Kōkatsu had transmitted the arts of *sarugaku* was Hada no Ujiyasu. It was he who performed the sixty-six *sarugaku* pieces in the Shishinden Hall. At that time, the acting governor of Ki was a man of high intelligence. He was the husband of Ujiyasu's younger sister, and he performed *sarugaku* with him.

Thereafter, it proved impossible to perform all sixty-six pieces in a single day, so they selected from among them and settled on these three: the Inatsumi no Okina (Okina mask), the Yonatsumi no Okina (Sanbasō), and Chichi no Jō.[52] The *Shikisanban* that we perform today are these. They are patterned after the Three Bodies of Buddha, namely, the Dharmakāya, the Sambhogakāya, and the Nirmāṇakāya.[53] An oral transmission regarding the Shikisanban can be found in separate written instructions.

Counting from Hada no Ujiyasu, the line extends twenty-nine generations to its distant descendants, Mitsutarō[54] and Konparu.[55] This is the Emai

49. Probably an imaginary source, although Emperor Murakami (926–967, r. 946–967) was an actual sovereign.

50. That is, the Kushan empire in what is the extreme western extent of modern China.

51. An old word for China, from the Sanskrit *cīnasthāna*.

52. Inatsumi no Okina (more simply, Okina), Yonatsumi no Okina (Sanbasō), and Chichi no Zeu (mod. J. Chichi no Jō) were the three old men who originally appeared in the ritual play *Shikisanban*. The earliest masks used for these characters predate the development of *sarugaku* and are the earliest direct examples of nō masks.

In modern performance, the character Chichi no Jō no longer appears but has been replaced by another role, that of a young man known as Senzai.

53. Dharmakāya, Sambhogakāya, and Nirmāṇakāya are the Sanskrit names of three aspects of a buddha's existence according to Mahāyāna scholasticism. Generally, the first (J. *hosshin*, 法身) represents the ultimate or absolute reality of the Buddha, the second (J. *hōjin*, 報身) a manifestation of him in a paradise, and the third (J. *ōjin*, 應見), his earthly and salvific form.

54. Mitsutarō (orth. Mutsutarau) is the twenty-seventh head of the Enman'i, or Emai, guild (orth. Yenman'yi-za) and the son of Bishaō Gonnokami (orth. Bishawau Gonnokami). His performance of demon roles is mentioned in *Conversations on Sarugaku*, *ZZ*, and, in translation, Erika de Poorter, *Zeami's Talks on Sarugaku: An Annotated Translation of the Sarugaku Dangi, with an Introduction on Zeami Motokiyo* (Amsterdam: Gieben, 1986).

55. Konparu here refers to Konparu Yasaburō (orth. Yasaburau), son of Mitsutarō's younger brother Konparu Gonnokami and father of Zenchiku.

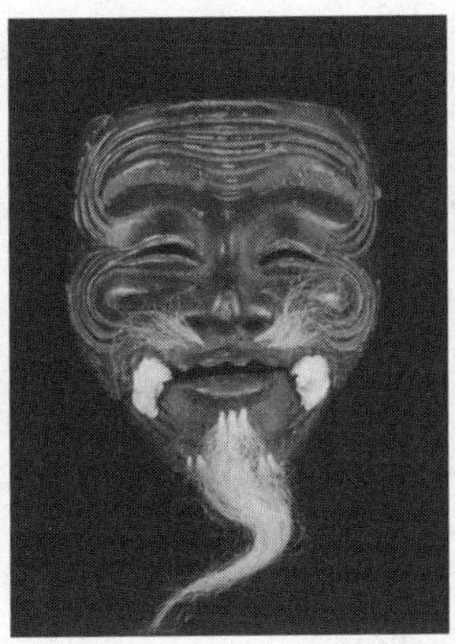

Three masks for the play *Shikisanban*: (*left to right*) Okina, Sanbasō, and Chichi no Jō. In Zeami's account of the origins of *sarugaku*, he mentions three plays chosen to represent a total of sixty-six plays supposedly performed in the distant past by Hada no Ujiyasu. Those three plays are conflated with three roles and three masks: Inatsumi no Okina (or, simply, Okina), Yonatsumi no Okina (or Sanbasō), and Chichi no Jō. The first two mask types continue to be used in *Shikisanban* as performed on the modern nō stage, but the role of Chichi no Jō has been taken over by a character who does not wear a mask. Some old Chichi no Jō masks, nonetheless, still exist. All three masks are listed as Important Cultural Properties by the Japanese government. The Sanbasō was carved by Nikkō, and the other two by Miroku. Although little is known about these mask carvers (reputed to have lived in the tenth century), both are mentioned in *Conversations on Sarugaku* and are counted among the best carvers in the tradition for these masks. (Photographs from the collection of Kanze Bunko Foundation)

guild in Yamato. This house has inherited three items from Ujiyasu, a demon mask carved by Prince Shōtoku, the Kasuga portrait of His Divine Visage, and a relic of the Buddha.

• In the current generation, on the occasion of the Vimalakīrti Lectures at Kōbukuji in Nara,[56] *ennen* dances are performed in the refectory, and rituals are performed in the lecture hall. This is to mollify the heathen and pacify demonic activity. At this time, the Vimalakīrti Sutra is expounded in front of the refectory. This is based on auspicious precedent at the Jetavāna Monastery.

56. The Vimalakīrti Lectures were held annually for a week beginning on the sixteenth day of the tenth month at Kōbukuji (called Kōfukuji today) temple in Nara. They consisted of a full reading of the Vimalakīrti-nirdeśa Sutra, a Mahāyāna scripture expounding nonduality through the words and deeds of the celebrated lay saint Vimalakīrti.

Kasuga (mentioned immediately after) and Kōfukuji are considered separate institutions today, the former a Shinto shrine and the latter a Buddhist temple. But when they were founded and during Zeami's day, they were a single institution with both Shinto and Buddhist significance as well as political weight, as the tutelary shrine/temple of the Fujiwara clan.

The services to the gods at Kasuga and Kōbukuji in the province of Yamato are performed in the temples there on the second and fifth days of the second month and comprise the beginning of religious observances for the year for the four *sarugaku* troupes.[57] They are prayers for peace in the realm.

- The four *sarugaku* guilds responsible for religious services at Kasuga in the provinces of Yamato: Tobi, Yūzaki, Sakado, Emai.[58]
- The three *sarugaku* guilds responsible for religious services at Hie in the province of Ōmi: Yamashina, Shimosaka, Hie.[59]
- At Ise, two guilds responsible for *shushi*[60] performances.
- The three *sarugaku* guilds participating in the New Year's Rectification Prayers at Hosshōji:[61] Shinza (resident in Kawachi),[62] Honza (Tanba), Hōjōji (Settsu). These three guilds are likewise responsible for religious services at Kamo and Sumiyoshi.

Ultimate Achievement

Now, I have written down the various notes of *Transmitting the Flower Through Effects and Attitudes* in large part for the instruction of our de-

57. "Troupe" is my translation of the Japanese *za*, a term for the professional organizations of artists and craftspeople characterizing the economy of artistic production in medieval Japan. The *za* bears some resemblance to a guild. Many of the arts of medieval Japan are carried on professionally by *za* and are thus termed *za no geijutsu* (arts of the *za*).

58. The four *za* of *sarugaku* performance that arose in Yamato and are identified as the progenitors of the oldest schools of *shite* acting are Tobi for the Hōshō, Yūzaki for the Kanze, Sakado for the Kongō, and Emai for the Konparu. The fifth modern school is the Kita, an offshoot of the Kongō that became independent in the early seventeenth century.

59. The three Ōmi (orth. Afumi) *za* that were active in Zeami's day. The Yamashina and Shimosaka *za* were resident in the so-named areas of modern-day Nagahama City. The Hie (orth. Hiye) *za* was located near the Hie Shrine on the western shore of Lake Biwa. It counted among its members the celebrated actor Inuō Dōami (orth. Inuwau Dauami), about whom Zeami speaks in *The Flower in . . . Yet Doubling Back* and *Conversations on Sarugaku*, in *ZZ*, pp. 261–66, passim. After Inuō, all the Ōmi *za* seem to have declined in popularity, and by the late sixteenth century, their more capable performers had been absorbed by the various Yamato *za*. See Omote's detailed note, in *ZZ*, pp. 434–35n.18.

60. *Shushi sarugaku* originated in performances of an apotropaic or esoteric character by priests at the Tōdaiji and Kōfukuji temples, but by Zeami's time, the magical elements in the performances seem to have diminished in place of a greater emphasis on entertainment.

61. Hosshōji temple was located in eastern Kyoto, in the Okazaki District, but the temple fell into disuse in the mid-fourteenth century. The three *za* mentioned here by Zeami were apparently the most important in Kyoto in days before Zeami. The Shinza (not to be confused with the *dengaku* Shinza) was based in Settsu Province, in modern Osaka. The Honza (also called the Yata *za*) was based in modern-day Kameoka, and Hōjōji (orth. Hohujauji) of Settsu Province was based in modern-day Ibaraki City. Again, see Omote, in *ZZ*, pp. 434–35n.18.

62. Zeami is mistaken here. The Shinza was actually from Settsu. See *ZZ*, p. 41n.

scendants, despite my anxiety that they come to outsiders' attention, but my fundamental intention in doing so comes from my observation of the members of our vocation who neglect the disciplines of our art and occupy themselves with unrelated activities, and, when they do chance to turn to our proper art, they forget its source and lose sight of its course, treating it as merely the opportunity for a cheap laugh,[14] tainted as they are by an ephemeral wish for celebrity. I wonder whether the Way isn't already in decay and constantly feel sorrow. In any case, if you devote yourself to the vocation and hold the art in high esteem, without selfish interest, then how could you fail to achieve its benefits? Although this art entails handing on the effects of tradition, there is also, in particular, something about it that stems from individual capacity, which is therefore beyond words. I call it *Transmitting the Flower Through Effects and Attitudes* because it is a matter of the flower's being transmitted from mind to mind through the attainment of its effects.

In general terms, the acting styles of Yamato and Ōmi[63] are different. In Ōmi, they emphasize the realm of *yūgen* and relegate dramatic imitation to second position, making expressive grace fundamental. In Yamato, it's dramatic imitation we emphasize, maintaining as broad a repertory as possible but in such a way that *yūgen* is apparent in our acting style. Nonetheless, a truly talented actor lacks nothing, no matter what his acting style. Concentrating all one's attention on a single style of acting is the approach of an actor who has not really arrived at full mastery.

In Yamato, therefore, the acting style takes dramatic imitation and discursive ingenuity[15] as fundamental, and we specialize in roles of impressive bearing or in the exercise of demonic fury; these are the kinds of roles at which we are considered masters, and the majority of our effort goes toward them; but at the height of his fame, my late father was celebrated for his acting style on the basis of roles like the play with Shizuka's dance[16] or the dramatic imitation of a deranged woman at the great *nenbutsu* recitation at Saga;[17] it was because of this kind of acting that he gained fame and appreciation and was known throughout the land. Nothing is more important than *yūgen* in an acting style like this.

Also, the expressive manner of *dengaku*[64] is a particularly distinctive, and all audiences are accustomed to think that it doesn't measure up to the criti-

63. Yamato Province is the area around Nara, and Ōmi Province is the area around Lake Biwa.

64. By Zeami's time, *dengaku* was a performing art much like *sarugaku*, although its origins were in music and dance associated with planting and agricultural activities. It was partially professionalized and came to include various feats of strength and acrobatics.

cal standards of expressiveness in *sarugaku*, but Itchū of the Honza,[65] who in recent times was considered a veritable saint in this vocation, offered a broadly diverse repertory and was known for his portrayals of demons and gods and the exercise of demonic fury. Why, I've heard that there wasn't anything missing from his expressive manner. And it's true that time and time again my late father said that Itchū was his real master in regard to expressive manner.

Each person in his own way, whether out of arrogance or inability, learns only a single manner of expression and fails to understand the importance of diversity, and is averse to the expressiveness employed by other troupes. Actually though, these people are not so much averse to the other types of expression as they are arrogant because they haven't mastered them. Since they are unable to master the other styles, even though they may at one time have been recognized for their skill in one particular style, they will not be able to sustain a long-lasting flower and will not gain the recognition of the powerful. Those who have gained the recognition of the powerful because of their skill will have something interesting in whatever manner of expression they may choose. Although forms of expression and models for emulation are diverse and varied, interest is common to all of them. It must be the arousal of this interest that is the flower. This is something that is not missing in Yamato, Ōmi, or *dengaku*. Unless you are an actor who has control of this capacity for not missing something, you are not likely to win the recognition of the powerful.

In contrast, there are expert actors who, even though they haven't mastered every type of role, probably do command control of about seven out of every ten and who have, moreover, polished a particular style among these so well that it becomes a model for their students; these actors, too, may well become famous throughout the realm if they bring their creativity to bear. But if there is some aspect in which they remain insufficient, their reception will be mixed, depending on whether the audience is in the city or the country and whether it is discerning or not.

All told, there are many different ways to gain fame in performance. It may be difficult for the expert to satisfy the perceptions of an insensitive audience. The mediocre will not gain the approval of the connoisseur. Now it should not be a surprise that the mediocre cannot satisfy the expectations of the connoisseur. When it's a case of the expert's being unable to gain the approval of the insensitive, it's because the perceptions of the insensitive aren't up to the task, but all the same, a truly accomplished and creative actor should be able to perform in such a way that even the insensitive will re-

65. The Honza was a *dengaku* troupe from the Shirakawa area of Kyoto and was, along with the Shinza in Nara, the representative *dengaku* troupe of the mid-fourteenth century. Itchū was its most famous actor and is discussed further in *Conversations in Sarugaku* and in Poorter, *Zeami's Talks on Sarugaku*.

gard the performance as interesting. We should regard an actor of such creativity and skill as a master of the flower. A performer who has truly risen to such a rank, no matter how old, will not prove inferior to the flower of youth. An actor like this who has attained such a rank is praised throughout the realm and regarded as interesting by everyone, even in the most distant and countrified places. An actor of such creativity is skilled in the full diversity of roles whether in Yamato or Ōmi—even, indeed, in the expressive manner of *dengaku*—all in accord with the preferences and expectations of the audience. I have written *Transmitting the Flower Through Effects and Attitudes* in order to make clear this fundamental insight regarding this endeavor.

That said, however, there's certainly no prospect for your performance if you neglect the model on which your own manner of expression is based. That surely makes for a weak actor. It is only in mastering the model for your own manner of expression that you will be able to understand the full range of acting styles. The actor who says that he has in mind the full range of acting styles and does not enter into the expressive manner of his own troupe not only fails to understand his own manner of expression but stands an even smaller chance of coming to a clear understanding of another manner of expression. For this reason, if your performance is weak, you will not have the flower for long. If you do not have the flower for long, that must be the same as not really knowing any manner of expression at all. For that reason, in the section on the flower in *Transmitting the Flower*, I said, "After you have given your all to a diverse repertory and made the fullest use of your creativity, then you will know the kind of flower that doesn't fade."[18]

With regard to secret matters,[19] the performing arts generally exist to mollify people's hearts and create excitement in the high and low; they are the foundation for long-term prosperity and increase, the means of gaining longevity. Indeed, it is said that all the vocations promote prosperity and longevity when fully mastered. When rising to the fullest rank and securing the family name a place in posterity, this art in particular gains the recognition of the powerful. This is long-term prosperity and increase.

There is, however, a fine point to consider here.[20] When an actor appears before people of discernment and intelligence, they respond appropriately to his mastery of artistic stature and rank, with no particular complication. The eyes of the dull, the rural, and the countrified may not have adequate sensitivity to appreciate such stature and rank. What should you do about this? This art is dependent on the affection and respect of the masses for the long-term prosperity of the troupe. For this reason, if you put too much emphasis on forms of expression that are difficult to access, you will fail to draw the appreciation of the people at large. Therefore, from time to time in certain places, your long-term prosperity will depend on your not forgetting your own initial intent as a beginner and performing in such a way as to appeal to the eyes of the dull. Carefully scrutinize the dynamics of interaction between actor and audience, from the exalted aristocrats and great temples to the countryside and hinterlands (including festival occasions at various shrines): isn't it true that the actor who can perform in all these circumstances without disparagement is the real virtuoso with long-term prosperity? Therefore, no matter how expert you may be, if you lack the affection and respect of the masses in some circumstances, you cannot be called an actor of long-term prosperity and increase. That is why my late father performed the art in such a way that no matter how far away he was in the country, in no matter what remote corner of a mountain village, he retained sympathy for the frame of mind of the people there and made their attitudes his most important concern.

That said, however, the beginning actor should not become discouraged, thinking it too difficult to attain such mastery. You should take these notes to heart and use little by little the principles they contain, and put your personal capacity to work with your understanding of them and use your creativity.

For the most part, these notes are even more applicable to the careful consideration and creativity of the expert actor than to the beginner. I lament the fact that there are many who, even though they are actors of considerable attainment, because they rely on their own power and are bedazzled by their fame, don't have this as reference and fail to acquire long-term prosperity, despite their celebrity. Even though they may have skills, without creativity they won't be successful. To have skills, on the one hand, and to give your utmost creatively, on the other, is like holding onto both the seeds and the flower.

If by some chance, such an actor as has won the recognition of the powerful should, through circumstances over which he has no power, face a time when his success diminishes, then so long as the flower of appreciation from the rural and rustic has not disappeared, there is no danger of the vocation itself coming abruptly to an end. As long as the vocation has not ended, then surely there will come a time when he will again be successful in the realm at large.

• The discipline required for long-term prosperity and increase is completely in accord with the principles of the world at large, and if you cling to selfish advantage, then this above all else will have the effect of destroying your vocation. Long-term prosperity and increase will come to those devoted to the vocation. If instead your efforts go toward prosperity, then that will surely destroy your vocation. If your vocation is destroyed, then that's the end for prosperity as well, isn't it? Focus on the causal relationship in which integrity and clarity[21] lead to the blossoming of the wondrous flower,[66] replete with its myriad virtues.

What I have written in *Transmitting the Flower*, from "Training Through the Years" through its various notes, is not the result of my own personal

66. *Myōka* (orth. *myaukwa*) was an important term in Zeami's later treatises. This is its first appearance and indicates a level of marvel or wonder in performance.

erudition at all. It is what I have learned from my infancy onward into adulthood, through the power of my late father and the more than twenty years since, from what I managed to retain of the things I have seen and heard; I have done this for the sake of our vocation and our house, as a steward of this tradition—how could it be from merely private interest?

In the ninth calendar year of Ōei [1402]:3:2
hastening my brush to completion
Zea (with seal)[67]

Written Preparations for the Flower

• Writing plays is the very life of our vocation. Even if you don't have unusual erudition, use your ingenuity and you will be able to write a good play.

The overall feel of a play is apparent in the section on *jo-ha-kyū*. When writing plays to be performed at the beginning of the day, you should be strictly faithful to the sources and write in such a way that from the first line of the play, those sources are immediately recognizable to the audience. Write in a generally straightforward manner in order to start off the day's performance in a lively and colorful way; you need not take advantage of every last detail for presentation. Then, once you have gone further into the day's sequence of plays, write subtly, taking fullest advantage of every turn of phrase and every opportunity for visible presentation.

Specifically, if the title of the piece relates to a famous place or legendary site, you should probably use Chinese and Japanese poems about the place, familiar poems, in points of concentrated interest in the play. Don't squander key phrases in places irrelevant to the *shite*'s[68] lines or stage business. Try as you may, the audience will pay no attention to high points in a play, whether visual or aural, unless they are well presented. In fact, excitement stirs when interesting words from the troupe's star performer come front and center in the viewer's mind and his actions capture the viewer's gaze; this is the first rule in writing nō.

Be sure, though, to choose poetic language that is appealing and readily comprehensible when heard. Strangely enough, when appealing language is matched to the actor's movements, the character portrayed takes on a tone of *yūgen* all of its own accord. Difficult language doesn't match the movements. There are, however, places where difficult and unfamiliar words may be employed. They are suitable when they match the material from

67. One manuscript includes the notation that Zeami attached his signature here, although that manuscript does not attempt to reproduce the signature proper, instead using the notation "with seal."

68. *Shite* is used here, rather unusually, to refer to the principal character, as in modern nō. But Zeami more frequently uses the word to mean actor rather than principal character.

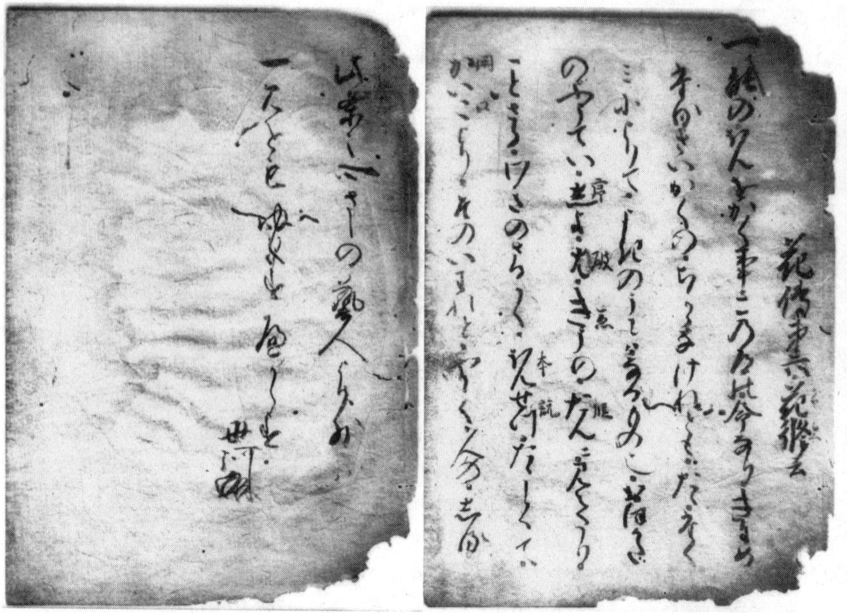

The first leaf (*right*) and the last leaf of Zeami's autograph manuscript of "Written Preparations for the Flower," from *Transmitting the Flower Through Effects and Attitudes.* The latter includes Zeami's admonition that the text not be shown to anyone other than serious professionals, as well as his signature, consisting of the two graphs *Ze-a* and his *kaō*, or cipher. (Photograph from the collection of Kanze Bunko Foundation)

which the character in question is derived. A distinction should be made according to whether the story is based on Chinese or native sources. When you use vulgar or common language, though, the expressive capacity of the play is impoverished.

So the best kind of play is one that is faithful to its source, fresh to the eye, has places of high interest, and a tone of *yūgen*. The second best is one that, though not particularly fresh in its manner of expression, isn't obviously flawed either and proceeds in a straightforward manner, with points of interest. These are general guidelines. But a play that has something to catch the eye should be interesting, something that, in the hands of a talented actor, can be turned to advantage. When one has gone through all sorts of different plays, day after day, then even a poor play may be made to appear interesting because the actor has injected a bit of color by changing the performance here and there. The success of a given play depends on when it's performed and how it falls in the overall program. You should not abandon a play on the grounds that it isn't any good. It has a great deal to do with how the actor handles it.

There is, however, something worth noting here. Certain kinds of plays should not be performed at all. No matter how much it may be a matter of dramatic imitation, you should not perform in wild derangement or anger when, for example, you are playing an elderly nun or an old woman or an elderly priest. Likewise, there should be no dramatic imitation with *yūgen* in an angry role. This is not real performance but frivolity.[22] I discussed the essence of this in the note on deranged roles in the second section.

Also, as in all things, without balance there will be no consummation. What I mean by balance is a play based on good material performed by a talented actor with a successful outcome. Accordingly, people are used to thinking that with a good play and a good actor, things could hardly turn out badly. Strangely, on some occasions, even in these circumstances, things don't turn out well. The discernment of a connoisseur will detect such a case, and he will understand that even though it is not the actor's fault, the general viewer may still conclude that the play isn't any good and the actor, nothing special. What is the problem when a talented actor performs in a good play and it still doesn't succeed? I wonder whether it doesn't have something to do with a disharmony in yin and yang at the time. Or is it because there's hasn't been adequate thought given to the flower? I remain puzzled by this.

Here is something requiring discernment on the part of the writer: Both an exclusively musical play based on a consistently quiet subject and a play centered mainly on dance and movement are easy to write because they are one-dimensional. What we need are plays in which the movement is matched to the singing of the text. This is a matter of great difficulty. These are the plays that really excite an audience's interest. The language should be easily understood, and individual words should hold interest; the melody should be attractive, and the flow from word to word, graceful; special care should be taken to include points of concentrated interest that can be enacted with strong visual appeal. This is how to write. When all these elements are suitable to one another, the entire audience is excited.

That being the case, some things you must know about in detail. The actor who uses the movements to set a meter for the singing is a beginner. When the movements are created from the foundation of the singing, it is because the actor is well seasoned. The singing is what is heard; the movements are what is seen. It stands to reason that it is only by following the path laid out by the story that everything is transformed into actual movement on stage. The language expresses that story. Therefore, the singing is the Substance and the actions are the Instance.[69] The proper order is that the actions should be born of the singing. Making the singing dependent on the actions is backward. In all vocations, as in things in general, precedence is given to the proper order

69. The conceptual binarism *tai/yū* (orth. *tai/yufu*, Ch. *ti/yong*) is introduced here, to be taken up again later, most extensively in *A Course to Attain the Flower*. See the introduction.

rather than an inversion. It is not the inversion that takes precedence over the proper order. Again and again, you must make the text of the singing the standard by which you bring out the color of the movements.[70] This is the training in which the music and the movements reflect a single frame of mind.

There is still another matter to consider when writing plays. In order to write in such a way that the movements proceed from the singing, you must write with the movements as the basis. If you make the movements the basis for writing, when those words are sung, they will naturally give birth to the movements. Therefore, when writing, make movements your priority, and also figure out how the melody can be made pleasant. Then when you reach the actual performance, you again should give priority to the singing. Once you acquire experience with such considerations in mind, the chanting will become the movements; the dancing will become the singing; and you will master the unity of a myriad forms of expression within a single mind. This leads, moreover, to great fame for the writer.

• On knowing the strong and *yūgen*, and the weak and the coarse, in performance. This is something that usually is visible, so it seems easy, but many actors are weak or coarse because they do not really understand it.

First, you should know that in all dramatic imitation, one becomes coarse or weak through imposture. With adequate consideration, you should be able to tell the difference. This is something you should grasp firmly in your mind.

First, to make something strong that is by rights weak is imposture and therefore coarse. That something strong will be strong is strong. It is not coarse. If you try to imitate an object, intending to invest something strong with *yūgen*, but it only resembles it, then it is not *yūgen* but weakness. Therefore, if you simply devote yourself to dramatic imitation and enter fully into the object without imposture, then there is unlikely to be any coarseness or weakness.

In addition, if something that is strong is performed too strongly, it will turn out to be particularly coarse. If you make something that is *yūgen* gentler still in its manner of expression, it will turn out to be particularly weak.

When you look carefully at the distinction, you will see how one goes astray by concluding that *yūgen* and the strong are separate; they are in the

70. Here and in two other places in this chapter of the text, Zeami uses the honorific verbal auxiliary *-tamau* (orth. *tamafu*). Omote suggests a particular relationship between Zeami and the person for whom he initially intended *Transmitting the Flower* but doesn't specify what this relationship might be. It remains a mystery, especially if it was intended for transmission to his sons, although it is unlikely he would use honorific forms for them.

substance of the thing. All sorts of things express *yūgen*: in the class of "people," they could be empresses and royal consorts or dancers, beauties and handsome men; in the class of "plants and trees," they could be the blossoms. Shouldn't we similarly label as strong such things as warriors and savages, or demons and gods, or the pine or cedar (if it's a matter of plants and trees)? If you skillfully imitate various things like these from among the myriad things in the world, then the imitation of something possessing *yūgen* will turn out to have *yūgen*, and something strong will, as a matter of course, be strong. If you don't fully recognize this but simply try to make everything express *yūgen*, then you will be giving short shrift to the imitation itself, and it won't resemble its object. To imagine that your performance expresses *yūgen* without realizing that it doesn't resemble the object of imitation is weak. So if you imitate a dancer or handsome man, as a matter of course you should express *yūgen*. You should just think of imitating your object. Also, if you effectively imitate something strong, you will produce, as a matter of course, a strong performance.

There is, however, something you should be aware of. Since this vocation regards the audience as fundamental, you should, in accordance with the times, adjust the imitation of something strong a bit toward the direction of *yūgen* when you are in front of an audience that enjoys *yūgen*.

There is something that the writer, too, should keep in mind about this strategy. When writing, he should focus on choosing characters that can be treated with *yūgen* and, all the more, keep his intent[71] and language elegant. If there is no imposture, he will naturally appear to be an actor who expresses *yūgen*. When you have completely understood the principle of *yūgen*, you will also understand what is strong. And as long as you truly resemble the object of imitation, you will have nothing to worry about in the way you appear to others. When you have nothing to worry about, that is strength.

Likewise, in the very resonances of unobtrusive words such as *nabiki* [sway], *fusu* [lie down], *kaheru* [return home], and *yoru* [approach] are opportunities for a gestural echo, because these words are gentle. *Otsuru* [fall], *kudzururu* [crumble/collapse], *yabururu* [be broken/defeated], *marobu* [topple/fall down], and so on all have strong resonances, so their accompanying movements should be strong, too.[23]

Because of this, you should know that strength and *yūgen* are not discrete phenomena but stem from directness in dramatic imitation and that weakness and coarseness result from divergence from dramatic imitation.

71. The concern here for intent (*kokoro*) and language (*kotoba*) reflects the age-old concerns of *waka* poetics.

Given this consideration, a writer is wrongheaded to insert coarse words, arcane and outlandish Sanskrit spells, Chinese collocations, and the like in opening lines such as for the *issei* and *waka*, the very places where he is aiming for gestures evocative of, and opportunities for the expression of, *yūgen*. To be sure, in some situations it would be out of character to perform exactly as the words of the text prescribe. A really accomplished person, however, understands these inconsistencies and maneuvers through them deftly, with creativity and ingenuity. Such comes from the genius of the actor. This doesn't mean we should simply overlook wrongheadedness in the writer. Then again, even though the writer may write with understanding, if the actor is oblivious to the potential, then that's another question altogether. That's how it is.

Also, some plays should not depend so much on language and discursive ingenuity and should be performed expansively, depending on the play. In such a play, you should dance and sing in a straightforward way and perform the stage business smoothly and expeditiously. To fuss and fidget over such a play, moreover, is the technique of a poor actor. You should know as well that this is the way such a play is diminished. Consequently, a search for choice language and gestural echoes should be reserved for plays with discursive ingenuity and points of concentrated interest. In a straightforward play, even if a character with *yūgen* is given difficult language to sing, it should work out well as long as the melodic structure is clear-cut. These, then, are matters that you should understand as basic guidelines for plays. Once you have thoroughly understood these notes, you will need to perform with poise and self possession, or all this instruction will be for naught.

• In regard to the success or failure of a play, you should know how suitably it is matched with the rank of the actor. There should be expansive plays of quite high rank, not particularly polished in terms of language or general tone, but strictly faithful to their source. Such plays may not have anything worthy of particularly detailed scrutiny. A generally expert actor may not be quite right for such plays. Even if the actor is an unsurpassed master of a level fully suitable to such plays, unless the play is performed for an audience of connoisseurs in a grand venue, it will not always be such a great success. Unless there is a high degree of suitability among the rank of the play, the rank of the actor, the audience, the venue, and the occasion, all these things, it will not be all that easy to succeed in performance.

There are, as well, unprepossessing little plays without a particularly impressive source, which nonetheless display *yūgen* and have a certain delicacy. These are often very good for beginning actors. For venue, they are likely to be suitable to religious festivals in out-of-the-way places or nighttime performances. Sophisticated members of the audience and good actors as well, beguiled by their interest in country performances or unobtrusive venues elsewhere may bring them to the stage with similar intent in grand venues, before aristocrats and such or on occasions meant to highlight a particular performer, only to find that they don't turn out well and that as a consequence, the actor's reputation is damaged and the sponsor loses face, too.

So unless an actor is such that he is unlimited in his choice of repertory or performance venue and there is no better or worse among his performances, he cannot be called a fully expert master of the peerless flower. When it comes to an expert who is suitable to any sort of performance context, there is no need to tell him what is right and what is wrong.

Also, some actors do not have a knowledge of performance commensurate with their skill in performing, and some actors know more about performance than their skill would suggest. The former, though successful before aristocratic audiences and in grand venues, may misunderstand performance and be stymied in other cases, because they don't know it. Then again, there are actors whom one might call beginners, who don't have that much real skill and command only a limited repertory but who don't lose the flower in important venues, who gain increasing appreciation from all, and who show hardly any inconsistency in their performances; this must be because they know performance disproportionately better than their actual skill therein.

Opinions are divided regarding these two types of performers. All the same, one's renown is likely to last longer if one's performances are successful each time before aristocratic audiences and in grand venues. And if that is so, isn't it also true that a troupe leader who has a clear knowledge of performance (even if he is lacking in certain respects as a performer himself) is preferable to one who doesn't really know performance as well as his skill would suggest? The performer who truly knows performance also knows where his own skill is wanting, so in an important performance, he refrains from something that is unlikely to succeed and emphasizes that manner of expression at which he is skilled; since the outcome is good, there is unfailing appreciation among his audience. You should thus use performances in unobtrusive and out-of-the-way venues to accustom yourself to aspects of your performance that don't always go as you wish. If you train in such a way, there will eventually come a time when those unsatisfactory aspects will turn out more to your satisfaction. In the end, then, your performance will gain grandeur, the grime will fall away, and your own fame will prosper, as will the troupe's, and then, certainly, the flower will remain with you as long as your years may last. This is because right from the beginning, you know performance. If you employ every bit of your ingenuity through a mind that knows performance, then you will know the seeds that produce the flower. In any case, people have their own opinions about these two types of performers and will determine which is better, as they are pleased to do so.[72]

"Written Preparations for the Flower," complete as above.
These notes should not be shown to anyone other than serious professional aspirants.
Zea (signature)

Separate Pages of Oral Instructions

On the matter of knowing the flower, read through these oral instructions. First, you might, say, look at a flower in bloom and you will understand the reason why in all things, we have come to use the flower for comparison.

A flower, you see, is particularly appreciated for its rarity when its time comes, since it among all the trees and grasses blooms in response to the change of seasons. In *sarugaku* as well, the mind perceives as interesting what it knows to be rare. The flower, what is interesting, and what is rare, these three all mean the same thing. Is there any blossom, after all, that does not scatter but lasts on and on? Precisely because it scatters, a blossom is rare when in bloom. In performance as well, we should, above all, recognize what does not stay the same as the flower. Rarity comes from not clinging to the same but moving on to other forms of expression.

There is, however, something worth noting here. This does not mean that you should dredge up some form of expression that has no place in the world merely on the pretext that it is rare. What you should do is complete a comprehensive training in accordance with the various notes presented in *Transmitting the Flower*, and then when you are ready to put on *sarugaku*, you should choose from the repertory in accordance with your particular circumstances. Is there any rare flower in the world apart from those that bloom in accordance with their time and season? Also, once you master the many roles that you have undertaken to learn, you should select a manner of expression that suits the season and occasion and reflects people's preferences; this is like keeping an eye out for seasonal flowers in bloom. That flower I speak of, moreover, comes from the seeds of last year's flowers. So in performance, even though various sorts of expression have been seen before, it takes a long time to exhaust your repertory once you have mastered a diversity of roles. Thus it is that something is rare when you see it once again after a long time.

72. *Seubu woba sadametamafu beshi.* The use of the honorific *tamafu* here (and two other places in the sixth book) may indicate that this book was intended for transmission to someone other than the person for whom the earlier books were written. See Omote, in *ZZ*, pp. 54n, 552.

What's more, people's tastes vary, and whether it's a matter of song or movement or dramatic imitation, they are different from place to place, so it is necessary to master many different forms of expression. Mastering a truly diverse repertory, then, is like having in your hands the seeds necessary to bring into bloom any flower from the full year's cycle, from the plums of early spring to autumn's chrysanthemums.[73] Then no matter what flower it may be, you can bring it out according to the wishes of your audience and the season. If you do not master such a diverse repertory, then at times you will fail to bring a particular season's flower into bloom. How, for instance, will an actor who knows only how to bring the flowers of spring into bloom manage when spring has passed and it's time to appreciate the flowers of summer plants? How will he bring into bloom that season's flowers when all he has to offer are the flowers of spring? There, that should make it clear.

Now as for the "flowers": the flowers in question are what is seen to be rare in the minds of your audience. These oral instructions, then, are what I referred to earlier in a passage from *Transmitting the Flower* where it says that after you have made the fullest use of the repertory and used every bit of your creativity, you will know the kind of flower that doesn't fade. When I refer to the flower, then, it's nothing particularly special. Giving your utmost to the repertory, finding a way to use your creativity, and understanding what creates the excitement of rarity: that's what the flower is. This is what I meant when I wrote, "The flower is the mind, the seed, the techniques of performance."

In the section on demons from "Notes on Dramatic Imitation," I even said, "The actor who only does demons well must not understand what's interesting about demons."[74] When an actor who has mastered a diverse repertory chooses to perform the role of a demon once in a great while, then, because of its rarity, it becomes the flower and is likely to be interesting. If you think someone is good only at portraying a demon, without other forms of expression, then even though it may appear that he performs that role well, there is nothing particularly unusual about it, so there is not likely to be a flower in what the audience sees. As when I said the role was "like a flower blooming out of a boulder," unless you make the demon strong and terrifying and bloodcurdling, then you don't have the basic manner of expression right. That is the boulder. What I mean by the flower is the sense of rarity experienced by your audience; they are accustomed to the actor in question and know him to be fully versed in all forms of expression, with a supreme

73. "Plum" is a conventional appellation for *Prunus mume*, sometimes also called a Japanese apricot. It is not the same tree as produces a sweet and fleshy fruit in midsummer.

74. This isn't exactly what Zeami said in the place mentioned; the text there reads, "The actor who does only demons well can hardly be one who understands the flower."

command of *yūgen*, yet here he is performing a demon!—that is the flower. The actor who performs only the role of the demon is merely a boulder; there won't be any flower there.

• It has been said, in detailed oral instruction, that singing, dance, vigorous exercise, stage business, and bearing all are of a single frame of mind. This means that when you perform the usual movements and sing in the usual way, people think to themselves, that's just what I expected; but you don't permit yourself to cling to that, and instead you set your sight on performing the movements (even though they are the same old movements) ever so lightly, or maybe you tax your ingenuity over precedents in order to sing (even though it is the same old song) with a certain something extra, paying additional attention to the timbre of your voice; then you will perform the action or singing at hand with great concentration, aware in your own mind that you've never devoted so much attention to it before, and your audience will be impressed, saying the performance is even more interesting than usual. Isn't this that very rarity in the frame of mind of your audience that I have been talking about?

So although the singing and overall bearing are the same, what a talented actor aims to do should be interesting in a particular way. A poor actor has no thought of the unusual, since he performs just those notes that he remembers learning. The talented actor performs the same melody, but he is aware of a certain twist.[75] What I mean by a "twist" is a flower in the melody. Among the same talented performers, with the same dramatic flower, the one who has given the most consideration to this problem knows, moreover, the flower of victory. In general terms, singing the melody is a fixed pattern, whereas the "twist" is something particular to the talented performer. In dancing, the movements represent a learned pattern, but a graceful bearing is something particular to the talented performer.

• In dramatic imitation, there is, surely, a rank of no imitation. Once you have brought dramatic imitation to its limits and have truly entered into the object of imitation, you have no intention of imitating. Therefore, if you make the places of interest your central consideration, how could there not be a flower in your performance? If, for example, it is a matter of imitating an old man, an accomplished actor will approach the role with the same intent as that of an ordinary old man who has gotten himself up in fancy dress to dance the *furyū-ennen*.[76] Being an old man to begin with, the actor has no

75. Zeami introduces a subtle distinction here among the prescribed (and sometimes notated) musical notes (*fushihakase*), the melody indicated by them (*fushikakari*), and a certain interesting "twist" (*kyoku*) given to it by a skillful actor.

76. The *furyū-ennen* were colorful dance celebrations performed widely by the people of Kyoto from the late Heian through the Muromachi period. *Furyū* were parades of people in bright costumes connected with the Gion Festival of the Yasaka Shrine or other religious festivals intended

need to imitate an old man. No, instead he concentrates all his efforts on the role he performs in dramatic imitation suiting the occasion.[77]

Also, the oral instructions regarding the way to seem old and still bring your performance to full dramatic flower are as follows: First of all, don't set your mind on the decrepitude of age. Both Dance and Sparring are performed in time to music, and the actor is to stomp his feet, extend and draw back his arms, perform his movements, and reflect in his attitudes the beat of the music. The fact is, though, that when you grow old, you stomp your feet, extend and draw back your arms, perform your movements, and strike your bodily attitudes just a little late, falling slightly behind the rhythm, a bit later than the *taiko* drum, the chant, and the main beats of the *tsuzumi* drum.[78] This more than anything else serves as a point of reference for portraying an old man. Just keep this consideration in your mind, and otherwise act as you would usually but with much more color and vividness. Generally in the mind of an old person is the desire to do everything just as if he were young. Unavoidably, however, his limbs are heavy, his hearing is slow, and although the heart is willing, the movements of his body don't make the grade. If you understand the truth of this, then that is genuine dramatic imitation. The techniques of performance should be carried out as the old man would wish, with a youthful attitude. This, I would say, is because in an old man's mind, the young are to be envied and their attitude is to be imitated, isn't that so? But even though the old man may try his hardest to act as if he were young, the fact is that he unavoidably falls behind in the rhythm. An old man acting as if he were young contains the principle of the rare. It's like a flower in blossom on an ancient tree.

• On mastering the ten styles[79] in performance. The actor who has mastered the ten styles can run through the same things sequentially time and time again, but since it takes a while to complete the cycle, he will always

to eradicate epidemic disease. *Ennen* were celebrations at which originally priest performers and later professional performers danced and displayed their talents for the increased longevity of the participants. Like *furyū*, *ennen* seem to have begun in the late Heian period. They became prevalent in the Kamakura and Muromachi periods, and were connected with charismatic Buddhist sects.

77. Compare Fujiwara no Teika on the celebrated poet Ariwara no Narihira: "When composing a love poem, abandon your ordinary self, and imagining how Narihira would have behaved, compose your poem as if you were Narihira" ("Kyōgoku chūnagon sōgobun," in Hisamatsu Sen'ichi and Nishio Minoru, eds., *Karonshū nōgakuronshū*, vol. 1, *Chūsei no bungaku*, NKBT, vol. 65 [Tokyo: Iwanami shoten, 1965], p. 333, trans. David Bialock, "Voice, Text, and Poetic Borrowing," *Harvard Journal of Asiatic Studies* 54, no. 1 [1994]: 212–13).

78. The *taiko* is a stick drum used in roughly 15 percent of the modern nō repertory. The *tsuzumi* is an hourglass-shaped drum used in nearly all nō performances. For further detail, see the introduction and appendix 1.

79. *Jittei* (lit., "ten styles") does not mean ten different categories of performance but is a way of encouraging a broad repertory.

seem to have something rare to offer. The person who has mastered the ten styles will, in his ingenuity and creativity in them, be able to spread out into a hundred different varieties of expression. He probably will have the breadth of consideration to vary things for rarity of expression, running through his repertory piece by piece without repetition for three to five years. This gives him a broad and confident position from which to perform. Also, during the course of the year, you should be clearly aware of the four seasons. And when it's a matter of *sarugaku* performed over several days, it goes without saying that you should think carefully about the sequence and variety of the plays you perform. If, in this way, you think over everything, beginning with matters of great importance and extending to little details, you should not lose the flower throughout your career.

Also, it has been said that rather than[24] knowing the ten styles, make sure you don't forget the flower that comes and goes, year in and year out.[25] As for the flower that comes and goes, year in and year out . . . —well, for instance, the ten styles are the varieties of dramatic imitation—what comes and goes, year in and year out, that is a matter of having all the various means of expression in this art under your control at one time, from the visual charm of a child, through the technique acquired by a beginner, to the movement of a mature young actor, to the manner of expression of an actor grown old. At one time in performance you may appear to be a boy or youngster; at another time, a man in his prime; at still another a fully mature and much seasoned performer, performing in such a way that you don't appear to be the same person from occasion to occasion. This is the principle of commanding all the artistic skills of a lifetime at one time, from the time of your childhood until past your old age. That is why we speak of the flower that comes and goes, year in and year out.

I have not, however, either seen or heard of an actor who reached this rank, whether long ago or more recently. I have heard only that in the prime of his youth, my late father was particularly accomplished in a manner of expression suggesting long experience in performance. I have no doubt about this, since I was well accustomed to seeing him in his forties. When he took the role of Lay Priest Jinen,[80] the way he performed on the preacher's dais created such a stir that the people who saw it said he looked like a sixteen- or seventeen-year old.[81] This is something that I actually heard from other people and witnessed with my own eyes, so I am confident that he was such a master fully suited to this rank of performance. I have neither seen nor heard

80. Although Lay Priest Jinen (or Jinen Koji, as mentioned here) refers to a character, a play of that name exists and could plausibly be attributed to Kannami. It is about a young Buddhist aspirant who saves a girl from slave traders by dancing and performing other entertainments.

81. Note Zeami's inconsistency in his later report of the occasion, in *Conversations on Sarugaku*, where he says Kannami looked only twelve or thirteen (*ZZ*, p. 265).

of another actor who, in this way, mastered in his youth the manner of expression of a long seasoned master actor and also sustained in his body after he had aged the manner of expression that he had been able to command in the past.

You should not forget any of the various elements of the art, starting from what you learned as a beginner, but pick and choose what you need on a particular occasion. Is it not wonderfully rare to be able to perform as a long-seasoned actor when you still are young and to sustain the attractions of your prime even when you have aged? For this reason, if once your artistic rank rises, you abandon and forget one by one the means of expression you used to employ, it will be just like throwing away seeds for the flower. What you will have then are just the flowers of those individual occasions; without seeds, they're nothing more than plucked flowers. But if you have seeds, how would you not be able to respond to the needs of each season, year after year? Above all, you must not forget your initial intent. It is for this reason that it is so common to hear statements of praise like "Hasn't he grown up quickly!" or "Look at how experienced he's become!" with reference to young actors, and "My, how youthful he looks!" with reference to old actors. Doesn't this show the rationale for rarity? If you use the ten styles to color your performance, it will give you a hundred colors to choose from. If in addition to this, you retain in your personal performance style the elements of performance that come and go, year in and year out, what a great flower you shall command!

• On being attentive to all things in performance. When, for example, you perform in a manner expressive of anger, you must not forget gentleness of mind. This will give you a method of acting as angry as you wish without becoming coarse. To maintain a gentleness of mind when angry is the principle of rarity. Again, in dramatic imitation requiring *yūgen*, you must not forget the principle of strength. This exemplifies the principle of, in all things, resisting the urge to cling, whether in Dance, in Sparring, in dramatic imitation, in anything.

Also, there must always be intent in making the use of the body. When you move your body strongly, you should hold back in stomping your feet. When you stomp your feet strongly, you should carry your body quietly. It is difficult to convey this in writing. It is something for face-to-face oral instruction. [This is discussed in detail under the titled sections of *Learning the Flower.*][82]

82. *Learning the Flower* (*Kashū*, 花習, orth. *Kashifu*) is the earlier form of the treatise that later was entitled *Kakyō* (orth. *Kakyau*), translated here as *A Mirror to the Flower. Kakyō* consists of six "titled" sections, each beginning with a catchphrase in addition to several subsequent sections, also with titles. These were not catchphrases but individual titles, each ending with the word *koto* and thus termed *kotogaki*. See Omote, in *ZZ*, p. 89n.

• On knowing the flower of secrecy: "When you keep it secret, it's the flower. Unless you keep it secret, it cannot be the flower," that's it. To understand this distinction is a flower of crucial importance.[26]

That is, in the houses of the various artistic vocations, the assertion by a given house that something is a matter of secrecy has a great effect, specifically because it is kept secret. For that reason, when these secrets are made known, they are not things of particularly great consequence. But the person who admits they are nothing of great consequence does so because he doesn't really understand the great utility of secrets.

For instance, if everyone knew that the flower is merely what is fresh, as these oral instructions explain, then, before an audience of people who would be expecting to see something fresh, even if you were to perform something fresh, they would not likely perceive it in their minds as particularly fresh and exciting. It becomes the flower for the actor precisely because the viewers do not know that it is the flower. Instead, the viewers just see the actor and think that he is surprisingly interesting, and the fact that they are not conscious of this as the flower in itself becomes the actor's flower. To just this extent, then, the plan to evoke unexpected excitement in people's minds—this is the flower.

For example, among the plans of those in the vocation of arms, the stratagem of a great general may, by employing an unexpected plan, result in victory over a powerful rival. What is this, in fact, other than that the defeated party loses because it has been fooled in accord with the principle of freshness? In all matters, this is the principle by which victory is attained in contests in the various artistic vocations. A plan like this would be easy to defend oneself against, after the fact, when one understands with hindsight: Ah, so that's what it was all about, but at the time, one loses because one doesn't yet understand it. For that reason, one preserves these things carefully, for the good of the line, as secrets.

In light of the preceding, know this. Not only should you not reveal secrets, but you should not even be identified as someone who knows such secrets. When you end up having your intent known to someone else, then, provided your rival is not negligent but alert, it will warn him to be wary. When your rival is not wary, it still should be easy for you to prevail against him. Is it not, in fact, a great effect of the principle of freshness to be able to win, having lulled your rival into neglectfulness? For that reason, you gain a lifelong mastery of the flower when you keep others from knowing some-

Kashifu should be distinguished from section 6 of *Transmitting the Flower*, 花修云, "Kashiu ni iwaku" (translated here as "Written Preparations for the Flower"), even though in modern Japanese, both Kashifu and Kashiu are pronounced similarly: Kashū and Kashu.

thing because it is a family secret. When you keep it secret, it's the flower. Unless you keep it secret, it cannot be the flower.

The ultimate is knowing the flower of cause and consequence. Everything is dependent on cause and consequence. The many things that one learns in the art as a beginner and thereafter are the cause. Performing with expertise and gaining fame are the consequence. When, therefore, you are indifferent to cause (in your training, that is), it will also become impossible to realize the consequence. You must be fully aware of this.

Also, you must respect the occasion. If last year all was at its peak, this year, you should be aware that there may be no flower. Each brief moment may be either male time or female time.[83] No matter what you may do, if there are good times in performance, then there are certain to be bad times as well. This is a cause and consequence over which you have no power. Be well aware of this, and when you are performing *sarugaku* on an occasion that is not all that important, you may hold back in performance, not knocking yourself out to be victorious in competition, not breaking your neck, and not being particularly worried if you lose; then just as the audience has started to lose interest, thinking, What is this all about, just then, on the day of an important *sarugaku* performance, you change your plan, and perform a hallmark play expertly, displaying your virtuosity, your audience will be taken by surprise, and you will certainly prevail with a great victory in an important contest. This is the great effect of the fresh. The disappointments of recent days can thereby be causes that lead to good consequences.

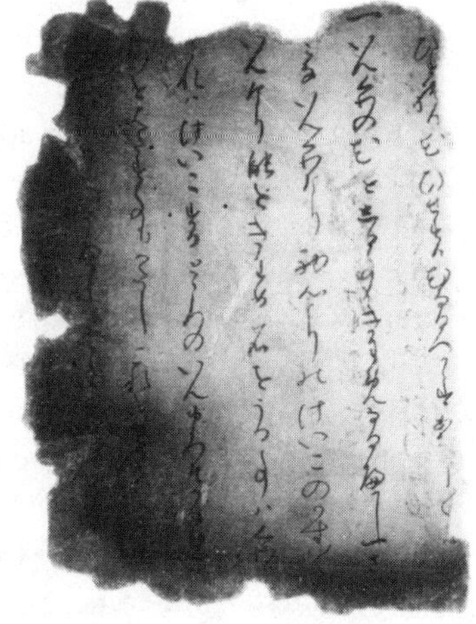

A leaf from Zeami's autograph manuscript of "Separate Pages of Oral Instructions," from *Transmitting the Flower Through Effects and Attitudes*. The second line from the right begins the section reading, "The ultimate is knowing the flower of cause and consequence. . . ." Although nearly invisible in a black-and-white image, the text includes some interlinear notes in red. It was badly damaged in a fire, but what remains is invaluable both because it is in Zeami's hand and because it preserves the earliest form of the text, for transmission to Zeami's younger brother, Shirō. (Photograph from the collection of Kanze Bunko Foundation)

83. As becomes clear in a later passage, *odoki* (orth. *wodoki* [male time]) is considered advantageous, whereas *medoki* (female time) is considered disadvantageous to the performer.

Now then, when you have three *sarugaku* performances on three consecutive days,[84] you should hold back on the first day and blend in with the rest of the performance, and then, on the day you feel is the most important of the three, choose a good play, a showcase for your particular talents, and perform it with striking intensity.[27] If on the very first day you are faced with the disadvantage of female time during a match performance, hold back at first, and then, once your opponent's advantage in male time has declined to the disadvantage of female time, perform a good play with vigor and concentration. This is the opportunity to take back the male time for your side. If this play turns out well, it should give you first place for that day.

This business of male time and female time means that in every competition, there is bound to be a time when you may show yourself to advantage. This is considered male time. If the competition extends over several performances, the advantageous time will switch back and forth between the rivals. A certain text[28] has it that "the gods of victory and defeat, the so-called *shōbujin*, preside over performance venues and keep watch. This is considered a particular secret among warriors." If your rival's *sarugaku* comes off well, you should be aware that the god of victory is with him, and be wary. Two gods oversee the moments of cause and consequence, and they alternate back and forth, so when you believe that it has become an advantageous time for your side, you should perform a reliable play. This is none other than the cause and consequence of venue. Take care not to ignore it. If you have confidence, you shall gain the advantage.

• We have it that there are good and bad occasions, which we refer to in terms of cause and consequence, but if we consider this problem comprehensively, it will resolve into a simple matter of two things: what is fresh . . . and what is not. You may watch the same talented actor in the same play yesterday and today, but what appeared so interesting before will not be interesting at all now; what you had been accustomed to think of as interesting yesterday appears uninteresting, and therefore bad, today. Then later on, on some occasion when it seems good, it is because earlier you had in your mind thought of it as not so good, but it changed into something fresh and became interesting. Therefore, once you have attained real expertise in this vocation and learned its ins-and-outs, you will understand that what we call the flower is nothing in particular. Unless you have become expert in the ultimate accomplishments of this vocation and come to see the principle of freshness in all things, there can be no flower.

It says in a certain sutra, "Good and bad are not two, false and true are a single reality."[85] Fundamentally, what are we to use to determine good and

84. Standard for *kanjin sarugaku* subscription performances.

85. 善悪不二、邪正一如. The sentence sums up the doctrine of nonduality as it is expressed in, for example, the ninth chapter of Vimalakīrti-nirdeśa Sutra, "The Dharma-Door of Nonduality"

bad? It is merely a matter of regarding as good what suffices and as bad what is insufficient at a given time. So, too, regarding various forms of expression: those forms that you select in consideration of the prevailing tastes of people at a given time, in a particular place—those are the flowers that aptly serve your need. If one style of expression is enjoyed here, then another style will be appreciated there. This is the flower of various different people and their minds. Which of these is to be counted authentic? You should know as the flower what serves the interests of the given occasion.

• These "Separate Pages of Oral Instruction" are of great importance to the house in this art and are to be transmitted to a single person in each generation. If your sole descendant is someone without talent, then you should not transmit this to him. It is said, "A house is not, in itself, a house. It is made a house through its transmission from generation to generation. A person is not, in himself, a person, but he becomes a person through knowing."[86] This is the means to the wondrous flower for the fulfillment of the myriad virtues in this art.

• The notes in these "Separate Pages" were transmitted to my younger brother Shirō[87] some years ago, but there are adequate grounds for their transmission hereby to Mototsugu,[88] since he has proved himself to be a master of performance. Secret transmission, secret transmission.

Ōei 25 [1418]:6:1, Ze (signature)[89]

Notes

1. In one possible reading of this passage, the term translated as "promotion of long life" (*ennen*) is taken to refer to a distinct performing art of the middle ages. Omote rejects this view in favor of the version on which this translation is based, that of *sarugaku* as a "life-stretching art."

(Robert Thurman, trans., *The Holy Teaching of Vimalakīrti* [University Park: Pennsylvania State University Press, 1981]), but the phrase itself is not found there. Tanaka also cites *Shuzen jiketsu* 4, attributed to Saichō, and *Mineaiki*, where it is mentioned as encapsulating the Tendai doctrine of *isshin sankan*.

86. The source of this quotation has not yet been identified. It appears in identical form in Shinkei's *Sasamegoto*, possibly through transmission by Zenchiku from here.

87. Zeami's younger brother, the father of Saburō (orth. Saburau) Motoshige—that is, Onnami. Note that the existence of the *Sōsetsu-bon* text, with its colophon for Motoshige, contradicts or at least complicates Zeami's injunction that the text is to be transmitted to only one person per generation.

88. It is unclear to whom this refers. Tanaka suggests an elder brother of Motomasa named Gorō (orth. Gorau), whose religious name was Gensen shami, whereas Omote suggests that Mototsugu was an earlier name of Motomasa himself. See Tanaka Yutaka, ed., *Zeami geijutsuron shū*, vol. 35 of *Shinchōsha koten shūsei* (Tokyo: Shinchōsha, 1976), and *ZZ*, p. 65.

89. The "signature" in question is a *kaō*, a presumably unique monogram generally composed of graphs from the writer's name and used much as we use a signature.

2. I use "dramatic imitation" to translate Zeami's *monomane*, a technical term for the representation of specific characters or character types on stage. See also the introduction.

3. Zeami uses the term *kōan* here (my "problem"), taken from the vocabulary of Zen Buddhism. In Zen, especially Rinzai Zen, the term might more appropriately be translated as "case." Kōan often are paradoxical or seemingly nonsensical but are purportedly used to jar the practitioner into a deeper level of understanding. Such a meaning is not completely unlike Zeami's use of the term, but at the same time he seems to use it in a less technical and less dramatic way, to mean something more like "a matter for serious consideration."

4. *Kokuō* (orth. *Kokuwau*), which I have translated as "king," is ambiguous. Although it might be taken to mean the "heavenly sovereign," conventionally called the "emperor" (*tennō*), it is more likely to mean the reigning shogun. Recall Yoshimitsu's acceptance of the title *Nippon kokuō* from the Ming court.

5. Zeami's text mentions two articles of clothing here. The first, *kinu*, is a generic term for robes as well as the word "silk," indicating the most desirable cloth for such robes. The second term, *hakama*, is a word referring to the broad trousers that both men and women might have worn on certain occasions. In modern nō, the most common "robe" worn is a specific type of short-sleeved kimono, the *kosode*, and the specific type of *hakama* is generally the *ōkuchi*, very broad trousers with wide openings on the sides of the body at the hips. For details on *sarugaku* and nō costuming, see Sharon Takeda, in collaboration with Monica Bethe, *Miracles and Mischief: Noh and Kyōgen Theater in Japan* (Los Angeles: Los Angeles County Museum of Art, and Tokyo: Agency for Cultural Affairs, Government of Japan, 2002).

6. Omote reads *sono michi* here and earlier in the same article to refer to professional prognosticators and fortune-tellers, and I have followed his lead. Konishi Jin'ichi (*Zeami shū*, Nihon no shisō, vol. 8 [Tokyo: Chikuma shobō, 1970], p. 53) and Yamazaki Masakazu (*Zeami*, Nihon no meicho, vol. 10 [Tokyo: Chūō kōronsha, 1969]) read it as a reference to nō acting with, consequently, different results. Omote is persuasive in that in all the treatises, Zeami uses the demonstrative adjectives very selectively. Clearly, when he says *kono michi*, he means this vocation of *sarugaku*, but he uses *sono michi* only twice, both times in this question-and-answer format. Accordingly, I have distinguished the usages by referring to *sono michi* as "business" and *kono michi* as "vocation." The inconsistency in translation is justified by Zeami's apparent skepticism about prognostication.

7. Following Omote's reasoning in reading the first *kanji* in the line as *hi* rather than *shi*. See *ZZ*, p. 438n.22.

8. *Ageku* (挙句), borrowed from the vocabulary of *renga*, where it signifies the last 7–7 verse of the sequence. Here the term does not refer to so brief a passage but borrows a similar sense of cadence or finality.

9. *Take* (長) is translated as "stature," and *kasa* (嵩) as "grandeur," in contradistinction to *kurai* (位). Zeami is, it seems, inconsistent in his explanation.

10. In his first reference to the word, Zeami uses a perfective verbal form, *shihoretaru*, but in translating it, I found it preferable to pretend the word is a nominal *shiore* (Zeami's spelling is *shihore*), since that is the way he later treats the concept. There is no agreement on the interpretation of the word. The word is written consistently in *kana* and may be close to the modern *shiore*, 萎れ (and which should be written in *kana* in more orthodox traditional orthography as *shiwore* rather than *shihore*). This word means something like "wilted" or "withered." But as Konishi Jin'ichi says, it may be more appropriately interpreted according to a now obsolete meaning, 霑 (drenched), which would correctly be written *shihore* ("Shihori no setsu," in *Bashō*, Nihon bungaku kenkyū shiryō sōsho, vol. 32 [Tokyo: Yūseidō, 1969], pp. 241–49).

11. The syntax of the first sentence here is ambiguous and has been taken to mean that Zeami disregards the censure of the world at large for writing down material that should, by rights, be transmitted only orally. I have tried to retain the ambiguity of the passage in translating it but follow Omote and Katō in their assertion that the censure referred to is what the world at large directs against actors who let their vocation fall into decline. See *ZZ*, p. 433n.15.

12. *Seinō* (細男, orth. *seinau*) The word used normally refers to a performer of interludes in *kagura*, but I follow Omote's note here, reading the word as a reference to performance rather than to performer.

13. *On'omote shirokarikeri* (Their august faces shone white) is the folk etymology of the word *omoshiroshi* (mod. J. *omoshiroi* [interesting]) an important term in Zeami's aesthetic vocabulary.

14. The word *keseu* is uncertain and has been the focus of various conjectures, ranging from 見証 (enlightenment) to 見所 ([critical praise from] the audience). Here I have followed Kōsai Tsutomu's suggestion, 戯笑 (*Zeami shinkō* [Tokyo: Wan'ya shoten, 1962], pp. 233–36).

15. *Giri* (儀理): Omote suggests that this means a kind of linguistic interest or interest in argumentation exemplified by the dialogue in the first half of *Sotoba Komachi* or the Zen dialogue in *Hōkazō*. See *ZZ*, pp. 437–38n.21.

16. Probably an early form of the play now entitled *Yoshino Shizuka*.

17. Perhaps an earlier incarnation of the play *Hyakuman*.

18. A slight variation on a passage at the end of the section "Notes in Question-and-Answer Form."

19. The extant texts give two variants at this point. The *Konparu-bon* and *Sōsetsu-bon* texts read *shigi in iwaku*, 私義云 (regarding private matters), rather than *higi ni iwaku*, 秘義云 (regarding secret matters). But when written in a cursive hand, the two Chinese graphs *shi* and *hi* are fairly similar, and there is a good chance that *shigi* is a mistranscription of *higi*. See *ZZ*, p. 438n.22.

20. According to Omote's suggestion, reading *koko ni* for *koto ni*.

21. *Shōjiki enmyō* (orth. *shyaudjiki yenmyau*) is unclear. *Shōjiki* is relatively comprehensible as "honest," "straightforward," or the like, but *yenmyau* has been parsed with the *kanji* 延命 and 円明. The latter combination seems more likely (see *ZZ*, p. 46) but still leaves us uncertain. *En*, as "round," suggests plenitude or well-roundedness, and *myō* suggests "luminosity" or "brilliance." But as a compound the word seems unattested elsewhere in Zeami's oeuvre, and we can only speculate that it means something like "clarity."

22. *Kyausau* is obscure but Omote sees it as meaning "crazy" or "frivolous." See *ZZ*, p. 49nn.

23. Not many of the words Zeami lists here appear in his plays, but for reference, the following is a sample of their occurrences in plays closely associated with him:

Kami no megumi ni *nabiku* ka to harumekiwataru (*Oimatsu*), "Spring begins to dawn everywhere, as if under the *sway* of the gods' blessings."

Itoma maushite *kaheru* yama no haru no kozue ni saku ka to machishi hana (*Yamanba*), "Taking my leave I *return* to the mountains in spring, for the flowers I've awaited seem about to bloom on the twig tops."

Iki to shi ikeru monogoto ni Shikishima no kage ni *yoru* to ka ya (*Takasago*), "Each and every living thing *draws under* the shelter of Shikishima."

Yasakebi shite *otsuru* tokoro wo I-no-Hayata tsutto yorite tsudzukesama ni kokono katana zo saitarikeru (*Nue*), "The arrow whistled through the air, and I-no-Hayata raced to the spot where it *fell*, and stabbed the beast nine times."

Sono yume wo *yaburu* na, *yaburete* nochi ha kono koromo tare ka kite mo tofu beki (*Kinuta*), "Don't *tear* me away from this dream, for once I'm *torn away*, who will come to see me, who will don these lover's robes?"

24. There has been some controversy about how to read *yori ha* here. In some cases, the word can indicate the time *from which* something happens, but in that case we would expect a perfective before *yori* rather than the *mizenkei+mu* (*n*) auxiliary found here, so it is unlikely that this was the intended usage (despite the modern Japanese translations by Yamazaki [*Zeami*], Konishi, and Tanaka). Omote chose the comparative *yori*, and I have followed him. See *ZZ*, p. 440n.26.

25. Here, on first appearance, Zeami uses a Sinified reading of the expression, as *nennen kyorai no hana*, but at the end of the paragraph, he nativizes it as *toshidoshi sarikitaru hana*.

26. *Kan'yō no hana* is syntactically inverted, if we are to believe the glosses by Konishi (*hana no yōketsu de aru*), Yamazaki (*hana ni tsuite no jūdai na kadai na no de aru*), and Omote (*hana no kan'yōji de aru*). But perhaps Tanaka's syntactically stricter rendering is closer to the mark. He says that because of secrecy, understanding the distinction between what is and is not a flower is itself a flower of particular importance (*sore wa hana no naka de mo toku ni jūyō na hana de aru*).

27. The primary manuscript reads *tansei*, but I have followed Omote in his reliance on supplementary manuscripts reading *gansei* and *ganzei*, respectively. The word comes from Zen texts like *Hekiganroku* (Ch. *Biyanlü* [*The Blue Cliff Record*]) in the expression *gansei tosshutsu* (Ch. *yanjing tuchu* [the pupils pop out]) and indicates strength of personal commitment in the performance of an action.

28. アルモノニイハク (lit., "in a certain *thing* it says"). The thing is assumed to be a text by Omote, and I have followed him, but perhaps it means "a certain person says. . . ." In either case, it remains unidentified. Where the quotation ends is uncertain as well. Omote and Tanaka include only the first sentence; Konishi and Yamazaki, two sentences.

An Extract from *Learning the Flower*
花習内抜書, 1418

Learning the Flower is presumed to have originally been a larger text, of which only this extract survives. Some of the text, very slightly revised, is repeated in *Mirror to the Flower.* The content focuses on the central structural principle in Zeami's plays and performance, *jo-ha-kyū*, which was described in the introduction. In discussing how play and performance structure work, Zeami takes time to comment on what happens when this structure is disrupted by the arrival of important spectators after the performance already has begun. His advice for such a situation is practical and directed toward what the actor may do to remedy the disruption, but we also see here some indication of Zeami's relationship with his patrons.

❁

Jo-ha-kyū in Performance

Although *The Transmission of the Flower* discussed *jo-ha-kyū* in general terms, a few items remain for more detailed examination. First, since all things have their particular *jo*, *ha*, and *kyū*, it follows that you should determine them accordingly in writing plays.

Since it comes at the beginning, what I mean by the *jo* is a sense of foundation. It is, for this reason, correct and frontal in attitude.[1] In *sarugaku* then, the *waki* play[1] is *jo*. Its appeal should come from a thematically straightforward play, auspicious and without particular subtlety, proceeding correctly. Stage business should consist of just song and dance, alone. Song and dance should provide the basic expressive matter in this vocation. Consequently, a play for the *jo* should be constructed with song and dance. The next play should be one that differs in tone from the *waki* play; while faithful to its source and strong, it should create a deliberate, settled impression. Although this second play is different in tone from the *waki* play, it still uses

1. Zeami usually uses the term "*waki* play" to refer to the play that comes after (*waki* [lit., "alongside"]) *Shikisanban*, the ritual play with which formal full-day presentations were begun. *Shikisanban* wasn't performed in every performance, however, so the *waki* play came to mean more or less the same thing that it means today, the first play in a performance of several, treating straightforward and auspicious events in a clear and uncomplicated way.

the expressive effects of the *jo*, in that it is not a time for intricate technique and should not be too detailed.

One should enter into the *ha* with the third play. The word that I pronounce *ha* is written with the graph for "break."[2] This signifies the basic expressive effect and straightforward, orthodox style of the *jo* moving into a level of greater intricacy. What I mean by *jo* is a basic attitude, as it is; *ha* imparts a sense of explanation, softening that tone. That being the case, you should apply your technique with subtlety, your manner of expression based on imitation. This should be the most important play of the day. For the fourth play, you might stage some kind of discursively oriented play in a manner of expression that accomplishes its ends through dialogue and witty argumentation, or you might find it especially advantageous at this point to perform the kind of play that brings the audience to tears. The fourth or fifth play should still fall within the bounds of the *ha*.

What I mean by the word *kyū* is the last verse.[3] Since it gives the final impression for the day, this is in a manner of expression that creates closure. *Ha* is, as I said, the attitude that "breaks" the *jo*, exhausts a diversity of material in detail, and reveals things in all their particularity. What I mean by *kyū*, then, is what remains as a last impression once the *ha* has been thoroughly played out. For that reason, the *kyū* should be forceful and compact, with a startling visual character, with expressive effects focused on a swift, unconventional dance or Sparring.[2] The forcefulness of which I speak is for this time in a performance.

Generally in the past, a program of plays would not contain more than four or five pieces. Accordingly, the fifth play was, without exception, *kyū*, but now, with so many plays performed in a single program, that may be too early for the *kyū*; if the *kyū* is too long, the play probably won't turn out well. In performance, it is the *ha* that should last a long while. In the *ha*, one offers up the full variety of performance, so the *kyū* should be devoted exclusively to the climax. But when one is performing at the behest of an exalted person, the standard way of doing things may not apply because the sequence in performance may be out of the ordinary. Even in a case like this, maintain a clear awareness of the performance, and although you may have been asked to stage a play normally reserved for the *kyū*, if the play you are performing will be followed by something else, then you must hold back and restrain your physical performance to seven parts of ten (the mind, they say, is engaged for a full ten parts; the body engaged for seven parts of ten),[3] so as to hold something in reserve for the end.

2. Zeami indicates that the Chinese graph used to write *ha* is the one (破) in native Japanese pronunciation that means "break" or "split."

3. *Ageku* (挙句 [last verse]) is, in *renga*, the last 7–7 syllable link in a full sequence, and that sense is related to Zeami's intention here, although he is not so specific and certainly doesn't limit the *kyū* to fourteen syllables of text.

Herein lies a matter of great concern: Sometimes quite unexpectedly, an exalted person will arrive when you have already reached the time of the *ha* or *kyū* in your performance. So, although the *sarugaku* will already have proceeded as far as the *kyū*, that person's frame of mind will still be in the *jo*. In such a case, if that person watches your performance at the *kyū* while his frame of mind is in the *jo*, the performance will not meet his expectations. The people who have been watching all along will grow all the quieter because of the appearance of that person, and a peculiar change will come over the house, so that all the people and the house itself will appear to have been carried back to the *jo*. It is very difficult to make a success of the performance on such an occasion. In such a case, you might suppose that it would be appropriate to return the performance itself to the stage of *jo*, but for some reason, such a performance will turn out badly. This is really very difficult. Watch for the occasion when this is likely to occur, and choose a play suitable to the *ha*, but perform it with something of the *jo* in mind, then you might, with calm self-possession, be able to capture the attention of the person in question. In this way, having brought the intent of the exalted person under your influence, you might be able, with appropriate expertise, to direct the house gently through the *ha* and *kyū*. But even though you put all your ingenuity to work, it may not suffice in this situation.

You may also find yourself summoned to perform *sarugaku* unexpectedly before an elite audience at the last minute, when, for example, they have been drinking.[4] Now, in a situation like this, your audience will have already reached the *kyū*. The performance you are about to undertake will be at the *jo*. This, too, is of great difficulty. When performing on an occasion like this, even though the play is staged within the limits of *jo*, you should frame your intent with something of the *ha* and *kyū* in it and maintain a light touch, not dragging it out too much, so as to move fairly quickly into the *ha* and *kyū*. This case tests your expertise in performance, but sometimes the performance, though demanding, will be successful. That performance I mentioned before, when the exalted person comes late: it won't be easy to carry that one off. That's a difficult business.

The same considerations apply when you perform for a drinking party. When you sense that the party has almost reached its high point, you should look out for the right opportunity, use your fan to beat the rhythm, sing a few short auspicious pieces, and perform the singing and dancing,[4] building in an appropriate sequence that should proceed according to plan, since you've been watching for the right moment. If some exalted person should arrive unexpectedly in the middle of the party, then considering what I said before, you should return the *kyū* in some degree to the *jo*, using your expertise in

4. In these two paragraphs, Zeami appears to distinguish between *ohogoshu* (大御酒) and *sakamori* (酒盛り). Both seem to refer to performing for audiences that have been drinking. The distinction between the two doesn't seem to be the degree of drunkenness but the amount of the actor's advance preparation. In the former case, it seems that an elite audience suddenly calls for *sarugaku*, whereas in the latter, the occasion seems designated in advance as a drinking party.

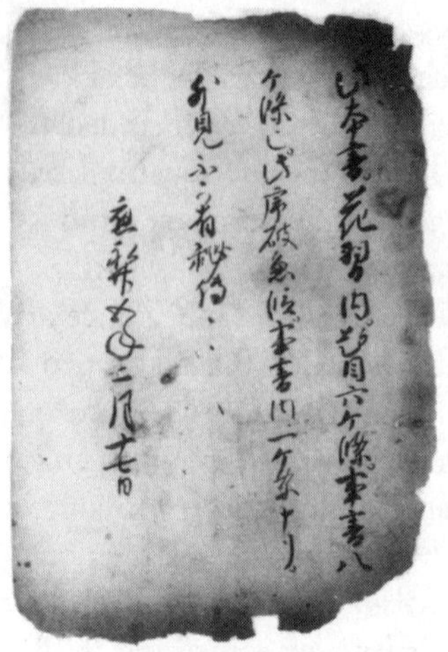

The final leaf from Zeami's handwritten manuscript of "An Extract from *Learning the Flower.*" Although the text does not bear Zeami's signature, part of it is written in *katakana* showing particularities also found in Zeami's autograph play scripts, attesting to its authenticity. (Photograph from the collection of Kanze Bunko Foundation)

performance. And if you yourself should arrive when the party has already reached the *kyū*, then take account of the advice I gave earlier, and perform the *jo* in a frame of mind directed somewhat toward the *kyū*.

So then as you consider *jo-ha-kyū*, whether in a grand formal performance, at a party, or even in a modest little musical gathering, be aware of the appropriate sequence.

Here above, the extract of a single article.

The original text for this, from *Learning the Flower*, consists of six articles with aphoristic titles and eight articles on specific matters.[5] This section on *jo-ha-kyū* is one of the articles on specific matters. This should not be shown to outsiders. It is a secret transmission; I repeat: a secret transmission.

Ōei 25 [1418]:2:17

Notes

1. *Omote naru sugata*, implying a (primarily) visual configuration from the front, in the sense of most recognizable, most proper, most formal, and most basic.

2. Sparring is, as noted earlier, a vigorous form of dance frequently mentioned in the *Performance Notes* (see appendix 1). What I have translated as a "swift, unconventional dance" is *ranbu* (乱舞), a term that occurs only twice in the *Performance Notes*, here and, in an almost identical passage, in *A Mirror to the Flower.*

3. This statement written here in parentheses is found between the lines to the right of the previous phrase in the original. See the section similarly entitled in *A Mirror to the Flower.*

4. *Shiugen no onkyoku* (祝言ノ音曲) refers apparently to short auspicious pieces characteristically used as party entertainments (even in some circles today). *Tachihataraki* (立チハタラキ) seems to mean the abbreviated excerpts from dance pieces that today go by the name *shimai*. See Omote, in *ZZ*, p. 71n.

5. The distinction between "articles with aphoristic titles" (*daimoku*, 題目) and "articles on specific matters" (*kotogaki*, 事書) is clear in the titles of the individual articles in *A Mirror to the Flower.*

Oral Instructions on Singing

音曲口伝, 1419

This text is a brief but technically challenging account of various aspects of singing and marks the beginning of Zeami's attempt to typologize singing styles. It also provides fairly lengthy examples of songs in the two types of singing, the *shiugen* and *bauwoku*, that he first distinguishes in his evolving understanding.

Zeami's first topic is the proper way to produce the voice. He insists that the actor listen to the pitch of the flute and then gather his "vital force" before finally breaking into song. The word I have translated here as "vital force" is the Japanese *ki*. Zeami uses the graph 機 for this word, but modern commentators stress its connection to the widespread East Asian concept typically written with the graph 気. This is a central element in East Asian psychological and physiological theory. It is pronounced *qi* in Chinese and has a distinct relation to breathing but also implies a flow of energy within the body. Although Zeami's use of the word does not seem inconsistent with this interpretation, his choice of the graph he uses to write *ki* is intriguing. It suggests a range of meanings related to "opportunity," "choice moment," and "vital force." Accordingly, I have chosen to leave this word in untranslated romanization.

After discussing vocal production, Zeami turns to proper elocution—when it does and does not matter—and then to comments on training the voice. In this section of the text, he introduces an important, but unfortunately rather obscure, typology of individual voices: "*wau*," "*shu*," and "doubly proficient." This terminology was apparently not widely used in the fourteenth century, and it is not in current use today. Some examples of these terms can be found in medieval discussions of Buddhist chant (i.e., *shōmyō*), but there, too, the discussion is not specific enough to be of much help. The main terms in question are *wau no koye* (わうのこゑ, mod. J. *ō no koe*, written with the graphs 横の声) and *shu no koye* (しゅのこゑ, mod. J. *shu no koe*, written by Zeami in *kana* or as 主の声). Omote surmises that the former is a broad, strong and masculine sort of voice, whereas the latter is a more slender and weaker feminine sort of voice.[1] The predictable objections to gender characterizations may have some validity here, although the actors to which Zeami refers were exclusively male, and so the characterizations may in fact have some practical validity. But the contrast still remains puzzling. The *wau* voice is further paired with music in the *ryo* (呂) modes, whereas the *shu* voice is matched with music in the *ritsu* (律) modes.[2]

A performer able to perform well in both styles is characterized as *ahiwon* (あひをん, 相音, mod. J. *aion*), "doubly proficient [at singing]," but all performers, regardless of the natural propensity of their voices, are encouraged to become proficient in both types of singing.

A binarisim like *wau no koye / shu no koye* invites comparison with a common binarism in contemporary practice, that of *tsuyogin / yowagin*, but no direct connection has been uncovered. (The discussions of these vocal styles in the Buddhist sources just mentioned use the graphs 横 for the former and 竪, or the simpler 竪, for the latter.)

Zeami's discussion of *shiugen* singing and *bauwoku* singing occupies the last of his explanatory passages here, and it also introduces a distinction between *kusemai*-style singing and *tadautai* singing (the distinction between the two, unlike that between *wau* and *shu*, is clearly understood today and pertains to the rhythmic configuration of the singing).[3] This final discursive passage is followed by extensive quotations from three songs that apparently are characteristic of the two styles. The first, a piece left untitled here, is known as "Ashibikiyama" in the later text, *Five Sorts of Singing*, from the *Notes*. In place of a title, the piece is introduced by the word *shiugen*.

Following "Ashibikiyama" comes a piece entitled here "Shihogama" (mod. J. "Shiogama"), which is known today from its place in the play *Tōru*. After this song, a third piece, identified as "Komachi," is quoted, preceded by the category *bauwoku*. The "Komachi" song is to be found today in the play *Sekidera Komachi*.

These three fairly long quotations comprise the oldest extant *sarugaku* texts, which, in addition to the words, contain some basic musical notation. I have transcribed the original texts into romanized Japanese, along with the translations, and have romanized the musical notations.

First Pitch, Second *Ki*, Third Voice

It is the *ki* that sustains the pitch. If you focus on the pitch of the flute first and use this occasion to match the *ki* with it, then close your eyes, draw in a breath, and only after that produce the voice, your voice will come forth from within the pitch from the start. When you focus exclusively on the pitch and let your voice loose without having first matched it to the *ki*, it is difficult at first for the voice to come forth from within the pitch. Since we best produce our voice only after having established the pitch within the *ki*, we say, as a rule, "First pitch, second *ki*, third voice."

Also, they say that the *ki* is to sustain the pitch, the voice is to come forth by means of the pitch, and the words are to be distinguished by means of the lips. Such a melodic articulation as cannot be effectuated syllable by syllable[4] should be performed by shaking the head.[1]

The *Classic of Songs*[2] says, "Feelings come forth in the voice, the voice forms a pattern, and one calls this a sound."

• There seem to be two disciplines in learning song: the first is that the person who writes the text of a play must be cognizant of the music and create graceful movements from syllable to syllable. The other is that the singer should clearly distinguish the syllables when setting them to music. The melody should be set in such a way that an appealing effect is created through the words, the elocution is correct, and the transition from phrase to phrase sounds fluent and smooth. Then when it is sung, provided you sing with a clear understanding of the music, the way the music is set and the way the words are sung will be well matched and will create interest and excitement.

Thus, the way the music is set should serve as the standard for the singing. Graceful movement from word to word and concord between the melody and the articulation of consonants in the text produce an appealing effect. The melody provides the outline; the vocal style relates to the movement from word to word; and its expression is a matter of the mind.[3] In effect, the breath is the same as the *ki*, and although the words *fushi* and *kyoku* can be written with the same graphs,[4] in singing the way they are to be learned is different.

1. With minor variations in orthography and one small circumlocution, the preceding is repeated in full in *A Mirror to the Flower.*

2. The *Classic of Songs* (詩経, *Shijing* [*Classic of Odes, Classic of Poetry*]) is one of five canonical books dating from very early in Chinese civilization. A royal commission's collection of folk songs and ritual songs was culled, supposedly by Confucius, to produce an anthology of more than three hundred individual pieces, which became the *Classic* itself. The book was eventually given a "Great Preface," the source of important early statements about poetry in East Asian civilization. The *Classic* was also known as the *Mao Poems* (毛詩), the name that Zeami uses for it. His occasional references to it come primarily from the preface, this one included.

3. Zeami frequently formulates his observations in tripartite sequences of (implied or explicit) formulas, which can be used as titles or summaries. "First Pitch, Second *Ki*, Third Voice" (一調、二機、三声), from the beginning of *Oral Instructions on Singing* and *A Mirror to the Flower*, is one such formulation. Another such formulation is found here: *fushi ha katagi, kakari ha mojiutsuri, kyoku ha kokoro nari* (節は形木、かゝりは文字移り、曲は心也). This typology of musical elements is interesting but also quite challenging. *Fushi* seems to indicate a prescribed configuration of pitches, a melody with a relatively strong sense of abstraction and a link to musical setting and notation. *Kakari*, a notoriously difficult word, seems to mean here a pleasing vocal delivery that is dependent on elocution and transition from syllable to syllable, word to word, and phrase to phrase. Finally, *kyoku*, which seems to be the most individual and perhaps most virtuosic element, is related to the heart or mind of the performer.

4. Both words may be written with the graph 曲 and are indeed so found in the preceding paragraph, as Omote reads it. See *ZZ*, pp. 440–41n.29, and the introduction.

During training, one says, "Forget voice and know expression; forget expression and know pitch; forget pitch and know rhythm."

Also, the matters to be learned for singing are first to memorize the words and, after that, to master the song; after that, to create distinction in the melody; after that, to understand the rank of your voice; after that, to grasp the intent. The rhythm must be understood throughout, at the beginning, in the middle, and at the end.

• On mispronunciation in singing: Mispronunciations pertaining to melodic inflections are of no consequence. Mispronunciations pertaining to words are problematic.[5] What I mean by "mispronunciations pertaining to words" is related to the fact that all proper words have an accent that, if incorrect, results in mispronunciation. What I mean by mispronunciations pertaining to melodic inflection has to do with the accent of particles like *te*, *ni*, and *ha*. When the accent of these particles *te*, *ni*, and *ha* is altered in favor of a more euphonic flow in the delivery of the text, there should be no problem so long as at least the melody is acceptable. This distinction should be clearly grasped and transmitted orally.

Regarding what I've been referring to as suffixes[6] like *te*, *ni*, and *ha*: when the accent[7] on words like *ha*, *ni*, *no*, *wo*, *ka*, *te*, *mo*, and *shi* is only slightly incorrect, it should be of no consequence so long as the melody is attractive. What I mean by melody pertains largely to the accent on *te*, *ni*, and *ha*.

As a general principle, the singing should not be in a singsong monotony. Proper words should be sung in coherent units, and the rhythmic elements should be stretched and condensed using particles like *te*, *ni*, and *ha*.[5]

There is an oral transmission that is relevant here. (The four tones *ping*, *shang*, *qu*, and *ru* correspond to the Five Pitches.)[6]

• On training the voice. You should train the voice being determined not to miss those times in which it is most amenable to that purpose. You should take a tonic for the voice after training.[7] This seems to be the way to improve it.

5. This comment is tantalizing in its suggestions about the rhythm of *sarugaku* chant in Zeami's day. Perhaps this indicates fifteenth-century roots for the ingeniously elastic and dynamic rhythms of singing in modern nō. For further discussion, see appendix 2.

6. These two sentences are written in pseudo-Chinese form and purport to connect the tonal system of Chinese (thus, the four classical tone designations: *ping*, *shang*, *qu*, and *ru*) with, apparently, the five pitch and modal categories of Chinese music, such as those mentioned in the introduction and appendix 1.

Zeami's attempt to link the four tones of orthodox classical Chinese poetics with Japanese pitch accent is doomed from the start, and his understanding of the five pitch and modal categories of Chinese music theory also is insufficient. Consequently, these two sentences tell us less about the music of *sarugaku* in Zeami's day than about his interest in establishing musicological credentials related to the older arts of *gagaku* for his new music of *sarugaku*.

7. Zeami mentions a powdered tonic, or medicine, for the voice, known also from other contemporary medical documents, in *Conversations on Sarugaku*, in *ZZ*, p. 311; and Erika de Poorter,

The training of a voice apparently depends on its propensities. It seems to depend on the power of the breath as well. We nurture a *wau* voice in training it but discipline a *shu* voice in training it. Some voices are better when they train us; other voices are better when we train them. Those voices that are both *wau* and *shu* are labeled "doubly proficient."[8]

On evening and morning: In the evening, practice a full range of vocal types, but in the morning, use some restraint in practicing. In particular, regarding the *wau* voice: in the morning it may be better to be trained by the voice and to take great care with it, taking as your basis the *osamegoye*.[9] Above all, you should take great care not to miss those times when you think the voice is most ready for the purpose.

• On knowing the difference between the voice of *shiugen* and the voice of *bauwoku* in singing. This originated from the pair *ryo* and *ritsu*. *Ryo* is the voice of joy, the voice of breath exhaled. *Ritsu* is the voice of sadness, the voice of breath inhaled. This is the way you might best understand the basic difference.

The voice of *shiugen* is produced by taking the *ki* as its Substance and fitting the voice to the *ki*. It is a strong singing voice. This is a disposition toward the voice of *ryo*. A strong voice swelling with the *ki* should meet the standard for breath exhaled. This is the voice of *ryo*, the voice of joy. It is, therefore, *shiugen*. The voice of *bauwoku* makes the voice itself the Substance, gently holding back the *ki*. It is at heart soft and frail. The essence of the inhaled voice is to hold the *ki* gently. This is the standard for *ritsu*, the disposition to tenderness. For this reason, it is termed *bauwoku*.

So then, since the voice of *shiugen* swells the *ki*, there is a tendency to go sharp. Since the voice of *bauwoku* gently holds back the *ki*, there is a tendency for the pitch to fall. Be aware of this.

• On knowing the difference between *kusemai*[10] and regular singing [*tadautai*]. *Kusemai* is something that developed out of a discrete performing art, so it is as different from regular singing as black is from white. In this case, with regard to the terminology, the word "dance" [*mai*] is suffixed to the word *kuse*. Although as a general matter we are speaking of singing, it should be apparent by my writing the term *kusemai* that there are important distinctions here.

Zeami's Talks on Sarugaku: An Annotated Translation of the Sarugaku Dangi, with an Introduction on Zeami Motokiyo (Amsterdam: Gieben, 1986), p. 135.

8. Zeami's technical vocabulary for the voice dominates this passage. See the introductory note to *Oral Instructions on Singing*.

9. おさめごゑ (mod. J. *osamegoe*). Omote says this seems to be synonymous with the *shu* voice on the basis of its use in the *A Collection of Jewels in Effect*.

10. *Kusemai* (曲舞, orth. *kusemahi*), was, in Kannami's time and earlier, a separate performing art danced and sung by female itinerants. See appendix 2.

The difference between the two is that rhythm occupies the Substance of *kusemai*. With regular singing, it is the voice that occupies the Substance, and the rhythm is added as an Instance of it. Thus, since rhythm controls the Substance of *kusemai*, we add the word "dance" to the word *kuse*. That's why we call it *kusemai*. It is an art form that is sung standing. It is singing that stems from visual effect.

Now in the past, *kusemai* was something discrete unto itself and was performed by *kusemai* performers alone and not sung in a more general way, but more recently it has been sung with a mixture of *koutabushi*[11] and in that context is particularly interesting. Because it is so interesting to listen to, this semi-*kusemai* style has become far and away the most popular sort of singing. The reason that this kind of music has spread so well is because my late father took it up and began to sing it in *sarugaku*. The first piece to be performed like this was the *kusemai* in *Shirahige*.[12] For this reason, singing in the style of *kusemai* has come to be associated with the singing of Yamato.

In this context, the rigidity of *kusemai* singing has been softened in its combination with *koutabushi*, and the styles have themselves gradually changed over the years, but most people don't realize this. If the melodies of *koutabushi* have been blended with *kusemai*, *koutabushi* has, for its part, taken on the style of *kusemai*. Since in the end it's musical interest that matters most, I cannot fault this. All the same, it would mean turning one's back on a fundamental matter if failing to understand this difference resulted in breaking the line of masters who had a full understanding of the vocation.

So as I was saying, the difference between *kusemai* singing and regular singing is that *kusemai* is a kind of singing in which rhythm occupies the Substance of the performance, so the words are borne by the rhythm, and the words and the transitions between phrases are to be light. Moreover, since the words and phrases are carried along by the rhythm, there are mispronunciations in the vocalization here and there. Even though they are mispronounced, they sound attractive musically, and they create an interesting impression when they are heard. This is a disposition toward rhythmic interest, so even though the pronunciation is somewhat distorted, it sounds like part of the music. This is the attraction of *kusemai* when it is heard.

For its part, "regular singing" is not dressed up by the rhythm but is sung just as it is said, so there should be no distortion in the pronunciation of the words. Because of this, its melodic essence is readily apparent from the briefest *sashigoto* or *tadakotoba* section, from the single phrase to the entire piece;

11. *Koutabushi* (こうたぶし), a widespread musical genre in the mid-fourteenth century and the primary musical form in *sarugaku*. It is synonymous with *tadautai* (regular singing).

12. *Shirahige* (*White Beard*), a *waki* nō about a Shinto–Buddhist syncretic deity, remains in the current repertory but is infrequently performed. This piece is extensively quoted in *Five Sorts of Singing*.

performer and audience member alike, listening distinctly with a clear head, should be of one mind in response to the feeling provoked by the music; in a word, this is the way the proper response is effected. The *Classic of Songs* says, "Rectifying gain and loss, budging heaven and earth, exciting the empathy of demons and gods: this we call excitement."[8] What they speak of here is this very "excitement." In this way, they say that gain and loss are made apparent because of appropriate excitement; they speak of rousing body and mind as moving heaven and earth; they call the pacification of enemies exciting the empathy of demons and gods. For this reason, because they express the true orthodox style, the words and transitions between phrases should be correct.

What we call expert technique here is the successful embodiment of this correctness. Correctness has no pattern. But what we mean by "talented" entails the autonomous musical expression of the pattern of formlessness out of the rank without pattern. This means that the voice creates the pattern. Expression amounts to a pattern made manifest and thus creates the pattern in those things that have a pattern. That voice should create a pattern without form—that must be the miraculous sound of the true professional. It is the pattern without pattern. This rank is what we refer to as the place of the miraculous.

SHIUGEN[13]

SASHIGOTO[14] Ashibiki no yamashitamizu mo taezu,
Hama no masago no kazu tsumorinureba,
Ima ha Asu[GE] kagawa no se ni naru urami mo kikoezu,
[GE]Sazareishi no ihaho to naru yorokobi nomi zo arubeki,
[GE]Shikareba ten ni ukameru nami no ittcki no tsuyu yori okori,
Sanka saumoku megumi ni tomite,
Kokudo anseyi no taudai nari.

GE, UTAU9 Chiyoki no kaze mo shidzuka nite,
Teubo no kumo mo osamareri.

13. Konishi Jin'ichi notes the presence of the following excerpts from plays and songs but doubts that they are part of Zeami's original manuscript, suggesting that instead they may be fifteenth-century additions (*Zeami shū*, Nihon no shisō, vol. 8 [Tokyo: Chikuma shobō, 1970], p. 138). Omote argues, to the contrary, that those manuscripts of *Oral Instructions* that do not include the excerpts are newer versions. See *ZZ*, pp. 446–47n.35.

14. Zeami includes some musical notation in this and other direct quotations from plays in the *Notes*. Although this notation does not correspond exactly to modern performance practice in nō, in many cases it is instructive and seems worthwhile to maintain in the romanized or original Japanese citations of the play texts.

[JŌ]Iza koko ni,
Waga yo ha henan sugahara ya,
Waga yo ha henan sugahara ya,
Fushimi no sato ha hisakata no,
Amaterasu hi mo kage hiroki,
[GE]Midzuho no [HARU] kuni ha yutaka nite
[JŌ]Tami no kokoro mo i-[GE]sami aru,
Miyo [GE] no osame ha arigata-[GE]ya,
Miyo [GE] no osame ha arigata-[GE]ya,

[SASHIGOTO]Below the trudging mountains, water flows unendingly,
grains of sand upon the beach, their number piled so high that
no complaint of shallows in the Asuka River is ever heard,
nothing indeed but the joy of pebbles swelling into boulders:[15]
Just as waves rise to the heavens swollen out of a single drop of dew;
mountains, rivers, grass, and trees are rich with blessings;
this age of ours brings peace and reassurance throughout the realm.

The wind in the millennial pine is calm,
clouds at dusk and dawn are quieted.

Here then,
will I pass my days, O Sugahara Moor,
will I pass my days, O Sugahara Moor!
The village of Fushimi lies beneath a wide expanse
of sky, filled with sunlight, under the sway of Amaterasu.
This land of ripened sheaves of grain is rich,
the people's hearts are valiant.
How propitiously peace spreads throughout the realm!
How propitiously peace spreads throughout the realm!

Shihogama

[SASHIGOTO]Michinoku ha idzuku ha aredo Shihogama no,
Uramite wataru oi ga mi no,

15. The conceit of "pebbles growing into boulders" is old in Japanese poetics, with a famous locus in *KKS* 7:343: *Waga kimi ha chiyo ni yachiyo ni sazareishi no ihaho to narite koke no musu made* (A thousand generations, no, eight thousand generations to you, My Lord, 'til pebbles should to boulders grow, and moss bedeck the top). It envisions the possibility that rocks might grow vegetatively over a very great length of time and thus turns up in wishes for enduring political stability and longevity.

[JŌ]Yorube mo isa ya sadame-[GE] naki,
[GE]Kokoro mo sumeru midzu no omo ni,
Teru tsuki-[HARU]nami wo kazofureba,
Koyohi zo aki no monaka naru,
Ge ni ya utsuseba Shihogama no,
Tsuki mo miyako no monaka kana.

[GE, UTAU][10]Aki ha nakaba mi ha sude ni,
Oi kasanarite moroshiraga.

[JŌ]Yuki to nomi,
Tsumori zo kinuru toshitsuki no,
Tsumori zo kinuru toshitsuki no,
Haru wo mukahete aki wo sohe,
Shigururu matsu no kaze made mo,
Waga mi no uhe to kumite shiru,
[JŌ]Shihonaregoromo [GE]sode samuki,
Uraha no aki no [HARU]iube kana,
Uraha no aki no iube kana.

[SASHIGOTO]Tori ha shukusu chichū no ki,
Sou ha tataku gekka no mon,
Osu mo tataku mo kojin no kokoro,
Ima mokumae no shiubo ni ari.

[JŌ, UTAU]Ge ni ya inishihe mo,
Tsuki ni ha Chika no Shihogama no,
Tsuki ni ha Chika no Shihogama no,
[JŌ]Uraha no aki mo nakaba nite,
Matsukaze mo tatsu nari [GE]ya,
Kiri no magaki no [GE]shimagakure,
[JŌ]Iza ware mo tachiwatari,
[JŌ]Mukashi no ato wo [GE]Michinoku no,
[GE]Chika no urawa [*sic*] wo [HARU]nagamemu ya,
[GE]Chika no urawa [*sic*] wo nagamemu ya.

[TADAKOTOBA]Somosomo kono Shihogama to mausu ha,
Ninwau gojifu-ni dai no mikado,
Saga no tenwau no miko Toworu no Otodo to maushishi hito,
Michinoku no Chika no Shiogama no teubau wo kikoshimesare,
Kono tokoro ni Shihogama no kata wo utsushi,
Naniha no Mitsu no ura yori higoto ni shiho [wo] hakobasete,
Koko nite shiho wo yakase isshyau gyoyū no tayori to shitamafu.

Sono nochi ha sauzoku shite moteasobu hito mo nakereba,
Ura ha sono mama hishiho to nate [*sic*],
Chihen ni yodomu tamarimidzu ha,
Ame no nokori no furuki e ni,
Ochiba chiriuku matsu no kage,
Tsuki dani sumade akikaze no,
Woto nomi nokoru bakari nari.
Sareba uta ni mo [GE]kimi masade,
[YURU]Kemuri tae-[GE]nishi Shihogama no,
Urasabishikumo miewataru kana to,
[HARU]Tsurayu-[GE]ki mo nagamete safurafu.

[GE, UTAU]Ge ni ya nagamureba,
Tsuki nomi miteru Shihogama no,
Urasabi-[IRU, GE]shikumo arehatsuru,
[HARU]Ato no yo made mo Shihojimite,
Oi [GE]no nami mo kaheru yaran,
[GE]Ara mukashi kohishi ya.

[AGEUTA]11

Kohishiya [JŌ]kohishi ya to
[GE]Shitahedomo negahedomo,
[JŌ]Kahi mo nagisa no [GE]urachidori,
Ne wo nomi naku [HARU]bakari nari,
Ne wo nomi naku bakari nari.

The Salt Kiln

[SASHIGOTO]"However it be elsewhere in the Hinterlands,
gazing out here at the coast of Shiogama,"[16]
I am filled with chagrin to be so old;
where am I to find cover, in this
uncertain state of mind? Yet all the same
that clarity on the face of the water,
where the moon shines, may yet clear my head.
To count from moon to moon, from month to month:
ah, this night is autumn's very heart,

16. Based on *KKS* 1088, an Azumauta poem: *Michinoku ha idzuku ha aredo shihogama no urakogu fune no tsunade kanashi mo* (However it be elsewhere in the Hinterlands, here on the coast of Shiogama, the fisher's net pulls at the heartstrings as he plies the surf).

and with the transfer of that place to this,
the moon of Shiogama shines right into the center of Miyako.

GE, UTAU Autumn's at its midpoint, but as for this old soul,
age lays on, the hairs are now all white,
JŌ as it were snow
come drifting, piling months on years,
come drifting, piling months on years.
I welcome the new spring, but soon enough tally yet another autumn
    to the count;
gather me in and you will know me, then,
waiting, in the pine-blown wind, under a drizzle,
dipping brine in my salt-stained robe; the cold gets in at the sleeve:
Yes, this is autumn in the dusk along this arc of coast,
Yes, this is autumn in the dusk along this arc of coast.

SASHIGOTO "Birds take lodging: trees along the lake.
A priest comes to knock: a gate beneath the moon."
Whether "to knock" or "push the door ajar?" This: the sensibility of
    those of old,—[17]
still present in the autumn dusk, here before our eyes.

JŌ, UTAU In times gone by,
Shiogama in Chika was thought nearer to the moon,
Shiogama in Chika was thought nearer to the moon.
With autumn at midpoint along the coastal arc,
the pine-blown wind arises.
The mist arises too, fencing off Magaki Isle
and now I must arise as well, and go across
and see for myself the traces of times past.
Let me gaze out on the coastal arc of Chika in the Hinterland,
Let me gaze out on the coastal arc of Chika in the Hinterland.

17. An old Chinese anecdote included in the collection *Shiren yuxie* describes the poet Jia Dao (779–843) riding a donkey in the marketplace, so deeply engaged in his consideration of the choice between "push" (*tui*) and "knock" (*qiao*) in the line "In moonlight, a monk [knocks at, or pushes] a gate" that he collides with a sedan chair carrying the eminent official Han Yu, who also was a celebrated literatus. When Jia Dao apologizes, Han Yu waves off his apology and opts for the word "knock," thereby alleviating Jia Dao's confusion. The phrase "push or knock?" has since become identified with broader concerns about getting the *mot juste* in poetry. See Mike O'Connor, *Selected Poems of Chia Tao: When I Find You Again, It Will Be in Mountains* (Boston: Wisdom Publications, 2000), p. 4.

TADAKOTOBA Well now, as for this coast of Shiogama,
a man called Minister Tōru,
scion of Emperor Saga, fifty-second in the line of earthly kings,
heard of the famous view of Shiogama in Chika of the Far North.
He transferred the features of Shiogama here,
and from Naniwa's distant Mitsu Coast,
each day he had brine carried here
and had salt water boiled.
He took lifelong pleasure in the scene.
Afterward there was no one to carry on with this diversion
and the banks were barren at ebb tide.
What water remained where lakes had been
was only what was left by passing rain, fallen in the ancient cove.
Dead leaves scattered down, to float across the reflection of the pines,
where even the moon no longer shines, and only
the rush of the autumn wind remains.
It was just as in the poem
that Tsurayuki himself intoned:
"With you no longer here,
The trails of smoke at Shiogama fade.
I gaze across the lonely banks and sigh."

GE, UTAU And when I gaze out there, it's true,
Shiogama's kettles are filled with nothing but moonlight,
all is gone to desolation and stark ruin,
but here I stay, soaked with a tide of tears even in these latter days,
the waves of age crash down upon me still.
Oh, how I long for the past!

JŌ "How I long, how I long for the past," I sigh,
but my yearnings and complaints
come to no end, and at the water's edge,
the plover cries and cries,
the plover cries and cries.

Bauwoku

Komachi

TADAKOTOBA Ashita ni ichihatsu wo ezaredomo motomuru ni atahazu,
Saui yufube no hadahe wo ka-GE kusazaredo-GE mo oginū ni tayori nashi,
GE Hana ha ame no suguru ni yote kurenayi masa ni oitari,

[GE]Yanagi ha kaze azamukarete midori yauyaku tareri,
[GE]Hito sara ni wakaki koto nashi,
[GE]Tsuhi ni ha oi no uguhisu no,
[GE]Momosahedzuri no haru ha kuredomo,
Mukashi ni [HARU]kaeru aki ha nashi,
[GE]Ara koshikata kohishi ya,
Ara koshikata kohishi ya.

[JŌ, SASHIGOE]Kono futauta ha chichihaha to shite tenarafu hito no hajime to narite,
Warera gotoki no sojin made mo,
[JŌ]Sukeru kokoro ni Afumi no umi no.

[JŌ, UTAU]Sazanami ya,
Hama no masago ha tsukuru tomo,
[JŌ]Yomu koto no ha ha yo mo tsukiji,
[JŌ]Awoyagi no ito taezu,
Matsu [GE]no ha no chiriusenu,
Tane ha [HARU]kokoro to [GE]oboshimese,
[JŌ]Tatohi toki utsu-[GE]ri koto saru tomo,
[JŌ]Kono uta [GE]no moji araba,
Tori no [GE]ato mo tsukiseji ya,
Tori no ato mo tsukiseji ya.

[TADAKOTOBA]In the morning, nothing gained to fill my begging bowl, a further search is useless;
in the evening, failing to hide my nakedness in a cloak of grass, all remedy is vain.
Now the rain is passed, the crimson in the flowers fades with age.
Blue willows, once enticed by the wind, soon enough hang limp;
people are never young again,
and in the end even spring grows old, its warbler's songs heard a hundred times.
The spring may well return,
but there's no return of an autumn now passed on.
Oh, how I long for times gone,
oh, how I long for times gone!

[. . .][18]

JŌ, SASHIGOE These two songs, as "the mother and father" of poetry, are
the first exemplars for writing,
even for commoners like me and my kind,
who have a taste for poetry; "On the great lake of Ōmi,

JŌ, UTAU O, the rippling waves,
though you exhaust the very last grain of sand,
there's no exhausting the leaves of speech in poetry,"[19]
no end to the tendrils of blue willow;
the needles of the pine never fall away to bare the tree.
Concentrate on the heart, as seed,
and though times pass and things change,
as long as poetry perdures,
there'll be no end to the "footprints of the birds,"[20]
there'll be no end to the "footprints of the birds."

These articles reach into the very heart of music, in Zea[mi]'s sense, and they are recorded here for personal use. These are things not to be shown to outside eyes.

Ōei 26 [1419], a day of the sixth month

Zea (seal)

Notes

1. See *ZZ*, pp. 443–44n.32.

2. For discussions of *ryo* and *ritsu*, see appendix 2.

3. See the introduction and the glossary.

4. 文字にもかからぬ . . . *Moji* here has a specifically written sense that might imply "words" but probably is to be taken most strictly to mean individual "letters"—that is, *kana*—which in the Japanese writing system implies syllables.

5. *Fushi-namari ha kurushikarazu. moji-namari ha warushi* (節訛りは苦しからず。文字訛りは悪し). This item is concerned with problems of pronunciation in singing and operates in accord

18. The quoted text leaves out the first part of a *mondō* dialogue between the *waki* and the *shite*, at the end of which two famous *waka* poems are mentioned, subsequently referred to as "the mother and father of poetry." The first of the poems is *Nanihazu ni saku ya*, quoted in full in *Figure Drawings of the Two Arts and the Three Modes*. The second, *MYS* 16:3807, reads: *Asakayama / kage sahe miyuru / yama no wi no / asaki kokoro wo / waga omohanaku ni* (The reflection of Mount Asaka / is clear to see / here in this mountain spring. / The spring may shallow be, / but shallow not, my love for thee).

19. Probably an allusion to the assertion, in the last lines of the *Kana* preface to *Kokin wakashū*, that no matter how the times change, we still will be faced with happy times and sad ones and therefore will be compelled to express our feelings in poetry.

20. Bird tracks were an ancient metaphor for writing, especially for writing poetry.

with a binarism: *fushi-namari* and *moji-namari*. *Fushi-namari*, which literally means "mispronunciation in the melody," as Zeami explains later, is the mispronunciation of grammatical particles for melodic effect. *Moji-namari* is the mispronunciation of "independent words"—that is, nouns, verbs, and so on. Zeami's *moji-namari* has a specific graphic relation. *Moji* are "written words," which might be expressed with Chinese graphs, whereas the grammatical particles subject to *fushi-namari* usually are single syllable particles written with *kana*.

The terminology Zeami employs here is confusing in that his *fushi-namari* is a small matter, whereas the *fushi* mentioned in the previous item as "the model" (i.e., *katagi*) for singing seems quite important.

6. Zeami's word *oharigana* (mod. J. *owarigana* [ending letters]) is somewhat imprecise in that although all the particles in question do follow another word, they usually do not end an utterance. Instead, for the most part, they are case markers or emphatics. Perhaps a more apposite translation would be "enclitics," but that seems too technical for our purpose.

7. Zeami writes in *kana* the word *shyau*, which I have translated as "accent," and Omote justifiably parses it with the graph 声 (voic[ing]). It's worth noting, though, that in the nearly identical passage in *A Mirror to the Flower*, Zeami writes the graph 正 (correct), thus betraying his prescriptive attitude toward accent in the language.

8. 正得失、動天地、感鬼神、謂之感. The "Great Preface" to the *Classic of Songs* actually follows the line 感鬼神 with 莫近於詩, rendering the full quotation as "For rectifying gain and loss, moving heaven and earth, impressing demons and gods, there is nothing closer to hand than poetry." The source of the final line in Zeami's quotation has not been identified.

9. The musical annotation here, 下ウタウ, is somewhat unusual, but Omote's suggestion that 下 indicates a drop in pitch and that ウタウ represents the change from *hyōshi awazu* delivery to *hyōshi au* delivery is persuasive. The passage comes, moreover, at a point where we might well, by analogy with other nō texts, expect to find a *sageuta*—that is, 下ウタ or 下哥.

10. Again, the unusual musical annotation.

11. Omote inserts this marking. It is useful to retain it here because it provides an informative comparison with modern performance practice.

A Mirror to the Flower
至花道, 1424

A Mirror to the Flower is a central text from the middle period in Zeami's writing about performance. The six articles with which the text opens have aphoristic titles like "First Become the Thing, Then Imitate the Way It Acts." These are followed by an additional twelve articles identified by topic, among which are important statements about the performative ideal *yūgen*. In *A Mirror to the Flower*, the manifestation of Zen Buddhism in Zeami's performance theory becomes more pronounced and self-conscious, and the proportion of Chinese graphs (*kanji*) to phonetic *kana* in the text dramatically increases.

Three of the articles in *A Mirror to the Flower* have antecedents in earlier texts. The articles, "First Pitch, Second *Ki*, Third Voice" and "On Studying Singing" first appeared in *Oral Instructions on Singing*, and "On *jo-ha-kyū*" can be found in an earlier version in *An Extract from* Learning the Flower. There are small differences in orthography between the earlier incarnations of these articles and those in *A Mirror to the Flower*, as well as more significant differences. In each case, the article here has been expanded from its earlier form and has a somewhat greater degree of consistency in technical terminology.

For example, in the article on *jo-ha-kyū* in *A Mirror to the Flower*, Zeami changed the term *fuzei* to *fūtei* in two places. Both terms are difficult to pin down in English (I have used "tone" for the former and "expressive effect," generally, for the latter), but apart from the subtle semantic shift that the change shows, it is important in that it reveals Zeami's attempt to be more consistent in his discussions. In subsequent texts, *fūtei* is, in fact, far more commonly found than *fuzei*. The close connection between *A Mirror to the Flower* and these earlier texts, however, shows that like the last books of *Transmitting the Flower*, this text was composed over a number of years, representing a record of notes on experiences and lessons learned during an extended period.

A Mirror to the Flower shows a far greater interest in relating Zeami's theories of performance to broader issues in East Asian philosophy and aesthetics. He cites more frequently from Chinese sources and Buddhist texts of various sorts than earlier. Zeami also develops more abstract arguments about aesthetics here than was the case in *Transmitting the Flower* or the other short texts written between its completion in 1418 and the completion of *A Mirror to the Flower* in 1424. Here, for example, we find a full article devoted to *yūgen* and also the first mention of a particular type of transcendent virtuosity that becomes central to Zeami's late aesthetic. (Here, specifically, it comes in reference to *taketaru kurai*, in the last paragraph of the article "On Wondrous Places." It also appears later, either in that form or with the Sino-Japanese reading *ran*, as in *ran'i* and *rangyoku*.)

The last four books of *A Mirror to the Flower* follow a couple lines of text that seem like closing remarks, the first an admonition to secrecy and the second the statement "Training resides in making effort with urgency." As Omote notes, "One recognizes that various addenda have been made since the time of *Learning the Flower* [1418]." He goes on to note that the discussion in some of the books here tends to depart rather significantly from the title given to the book in question, and he points out certain changes in vocabulary.[1]

First Pitch, Second *Ki*,[2] Third Voice[3]

It is the *ki* that sustains the pitch. If you focus on the pitch of the flute first and use this occasion to match the *ki* with it, then close your eyes, draw in a breath, and only after that produce the voice, your voice will come forth from within the pitch from the start. When you focus exclusively on the pitch and let your voice loose without having first matched it to the *ki*, it is difficult at first for the voice to come forth from within the pitch. Since we best produce our voice only after having established the pitch within the *ki*, we say, as a rule, "First pitch, second *ki*, third voice."

Also, they say that the *ki* is to sustain the pitch; the voice is to come forth by means of the pitch; and the words are to be distinguished by means of the lips. Such musical expression as cannot be effectuated syllable by syllable should be performed by shaking the head. This is something you should take to heart and concentrate on[4] intently.

1. See the introductory remarks to the excerpts from *A Mirror to the Flower* included in Omote Akira et al., eds., *Rengaronshū, nōgakuronshū, haironshū*, Nihon koten bungaku zenshū, vol. 51 (Tokyo: Shōgakukan, 1973), p. 300.

2. See the note on *ki* at the beginning of *Oral Instructions on Singing.*

3. The first two paragraphs of this article are nearly identical to the article of the same name in *Oral Instructions on Singing.* Such differences as there are, are often slight orthographic and syntactic variations that can hardly be reflected in translation. The final sentence of the second paragraph here, however, does not exist in the *Oral Instructions on Singing* version.

4. *Nenrō* (念ろう), sometimes written 念籠, probably derived from a Zen term, 拈弄, meaning "to reflect intently on and interpret a classic dictum."

Rising and falling through *do* and *re*, the voice makes a pattern; this we call "sound." *Do* is yin; earth, *ryo*, the exhaled breath. *Re* is yang; heaven, *ritsu*, the inhaled breath. *Ryo* and *ritsu* come together in the ascent and descent of the voice; we call this the voice pattern. In distinguishing the five tones, we create the twelve modes, six of them *ryo* and six *ritsu*.[5]

Move Ten Parts of the Mind, Move Seven Parts of the Body

This is what I mean when I say "move ten parts of your mind and move seven parts of your body": in your training, once you have mastered stretching out your arms and moving your feet as your teacher has directed, you should then restrain the movement of your arms a bit more than that of your mind, and pull them inward intently. This doesn't necessarily apply just to Dances and Sparring. In all the movements of your body, when you restrain the body more than the mind, the body becomes the Substance and the mind the Instance;[6] this will surely produce interest and excitement.

Move the Body Vigorously, Stomp the Feet with Restraint, Stomp the Feet Vigorously, Move the Body with Restraint

In this, too, my intent is largely that of moving ten parts of the mind, as I just stated. When the body and the feet move in the same manner, it looks coarse. When you put the body into motion but hold the feet in check, you may appear to move wildly, but it will not be coarse. When you stomp your feet vigorously but move the body quietly, the stomping may be loud, but because the body is quiet, it will not appear coarse. The discrepancy between what is seen and what is heard actually brings the two components into concord and produces interest and excitement.

5. Although the general purport of this paragraph seems relatively straightforward, there are a number of obscurities in the way it is written. I take it to mean that vocal patterns—that is, melodies and the musical expression founded on them—are produced as the voice ascends and descends in pitch and that these ascents and descents have a particular relation to inhalation and exhalation, yin and yang, heaven and earth, and the terms *ryo* and *ritsu*. The pseudo-Chinese form into which it is cast appears from time to time in the *Performance Notes*, but in addition to that Zeami uses the technical vocabulary of Chinese music here without plausibly relating the content to known Chinese sources. See appendix 1.

6. Zeami refers here to a widely discussed binarism of Chinese philosophy: *tai/yū* (Ch. *ti/yong*), my "Substance" and "Instance." See the introduction.

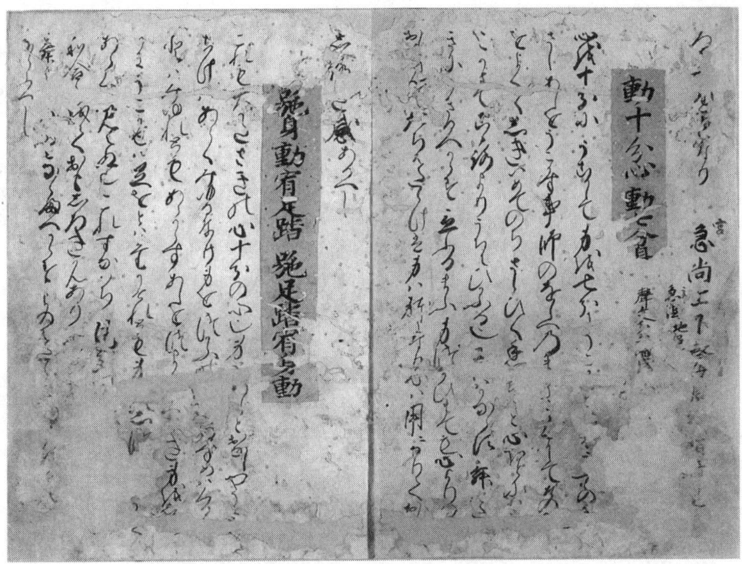

Two leaves from *A Mirror to the Flower*, showing the sections "Move Ten Parts of the Mind, Move Seven Parts of the Body," and "Move the Body Vigorously, Stomp the Feet with Restraint." This manuscript appears to be in the hand of Konparu Zenchiku and is the copy that Tsurauji (probably an early name of Zenchiku) rejoices in having in his colophon. Titles for the individual sections have been written on separate slips of paper and inserted into the manuscript, which accounts for the different color of the paper surrounding those titles. The contrast between the Chinese titles and the text proper, most of it written in *kana*, is easily seen. Note as well the corrections added to the Chinese in the lower half of the first line on the right. There, Zeami originally wrote the graph *kyū* (as in *jo-ha-kyū*), as the pitch *kyū*, which has been corrected to the right of Zeami's version. (Photograph courtesy of Hōzanji temple, Ikoma, and the library of Nara joshi daigaku).

For the most part, while learning how to stomp your feet, you should not do so in dancing Dances. You should learn to stomp in other kinds of Sparring and in dramatic imitation.

First Hear, Then See

The effect of every type of dramatic imitation depends on seeing and hearing what the text states. Some actors create the visual effect simultaneously with the words of the text or even in advance of the words. It is what is heard, though, that should take precedence over what is seen. If you first give to the audience's ear access to what it is to hear and then follow with the visual effect a bit later, the transition from what the mind apprehends on hearing to what in a moment appears before the eyes brings a sense of excitement that both what is seen and what is heard have come to consummation.

For example, if it is a matter of weeping, then let the people hear the word *weep*, and a little bit after the word has been uttered, press your sleeve to your face and bring the matter to completion with the visual impression.[7] Should you press your sleeve to your face before they have had the chance to grasp the word weep, the word will seem like an afterthought, and the matter will be brought to completion on the word. That way, the visual effect will already be over, and there will be a sense that the word is left hanging. So since it is better to bring things to a close with the visual impression, I say, "First let them hear it, and then let them see it."

First Become the Thing, Then Imitate the Way It Acts

"First become the thing" refers to the various types of dramatic imitation in *sarugaku*. If you are to become an old man, then because the figure is aged, you should bend at the waist, be unsteady in gait, and reach out and draw back your arms only a short distance. You should first adopt that attitude and dance your Dance and perform your Sparring and singing from within that form as well. For a woman, you should hold your waist fairly straight, reach out and draw back your arms rather high, be mindful of not using force (so that the limbs each move gently), and employ the body gracefully. It is, then, in that attitude that you perform the stage actions: your Dance, your Sparring, and your singing, too. If the role in question is a violent one, then set your mind on force, carry your body powerfully, and perform your Sparring likewise. In addition to these, for all the other characters in dramatic imitation, the first thing to learn is how to become the character in question. After that, do what the character does.

The Dance Has Its Root in the Voice

Unless the dance emerges from the singing voice, there is unlikely to be any excitement. In the transition in which one moves from the atmosphere of the *issei* into the dance, there should be a wondrous energy. Again, where the dance comes to resolution, it resolves at the rank[8] of excitement in the singing.

7. It is interesting to note that the representation of weeping in modern nō does not entail pressing the sleeve to one's face as Zeami stipulates but, instead, positioning the hand with the palm toward the face and fingers outstretched and with all the fingers closed together.

8. *Kurai* (orth. *kurawi*). The word was commonly used earlier in Japanese history to refer to the officially sanctioned status rankings bestowed by the royal court. Zeami thinks of achieve-

In effect, you see, song and dance issue from the *tathāgata-garbha* and such.[9] First, the breath that emerges from the five chief organs is divided into five different sorts to become the five pitches and the Six Modes.[10] *Sōjō*, *ōshiki*, and *ichikotsujō* are the three *ritsu* modes. *Hyōjō* and *banshiki* are the two *ryo* modes. *Mujō* is an application of the voice that emerges from both the *ritsu* and the *ryo* voice. Thus the inception of the dance is to be found in the way the character moves the Five Bodily Components[11] in response to the voice that emerges from the Five Vital Organs.[12]

Thus, what is meant by "the mode of a particular time" refers to the particular time to which each individual mode corresponds (whether *sō[jō]*, *ō[shiki]*, *ichikotsu[chō]*, *hyō[jō]*, or *ban[shiki]*), as it is distinguished according to the four seasons or the twelve hours of day and night. Then again, some say that it refers to the mode of a particular time, the occasion of song and dance among the heavenly beings, which excites a sympathetic response here below, which consequently is the "mode of the time." It would seem that both definitions are applicable, since it is unlikely that occasions of dancing and singing in the heavens would be arbitrary. Now, with regard to the Suruga Dance,[13] it has come down to us as a secret piece in this land ever since its inception when a heavenly maiden descended to earth and left it here. This matter is too complicated to write out in full.

Let it be enough for you to understand that unless there is sufficient power in the singing, the Dance will not create excitement. Now even if you perform an ordinary dance to the singing of a *kusemai* or the like, you should find enough indications of how to dance it. It's not likely you'll be able to dance it

ments in performance in terms of similarly constituted ranks and uses the term throughout *Performance Notes*. See the introduction.

9. Zeami uses the technical vocabulary of scholastic Buddhism here in his reference to the *tathāgata-garbha*, or *nyoraizō* (如来蔵). The term, which might be translated as "womb of buddhahood," refers in a general way to the potential for enlightenment residing in all sentient beings. (Such a characterization of it may not be adequate to technical buddhological discussions, but Zeami's reference itself seems rather loose, as indicated by the final clause in his sentence, *to unnun* ["and such" or "and so on"].)

10. Five-Element theory here is compounded with Six-Mode musical theory. See the introduction and appendix 1.

11. The Five Bodily Components, or "five limbs," most likely means the head, both arms, and both legs here, but in some cases the term means the tendons and sinews, the vascular system, the flesh, the bone, and the hair or fur.

12. The Five Vital Organs are generally construed as the spleen, lungs, heart, liver, and kidneys. Five-Element theory was widespread in medieval Japan, and here we see elements of this typology as they relate to musical pitches and modes. See appendix 1.

13. The Suruga Dance occupies an important place in the lore of *sarugaku*'s origins and is related to the celebrated legend of the angel who descended to earth and was temporarily deprived of her cloak of heavenly feathers. That legend is at the heart of the nō *Hagoromo*. Zeami takes up the Suruga Dance once again in *The Flower in . . . Yet Doubling Back*.

without flute and drum to keep the beat. Doesn't this mean that you dance through the power of sound?

They say, moreover, that dance has five precepts. First is the Precept on Gesture; second, the Precept on Dance; third, the Precept on Mutual Implication; fourth, the Precept on Gestural Focus; and fifth, the Precept of Focus on Dance.

1. The Precept on Gesture refers to the mastery of a course of performance in which the dance is to be danced within the contours of *jo-ha-kyū*, from the praying hands posture to the movement of all five limbs and the extension and drawing back of the arms.[14]
2. Although gesture is, of course, a part of the dance, in the Precept on Dance, it's not a question of the hands and feet. Instead, visual grace is the matter of concern, and one conveys an impression without relying on a particular gesture or style. Metaphorically, you should evoke the impression of a bird flying along in the wind. This is the Precept on Dance.
3. The Precept on Mutual Implication results from the addition of dance to the aforementioned Precept on Gesture within the contours of *jo-ha-kyū*. Performing the gestures is an effect of pattern, and performing the dance is an effect of no pattern. When you have harmonized the patterned and unpatterned activities into mutual implication, you will have it: the vision is complete. This is the expressive domain in which one perceives interest. To perform the dance having grasped these two courses is called the Precept on Mutual Implication.
4. The Precept on Gestural Focus entails the following: once the patterned and unpatterned are harmonized in mutual implication, they create an effect of expressive concentration in which the gestures become the Substance and the dance is the Instance. To apprehend things in this way is termed the Precept on Gestural Focus.
5. The Precept of Focus on Dance is the effect of expressive concentration in which one makes the dance the Substance and gesture the Instance. This is beyond form.[1]

If we compare these in a general way with the forms of the Three Modes, I suppose that the Man's Mode[15] might correspond to the knowledge of ges-

14. "Praying hands posture" (*gasshō*, orth. *gasshyau*) remains a common gestural figure at the beginning of many dances in nō, although it is now known by the technical term *tappai* (達事).

15. The mention of *nantai* (男体, Man's Mode) is not fully consistent with the Three Modes (Aged Mode, Woman's Mode, Martial Mode), but occasionally Zeami does use this general term, apparently to combine the Aged Mode and the Martial Mode.

tural focus. The Woman's Mode would probably be better with the knowledge of focus on dance. Let me say it yet again: you have to adjust the character of the performance to accord with the object of dramatic imitation.[16]

Also in Dance, we say: eyes ahead, mind behind. That is, "look to the front with your eyes; put your mind to the back." This is the cognitive manifestation in your manner of expression on the basis of the aforementioned knowledge of dance. As seen by the audience, your attitude is a vision apart from your own, but what your own eyes see is your own vision. It is not a Vantage from Vision Apart. To see with the Vantage from Vision Apart is, in effect, to see with the same mind as the audience does. At that time, you achieve a vantage on your own attitude. If you can clearly see yourself, you also will see what is to your right and left, what is before you, and what is behind. Although you already know about seeing in front and to the right and left, have you failed so far to see your attitude from the back? Unless you perceive how you look from the back, you will be unable to tell what is vulgar in your attitude. For this reason, you need to present a graceful form through your entire body[17] by seeing from the Vantage from Vision Apart, taking on the same vision as the audience and learning how you look in places where you cannot yourself see. Isn't this what it means to speak of putting your mind to the back? I'll say it over and over again: achieve the clearest possible Vantage from Vision Apart; be aware that the eye cannot see itself;[2] and gain a sound vantage on left, right, front, and back. With your own two eyes, you shall see your proof in attaining to *yūgen* in dance, with the flower brought into form, the jewel into grasp.[3]

Everything, right up to Dances and Sparring, is to be managed in terms of left, right, front, and back, as in the example of the guy with a plank over his shoulder.[18,4]

The six articles with aphoristic titles are as above.[5]

On Fitting the Moment to the Excitement

When you appear in a *sarugaku* performance, you will have an opportunity to begin singing the *sashigoto* and *issei*. It isn't good to begin too soon. Nor should

16. Zeami paraphrases himself, more or less; compare *Transmitting the Flower.*

17. *Gotai*, or "five [parts of the] body," as in note 11.

18. When one is carrying a plank, anything beyond moving straight ahead is fraught with uncertainty and potential injury to others. As an example of one kind of movement, pragmatic but obstructed, this might serve here as a limit in the direction of simplicity, whereas the Dances and Sparring mentioned immediately afterward speak to the limit of complexity and formal figuration. Thus this final line of the chapter emphasizes the importance of knowing where you are and how you look from every direction, whether in some simple movement or in the formal dancing of *sarugaku*.

you be too late. You should, I'd say, emerge from the green room, take a few steps onto the *hashigakari*, direct your attention all about, and begin to sing at that very moment when the audience waits in anticipation, all as one, with the thought, "Look, he's just about to begin singing." This way of responding to the intent of the audience and singing right then is how you fit the moment to the excitement. Once this moment has passed by, even by a little bit, the intent of the audience slackens, and if you begin then, belatedly, it will not match their excitement. This moment finds its opening with the spectators. What I mean in saying that the moment finds its opening with them is that this is an opportunity the actor should use his intuition to watch for. This is an opportunity for the actor to pull into his own mental vision the visual intent of the entire audience. It is the most opportune moment in the entire day.

Now you should begin singing the *issei* about two-thirds of the way along the *hashigakari*. The *ninoku* should be sung at the end of the *hashigakari*, where it joins the stage proper. You should hold your head at about the level of the seats in the stands,[19] but you should not stare in that direction. As for the way you hold your head, it should be directed toward the exalted members of the audience, at about the same height. In chamber performances indoors and at drinking parties, you should likewise direct your head toward the honored guests at about the same height, without staring at them. The way you carry your arms in dancing is a matter of how you extend your sleeves to match the way you hold your head, so if you move on stage with these considerations in mind, your bearing will be suitable in large halls, small chamber performances, and even drinking parties.[20] Consider this carefully.

Also in regard to stage performances, you should stand at a distance of about one-third of the depth of the stage in front of the musical ensemble. Again, in dances, both when you begin to dance and when you conclude the dance, you should have about one-third of the depth of the stage behind you. Furthermore, for *sarugaku* in large venues, you should try to bring the more exalted members of the audience closer. In smaller venues, you should keep them at some distance. In performances indoors, especially, you should make every effort to keep some distance between yourself and the august members of the audience.

Also, in musical performances and the like indoors, there will be a certain time when you can capture the intent of the members of the audience. It won't work to do it too early, and doing it too late is even worse. Wait atten-

19. In some cases, *sarugaku* was performed before audiences in stands (*sajiki*), which held the seats of the highest-ranking members of the audience. *Taikeiki* relates the tragic circumstances of the collapse of such stands in 1349, with fatalities. The performance on that day is mentioned in *Conversations on Sarugaku*, in *ZZ*, p. 272.

20. This division into large halls (*ohoki naru zashiki*), small chamber performances (*chiisaki zashiki*), and even drinking parties (*sakamori*) suggests that stage performances were not necessarily the standard and that other venues were of considerable importance.

The nō stage at Nishi Honganji temple. Although not contemporary with Zeami, this is one of the oldest extant stages, dating from 1581, and was moved here from its original site in Toyotomi Hideyoshi's villa, Jurakutei. To the left in the back is the *hashigakari*, a bridge between the stage and the green room that serves an important role in performance. The area of the stage to the viewer's right, flanked by a low wooden wall, is where the chorus is seated. The white stones in the courtyard around the stage serve to light the stage during daytime performances. At night, bonfires or braziers in the courtyard would serve the same purpose. (Photograph courtesy of the translator)

tively for the time when they're thinking, "Look, he's just about to begin singing," and given that opportunity when the mind's ear has just settled to attention, you should begin to sing. This is the point at which you produce your voice, thinking, "first pitch, second *ki*, third voice."

On *Jo-ha-kyū*

Since it comes at the beginning, what I mean by the *jo* is the basic expressive attitude.[21] The *waki* play[22] is *jo*. Its appeal should come from a thematically

21. This article is very close to the article of the same name in "An Extract from *Learning the Flower*," and many of the notes on that passage, though relevant here, have not been duplicated.

22. Zeami usually uses the term "*waki* play" to refer to the play that comes after (*waki* [lit., "alongside"]) *Shikisanban*, the ritual play with which formal full-day presentations were begun. *Shikisanban*, however, wasn't performed in every performance, so *waki* play comes to mean more or less the same thing it means today: the first play in a performance of several, treating straightforward and auspicious events in a clear and uncomplicated way.

straightforward source, auspicious and without particular subtlety, proceeding correctly. Stage business should consist of song and dance alone. Song and dance are to provide the basic expressive effect in this vocation. The next performance should be one that differs in expression from the *waki* play; while faithful to its source and strong, it should create a deliberate, settled impression in its expressive effects. Although this second play is different in tone from the *waki* play, it still uses the lingering expressive effects of the *jo*, in that it is not a time for terribly intricate technique and should not be too detailed.

From the third play on, one is in the *ha*. This style carries over the basic expressive effect and straightforward, orthodox style of the *jo*, but with greater detail. What I mean by *jo* is a basic attitude, as it is; *ha*, then, imparts a sense of explanation, softening that attitude. That being the case, you should apply your technique with subtlety, your manner of expression based on imitation. This should be the most important play of the day. Similarly, the fourth or fifth play still falls within the bounds of the *ha*, so you should perform a diverse range of material.

What I mean by the word *kyū* is the last verse.[23] Since this gives the final impression for the day, it should create an effect of closure. *Ha* is, as I said, the attitude that "breaks" the *jo* and sets out in detail a whole range of material. What I mean by *kyū*, then, is what remains as a last impression once the *ha* has been thoroughly exhausted. For that reason, the *kyū* is to be forceful and compact, with a startling visual character and expressive effects focused on a swift, unconventional dance or Sparring.[24] The forcefulness of which I speak is for this time in a performance.

Generally in the past, a program of plays would not contain more than four or five pieces. Accordingly, the fifth play was, without exception, *kyū*, but now, with so many plays performed in a single program, that may be too early for the *kyū*; if the *kyū* gets too long, it isn't the *kyū*.[25] In performance, it is the *ha* that should last a long while. In the *ha*, one offers up the full variety of performance, and the *kyū* should be devoted exclusively to the climax. But when one is performing at the behest of an exalted person, then the standard way of doing things does not apply because the sequence in performance is out of the ordinary. Even in a case like this, maintain a clear aware-

23. *Ageku* (last verse) is, in *renga* poetry, the last 7–7 syllable link in a full sequence and in that sense is related to Zeami's intention here, although he is not so specific and certainly doesn't limit the *kyū* to fourteen syllables of text.

24. Sparring is a vigorous form of dance frequently mentioned in the *Performance Notes* (see appendix 1). What I have translated as a "swift, unconventional dance" is *ranbu* (乱舞), which occurs only twice in *Performance Notes*, here and in "An Extract from *Learning the Flower*," in an almost identical passage.

25. *Kyū* means "fast."

ness, and although you may have been asked to perform a play normally reserved for the *kyū*, if the play you are performing will be followed by something else, then you must hold back and not to be too forceful, but restrain your physical performance[6] to seven parts of ten, to hold something in reserve for the end.

Herein lies a matter of great concern: Sometimes quite unexpectedly an exalted person will arrive when you have already reached the time of the *ha* or *kyū* in your performance. So, even though the *sarugaku* will already have proceeded as far as the *kyū*, that person's frame of mind will still be in the *jo*. In such a case, if that person watches your performance at the *kyū* while his frame of mind is in the *jo*, the performance will not meet his expectations. The people who have been watching all along will grow all the quieter because of the appearance of that person, and a peculiar change will come over the house, so that all the people and the house itself will appear to have been carried back to the *jo*. It is very difficult to make a success of the performance on such an occasion. In such a case, you might suppose that it would be appropriate to return the performance itself to the stage of *jo*, but for some reason, such a performance will turn out badly. This is really very difficult. Watch for the occasion when this is likely to occur, and choose a play suitable to the *ha*, but perform it with something of the *jo* in mind, then you might, with calm self-possession, be able to capture the attention of the person in question. In this way, having brought the intent of the exalted person under your influence, you might be able, with appropriate expertise, to direct the house gently through the *ha* and *kyū*. But even though you put all your ingenuity to work, it may not suffice in this situation.

You may also find yourself summoned to perform *sarugaku* unexpectedly before an elite audience at the last minute when, for example, they have been drinking.[26] Now, in a situation like this, your audience will have already reached the *kyū*. The performance you are about to undertake will be at the *jo*. This, too, is very difficult. When performing on an occasion like this, even though the play is staged within the limits of *jo*, you should frame your intent with something of the *ha* and *kyū* in it and maintain a light touch, not dragging it out too much, so as to move fairly quickly into the *ha* and *kyū*. In this case, it's a matter of your expertise in performance. Under these circumstances, your performance should be successful.

26. In these two paragraphs, Zeami appears to distinguish between *ohogoshu* (大御酒) and *sakamori* (酒盛り). Both seem to refer to performing before audiences that have been drinking. The distinction between the two doesn't seem to pertain to the degree of drunkenness but the amount of the actor's advance preparation. In the former case, it seems that an elite audience suddenly calls for *sarugaku*, whereas in the latter, the occasion seems to be designated in advance as a drinking party.

The same considerations apply when you perform for a drinking party. When you sense that the party has almost reached its high point, you should look out for the right opportunity, use your fan to beat the rhythm, and sing a few short auspicious pieces, carrying through in a manner of expression appropriate to the sequence of performance. This should go according to plan, since you've been watching for the right moment. If some exalted person should arrive unexpectedly in the middle of the party, then considering what I said before, you should return the *kyū* in some degree to the *jo*, using your expertise in performance. And if you yourself should arrive when the party has already reached the *kyū*, then take account of the advice I gave earlier, and perform the *jo* in a frame of mind directed somewhat toward the *kyū*.

So then as you consider *jo-ha-kyū*, whether in a full-fledged formal performance, at a party, or even in a modest little musical gathering, be aware of the appropriate sequence.

On Knowing How to Study the Vocation

If you have studied the performance of an actor who has attained great mastery, then you may try to imitate him. But if you have not studied under him, you should not try to imitate him. The manner of expression of a master who has already come to the deepest understanding of the art and has at last attained the rank of full confidence is of great interest to those who see him, but a beginner who concludes that this simply is a matter of interest and nothing more and imitates him may resemble him in performance but will provoke no interest or excitement. When a beginner sees the performance of a master who has, over the years, trained both his mind and body to the fullest attainment of learning and who performs consummately with the restraint of "moving seven parts of the body," that beginner will imitate the master without having learned under him and consequently will move only seven parts of his mind as well as seven parts of his body. In such a case, his performance will stagnate.

For this reason, when instructing younger actors, the master should train them not to his own current level of performance but to the level he himself commanded when he was a beginner, teaching them to use both body and mind to a full ten parts. Only after he has finished training them and they gradually attain mastery on their own and reach a rank of full confidence should they restrain the body in performance little by little so that they arrive at "moving seven parts of the body" naturally.

In general terms, there is no way to imitate the rank of full confidence in performance. When one merely imitates, it creates great difficulty. There are, to be sure, ways of imitating what is of great difficulty. As they say, "Is there a resemblance? Yes, there is a resemblance. But is it the real thing? No, it's not the real thing."[27] Is there any method for imitating the real thing? Great difficulty and full confidence are two sides of the same coin.[28] There are oral instructions about this.

• In the matter of becoming a teacher or becoming a student, I have nothing out of the ordinary to say regarding instruction in general matters, but when it comes to the rank to which a teacher gives access, then in my view you must not give such access unless you have a penetrating view of the student's artistic grounding and his mind.[7] The [*Classic of*] *Changes* says, "If it is not the proper person to whom the proper text is transmitted, this is deplorable to heaven."[8] When the student's grounding is inadequate, it is inappropriate to give him access. Here is why: when you grant access to someone who is not adequate to it, then the rank is too high to allow access. The student's talent doesn't reach that far, and since the student and the rank are badly matched, it doesn't work out right. Since it doesn't work out right, the access granted in the first place is counterfeit, and the student should not be granted access at all, since it will prove detrimental.

In sum, then, there are three requirements for becoming "the very thing." A talent that is appropriate to your grounding is one. An artistically receptive mind, a mind capable of wholehearted devotion to the *samādhi* of this vocation[29] is another. A teacher who can teach you this vocation is the third. Unless you have all three of these, you are not likely to become "the very thing." What I mean by "the very thing" is the attainment of a rank of great mastery, a rank at which you will be recognized as a teacher yourself.

Also, I have noticed in the performing styles of young actors these days a tendency to skim the surface.[9] This, too, is because they imitate without having really learned. If you pursue a gradual course of training, moving from the Two Arts into the Three Modes[30] and studying over the years according to what is appropriate at a given stage of training, you will enter every field and master each artistic style one by one, but if you simply imitate one thing or another here and there in your study and do only what serves the moment's purpose, then it seems from my experience that you are likely to merely skim the surface. First, while you are studying the Two Arts, you should not study

27. *Nitaru koto ha nitaredomo, ze naru koto ha ze narazu.* This proverb is found in several places in the collection of Zen kōans entitled *The Blue Cliff Record* and also in the *Taiheiki.*

28. Nijō Yoshimoto, *Hekirenshō*: "In *renga*, what is easy is of great difficulty, and what is of great difficulty is easy" (Omote et al., eds., *Rengaronshū, nōgakuronshū, haironshū*, p. 33).

29. The language is explicitly Buddhist, equating devotion to the profession (vocation) of nō with *samādhi*, or complete engagement in meditation.

30. The Two Arts are singing and dance, and the Three Modes are the three basic role types from which, in Zeami's view, all acting proceeds: the Aged Mode, the Women's Mode, and the Martial Mode. See *The Three Courses.*

the Three Modes. And even once you've begun to study the Three Modes, you shouldn't study the Martial Mode for a while. And when you come to study the Martial Mode, you should hold off studying the Modes of Intricate Movement and Violent Movement[31] until you have reached an age when it is appropriate to study them. What extraordinary difficulty there would be in learning them all at once or imitating them all at once. I think that would be entirely unimaginable. If a young actor, misled by his accomplishment, should merely skim the surface like this in his performance, it would produce only an ephemeral flower. Then as he grew older, his performances would be likely to decline. Even if they didn't decline, there's hardly any chance at all that he would become a great actor. Keep this in mind.

There is something else you should keep in mind about skimming the surface. If you show too much preference for fresh, new plays and abandon the old plays one by one and thereby fail to own the repertory, that too is a kind of skimming in performance. You should settle on a stable repertory of plays that you have under complete control, and mix new plays in among them. If you simply skip from one fresh play to another, you will forget the most basic plays, and in this way, the rank of your performance will suffer from superficial skimming. To perform only fresh new plays itself lacks freshness. But if you mix old and new performances, then both the old and the new will exhibit a certain freshness. This will surely be the true flower. As Confucius said, "Warm to the old and know the new. Therewith shalt thou be a teacher."[10]

On an Expert's Grasp of Excitement

When his Singing, Dance, and Sparring are complete, we call an actor expert. When he is not fully accomplished in these, he undeniably remains inadequate in some ways, but his expertise exists on its own, all the same. This is evident in the fact that some actors do not become real masters, even though their voice is fine and their Dance and Sparring fully competent. Some also are perceived as talented by all the world, even though their voice is not so good and their command of the Two Arts not particularly accomplished. This is because Dance and Sparring are matters of technique. The main concern, though, is the mind. Or again, the authenticity of rank. Thus, there are those who know the savor of interest, perform plays with the mind, and gain fame for their expertise, even though they are not fully accom-

31. The Mode of Intricate Movement and the Mode of Violent Movement are two styles of acting that derive from the Martial Mode but are used primarily to portray demons, the former a demon with a human heart and the latter a full-fledged demon-hearted demon. Zeami eventually seems to reject the latter entirely in his troupe's performances.

plished. Gaining a name for true expertise, then, does not depend on a complete mastery of Dance and Sparring. I have the sense that excitement might come, plain and simple, from the happy effect that the actor's mind creates in its authenticity of rank. True expertise resides in understanding this distinction. Thus even an actor who is accomplished in the whole range of fields may not have that certain something that creates interest. There are also those actors who create that certain interest even as beginners. So then, even though you may graduate from beginner to 70 or 80 percent expert, eventually to attain a rank of full expertise, that's still different from really being thought interesting.

Also, even above the rank at which an actor is thought interesting is a level at which people say "Ah!" without themselves being conscious of it. This is excitement. Since it occurs without conscious awareness, this is a level of excitement at which you don't even realize that it's interesting. This could as well be called "unmixed." That's why, in the *Classic of Changes*, the word for excitement [感] is written without the graph for mind [心] at the bottom, thus 咸, pronounced "kan."[32] That's because with true excitement, one has ventured beyond the conscious mind.

This is how it is with an actor's rank. From the level of a beginner, one continually advances in one's learning until one is called a good actor. This is the rank at which one has attained real expertise. Above this is the rank of true interest, already the rank of a famous actor. Above this, when one possesses the kind of excitement that transcends the mind, one is at a level at which one gains fame throughout the realm. It is important to learn these various levels well and make the most of your ingenuity, so you can get all the way to the very top in your performance.

On Depth

There is a matter in performance that you should take to heart and give due consideration. If it isn't finely constructed, then it won't be interesting. But if you set your mind on finely constructed meaning, then you will run the risk of looking small in performance. In contrast, if you set your mind on expansiveness, there won't be much to catch the eye, and you'll tend to look plodding. The distinction is of very great importance.

32. The locus classicus is found in the *Classic of Changes* under the hexagram *xian* (Wilhelm Baynes, trans., *The I Ching or Book of Changes*, Bollingen Series 19 [Princeton, N.J.: Princeton University Press, 1961], no. 31, p. 540). The interpretation in which *xian* is seen as a kind of excitement or stimulation without conscious intent or awareness had its antecedent in the Neo-Confucianism of Zhuxi, according to Omote, in *ZZ*, p. 95.

You should, I imagine, treat the places that are finely constructed ever so finely and perform the places that should be expansive expansively. The distinction between the two will be difficult to discern unless you understand performance very well. You should inquire carefully of your teacher and make the difference clear. Nonetheless, though, there is a particular situation you should be aware of overall. Whether in the Two Arts, in your gestures, or in the atmosphere of your performance, your mind should be finely attuned in every respect, whereas your body should be expansive. Give this very careful consideration and maintain your intent resolutely.

In general terms, if your training for performance has been based on expansive models, it should move in the direction of fineness. If your training in performance has grown up on the basis of a small model, it is unlikely to move in an expansive direction without great effort. Within the great, there is the small. Within the small, there is no great. This is where you must be particularly creative. A performance that comprehends both the great and small is spacious. Just as the ice from a great freeze melts, so does the ice from a small freeze.[11]

On Crossing into the Realm of *Yūgen*

The expression of *yūgen* is accounted the greatest achievement in many vocations and endeavors. In this art particularly, the expression of *yūgen* is considered foremost. In a general sense, it is something you can see, and members of the audience take particular delight in it, but an actor with *yūgen* is not all that easy to find. This is because few truly know the savor of *yūgen*. When that is the case, no actor crosses into its realm.

Now then, I wonder what sort of place we speak of when we talk about the realm of *yūgen*. First, we look to various classes of people with regard to their appearance in public, to find that the demeanor of aristocrats shows exalted rank and a manner of appearance different from others; is this, then, what we call the rank of *yūgen*? If so, then the basic style of *yūgen* is a beautiful and gentle style. The display of a tranquil and collected personal style is *yūgen* in an individual's demeanor. Similarly, if you observe with great care how elegant the spoken usages of nobles and courtiers are and learn to speak gently and elegantly, even in the most casually uttered expressions from your mouth, that will be *yūgen* in speech. Or again, with regard to singing, when the melody comes down beautifully[33] and sounds graceful, that must be *yūgen* in

33. *Fushikakari utsukushiku kudarite: kudarite* means "go[ing] down" or "descend[ing]." It seems somewhat odd that this particular direction in melodic structure should be emphasized, and yet overall, the change in pitch in a nō song usually moves from an upper register to a lower register. This is true in other varieties of Japanese music as well, for example in the celebrated *otoshibushi* of Shinnai.

singing. If the dance is thoroughly internalized, the individual demeanor beautiful in its style, quietly manifested, and interesting in the high points, that then must be *yūgen* in the dance. Or again, with regard to dramatic imitation, when the palpable quality inherent in the Three Modes is beautifully realized, this must be accounted as *yūgen*. Or with a display of anger in representing a demon, even though you may carry your body with a certain forcefulness, if you do not forget about visual beauty, endeavor to "move ten parts of the mind," and "vigorously move the body while stomping the feet with restraint" so as to present yourself with beauty in your individual demeanor; that, then, should amount to the *yūgen* of a demon.

Turn your mind to the clearest possible apprehension of these several objects, and in making yourself into one of them, do not depart from *yūgen*, no matter what the station of the object of your imitation. Whether highborn lady or maidservant, man or woman, priest or layman, bumpkin or lout, even beggar or pariah, they should, every one, be made to appear as if they were carrying a spray of blossoms. They should elicit acclaim: "What beautiful blossoms," no matter the difference in their social stations, for the flower of performance is the same for every one. This flower comes from individual demeanor. What displays the attitude beautifully is the mind. The mind of which I speak must understand that the seed of *yūgen* comes from clearly discerning the underlying principles—studying poetics so that the words possess *yūgen*, studying the proper standards of expression in dress so that the attitude possesses *yūgen*—from having a specific sense of what is beautiful, even though the object of imitation may vary.

If you don't watch out, though, you might conclude that the discrimination of such and such an object of imitation is the ultimate achievement and forget about your visual attitude; in that case, it will be no small matter for you to cross into the realm of *yūgen*. Unless you enter the world of *yūgen*, you will not attain the greatest achievement. If you fail to attain the greatest achievement, you will not be celebrated for your talent. So, then, to become a famous performer is no small matter. Train hard, and be resolute in your commitment[12] to the importance of this style of *yūgen*.

What I mean by the greatest achievement is beauty and palpable quality. Make very sure you take great care with the appearance of your attitude. If you do, and exert yourself to the furthest extent and, from the Two Arts through every variety of dramatic imitation, present a beautiful visual form, then each in its turn should result in the utmost achievement. But if your visual attitude is bad, then each of these is likely to be vulgar. You must realize that *yūgen* resides in being beautiful in the broadest way—in visual attitude and in aural attitude. Use your creativity in your own way regarding this principle, master it, and you will be known as one who has crossed into the realm of *yūgen*. If you fail to use your creativity in these various matters, and—need I mention?—fail to make them your own but simply think this or that should produce *yūgen*, then never in your entire life will you find *yūgen*.

On a Matter to Take to Heart Regarding Experience

I call it the benefit of long-term experience when as you train and study this art and gain a name for your expertise, your rank improves. Sometimes, however, your long-term experience may change in accordance with where you find yourself. Fame can be gained only by earning appreciation in the capital. Someone like this, though—once he's returned home, determined though he may be, even there in the country, not to forget the manner of expression he employed in the capital—for all his efforts not to forget the good things experience taught him, fails in the end to realize that his positive expressive capability has gradually grown overbearing, and in the longer term, it becomes a burden of experience. Such "stagnant experience" should be avoided.

In the capital among sharp-eyed critics, any tendency to grow stagnant quickly becomes apparent in the attitude of the audience, even if the actor himself is unaware of it; when, moreover, one's ears are struck both by praise and deprecation, he eliminates weaknesses one after the other, gains only good experience, and stores that experience away, polishing it to a high sheen just as if it were a fine gemstone. As they say, when crooked wormwood grows with hemp, it comes out straight, even though untrained; white sand in the dirt is black at heart.[34] When you live in the capital, you are in good surroundings, so naturally there are no bad elements. When bad elements are removed little by little, that amounts to good long-term experience. Good long-term experience is not something that piles up on its own. Take to heart, with greatest care, how the accumulation of good long-term experience may turn into bad long-term experience.

So then, when a quite good and talented actor goes stale as he grows older, that's the kind of experience I'm talking about. When an actor doesn't recognize something in his performance that people dislike and persists in thinking, I made my name in the past for just this very thing—the thing they dislike seeing—he ends up stumbling through his swan song,[35] that is,

34. A proverbial expression; compare *Dadai Li*: "Master Zeng [Can] said, 'When wormwood grows with hemp, it comes up straight without training; when white sand is in the mud, it mixes with it, and all turns black'" (quoted by Omote, in *ZZ*, p. 99, headnote).

35. Zeami's term here, *irimai* (入舞, orth. *irimahi*), refers to the last elements of a *bugaku* piece before the dancers leave the stage. "Swan song" is only a rough equivalent.

through and through, the kind of experience I'm talking about. Take this very carefully to heart.

On Binding the Many Arts with a Single Intent

In their critiques, members of the audience often say that the places where nothing is done are interesting. This is a secret stratagem of the actor. Now the Two Arts, the different types of stage business, and varieties of dramatic imitation all are techniques performed with the body. The gap between is where, as they say, nothing is done. When you consider why it is that this gap where nothing is done should be interesting, you will find that this is because of an underlying disposition by which the mind bridges the gap. It is a frame of mind in which you maintain your intent and do not loosen your concentration in the gaps where you've stopped dancing the dance, in the places where you've stopped singing the music, in the gaps between all the types of speech and dramatic imitation, and so on. This internal excitement diffuses outward and creates interest.

However, should it be apparent to others that you have adopted this frame of mind, that is no good. If it becomes apparent, then it is likely to turn into a dramatic technique in itself. Then it is no longer "doing nothing." At the rank of no-mind, one bridges the gaps between what comes before and after with such a stratagem, so that one's intent is even hidden from oneself. This, then, is "Binding the Many Arts with a Single Intent":

> Life and death, come and go: marionettes in a puppet show.
> If a single string should snap, tumble, tumble, down they go.[36]

This is a comparison with the situation of a person trapped in the karmic cycle of life and death. The manipulation of a marionette on a stage may produce various visual effects, but the puppet doesn't actually move on its own. It functions because of the strings used to manipulate it. The sense, then, is that if a string should break, it all will collapse into a heap. In *sarugaku* as well, dramatic imitation is a kind of puppetry. The intent is that the puppeteer hold the performance together. The intent should not be visible to the

36. A verse from *Gettan oshō hōgo* (orth. *Gettan Wosyau hohugo*), a collection of homilies by Gettan Sōkō (月菴宗光, orth. Soukwau, 1326–1386), a Rinzai priest from Mino who eventually came to reside in Tajima and was the religious adviser to the Yamana clan. As Tanaka Yutaka points out, the implied comparison is with the uncertain believer who, when doubt arises, finds before his eyes the panorama of unenlightened existence and is in jeopardy of falling into it for untold aeons (*Zeami geijutsuron shū*, Shinchōsha koten shūsei, vol. 35 [Tokyo: Shinchōsha, 1976], p. 145).

audience. If it is, then it's as if they could see the puppet's strings. You should make every effort that your intent serves as the strings binding the many arts of performance without the audience seeing them. If you can do this, then your performance will have life.

In the most general terms, you should not limit this to the actual occasion of performance. Day after day, night after night, whether coming or going, sitting up or lying down, you should not forget about this intent; you should bind your experiences together with a resolute mind. If you employ your creativity in this way without negligence, your performance will improve evermore.

This article is a transmission of the greatest secrecy.[13]

Training resides in making effort with urgency.[14]

On Wondrous Places

By "wondrous" I mean what is marvelous.[37] By "what is marvelous" I mean an attitude without a figure.[38] In its formlessness, it is a wondrous style.

Now then, in the performing arts, what I am calling wondrous places should be found, starting with the Two Arts, in every sort of action and such on stage. If, then, you try to say where they are, there will be nothing to say. I would venture that an actor who has in his capacity such wondrous places must be the very thing, unsurpassed.[15] But then again, there are cases in which one can see a presentiment of such wondrous style innate in some even from the time when they are beginners. It is not known to the actor himself, but it should be apparent to the penetrating eye of a discerning member of the audience. To the more typical member of the audience, though, he may present a sight of no particular interest. Even a greatly accomplished actor is aware only that this exists somewhere in his manner of expression. He is not likely to know just where to find it. What makes it a wondrous place is not knowing. If it were, even in part, explicable, then it would not be wondrous.

All the same, put your ingenuity to work on this: isn't it the case that in bringing one's performance to its utmost to become the most expert of actors

37. *Meu to ha tahe nari.* Zeami redefines *meu* (妙, mod. J. *myō*, my "wondrous") a loanword from Chinese with strong Buddhist connotations, with *tahe* (mod. J. *tae*, my "marvelous"), a native Japanese word redolent of the world of *waka* poetry and *Genji monogatari.* Both have the sense of something inexpressibly beautiful, but in the former case (etymologically, apparently, a mysterious and beautiful woman and, in a derivation, "unfathomable"), there is probably a stronger sense of the mysterious and surprising, whereas in the latter case, the word has a fairly strong sense of sacredness, with a visual display in pristine beauty, by association with *shirota(h)e*, white cloth made with mulberry fiber. It's open to question how much of this Zeami intends. It could be that he is simply Japanizing a rather Chinese-sounding word.

38. *Katachi naki sugata nari.* Because this is a paradox, it of course eludes precise translation.

and in entering completely into a position of the fullest confidence in the rank of great virtuosity,[39] one does not rely in the slightest on the techniques of performance but aspires to a visual style of the rank of no-mind and no-style—isn't this what constitutes these wondrous places? I would venture to say that the virtuosic fulfillment of *yūgen* in one's manner of expression must be fairly close to these wondrous places. You should look into this very carefully in your own mind.

On Criticism

Now then, with regard to criticism of performance, people's tastes are different. It is, consequently, nearly impossible to appeal to the sensibilities of everyone. You should therefore take as your model an accomplished master who achieves broad commendation in the realm.

First, you will know this by carefully discriminating by sight and sound between those performances that succeed and those that fail in actual performance. The three varieties of success in an actual performance are sight, sound, and mind.

In a performance that is successful on the basis of sight, the house is filled with color right from the very beginning; the dancing, the singing, and the tenor of performance are interesting; members of the audience, both high and low, give voice to their excitement; and the occasion has a visual splendor; this is a performance that succeeds on the basis of sight. A success like this is evident to all alike, from the visually discerning (it hardly needs mention) even to those people who don't really know much about performance—all are taken by how interesting the occasion is. There is, however, something an actor should be aware of regarding a performance like this. It can achieve such a momentum that everything you do is interesting, and then the viewer's minds become so roused that their eyes and their minds become overburdened, and the performance shows signs of going a bit astray. The actor's own mind may be caught up in it and exhaust every last possibility for visual appeal, at which time the minds of both actor and audience grow overloaded and lose the basis for discrimination; the performance leans toward ostentation and shows signs of debasement. This I consider the malady of overperformance. In a time like this, restrain your performance somewhat; rein in your expression and display; give the eyes and minds of your audience a chance to rest; open up some space; let them breathe; perform the interesting parts quietly; and then when

39. *Taketaru kurawi* (mod. J. *kurai*), also *ran'i* (or, in Zeami's day, probably *ranni*), one of the earliest references to this level of consummate artistry, which becomes exemplary of the fullest artistic achievement in the aesthetics of Zeami's late writings.

their interest mounts once again, the performance will grow ever stronger; and with each subsequent play there will be excitement enough to last. A success in *sarugaku* like this I call a performance that succeeds from sight.

In a performance that is successful on the basis of sound, there is from the very beginning a penetrating depth; the singing comes to proper pitch immediately[40] and creates a graceful interest. This is, above all, an excitement produced by singing. It is a palpable kind of excitement characteristic of those of unsurpassed talent and accomplishment. The flavor of a performance developed in this way is not especially highly regarded by countryside critics. A performance like this becomes more and more interesting as a diversity of expression emerges, by itself, from an actor of unsurpassed expertise. If a performance like this is undertaken by a second-rank actor of limited sensibility, then it's likely to grow weaker as the performance proceeds. If the performance is achieved with icily quiet beauty, then with each subsequent play, the mood of the performance is likely to show signs of dragging. Should you become aware of this, inject your sensibility into the performance, and make an interesting display here and there to arouse the minds of the audience and thereby adjust the manner of expression. For someone of unsurpassed expertise, this is where, as a matter of course, his diversity in dramatic imitation, his bodily skill and mental creativity, will be palpably manifest from the perspective afforded by his training and experience so that the performance will grow more interesting by the moment. An actor of middling accomplishment must have a very clear understanding here and be conscientious so that the performance is not allowed to drag as the day's program proceeds. And yet the audience must not perceive that he is making particular efforts to keep the program from dragging. He must arrange it so that the audience simply thinks, Look how interesting it's getting! I count this a professional secret and fine point among actors. Such a success on the occasion of a performance like this, I call a performance that succeeds on the basis of sound.

A performance that is successful on the basis of mind can be found, after other diverse plays have been performed, in *sarugaku* by an actor of unsurpassed expertise performing a play with nothing particularly noteworthy in the Two Arts or in dramatic imitation, with no particularly ingenious dia-

40. *Yagate ongyoku teushi ni ahite.* The mention of *teushi* (mod. J. *chōshi*) raises interesting questions and a paradox. If the word is intended to indicate a pitch, as is generally believed, and referring to the first article in *A Mirror to the Flower*, in which the actor's lock on pitch is supposed to come before the utterance of any sound at all, then this remark would seem to be superfluous and would not be a meaningful comment on the particular virtues of a performance based on sound. If, however, performance in Zeami's day was like modern performance practice, in which the chant begins at a somewhat lower pitch than it is destined for as the individual song proceeds, the comment is more instructive.

logue, where there is, within a quiet understatement,[41] an indescribable mental excitement. One could also call this the music of chilling beauty. Even the better sort of visually discerning critic may not be able to see this rank of achievement. And of course, it would hardly even occur to a countryside critic that such a thing exists. In my experience, this is the happy effect of an actor of unsurpassed expertise. This, I call a performance that succeeds on the basis of mind or a performance of no-mind or, again, a performance of no pattern.

You must be able to understand and discern among these several types of subtly differing expressive effects.

There are, all in all, people who possess only a discerning eye and who do not know performance. There are also those who know performance but who do not have a discerning eye. If one's knowledge and one's eye are well matched, then one is likely to be a fine critic. One should not base one's critical judgments on occasions when an expert actor's *sarugaku* does not succeed or occasions when a mediocre actor's *sarugaku* does succeed. Our expectation for an expert actor is that he will succeed in an important festival performance or a grand performance before the elite. Our expectation for a mediocre actor is that his performance will succeed on modest occasions or in country performances and the like. The actor who understands how to arouse the interest of his audience should have an advantage in performance. A member of the audience, moreover, who watches the performance with discernment vis-à-vis the actor's mind is one who knows performance. With regard to criticism one says, "Forget about whether or not it succeeds and watch the performance. Forget about the performance and watch the actor. Forget about the actor and watch the mind. Forget about the mind and know the performance."[42]

On Studying Singing

Two disciplines are involved in studying this: One is that the person who writes the text of a play should be aware of the music and create graceful movement from syllable to syllable.[43] The other, then, is that the singer should clearly distinguish the syllables in setting them to music. The melody should

41. *Sabisabi to shitaru naka ni. Sabi* is the much discussed late-medieval ideal of understated, monochromatic, somewhat deteriorated, rustic beauty. Here, reduplicating the word and turning it into an adverb (via *to*), Zeami refers to an atmosphere in which nothing in particular stands out but from which a profound mental (cognitive, intellectual, emotional?) beauty is born.

42. This final line is couched in the quotative mode that one might be inclined to use when citing Confucius, say, or a revered sutra, but is assumed to be Zeami's own dictum.

43. This passage is, with certain exceptions noted later, identical to a passage in *Oral Instructions on Song*. In *Oral Instructions on Song*, the passage is appended as two separate articles.

be set in such a way that an appealing effect is created through the words; the elocution is correct; the transition from phrase to phrase sounds fluent and smooth. Then when it is sung, provided you sing with a clear understanding of the music, the way the music is set and the way the words are sung will be well matched and will create interest and excitement. Thus the way the music is set serves as the standard for the singing. Graceful movement from word to word and concord between the melody and the articulation of consonants in the text produce an appealing effect. The melody provides the outline; vocal style relates to movement from word to word; and expression is a matter of the mind. You should be very careful to understand the distinction between the breath and the *ki*, and *fushi* and *kyoku*.[44] During training, one says, "Forget voice, and know expression; forget expression and know pitch; forget pitch and know rhythm."

Also, about the order in studying singing: first memorize the words, and after that, master the song; after that, create distinction in the melody; after that, discern the proper accent for the words;[16] after that, grasp the intent. The rhythm must be understood throughout, at the beginning, in the middle, and at the end.

Also, with regard to mispronunciation in singing: mispronunciations affecting melodic inflections are of no consequence. Mispronunciation affecting words are likely to be more problematic. The distinction between the two is important. You should learn it well. What I mean by "mispronunciations pertaining to words" is related to the fact that all proper words have an accent that, if incorrect, results in mispronunciation. Mispronunciations pertaining to melodic inflections has to do with the accent of *kana* like *te*, *ni*, and *ha*. When the accent of these particles *te*, *ni*, and *ha* is changed a little on account of the melodic configuration of the text, it should not be jarring to the ear as long as the melody is acceptable. "The lightness or heaviness, the voicing or lack of voicing of a word depends on the preceding text," as they say. Or they refer to euphonic elisions. This is to be clearly transmitted orally.

Regarding what I've been referring to as suffixes like *te*, *ni*, and *ha*:[17] when the accent on words like *ha*, *ni*, *no*, *wo*, *ka*, *te*, *mo*, and *shi* is only slightly incorrect, it should not be jarring to the ear as long as the melody is attractive. What I mean by melody and expression is largely the resonance[18] of the letters *te*, *ni*, and *ha*.[19]

44. *Oral Instructions on Song* reads, "In effect, the breath is the same as the *ki*, and although the words *fushi* and *kyoku* can be written with the same graphs, the way they are to be learned in singing is different." Zeami himself seems aware of the seeming paradox here by calling attention to the confusion between the different Chinese graphs, which can be read *fushi* in Japanese. In his continued discussion of the distinction between *fushi* and *kyoku*, he seems to make an increasingly clear distinction between the former, an abstract formal structure that is unambiguous and provides the same "outline" for each singer, and the latter, which is unique to the individual performer and impossible to imitate. See the introduction.

As a general principle, the music is not to be sung in a singsong monotony. Proper words should be sung in coherent units, and the rhythm should be stretched and condensed using particles like *te*, *ni*, and *ha*.[20] The four tones *ping*, *shang*, *qu*, and *ru* should match correctly.[21]

The *Han shu*[45] says, "The twelve musical tones were transferred into the *ritsu* scale and *ryo* scale[46] when Lü Lizi went to Mount Kunlun and heard the call of the male phoenix and the call of the female phoenix," and so forth.[22] The *ritsu* scale is the voice of the male phoenix and is yang. The *ryo* scale is the voice of the female phoenix and is yin. The *ritsu* scale is the voice that descends from above and is inhaled breath. The *ryo* scale is the voice that ascends from below and is exhaled breath.[47] The *ritsu* scale is the voice emerging from the *ki*; the *ryo* scale is the voice emerging from the breath. The *ritsu* scale is being; the *ryo* scale is nothingness. This probably means that the *ritsu* scale is vertical and the *ryo* scale, horizontal.[48]

The *Analects*[49] says, "Bear, tiger, and leopard skin make good targets for archery. Tiger, for the Son of Heaven; leopard, for the various dukes; bear for the great ministers." Since that is the case, they should be listed as tiger, leopard and bear, but they are listed as written above, so that the order proceeds euphonically, and so forth.[50]

45. Material of similar content is to be found in *Han shu*, *Lülizhi* (漢書、律暦志), although Zeami apparently mistakes the chapter title, "Lü Lizi," for a personal name. The chapter in question concerns the myth-history of musical tones and calendrics.

This, the previous line about the four tones, and the following paragraph are appended to the main body of the text as notes.

46. For *ritsu* and *ryo*, see the article "First Pitch, Second *Ki*, Third Voice."

47. A mechanical means of determining pitch intervals, termed the *sanbun-son'eki-hō*, specified the use of a tube of a given length (and pitch) that was divided in thirds. A second shorter tube, of two-thirds the original tube's length, should then produce a pitch a perfect fifth higher than the original pitch. A third longer tube, of four-thirds the original tube's length, should produce a pitch a perfect fourth lower than the original pitch. On this basis, the physical relationship of various pitches was mathematically determined. When working with *ryo* pitches, complementary harmonics apparently were determined on the basis of a low root note, whereas when working with a *ritsu* pitch, a higher tone was regarded as fundamental, and lower consonant pitches were determined on the basis of the higher tone. See appendix 1, and Omote, in *ZZ*, p. 442n.31.

48. "Vertical" and "horizontal" as translations are surmises on the basis of Zeami's use of 横. His 主 as the former is accounted an *ateji* that would more precisely be written 竪 (or, better yet, 豎). These terms, though far from clear to modern scholars, are discussed in more detail by Zeami in *A Collection of Jewels in Effect*.

49. The quoted passage cannot be found in the *Analects*, but there is a similar passage in *The Rites of Zhou* (specifically in *Zhou li, Tianguan, zhongzai*), although there it says that the Son of Heaven, the emperor, is to have a target of tiger, bear, or leopard; the various lords (諸侯) to have a target of bear or leopard; and the ministers and great officers (卿大夫) to have a target of reindeer. The *Shuo wen* lists the order as "bear, tiger, leopard."

50. Zeami is interested here in the discrepancy between a listing according to civil rank, which would place the tiger, as the skin used for the emperor's targets, before the leopard and bear, and

The Innermost Section

The whole of this volume is contained more or less in the aforementioned articles. There should not be any other matters for instruction. In effect, there isn't anything else but to know performance. Unless you discern what it means to know performance, all these articles will be useless. If you really and truly intend to know performance, then you first must push aside all other vocations and concerns, enter completely and exclusively into this art, practice continually to refine what you have learned, and lay down layer upon layer of experience, at which point it will take shape in your mind of its own accord; then you will be sure to know it.[23]

You should assuredly have confidence in what your teacher tells you and focus on it in your mind. What I mean by what your teacher tells you is to strive intently in your study of the articles in this volume, to apprehend them firmly in your mind, and then, when it comes to an actual performance, to try putting these articles into practice, and if they are effective, then to respect them for their value, to have all the more reverence for the vocation, and to lay down your experience over many years; this is of the greatest efficacy in knowing performance. In every artistic vocation, there is a proper way to proceed: you should learn and learn, study and study, and then bring it into effect. In *sarugaku* as well, you should learn and should study, then you will be able to bring into effect every one of these articles.

In secret[51] it is said that the performance is to be studied continuously from youth through old age.[24] What I mean in saying that it should be studied through old age is this: once you have learned what is appropriate to each stage of your life, from the time you were a beginner through your prime, you should then, after forty, perform with restraint and adopt a manner of expression made increasingly spare. This then is what it should be to study the manner of expression from forty on. From somewhat after the age of fifty, you should mainly make it your method to do nothing.[52] This is a transition of great difficulty. Regarding what you are to study during this period, you first should reduce your repertory. Make singing the basis of your performance; use your expressiveness sparingly; and reduce

the listing with which he begins the paragraph, which proceeds according to euphony in Mandarin, *xiong*, *hu*, *bao*, and in Japanese, *iu*, *ko*, *hau*.

51. In some manuscripts, the words "in secret" are written as a section head, roughly comparable to "The Innermost Section."

52. Compare *Transmitting the Flower*: There's probably no better method around this age than to do nothing.

the figures in your Dance[53] so as to show just a hint of your earlier performance style. It is likely that in singing you will find a certain twist of interest for your performance as an old man. Any raw immaturity has been leached out of the aged voice, and in the remaining voice, whether *wau* or *shu* or doubly proficient,[54] there should be a certain twist, which allows for interest and excitement in sound. This will give you one advantage. On the basis of our understanding of all this, what I mean is that you should adopt a manner of expression in old age in which you endeavor to strip one figure away.[55]

Dramatic imitation based on the two modes, the Aged and the Woman's, should be suitable for imitation in the art of an old actor. It will, however, depend on those things at which the actor is physically adept. An actor who is adept at quiet forms of expression is likely to match well with the Aged Mode. If, however, he is adept at techniques for representing madness and frenzy, then he is unlikely to suit the part. Nonetheless, if he understands that Dance or Sparring, which would ordinarily be performed at a full 100 percent, should in this case be performed at 60 or 70 percent, then he might undertake the part, on the specific understanding that he only "move seven parts of the body." This, you should know, is what should be studied in old age.

Now then, there is a phrase among our troupe that sums up many accomplishments in a single virtue, to wit:

> Do not forget your initial intent.[56]

Oral transmissions concerning this phrase are contained in three separate articles:

> Do not forget your initial intent, right or wrong.
> Do not forget your initial intent on each occasion.
> Do not forget your initial intent in old age.

53. *Te* are probably the gestural figures in a particular Dance that give it its unique character and that occur at focal points during its predictable choreographic course. They correspond structurally to the *te*, or melodic figures, in the flute parts of Dances, although they do not necessarily occur at the same point.

54. See *Oral Instructions on Singing.*

55. *Hitote toranzuru koto* does not, I think, mean a particular figure but to reduce by one the "figurality" of the performance.

56. 初心不可忘, perhaps Zeami's most famous saying.

• What I mean by "don't forget your initial intent, right or wrong" is that there are many advantages to be had once you've grown old as long as you don't forget your first intent while you were young but keep it with you all along.

> "In knowing an earlier wrong," as they say, "you're laying a claim on what's right later on."
>
> "The place where one cart overturns repays the next one's keen concern."

To forget your initial intent, doesn't that mean forgetting your retrospective intent as well? When your long experience prevails and you gain fame, that's the effect of your performance improving. If you forget how this improvement has happened, then you'll fail to know when your mind regresses to your initial intent. But regressing to your initial intent surely means your performance is declining. You must, therefore, contrive a way not to forget your initial intent, in order not to forget your current rank of attainment. Make every effort to understand this principle: if you should forget your initial intent, you will regress to it. If you don't forget your initial intent, then your subsequent intent should be correct. If your subsequent intent is correct, then the techniques by which your art has improved will allow no regression.

This is the rationale by which you may distinguish the right from the wrong.

Also, a young person must have an accurate perception of his rank of artistry at present and must concentrate intently on the fact that "this is the measure of my initial intent. In order to know higher levels of artistry, I must not forget this initial intent." If he forgets his initial intent, he will not recognize the opportunity for improvement, and his performance will not improve. This is why a young person must not forget his initial intent now.

• What I mean by "don't forget your initial intent on each occasion" is that you should take great care in the manner of expression appropriate to your artistry at any particular stage from your initial intent through your prime until you have attained old age; this is your initial intent on each occasion. For should you forget the artistry associated with each particular stage in your career, abandoning it as you move along, then you will have nothing in your control but the artistry of your present stage. If you retain your present capability of performing in each style you mastered in the past, then you will have great diversity at your disposal and will never deplete your repertory. The dramatic expression of each of these occasions in the past comprises the initial intent on each occasion, so it follows, doesn't it, that maintaining these in your current performance amounts to not forgetting your initial intent on each occasion? There you have him, then: an actor with real diversity. Do not, therefore, forget your initial intent at each stage.

• What I mean by "don't forget your initial intent in old age" is that life has its term, but performance should have no bounds. Having mastered each particular style in its time, you then learn those forms of expression appropriate to old age; this is your initial intent in old age. Since this is the initial intent in old age, your earlier performances entail retrospective intent. I have said that from fifty on, "there is no better method than to do nothing."[57] That one should undertake in old age to do something as difficult as making a method of doing nothing—doesn't that amount to initial intent?

If you pass your entire life in this way without forgetting your initial intent, you will sing your swan song in old age in the full possession of your powers, and your performance will never diminish. You thus will end your life without laying bare any limitation in your performance; this is the ultimate teaching among our troupe, a secret transmission for the instruction of our children and grandchildren. I make this my plan for the art: to hand down the full depth of my understanding as the transmission of the initial intent to coming generations. Once you have forgotten your initial intent, you cannot transmit it to your descendants. Do not forget your initial intent; make it the inheritance of generations.

There may, in addition to this, be different views, depending on the insights of the perceptive.

The various chapters of *Transmitting the Flower Through Effects and Forms*, from "Notes on Training Through the Years" through "Separate Pages of Oral Instructions," represent a secret treatise that makes our vocation known from the point of view of the flower. It is a record of articles on various of my father's teachings as I mastered them over a period of more than twenty years. This volume, *A Mirror to the Flower*, is a summary in six chapters and twelve articles of what I myself have learned about the art now and then, from the time I was a little over forty until my old age, and I have written it out in a single text to leave it as a record of the art.

Ōei 31 [1424]:6:1[58] *Zea (seal)*

This volume was transmitted to Zeami's grandchildren's household[25] and was not to be given out to anyone else, but my devotion to the vocation met with divine favor, and I was therefore able to get access to the text. For this reason, I have copied it out myself for the sake of our vocation and for the

57. See *Transmitting the Flower.*

58. The sixth lunar month would appear to have been one of Zeami's favorite times for writing. (It corresponds to midsummer, perhaps not a favorite time for full performances. Indeed, nō performers perform infrequently in July and August except in celebratory—or commercial—*takigi* performances, which take place outdoors, generally at night.) Note that the colophon to *Oral Instructions on Singing* also specifies a day in the sixth month and *Transmitting the Flower* is dated to 1418:6:1.

sake of our house because it is an auspicious relic for our troupe. Praise be! Praise be! It is not to be shown to anyone else.

A day in Eikyō 9 [1437]:8 Tsurauji (seal)[59]

Notes

1. Literally, without shape or form, but "shapeless" or "formless" hardly conveys the valence here. Compare Omote: "a wondrous figure in Dance which is beyond description" (*ZZ*, p. 88).

2. Apparently a rephrasing of 眼不能見其睫 (The eye cannot see its own eyelashes) from 顔氏家訓.

3. Zeami's phrase is 花姿玉得の幽舞, which might be more literally translated as the exquisite beauty in dance of "blossoming form and jewel attained." 幽舞 readily suggests *yūgen* (幽玄), and 花姿玉得 seems to be Zeami's own coinage, or a compound created within the circle of *sarugaku* intellectuals at the time. The terms used are encountered among the titles of certain pieces in his *Notes* (e.g., 風姿花伝、拾玉得花) and often are elements in his technical vocabulary when discussing the aesthetic desiderata of performance. My thanks to Susan Matisoff for her insights regarding this passage.

4. The meaning of the final line of this chapter seems somewhat incongruous and, even after the considerable reflection given it by the major commentators, remains open to some doubt. 担板 seems relatively settled as an expression from various Zen sources referring to someone carrying a plank over his shoulder or on his back and having, therefore, an obstructed view of things. 担板感, though, has been read as 担板漢 (a guy with a plank over his shoulder) (Omote, in *ZZ*, pp. 89, 449–50, based on an earlier interpretation by Kawase Kazuma in a manuscript autographed by Kanze Kiyochika from 1723) and as 担板箴 (an admonition for one carrying a plank over his shoulder) (Konishi Jin'ichi, *Zeami shū*, Nihon no shisō, vol. 8 [Tokyo: Chikuma shobō, 1970], p. 199). I follow Omote, accepting his reasoning that 箴 would be a *hapax* in Zeami's *Notes* and therefore an unlikely emendation.

Yamazaki Masakazu reads 感 as both 漢 and 箴 (i.e., いましめ [ていう]), expands the sentence into a paragraph, and interprets the "guy with the plank over his shoulder" as a self-deprecating reference by Zeami to himself: "Even a person like myself, with a plank over my shoulder, and consequently blind for some 180°, takes care to act with attention to left, right, front, and back" (*Zeami*, Nihon no meicho, vol. 10 [Tokyo: Chūō kōronsha, 1969], p. 174).

I accept Omote's emendation of 動 as はたらき, augmenting the graph to give what in modern Japanese would read as 働. In many cases in the *Notes* this is a highly plausible emendation.

5. All of the first six articles in *A Mirror to the Flower* are expressions in *kanbun* that can be read as sentences in the indicative or imperative. The rest of the articles in *A Mirror to the Flower*, with the exception of the final one, end with the nominalizing graph 事, resulting in a rendering of "The matter of . . ." and Zeami makes explicit reference to the distinction here.

6. Zeami writes 心七分動 here but clearly mistakes 心 (*shin*) for 身 (*shin*), as articulated in the previous article 動十分心、動七分身, "Move Ten Parts of the Mind, Move Seven Parts of the Body."

7. Zeami's reference to "rank" (位) raises significant questions. In previous uses of this word, he seems to have been referring to the level of a performer's attainments, but here the usage implies something that a teacher can allow or entrust to a student. Omote conflates this with Zen seals of enlightenment (*inka*, 印可) and artistic licenses (*menkyo*, 免許) such as are awarded to performers in a wide variety of traditional arts at milestones in their training (usually for a significant fee). See *ZZ*, p. 93n. It seems doubtful, though, that the systematization of artistic pedagogy

59. 貫氏. Tsurauji is apparently an early name of Komparu Zenchiku, Zeami's son-in-law. Zenchiku was thirty-two in 1437.

had reached this level of development in Zeami's day, and it is probably worth noting that Zeami's reference here is not to any object but to the action of permitting or allowing (the rank is "allowed" or "permitted," or even perhaps "made accessible" to the student in the verb *yurusu*).

8. 易云、非其人伝其書、所天悪. The sentence is written between the lines of the primary manuscript Omote that uses (the *Tsurauji-bon*, in the possession of Hōzanji temple in Ikoma), with a notation that it is to be inserted after the previous sentence. It also is inserted at the end of *A Course to Attain the Flower*, along with other Chinese citations, citing the *Classic of Changes*, yet the line cannot be found in the *Classic of Changes* and has not been identified precisely elsewhere either, although similar sentiments were widely expressed in medieval Japan.

9. Zeami uses the word *tendoku* 転読, a form of abbreviation sometimes practiced by Buddhist clerics in which they skip from passage to passage, skimming over the intervening text. He borrows the term here to describe the acting style of young performers who borrow aspects of masters' performances without the training that led to those aspects, as warned against in a previous passage.

10. 温故新知。可以為師 is a slight mistranscription of *Analects* 2.11, which more accurately is read 子曰、温故而知新。可以為師矣. The English translation of the latter would not vary noticeably.

11. Zeami's text reads 大寒氷解、小寒云々, but I am persuaded by Omote that his use of the final two graphs here is eccentric and should be understood to represent a repetition of the final two graphs in the preceding line: 大寒氷解、小寒氷解, thus the translation. Apparently a proverb, the source has not yet been identified.

12. Zeami writes 感用, and Omote suggests quite plausibly that this is his own idiosyncratic rendering of a word that would normally be written 肝要. The latter, though, seems merely to be a synonym for 大切, which Zeami also uses earlier in the sentence (although using *hiragana*, not *kanji*). I have assumed that Zeami's choice of the particular graphs 感用 is related to the affective importance of the word 感, as he discusses it earlier in *A Mirror to the Flower.*

13. In some texts, the word "article" is reduplicated, making it uncertain whether this instruction is to be applied to this article alone or to all of *A Mirror to the Flower* up to this point.

14. 稽古有勧急. The meaning of this sentence, in *kanbun*, is not immediately clear and is open to various interpretations. Those who read it as written suggest versions like the translation I have given (for a Japanized 稽古ハ急ニ勧ムルニ 有リ) or "Training resides in promoting urgency" (for 稽古ハ急ヲ勧ムルニ 有リ).

It is possible that the graph 勧 is a mistranscription for 勤, which would suggest a translation like "Training resides in working hard with urgency." Or, if 勧 is to be taken as an ad hoc representation (i.e., *ateji*) of 緩, then one could translate the sentence as "Training may be undertaken at leisure or with urgency" (the latter being preferable). Or again, given the same emendation but a different nuance: "Training has its times of leisure and times of urgency."

Again, it could be that 急 is a mistranscription for 志, which would lead to something like "Training resides in promoting ones intention."

Omote lays out the numerous possibilities and discusses their various proponents, as well as possible links to *Gettan oshō hōgo*, in *ZZ*, pp. 451–52n.43.

15. *Mujau no sono mono naru beshi* (mod. J. *mujō no . . .*). "The very thing" seems frustratingly vague, although perhaps it accords in Zeami's way of thinking with the ineffable quality of these "wondrous places. Note earlier, in "On the Matter of Knowing How to Study the Vocation," how he speaks of "the very thing" and defines it as "the attainment to a rank of great mastery, a rank at which you will be recognized as a teacher yourself."

16. In the corresponding position in *Oral Instructions on Song*, Zeami says instead, "understand the rank of your voice."

17. As stated earlier. Zeami's word, *oharigana* (mod. J. *owarigana* [ending-letters]) is somewhat imprecise in that although all the particles in question do follow some other word, they do not, in most cases, end an utterance. They are, for the most part, case markers or emphatics. Perhaps a more apposite translation would be "enclitics," but that seems too technical for our purposes.

18. *Oral Instructions on Song* reads こゑ, which in context I translated as "accent" rather than ひびき, my "resonance" here.

19. Here, Zeami revises the otherwise nearly identical passage from *Oral Instructions on Singing* in order to mention both "melody" (*fushi*) and "expression" (*kyoku*), whereas earlier he spoke only of *fushi*. Note the fine distinction between the two, mentioned earlier.

20. The wording in *Oral Instructions on Song* is slightly different: "the rhythmic elements should be stretched and condensed using particles like *te*, *ni*, and *ha*."

21. In *Oral Instructions on Song*, Zeami says, "The four tones *ping*, *shang*, *qu*, and *ru* correspond to the five pitches." This is puzzling, as noted in the footnote to that passage. Here he says rather laconically, 平声 [*sic*, for 上] 去入四声可合, my "The four tones *ping*, *shang*, *qu*, and *ru* should match correctly." Presumably he means that the execution of the particles in question should accord with their "tone," borrowing, as he does, the idea of tone from Chinese.

22. "Phoenix" is an expedient rendering of the name of a Chinese mythical species of bird, the *fenghuang* (鳳凰), which appears in the world in tandem with a sage emperor.

23. 是をしるべし. The antecedent for 是 is not clear. Probably it means 能, my "performance" in the previous sentences.

24. There is some uncertainty as to the reading of this line. It seems to be written as a cursivized form of the graphs 私義云, but for reasons that Omote details, it is probably intended to read 秘義云. See *ZZ*, p. 438n.22. In either case, it alerts the reader to the confidentiality of the following passage.

25. One of the graphs in this passage is difficult to decipher, but I have accepted Omote's reasoning for parsing this as 世子、孫之家ニ伝. See *ZZ*, p. 454n.48.

A Course to Attain the Flower

至花道, 1420

A Course to Attain the Flower is a brief but important text from Zeami's middle period. Its five primary articles concern the qualities of successful and unsuccessful actors and the way that an actor should take individual control of performance. As he does in *A Mirror to the Flower*, Zeami reaches to Chinese and Buddhist classics to bolster his assertions. Indeed, the final article, "On Substance and Instance," takes its inspiration from a well-rooted binarism in Chinese philosophy, and Zeami's understanding of the pair contributes a new and important practical significance to this abstract concept.

A Course to Attain the Flower is more closely focused on a single matter, that of the actor' s training, than are, say, *A Mirror to the Flower* and *Transmitting the Flower Through Effects and Attitudes*, both of which cover a wide range of concerns. In part, because of the existence of diversely ambitious works like these, Zeami can afford to concentrate on a particular area of interest for intensive treatment here, but his focus also shows an increasingly theoretical weight in his interests and, in the rest of his writing, shorter and more single-minded texts

Although *A Course to Attain the Flower* has an earlier date than *A Mirror to the Flower*, I follow Omote in situating it here after the latter text, because I am persuaded by his arguments that most of *A Mirror to the Flower* was written before *A Course to Attain the Flower. A Mirror* seems to have been the major text of the middle of Zeami's career and to have been written over a period of years after the completion of *Transmitting the Flower.* After *A Mirror* was relatively well settled (except, perhaps, for the last four sections), Zeami apparently wrote this text, which, in any case, bears a close relation to *A Mirror.*

- On the Two Arts and the Three Modes
- On Failing to Bring the Subject into Effect
- On the Rank of Great Virtuosity[1]

1. *Taketaru kurawi* (mod. J. *kurai*), or in Sino-Japanese, *ran' i*, is a central attainment, perhaps the ultimate attainment, of the actor, discussed at length for the first time here. See also the introduction.

- On Skin, Meat, and Bones
- On Substance and Instance[2]

• Various articles regarding training in this art. Although there are many forms of expression [in *sarugaku*], the first steps taken in an actor's training should not depart from the Two Arts and the Three Modes. The Two Arts are singing and dance; the Three Modes are the roles in dramatic imitation.[3]

A child should first learn music and dance very thoroughly from his teacher, and from about age ten until he puts aside a child' s attire,[4] he should not study the Three Modes. Whatever his role, the effects of his performance are to be presented from the attitude of a child. He should not wear a mask; any dramatic imitation should be done in name alone; and his attire should be such as befits a child. Just as in the dances of *bugaku*, in which, if it's a child who is dancing, he wears no mask and is dressed as befits a young boy, and if the dances Ryō-ō and Nasori are performed, they are performed only in name.[5] This is the root through which *yūgen* may be sustained in his art into the distant future. (As it says in *Daxue*, "When the roots are in disorder, there is no ordering of the branches.")[6]

Once the child has "donned his trousers" and assumed the role of a man, he then may wear a mask and assume diverse attitudes on stage, with their corresponding costuming; all the same, the first steps leading him to artistic styles of the greatest achievement are simply the Three Modes. They are these three: the Aged Mode, the Woman's Mode, and the Martial Mode. There's

2. The conceptual binarism *tai/yufu* (mod. J. *tai/yū* or *yō*; Ch. *ti/yong*), first mentioned in *Transmitting the Flower*, is treated most extensively here. Also see the introduction.

3. The Three Modes are discussed in detail in *The Three Courses*. See also *ZS*, chaps. 3–5.

4. In other words, as long as he continues to wear his hair loose as a child characteristically does and doesn't take to wearing *hakama* trousers. Traditionally, upper-class male children underwent the ceremony of *genbuku* (donning trousers), which marked the social threshold at which they entered adulthood.

5. *Bugaku* is a type of dance associated with the royal court, which was imported into Japan in the sixth through ninth centuries along with *gagaku*, the music used to accompany it. Among its most famous pieces are Ryō-Ō (陵王, orth. Reuwau, also Ryō or Ranryōō) and Nasori (納蘇利, orth. Nassori). Ryō-Ō is said to be a dance of celebration after a battle in which the king of Qi, Chang Gong, who was extraordinarily handsome, donned a grotesque mask and achieved a major victory. The mask used in Ryō-Ō today is, indeed, grotesque and fascinating, and it is hard to imagine a child dancer wearing it.

Ryō-Ō is traditionally paired with Nasori in full *bugaku* performances. The later piece is thought to represent the dance of a pair of dragons, one male and one female. Again, the masks used are quite exotic.

6. The quotation from *Daxue* is not exact. It should be 其本乱而末治者否矣 (There is no such thing as branches being well ordered when the roots are tangled). Zeami quotes the passage, in his version, twice elsewhere in the *Notes*. He perhaps transcribed it from an acquaintance's oral version. In the text here, there is a mistranscription as well as the oral paraphrase just referred to. For further details, see Omote, in *ZZ*, p. 455n.50.

really no other system of training in this vocation apart from learning everything you possibly can about these three—that is, the study of roles in which you become an old man, the study of roles in which you become a woman, and the study of valiant roles—and imbuing every one of them throughout with the Two Arts of singing and dance, which you have internalized since you were a child.

The other attractions of performance, each and every one, are derived as a matter of course from the Two Arts and the Three Modes, and you should wait patiently for them to develop. The display of sacredness and utter tranquillity is an adaptation of the Aged Mode; the elegant grace of *yūgen* is an adaptation of the Woman's Mode; and an energetic vitality in performance, vigorous movement, and the stomping of feet is an adaptation of the Martial Mode; in this way, the scene you have in mind should, on its own accord, unfold visually.[7] For some reason, if your artistic power is inadequate to this and these adaptations fail, you still can be an actor of the greatest achievement as long as you have made the most of the Two Arts and the Three Modes. (I call these Two Arts and Three Modes the ground that ensures a foundational expressive capacity.)

I have observed in this context that in *sarugaku* training these days, everybody is learning all sorts of dramatic imitation and eccentric forms of expression without having first committed themselves to the Two Arts and Three Modes, so of course they end up failing to bring the subject into effect; their performance is weak; they look inferior on stage; and not a single one gains a name as an artist. I'll say it again and again: if you don't take your first steps [in this vocation] in the mainstream of the Two Arts and Three Modes but put your efforts into peripheral kinds of dramatic imitation, your training is sure to diverge into trivialities and end up without substance. Understand that the first graceful beauty in a child's attitude is to remain in the Three Modes, and the various adaptations of the Three Modes are to produce a generative scene for a myriad forms of expression.[8]

• Something you should avoid in this art is, namely, failing to bring the subject into effect. Take care to understand this well. It could be that one should have a mastery by virtue of one's innate artistic grounding. Then again, it could be that one's grounding comes as a matter of course, as the result of long experience in training.

7. The point being that a full competence and mastery of the Three Modes imbued with the artistic quality of the Two Arts will enable the performer to bring the scene within his mind, whatever it may hold, into fruition on stage.

8. *Bankyoku no seikei*, the phrase recurs in *Figure Drawings of the Two Arts and the Three Modes*. *Seikei* is the generative ground, or "scene you have in mind" (*ichū no kei*), from which any type of performance can be assembled.

Apparently, even in singing and dance, as long as you are still engaged in mimicry, you will fail to bring the subject into effect. Even though such mimicry may for a time resemble its object, unless you really have made it your own, your expressive power will prove inadequate, and your performance will not improve, since as such an actor, you will be without an effective subject. If, however, you have learned well, imitating your teacher, have captured what he teaches with your eyes and fully absorbed it both mentally and physically, and have come to be an accomplished actor of the rank of consummate ease, then that is what it is to be a master. That, surely, is a living performance. To have studied and trained and, on the basis of the artistic power in your grounding, gained a commensurate capacity for performance and become "the very thing," that is surely what it means to be an actor who has mastered how to bring the subject into effect. I'll say it over and over again: achieve the clearest possible view of the distinction between bringing the subject into effect and failing to bring the subject into effect. As they say, "What's hard is not doing something, but doing it well."[9]

• Occasionally in this art, an expert actor has arrived at the peak of his artistry and, from the rank of great virtuosity of intent, manifests from time to time strange forms of expression; beginners sometimes try to emulate this. The expressive mastery made possible by this kind of virtuosity is not so easily imitated. What sort of understanding would, indeed, make it possible to imitate this?

You see, the technique of this rank of great virtuosity is a form of artistry that occasionally appears through the power of intent of an expert actor who, over years of training from his youth all the way to advanced age, has, in an exhaustive mastery, distilled the right and eliminated the wrong and raised himself above it. It's a matter of tempering the right way to perform with the admixture of a small degree of the wrong way to perform, which the actor has managed to isolate and eliminate from his performance through the long years of his training. Why, you ask, should an expert actor perform in the wrong way?—this relates to the ingenuity of the expert actor. He would not be an expert unless he performed in the right way. That being the case, though, there's nothing fresh about his performing correctly, and the audi-

9. A similar phrase is quoted in *Pick Up a Jewel and Take the Flower in Hand*, where it is attributed to the *Mencius*. The phrase, however, is not found there, but phrases of similar meaning (though not identically expressed) can be found in numerous medieval Japanese texts. Omote quotes *Shasekishiu*, *Shōbōgenzō zuimonki*, and Nijō Yoshimoto's *Renri hishō*. See *ZZ*, p. 455n.51. The phrase and its variants seem to have circulated as proverbs with textual antecedents in the *Wenzhuan*, where it takes the form 蓋非知之難、能之難也 (Now this is not difficult to know, but it is difficult to be able [to do]), and the *Shujing*, where it reads 非知之艱、行之惟艱 (This is not difficult to understand; it is merely difficult to carry out). In Zeami' s citation, the graph 堅 is a substitute (*ateji*) for 難 or 艱.

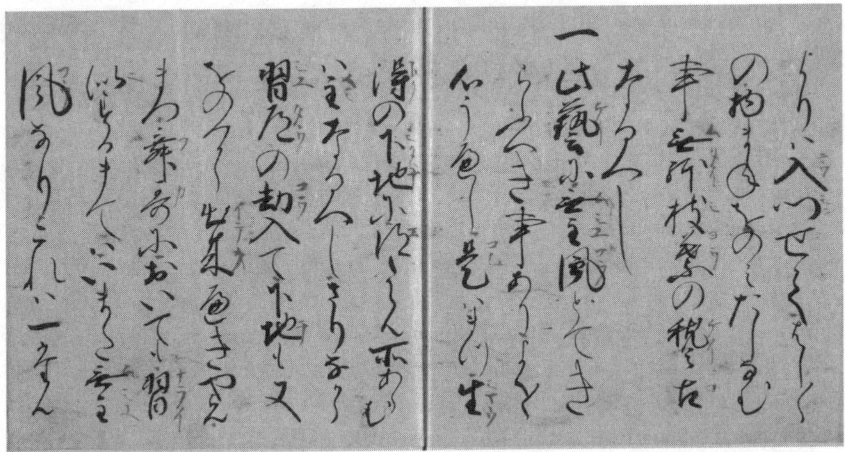

Two leaves from *A Course to Attain the Flower.* From the middle of the leaf on the right is the section on failing to bring the subject into effect. Although once considered an autograph manuscript by Zeami, it actually dates from the late Muromachi period (1333–1573) and is in the same fluent hand as an important manuscript of *Transmitting the Flower.* The text shows a higher percentage of Chinese graphs (*kanji*) to *kana* than in earlier texts in the *Performance Notes*, which perhaps necessitated the extensive use of Japanese glosses, in red. (Photograph courtesy of Hōzanji temple, Ikoma, and the library of Nara joshi daigaku)

ence is likely to grow rather too familiar with how he looks, but on the rare occasions when he mixes in something wrong, it serves as a fresh attraction precisely because he is an expert. There is, then, contrary to expectation, a perspective afforded by distance in which the wrong style turns into the right style. This is a form of display in which the wrong is transformed into the right through the expressive power of the expert actor. And it is also an interesting manner of expression.

When a beginner, though, concludes that this is an interesting technique and sets about to imitate it with the thought that it is worthy of emulation, then he mixes techniques that are, by their very nature, inadequate to his as yet scant artistic foundation, as if he were throwing wood on the fire. He fails to understand, doesn't he, that this virtuosity is not a technique per se but a matter of the expert's mental rank. You must take care to understand this thoroughly. There's a difference as stark as black and white between the expert who does this, understanding what is wrong about it, and a beginner who imitates it, misunderstanding it as right. How, in such a situation, could anyone without long experience, much less a beginner, ever attain the rank of great virtuosity? In such circumstances, the beginner's imitating what the expert does in his great virtuosity amounts to imitating what is wrong, so what he attains is a hard-won mediocrity, isn't that right?

"To look for what you desire by doing what you are doing is like resorting to a tree to look for a fish."[10] They also say, "Resorting to a tree to look for a fish is merely foolish. There is no great loss. To do what you are doing, in the pursuit of what you desire, though, will entail a great loss." From *Mencius*.[11]

This virtuosic technique of the expert, the technique in which the wrong is flipped over into the right, is a twist[12] that the expert has at his command. It is not the sort of technique a mediocre actor has at his command. As a consequence, it undoubtedly will result in failure should a mediocre actor, given the capabilities at his command, seek to employ capabilities that are not at his command. It will be like "seeking for what he desires by doing what he is doing." If it's a matter of high-quality performance within the parameters of a foundational expressive style, then when it's close but doesn't quite work, that in particular doesn't constitute a failure. This is on a par with resorting to a tree in searching for a fish. I'll say it over and over again: one cannot *learn* the wrong way to perform and the twist of eccentricity to which an expert may have access in his virtuosity. That would be to train toward loss. Keep this in mind.

Generally, as a beginner you should stay close by your teacher, raise questions about what you don't understand, and dutifully ask for clarification of your progress in the ranks of the art. Even on occasions when you may observe such mysteries of the art as these, you should turn back again and again to the primary foundational techniques of the Two Arts and Three Modes until you have achieved the clearest possible view. (Think carefully about what it says in the Lotus [Sutra] about "contriving an understanding without yet having understood, and contriving enlightenment without yet being enlightened.")[13]

• There are skin, meat, and bones in the constitution of this art. All three have not yet come together (in a single actor). And according to tradition, for

10. 若所為、求若所欲、猶縁木而求魚也。An exact quotation of *Mencius*, Liang Huiwang I, A, vii, 17, except for the omission of the first graph there, 以.

11. After the restatement in Japanese of what had been quoted in Chinese, Zeami proceeds, again quoting *Mencius* relatively closely, 縁木求魚、雖不得魚、無後災、以若所為、求若所欲、尽心力而為之、後必有災 (Resorting to a tree to look for a fish, though it results in no fish, does not entail a disaster afterward; doing one thing in the search for something else, exhausting the power of your mind in the process, will inevitably lead to disaster).

12. *Kyoku* is a "turn," a "bend," or a "twist." Zeami uses this metaphor as an indication of something uniquely attractive in a talented performer, and it becomes the linchpin in this theory of expression. See the introduction.

13. The line is a variation on a line from the *upāya kauśalya* or *fangbian* (J. *hōben*) chapter of the Lotus Sutra (Saddharma puṇḍarīkā Sūtra). The original Chinese reads 未得謂得、未証謂証 (calling it an understanding without yet having understood, and calling it enlightenment without yet being enlightened). The form in which Zeami quotes the lines already was in Fujiwara no Shunzei's colophon to *Minbukyō utaawase* and his twenty-first judgment in the *wakakusa* section of the *Roppyakuban utaawase*. See Tanaka Yutaka, ed., *Zeami geijutsuron shū*, Shinchōsha koten shūsei, vol. 35 (Tokyo: Shinchōsha, 1976), p. 107n.13.

that matter, it's only in the writing of Kūkai that all three come together, even in calligraphy.[14]

Now, in indicating where in the constitution of the art one is to find this skin, meat, and bones, I believe I would say that the bones are the visible display of innate talent that comes into being with its own felicitous spontaneity in the expert actor. I would say the meat is clear to see in the full expression of a mastery of dance and singing. I would say that the skin is the expressive form in its fullest fluency and beauty, developed to maturity from these qualities. Or if you were to analogize these to vision, hearing, and mind, then I suppose you would say that vision is the skin, hearing is the meat, and mind is the bones. One should also be able to identify these three in the singing alone. (The singing is the skin, the expressiveness is the meat, and the breath is the bone.)[15] You should be able to find them in dance alone, as well. (The attitude is the skin, the gesture is the meat, and the mind is the bone.)[16] Keep these distinctions in mind.

In this context I have observed among actors these days not only that no one possesses all three of these, but no one even seems to be aware of their existence. The only reason I am aware of these distinctions is because of the secret transmission of my late father in this regard. As far as I can see among actors today, there's some evidence of skin and not much else. This, too, is not real skin. And in imitating an expert, it also is only the skin they imitate. For this reason, they are actors with no effective subject.

But even an actor who might have these three in hand must know something more. What you have acquired as innate grounding may be bone; your expressive mastery in song and dance may be meat; and the *yūgen* in your individual demeanor may be skin, but simply having them is not enough. In such circumstances, it still would not be possible to say that the actor "has them ready." The rank at which you might say you "have them ready" is when you have developed each and every one of these elements of happy effect to its utmost, attained the peak of expertise, and entered comfortably into the rank of effect in nothingness, so that your form of expression on the occasion of performance is inexplicably interesting and the audience loses itself in your wondrous appearance; from the sound vantage point of later reflection, they

14. The treatise on poetics, *Guhishō*, spuriously attributed to Fujiwara no Teika, states that skin, meat, and bones are found in the art of calligraphy but are found together only in the work of the great Shingon patriarch Kūkai. See Tanaka, ed., *Zeami geijutsuron shū*, p. 107n.15.

15. The parenthetical remarks are a marginal annotation in the original text. "Singing" (声 [lit., "voice"]) seems to mean the actual manifestation of sound; "music" (曲), the underlying artistic structure; and "breath" (息), the phys(iolog)ical grounding.

16. Again, the parenthetical remarks are a marginal annotation. In this case, "the attitude" seems to mean the actor's overall appearance on stage; "gesture" means the particular vocabulary of movement at his command; and "mind," his intent in the performance, assuming the basis of training and experience on which that intent is based.

will then put together in their thoughts all these things that have only now become apparent in their Vantage from Vision Apart: The excitement aroused from your artistic experience in its bones would mean there wasn't a weak spot, no matter where they looked; the excitement aroused from your artistic experience in its meat would mean that whatever they looked at proved boundless; and the excitement aroused from your artistic experience in its skin would mean that whatever they saw showed *yūgen*; then they would be certain to say, Aha, this is a performer with bone, meat and skin already in control.

• You must know about Substance and Instance in performance. It's as if Substance were the flower and Instance its fragrance. Or as if they were the moon and its reflection. If you have fully understood the Substance, then its Instance will appear of its own accord.

Now, on seeing a performance, those who know see with the mind, and those who don't know see with the eyes. What you see with the mind is Substance. What you see with the eyes is Instance. As a consequence, beginners see the Instance and imitate it. In effect, this amounts to imitating without knowing the principle of Instance. There is good reason not to imitate the Instance. Those who know performance because they see with the mind imitate the Substance. In imitating the Substance well, the Instance is present. Those who don't know imitate the Instance under the impression that it is a manner of expression that can be brought into effect, and they fail to realize that if you imitate the Instance, it becomes the Substance. Since this is not really the Substance of a performance, there is, in the end, no Substance and no Instance either, so the spirit of the performance goes to pieces. This sort of thing is called a performance with neither rhyme nor reason.

When we talk about Substance and Instance, we have a pair. When there is no Substance, there also can be no Instance. It follows that since Instance is not a thing in itself, it contains nothing to take as an object of imitation, so there is no way you can get Substance by taking this nothing as something that can be imitated. What I mean by knowing this is to be aware, through your understanding that Instance is resident in Substance and that they are not separate things, that there is no principle by which something that is not there can be imitated; this is, in effect, to know performance. Thus, since there is no principle by which you can imitate Instance, you should not imitate it. You must understand that imitating Substance is not separate from imitating Instance. I'll say it again and again: if you confidently grasp the principle of what happens to Substance when you imitate Instance, then you will become an actor who has a clear understanding of the distinction between Substance and Instance. Someone has said, "What you want to imitate is the expert; what is not about to be imitated is the expert." If so, then I wonder whether imitation might be a matter of Instance and real resemblance a matter of Substance.[1]

• The various articles regarding training in this, both shallow and profound, were not so much in evidence in the old days. Among performers in the antique style were a few greatly accomplished actors who attained this sort of artistic strength on their own. In those days, in the assessments of aristocrats and the exalted, the good alone was noticed and celebrated, and the bad, for its part, was not criticized. These days, however, the critical eye of the audience is highly refined, and they criticize the slightest fault, so unless the play is an elegant one,[17] a polished gem or carefully selected flower, it is not likely to conform to their standard. As a consequence, there are few really accomplished actors. I fear that the vocation is already waning, and if we neglect instruction of this sort, the vocation might be discontinued, so I have simply made a general statement of those matters in the art that are in my purview. There are still, in addition to this, secret transmissions to be made face to face to those aspirants in the art who have a capacity to understand them.

Ōei 27 [1420], a day in the sixth month, written by Zea

(In the *Analects*, it says, "When someone is to be spoken to, and you fail to speak to him, you waste a person. When someone is not to be spoken to, and you speak to him, you waste your words."[18]

In the [*Classic of*] *Changes* it says, "If it is not the proper person to whom the proper text is transmitted, this is deplorable to Heaven."[19]

As you gain long experience in the fine play of performance,[20] if you find that Instance has produced Substance anew, then there surely will be a wonderful visual display.[2] Once you have created visual display in which the expressive attraction attains the greatest achievement, then there will be no distinction between Substance and Instance. When this happens, and the performance rank of long experience is such that the Instantiated expression of all manner becomes none other than the Substance of performance, that, I believe, must be the wondrous style. Again, all visual display going by the name of expressive grace is of a nature impossible to situate precisely. It simply emanates, as if it were a fragrance, from the Substance into the visual

17. The word *yūkyoku* is used elsewhere to designate a particular genre of play, but in this case, it seems to indicate a level of accomplishment in performance rather than a generic designation. One wonders whether Zeami is making a veiled reference to the artistic interests of the shogun, Ashikaga Yoshimochi, who did not prove to be a reliable patron for him but, rather, a strong supporter of a rival, Zōami, an actor specifically noted for his elegance. See *ZS*, pp. 26–28.

18. *Analects* 15 (Wei Ling Gong), 7.

19. The line is not actually in the *Classic of Changes*, but it also is quoted in *A Mirror to the Flower*.

20. *Yūgaku* (遊楽) is an unusual term that is rather difficult to translate and is discussed in more detail in the introduction. In this particular case, we could interpret it as a synonym for *sarugaku*.

display. Expressive grace is, therefore, resident in Substance but visible in Instance.

The white bird holds a flower in its beak; is this the form of *yūgen*?)[21]

Notes

1. This is seemingly a contradiction (Omote admits it is difficult to understand). The differential must be in the contrast between *nisuru* (似する) and *nitaru* (似たる). How should that to be constructed? The former may be inceptive or may indicate an unsuccessful attempt, whereas the latter, with its perfective termination, may indicate success in the undertaking. Zeami himself seems to be speculating about the underlying logic.

2. As an example of Zeami's eccentric attempts to write in Chinese, this entire passage contains many ambiguities. I followed the *Yoshida-bon* as the basis of my translation of the line 用又体ニ成レハ見風可有 (as also with Konishi Jin'ichi's modern Japanese parsing in *Zeami shū*, Nihon no shisō, vol. 8 [Tokyo: Chikuma shobō, 1970], p. 152, and Kanze Hisao's paraphrase in Yamazaki Masakazu, ed., *Zeami*, Nihon no meicho, vol. 10 [Tokyo: Chūō kōronsha, 1969], pp. 212–13). Omote and Tanaka Yutaka (*Zeami geijutsuron shū*, Shinchōsha koten shūsei, vol. 35 [Tokyo: Shinchōsha, 1976]) have preferred to follow the *Hosokawa-bon* here, with its reading 用又体ニ成見風可有. It seems indeed possible to construe even this version as in my translation, especially given the anomalies that Zeami introduces into his Chinese syntax.

Omote and Tanaka, however, read the *Hosokawa-bon* line more conventionally (taking 成 as the verb in a phrase modifying 見風, rather than as the verb in a dependent conditional or temporal construction), and if we strictly follow their reading, the translation would more plausibly be something like "As you gain long experience performing this festive art, there should be visual display in which Instance further transforms into Substance."

The ambiguity would be a minor technical matter were it not for the fact that this sentence contradicts what Zeami has just said about "Instance" being incapable or serving adequately as "Substance." Given (1) the supplementary nature of these comments, attached as they are in an unusual stylistic form at the end of the manuscript, and (2) the apparently contradictory nature of what they express, they seem to be a revision or careful exception to the general statements of the text. In that light, they may be seen as highly significant foreshadowings of the trangressive and superlative artistic freedom that is more fully discussed in late texts such as *The Flower in . . . Yet Doubling Back.*

21. The entire passage after the colophon (in parentheses here) is not found in the central text that Omote (and I) have used, but it does plausibly seem to be an addition to *A Course to Attain the Flower* by Zeami himself and has been appended here from the *Yoshida-bon*. In the basic text used in this study, the *Five Ranks*, is appended here, but I have treated that as a discrete text in its own right and translated it here.

Figure Drawings of the Two Arts and the Three Modes
二曲三体人形図, 1421

Figure Drawings opens with a reference to *A Course to Attain the Flower* and supplements that text with sketches illustrating the primary characteristics of three modes of dramatic imitation that Zeami developed in the middle period of his thinking about performance. Those Three Modes focus on the portrayal of old men, women, and warriors, and in his discussion of each of them, Zeami remarks on the mode itself and the form of dance or movement that characteristically accompanies it. He goes on to identify three separate applications of the Three Modes with which one can approach demonic roles and the musically unique role of the Heavenly Maiden.

Near the end of the text, we find an attempt to notate onomatopoetically the footwork of an actor performing Sparring in the Style of Intricate Movement. It is as puzzling as it is fascinating. The sketches reproduced here are taken from Zenchiku's handwritten copy of the text and are presumed to closely reflect the originals by Zeami.

Although I gave a detailed account of the disposition of the Two Arts and Three Modes in *A Course to Attain the Flower*, there is no visual representation of them to be seen there, so it is difficult to gain a full apprehension of their appearance; I therefore have transferred them into figure drawings, to display their material essence.

Epigraphs[1] have I attached to each of the forms of the Three Modes in that they take their visual effect from a scene within the mind.[1] The point here is to gain a careful visual impression so that you can attain a clear and precise subjective effect in the corpus of performance.

I have, moreover, displayed the figures of the Three Modes naked in line drawings so that you may more carefully discern the correct visual Substance. Clarify in every respect your visual understanding so that you understand the meaning of the epigraph.

1. The awkward syntax of the translation is intended to reflect the ersatz Chinese of the original. See appendix 3.

- The Fine Play in Dance[2] in the Attitude of a Child: the basic expressive effect for the Two Arts
- The Aged Mode, the Old Man's Dance: the first of the Three Modes
- The Woman's Mode, the Woman's Dance
- The Martial Mode
- The Demon of Intricate Movement
- The Demon of Violent Movement
- The Heavenly Maiden
- Stomping the Feet with Intricate Movement

"When a single flower opens, it's spring throughout the realm," as they say. They also say,

Nanihadzu ni saku ya ko no hana fuyugomori
Ima ha harube to saku ya ko no hana[2]

The trees have blossomed, hey,
in Naniwa,
after winter's long seclusion.
Now it's springtime,
the trees have blossomed, hey!

On this basis, the plum blossom is considered the first flower of the new year. Thus, since the Two Arts are the first flower of the fine play in expression[3] in the figure of a child, the plum blossom is to be considered a vision of *yūkyoku*.[3] From the Two Arts to the Three Modes, up to the energetic vitality in performance that comes from vigorous movement and the stomping of feet, through it all one should display the expressive coloration of the [plum] blossom. Be very careful to attain a clear visual impression.

A Figure Drawing of the Two Arts

The Child's Dance

A Course to Attain the Flower says, "The first graceful beauty in a child's attitude is to remain in the Three Modes, and the various adaptations of the

2. The poem is quoted prominently in the preface to *Kokin wakashū*, exemplifying the first of the "Six Styles" of poetry, the so-called *soheuta* (mod. J. *soeuta*). Zeami alludes to it in *Oral Instructions on Singing*, too.

3. *Yūkyoku* (幽曲), which becomes the name of a particular class of singing in *Articles on the Five Sorts of Singing*. See the introduction, Zeami' s own more detailed discussion in *Articles on the Five Sorts of Singing*, and the examples of such singing that he quotes in *Five Sorts of Singing*.

"The Child Dancing," from *Figure Drawings of the Two Arts and the Three Modes*. The sketch of the child is squeezed into an open space on the last page of the opening statement in the text. The figure shows a boy in *kariginu* and *hakama* trousers, holding a fan and dancing and possibly singing under a sprig of blossoms. The text above the figure reads, "A figure drawing of the Two Arts, the Child's Dance," and the text to the far right comes from the opening statement. (Photograph courtesy of the Noh Theater Research Institute, Hōsei University)

Three Modes are to produce a generative scene for a myriad forms of expression."[4] The figure of the child embodies *yūgen*. His arts are Dance and singing. Once you have mastered these two arts, they merge into each other, and you become an accomplished actor of lifelong promise and lofty performance. Thereafter, if you transpose the figure of the child into the Three Modes to dance and sing, *yūgen* will be manifest in the Three Modes. Not performing the Three Modes as a child while preserving the overall attractiveness of a child throughout the Three Modes is a profound strategy. Once you have mastered those Two Arts in the figure of a child, you can safely attain an enduring and lofty subjective effect, which thereafter will remain in your applications of the Three Modes to be realized in a myriad forms of expression.

Figure Drawings of the Three Modes

The Aged Mode

With tranquil intent, a distant gaze.

This is the essential appearance [of the Aged Mode], which is to be clothed appropriately. You should fix this image carefully in your mind and shape your actions accordingly. *A Mirror to the Flower* says, "First become the thing, then imitate the way it acts." Here you have it. Don't forget this.

4. *A Course to Attain the Flower.*

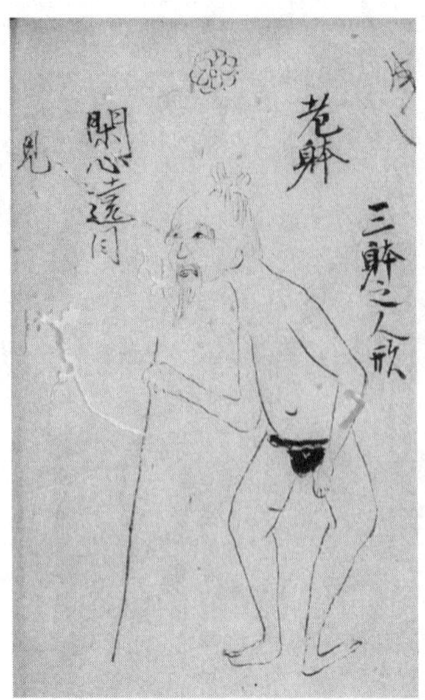

"The Aged Mode," from *Figure Drawings of the Two Arts and the Three Modes.* The sketch of an old man, shown undressed to better illustrate his posture, is labeled "Figure Drawings of the Three Modes," and then "The Aged Mode." The man stands directly under a blossom and gazes through the words "With tranquil intent, a distant gaze," toward a graph that reads "see." This seems to illustrate Zeami's insistence that the actor understand how to use a gaze into the distance for dramatic effect. The figure is not clearly wearing a mask, but his face is depicted in a way reminiscent of the genre of old men's masks (*jō no men*) in nō. (Photograph courtesy of the Noh Theater Research Institute, Hōsei University)

The Old Man's Dance

The demeanor here is particularly difficult. The way that refinement and a fine play in expression are brought into effect out of an utterly tranquil Substance is like a blossom coming into flower on an old tree. Tranquillity of intent must be continuous in the demeanor of the dance.

Aged nuns and old women are the same. The instantiation of this effect for a display of sacredness and utter tranquillity originates here.

"The Aged Dance," from *Figure Drawings of the Two Arts and the Three Modes.* The old man is shown dressed, like the boy in "The Child Dancing," in a *kariginu* and *hakama* under a sprig of blossoms. He wears a court hat (*eboshi*) and holds an open fan. (Photograph courtesy of the Noh Theater Research Institute, Hōsei University)

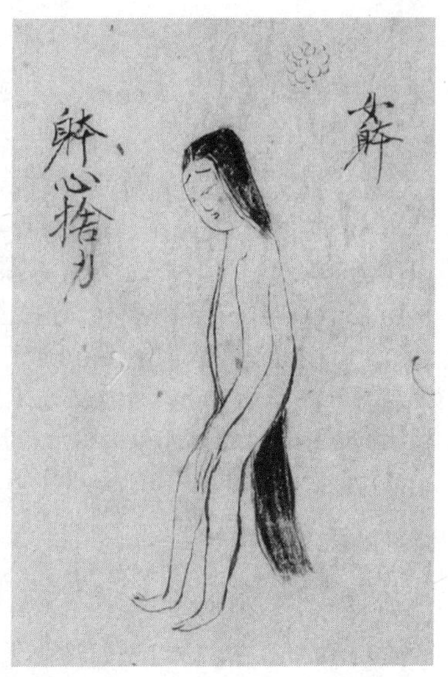

"The Woman's Mode," from *Figure Drawings of the Two Arts and the Three Modes*. The figure is unclothed to allow a clearer view of posture, exemplified in the inscription to the left, "With intent as Substance, cast force aside." Again, the character stands beneath a sprig of blossoms. (Photograph courtesy of the Noh Theater Research Institute, Hōsei University)

The Woman's Mode

With intent as Substance, cast force aside.

Be very careful to attain a clear mental impression of the consideration that the Substance is intent and that force is to be cast aside. The most difficult elements of dramatic imitation are here. This is, moreover, what we call the foundational expressive effect for *yūgen*. I'll say it again and again: don't forget the body.

"The Woman's Dance," from *Figure Drawings of the Two Arts and the Three Modes*. The actor dances in the Woman's Mode, with a fan, a court hat (*eboshi*), *hakama* trousers, and, apparently, a *maigoromo* robe. The blossoms above her, probably plum blossoms, are more numerous than those accompanying any of the other characters, except for the Heavenly Maiden. The line to the left reads, "The elegant grace of *yūgen* originates here." (Photograph courtesy of the Noh Theater Research Institute, Hōsei University)

The Woman's Dance

The elegant grace of yūgen *originates here.*

Dance in the Woman's Mode is of a particularly lofty demeanor, given the perspective afforded by the wondrous Substance of *yūgen*. Among the visual effects of the Two Arts in the figure of a child, and the Three Modes as well, the Woman's Mode should be considered the greatest achievement. Do not forget that the intent is to be the Substance and that force is to be cast aside; the forms for singing and dance are to be linked throughout by the mind. This is the supreme performance of this art. The wondrous excitement of singing and dance, made one through the mind, is to be found in this elegant expressiveness.

The Martial Mode

With force as Substance, make the intent intricate.

Although this is the Martial Mode, it still partakes of the lingering flower of the Two Arts in the figure of a child because it retains in visible effect the cherished beauty of the scene.[4] Be very careful to obtain a clear mental impression of the consideration that force is Substance, and make the intent intricate. Clarify your visual understanding of the details of intent and Substance in the figure.

The figures of the Three Modes are as earlier. Now we will turn our attention to that energetic vitality in performance that comes from movement of the body and stomping of the feet.

"The Martial Mode," from *Figure Drawings of the Two Arts and the Three Modes.* The figure for the Martial Mode holds a sword as well as a fan and wears a different type of *eboshi* from those seen in previous sketches, with a headband characteristic of martial roles on the nō stage. He stands under a single blossom. Note how markedly his legs differ in posture from those of previous characters, especially in the Woman's Mode. The inscription to the upper left reads, "With force as Substance, make the intent intricate," and that to the lower left is the opening of the description of the Martial Mode. (Photograph courtesy of the Noh Theater Research Institute, Hōsei University)

"The Style of Intricate Movement," from *Figure Drawings of the Two Arts and the Three Modes.* The figure dances in a *happi* jacket and *hakama*, apparently wearing a demon's mask with an open mouth, perhaps in the line of the *tobide* masks in nō. He also seems to be wearing a *kurogashira* wig and carrying a whip, or scourge, on his back. The inscription on the left reads, "With form demonic, the intent is human," and then, "Energetic vitality in performance that comes from movement of the body and stomping of the feet originates here." There are, interestingly, more blossoms above this character than above the figure representing the Martial Mode. (Photograph courtesy of the Noh Theater Research Institute, Hōsei University)

The Style of Intricate Movement

With form demonic, the intent is human.

Energetic vitality in performance that comes from movement of the body and stomping of the feet originates here.

In this Style of Intricate Movement, you should shape your actions so as not to hold too much force in the body, for although the form of the role is demonic, its intent is human; consequently, movement should be careful and intricate. The circumstances by which you do not fill your mind and body with force but carry yourself lightly amount to the personal style of intricate movement. Overall, what I mean by Sparring is to make this Style of Intricate Movement the foundation and to maintain, whether for old or young, boy or man, or even madwoman, this Intricate Movement in your intent. *A Mirror to the Flower* says, "Move the Body Vigorously, Stomp the Feet with Restraint, Stomp the Feet Vigorously, Move the Body with Restraint."

"The Style of Violent Movement," from *Figure Drawings of the Two Arts and the Three Modes.* The figure dances in *kariginu* and *hakama*, apparently wearing a demon's mask with a tightly closed mouth, perhaps in the line of the *beshimi* masks in nō. Instead of an *eboshi*, he wears a *tōkamuri*, or Chinese-style court cap, with its characteristic long tails. He holds a whip, or scourge, in his hand. His shoes are *kegariha*, with feathers implanted on top, giving a much heavier impression than the rather dainty feet of the demon of intricate movement, appropriate to the kind of stomping characteristic of the role. The inscription on the left reads, "Power, form, and intent are demonic." Even this fearsome character dances under blossoms, although in one manuscript, they have been omitted. (Photograph courtesy of the Noh Theater Research Institute, Hōsei University)

The Style of Violent Movement

Power, form, and intent are demonic.

This is a style in which you move vigorously, the Substance being mere force, so there is not likely to be anything of quality to see. Since the intent is that of a demon, all visual display comes from rage, so little of what appears is interesting. After various performances have been given, however, and all manner of expression has been tried, then when a brief view of this style is shown in the effect of the *kyū*, it incites a momentary enthusiasm, startling the spectators' vision and shaking up their minds. Accordingly, it should not be used more than once. Be aware of this.

The Dance of the Heavenly Maiden

Intent riding on the music.

In the Dance of the Heavenly Maiden, assign musical effect as the central nexus;[5] fill all the limbs with the force of intent; dance the Dance; be danced

"The Dance of the Heavenly Maiden," from *Figure Drawings of the Two Arts and the Three Modes.* More blossoms surround this figure than any of the other figures in the text, and the petal shapes seem to indicate that these are cherries, rather than the plum blossoms (most likely) in the other drawings. The figure dances vigorously in a *maigoromo* robe, with an open fan like that of the figure in "The Woman's Dance," but here wears a *tenkan* crown, gold with openwork. The inscription on the left reads, "Intent riding on the music." (Photograph courtesy of the Noh Theater Research Institute, Hōsei University)

by the Dance; make manifest the full dimensions of performance; like flowers and birds on the winds of spring, you are to effect a perspective of wondrous expression and musical elegance, and blend the skin, meat, and bones throughout the performance in the body of a single expressive power.[6] I'll say it again and again: you are to dance expansively. Make certain your training and study are extensive.

• Since the fine play of the Dance of the Heavenly Maiden is not a matter of human expression, it falls outside the Three Modes. Nonetheless, it has the expressive characteristics of the Woman's Mode. Since this is a grand Dance entailing fine play in musical expressiveness,[7] there should be no objection if, having understood it in general, you draw it into the sphere of human expressiveness.

All in all, since the Dance of the Heavenly Maiden requires a fine play in expression in which the style of performance comes into being through forms of genuine power, omitting neither body nor mind nor a single limb, it is the foundation of training and study.[8]

There are five sections of *jo-ha-kyū*: the single section of *jo*, the three sections of *ha*, and the single section of *kyū*. On some occasions, however, one dances in the order *ha-jo-kyū*-extension. This is a particular adaptation for a given occasion. A standard abbreviation, I call it. This should be transmitted in person.

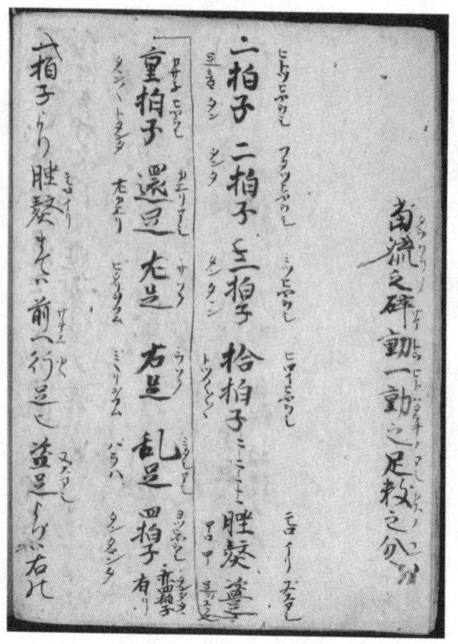

A leaf near the end of *Figure Drawings of the Two Arts and the Three Modes* illustrating the passage about stomping. The names of particular footwork techniques are written in boldface Chinese graphs, with Japanese glosses on the right and onomatopoetic characterizations on the left, the Japanese in *katakana*. (Photograph courtesy of the Noh Theater Research Institute, Hōsei University)

The Part for Dance Steps for One Cycle of Sparring Using Intricate Movement According to Our Troupe

	1 beat	2 beat	3 beat	pickup beat –"–"–'–'–'–'
with the feet:	*tan*	*tanta*	*tantatan*	*totsu totsu totsu totsu*
moroiri *horoho*	*nusuashi* pull the feet out	*kasanebyōshi* *tatan tatan to tanta*	*kaeriashi* a turn to the left	left foot stomp left
right foot stomp right	*midareashi* *haraha*	four beats *tan tatan ta*	then there are another four beats[5]	

From 1 beat until *moroiri*, the steps go forward. From *nusuashi*, bend the body around to the right, in a great circle move around toward the back right; and from *kasanebyōshi*, move to the right side of the stage, stomp the *kaeriashi* pattern; then after *midareashi*, with the left foot and the right foot, move the body forcefully; then bring the Sparring to an end with the four beats of *yotsubyōshi*. Details should be conveyed in an oral transmission.

5. In most manuscripts of the text, the highly intriguing, and as yet only vaguely understood, technical terms ("1 beat," "2 beat," . . . "*moroiri*," etc.) are connected with vertical lines, one after the other. Glosses with what seem to be onomatopoetic renderings ("*tan*," "*tanta*," . . . "*horoho*," etc.) and stage directions ("pull the feet out") are written alongside the terms themselves. Terms using the word *-byōshi* here and later are written *byaushi* in the original orthography.

In addition to these, any number of rhythms can be produced depending on the demands of the character of the performance, among them the *yose-byōshi*, *moroashi*, *okiashi*, *haneashi*, and so forth. There also are ways of turning to the left and the right, such as "turning without stepping" and "circling without stepping." These are ways to turn the step without stepping.

In this troupe, we do not beat the rhythm with the knees or in kneeling turns. I would warn against the use of acrobatics in general. That is because these moves did not appear in the Intricate Movement of my late father.

Ōei 28 [1421], a day of the seventh month

Notes

1. The term 風名 is unfamiliar and has been taken to refer to the names of the Three Modes themselves, but as Omote points out, it seems inconsistent that while writing *Figure Drawings of the Two Arts and the Three Modes* in 1421, Zeami should note that he had given names to things that he already had clearly named in 1420 when writing *A Way to the Flower Attained*. See *ZZ*, p. 458n.57. On that basis, Omote surmises that the 風名 are not names for the Three Modes but the motto-like "epigraphs" that he attaches to the pictures of each of them, for example, 閑心遠目 for the Aged Mode.

2. *Yūbu* (遊舞, orth. *iubu*). This term is unusual, occurring in only two compounds in this text (児姿遊舞 and 天女之遊舞) and in *Pick Up a Jewel and Take the Flower in Hand*, where we find two instances of the first compound. All the same, the term is important and is clearly related to Zeami's notion of "fine play." See the introduction and appendix 3.

3. *Buga yūbū* (舞歌遊風, orth. *iubū*) is probably Zeami' s own coinage and is obviously related to *yūbū* (fine play in expression) and the important aesthetic attainment *yūgaku* (orth. *iugaku* [fine play in performance]), which is discussed in the introduction.

4. *Chōkei no kenpū* (寵景之見風 [lit., "the visual effect of the cherished scene"]), a puzzling phrase. It seems to condense into the word "scene," an interest in the visual beauties of nature—especially blossoms, colored leaves, birds, the moon, and the like—but, following in a long tradition, also goes on to equate those beauties with the graces of poetry and music. The discussion of the *shura* role in *Transmitting the Flower* is helpful here in that it specifies that this role should "bring out the connection between [that role, or character] and poetry and music."

5. *Taikau* apparently should be written 大綱 (a great rope) and is understood to mean "fundamentally" or "generally" (Omote parses it as *konpon*).

6. *Hi-niku-kotsu wo bantai ni fūgō* [orth. *fūgafu*] *renkyoku subeshi* (皮肉骨を万体に風合連曲可レ為). The line is not entirely clear. One text (the *Yoshida-bon*) reads it 万体 rather than the 一力体 that is found in other manuscripts and has most generally been adopted by modern editors. In text written vertically, as this text originally was, 万体 could easily be miswritten as 一力体, and vice versa, so Omote's hesitation about a definitive reading is well justified. See *ZZ*, p. 461n.56.

7. *Yūkyoku* (遊曲, orth. *iukyoku*) is clearly related to *yūgaku* (遊楽), *yūbū* (遊風), and their variations, but in order to maintain at least the graphic distinction of the original, I have translated this as "fine play in musical expressiveness." For a detailed discussion, see appendix 3.

8. The sentence is frustratingly obscure. In addition to the fairly common difficulty of Zeami's abstractness, the word 正力体 presents some particular difficulties. It is a hapax legomenon, and, as Omote says, "正力体 [my "forms of genuine power"] is Zeami's neologism and is not to be understood literally in isolation. So although I have interpreted it as noted in the headnote [*ZZ*, p. 131], this is nothing more than a conjecture referring to the more extended discussion of the picture [of the heavenly maiden]" in a supplementary note (*ZZ*, p. 461, n. 65). The headnote in question interprets 正力体 as "a configuration in which the power of mind swells to the brim throughout the entire body"—that is, 心力が全身にみなぎった姿, *shinriki ga zenshin ni minagitta sugata*.

The Three Courses

三道, 1423

The Three Courses[1] is Zeami's most detailed treatment of the composition of plays. He begins by discussing the three components of any play (the Seed, the Structure, and the Writing proper) and then goes on to discuss in yet greater detail the three primary modes or genres of play in *sarugaku*, with specific remarks about each. This is followed by a similar discussion of important types of plays that fall outside those three modes and then a list of plays that found favor with his audiences in his career up to that point. This is the most extensive list of plays to date in the *Performance Notes*, and it has been an important resource for those interested in the authorship of nō plays.

Zeami's most detailed remarks concern the structure and prosody of plays. He even remarks on the particular number of lines that a given song might have. Clearly, he is greatly concerned with the development of musical form in plays and its interaction with the play script. The terminology he uses shows some small distinctions that may indicate musical differences otherwise difficult to discern in what we know about *sarugaku* performance in these early days. In his remarks about plays in general, he first speaks of how much *ongyoku* (*ikahodo no ongyoku*) should be included. Later he asks how much of each of three types of *ongyoku* (*miiro no ongyoku ikahodo*) and, for the final *dan*, how much of an appropriate *kyokufū* (*kiu ni niahitaru kokufū ikahodo*) should be included. From its usage earlier in the *Notes*, *ongyoku* seems to apply most specifically to singing, rather than to music in a general sense. (This is not to imply that the flute and drum were not played in accompaniment to this singing, but whatever instrumental music had a place in performance at this point is unclear from Zeami's remarks.)

The distinction among the "three types of *ongyoku*" mentioned for the *ha* section of a play seems to depend on how the syllables of text are musically disposed vis-à-vis the rhythmic structure and perhaps the degree of melodic inflection for each type. Zeami clearly distinguishes among the singing styles *sashigoe*, *tadauta(h)i*, and *kusema(h)iuta(h)i*, and he also mentions specific song types, such as the *issei* and *shidai*, which have their own characteristics. A more detailed understanding of these types of music can be gleaned from the remarks he makes regarding the construction of plays in each of the Three Modes later in the text, but it still remains rather unclear what specifically the "three types of *ongyoku*" are. The use of the word *kyokufū* may indicate an awareness of the importance of instrumental music in this section of a play. Certainly the distinction between Sparring and Dance is relevant here, and the types of music used on the modern stage to accompany these different genres of dance are themselves distinct and, even within the individual genre, rather diverse.

The fact that this text was transmitted to Zeami's second son, Motoyoshi, is noteworthy, and, as Omote notes, may point to a tradition of playwriting among performers other than the head of the troupe in the Kanze guild. Three generations later, the *ōtsuzumi* drummer Kanze Kojirō Nobumitsu became known as a fine playwright as well. Unfortunately, though, we have no record of the authorship of a play by Motoyoshi, and he himself retired from *sarugaku* performance and took the tonsure in 1430 after having recorded Zeami's artistic memoirs, *Conversations on Sarugaku*. When Motoyoshi's elder brother, Motomasa, died two years later, Motoyoshi may have returned to performing, as a drummer, for Motomasa's young heir.

❁

Articles on the Composition of Plays

1. First, then, we proceed along three courses, the Seed, the Structure, and the Writing: (1) Understand the Seed of the play; (2) Lay out the Structure of the play; and (3) Write the play.[2] Get a firm grasp on the Seed as it appears in its original source; arrange the Structure in five sections according to the three principles of *jo*, *ha*, and *kyū*; then write out the play, pulling the text together and setting the melody.

• What I mean here by the Seed is that person who performs the action in the source on which the play is based; you must be aware that this is of great significance for the dance and singing in the play.[3] You see, what gives the fine play of performance in this art its character is Dance and singing. If the Seed is a person who does not sing or dance, there will be hardly any way of making a visual display in the performance, no matter what sort of legendary hero or great star he or she may have been. Make sure you have a firm grasp on the rationale here.

For example, as character types for dramatic imitation, heavenly maidens, goddesses, and shrine priestesses all are amenable to the dance and singing of *kagura*.[1] For male roles, consider Narihira, Kuronushi, Genji, and spirited nobles like them, and for the Woman's Mode, Lady Ise, Komachi, Giō, Gijo,

1. *Kagura* was originally the music and dance performed in "Shinto" shrines to placate the deities of Japan's indigenous religion. For a fuller account, see the glossary.

Shizuka, Hyakuman, and graceful ladies of their kind;[2] all these persons have a reputation for a fine play in expression through dance and singing, so there should be, as a matter of course, ready opportunities for visual display through the fine play in performance when you select one of them for central treatment in a play. Or again, among clerical players[3] are charismatic figures like Lay Priest Jinen, Kagetsu, Lay Priest Tōgan, and Lay Priest Seigan,[4] but also men and women, persons young and old of no particular fame; in each and every one of these cases, you should be able to compose plays in such a way that these persons are made amenable to treatment with dance and singing. What I call a "Seed" is a person like any of them who offers a ready opportunity for the focus of a play.

Sometimes also, a new play, what I would call a "play script from scratch," is written without any original source whatever and, when performed, creates great excitement throughout the house with its visual display, relying on such connections as can be made with famous places and legendary sites. This is a job for an accomplished master with his erudition.

2. The Structure of the play refers to that determination—once one has found the right Seed—of what action should take place where.

First, there should be five sections, or *dan*,[5] organized into an introduction or "*jo*," a development or "*ha*," and a conclusion or "*kyū*": the *jo* consists of

---

2. All the spirited nobles and graceful ladies mentioned here are characters in at least one nō play. Many of them figure in *sarugaku* plays by Zeami or contemporary with him. Some of them are historical figures: (Ariwara no) Narihira (825–880) and (Ōtomo no) Kuronushi (late ninth century), Lady Ise (late eighth to early ninth century), (Ono no) Komachi (fl. ca. 850), and Shizuka (orth. Shidzuka, late twelfth century), whereas others are fictional: Genji, of course, as well as probably Giō (orth. Giwau) and Gijo (orth. Gidjo, alternatively Ginyo).

3. *Hōka* (orth. *haukasō* or *hauka*) were street performers, often in priestly dress, who sang and danced accompanying themselves on *kokiriko* or *sasara* (rhythm sticks or clappers). Sometimes they did magic tricks and acrobatic tricks as well. The popular nō play *Hōkasō* is about two brothers who disguise themselves as *hōka* performers in order to get close enough to their father's killer to exact revenge on him.

4. Lay Priest Jinen, Kagetsu (orth. Kwagetsu), Lay Priest Tōgan, and Lay Priest Seigan presumably are fictional characters, all young aspirants to Buddhist orders but not yet ordained. Plays about them have a variety of singing and dancing. They seem to have something of the air of religious charismatics. There are eponymous plays in each case, although *Seigan koji* is no longer performed.

My translation, "lay priest," is for the Japanese *koji*. The term can mean a male religious aspirant who pursues his devotions outside a formal religious establishment, but here it is a title for young men associated with temples who have taken some vows and been given Buddhist names, such as Jinen, but who have not yet been ordained.

5. The structural term *dan* is widely used outside *sarugaku* and nō, in both music, such as *jōruri* and *sōkyoku* (for the koto), and literature, where it means "passage," "paragraph," or "episode." Zeami uses the term frequently, and I will henceforth treat it as an English word.

one section; the *ha*, three sections; and the *kyū*, one section. In the first *dan*, the opening player[6] comes on stage to sing his *sashigoe*, *shidai*, and *hito-utai*.[7] (The *ha* follows.)[4] The *shite* now emerges and sings from the *issei* through his *hito-utai*: one *dan*. After that is a *mondō* with the opening player and a *hito-utai* in unison:[8] one *dan*. Then after that is a musical passage, either a *kuse-mai* or a piece in normal *tadautai* style: one *dan*. (The *kyū* follows.) After that, another *dan*, whether a Dance or Sparring, or *hayabushi* or *kiribyōshi*, or the like. These are the five *dan* of a play. Sometimes, depending on the way in which the original source is divided, six *dan* may be needed. Then again, plays may have four *dan*, lacking one *dan*, depending on the material. The basic pattern, however, has five *dan*.

In setting out these five *dan*, ask yourself how much singing should be allotted to the introduction, how much of each of the three types of singing is needed for the three *dan* of the development, and how much music and dance would be appropriate to the conclusion; this determination of the number of lines in the piece and the laying out of its overall structure are what I mean by the word *Structure*. The musical composition should vary through the *jo*, *ha*, and *kyū*, according to the type of play being written and the mood it is to evoke. The length of the play should be measured by the number of lines of its music.

3. In Writing, you should get a firm grasp on the sort of person you are dealing with, from the very beginning all the way through, asking yourself, "What kind of language is most appropriate for a person like this?" Assign phrases from poetry expressive of *shiugen*, *yūgen*, love, complaint, or *bauwoku*,[9] according to the type of person being depicted.

A play should have a place where the original source is pointed out. If it is an evocative and famous place or legendary site, then you should take lines

6. *Kaikōnin* means, literally, "the one who opens his mouth." This refers to the first actor to speak or sing in a play (in modern performance, almost always after the entrance music played by the ensemble). In the great majority of cases, this actor is the *waki*. In some cases, however, another actor performs this task, such as the *aikyōgen* actor in the play *Kantan*, so I have adopted the translation "opening player."

7. These are the names of individual song types, or *shōdan*, as are numerous italicized terms in the following passages. The individual *shōdan* are identified briefly in the glossary. For a more detailed discussion, see *ZS*, pp. 3–6, 291–300.

8. That is, with the chorus. In modern performance, the chorus alone sings this song, but in historical performance practice, the *shite* or *waki* seems to have sung along.

9. *Shiugen*, *yūkyoku*, *koi*, *shukkwai*, and *bouwoku* (the last is spelled *bauwoku* or *bauoku* elsewhere. I have changed it here for clarity of understanding). These five terms represent one stage in Zeami's evolving typology of singing styles. See the discussion in the introduction and appendix 1.

from well-known poems about the place, in Chinese or Japanese, and write them into concentrated points in the three *dan* of the *ha*. These become important places for action. In addition to this, you should work distinguished sayings and famous lines into the *shite*'s language.

Working through these articles in this manner is what I mean by composing a play.

The three courses of Seed, Structure, and Writing are as mentioned.

Articles on Composition for the Three Modes

(The Aged, the Woman's, and the Martial—these are the Three Modes.)

• The Aged Mode. (This generally has the expressive manner of the *waki* play.)[10] First, in the *shiugen*, or "congratulatory" style, a play takes the following configuration: The opening player appears and delivers the first section from the *shidai* through the *hito-utai* singing in a meter of 5–7–5/7–5/7–5, and so on, for a total of seven to eight verses. One verse consists of a seven-syllable line and a five-syllable line, but a standard *waka* poem (5–7–5/7–7) counts as two verses.

Then the *shite* appears. (From here on comes the first *dan* of the *ha*.) As in the instance of the old couple,[11] after an *issei* of 5–7–5/7–5 and a *ninoku* of 7–5/7–5, the *sashigoe* proceeds for about ten verses of 7–5/7–5. There are about ten verses in the *hito-utai* from the part in a lower register through the part in a higher register. (Next comes the second *dan* of the *ha*.) Now there is a *mondō* between the opening player and the *shite*, which should not be more than four or five exchanges between the two. (In this *mondō*, the old couple are asked about the area, and they make their explanations. This should not be more than two or three exchanges apiece.) Then in the upper register, from the point where the chorus join in (this might be an ear-opening point), through the point where they stop, there should be about ten verses sung in two strains. (From here on comes the third section of the *ha*.) Thereafter, if there is a *kusemai*, there should be about five verses of *agurukoe*,[5] five of *sashigoe*, and then, in the lower register, about five to six verses to the cadence.

10. In modern terms, "*waki* nō" refers to those plays of a congratulatory or an auspicious character that occupy first place (after the ritual piece *Shikisanban*, known today often as *Okina*) in a full day's performance of nō (consisting of six nō plays, including *Shikisanban*, and four kyōgen). They also are known as "god plays" (*kami-nō*), common examples being *Takasago*, *Oimatsu*, *Yōrō*, *Kamo*, and the like. Zeami's terminology overlaps considerably with this but, strictly speaking, refers to those plays that come "to the side" (thus *waki*, 脇) of *Shikisanban*. This means the plays coming after *Shikisanban* in a full day's performance.

11. Zeami is referring here to the old couple who are the *shite* and *tsure* in his play *Takasago*, perhaps the finest of all *waki* nō. See *ZS*, pp. 69–103.

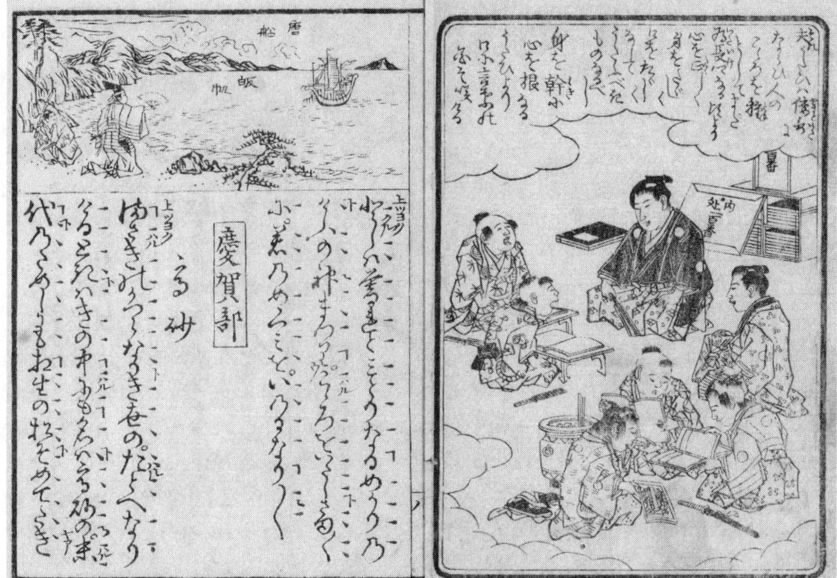

Terako koutai shiki no tomo, "Nō songs for the temple school: a companion for all seasons," 1842. Chanting excerpts from nō plays was a widespread pastime in the Edo/Tokugawa period, and brief passages from these excerpts were even used in elementary education for commoners in the *terakoya* (temple schools) of the period. The frontispiece to the text, on the right, claims that learning to chant makes the body, mind, and mouth correct and that "the flower of words comes into blossom in the mouth through chanting." On the left is a brief passage from the play *Takasago*. (Photograph from Kōzan bunko, courtesy of the Noh Theater Research Institute, Hōsei University)

The *kusemai* should [perhaps] consist of twelve to thirteen verses initially and then the *kōnomono* of [perhaps] twelve to thirteen. Then there should be two to three exchanges in the [*utairongi*], which should close briskly and lightly.

(Now comes [the *kyū*].) Here the *shite*, whether a heavenly maiden or a male role, sings a *kōnomono* or *sashigoe* flowingly from the *hashigakari* and delivers the *issei*, the last verse of which is accompanied by the chorus and sung expansively and brought down to cadence. The two or three exchanges in *semerongi* are sung rhythmically and lightly with increasing speed. In some cases, depending on the sort of dance the *shite* does in character (the eye-opening point is not fixed in a particular place), the play should close with a *kiribyōshi* section. In any case, it should not be too long. One should plan the length by the number of verses to be sung.

The shape of a play in the style of the *jo* follows this general outline. Since it is most appropriate for an old man to appear in a *waki* play like this, this category is classified as the Aged Mode. The Aged Mode can be used in other ways as well, depending on the material.

Plays of a congratulatory nature in the Women's Mode also take the same five-*dan* configuration.

• The shape of a play in the Woman's Mode. One must write making allowances for visual display in the manner of expression. This is where singing and dance have their primary expressive effect. Among the plays of this category, one finds expression of the very highest order. For instance, in writing of women of exalted rank, such as queens and royal consorts, Ladies Aoi, Yūgao, and Ukifune,[12] and the like, the writer must remember that the noble bearing of such persons exhibits a grace and elegance unparalleled among ordinary people. For this reason, the writer must carefully consider the music and appearance appropriate to the characters and be careful not to fashion them after professional entertainers. A person of such rank should be of the most refined stature, entrancing and of the highest level of mysterious beauty; the quality of her voice, her movements, and the very atmosphere of her presence should be without parallel. The slightest deficiency will spoil the effect.

In such a person, one finds, as it were, a jewel among jewels. Over and above the sheer beauty in the visual display of such noble persons, one has rare and valuable material here: Lady Aoi bewitched by Rokujō,[13] Yūgao captivated by a malevolent spirit, the possession of Ukifune—in these and similar situations is a Seed that can manifest the blossoming of mysterious beauty, of rare expressive potential. It is the Seed for a flower even more wonderful than that mentioned in the old poem, which "blends the scent of plum and the blossom of cherry and sets them to bloom upon a willow branch."[14] That being the case, you could probably say that a performer who suitably manages such a style is an unsurpassed master of wondrous excitement.

12. Lady Aoi (orth. Afuhi), Lady Yūgao (orth. Yufugaho), and Ukifune are three prominent characters in *The Tale of Genji*. Lady Aoi was, as Zeami indicates, a woman of high social rank, the daughter of the minister of the left, the highest civil post in government at the beginning of the tale. The other two, by virtue of their presence in *The Tale of Genji*, have been afforded a social prominence in Zeami's eyes that they didn't originally have: Yūgao was born of high-ranking parents, but they both died young and she never had the kind of backing she needed for social prominence of her own. Ukifune's father was a royal prince, but her mother was only the niece of his chief wife. She had only an ephemeral relationship with the prince and went on to marry a provincial governor.

13. In *The Tale of Genji*, Lady Rokujō (orth. Rokudeu) was the consort of a deceased crown prince and a woman of truly exalted rank. Her jealousy provokes her spirit to take possession of Lady Aoi while the latter is in childbirth. The story provides the material for the celebrated play *Aoi no ue* (orth. *Afuhi no uhe*).

14. An almost complete quotation of Nakahara no Munetoki, *Goshūi wakashū* 82: *Mume ga ka wo sakura no hana ni nihohasete, yanagi ga eda ni sakase* [*teshi gana*] ([If only I might] blend the scent of plum with the blossom of the cherry and set them to bloom upon a willow branch).

In addition to this are such persons as Shizuka, Giō, and Gijo. Their manner of expression stems from their role as *shirabyōshi* dancers, so they should chant a *waka*, intone an *issei*, and sing in a high *sanjū* register,[15] staying strictly in time; then stamping out the *seme* pattern with their feet, they should make their exit dancing. It is appropriate for such persons to leave the stage with the feeling of a quiet *kiribyōshi*. Then again are persons like Hyakuman and Yamanba,[16] who are fairly easy to create because they are *kusemai* dancers. Of the five *dan* of the play, the *jo* and *kyū* can be shortened, making the *ha* into the body and putting the *kusemai* into a prominent place; the second half of a two-part *kuse* is compacted, and the part is written carefully, just like a professional *kusemai*; the dancing should come to an end with a *shidai*.

There are also plays in the madwoman style, and since these are, after all, about people of deranged sensibility, it is best to take pains with the expressive potential and write the music with attention to details suitable to the movements to be performed; as long as the person possesses *yūgen*, whatever is done should be interesting. Write with the awareness that the person's appearance should be beautiful, the melody skillfully inflected, the actor's technical skill pushed to its limit, and the play colorful.

The writer who makes distinctions according to the person portrayed—whether she is a paragon of elegance and beauty, a noble lady, a *shirabyōshi* dancer, a *kusemai* dancer, or a madwoman—and furthermore assigns the appropriate artistic qualities to the role is a writer who truly understands the vocation of performance.

• The shape of a play in the Martial Mode. If, say, the play is to be created around a famous general of the Genji or the Heike, you should take special care to write the story just as it appears in *The Tales of the Heike*.

In this, too, you should calculate the arrangement of the five *dan* and the musical proportions. Also, if the *shite* is to leave the stage partway through the play to reappear later in a different guise, then the *kusemai* and so on should be set in the latter half of the play. In this way, the *ha* runs over into the *kyū*. Such a play may also be written in six *dan*. Again, if the *shite* does not leave the stage, it may be written in four *dan*. It depends on the particular play. The first half of the play should be compressed and written so to be as short as possible.

15. *Sanjū* (orth. *sandjū*) is a specific melodic form in a high register in some types of performance contemporary with *sarugaku*, notably in the recitation of *The Tales of the Heike*. The term is no longer commonly used in nō but must reflect a high pitch here.

16. Yamanba (orth. Yamauba) is the name of an elderly and uncanny *kusemai* dancer who figures in an eponymous nō play, in which she portrays a threatening and powerful (but apparently benevolent) supernatural spirit.

The expressive character of a play in the Martial Mode varies considerably according to the original source, and there is no single specific way to write it. You should write the musical passages so they are brief, and in the *kyū*, the *shite* should make his exit in *hayabushi*[17] of the *shura* style. In certain cases, it is appropriate to portray a character with demonic fury. The melody should be compact in a heroic style. When the *shite* appears dressed as a warrior, he should definitely make a self-introduction in a *nanori.* Take care in the writing.

The construction of plays for the Three Modes is as just noted.

• Clerical players. These roles stem from the Martial Mode and require an expressive attitude of Intricate Movement.[18] Whatever the role, whether Lay Priest Jinen, Kagetsu, male mad roles, and even some female mad roles, there should, in accord with the type of play in question, be something useful to draw on based on Intricate Movement.

After the first *dan* of *jo*, where the opening player appears, everyone waits while the drums play, then an actor appears dressed as a clerical player and delivers a *sashigoe* expansively from the *hashigakari*—whether an old poem or a famous saying or whatever, the words should be readily recognizable and interesting—and as this *sashigoe* blends into the recitative of *tadakotoba*, he delivers seven or eight verses with increasing speed to begin the *issei.* The dramatic imitation at this point should make the most of the expressive display as the actor uses the perspective afforded by the *hashigakari*, singing engagingly and with attractive wit.[6] You should be aware of this much when you set out the structure and write the part, researching the language and inquiring into the character of the role. Now then, what you sing in the *jo* of the *sashigoto* section should be sung briefly and lightly. It should be as long as the singing in the usual *jo* section.[7] Then, in the exchange between the *shite* and the opening player, you should set the music with lightness and animation: where the conversation hinges on logical problems, there should be about four or five exchanges in *kotoba rongi* and then a *kōnomono* song of about ten verses. From the Dance through the *kusemai*, it should be compact. In the *kyū*, you should color the performance ingeniously, using *hayabushi* and *otoshibushi* and the like, and dress up the expressive capacity.

In plays like this, the ending often brings resolution in the form of a long-sought reunion of parent and child, husband and wife, or brother and sister.[19]

17. *Hayabushi* probably corresponds to *chūnori* in nō, a musical rhythm in which two syllables of text are allotted to one beat of the music.

18. Zeami's term is *saidō*, which comes to have particular significance in the context of demon plays.

19. Meetings like these abound in the so-called mad plays and their variations, such as, for parent and child, *Hyakuman*, *Sakuragawa*, and *Miidera*; and for husband and wife (or for two lovers who are not married), *Ashikari*, *Hanagatami*, and *Hanjo*. For "elder and younger brother," the

In that kind of play, you should write a climax into the third *dan* of the *ha* and use the final *dan* for an *utairongi*, and if the reunion brings parent and child or siblings together, you might bring it to a close with something of the expressive character of a tearful melodrama.[20] The expressive manner in plays like these has, in general, the same potential for visual display as the mad plays do.

• The structure of plays about demons of Intricate Movement. (These roles are an expressive application stemming from the Martial Mode. Their form is demonic, and their intent is human.)

Plays of this type are, for the most part, composed in two parts. In the first part, whether of three *dan* or two, you should write briefly; the character who appears in the second part should be a ghost in demonic form. The *sashigoe* delivered from the *hashigakari* should consist of four or five vivid verses, and once these have been delivered and the actor moves onto the stage itself with the *issei*, he should move his body and legs intricately and say one thing and then another, bringing the song to a close with a falling cadence.[21] Then there should be about ten verses of *kōnomono*, sung briskly and lightly in unison with the chorus, or perhaps three or four exchanges in *semerongi* style. The *kyū* should be composed with either *hayabushi* or *kirufushi* lines one right after the other. There should be opportunities using the musical composition to create a visual display that blossoms expressively in Sparring. Make sure you have a firm grasp on the musical style when you write this.

There is, in addition to this, the demon of Violent Movement. (The demon of Violent Movement is demonic in power, form, and intent. Such a character entails a strange form of expression showing a vision of rage. This form of expression is not acceptable in our troupe. When it comes to demons, we consider only those in the style of Intricate Movement worthy of display in performance.)

• You should construct your plays and write them out with a careful visual impression of what is contained in these various articles.

Here is something else to be aware of: in a play, in either the *ha* or the *kyū*, there is to be an ear-opening point and an eye-opening point. The ear-opening point is where two kinds of hearing come together in a single strain

literal meaning of the word *kyōdai*, which Zeami uses here, I am rather hard pressed to find well-known plays that literally involve the reunion of brothers, but the play *Semimaru*, for example, reaches its climax in the temporary and tragic meeting of a sister and brother, and *kyōdai* is often used simply to mean "siblings."

20. *Sukoshi naki-nō no ifū no keshiki.* Omote calls these plays *higeki*, which is the Japanese translation of "tragedy." But tragedy in the classic theatrical sense isn't really the issue here, apart from exceptional plays like *Semimaru* and *Sumidagawa*.

21. *Otoshibushi* is apparently a melodic figure in which the voice drops quickly from a higher register to a lower register, although the term is mentioned only twice in the *Performance Notes*, both times in close proximity in *The Three Courses*.

of enchantment. On the one hand, there is a certain kind of hearing in which the sense behind the original source of the play becomes apparent to the mind's ear throughout the audience, and the words in which this sense is expressed are, for their part, matched perfectly with the vocal music, so that sense is wedded to sound for a single strain's enchantment, and there is such excitement that one earns the appreciation of the whole audience. This world in which hearing the sense and hearing the sound come together into a single moment's enchantment is what we call the ear-opening point.

Likewise, the eye-opening point should be that place within a play where the visual display comes together to create an exciting response in the eye. It amounts to the situation in which a wondrous excitement is created in the whole audience at once through the types of expression used in dance and movement. This comes from the *shite*'s expressive power to create excitement. Even though this would not seem to be within the purview of the author as he creates the play, it won't happen unless a place has been prepared to express such visual attractiveness. For this reason, you must construct your plays and write them out with a firm grasp on the spots where action might be turned to the attraction of dance. Since such a place is the wondrous point where the eyes are opened for the entire play, we call it the eye-opening point.

Thus the ear-opening point is apparently the responsibility of the writer, and the eye-opening point seems to depend on the actions of the *shite*. When both tasks are taken in hand by a single accomplished master, there should be no problem. There may also be a wondrous moment where [ear] and eye are opened together.[8] This is for oral transmission. Inquire about it.

• There are certain things to be aware of when creating plays for child actors. Because of the natural physical resemblance, there should be no difficulty when a child actor takes the role of the son or daughter as the subordinate of the principal character.[22] If the child is to perform on his own, you should not expect forms of expression from him that are implausible. By implausible I mean, for example, having him take the role of a father or mother in a play about a child and presenting him in the mournful search for the child, having

22. The sentence seems to point to an advantage of natural physical resemblance to be gained when central actors put their own children in subordinate roles, provided that those are the roles of the sons or daughters of the central characters themselves. This seems entirely reasonable, and it is the reading that Omote, Konishi Jin'ichi (*Zeami shū*, Nihon no shisō, vol. 8 [Tokyo: Chikuma shobō, 1970], p. 182), and Yamazaki Masakazu (*Zeami*, Nihon no meicho, vol. 10 [Tokyo: Chūō kōronsha, 1969], p. 265) all take from the passage, but the syntax of the sentence does contain some ambiguities. What I have translated as "the role of the son or daughter" might imply that sons or daughters of actors could appear on stage in these roles, thereby sanctioning the appearance of female children on the *sarugaku* stage. This would be surprising, given the exclusion of women from the stage in *sarugaku* (and, for the most part, in nō performance as well), but at least grammatically, it is a possibility. The word "subordinate" translates *waki* in the original. In nō, the role in question would be not a *waki* role but a *tsure* role.

made a yet younger actor take the role of that son or daughter; in a play about the eventual reunion of a parent and child, the sight of them hugging and clinging and weeping and carrying on would appear really very tawdry to viewers. When people shun plays about children and say that even when they're done well, they have certain rather distasteful aspects and such, it's because of plays like this. If the play is to be about a child out on his own, he should be cast as someone's child or younger brother in search of his lost parent or bereft at being parted from his older brother. This kind of character is appropriate to such a manner of expression. Even if the play is not about a parent and child, it still would be inappropriate to expect a child to carry off a dramatic imitation in the Aged Mode.

There is also something an old actor should be aware of. When you are to wear a mask and transform your attitude into that of a given character, then there shouldn't really be a problem with any sort of dramatic imitation, but if you are too advanced in age, then your attempt to perform in an inappropriate style will simply not look to viewers like what you're aiming for. There may not be any particular problem when a young actor takes on the role of an old person. When an actor of a certain age, however, plays someone's little girl or an aristocratic young general like Atsumori or Kiyotsune, then it simply doesn't come off. You should be aware of this.

One of the most difficult things in writing plays, then, is assigning to a given actor a role that is appropriate to his expressive capacity. Unless you understand a certain play, after discerning the happy effects of which the actor is capable, it won't come off. This is one of the most difficult things for a writer.

• Various plays that have made a good impression with the public in recent years from the Three Modes and the like:

In the Aged Mode: *Yawata, Aioi, Yōrō, Oimatsu, Shiogama, Aritowoshi,*[23] and so forth.

In the Women's Mode: *Hakozaki, Unoha, Mekurauchi, Shizuka, Matsukaze Murasame, Hyakuman, Ukifune, The Woman of Higaki, Komachi.*[24]

23. All these plays remain in the nō repertory, although some are known by different names. *Aioi* (orth. *Ahioi*) is today known as *Takasago*, and *Shiogama* (orth. *Shihogama*) is today's *Tōru*. The traditional orthography for *Yōrō* is *Yaurau*; *Yawata* is presumably *Yumi Yawata* (orth. *Yahata*). *Aritowoshi* was originally spelled *Aritohoshi*, which is significant because it contains a pun relevant to the theme of the play, which is discussed in connection with the lengthy quotation from the play in *Five Sorts of Singing*. The modern spelling, *Aridōshi*, obscures the pun even more than Zeami's misspelling, so I have used Zeami's orthography.

24. Both *Hakozaki* and *Unoha* are celebratory plays in the Women's Mode that were dropped from the repertory during the Edo/Tokugawa period. *Mekurauichi* (*The Blind Man Strikes*) is lost but was likely a vendetta piece with a blind hero (or a hero pretending to be blind), perhaps an early version of the play *Mochizuki*. *Shizuka* (orth. *Shidzuka*) was apparently an early version of

In the Martial Mode: *Michimori, Satsuma no kami,*[25] *Sanemori, Yorimasa, Kiyotsune, Atsumori.*

For the fine play of charismatics: *Tango monogurui, Jinen koji, Kōya, Ausaka.*[26]

In the Style of Intricate Movement: *Koi no omoni, Sano no funabashi, Shii no shōshō, Taisan Moku.*[27]

These several plays should be taken as models for new creations.

I would venture to say that several plays created recently are in a new style that has taken something from the old style. One of these is now *Hyakuman*, which used to be *Saga monogurui no kyōjo*. There's an older play behind *Shizuka. Tango monogurui* was once *Fue monogurui. Matsukaze Murasame* was once *Shiokumi. Koi no omoni* was once *Aya no taiko*. There are older and newer versions of *Jinen koji*. There's an older version of *Sano no funabashi*. Each one of these is thus a new version of an older play. Language has been amended and music revised, adapting each play to its time, to serve as seeds for a flower that comes and goes, year in, year out. This is the way in which you might expect things to change for years to come.

The evaluation of plays is not, for the most part, a matter of individual judgment. This is an art that has gained fame in the city as well as the country, near home as well as far away, so its standards should be no secret. Thus, even though you might well expect that the character of the performance of a given play would change from an older style to one more contemporary, in each case, when it comes to those accomplished masters who have gained unique fame in the realm, their manner of expression has possessed the grace of *yūgen*. In the old style, it was the *dengaku* actor Itchū, in the more recent

---

the play *Yoshino Shizuka. Matsukaze Murasame* is now known as *Matsukaze* and is one of the most celebrated plays in the nō repertory. It, or an antecedent to it, was once entitled *Shiokumi* (orth. *Shihokumi*). *Hyakuman* (orth. *Hyakumamu*) is also a famous play. The text of *Ukifune* remains in the repertory but is not frequently performed. *The Woman of Higaki* is known today simply as *Higaki*. Of the four plays in the repertory about Ono no Komachi, the one referred to here is apparently an early version of *Sotoba Komachi* (*Komachi on the Stupa*).

25. *Satsuma no kami* (*The Governor of Satsuma Province*) is now known as *Tadanori*. It, and the other plays mentioned here, are actively performed today.

26. *Tango monogurui* (orth. *Tango monoguruhi* [*The Madman of Tango Province*]) was dropped from the repertory in the early Edo/Tokugawa period. *Kōya* (orth. *Kauya*) is likely the old name of *Kōya monogurui* (*The Madman of Kōya*). *Ausaka* (orth. *Afusaka*) is probably the play *Ausaka monogurui* (*The Madman of Ausaka*), based on the same material as the more successful *Semimaru*. See Susan Matisoff, *The Legend of Semimaru, Blind Musician of Japan* (New York: Columbia University Press, 1978), pp. 79–81.

27. All these plays remain in the nō repertory. *Koi no omoni* was originally spelled *Kohi no omoni* (*The Heavy Burden of Love*). *Sano no funabashi* is now known simply as *Funabashi* (*The Pontoon Bridge*). *Shii no shōshō* (orth. *Shiyi no seushyau* [*Lesser Captain of the Fourth Rank*]) is now known as *Kayoi Komachi. Taisan moku* is called *Taisan bukun* today.

past the late master of our troupe, Kanze,[28] and Inuō of Hie[29]—all these made *yūgen* in dance and singing the basis of their style, and all were accomplished masters of each of the Three Modes. There were, apart from them, actors who made a name for themselves at some time for the Martial Mode or for Intricate Movement, but none of these gained lasting fame. For that reason, it would appear that the rank of the greatest achievement on the basis of true *yūgen* does not look different from age to age.

You should, therefore, create plays that make their basis the seeds for the flower of *yūgen*. I'll say it again and again: although expert actors have been diverse in the past, as they will be in the future—in old times and new, come and go, year in, year out—for the actor who would capture fame throughout the realm, supreme and perennial, there is only *yūgen*. The real proof of an expert artist—one who was famous long ago, who is singled out yet today, who has gained a name for himself consistently both in the city and out—that proof does not stray from the expressive flower of *yūgen*.

Given what I have written here in general terms and based on my observations of recent years, I would venture to say that judgments of the several plays written during the Ōei era will remain consistent even in ages to come. You should be certain to get a firm hold on these articles.

I hereby make a secret transmission of this manuscript to my son Motoyoshi.

Ōei 30 [1423]:2:6.
Zea (signature)

Notes

1. Much of my translation is based on my earlier work on *The Three Courses* in *ZS*. There I refer to the text by the title *Sandō*. The translation here is complete, whereas in *ZS* it was abridged, and here I have been much more "literal" in keeping with the approach adopted in this volume. The detailed information in *ZS*, however, is still accurate and relevant, for the most part, and the reader wishing more detailed structural analysis may turn there.

2. 能作書条々. Perhaps a mistranscription of 種作書条々, this subhead is parallel to one later in the text reading, 三体作書条々, "Articles on Composition for the Three Modes."

3. The manuscript on which this translation is based reads "*shu to ha, geinō no honzetsu ni sono waza wo nasu jintai ni shite, buga no tame taiyō naru koto wo shiru beshi.*" In Zeami's usage, the word *taiyō* is ambiguous. It may mean "important" or "efficacious," although in the latter case, it should probably read "*taiyō aru*" rather than "*taiyō naru.*" There has been disagreement about whether the person chosen as the central figure in a play should also have a direct connection to singing and dancing in the original source. (Some of the characters Zeami mentions later certainly had such a connection, but others, in highly respected plays, did not.) Some manuscripts read "*. . . nasu jintai ni yo[t]te*" rather than "*. . . jintai ni shite,*" but this reading makes the sen-

28. Orth. Kwanze—that is, Kannami.

29. Inuō Dōami (orth. Inuwau), a celebrated actor of Kannami's generation in the Ōmi style of *sarugaku*.

tence more ambiguous still, and the newly discovered traced copy of the Matsunoya manuscript reading "*jintai ni shite*" strengthens the position of scholars like Omote and Konishi Jin'ichi (*Zeami shū*, Nihon no shisō, vol. 8 [Tokyo: Chikuma shobō, 1970], p. 167), who have preferred this reading all along. There is a further complication in that "*shu to ha*" may mark the subject of the sentence or may mark, less precisely, the topic of the sentence. In the latter case, the sentence might be interpreted as something like "the Seed resides in the fact that there is great significance for the song and dance [in a play], depending on [reading "*jintai ni* yo(*t*)*te*"] the choice of a person who performs these actions [in the original story]."

4. The remarks enclosed in parentheses here and in the rest of the *Three Courses* are written in smaller script.

5. 上声. This corresponds to the *shōdan* known later as the *kuri*, a short song in noncongruent rhythm, mostly in a higher register, which occasionally reaches the highest pitch commonly used in nō, the "*kuri* pitch."

6. *Seimon'ikyoku* (声聞意曲). The compound occurs only here in Zeami's *Notes* and rarely, if ever, elsewhere; it seems to connote beauty in singing and wit in meaning.

7. *Yo no tsune no jobun no ongyoku* (よのつねの序分の音曲). There is disagreement about what sort of "*jo* section" is in question here. Some suggest the first *dan* of a play, but Zeami's understanding of *jo-ha-kyū* entails a kind of fractal structure in which the three elements in question are to be found in every structural element of performance, from a full day's program to a single word of an aria. That is the rationale, I assume, that Omote uses in his persuasive contention that the *jo* in question here is the opening part of the second *dan* of a play. See *ZS*, pp. 109, 273n.48, 274n.49.

8. 開眼一開{之}妙所可有. I follow Omote's emendation of 開眼 to 聞眼.

Technical Specifications for Setting a Melody
曲付次第

Technical Specifications for Setting a Melody is undated and cannot be precisely situated among the *Performance Notes*. It is concerned throughout with how melodies are to be composed for *sarugaku* and, in that connection, seems to complement *The Three Courses*, but there is no mention of *Technical Specifications for Setting a Melody* in that text and likewise no mention of *The Three Courses* in this one.

The text is indeed highly technical but also pragmatic. Zeami's specifications for setting melodies are explicitly directed toward success in performance and understanding different varieties of music in concrete terms. It is toward this end that he introduces a large number of technical terms, some of which are incomprehensible to us today. His emphasis on the importance of rhythm is exemplified in the formulation "Forget the voice and you'll know the pitch. Forget the pitch and you'll know the expression. Forget the expression and you'll know the rhythm," which conforms well to the general characteristics of music in nō today. His comments on breathing are applicable to other types of singing and musical performance as well.

❁

When it comes to singing, a person must have mastered two or three matters before I find it possible to say that he is fully competent: He must excel in elocution[1] and the Six Modes;[1] he must render the accent of words correctly and must set the melody with attention to the weight of the text, that is, to the voicing and nonvoicing of consonants.

Be that as it may, since there isn't one person in a million who is truly accomplished in elocution, one tends to try for a general sense of the matter, relying on one's ear or drawing on the expertise of someone practiced in composition; and so one sets the melodies and writes the lyrics. Since that, then, is all it takes to excite the interest of the average listener, it's enough to get you noticed for a time.

But what I mean by a person truly accomplished in elocution and the Six Modes and what I mean by someone who is expert at singing are two

1. The Six Modes come from Japanese adaptations of Chinese musical theory. See appendix 1.

different things. Some people understand elocution but don't know about singing. Some experts in singing are not accomplished in elocution. That said, though, once they have risen to a rank of true expertise, some people are, as a matter of course, fully competent with regard to elocution, even without receiving a formal transmission in the subject. Someone once said, "Neither the teacher nor the student really knows the way elocution and musical modality work. Rather, they exist of their own accord in the hands of a truly accomplished master." In the *Rites* they speak of "hearing without there being a voice and seeing without there being a form."[2]

Therefore, since it's almost always the case that what is appreciated is what the greatest number of people find exciting to listen to, let us, for the time being, take this as our assignment; in setting the melody, one proceeds with lines of the syllable count 5–7–5, 7–5, 7–5. You should not put words of the same accent[3] in the opening syllables in the 7–5, 7–5 verse lines where you begin to sing. If you repeat the same accents there, it sounds redundant. If, say, you begin to sing with an accent of the "falling tone," then you should distinguish the second verse with an accent of "entering tone."[4] Similarly, the final words in the line will sound particularly redundant if the same accent is allowed to carry through. But then again, when you try to bring the song to a close on a different accent, it is not by any means a simple matter to find a word in which the accent conforms to the melody.[5] You should look for words with accents that fit the contours of the melody and write it out using them. You are likely to produce the best melodies with words accented in a way that naturally fits the melody. You can also generally achieve a good result with transitional phrases in which the word accents fit well with the melody. You should be able to distinguish what's correct and incorrect in the resonances between one word and the next as they operate according to the

2. Unlike many of Zeami's putative references to the *Rites* (*Record of Rites* [*Li ji*]), in this case there actually is a similar phrase to be found in the Chinese text, in *Qu li* I, 2, iv.12, but the text there seems to refer to a filial son's ability to hear his parent's voice before any words are spoken and to understand his parent's intention before it takes form in expression. Zeami reinterprets this. See Omote, in *ZZ*, pp. 464–65n.76.

3. Like other theoreticians of his time, Zeami borrows the idea of tones from Chinese, even though Japanese is not a tonal language. He seems to refer in concrete terms to accent.

4. The "falling tone" (Mandarin *qusheng*) and "entering tone" (Mandarin *rusheng*) are traditional technical designations for the pronunciation of Chinese tones. The precise import of Zeami's usage here is uncertain, but perhaps he means that consecutive 7–5 verses should begin with words having different pitch accents. In any case, the more general point about redundancy is clear.

5. As in his earlier text *Oral Instructions on Singing*, Zeami is very concerned about pitch accent in the text as well as more narrowly defined musical issues. His dilemma here is finding a word that is both natural in Japanese (and thus displays certain accentual characteristics at the end of an utterance) and also provides sufficient diversity of "accent" to avoid the redundancy he mentions.

four accents and the modal structures of *ryo* and *ritsu*.[6] Give careful consideration to the details. Then people will not be able to discern small discrepancies in the way the melody sounds. A real master, though, is likely to pick them out.

You must be aware of how to set a melody to a text that fits well, as well as to a text that doesn't fit so well. In cases in which it is particularly difficult to set the singing voice to the text, you should ask someone who is well versed in the Five Sounds[7] and then consider carefully how you might assign the text to your singing, putting all your ingenuity into setting the melody. Once you have picked out the melody, having carefully decided how it fits with the Five Sounds and the Four Accents, it should be beautiful and flow smoothly and have a certain grace on the hearing that is not obtrusive, as if to insist, "Here's a good tune." That, you will recognize, is the best type of melody. You should keep in mind the saying that "the profoundly deep is close to the shallow."

That being the case, don't think that the most difficult thing about setting the melody is simply setting the melody. You will have a secure understanding of what's most difficult only once you have taken great pains to set the words of a text so that the accents accord well with the contours of the melody and laid it out in 7–5 meter; only then, when you try singing it in rhythm, will you discover that with its beauty, its virtuosity, and the interest they excite, it holds great appeal for the listener. You must then make every effort to seek out critics and connoisseurs to find out what was right and what was wrong in your singing. The *Rites* says, "A real master hears the Dao and exerts himself to study it. A middlebrow hears the Dao, and sometimes it's there, sometimes not. A common fellow hears the Dao, claps his hands, and lets out a great guffaw. If this last guy doesn't laugh, then be assured, it cannot be the Dao."[8, 2]

• You should not repeat words of the same pronunciation in adjacent 7–5, 7–5 syllable verses. Even if they are the same words with different accents, they will sound redundant. If the last word in the melody of the final line is to be sung resolutely, then the last word in the previous line should be sung so lightly that it is almost dropped.[3] Musical relations between the last words of

6. The "four accents" mentioned in the text are, in Zeami's terminology, identified as "four tones" (as in Chinese). *Ryo* and *ritsu* are discussed in appendix 1.

7. Omote reads the word here, 五音, as *go in*, distinguishing the term from *go on*, the Five Sorts of Singing, which is written with the same Chinese graphs.

8. The quotation is actually not from the *Rites* but from Laozi, *Dao de jing* 41, with some lexical discrepancies, emendations, and variations among the manuscripts of *Technical Specifications for Setting a Melody*. The most widely available texts of the *Dao de jing* read, "A person of high capacity hears the Dao and exerts himself to practice it. A person of middle capacity hears the Dao: sometimes it's there, sometimes it's not. A person of low capacity hears the Dao, lets out a loud guffaw over it. If he didn't laugh, it would not suffice to be the Dao." The citation also is found in *Pick Up a Jewel and Take the Flower in Hand*.

adjacent verses like this are particularly common in noncongruent songs[4] and *kudoki*.[9] "The transition from verse to verse" refers to the sound of your vocal pattern from 7–5 verse to 7–5 verse. "The transition from word to word" is of particular concern as you move from the last word in one verse over the boundary into the next verse. You should not use the same vocal pattern, the same accent, or the same words in the transition from one 7–5 verse to the next. If, say, it's just a matter of using the same accent in two adjacent verses, that shouldn't cause a serious problem. If that repetition continues for three verses, though, it will be conspicuous to the ear and sound redundant. You should be careful to use word choices and accent for distinction in sound.

• On rhythm in singing: this is the life of musical expression. They say, "Forget the voice, and you'll know the pitch. Forget the pitch, and you'll know the expression. Forget the expression, and you'll know the rhythm."

In some cases, a song divides into two parts as the singing proceeds through 7–5 verse lines and you beat out the rhythm. In such cases, the second part should be brought to a close more lightly and with a more compact rhythm than the first part. Sometimes the 5–7–5 metrics are altered in such a way that what would be five syllables ends up being six and what would be seven ends up as eight or nine. In verses with extra syllables like these, you may elide syllables in the words. The rhythm is fixed in its extent. If you make the standard rhythmic allotment to a text with more syllables than usual, there will be too many syllables to fit the beats of the music. If you stretch out the rhythm to accommodate the text, then the singing will drag. In such a case, you should make the rhythm your first priority and compress or elide the text to fit it. There also may be cases in which there are not enough syllables in the text. In such a case, you can extend the beat in such a way that it holds the place where there are not enough syllables in the text, and if you go on beating out the rhythm as if there were enough syllables, then sometimes you will achieve an unusual effect in the expression that generates excitement. You should make a careful study of how to make the singing and the rhythm suitable to each other like this and set your melodies accordingly. In some cases an excess of syllables creates a quite unexpected effect in singing. You should use your ingenuity in setting the melody this way and that, assigning it boldly,[5] extending the beat or packing it tightly together, or opening it up, or stretching out the text.[10] Not all will go into writing.

9. The modern *kudoki* is a noncongruent *shōdan* centered on the lower register. See the glossary.

10. *Hyaushi wo koshitsu, tsumetsu hirakitsu, moji wo nobetsu.* Flexibility in the relationship between the text and the rhythm is obviously a primary concern for Zeami here, but some of the terms he uses may also refer to specific technical means of dealing with discrepancies between prosody and rhythm. Some of these terms, such as *koshi* and *tsume*, are used in modern *utai*.

• On rank in musical expression: As I said earlier, what sounds so appealing when the word accents are treated with precision, and the beauty and virtuosity of the singing sound spontaneous and unaffected, is the exhaustively trained, wondrous voice of the rank of full confidence. The best musical expression, then, must be an unaffected sort that appeals spontaneously to one's excitement when heard. When the musical expression arouses the mind's ear and makes a person aware that he is listening to good singing, that must be accounted second best. This would be the greatest extent possible within the rank of aural excitement aroused through formal patterns.

Also, however good a strain of musical expression is, if it appears twice in the same song, it will sound redundant and should be avoided. As it says in the *Rites*, "Exceeding falls short."[11]

• Various types of singing. First, the singing of *shiugen*: from the *sashigoe*, you sing verses in 5–7–5 metrical structure some six or seven times smoothly (a 5–7 couplet counts as one verse, but a *waka* poem counts as two verses),[6] and from the point at which the singing drops to the lower register as far as the *kōnomono*,[12] you should sing about ten verses. You shouldn't use a melody that is likely to draw particular attention here. It should be sung smoothly and unobtrusively and then brought to a close; there should be a place where it is sung in *kan no koe* (this refers to the *nijū no kan*)[13] with a gentle grace and fluent transitions from word to word in a full-throated melody.

Now, such treatment should not be limited to *shiugen* songs. Any more or less independent song[7] should be closely matched to the rhythm in 7–5 verses and should be written straightforwardly and confidently. Rhythmic variants such as *matsufushi*, *yarufushi*, *koshite matsufushi*, *kirufushi*, *kasanebushi*, *semebushi*, *hayafushi*,[14] and other such sequences and tunes should not be used in a song in the *jo* section. These kinds of tunes should appear as needed in setting the melody later on, deeper into the piece, in accordance with the position in question. They should not be isolated in a given song.[15] In particular, *kirufushi* and *tatamufushi* should not be overused. The same vocal pattern

---

11. Actually, the quotation is not exact and is not from the *Rites*, but from the *Analects* 11.15, where the text reads, "Exceeding is just like falling short."

12. A *kaunomono* (more correctly spelled *kafunomono;* mod. J. *kōnomono*) is, in general terms, "a higher part" and sometimes refers to part of a *kuse* in a higher register, as in, for example, *Three Courses*. Here, though, Omote specifies an *ageuta*.

13. A parenthetical note with the technical term *nijū no kan* (a twofold *kan* pitch). Apparently a technical term for some kind of melodic pattern or embellishment, *nijū no kan* remains unexplained.

14. These technical terms are not clearly understood at present. *Hayafushi* indicates *chūnori* rhythmic style (in which one beat in the music is allotted to two syllables of text, but here it seems to indicate a particular type of melody or melodic embellishment).

15. Zeami seems to be saying, don't use one of these patterns or riffs unless you can use it more than once. But that seems somewhat at odds with the next sentence.

should not be repeated in 7–5 sequences. The *kan no koe* should appear once in a *kōnomono.* Occasionally, however, depending on the location in question, you might rise to the level of *kan no koe* more than once. Knowing where to find such a place is a matter of expertise in composition coming from the composer's knowledge. Again, depending on the verse in question, there may be places where it is not set in 5–7–5 meter.

• *Kusemai*: This line of singing is different from the typical sort. First and foremost, it takes rhythm as its Substance and should proceed expeditiously, relying on rhythm. The melody[8] should be set in such a way that it passes across beats in the rhythm, shrinking and opening up to the movement through the 7–5 verses as it is counted out in the mind, and adjusting this way and that in sequences of *matsufushi*, *kasanebushi*, and *kirite yarufushi.*[16]

These days, however, one often hears *koutabushi-kusemai*, which is a combination of standard singing in *tadautai* style with *kusemai*. This is smooth and has the grace of *yūgen*. Singing like this may be a type of *kusemai*, but it cannot be called *kusemai* music in the original sense.[9] Although the melodic structure does not, strictly speaking, match the original genre, it is interesting because it allows for a graceful transition from word to word and verse to verse, so these days you should set melodies according to this manner of expression.

Also, one sometimes hears *kusemai* songs closing on a repeated line. Although this is not really the way it should be done, in recent times, one frequently hears songs brought to a close with this repetition. Were these real *kusemai*, they wouldn't end with a repeated line.

Kusemai take rhythm as their primary matter, and they take this rhythm as their primary matter because they are of a musical style in which one sings to the dance. This is, in fact, the reason that they are called *kusemai*, because one word for singing is added to the word for dance in their name.[10] In setting melodies, you should be acutely aware of this distinction.

• On breathing in singing: This is the basis on which you are able to continue to sing from phrase to phrase. Setting melodies in such a way as to facilitate the breathing must therefore be the way to musical expression.

First of all, you should breathe on the caesura between the 5–7–5 and the 7–5, 7–5 lines in transition from verse to verse. In the *jo* section, as long as you are singing in *sashigoe* style, you generally should breathe between each pair of 7–5 verses. When you begin singing congruent songs, then sometimes you should sing for two full verses without drawing a breath, depending on the performance style.

In effect, what maintains the transition from verse to verse and word to word is the breath. You should not draw a breath just as you have finished

16. The text means "cut and extended" sequence or tune, but it has not been pinned down specifically.

singing a phrase. You should, rather, sustain your breath, and bring your singing to resolution while you still have plenty of breath. If your breath is insufficient and you finishing singing a phrase with your breath exhausted, the words won't settle properly. It is only during the lingering resonance after the words have been sung that you should draw the next breath. Make sure you keep this in mind.

Also, there is the matter called "dropping the voice," when you proceed to the next verse having dropped the last words of the previous verse or the transition to the next. At this time, you purposely abandon the breath before finishing the enunciation of a word. This amounts to dropping a word as you draw your next breath. It is a musical technique used in *kusemai.* This stems from a rank of musical performance of great virtuosity. You should know that this is a very special and secret type of singing. In the normal experience of singing, you should always finish what you are singing before your breath runs out.

Now then, there is an oral transmission regarding the voice as you begin singing. The correct use of the voice as you begin singing is a matter of breathing. Singing in the appropriate register is also a matter of breathing. Maintaining the correct pitch as you sing is also a matter of breathing. Expressive manner in singing, too, is a matter of breathing.

For the most part, you should take your breath between verses, but that said, in some places it is possible to steal a breath, depending on context. What I mean by "stealing" a breath is taking a breath in circumstances when it isn't noticed. Then again, there assuredly are places where, according to the rhythm, you should rest between words but where even though the text breaks off, you should maintain your breath. This should be transmitted in one's training in singing. A master who is accomplished in singing, however, will surely know this even without being given the transmission.

Thus, since breathing is the base that sustains the comprehensive matter of singing, you should be aware of it and find opportunities in setting melodies to assist the breath and allow the performer to take a breath. I'll say it again and again: Setting melodies and constructing phrases without allowing for a place to take a breath is entirely unreasonable. You must understand that the path to singing cuts across the ground of breathing.[17] You take the breath; don't let the breath take you.[11]

In general, the articles on setting melodies are complete as mentioned. Apart from this, the expressive grace of the wondrous voice of no-singing is not a matter to be written down.

In secret: The consummate practice in singing should entail composition well matched to the language of *waka* poetry. The first reason for this is that the basic matter is to be set to verses of 5–7–5. The chanting of poetry,

17. Compare *A Collection of Jewels in Effect.*

moreover, cannot help but conform to singing, since as a variety of chant at heart, it entails a continuous delivery of the text as poetry and is therefore amenable to the musical theory of the Five Sounds and subject to the constraints of correct enunciation. Thus when you consider how a *waka* poem is sung, you should find nothing at odds with the expressive grace of the melody. This is how you know that the basis for grace in a melody lies in the proper pattern of enunciation.

If, moreover, you carefully examine the words, then even though you may gain the impression that they don't conform precisely to the accent, in certain cases they do nonetheless match the chant of the singing voice. These should simply be handled in such a way that chant is their basic matter. Although the accents may not conform completely on account of elisions in pronunciation, there should be no adverse effect, because a song text, written out as a whole, will, under the influence of chanting as poetry, sound melodious and flow gracefully. "The lightness or heaviness, the voicing or lack of voicing of a word depends upon the preceding text," as they say.[18]

Vocal phrasing in singing is, for the most part, like water flowing over the contours of the ground. When a river flows over level ground, the surface of the water is calm and flows away swiftly. When it flows over a rocky and uneven place, the rivulets twist and curl in patterns, raising little ripples and flowing back upon themselves, whether coming or going, but in the end, the stream does go over the ground, conforming to its shape. So, too, singing in a straightforward manner of expression follows the beat in 7–5, 7–5 verses, conforming to the standards of vocal music and proceeding calmly and mellifluously. Some of the verses are long and some short; the words are diverse in character; and the pattern of the voice twists and turns, creating an effect of the new and unusual; but the accentuation of the singing voice in its transitions from word to word and the conformity of the chant as text sung continuously with proper elocution are the same as rivulets of water following the lay of the land. If by chance you should simply set a melody and try to force the expression from it, heedless of the rationale for chanting according to the proper elocution in the continuous production of voice, then the music you produce will be like raising waves in water flowing over a flat surface or, again, like a puddle of rain in the garden which, though it may indeed show ripples in the pattern on the surface of the water for a short time, will in the end dry up into nothing.

Chōmei says, "Now the course of a living river flows on unceasingly, yet never with the same water as before."[19] In figural terms, the voice might be

18. It is unclear where this quotation comes from, but Zeami also quotes it in *A Mirror to the Flower.*

19. The much celebrated opening line of "Hōjōki" (A Record of My Ten-Foot-Square Hermitage), by Kamo no Chōmei (1153–1216), except that Zeami has added an inceptive *sore* (my "Now")

water, and the expression, its flow. If so, then the way the expression courses along, one way or another uninterrupted, without sounding redundant, might be considered "flowing on unceasingly, yet never with the same water as before." Setting a melody then might combine all the things that water does in a lake in the garden, swirling in eddies, rising up against rocks in its path, pooling and falling in a curtain, weaving fallen leaves into a watery brocade. In the same way, you must be aware that the voice, like water, takes the Five Sounds of proper elocution and the four accents as its ground, and its flowing course follows that ground, so if the reverberations of even a word or a syllable should fail to conform to the ground of the proper pitch and accent, the flow of the voice will be impeded. Using the voice and taking the proper medicine for it in training is a matter of purifying the waters. Keeping the expression correct and being cognizant of musical pitch corresponds to laying out the course of water in a garden. Again and again: you must be aware that the expressive rationale for a pattern in the voice "flows on, uninterrupted, yet not with the same water as before," thus avoiding redundancy.

Notes

1. 五音. Although the term is ambiguous, given Zeami's interest in "five sounds" (see, for instance, the two texts later in the collection with the words "Five Sounds" in their title), here his concern must be the elocution and accent of words, as evidenced in what follows. In such a context, this should be pronounced *go in* rather than *go on*. See also *Oral Instructions on Song*.

2. The more prominent discrepancies in the text are Zeami's replacement of "study [the Dao]" for "practice [the Dao]" and his embellishment of the reaction of the common fellow upon hearing the Dao. The consistent use of 子 rather than 士 for the subjects of the first three sentences doesn't seem to alter the meaning greatly, although I have given different translations for the words in question. These could merely be mistakes in the Japanese reading of a Chinese text, since the words are homophones in Japanese. So, too, the graph 損, which means "damage" or "impair," in this case seems merely to be a quasi-homophonic replacement of 存. Omote details the rather complicated textual state of the line and points to the quotation of a similar version in Zenchiku's *Kabu zuinau no ki*. See *ZZ*, p. 466n.78.

3. Zeami distinguishes here what appear to be technical terms. If the last word is to be sung resolutely (lit., "placed firmly" [*kyoku wo suete wokitaraba*]), then the "last word in the previous line" can be "abandoned in the saying" (*ihisutete wokubeshi*). *Sue*[*ru*] remains a technical term in modern nō chanting, signifying a drop in pitch at the end of a *tsuyogin* passage. Although the degree of drop is not specified, it usually is not very great. For a basic explanation relevant to the modern Kanze performance of this vocal figure, see Miyake Kōichi, *Fushi no seikai*, rev. ed. (Tokyo: Hinoki shoten, 1977), p. 109.

4. *Ji no mono* (orth. *dji no mono*); the term is not familiar from modern *utai*. Omote asserts that it is not a chorus part, as one might assume, but probably a *sashi*-style song, thus in noncongruent rhythm.

---

at the beginning of the line, just as he does in quoting a somewhat longer passage from the same place in his play *Yōrō*.

5. The text reads それらをば大にあてがひて . . . at this point and doesn't make good sense. Perhaps 大 is a mistake or an incomplete writing of some compound. I wonder whether something like 大様 was intended, thus my "boldly."

6. In the primary manuscript on which Omote bases his text, this passage, in smaller type, is written as a note alongside the main text. It helps clear up the ambiguity of the earlier line in which, even though Zeami specifies six or seven repetitions of 5–7–5 lines, he probably means six or seven units of 7–5 couplets. But since these songs often begin with the first section of a *waka* poem (5–7–5), the combination 5–7–5, 7–5 should be counted as two verses. Compare this with the discussion in *Three Courses*.

7. 一句うたい, a hapax legomenon, of uncertain meaning. I follow Omote's suggestion in the headnotes to *ZZ*, p. 150, and pp. 489–90n.140.

8. Following Omote's parsing of 曲 here as *fushi*.

9. Zeami distinguishes the two homophones in the graphs with which he writes them, the first 曲舞 and the second 節曲舞 (の曲).

10. Zeami's etymology is based on the perfectly conventional use of the word for "dance," 舞 (*mahi*, mod. J. *mai*), with an unusual word for "music," 曲 (pronounced *kuse* as a single graph, but *-gyoku* in the compound words like "singing" [*ongyoku*]).

11. The main text here reads 息次息次 , in Chinese. As such, it is redundant and ambiguous, but it has been pointed with an archaic negative imperative in the second clause, presumably by Zeami, so it can be read in Japanese as "*iki wo tsuge, iki ni tsugare so.*" I have followed the pointing in the translation.

A Collection of Jewels in Effect

風曲集

A Collection of Jewels in Effect seems less pragmatic than *Technical Specifications for Setting Melodies*, perhaps because we simply don't know what Zeami intends by some of the technical vocabulary he frequently uses in the text. His distinction between the *wau* voice and the *shu* voice, for instance, remains opaque, and his emphasis on *ryo* and *ritsu* is also difficult to understand, whether from their earlier musicological meaning in China and Japan or from modern performance practice. Nevertheless, his advice about how to practice (as if every practice session or performance off the beaten track were a performance of great importance) is eminently practical and applicable beyond the confines of *sarugaku* or nō performance. The discussion at the end of the text of patternlessness and beauty has palpable ties, through Zen, to other celebrated arts of the fifteenth century, foreshadowing the aesthetics of the "Higashiyama era" of the latter half of the fifteenth century.

The remark at the beginning of the text, "The title was bestowed by His Majesty, from the Sentō Palace," suggests that *Jewels in Effect* was named by Retired Emperor Gokomatsu (1377–1433, r. 1382–1412). Zeami and his eldest son, Motomasa, were supposed to give a command performance for him in 1429, but Ashikaga Yoshinori, the shogun, prevented it from taking place. It is not known whether there is any relationship between *A Collection of Jewels in Effect* and that performance.

Remarks near the middle of the text in connection with "Priorities in training" include a tantalizing reference to the contraction and expansion of the verse between lines, which suggests that the rather subtle and complex rhythmic conventions of drumming in nō may have begun as early as Zeami's day.

❁

The title was bestowed by His Majesty, from the Sentō Palace.

On learning singing. There certainly are a great many things to account for in articles on training, beginning with the five sounds of proper elocution and the four accents[1] and culminating in a rank that ensures vocal expertise in the *ryo* and *ritsu* modes.[2]

---

1. The five sounds (*go in*) in this context seem to refer to medieval linguistic arcana, while the four sounds are adopted from the classical Chinese tonal system. Here, though, their application is puzzling. See the discussion in *Oral Instructions on Song* and *Technical Specifications for Setting a Melody.*

2. *Ryo* and *ritsu* are discussed in appendix 1.

First of all, it is important for beginners in the vocation to devote a certain amount of time to learning to distinguish specifications in vocal music, beginning with their introduction to "first pitch, second *ki*, third voice."[3] There are two types of singing voice, the *wau* voice and the *shu* voice.[4] In terms of *ryo* and *ritsu*, I suppose the *wau* voice would be *ryo*, and the *shu* voice would be *ritsu*. For tuning and warming up, you use the *shu* voice. Once you set the voice loose in singing, that's the *wau* voice. They say, "Sing with *wau* and bring the song to cadence with *shu*." Since, however, the voice comes into pitch in *shu*,[5] the word on which one begins to sing should be *shu*. The course the voice follows, then, begins as *shu* changes to *wau*, eventually coming to cadence with, again, *shu*. *Wau* is articulated with the breath exhaled; *shu* should be distinguished by the breath inhaled. You can create excitement in singing by assisting the voice with the use of inhaled and exhaled breath and giving the melody distinction. You should be aware that there is ingenuity in the use of inhaled and exhaled breath relating to the word or type of vocalization in question. This is the life of singing. "The path to singing cuts across the ground of breathing," as they say.[6]

There is something else you should know in this connection. Some people are born with singing voices predisposed to *wau* and others with voices predisposed to *shu*. Those with a natural propensity in both are called "doubly proficient." This is a good voice. A good voice should be used naturally from the *sashigoe* through the *kōnomono*,[7] and then once it has dropped to a lower pitch, the vocal pattern should settle into *shu* voicing and come to cadence in the resonance of inhaled breath. This is how the melody should be produced by someone with a good voice who is doubly proficient. For someone whose voice is inclined toward *wau*, it is better to direct the vocal pattern somewhat toward *shu* during the *kōnomono* and to sing through while constraining the voice. This exercises the ingenuity necessary to add the distinction of a doubly proficient performance of the song. For someone with a propensity toward *shu*, it is better to sing through in such a manner so as to open up the breathing for vocal patterning in the *wau* style. A voice in the upper register should be unrestrained, and a voice in the lower register should be restrained. The underlying disposition of the unrestrained voice should begin with *wau* and

3. The quotation comes from *Oral Instructions on Singing* and is repeated in *A Mirror to the Flower*. Here, Zeami demonstrates the direct link to the individual performer's mind, putting the most basic elements of his training at the heart of virtuoso performance before the most exacting audience.

4. See *Oral Instructions on Singing* and appendix 1.

5. Zeami understands the voice that results from listening carefully to the pitch of the flute and transferring that pitch into one's *ki* as a *shu* voice. It is not clear why this should be the case.

6. Quoted with a small grammatical change from *Technical Specifications for Setting a Melody*.

7. See the glossary.

come to rest in *shu*. Make sure you understand this. To speak of using the voice well means making distinctions like this in your deployment of the voice. This is the rank of the expert. Unless you understand the correct makeup of your own voice, it is impossible to sing with distinction and to bring the melody into effect in the musically correct way.

• Be aware of the accentuation of a given word, and don't use the same accentuation again at the outset of singing, the head, or the end of a verse. In transitions from verse to verse and word to word, aim for distinction and variety. For instance, if you have used the *shō* accentuation at the beginning of one verse, you should follow with *kaku* accentuation in the next verse.[8, 1] In this way, there is no redundancy from verse to verse. Similarly, when in transition from one word to another and the former is in falling accentuation,[2] the first word in the next verse should be distinguished by the use of an entering accentuation.[3] You should choose from among the four accentuation patterns and make a distinction in singing by changing from one to a different one as you progress. This is of crucial importance in singing. No doubt, on some occasions there is no alternative but to repeat the accentuation in the transition because of the words in question. In such cases, you should do what you can mentally to alter the vocal pattern in order to make a distinction. This is what it means to grasp the intent in singing. These all are precepts with regard to setting melodies.

Also, you should make allowance for expanding or contracting in singing in the transitions between 7–5 verses, in accordance with the rhythm beat out by the drum(s).[9] The matter of expanding or contracting the rhythm depending on a verse or a word is for learning by transmission from your teacher. Beginners should pay great attention to this transmission.

Priorities in training: First, you must have a clear understanding of how to pronounce the words in the singing; next, be comprehensive in performance styles; next, polish the accents in transitions from word to word; next, understand the expansions and contractions of the rhythm; next, know the intent. What that intent amounts to is, as I said before, taking the inhaled and exhaled breath as your grounding, helping your voice along, adding distinction to the melody, and residing in the rank of utter confidence through the undiminished yet irreplete[4] fact that the path for singing lies over the ground of

8. Zeami has borrowed extensively (though not always with clear intent) from the vocal principles used in chanting Buddhist texts (*shōmyō*).

9. Although it is not possible to point to concrete examples of what Zeami intends here, the comment is interesting in that it seems to point to, or at least foreshadow, the intricate rhythmic distinctions in modern nō chant, in which the singer begins a subsequent phrase at a specific point in the eight-beat measure by responding to the signal of the *otsuzumi* and *kotsuzumi* drum calls and beats. This is indicated in modern nō libretti by the use of the syllables *ya*, *wo*, and *ha* and the intervals at which the singer enters are called *ya-*, *wo-*, *ha-no-ma*, and the like.

breathing. By the way, articles on setting the melody can be found in another text.[10]

• Matters to take to heart in the training of beginners: When practicing alone, exercising the voice, and singing, even though you may be all by yourself, in private, you should, all the same, think of yourself as appearing before exalted persons, adopt the proper attitude for a full formal performance, and sing whatever you've chosen that way. Maintain a formal posture, establish the correct pitch from the start, and be confident in both mind and body that this is an appearance before an actual large audience. Don't for a minute think it's just a private matter, but take a mental vow and sing as if it were an occasion of the greatest importance. Once you have composed your intent in this manner, your training will proceed correctly and no matter how large the audience, you will not falter or suffer from stage fright; this is a method by which you may avoid blunders and misjudgments regarding the measure of your abilities.

Now in singing, you need to make suitable adjustments according to the occasion of a given performance. The things you do in an appearance ordered by exalted persons begin with auspicious songs of *shiugen*, and the singing follows *jo-ha-kyū*, so there should be nothing out of the ordinary from the procedures you have at hand. These are things at which expert performers are particularly skilled. Then again, on occasions that are not quite so formal but aren't drinking parties either but are simply regular performances, it is not necessary to limit yourself to *shiugen*. Then you may confidently undertake a piece with the appeal and expressive manner of *yūgen* such as may be appropriate to the occasion. One of the currently popular songs in the regular style or *kusemai* style should work well. You should have certain acts at hand for such occasions and have a repertoire of a number of songs on which you can draw. I would say that making reliable plans like these is a matter to take to heart in training.

As you train like this and study in the most comprehensive way, you should, as I said before, regard private practice or, for that matter, singing in any traveling performance off the beaten track, as if it were a formal performance before exalted persons; then when you are actually called on to give a command performance on an important occasion, you won't be worried about your exalted audience but instead will have confidence in the power of intent you have cultivated in mastering the matter of your training; you will be able to regard the perceptions of a vast audience with full confidence, as a single pair of eyes, and sing at liberty, thinking "first pitch, second *ki*, third voice."[11]

10. Zeami apparently is referring to *Technical Specifications for Setting a Melody.*

11. The quotation comes from *Oral Instructions on Singing*, repeated in *A Mirror to the Flower*, and was discussed earlier.

• There are two types of appeal and expression in singing. There are also different qualities in people's opinions. Some like a sequence of melodies, distinctions among the verses, and plenty of passages to display a brilliant musical texture. Then there are those who prefer an unobtrusive vocal texture and no melodies that draw particular attention to themselves, but merely an overall beauty and fullness of body in the vocal expression. It is not a question of one approach being superior to the other.

There are, however, different types of "unobtrusive texture." There is, on the one hand, a type of excitement that sounds like no melodic articulation and patternlessness and that comes from the long experience of the performer who has refined his command of melody and finesse in the treatment of accentuation to such a degree that he creates excitement in response to unadulterated interest in the vocal pattern without a sense of where that interest comes from; this requires the sublation of long experience of wondrous sound at the rank of complete confidence.[12, 5] On the other hand, one certainly does find tedious the singing of someone who is patternless out of his pure obtuseness, who in fact doesn't know anything about melody, who has not been taught about accentuation, whose "patternlessness" is simply vacancy of mind.

Now, a rank of patternlessness that is also interesting is the greatest achievement. There is nothing greater than that rank, in which one has comprehensively internalized all the articles of such training as this and has gained a full understanding of the four types of accentuation, transition from verse to verse and word to word according to the conventions of *ryo* and *ritsu* modes, and attained by sublation the rank of complete confidence so that all these things are resident in the disposition of his intent; what you hear, then, is purely the unobtrusive musical texture of his vocal pattern. Once you have attained this rank, singing can be in whichever performance style your intent desires, whether in the brilliantly textured or in the patternless.

There is thus a distinction in how you hear the melody, based on whether it is textured or patternless. When you listen to a singing voice of the patternless sort and the more you listen the more it sounds interesting but doesn't create much excitement, you should recognize that as insensible patternlessness. Then again, when something sounds like patternlessness but the excitement you feel as you listen grows greater and greater and the interest is inexhaustible, you should recognize this to be the patternlessness that has transcended brilliant texture. This is the rank of the wondrous voice in its greatest achievement. That being the case, this unobtrusive musical

12. Zeami's unusual word, *narikaheru* (to become, in turning back), has an almost Hegelian resonance, thus my "sublation." It may be related to his idea of *kyakurai* (doubling back), discussed in *The Flower in . . . Yet Doubling Back*.

texture is to be accounted best, because it contains the brilliantly textured. Since it has yet to reach that unsurpassed level, a brilliant musical texture is accounted second. "The one," as they say, "comprises great diversity; the two is nothing but a pair."[13]

Notes

1. Zeami's *shō* (orth. *shyau*) accentuation is written here with the graph 尚, but that is a borrowing for the more correct 商, which fits the graph for *kaku*, 角, as two of five degrees of the "scale" or "mode" in the set 商角宮徵羽.

2. 去正 for 去声.

3. 入正 for 入声.

4. 不增不減. The characterization may come from the Heart Sutra, which contains an identical phrase.

5. *Mukyoku mumon ni kikoete, kowagakari no omoshiroki bakari to shiru tokoro no, sono omoshiroki kan to ha, kyoku wo tsukushi, monshyau* [文正] *wo migakite nochi, yasuki kurawi no meumon ni narihaheru kofu no kan nari.* Zeami's syntax is unclear, particularly where *shiru tokoro no* is left hanging and following the topicalization of *kan to ha.* Some of the vocabulary, too, is explicitly paradoxical, here announcing the dramatic "Zen-like" discourse of his later texts.

13. Quoting the celebrated collection of Zen kōans, *Biyanlü* (J. *Hekiganroku* [*The Blue Cliff Record*], case 2), but with *ateji* substitutions for some of the graphs in the original.

An Effective Vision of Learning the Vocation of Fine Play in Performance
遊楽習道風見

An Effective Vision of Learning the Vocation of Fine Play in Performance is a brief but pithy text. Zeami takes a somewhat different tack here than in earlier texts. Although he is fond of allusions to and quotations of earlier texts in virtually all his writing, in this text he more explicitly bases his comments on quotations from the *Analects* of Confucius, the Mao preface to the *Classic of Songs*, and the Heart Sutra. His method of exegesis, with occasional misprision, provides a fascinating insight into how he read "the classics" and found practical meaning in them.

Again Zeami discusses *jo-ha-kyū* and the evaluation of a young actor. For the first time, he quotes *The Tendai Interpretation of "Wondrous."* The text has not been otherwise identified, but Zeami mentions it again in *Five Ranks* and *Six Models*.

❀

The Mao preface to the *Classic of Songs* says, "Wee, ho, prettie, ho, hooty-bird's brood.[1] 'Wee' and 'prettie' refer to a fine and dainty appearance. 'Hooty-bird' is the name of a bird."[2] The *Zheng Commentary* says, "The lords of Wei at first achieved some good, but failed to succeed in the end. They were like the hooty-bird."[3] The hooty-bird is the owl.

The owl is cute as a chick but later looks funnier and funnier, so they say. Similarly, in human arts, a fully effective artistic style in a child appears to be a sign that things are not likely to turn out well over the years. The reason for this is that consummation is achieved in the arts when the action on stage is well suited to the actor's physical substance. A fully effective artistic style is the consummation. If the question is what is well suited to a child's behavior

1. This is the first line of the last poem in a series of four entitled "Maoqiu" (Signal-Flag Mound), from the Beifeng in the *Classic of Songs*. The poem is enigmatic, but the subsequent lines in Zeami's quotation represent attempts by the Mao commentator and the Zhengxuan commentator to interpret its meaning.

2. A quotation from the Mao commentary on the *Classic of Songs*.

3. From the commentary by the Later Han Confucian scholar Zhengxuan (127–200) on the *Classic of Songs*. Zheng makes a characteristically political reading of the text, understanding it to refer to the initially promising experience of the lords of Wei, who eventually were defeated by Qin.

on stage, then I suppose we ought to say what we mean by well suited. In the way the young behave, an insufficient understanding, a deficient control of action, and an inadequate mastery of expression all are well suited to childhood. Then, of course, as the years pass and the child eventually grows up, his performance comes together and reaches maturity, and that is well suited to the performance of an adult. So then, during childhood, if the performance has already come together and to all appearances the actor is mature, should we not then say that this is not well suited to the behavior of a child? The artistic career of such a child does not proceed as expected because it is not well suited. If, however, a certain insufficiency is, in fact, well suited to a child's performance, then once this child has grown up, and his ability in a variety of roles finally comes together, he will be well suited to performance as an adult. That is why they say that an owl, pretty as a chick, has a distasteful appearance when it matures; it's because the prime of its life comes first.

That is the reason we should not teach the varieties of dramatic imitation in too much detail for a child's performance. You should devote your attention to getting right the Two Arts of Dance and singing. These are to be the vessels. That is because Dance and singing comprise the main attraction in all the performing arts. They are not the exclusive prerogative of this art alone. They are the underlying expressive bases throughout the fine play of performance. Once you have really and truly learned these Two Arts and developed a diverse repertory as you mature in order to attain a mastery of the Three Modes, then in whatever role you sing, there will be excitement, and whenever you dance, there will be interest—is this not the virtue of having filled up the vessels of Dance and singing in advance? Again and again: You must have a clear understanding that dramatic imitation is to be taken as the focus of study only after you have made the Two Arts into vessels of an underlying expressiveness.

Now let us consider more comprehensively why someone who appears so interesting as a child turns out to be inadequate when he gets older: If he has mastered dramatic imitation and a diverse repertory in his approach to this art as a youth, then the audience will be startled by what they see in his performance, and no sooner do they think, "That's brilliant," than they conclude he's a real expert. In most case, there are good reasons to believe that this is merely the flower of his appearance on that particular occasion and that it will likely be cut off later. One reason is the very regard he calls forth as, "Oh, so brilliant! What expressive mastery across the repertory in but a child!" Another is the particular flower of expression that is found in a child's grace. Another is the excitement that comes from a young voice. All these are ephemeral virtues. They won't last. The reason is that what is perceived as brilliant in a child's display of a diverse repertory will not be there for an adult. The grace of a child's figure won't be there in a man. The excitement of a young voice won't be there once the voice has changed. As for the dramatic imitation inculcated into the child, the achievements in forms of depiction will settle rigidly into him, and in an adult's body, they will be awkward and lack artistry, and as the body changes, they will not be of use. With that being the case, many of the vessels for expressing the flower at that time will be lost, and it will be like the sere winter vision of a stand of trees that earlier had been vibrant with leaves and flowers. Given this consideration, it is easy to understand why on reaching maturity, the fine play in expression fades and dissipates.

So then, in this context as well, as I said earlier, the actor is to be taught only the underlying expressive bases of the Two Arts of Dance and singing, and having made him skilled at these, you should leave him ignorant and wanting regarding dramatic imitation and impersonation during his childhood; then as he grows up and it is time for the Three Modes, you should introduce to him, one after the other, the varieties of roles in the repertory, and he will exhibit a manner of expression well suited to his maturity, and his ability to perform will be long lasting; there should be no doubt about this. The Two Arts of Dance and singing are the primary attraction in all vocations of performance and are of an expressive rank common to beginners, experienced performers, old and young, man and child. Dramatic imitation and impersonation are based on conventions exclusive to this art, and once one has settled into the particularities of a competence in them, one will not be able to comprehend a broader form of expression. This is all the more the case if the body into which those conventions have been inculcated is that of a child; then the artistic level of that time dominates the performer's career. To regard a youth's mastery of dramatic imitation as brilliant shows the flower of the moment.[4] It's like the prettiness of the hooty-bird's brood.

• The *Analects* says, "There are those that sprout but do not flower, and there are those that flower but do not set fruit."[5]

You should know this verse to be the *jo-ha-kyū* for your training in the forms of the art throughout your life.

Among the Two Arts as you have learned them since your youth, whether Dance or singing, there should be already, innately, the sprouts of your talent, perhaps in the interest you create when you dance, perhaps in the excitement you create when you sing. How, then, should these sprouts be nurtured? It appears that you simply have to water them and let them grow up as they will. Once these seedlings stand up straight, they can be transplanted, and after they have started to root, then you pull up any weeds, water, and wait for the rain, and then when they have at last leafed out well, it will be time for the bud to form. And then, about to set fruit, the bud begins to color; and now,

4. Compare *Transmitting the Flower.*

5. A quotation with small variations from *Analects* 9.21.

you don't want the rain that you had looked forward to earlier, but instead you look for the sun and expose the plants to the full sunlight, and in this way, you should be able to get them to set fruit.

In training in this art, we take the child while still young, as a seedling, and water him with the Two Arts, and once he's started to flower and show the visual attraction of a mature artist and get a stable command of the set forms, we take particular care with his appearance in those places that the mind doesn't normally perceive; with the passing years, right through to old age, he should remain mindful of what it takes to bring his audience to yet greater levels of excitement; this, then, must be what it is to know the setting of fruit. In Buddhism too, they say, "It's easy enough to receive the Dharma, but it's hard to maintain it." What's hard about preserving something stems from our propensity to go astray in our own subjectivity. You must be ever so careful about whatever faults may hide beyond your perception. Those who fail to notice whatever faults hide beyond their perception may find their performance changing for the worse. It's like a flowering head of rice that is spoiled by wind and rain and withers without setting fruit. These three stages of sprout, flower, and fruit are, as I said, the *jo-ha-kyū* of your training throughout life.

• The Heart Sutra says, "Form is emptiness, emptiness is form."

So too in all the arts can these two, form and emptiness, be found. Once the three stages of seedling, flower, and fruit are complete and you have attained the rank of complete confidence, then each and every attraction of performance finds full expression in the scene within your mind—is this not "form is emptiness"? But a view of performative intent that settles on this as the consummation of expression in nothingness[6] has yet to account for "emptiness is form" and would amount, I venture, to contriving enlightenment without yet having understood it.[7] There would yet be some hazard in the precautions regarding what is right and what is wrong that are beyond perception. I would surmise that "emptiness is form" is to be found in that rank of performance from which any such hazard regarding precautions is gone, and whatever the character of the performance, it is of great virtuosity; while it may strike one as a truly unusual display, it nonetheless is interesting and empty of right and wrong or good and bad. If both right and wrong are interesting, then there can be no judgment as to right or wrong. Nor can there be any precaution about what is beyond one's knowledge.

In the vocation of poetry as well, they warn against such ailments of poetry as the ailment of redundancy, but then there is this poem:

6. *Mufū* is likely a construction related to the discourse of negatives in Buddhism, especially Zen. Zeami also uses *mushin* (no mind), *mui* (no rank), and the like.

7. Compare *A Course to Attain the Flower*: "contriving an understanding without yet having understood, and contriving enlightenment without yet being enlightened."

Nanihadzu ni saku ya ko no hana fuyugomori
Ima ha harube to saku ya ko no hana[8]

The trees have blossomed, hey,
in Naniwa,
after winter's long seclusion.
Now it's springtime,
the trees have blossomed, hey!

In this case, the redundant words are perfectly obvious, but the poem has turned out to be a particularly good one; this goes to show that there is a rank at which poetic ailments and faults are not an impediment. Perhaps it's for that very reason that this is accounted the father of all poems.[9]

There is also a famous poem by Teika:

Koma tomete sode uchiharahu kage mo nashi
Sano no watari no yuki no yuhugure[10]

No hint of shelter
to rest my pony
or brush off my sleeves:
The Sano Ford,
where dusk descends over snow-filled skies.

Now with this poem, famous though it might be—and it certainly is interesting to listen to—I'm not sure what's so interesting about it. It sounds simply like the experience of someone at the roadside on a journey, with snow falling and no place to seek shelter. But since I am not an initiate in the Way of Poetry, I thought that perhaps there was some other reason for excitement that I was missing, so I asked a poet by vocation; all he told me, though, was that the poem should be taken at face value.

So then, what I got out of that was that there was no particular frame of mind in which the snow became the focus of appreciation, that it was simply an expression of what it is like to be on the road there at the riverside with re-

8. From the Japanese preface to *Kokin wakashū*, quoted in *Figure Drawings of the Two Arts and the Three Modes*.

9. In the Japanese preface to *Kokin wakashū*, the Nanihadzu (mod. J. Naniwazu) poem is accounted the father of poetry, and the following poem (*MYS* 16:3807), the mother: *Asakayama kage sahe miyuru yama no yi no / asaki kokoro wo waga omohanaku ni* (Though shallow be the mountain spring on Mount Asaka, mirroring reflections, / Think me not of a shallow heart in loving thee).

10. Fujiwara no Teika (1162–1241), *SKKS* 671.

ally no good place to take shelter from the storm and no perspective by which one might get his bearings, so the poet just gave voice to what was staring him in the face. So perhaps then, the task of a real master is this: to create an excitement that is not to be explained in such and such a manner. *The Tendai Interpretation of "Wondrous"* states, "There where the path of language is of no avail, where one cannot fathom the principle, and the operations of the mind founder; that is 'wondrous.'" This must be the sort of attitude we have before us. In this art of ours, when one has attained the rank of a real master and such, then just as with this poem, "No hint of shelter," there isn't the slightest bit of artificiality and no grasping in the mind after a particular manner of expression; instead an excitement that transcends excitement[11] becomes apparent in the Vantage from Vision Apart, and the fame of one's house spreads far and wide; this is what is meant by a truly accomplished master of the wondrous expressive capacity of the fine play in performance.

• In the *Analects* it is written, "Zi Gong inquired of the Master saying, 'What of me?' The master replied, 'Thou art a vessel.' (Kong Anguo says, "he means 'thou art an efficacious person.'") 'What manner of vessel?' 'A *hulian*.'" (Baozi says, "A *hulian* is a vessel for grain. It is a precious object for ancestral offerings.")

Now then, in terms of our art, this vessel must be the diversely accomplished master who has attained each and every attraction of performance, beginning with the Two Arts and the Three Modes, and who is thus a capable vessel. This consists of the artistic power in which one contains in one's being a full diversity of powers of manifestation, comprehending all manner of expression. The visual and aural attractions of the Two Arts and the Three Modes are pervasive in their creation of excitement and carry undiminished and yet unfilled potential;[12] as such, they are a vessel.

If you understand this in terms of being and nothingness, being is the visible phenomenon, and nothingness is the vessel. What manifests being is nothingness. For example, crystal is a pristine body, a colorless and patternless empty body, but from it come fire and water.[13] By what sort of causal relation can things of such diametrically opposed natures as fire and water both be born of colorless emptiness? There is a poem that reads:

11. *Mukan no kan*; earlier, Zeami spoke of *mushin no kan* (a kind of excitement that transcends the mind), and his assertions about an "excitement that transcends excitement" seem to be related. The various concepts prefixed with negatives such as *mushin* and *mukan* (*mu* being 無) are impossible to translate, as they pertain to the Zen dialectic that insists on ineffability. Whatever translations are used for them should be understood as heuristic and "sous rature." See "On Depth," in *A Mirror to the Flower*.

12. *Fuzō fugen*, a compound used in a familiar passage in the Heart Sutra, to which this passage may allude.

13. Crystal "produces" fire when sunlight is refracted through it and directed at something flammable. It "produces" water when dew forms on it.

Sakuragi ha kudakite mireba hana mo nashi
Hana koso haru no sora ni sakikere[14]

Take a cherry tree,
break it apart
and you will find no blossoms.
Blossoms come to bloom
out of the empty springtime sky.

What creates the seeds and flowers of every attraction in this fine play in performance is the intent that pervades the performer's power to excite. Just as crystal gives birth to fire and water out of the air, and a cherry tree bears blossoms and fruit out of its colorlessness, so does the accomplished master create the phenomenal manifestations of his art from the scene within his mind, and as such, he must indeed be a vessel.

The ornaments to graceful performance and inducements to long life, the attractions of nature and the fine sights in this art are of various sorts. The vessel that gives birth to all things, from the seasonal changes of flower and

14. Omote notes that there is a near match for this poem attributed to the Zen priest Ikkyū in *Mizukagami* (to be distinguished from the twelfth-century pseudohistorical text of the same title attributed to Nakahara Tadachika). The Ikkyū attribution is questionable, but the text in which the poem is quoted is as follows:

> A mind which aspires to the Way is that wherein all things are regarded as empty, each without a permanent being. . . . The emptiness of *śūnyatā* [*kokū*] is such that within it all things are nurtured, and it puts forth all forms [*iro*]. Since it is that *śūnyatā* that is not separate from all forms and from which all forms emerge, we call it "the paddy-ground of origination" [*honbun no denji*]. Should you ask why we say "origination," it is because all grasses and trees grow from the ground. All forms emerge from emptiness; thus by a provisional metaphor, we call it the paddy-ground of origination.
>
> Sakuragi wo kudakite mireba hana mo nashi
> Hana woba haru no sora ni mochikeri
>
> Take a cherry tree,
> break it apart
> and you will find no blossoms.
> Blossoms are contained
> in the empty springtime sky.
>
> You should be able to understand it from the meaning of this poem. It is not just the springtime blossoms that emerge, entirely, from the emptiness of *śūnyatā*. You can understand as well the transformations of all the plants of summer, fall, and winter likewise (quoted in *Chūsei no bungaku*, vol. 1 of *Karonshū nōgakuronshū*, ed. Hisamatsu Sen'ichi and Nishio Minoru, NKBT, vol. 65 [Tokyo: Iwanami shoten, 1965], pp. 560–61n.6).

leaf to the snow and the moon, the mountains and seas, the plants and trees, the sentient and even the nonsentient, is the universe. In taking these many things as the affective supplements to performance, our aim is to make the mind a vessel of the universe, establish that vessel of mind securely in the vast and formless empty Way, and attain the miraculous flower of attainment through fine play in performance.

Five Ranks

五位

Five Ranks is a very brief text that discusses five different effects produced by *sarugaku* performance. It is written in a kind of pseudo-Chinese, with Japanese pointing (*kaeriten*, etc.) In one manuscript, a later collator or editor has added extensive pointings in red ink (*kaeriten, okurigana, furigana*, etc.), but in many cases these are mistaken.

In its numerical typology, *Five Ranks* bears some resemblance to *Nine Ranks* (the text that follows it here), although the latter text has attracted far more attention and seems better integrated with *Performance Notes* as a whole. *Five Ranks* deals with the effects of performance, whereas *Nine Ranks* deals with training and levels of attainment in acting.

❁

We speak of five ranks of performative effects in the fine play of performance: wonder, excitement, intent, vision, and voice.

1. The Effect of Wonder

By wonder, I mean what exists apart from being and nothingness even as it comprises being and nothingness. Nothingness as Substance is manifest in the effect of vision. It is, therefore, beyond the reach of appreciation.

The Tendai Interpretation of "Wondrous" states, "Where the path of language is of no avail, one cannot fathom the principle, and the operations of the mind founder; this is 'wondrous.'"[1]

2. The Effect of Excitement

By excitement, what I mean is what startles intent and vision in its unexpectedness. The effect of excitement resides in aptness to the moment, aptness to

1. The same quotation appears in *An Effective Vision of Learning the Vocation of Fine Play in Performance.*

intent, and aptness to vision.[2] When the *ki* has been shifted, visual excitement will come into being through the vision apart.

The Mao preface says, "Rectifying gain and loss, budging heaven and earth, exciting demons and gods; this we call excitement."

3. The Effect of Intent

By intent, what I mean is that the effect of intent generated within is made manifest without to produce a supremely wondrous excitement.[1] Manifesting various degrees of depth, it produces the root from which all manner of expression is effected. This is the seed from which the flower of interest is made visible.[2]

The *Shiren yuxie* says, "There is a scene within the intent, there is intent within the scene."[3]

4. The Effect of Vision

By vision, I mean what is already evident in the effect of the dance; the gestures of the hands and the motions of the feet make evident to the eyes the visible proof of performance artistry.

The *Mencius* says, "There is a proper way to observe the waters. One must observe their billowing waves."[4]

5. The Effect of Voice

By voice, what I mean is that even if the effect of vision is in some measure wanting, the excitement of sound will penetrate the mind's ear, and a happy musical effect will create excitement in the audience.

The Mao [preface to the *Classic of*] *Songs* says, "Feelings come forth in the voice, the voice forms a pattern, and one calls this a sound."[5]

---

2. *Sokuza, sokushin, sokumoku*: The first of these also might be translated "spontaneity," but the way I have rendered it is to preserve the parallelism with the other two expressions.

3. See also *An Effective Vision of Learning the Vocation of Fine Play in Performance. Shiren yuxie* (*Jade Chips from the Poets*) is a compilation of poetic lore and criticism by Wei Qingzhi (fl. 1265–1274) of the Song dynasty.

4. After *Mencius* VII, 1, 24.2.

5. See *Oral Instructions on Singing.*

[. . . . name and substance of the fine play of performance. . . . truly penetrates the nature and mind . . . august illumination ought truly to make a mystery, indeed.

Kōmon . . . Jōkan][6]

Notes

1. 至妙成ㇾ感. The primary manuscript of *Five Ranks* includes a pointing, or a phonetic gloss, of "*shimyō nari, kan . . .* ," which would suggest a translation along the lines of "supreme wonder comes into being and excitement [manifests various degrees of depth]," but following Omote and in an analogy with the phrase 上手之知ㇾ感 in *Mirror to the Flower*, I read the clause in Japanese as 至妙の感を成す.

2. The antecedent of "this" is unclear from this sentence alone, but Omote interprets it as "intent" (*i*). This is consistent with a clearer Japanese rendering of essentially the same assertion in *hana ha kokoro, tane ha waza naru beshi*, from near the end of the third section of *Transmitting the Flower.*

6. The colophon appears to be a later addition. It is found only in the Hōzanji text and has been damaged by nibbling mice. Most of it is obscure. The names at the end are, in their original orthography, Koumon and Jaukan.

Nine Ranks
九位

Like *Three Courses*, *Five Ranks*, and *Six Models*, *Nine Ranks*[1] displays Zeami's penchant for numerically organized typologies. But unlike the largely practical orientation of *Three Courses*, with its detailed instructions on the composition of plays, *Nine Ranks* has an abstract and philosophical emphasis. Unlike *Five Ranks* and *Six Models*, *Nine Ranks* has attracted extensive critical attention and praise, and it provides, even given its abstraction and difficulty, numerous important insights into Zeami's aesthetic ideals and their relation to East Asian philosophy, especially Zen.

Nine Ranks is a brief and, at times, cryptic text that lays out a hierarchy of achievements in performance. Each of the ranks is characterized by a Chinese tag, often with traceable connections to Zen texts. After the tag comes a short (and sometimes cryptic) commentary on it, not unlike the structure of some of the collections of Zen kōans with which Zeami may have been familiar. The last half of the text delineates the path that an actor's training and experience should take through the nine ranks and lays the important

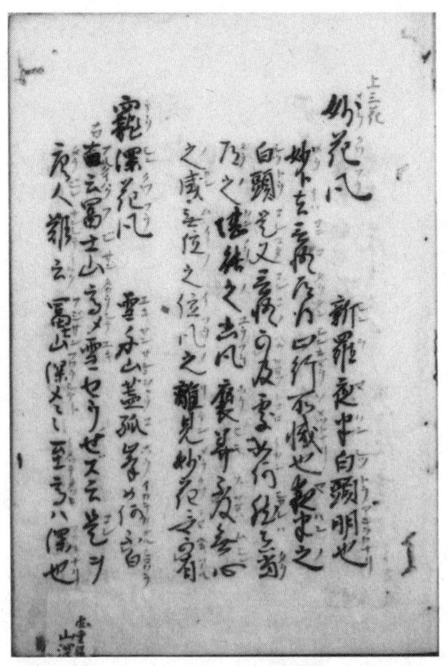

A leaf from the opening of *Nine Ranks*. The heavily Sinicized text, in black, is extensively glossed in red *katakana* in Japanese. The full text for the top rank and a few lines of the text for the second rank are shown. This manuscript dates from the mid–Edo/Tokugawa period and has been transmitted in the Kanze line, together with manuscripts of *Transmitting the Flower*, "An Extract from *Learning the Flower*," *Figure Drawings of the Two Arts and the Three Modes*, and *Learning the Profession*. (Photograph from the collection of Kanze Bunko Foundation)

foundation for Zeami's understanding of virtuosity in performance. Particularly noteworthy are his assertions that one does not start at the bottom of the nine ranks in training, but at the lowest of the three middle ranks, and that once one has attained the top rank of the upper three, one is free to descend to the lower three, performing in styles that would otherwise be uninteresting and artistically deleterious.

Nine Ranks is undated, but the typology of "nine ranks" is mentioned in *Six Models* (1428), which suggests that the text bearing this name was written at generally the same time.

❁

The Top Three Flowers

The Effect of the Wondrous Flower: Silla,[1] midnight: the sun is bright.[2]

> What I mean by wonder pertains to the severing of the path of language, the foundering of the operations of the mind. Is the sun at midnight a matter to which language can aspire? How does that happen? So then, the sublime effect of a true master in this vocation is beyond the reach of appreciation, an excitement that transcends the mind, a vision apart effected by the caliber of no-rank must most surely be the wondrous flower.[2]

The Effect of the Flower That Cherishes Depth: Snow blankets a thousand mountains. How is it that a solitary peak is not white?

> Of old someone said, "Mount Fuji is so lofty, its snows never melt." A Chinese criticized this, saying that it should be, "Mount Fuji is so deep, . . ." and so forth. For what is supremely lofty is deep. There is a limit to loftiness. Depth is fathomless. Therefore, the deep scene of snow on a thousand mountains, with one peak that is not white, may be commensurate with the effect of the flower that cherishes depth.

The Effect of the Tranquil Flower: Piling snow into a silver bowl.

1. A fourth- to ninth-century kingdom on the Korean Peninsula.

2. This image of the starkest paradox was popular with Zen writers, beginning with Dahui (in *Dahui pujue chanshi yulü*). It also occurs in the thirteenth-century Japanese Zen text *Chūshinkyō* (*Commentary on Mind Sutra*). Nose Asaji (*Zeami jūrokubushū hyūshaku* [Tokyo: Iwanami shoten, 1944]) and Mark Nearman ("Zeami's *Kyūi*: A Pedagogical Guide for Teachers of Acting," *Monumenta Nipponica* 33, no. 3 [1978]: 323) consider this the most likely source for Zeami's familiarity with the phrase, although it is also used in Musō Soseki's *Muchūmondō*, 93.

Piling snow into a silver bowl,[3] the palpable sensation of white light, pure and pristine, truly a vision of gentleness and harmony, must be called the effect of the tranquil flower.

[The Middle Three Ranks]

The Effect of the Correct Flower: The mist[4] is bright, the sun sets, ten thousand mountains are crimson.[5]

In the blue sky the single point of the white sun: ten thousand mountains fast and clear;[3] this is the perspective afforded by the effect of the correct flower. This surpasses the Effect of Expansive Subtlety and comprises the first penetration into the attainment of the flower.

The Effect of Expansive Subtlety: Exhausted in the recounting, the mind intent on mountain clouds and moonlight on the sea.

The mind intent on mountain clouds and moonlight on the sea—that is, exhausting in the recounting an expansive scene of green mountains as far as the eye can see—is just right for learning the Effect of Expansive Subtlety. This is the watershed between what comes before and what after.

The Effect of Shallow Patterns: What makes a path a path is not the eternal path.[6]

In treading the eternal path, you should know what makes a path a path. It is with the shallow that the pattern is first revealed. Therefore, we make this effect of shallow patterns the introduction to training in the Nine Ranks.

3. The phrase occurs in *Baojing sanmei*, by the Caotong (J. Sōtō) Zen patriarch Dongshan Liangjie (807–869), continuing as follows: "A silver bowl is filled with snow, the bright moon conceals a heron; they are similar, yet not the same, put them together and you know their proper place." The famous collection of kōans, *The Blue Cliff Record* (Ch. *Biyanlü*, J. *Hekiganroku*), 13, also uses the image: "A priest asked Baling, 'What is the teaching of *Kāṇadēva*?' Baling said, 'Piling snow into a silver bowl.'" See also *Pick Up a Jewel and Take the Flower in Hand*.

4. In Japanese poetry, mist (*kasumi*) is conventionally associated with spring.

5. Apparently the expression is associated with Zen (but as yet unidentified). The line occurs as well in the nō play *Hitachi obi*, a piece no longer in the repertory.

6. A quotation of the first verse of the Daoist classic, *Dao de jing*.

[The Bottom Three Ranks]

The Effect of the Strong yet Intricate: Reflections dance across the metal hammer, the light from the precious sword is cold.

> Reflections dancing across a metal hammer are the effect of strong movement. The coldness of light from the precious sword makes for a chilling performative effect. This even appears to be valid in a finely calibrated view.

The Effect of the Strong and Coarse. Three days after birth, a tiger cub would gobble down an ox.

> A tiger cub with such vigor only three days after birth means strength of will.[7] To gobble down an ox, that is coarse.

The Effect of the Coarse and Leaden. A tree rat with five [abilities].

> Confucius said,[8] "The tree rat has five abilities: to climb trees, to lunge into the water, to dig holes, to leap through the air, and to run. In none of these does his accomplishment surpass his lowly station. Art that is not fine in its movement is coarse and leaden."

[Articles on] the Sequence of Training in the Vocation in the Nine Ranks

Middle first, top second, bottom last, which is to say, in embarking on a career in the performing arts, one undertakes the articles of training in the two arts of singing and dance with the Effect of Shallow Patterns. The rank at which one gradually arrives on this path, by thoroughly mastering this and adding pattern to the shallow effect, is the Effect of Expansive Subtlety. What you arrive at in full fruition when you complete every aspect of training at this level

7. That is, *ki*.

8. Actually not Confucius, but *Xunzi* 1.6. John Knoblock paraphrases Guo Pu on this passage: "The five talents of the flying squirrel are its abilities to fly, climb, swim, dig, and run. They are deficient in that though it can fly, it cannot fly well enough to get over a roof; though it can climb, it cannot get to the top of a tree; though it can swim, it cannot cross a gorge; though it can dig, it cannot build a safe shelter; and though it can run, it cannot outdistance a man. Thus, no one of its talents amounts to a real ability" (*Xunzi: A Translation and Study of the Complete Works* [Stanford, Calif.: Stanford University Press, 1988], vol. 1, p. 270n.33).

and follow its course long and far is the Effect of the Correct Flower. This is the rank at which one arrives at the Three Modes through the Two Arts. This is the line to be crossed where it becomes apparent to audiences whether one has awakened to a serious understanding of the art and grasped the flower of this vocation, having attained a secure competence in exciting an audience. This is the [Effect of the Tranquil Flower][4] in which, in looking back on one's artistic accomplishments thus far, one transcends them through the secure attainment of the greatest achievement. Above this is the Effect of the Profoundly Cherished Flower, at which one embodies surpassing grace and elegance and visibly manifests a performance style that transcends the difference between being and nothingness. Above this is the Effect of the Wondrous Flower, a place where language is of no avail and one makes manifest the internal scene of wondrous nonduality. With this, the path to attain the ultimate accomplishment reaches the top.[5]

Now then, the point of departure in these articles is the Effect of Expansive Subtlety. This is the foundation for the performing arts and the place where the expansively intricate seed for the flower of universal efficacy is first made manifest. For that reason, the watershed between what comes before and after Expansive Subtlety is to be found here. Those who attain the flower at this point will proceed to the Effect of the Correct Flower, those who do not will fall to the lowest three ranks.

So then, the lowest three ranks are the swift undercurrents of this fine play in performance and are graduated accordingly but are not of great importance in training. However, once you have gone through the middle three ranks and succeeded to the upper three flowers to attain the secure rank of the Wondrous Flower, you may double back[9] and play freely in the bottom three ranks, and the activities you pursue even at these levels are harmonized aesthetically. In the past, some expert performers declined to resort to the three bottom levels, even though they had mastered the top three flowers. This is like the saying "The majestic pachyderm disdains the paths of rabbits." Only in the performances of my late father have I seen one who proceeded from the middle three ranks to the top three flowers and thereafter descended to the bottom three ranks, mastering all. Many others have come to the Rank of Broad Subtlety, but before they have attained the Effect of the Correct Flower, they have made the descent to the bottom three ranks; in the end, they do not succeed as performers. Moreover, these days some people in the art take the bottom three ranks as their introduction. This is not the proper order. Consequently, many do not properly enter into any of the nine levels of artistic accomplishment.

9. *Kyakurai,* a specialized term indicating the virtuoso's freedom to exercise artistic effects normally out of bounds. The concept is the focus of the text *The Flower in . . . Yet Doubling Back.*

So then, there are three types of paths for the bottom three ranks. Given the expertise of a truly accomplished actor, who has entered into his training from the beginning of the middle ranks, next learned his vocation proceeding to the upper ranks and finally to the lower ranks: even at those lower ranks, he effects a visual display of superior quality. Those who have proceeded from the Effect of Expansive Subtlety into the lower three ranks are most likely to find their powers commensurate with the Strong and Coarse or the Strong yet Intricate. In addition to these are actors who by mischance have entered their training from the lower ranks and who are unlikely to be classed in the nine ranks at all, given their undisciplined and unidentifiable artistic styles. Although they made their aim the bottom three ranks, they are of a rank that cannot be securely situated even there. It is difficult to imagine that they should attain any position in the middle three ranks.

Notes

1. Two manuscripts follow the title with the graph 住, which doesn't make sense. It appears to me a mistranscription of 註 (Notes).

2. 当道の堪能の幽風、褒美も及ばず、無心の感、無位の位風の離見こそ、妙花にや有るべき. The syntax of the sentence is uncertain. The central phrase, 無心の感, seems to float between the first and second clauses, which are relatively straightforward syntactically. Perhaps we are to understand it as the subject of the second clause, with 無位の位風の離見 grammatically parallel, as an appositive.

3. 早白. Manuscripts contain the gloss *ichishiroki*.

4. The primary manuscript has 開花風, clearly a mistranscription of 閑花風.

5. The primary manuscript reads 奥義の上の道 (the path over the ultimate accomplishment), but I follow Omote's reasoning in adopting the text of a variant manuscript: 奥義之上の道. This could also be read as *okugi* [or *augi*] *no ue no michi*, but the two graphs, 之上, are glossed as シジヤウ(*shijyau*). Omote's suggestion that 之上 should therefore be read as an allograph for 至上 (reaches the top) seems entirely reasonable.

Six Models
六義, 1428

Six Models is the most arcane of Zeami's numerically organized typologies. It is an attempt to link six "models" derived from Chinese poetics with some of the Nine Ranks. The very word from the title, which I translate as "model," is difficult to pin down in this context. In most contexts, the graph would be read as "principle" or "precept," but here it seems too vaguely defined for such a translation. Distantly derived from early Chinese poetics, the models are *feng* (風), *fu* (賦), *bi* (比), *xing* (興), *ya* (雅), and *song* (頌). They were first named in the *Rites of Zhou,* but Zeami's source is, instead, a commentary on the prefaces to *Kokin wakashū*, which in turn derived its references from the Mao preface to the *Classic of Songs*. The meaning of the six terms has varied over time, ranging from the sociopolitical to the rhetorical. *Feng*, for example, is sometimes translated "air" and, in the Mao preface, indicates a type of poetic composition intended to tactfully criticize government or society in order to bring about political change. Similarly, in the Mao preface the *ya* is supposed to illustrate the rise and fall of governments, with concomitant moral lessons, and the *song* is to eulogize exemplary virtue.

The *fu*, the *bi*, and the *xing* seem to be more aptly classified as modes of composition or rhetorical techniques, *fu* relating to description, *bi* to comparison, and *xing*, in Tim Wixted's words, to "evocative imagery."[1]

The references to these terms in the preface to the *Kokin wakashū* have not as yet proved particularly germane to the poetry in that anthology or to the classification of Japanese poetry in general. In Zeami's recontextualization, however, we might just see a reemergence of the earlier Chinese emphasis on the relation between literary and musical production, on the one hand, and the well-being of the state, on the other, a theme with which Zeami is more explicitly concerned in *Five Sorts of Singing* and *Articles on the Five Sorts of Singing*.

If the Six Models are not completely clear in their original Chinese context, in the prefaces to *Kokin wakashū*, they leave the reader, as Helen McCullough observed, "uncertain whether all six belong to a theoretical framework or whether *fu*, *bi* and *xing* are to be taken as rhetorical modes" (leaving *feng*, *ya*, and *song* as characterizations of the sociopolitical uses of poetry).[2]

In Japan, the use of the six terms in the prefaces to the *Kokin wakashū* does not clarify the criteria on which the typology was created. Zeami's use of them does not make them any clearer either but at least makes an explicit link with the first through the fifth and the seventh of his Nine Ranks, further characterizing them.

Six Models is brief and eclectic, referring frequently to commentaries on Chinese and Japanese poetry as well as *The Tendai Interpretation of "Wondrous,"* which Zeami holds to be a Buddhist text of the Tendai sect. The text has not been identified or is no longer extant.

The remarks in the translation in parentheses reflect rubrics written in a smaller script to the right side of the text in the original manuscripts.

❀

When I speak of the Six Models, I refer to the *Commentary on the Kokin wakashū*,[1] where it says, "In India, it was the *reimon*,[3] in China, *shi* and *fu*, in Japan, *waka*: poetry has edified each of these three lands. Thus we refer to poetry here as *Yamato uta*, that is, songs that edify in great measure" and so forth.[2] Each of these forms of poetry exhibits Six Models. They are *feng*, *fu*, *bi*, *xing*, *ya*, and *song*. I have adopted their intent and adapted them for use in training in this vocation of fine play in performance. Now, in the performance styles of this vocation, visual display happens to be classified according to the Nine Ranks. Thus it is our task to define the circumstances of each of these in comparison with the Six Models.

[1.][4] *Feng* Performance: This is the Effect of the Wondrous Flower (first of the Nine Ranks). As for *feng*, the *Commentary on the Kokin wakashū*[3] says, "Although neither its form nor its substance is visible, it is concurrent with the phenomenon in question and thus is regarded of as an effect thereof," and so forth. The wondrous is (as it states in *The Tendai Interpretation of "Wondrous"*) "where the path of language is of no avail, one cannot fathom the principle, and the operations of the mind founder; this is 'wondrous,'" and so on. It has, therefore, no substance. It simply exists concurrently with the character of the

1. *Six Models* is full of references to a certain *Kokin no chū* (*Commentary on the Kokin* [*wakashū*]), which has been identified by Miwa Masatane as *Kokin wakashu jo no kikigaki*, a composition by Teika's grandson Fujiwara no Tameaki. For details, see Miwa Masatane, "Kamakura jidai kōki seiritsu no *Kokin wakashū* jo chū ni tsuite, chū," *Bunko*, nos. 17–18, February 1968. See also Omote, in ZZ, pp. 473–74n.98.

2. Based on a quotation from the *Commentary on the Kokin wakashū*, this passage seems to be based on the idea that poetry has both edified the three cultures mentioned and been progressively refined in its development from India through China to Japan, so that in Japan it is consists of "songs that edify in great measure," a recondite and rather forced interpretation of the name for "Japanese poetry." The word here translated as "edify" can also be taken to mean "translate" or "render more easy to understand," which also would be applicable in that through the procession from India to China to Japan, poetry becomes more accessible to the Japanese-speaking population. A very closely related line occurs in the play *Hakurakuten*: "Now then, the *reimon* of India was taken together with the *shi* and *fu* of China and made into the *waka* in our kingdom. For that reason, we refer to poetry here as Yamato *uta*, which is to say, songs that refine in great measure in that the three lands have been refined in this way."

3. The *Commentary on the Kokin wakashū* says, "Although neither the form nor the substance of wind is visible, we recognize it when it plows against something. This poetic style is similar and is thus analogized as the 'wind' [i.e., *feng*] style poem."

performance. Moreover, when you try to identify it consciously, there's nothing to grasp. Therefore, I imagine that we should associate the Effect of the Wondrous Flower with *Feng* Performance.

[2. *Fu*] Performance: This is The Effect of the Flower That Cherishes Depth (second thereof). As for *fu*, the *Commentary on the Kokin wakashū*[4] says, "It is a poem in which there is a multiple intent." The Effect of the Flower That Cherishes Depth refers to a beautiful attitude. "Depth" pertains to the vantage from a vision apart, and "Flower" is a palpably manifest effect. The intentional scene accordingly is diverse. Therefore, I suppose we should associate the Effect of the Flower That Cherishes Depth with *fu* Performance.

[3.] *Bi* Performance: This is The Effect of the Tranquil Flower (third thereof). As for *bi*, the *Commentary on the Kokin wakashū*[5] says, "This pertains to the way two things resemble each other when they are lined up one next to the other." "Tranquil" is the mind's adaptability to excitement, whereas "flower" refers to the blossoming forth in the mind's perception. Neither "tranquil" nor "flower" takes priority with regard to the wondrous result. Therefore, I suppose we should associate the Effect of the Tranquil Flower with *bi* Performance.

[4.] *Xing* Performance: This is the Effect of the Correct Flower (fourth thereof). As for *xing*, the *Commentary on the Kokin wakashū*[6] says, "Posit two things and divide them through competition." The correct visible manifestation of the Correct Flower should amount to the attainment of the flower in this vocation. In other words, this is your strong point. If you have a strong point, then it would seem that you are likely to have a weak point. Is it for this reason that there is proof by competition in the arts? I suppose, therefore, we should associate the Effect of the Correct Flower with *xing* Performance.

5. *Ya* Performance: The Effect of Sidelong[5] Subtlety (fifth thereof). As for *ya*, the *Commentary on the Kokin wakashū*[7] says, "This refers to something properly ordered and correct," and so on. Is it not the case that in being expansive and subtle, the Sidelong and Subtle is properly ordered and correct? This, then, is a fully stable attitude. Therefore, I would say we associate the Effect of the Sidelong and Subtle with *ya* Performance.

[6.] *Song* Performance: The Effect of the Strong yet Intricate (seventh thereof). *Song* indicates celebratory intent.[8] For its part, the Strong yet Intricate

4. The *Commentary on the Kokin wakashū* says, "A *fu* is a poem in which there are many intents."

5. The *Commentary on the Kokin wakashū* says, "This type of poem pertains to the way that two things resemble each other when they are lined up one next to the other."

6. The *Commentary on the Kokin wakashū* says, identically, "Posit two things and divide them through competition."

7. The *Commentary on the Kokin wakashū* says, "This refers to something in which the intent and the diction are correct."

8. Zeami doesn't quote the *Commentary on the Kokin wakashū* here, but what he says is close to the terms used there: "A *song* poem is auspicious," auspicious being the familiar term *shūgen*.

means a mind that does not fail and thus is "strong," and an integrity that is resilient and thus is "finely calibrated." What is strong and resilient would be, then, what accords with one's intent. This is performance that accords with one's intention. If it is a performance that matches one's intent, then it must have an auspicious effect. Isn't this *shiugen*, then? Therefore I suppose we might associate the Effect of the Strong yet Intricate with *song* Performance.

There is, however, something that must be understood regarding "the strong." Of the five virtues of Benevolence, Integrity, Propriety, Wisdom, and Trust,[9] Integrity has been parsed as "resilience."[10] Therefore, to be resilient and not to fail should mean strength. The Mao [preface to the *Classic of*] *Songs* says, "The voice in a well-ordered age expresses joy in that it is confident," and so on. To be well ordered indicates the integrity of strength. Again and again, it appears that resilience is the way of strength. The substance of the text is thus.

The articles thus expressed are a written account of what it has been in the power of my study and understanding to grasp for the sake of this vocation.

Now, if you have been able to settle into a secure control of each of these six effects, one by one, and attained the level of a master in essence, with full confidence of your rank, then you may succeed in capturing all six effects in a single performance, to become a great virtuoso. It was in such a way, they say, that a great sage of Japanese poetry managed to compose a secret verse that instantiated all the Six Models into a single verse.[11]

Ōei 35 [1428]:3:9

The head of the Konparu troupe[12] *expressed a desire for this scroll, so I have transmitted it to him.*

Zea (signature)

9. The five cardinal virtues in Confucianism.

10. Zeami's source for such an interpretation has not been identified.

11. The single verse that supposedly instantiates the Six Models is quoted, not in the *Commentary on the Kokin wakashū*, but in *Gyokudenshū waka saichō*, another critical text attributed to Fujiwara no Tameaki. The poem in question is "On the First Day of Spring," by Ki no Tsurayuki (*KKS* 2): *Sode hidjite musubishi midzu no kohoreru wo haru tatsu kefu no kaze ya tokuran* (The spring water that once soaked my sleeves has frozen now. Will the wind today—the day that spring begins—melt the ice?). The relationship can be effected only by turning the Six Models into six thematic categories of Japanese court poetry (the four seasons, love, and miscellaneous), thus:

Sode hidjite [plunging sleeves]: miscellaneous
musubishi midzu no [water that soaked]: summer
kohoreru wo [has frozen]: winter
haru tatsu kefu no [the day that spring begins]: spring
kaze ya [will the wind . . . ?]: autumn
tokuran [melt]: love

12. At the time, Zenchiku was twenty-four years old, and Zeami was sixty-eight.

Notes

1. Tim Wixted, "The *Kokinshū* Prefaces, Another Perspective," *Harvard Journal of Asiatic Studies* 43 (1983): 228–30.

2. Helen McCullough, *Brocade by Night: "Kokin wakashū" and the Court Style in Japanese Classical Poetry* (Stanford, Calif.: Stanford University Press, 1985), p. 306.

3. *Reimon* is written 礼文 in the manuscripts of *Six Models*, but some of the sources for this quotation write the word 乱文 (disordered text). Some have assumed that 霊文 (divine writing) was intended, referring to *dhāraṇī* or *mantras*, but Omote's study of the sources suggests that 乱文 was indeed the intended writing. That leaves open, however, a more precise sense of the meaning. Omote opts for 梵音 (the sounds of Sanskrit).

4. The primary manuscript has suffered damage by rats, and the numerals and, in some cases, the headings are missing. They have been added based on a variant manuscript.

5. The text has 横精 (sidelong subtlety), rather than 広精 (expansive subtlety). Omote argues that this is merely an allograph.

Pick Up a Jewel and Take the Flower in Hand
拾玉得花, 1428

A central text of Zeami's late period, *Pick Up a Jewel* takes up again the question-and-answer form that he used in sections of *Transmitting the Flower*. As elsewhere in *Performance Notes*, Zeami is concerned here with what makes a truly consummate actor different from a merely competent one or, indeed, from a rough-and-tumble player of unreliable technique. In this case, though, Zeami takes a particularly philosophical and abstract approach to this concern. The text reveals a deepening interest in East Asian philosophical traditions, ranging from Confucianism to Zen to the philosophical reception of Shinto myth in medieval Japan.

Various interlinear annotations in red ink are found in *Pick Up a Jewel and Take the Flower in Hand*. Some are to the right of the phrase apparently so annotated, and some are to the left. There is disagreement about whether Zeami himself wrote the notes or whether they were added later by someone else, perhaps Konparu Zenchiku. Omote says they are not inconsistent with the main text and so may be Zeami's own annotations, whereas the NKBT text (edited by Nishio Minoru) suggests that they were written by Zenchiku. In my translation, I have put these annotations in parentheses.

Unlike *Transmitting the Flower* and *A Mirror to the Flower*, this text seems to have been written single-mindedly over a relatively short period of time. It was intended for transmission to Konparu Zenchiku (known by his youthful name, Ujinobu, in the note at the end), and it covers some of the same territory as earlier texts from the *Performance Notes*, which had been written for Zeami's brother and sons. Zenchiku was Zeami's son-in-law, but he belonged to a different troupe, albeit one long related to Zeami's, both aesthetically and probably by intermarriage. Although Motomasa apparently showed Zenchiku some text "of great moment"[1] at some point before Motomasa's death in 1432, it is not likely that Zenchiku had continued access to the texts written for Zeami's sons, so a certain amount of redundancy can be expected

1. Probably *A Mirror to the Flower*. See *The Flower in . . . Yet Doubling Back*. In addition, *Pick Up a Jewel* contains several references to *Figure Drawings of the Two Arts and Three Modes*, thus offering further evidence of that text's transmission to the Konparu line (the oldest copy of that text seems, indeed, to be in Zenchiku's hand).

in this text. Nonetheless, Zeami does not merely quote what he said before and leave it at that. Instead, he continues to rethink and deepen his understanding of the issues he raises, and consequently, *Pick Up a Jewel and Take the Flower in Hand* has much to offer.

One reason for the explicit references to Zen texts here may be that the text was addressed to someone himself deeply interested in Zen. (Zenchiku later became a student of the celebrated Zen master Ikkyū Sōjun, 1394–1481.)

❁

Q: In an effort to achieve freedom in performance in this art of ours, we exhaust both intent and technical expertise in training in the various articles of the discipline; we garner long experience and perform the art to the utmost capacity of our intent (personal capacity),[1] all in a fully serious way, yet sometimes we succeed and other times we fail. Why is that?

A: The distinction between success and failure resides in the event of performance. Although one may speak of a certain inevitability in the occasion, if you use your training and apply the right stratagem, how can you fail to understand the reason for success or failure? You may wonder whether it is perhaps a matter of inadequate or halfhearted endeavor, yet why should we see a discrepancy, depending on the occasion, such that the same skilled actor, performing in the same style, may fail today when he succeeded yesterday? Well might you wonder, and it's only natural that in aspiring to graceful performance and a long career, you should tax your ingenuity to understand why this should be so.

If the same skilled actor, acting in a style exhibiting the same consummate performative expertise as always, finds a discrepancy in outcome depending on the occasion, I believe this might be because of a disharmony between yin and yang. The specific *ki* on that occasion (i.e., the specific *ki* as it relates to "first pitch, second *ki*, third voice")[2] is not likely to be in harmony unless the performer's pitch, at a given time, accords with the musical mode from among the five sounds that is appropriate to that moment, whether morning or night, in whatever season[2], at dawn or dusk, before the elite or commoners, a large audience or small, in a big venue or a little one. The first step toward harmonizing with the moment is to give ample consideration to the way your personal intent is to be matched to the *ki* on a given day and to transfer the musical pattern in your singing to

2. Compare "First Pitch, Second *Ki*, Third Voice," in *A Mirror to the Flower*; the parenthetical note is in red in the primary manuscript.

the pitch of that particular time, thereby creating excitement in the audience sympathetically in sound.

I suspect, moreover, that there must be species of aural excitement that harmonize with a particular time, whether the warm season or the cold, day or night, dawn or dusk. The cold is the time of yin, the warm of yang, and you should consider what is exciting about the voice in such a way as to complement natural conditions of yin with yang, or to match conditions of yang with yin. What I mean by yin and yang is this: When the natural conditions are yin and there is a general atmosphere of subdued austerity, then you realize, ah, this is yin, and you mollify it with the complement of a yang voice (*shō* pitch)[3] harmoniously articulated[4]—

(The moon shines over the river, wind soughs through the pines; what are we to do on this long night, this pristine eve?)[3]

—you thereby create musical excitement; this is the affective complement in all present to the consummation of the performance. The material effect that this affective complement imparts in vision is, then, the affective complement of the audience as it exclaims, "Oh, how interesting!" I would say, then, that consummation through a harmony effected by musical excitement, like this, is what indicates a time of success in performance. In contrast, when you suspect that the audience is in a condition of yang, you should regulate the breath (whether or not it matches the *ki*)[5] in your singing voice, and make the yin voice (vocal pattern)[4] the Substance of your singing

(In deep night, the raven flies, enveloped in snow)[6]

to create excitement through pitch,

(Going up and down the scale, the voice produces a pattern; we call it sound.)[7]

and wield the power of your singing so as to bring the audience together by capturing the attention of the mind's ear in them. Again,

3. Interlinear note in red. The couplet, slightly misquoted, is by Yongjia Xuanjue (665–713), a disciple of Zen master Huineng who was particularly well versed in Tiantai philosophy and meditation practice, from his *Chengdaoge*. The couplet also is quoted in the play *Yoroboshi*.

4. Interlinear note in red alongside the word *yin*. It is difficult to gauge its meaning. although Omote conjectures that it might refer to the vocal patterning of the *shu* voice associated with yin. See *ZZ*, p. 475n.99.

although the close of autumn and the three months of winter are seasons of yin, you should still be able to achieve a consummation through the fine play in performance for all present if, given a bright sun and a good crowd gathered for the performance—even though they are difficult to settle, with their rustle and chatter—you sing right into their mind's ear with a full voice well balanced between yin and yang,[5] drawing the eyes and the intent of those present into focus on the central actor, bringing into effect that perspective in which the phrasing is transferred to expressive form, to excite as one the appreciation of every last person present in their affective response. This, I would venture, must be the border where one takes the first step from aural excitement to a visible manifestation. This was my intent in *A Mirror to the Flower*, under the subtitle "First Hear, Then See."[6]

There isn't the slightest difference in this consideration from when I told you to take account of the context of each individual occasion of performance, whether it be before exalted aristocrats, before a general audience or a small gathering, whether out in the open or indoors, or, indeed, whether it is the most informal sort of performance on the spur of the moment. A subscription performance or other such *sarugaku* for a large audience is subject to the three constituents[7]—heaven, earth, and human affairs—whereas in a performance in a private garden or indoors or the like, the Substance of the performance is likely to depend exclusively on human affairs, and the natural conditions are relegated to Instance.[8] I have the impression that the degree of success in performance depends on whether you have given adequate consideration to the occasion in question.

(An outsider asked the Buddha, "What sort of Dharma did You teach yesterday?" The All-Revered said, "I taught the unchangeable Dharma." The former asked once again, "And what sort of Dharma do You teach today?" The All-Revered said, "I teach the changeable Dharma." Yet again, the former said, "On what ground do You teach the changeable Dharma today?" The All-

5. It is not clear whether *kōshō* (orth. *kaushyau* [lit., "high voice"]) is high in pitch or, rather, loud. Again, the mention of *aion* does not seem intended in the highly technical sense of the "doubly proficient" voice of *Oral Instructions on Song* and *A Mirror to the Flower.*

6. *A Mirror to the Flower.*

7. A widespread East Asian typology of universal phenomena.

8. Zeami returns here to the binarism *tai/yū* (my "Substance" and "Instance"), which he frequently used earlier in the *Notes*. Interestingly, he also apparently writes the primary technical terms in the passage in *katakana*, whereas the rest of the text is in *hiragana* and *kanji*. Even so, in this case, the use seems relatively casual: human affairs are the center of more casual performances, and the broader cosmic manifestations are incidental.

Revered said, "Yesterday's unchangeable Dharma is today's changeable Dharma.")[9]

Q: There is, truly, no doubt that the degree of success in performance depends on the temper of the occasion.[8] An actor devotes himself to a long training, attains a rank at which his reputation is well known, and creates the kind of visual excitement that elicits great interest; this we regard as the reward for long experience, and yet on the other hand, we occasionally discern great interest in the figure of a child, from an actor who has barely attained a beginner's competence in the Two Arts through fine play in expression. Can that possibly be of the same rank as the interest elicited by an accomplished master with long experience? I don't understand.

A: An account of this is to be found elsewhere. I have compared the perception of interest to a flower. This entails the perception of freshness. To push this understanding to its greatest limit is what I mean by knowing the flower. This is to be found in *Transmitting the Flower.*

Now then, a flower is interesting in that it blooms and is fresh in that it scatters. Someone once asked, What is the essence of impermanence? The answer: The scattering of blossoms, the falling of leaves. Again, he asked, what is eternal and incorruptible? The answer: The scattering of blossoms, the falling of leaves, and so on and so on.[10] There is no fixed intent in the spontaneous visual perception of interest. Nevertheless, what provokes interest is regarded as evidence of skill in all the arts, and one who has long-term control over such interest is called an accomplished master of great repute. For that reason, the actor who maintains such interest through long experience appears to resemble the eternity of scattering blossoms and falling leaves. Then again, though, there are also actors who display a more generic kind of flower. In the Nine Ranks I delineated, it is readily apparent that the top three possess the flower—they are, indeed, designated as "the top three flowers"—but if interest is to be found in the middle and the bottom three ranks as well, then that must be due to the presence of a flower commensurate to such interest. For example, when a bumpkin or lout perceives interest in the blossoms on some scraggly tree or such, that should be accounted the visual sensibility of a

9. This brief dialogue is found in numerous Zen-related texts and comes, in its original Chinese version, from Wudong Huiyuan.

10. The source of this exchange has not been identified, but Omote notes a parallel in the play *Ebira*: *Hikwa rakuefu no mujyau ha mata, jyaujiu fumetsu no ei wo nashi* (The impermanence of scattering flowers and falling leaves is, in contrast, the glory of the eternal and incorruptible).

common fellow. To see interest in the top three flowers is the visual sensibility of the real master.

> (The *Rites*[11] says, "A real master hears the Dao and exerts himself to study it. A middlebrow hears the Dao and sometimes it's there, sometimes not. A common fellow hears the Dao, claps his hands, and lets out a loud guffaw. If he doesn't laugh, then be assured, it cannot be the Dao.")

Among both actors and audience, each possesses his own mental and visual sensibility.

I have my own personal considerations in this matter. I have come to think of two categories, the flower-in-its-very-nature and the flower-as-it-is-manifested. What I mean by the flower-in-its-very-nature would, I suppose, be the cherry. It is of a rank that matches the visual sensibility of the real master. I have designated the top of the middle three ranks as the correct flower, so it would be a cherry as well, but the flower at this rank need not be limited solely to the cherry. It might include various trees, among them the cherry, the plum, the peach, and the pear alike.[12] The sight of red and white plum blossoms is of a particularly elegant visual sensibility. That's why Lord Michizane[13] found them so worthy of praise. It also bears saying that what is of crucial importance to this vocation of ours, what makes it a vocation, is making an affective claim on the visual sensibility of all types of people. All the same, to regard this, in particular,[14] as interesting is proof of the person's being a real master. There are in the audience, however, differences in understanding. That freshness we remark in the fine play in expression in the figure of a child is, by analogy, a single-petaled cherry that blooms first in the spring and is an example of the flower-as-it-is-manifested. Those for whom such an affective claim can be made, those who regard this alone as interesting, have the visual discernment of the middlebrow or the common fellow and such. A real master also gains a fresh perception and appreciates it for what it is, but he doesn't see it as the genuine flower-in-its-very-nature. If we make an analogy between our art and the blossoms on an ancient or a cele-

11. The quotation is actually from Laozi, *Dao de jing* 41, with some lexical discrepancies and emendations. The same citation occurs in *Technical Specifications for Setting a Melody.*

12. The precise botanical identity of the trees mentioned is uncertain, although that seems rather unimportant, given the figural nature of their use here.

13. Sugawara no Michizane (845–903). Zeami refers to him by the name *tenjin* (heavenly deity), in accord with his apotheosis as a deity of learning.

14. The antecedent is not entirely obvious, but apparently it means "the flower in its very nature" mentioned earlier in the paragraph.

brated tree, or the blossoms at such famous sites as Yoshino, Shiga, Jishu,[15] or Arashiyama, then it is these latter ones that represent the flower of genuine success. The real masters are those who can understand this. Such must be the visual sensibility with which all sorts of different people, high and low, appreciate the beauty of many different types of flowers.[16] Real masters have a capacious vision, so it is unlikely that they will dislike different sorts of flowers just because they are different. Actors are like this, too. Thus we may speak of a masterfully versatile actor as one who doesn't leave any of the Nine Ranks untried. "The myriad dharmas return to the one. Whither returns the one? To the myriad dharmas," and so forth.[17] In this way, we can understand as various kinds of flower the diverse ways in which different objects of interest hold their particular appeal according to a given subject's capacity. But we can perhaps clarify the question of whether the interest created by the figure of a child and the interest created by an accomplished master with long experience come from the same perception, by distinguishing between flower-in-its-very-nature and flower-as-it-is-manifested.

Q: Tell me now, what is the reason that this experience was grasped in the first place with the term "interesting"? If it is by metaphor that we regard something as a flower, then how did it come about that in the absence of metaphor and without cognitive discrimination, someone was given to say "how interesting!"?[18]

15. In the temple precinct at Kiyomizu, in southeastern Kyoto.

16. The sentence is by no means clear, and its relation to the previous discussion is puzzling. Omote takes it as a justification for the diversity of taste in Zeami's audiences and relates it to a passage at the end of *Transmitting the Flower*: "So too, regarding various forms of expression: those forms that you select in consideration of the prevailing tastes of people at a given time, in a particular place—those are the flowers that aptly serve your need. If one style of expression is enjoyed here, then another style will be appreciated there. This is the flower of various different people and their minds." While this is possible, it seems to rely heavily on the context of the previous lines. The interpretations of Yamazaki Masakazu and others are somewhat different: that the performances of the truly successful actor, while understood only by great masters in the audience, are nonetheless appreciated by all audiences alike, just as the celebrated sites for cherry blossoms are appreciated by all, even though only certain select connoisseurs understand their aesthetic and historical significance (*Zeami*, Nihon no meicho, vol. 10 [Tokyo: Chūō kōronsha, 1969], p. 239). The latter alternative seems somewhat more natural, given the text.

17. The first two lines are widely attested in Zen writing, for example, see *The Blue Cliff Record* (Ch. *Biyanlü*, J. *Hekiganroku)*, 45. The third appears following the first two in the recorded sayings of Zen priest Tōzen Ken'eki (Ichige Tōzen Oshō goroku), from an encounter in 1411. Tōzen was the sixty-seventh abbot of Tōfukuji and the seventy-third of Nanzenji. See Kōsai Tsutomu, *Zeami shinkō* (Tokyo: Wan'ya shoten, 1962), pp. 215–17, and *Nōyō shinkō* (Tokyo: Wan'ya shoten, 1972), pp. 411–16.

18. The question here, as Omote notes, takes the form of a Zen dialogue more explicitly than is the case with this format elsewhere in the *Notes*. It seems to inquire into basic problems of knowing and discrimination.

A: This would, I suppose, be a matter for one who is already enlightened to the flower and awakened to the most profoundly significant of accomplishments in our vocation. These items I have spoken about, the interesting, the flower, and freshness—these three are a single matter with three names. Although they are spoken of as three—the wondrous, the flower, and interest—they are substantially the same, but with distinctions of high, middle, and low. "The wondrous" is where language is severed and the operations of the mind founder. "The flower" is the perception of this as wondrous. To mark it out as distinct is "interest."[19]

Now, this designation "interesting" derives from the happy occasion when the Great Goddess, captivated by the fine play in performance of *kagura* at Ama-no-kaguyama, deigned to push aside the boulder before her cave; she then could see the radiance of each and every one of the other gods' faces, and she was given to name this as white-in-the-face [i.e., "interesting"].[20] It cannot have been at that very instant that someone said, "Interesting." Rather, "interesting" was the name given to mark the experience as distinct. Before such a distinction had been made, what might one have possibly said?

In this connection, if we examine the issue with regard to performance strategies in our vocation, then the spontaneous perception by which something is regarded as interesting by means of the fine play in performance is excitement without intent.

> With regard to excitement without intent: since there is really no conscious intent in the spontaneous perception of excitement, in the *Classic of Changes*, the graph for "excitement" is written without the usual element "mind" at the bottom, and the resulting graph is parsed as excitement.[21]

19. This rather difficult passage seems to refer to different levels or stages or perspectives vis-à-vis a knowledge or objectification of experience: The wondrous entails a dissolution of identity into sublime (for lack of a better word) experience; the flower focuses on its perceptual categories; and "interest" pertains to a further objectification. Zeami is relying at least in part on a dialectical formula regarding the interpenetration of the absolute and the relative, called the Five Ranks of Caotong. See Omote, *ZZ*, p. 477n.102; Kōsai, "Zeami no Zen teki kyōyō," in *Zeami shinkō*, pp. 20–39; and Konishi Jin'ichi, *Nōgakuron kenkyū* (Tokyo: Hanawa shobō, 1961), pp. 228–29. Also helpful is Heinrich Dumoulin, *Zen Buddhism: A History, Japan* (Bloomington, Ind.: World Wisdom, 2005), pp. 222–30.

20. *Omoshiro* ("face white" or "white in the face"), which, in its adjectival inflection, *omoshiroshi*, has long meant "interesting" or "attractive." The story was recorded as early as the *Kojiki*, but Zeami's particular interpretation is from *Kogo shūi*.

21. This is an annotation to the text in black ink, referring to the graph 咸, which occurs in ancient Chinese documents as an alternative for the more common graph 感, omitting the element

Now, once the Great Goddess had closed off the heavenly cave with a boulder, earth and sea reverted to a state of timeless obscurity and were utterly dark; when in absence of any intent, it then became light, in that instant of awareness, was there not simply the perception of joy? This would be felicity in vision.[9] This would be the occasion of a spontaneous smile.[22] When she deigned to close off the cave with a boulder and it was utterly dark and language was severed, that was "the wondrous"; when it had become light, that was "the flower"; and when a distinction was made through conscious awareness, that was "the interesting." Is it therefore the case that excitement without intent, that is, spontaneous perception, is simply felicity in vision? On the occasion of a spontaneous smile, language is severed and there is truly nothing.[23] A situation like this is called "wondrous."[24] The mind's apprehension of this as wondrous is "the wondrous flower." That, then, is why we have made the wondrous flower the foremost of the Nine Ranks and defined it as the flower of golden essence.[25] There is a realm in which an excitation from the scene within the intent, startling the mind's ear through the attractions of dancing and singing, spontaneously arouses excitement in the audience—that is the wondrous flower. That is interest. That is excitement without intent. With these three aspects of excitement, it is truly a matter of an instant of no intent. What sort of thing is it that admits interest without a particular frame of mind? Essence admits nothing alien. It is therefore no pattern of visual attraction that excites the golden and silver essence at the top of the Nine Ranks. You must understand this. To smile spontaneously is merely a matter of joy. And as Master Gettan says,

---

心 because that element, "heart" or "mind," is post facto to the spontaneous experience of excitement. A similar passage can be found in *A Mirror of the Flower.*

22. Omote notes the connection to the Zen phrase *nenge mishō* (a smile on grasping the flower). See the discussion of this passage in the introduction.

23. Based on the Zen dictum, and third line from later versions of the celebrated verse of Huineng demonstrating his worthiness to be designated the sixth patriarch. That line reads *benlai wu iwu* (J. *honrai mu ichimotsu*). Earlier manuscripts of the line read, "Buddha nature is always clean and pristine." See Philip Yampolsky, trans., *The Platform Sutra of the Sixth Patriarch* (New York: Columbia University Press, 1967), pp. 132–33.

24. Compare *A Mirror of the Flower.*

25. There is no mention of a "flower of golden essence" in extant manuscripts of *Nine Ranks,* but several references to it occur in Zenchiku's treatises, leading to the indication that at some point Zeami's top three ranks were compared to gold and silver. Omote sees the current text of *Nine Ranks* as the result of a polished editorial process in which such miscellaneous associations were excised, certainly a possibility. Another possibility, though, is that a text on the *Nine Ranks,* including comparisons to precious metals, has simply been lost.

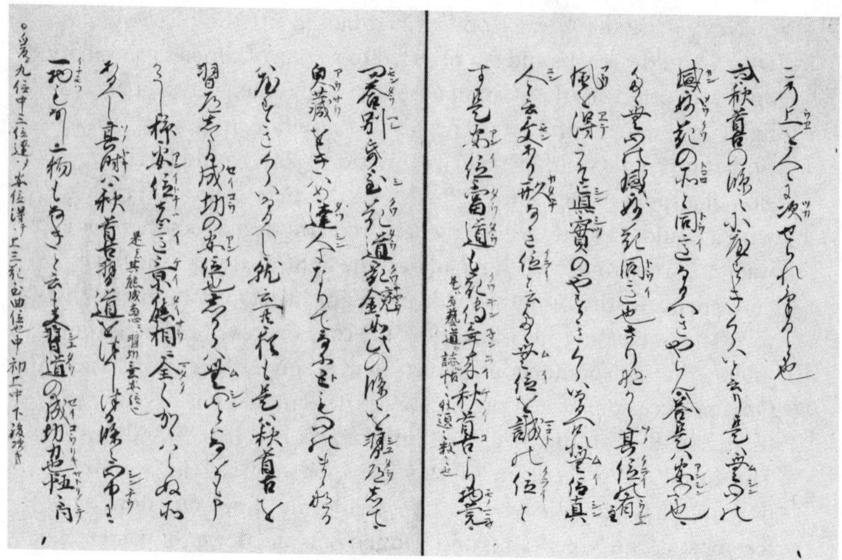

Two leaves from *Pick Up a Jewel and Take the Flower in Hand*, written out by Konparu Yasuyoshi (1588–1661), an actor and important collator of nō and *sarugaku* and the second son of the troupe's leader, Konparu Yasuteru. Yasuyoshi's writing contains various orthographic idiosyncrasies, such as the writing of the word *keiko* (稽古) as though it consisted of three graphs, 秋首古. (This can be seen here in the last line of the page on the right.) The manuscript is unique and was the last of Zeami's *Notes* to be made public, in 1955. It is written in a fluent hand in black, with extensive interlinear notes and glosses in red. (Photograph courtesy of the Noh Theater Research Institute, Hōsei University)

Ureshiki koto ha
iharezarikeri

The wherewithal of joy, you see,
cannot be rendered into words.

They say he used to add these lines to cap the verses he called on people to compose.[26]

Q: The articles on training mention "the rank of complete confidence." Does this perhaps mean the same thing as the business about "the wondrous flower" and "excitement without intent"?

26. "Master Gettan" (Gettan Sōkō, 1326–1389) was a Zen priest who eventually settled in Tajima, having practiced at Nanzenji in the capital and elsewhere in the countryside. A hymn by him is quoted in *A Mirror to the Flower*. The quotation conforms metrically to the last half of a *waka* poem. Apparently, first lines were solicited from Gettan's acquaintances and parishioners, and he would use the quoted lines to cap them.

A: This is a matter of confidence in intent. Excitement without intent means the same thing as the wondrous flower. But it is only in a mastery of subjective effect of a concomitant degree that one secures this rank of complete confidence. Consider the term "the authentic person, of no rank."[27] They call that a rank of no set form. That would mean that only no rank is true rank. This then is a rank of complete confidence.

In our vocation, then, this completely confident rank would mean a complete fluency in expressing your intent, being an accomplished master with a complete command of his treasure store within, on the basis of having learned the way through articles like "Training over the Years," "Dramatic Imitation," "Articles in Question and Answer Form," and "Separate Pages [of Oral Instructions]" from *Transmitting the Flower,* as well as *A Course to Attain the Flower* and *A Mirror of the Flower* (these being the titles of various manuscripts in which the vocation of this art has been recorded). That said, however, what we're talking about here is still a rank of complete confidence based on long experience in learning the vocation. If that is the case, then it remains impossible to say just what "being without intent" entails.

So, then, this rank of complete confidence must reside in something altogether independent of the scene within the actor's intent or his expressive form. (This is a rank of complete confidence in training, experience, and intent in the mind that brings expressive form into effect.)[10] At such a time, "there isn't a single thing in mind" when it comes to the articles that you have exhausted in your training and in learning the way. To say there isn't a single thing in the mind, moreover, is the consequence of long experience in learning the way. To be enlightened to enlightenment is tantamount to no enlightenment.[28, 11]

Master Zide has said (in the sixth of the Six Oxherding Pictures),[29]

27. *Mui shinnin* (also *mui no shinjin*), a term apparently coined by the patriarch of Rinzai Zen, Linji Yixuan (d. 866), to represent a person entirely free from psychological, corporeal, and social constraints.

28. A Zen saying after *Jingde chuandeng lü* or *Wudeng huiyuan,* where it is attributed to Dhṛtaka, the fifth patriarch of the Indian lineage of Zen, in a verse homily reading, "For the mind that penetrates to and attains the original Dharma, there is no Dharma, there is no non-Dharma. To be enlightened to enlightenment is tantamount to no enlightenment; there is no mind and again, there is no Dharma."

29. Zide Huìhui (1097–1183) was a Song dynasty Chan priest in the Caotong (J. Sōtō) lineage. The Six Oxherding Pictures belong to a genre of Chan or Zen text-image practice in which the stages of awareness in the search for enlightenment are compared to a herdboy searching for a lost ox. Far more common than the Six Oxherding Pictures are numerous versions of Ten Oxherding Pictures, and several sets with both text and image survive. Of the Six Oxherding Pictures, only the texts survive. The following quotations are from the texts originally accompanying the fifth and sixth pictures in the series. The text can be found in *Wanxu zangjing* 116 (*Chanzong yulü*

"When the root of life is cut and,
though severed once, is yet again reborn,
true to your type, you receive your being," and so on.

Again,

"Pure gold, though meeting with fire, alters not;
a pristine jewel, though mired in the mud, retains its selfsame integrity."

So it is with this art. From the middle three ranks, one brings the top three flowers to perfection, and then even in mixing with the bottom three, the actor's rank will remain secure among the top three flowers (here it is a question of the performance rank when one has attained the middle three of the Nine Ranks and a complete confidence in them and has reached as far as the upper three flowers. The order is first the middle, then the top, then the bottom). This is gold in the sand or a lotus in the mud: though mixed in with other elements, it is not tainted by them. It is the accomplished master of this rank who, we should tell ourselves, is at the real rank of complete confidence. Though such a person carries out all sorts of performances, no awareness of confidence will ever cross his mind. This is the attitude apposite to one beyond performative technique or intent. This is the rank we should call the miraculous flower of fundamental nothingness.

When, however, a beginning actor takes note of such confidence in the performance of an actor expert in the miraculous flower, his attempt to imitate the confidence expressed in it is like batting his hand around in the air to strike at the moon. This admonition should be taken seriously by actors of the middle and bottom three ranks as well. There should, however, be no objection when actors who have reached the middle three ranks find ease in performance in accord with those ranks or when players of the bottom three ranks find ease in their ranks commensurate with the force of their skills. What is of crucial importance in this art, with respect to modes of performance that have been acquired one by one, is that given the perspective afforded by some distance, actors effect in performance an expressive manner with confidence commensurate with the performers' capacities.[30]

tongjibu) (Taibei: Zangjing shuyuan, 1983), pp. 978–79. I am grateful to Bernard Faure for providing me with the text.

30. The passage is challenging partly because some of the terminology is not clearly defined, here or elsewhere in the *Performance Notes*. The word *kyokugei*, my "mode," for example, occurs only here in the *Notes*. It seems to refer to a particular range of performance techniques that are

Q: In each and every art and vocation, they speak of "consummation." Is this to be taken at face value, or does it have a more profound meaning? What about this?

A: "Consummation" means to come into a state of completion. In this art, then, it also appears to mean the perception of interest. This consummation conforms to *jo-ha-kyū*. The reason for this is that when things come into a state of completion, they fall into place. Without this falling into place, there can be no consummation in our minds. The visual manifestation is consummated at the moment of interest. A fluent progression through *jo-ha-kyū* is a consummation.

Upon careful consideration, it becomes apparent that all phenomena in the universe, positive and negative, great and small, sentient and nonsentient, are each equipped for *jo-ha-kyū*. Even the chirping of birds and the crying of insects—the way each cries forth with its own particular sense—is *jo-ha-kyū*. (This is none other than a consummation beyond mind, beyond rank.) This is why both these excite interest in the hearing and evoke tenderness in the mind. If they contained no "consummation," there could be neither interest nor pathos in their perception.

(As Chōnō said, "A springtime grove rustling in the eastern wind, autumn insects crying in the northern dew, both these are the matter of song," and so forth.[31] The voices of both sentient and nonsentient, therefore, chant poetry.[32] This is the excitement that favors the consummation of *jo-ha-kyū*.)

(The advent of the season when trees and plants, absorbing rain and dew, bear flower and fruit is *jo-ha-kyū* as well.)

(It also resides in the voice of the wind and the sound of the waters.)

---

subject to mastery by an actor. Such modes can, purportedly, be mastered by actors "one by one," as a body (Zeami's phrase is *ittai ittai* [lit., "body by body"]) and can give him a particular, but circumscribed, field of confidence. Such "modes" of competence should be distinguished from the "ranks" to which Zeami gives much more sustained attention.

31. Quoted as well, in slightly different form, in the *kuse* of *Takasago*. "Song" here is the translation of *waka*, which would more narrowly be taken as "Japanese poetry" or "poetry in *waka* [5–7–5/7–7] form," as elsewhere in this translation. Given the context, however, both these seem too narrow. "Poetry" would be a good translation, but I reserve that for the next sentence to reflect the difference between *waka* here and the term *shiika* used there, which indicates poetry in a general sense but with perhaps less sense of song.

Chōnō (orth. Chyaunō) was Fujiwara no Chōnō, and the quotation was purported to be from a work entitled "Chyaunō shiki" (Chyaunō's Personal Record). Such a text is no longer extant, and in any case, the quotation may be erroneously attributed. For further information, see *ZS*, p. 273n.48.

32. As noted in the previous footnote, "poetry" here is my translation of *shiika* ([Chinese] *shi* poetry and [Japanese] *uta* poetry).

Now, matters relating to *jo-ha-kyū* in the art of this vocation of ours are to be seen in detail in *Transmitting the Flower* and *A Mirror to the Flower*. For when the program on a given occasion has come to fulfillment and you earn the praise of the entire audience as one, that is because of the consummation of *jo-ha-kyū* on that day. Everything falls propitiously into place. This is the most fundamental sort of consummation, when the entire audience as one comes to spontaneous excitement then and there. Again, in the sequence of plays performed on a given day, each should have its own consummation through *jo-ha-kyū*. And again, in a single dance or a single sound, what is of interest is the consummation of *jo-ha-kyū*. There is *jo-ha-kyū* in a single gesture of the dancer's sleeve, in a single reverberation from the stomp of a foot. This is not something that can be exhausted by writing it out. Related oral transmissions exist. Interest resides in the *jo-ha-kyū* of the audience in its single vision; the single effect of something in its performance resides in the artist's *jo-ha-kyū*. There is a consummation in the single sound of an audience that in its excitement gasps, "Ah!" In the excitement of a particular moment, as well, the way a given pitch accords with the musical system of five pitches exemplifies *jo-ha-kyū* in the musical sense of *ryo* and *ritsu*. Should the mind not be engaged when the actor sings—even within the scope of a single note—and the sound fails to deliver its excitement, then it surely will not be interesting (this is covered in an oral transmission). This would probably be because the flow of the voice passed through *jo* and *ha* but failed to come to resolution in *kyū*. (This is like bringing a statue of the Buddha to completion without opening its eyes.)[33] How could this possibly result in consummation? It could not, therefore, be interesting. Without a grasp of the sense of this, the performative intent can find no consummation in *jo-ha-kyū*. As I have personally explained with the phrase "first pitch, second *ki*, third voice,"[34] pitch is *jo*. Coming forth into the *ki* is *ha*. The actual production of voice is *kyū*. The interest that results when these three effect excitement in the mind's ear is, then, consummation. Throughout all sorts of performance, the match of a given manner of expression or a particular sound with the *ki*, instantaneous as the flick of a finger, effects its consummation through *jo*, *ha*, and *kyū*.

As it says in the *Zhuangzi*,

33. "Opening the eyes" of a Buddhist image is the last step in its creation and coincides with its consecration to religious office.

34. *A Mirror to the Flower.*

> The mallard's legs may be short, but how he would grieve if you lengthened them! The crane's legs may be long, but how he would suffer if you cut them short![35]

Whether long or short, large or small, each is equal in being subject to *jo-ha-kyū*. If you have grasped the sense of this, then your own intent should find consummation in *jo-ha-kyū*. You should likewise gain a clear knowledge of the good and bad in your own performance style. Thus, once you have filled out the good and, knowing what is bad, eliminated it, you should become a performer of unsurpassed mastery in the art. (What I mean by mastery is an expressive capacity that can be effected with neither instruction nor advance planning.) It is at precisely this time that *jo-ha-kyū*, as the very nature of your intent, achieves in its consummation the clearest possible visual manifestation. Above all, you must know that what is interesting in all sorts of performance relies on the consummation of *jo-ha-kyū*. If it is not interesting, then you should know that this is because *jo-ha-kyū* has not come to consummation. What is cause for concern is whether or not one has really grasped the sense of this. In penetrating to the utmost degree the nature of your intent, if you have truly attained this wondrous vision, then you should, I think, be able to grasp this. (A visual manifestation of your secure grasp of it in performance is this: Interest comes to consummation in each thing heard and each thing seen. This is what is called expertise. What is not interesting and does not come to consummation, I call mediocrity.)

Q: Everyone who performs a given art has a grasp commensurate with the capacity of his intent. Is there anything special one should be aware of with regard to being "commensurate with the capacity of his intent?"

A: There are, in our vocation, many things you should be aware of with regard to being commensurate with the capacity of your intent in performance. In the Nine Ranks, for instance, the expressive manner in the top three ranks for an actor who may have reached them should be commensurate with his intent. This should already be understood as the greatest achievement. The middle three ranks, as well, are commensurate with the capacity of their intent. The bottom three ranks, inasmuch as each actor has attained the rank in question, will be commensurate with the capacity of his intent. In each case, if that's as far

35. After *Zhuangzi* 8, "Pianmu." "What is long is not accounted an excess. What is short is not accounted an insufficiency. Just so, though the duck's legs be short, should you lengthen them, how he would mourn! Though the crane's legs be long, should you cut them down, how he would suffer!"

as his understanding reaches, then he does not really know how to be genuinely commensurate with the capacity of his intent. You cannot really become commensurate with your intent unless you have completely entered into authentic dramatic imitation.

Among the Three Modes, in *Figure Drawings*, for example, I have given the epigraph "with tranquil intent, a distant gaze" to imitation in the Aged Mode. That means "maintain a tranquil intent and gaze into the distance." This is the manner of expression for the Aged Mode. (This expressive effect comes from an old man's vision being hazy and his perspective into the distance being unclear.) If you shape both your posture and your mental attitude to this, perform the Two Arts accordingly, and exhibit an artistic style in which you have fully transformed your body in this way too, then the result should be commensurate with your intent for the Aged Mode. For the Woman's Mode, I have used the epigraph "with intent as Substance, cast force aside." If you transform yourself in the consideration that the intent is the Substance and force is abandoned and then perform the Two Arts, the result should be commensurate with your intent for the Woman's Mode. (If you succeed in making your intent apparent in your attitude, then force will be cast aside.) Similarly, I have used the epigraph "with force as Substance, make the intent intricate" for the Martial Mode. (It is very difficult to make the intent intricate when the Substance is force.) If you give both body and mind careful consideration in accord with making force into the Substance and showing intricacy in intent and then perform the requisite actions, the result should be commensurate with your intent in the Martial Mode. Because the Martial Mode requires a manner of expression derived from the *shura*,[36] you should take particular care not to cross the line into coarseness but always maintain dignity in the way you carry yourself, preserving a clear frame of mind, whether in carrying a bow and arrows, advancing to attack, withdrawing to defend, parrying or evading the enemy's blows, striding resolutely or using a light step. The result should be commensurate with your intent for the Martial Mode.

It is all too easy to misconstrue this and to assume that all you need to do to be a woman is put on a pretty appearance. Thus, when it is time to assume a role in the Woman's Mode, you fail to take "intent as Substance, cast[ing] force aside" and move directly into the mimicry of a woman, even while remaining in the physical state that takes "force as Substance, mak[ing] the intent intricate"; in such a situation, the object of dramatic imitation withers away, indeterminate, result-

36. A supernatural being of warlike character. See *Transmitting the Flower*.

ing in a manner of expression of no genuine substance. Members of the audience may then admonish you, saying, "It's withered away, you know," and "Don't you see how weak it is?" But in such degree as you return body and mind to the Martial Mode, the performance grows coarse. How could these ever be called commensurate with your intent in the Woman's Mode? A typical woman in our world wouldn't try to mimic a woman. She is born a woman, and in accord with her position—whether the deportment of a lady or a commoner—it is her own particular behavior as she is that amounts to "behavior commensurate with the capacity of her intent." If someone takes it into his head to fabricate a pretty appearance, thinking that in that way, he'll achieve *yūgen*, it will never work. (It is particularly difficult to gain a real understanding of *yūgen*.) When someone tells an actor like that, "You know, it's awfully coarse," there's nothing he can do. And then when somebody asks him, "Why don't you do something with it?" his acting just gets coarser. It is only when you perform within the proper parameters of the role (this is where the bounds of what is commensurate with your intent are found) that any meaningful judgment can be made as to whether your performance is strong or weak. That's why it is so extraordinarily difficult to assume the role of a woman when you have the body of a man; that being the case, it is in adopting the model "with intent as Substance, cast force aside" that you find expressive effect so that both mind and body are transformed. This, then, is what it means to be commensurate with your intent in the Woman's Mode. But in contrast, if without any such consideration, you merely try to mimic a woman, that will never be commensurate with your intent in the Woman's Mode. Mimicking a woman is not being a woman. It is only in mastering how to effect the subject in a woman's role that you are commensurate with your intent as a woman. (The rank of mimicry is the failure to bring the subject into effect, and the rank of attainment is bringing the subject into effect. Then again, if you "double back" by way of a resurrection in rank, you may end up without an effective subject.)[12] Make sure you understand this distinction well. This is also true for the Aged Mode. Only if you have fully grasped "a tranquil intent, a distant gaze" and fully mastered the model is it possible to act commensurately with the capacity of your intent in the Aged Mode. All Three Modes are like this.

Also, when it comes to the matter of the deranged and the like, you wouldn't expect them to be counted among the characters appropriate to this vocation at all, since they involve laying one's shame open to public view, with no concern about the general regard, but actually this is the very stuff of *sarugaku*. Take, for instance, a woman who would normally be discreet and inclined to avoid attracting attention.

She may not offer much in the way of display in the normal course of things, but make her deranged and have her entertain by dancing a dance and singing a song, and the sight of her, elegant enough in itself, will be scattered over with blossoms and dressed up in color and fragrance, realizing an expressive effect more interesting than anything else. An actor who has attained such a rank as this is accounted to have grasped the greatest achievement.[13] This holds the greatest capacity for interest through intent.

Also, outside the Three Modes, the character of the demon and such make excellent material for imitation in *sarugaku*. There's no seeing genuine demons, though. There probably isn't any way of imitating either, for example, the shapes given to demonic characters depicted in pictures. That being the case, you should assume a general resemblance as your consideration and disengage from what might be, by rights, a coarse display, to mollify the movements with a certain intricacy and beguile the viewer with such ingenuity as you can muster. This is what it means to be commensurate with your intent for the character of the demon. This is what has been termed the Style of Intricate Movement (on the basis of its appearance) or again, what we mean when we say, "The form is demonic, the intent is human" (on the basis of its intentional activity). (There also are demons in the Style of Violent Movement. These, however, are not suitable for our troupe.) Get a solid grasp of this consideration and make the necessary differentiations in the right way; that should be commensurate with your intent for the character of intricate movement.

The matter of creating a corpus of performance without deceit, using diverse types of dramatic imitation, and learning the Way in the Two Arts amounts to being commensurate with the capacity of your intent for each discipline of performance. Should you try to carry things off with a general conjectural consideration without the particular considerations and appropriate distinctions, then that cannot be called commensurate with subjective intent. Thus, because there is in the end no clear intent regarding the model, the distinctive flavor of your performance will subside, and as age descends on you, your performance will degenerate. This is something to be understood clearly.

As it says in the *Great Learning*, "When the roots are in disorder, there is no ordering of the branches," and so on.[37] To achieve a fine likeness in accord with the object of dramatic imitation: this, of course, is fundamental. If you fail to master this genuinely, and your

37. The quotation from the *Great Learning* (*Daxue*) is not exact. See *A Course to Attain the Flower.*

performance techniques in imitation are slipshod, then you are not likely to be a master of subjective effect. The roots thus being in disorder, there will be no ordering of the branches. It has also been said that "exceeding is falling short."[38] That is, to be excessive is the same as failing to attain your goal. At the border of dramatic imitation, neither a slight deficiency nor an excess can be counted as adequate at base. If you have genuinely entered into a mastery of subjective effect, you should then have no intention to imitate.[39] (This matter of the rank of bringing the subject into effect and the failure to do so can be found in *A Course to Attain the Flower.*) This should be called genuine dramatic imitation and mastery of subjective effect. Only when you have truly entered into a mastery of the technical effects at the outermost edge of performance can it be called the rank at which the most fundamental effects commensurate with the capacity of your intent are in your control.

As it says in the *Mencius*, "It is not doing it that's hard, but doing it well that's hard."[40] For the most part, there should be no complication in learning how to imitate something; as for achieving an acceptable visual effect—you should manage that part of it without great difficulty. There are, however, few who have gained a name for genuinely entering into the very thing. This—doing the thing really well—is what is truly difficult. "Is there a resemblance? Yes, there is a resemblance. But is it the real thing? No, it's not the real thing."[41] ("Similar, yet never the same, put them together and you know their proper place.")[42] Strive hard to attain a lasting name as an accomplished master, the very thing, by making every effort to secure for yourself the level of the real thing.[14]

This notebook entails a secret transmission for learning the vocation of this art. Herewith, I approve its transmission, as above, to Konparu Dayū,[43] on account of the promise apparent in his performance.

Shōchō 1 [1428]:6:1

Zea (signature) (copying the seal as well)

38. A quotation, purportedly from the *Classic of Rites* but actually similar to the *Analects* 11.15. See *Technical Specifications for Setting a Melody.*

39. A similar observation can be found in *Transmitting the Flower.*

40. A similar phrase is quoted in *A Course to Attain the Flower.* The attribution to *Mencius* is spurious, but similar phrases can be found in the *Shujing* and *Wenxuan.*

41. See *A Mirror to the Flower,* where this proverb also is quoted.

42. See *Nine Ranks.*

43. Konparu Zenchiku. It is of great interest that a secret treatise, as Zeami designates this, was transmitted to Zenchiku some four years before Zeami's heir, Motomasa, died, as is the fact that Zenchiku acknowledges Zeami as his master (*shika* or *shike*) later here.

Moshihogusa kakioku tsuyu no tama wo miba
migaku kotoba no hana ha tsukiseji

Should you catch sight
of a gem of dew
in the brine-soaked sea grass raked up here,
then the flower of polished language
will never come to an end.

This notebook was transmitted to me in the lineage of the master in my youth.

a day in Kyōtoku 2 [1453]:8
Ujinobu[44] *(signature)*
(copying Zenchiku's seal as well)

Moshihogusa no hana mo tamamo mo kakiatsume
mireba kagami no ura mo kumorazu

Raking up together
flowers of the briny sea grass,
gem grass too,
I look it over to find,
even the back of the mirror remains unclouded.[45]

Konparu Hachirau, Hata Yasuteru[46] *(signature)*

Notes

1. In this particular case, Zeami writes 我意分 but may intend the word conventionally written in medieval Japanese with the graphs 涯分, which is written in red to the left of Zeami's spelling. Common translations for the latter might be "to one's fullest capacity" or "commensurate with one's position or station," but Zeami's choice of the graphs is not likely to have been purely arbitrary, so I have translated the word as "commensurate with [one's] intent."

2. The text reads 四気 (four *ki*), but it seems likely that the second graph is an allograph for 季, which in fact is added in an interlinear note in red.

3. This interlinear note is in red, apparently referring to the pitch *shō*, here written 尚, but more correctly written 商.

4. ヤウセイ«尚»・エイキョク . . . をアイヲンにキウソクして, parsed by Omote as 陽声«尚»永曲を相音に休息して. The mention of アイヲン here begs comparison with the technical term I trans-

44. Konparu Zenchiku.

45. The poems connected with the designation of Huineng as the sixth Zen patriarch are concerned with an unclouded mirror and may lie behind this *waka* by Zenchiku. See Yampolsky, trans., *Platform Sutra of the Sixth Patriarch*, esp. sec. 6, 9.

46. Head of the Konparu troupe six generations after Zenchiku, who died in 1621 at the age of seventy-two.

lated as "doubly proficient" in *Oral Instructions on Song* and *A Mirror to the Flower*, but such a specific technical meaning does not seem to be Zeami's intention here (as there is no mention of the complementary terminology of *wau no koye* and *shu no koye*), and, indeed, Konishi Jin'ichi, *Nōgakuron kenkyū* (Tokyo: Hanawa shobō, 1961); Omote, in *ZZ*; and J. Thomas Rimer and Masakazu Yamazaki, trans., *On the Art of the Nō Drama: The Major Treatises of Zeami* (Princeton, N.J.: Princeton University Press, 1984), seem to read the passage without the technical specification.

5. 機当不当: interlinear note in red alongside the word *breath* (息). The 機 may be an allograph for 気, as Omote suggests in *Ongyoku kuden*, *Oral Instructions on Singing*, n.1.

6. The chapter on Liang Shanguan in *Wujia zhengzongcan* records a verse from a hymn by Liang's successor, Taiyang Jingxuan, reading 夜放烏鶏帯雪飛. In the Sōtō lineage in Japan, the verse was read as it is here, apparently to provide an image of yin.

7. 急尚上下声成文、謂之音: interlinear note in red. The line is found in *A Mirror to the Flower* but has been mistranscribed here with 調 for 謂. As Omote points out, this doesn't make sense, so he, and I following his lead, substitute the line as quoted in *A Mirror to the Flower.*

8. The text reads ソノおりきげん, which Omote parses as 其折・機嫌. The *kanji* seem appropriate, but the relation between the two compounds is less certain. It might be "the given occasion *and* the temperament (of something unspecified)," but the question seems to follow directly after the previous answer, and so I have read the two compounds as related in a genitive construction.

9. The annotation glosses the native Japanese うれしき心 with the Chinese compound 観喜, but Omote, Konishi, and Yamazaki Masakazu (*Zeami*, Nihon no meicho, vol. 10 [Tokyo: Chūō kōronsha, 1969]) take this to be a miswriting of the homonym 歓喜, a word redolent with Buddhist associations (as in the name of the divinity, 歓喜天, Chinese for Ganeśa). Might it not be overhasty, though, to assume that Zeami (or whoever made the annotation) misnotated his intent? The compound makes good sense in the context of this discussion as the joy of seeing or, by extension, the joy of perception, and Zeami has a distinct penchant for neologisms.

10. 是者、其態成当心ニハ習功意安位也. The insistent Sinicization of the text in this note makes it difficult to know how it is to be read. Omote adds particles and a verbal inflection to achieve this result: 是者、其の態を成す当心ニハ習功意安の位也. This seems sensible, although there remains some discrepancy on the parsing of the last several graphs. Konishi opts instead for 習功意の安位なり at this point. My translation follows Konishi more closely. Omote's would read something like "This is a rank of complete confidence within the mind based on long experience in training, for the mind that brings expressive form into effect."

11. Zeami writes 未子 for 未悟.

12. 却来似スル位ハ無主風、ニ得ル位有主風也。又、甦位却来シテ無主風可レ至。 This interlinear note, appended to the right of "It is only in mastering how to effect the subject in a woman's role" is puzzling in two respects. *Niuru* (ニ得ル) is apparently Zeami's (or the annotator's) neologism and seems at least in part to appear as a rhyming counterpart to *nisuru*. The implied contrast seems logical from the previous discussion.

The final line is more difficult. The graphs 甦位 appear nowhere else in the *Performance Notes* and as "resurrection rank" don't make much sense, although the subsequent compound 却来 (my "double back") represents an important concept in Zeami's aesthetic from *Nine Ranks* forward. Konishi suggests that 甦 is an allograph for 向, that 位 is a mistranscription of 去, and that the intended phrase therefore is 向去却来 attested in *Articles on the Five Sorts of Singing.* As Omote points out, however, the idea of a mistranscription is not entirely persuasive, since the cursive script forms of the two graphs are quite different.

13. Reading 上果 for 上花, but as Omote says, 上花 could also mean 上三花, "the top three flowers" of the Nine Ranks.

14. 此是をよくよく安位して、達人長名の其物に至らん事を可レ得. This is a difficult sentence with an uncharacteristic verbal use of 安位 (して), with the abstract values of 此是 read "*kono ze*," and 其物 (*sono mono*) and the injunction framed unusually with 事を可レ得.

Articles on the Five Sorts of Singing

五音曲条々

The heterogeneous *Articles on the Five Sorts of Singing*, taken together with *Five Sorts of Singing*, represents the culmination of Zeami's thinking on genre in relation to music. This text names the five individual sorts of singing, then compares the five sorts to five trees, and illustrates each with a poem. Songs of each of the five sorts (one apiece) and a discussion of expressiveness in singing, with quotations from the *Great Learning* and the *Classic of Songs*, follow.

The text contains various annotations in red and black, but its original title is unknown. One manuscript begins with simply *Go ongyoku* (*Five Sorts of Singing*), but when Yoshida Tōgo first published the text in the modern era, he added the word *jōjō* (articles), and his title has remained with the text, usefully distinguishing it from the closely related text *Go on* (*Five Sorts of Singing*), which follows this one.

❁

There are five different classes of music: *shiugen*, *yūkyoku*, *renbo*, *aishyau*, and *rangyoku*.[1]

• *Shiugen* means the sound of peace and contentment. The delivery should be straightforward, proceeding with a light touch, in a tone that reflects the voice of order in the world. But then again, it is no simple matter to maintain great seriousness with a light and flowing expressive tone. (The sound is complete and orthodox in substance, at the rank of the sovereignty of heaven.)[2] Concentrate on this intently.

For its part, *yūkyoku* means adding graceful appeal to the *shiugen* just mentioned. The vocal rank is supple in delivery; vocal ornaments are thoroughly integrated; and the singing has a beautiful, yet correct surface. It's the prospect of blossoms and the moon there before you at dusk and dawn, together. From the viewpoint of Substance and Instance, this style makes In-

1. See the introduction.

2. The "sovereignty of heaven" (*tensei*) seems to derive from the older Daide articles in the *Classic of Rites*, where "the sovereignty of heaven is called orthodox, the sovereignty of earth is called life, and the sovereignty of man is called discrimination." See *ZZ* p. 478n.108.

stance the Substance and thoroughly integrates the Substance per se. One who has attained a rank such as this, who possesses such a vocal style, we can call an expert of unsurpassed accomplishment.

Renbo means adding tenderness to what is already gentle and quiet. It has a melodic appeal with a kind of excitement you can't quite pin down and a disquieting tenderness. You create musical appeal and express excitement by enlivening the words with a hint of mispronunciation and thoroughly integrating vocal ornamentation. You need to know just what I mean when I talk about mispronunciation in the voicing. There is, you see, considerable difficulty in this matter of mispronunciation. You shouldn't imagine mispronunciation to be uniformly undesirable. There would seem to be, in Buddhist chanting[3] and *gāthās*,[4] for instance, vocal articulations that require a degree of mispronunciation. When we say, "The lightness or heaviness, the voicing or lack of voicing of a word depends on the preceding text"[5] or refer to euphonic elisions and the like, these are Instances in sound that require such mispronunciation. You must have a clear knowledge of the distinction between mispronouncing appropriately and inappropriately, between what is permitted and what is to be avoided in diction. To mispronounce appropriately may contribute to the flower in singing. In that case, even though you actually mispronounce, it is not likely to be heard as such. To be able to hear the difference between what is permissible and what is to be avoided in mispronunciation must depend on the singer's finesse. Thus, the palpable quality of *renbo* may well be found in a mispronunciation bearing on melodic inflection[6, 1] thoroughly integrated into the gentleness and quiet, where the musical appeal reverberates with a disquieting tenderness. That being the case, one should sing with "the music as the Substance, the melody as the Instance."

Aishyau means that frame of mind that calls forth tears of excitement, also in response to tenderness (to the voice of passion, which expresses the tenderness just mentioned). The melodic appeal should come from a sound that makes one aware of impermanence. Now, since *shiugen* is accounted the foundation of everything in these times, this *aishyau*, which after all means "anguish," should be measured and discreet, whatever the melodic appeal that anguish may have. In performances of linked verse, as you know, the category of "anguish" has long since ceased to hold a place. So also in singing, the essential character of *aishyau* will have been evoked as long as the melody is palpably beautiful and there is such tenderness as is generally discernible to

3. That is, *shōmyō*.

4. That is, *kada* here but also known as *geda* or simply *ge*. These are Buddhist verses, sometimes based on sutras, and can be written in Sanskrit, Chinese, or Japanese.

5. Quoting *A Mirror to the Flower.*

6. *Fushinamari*. See the discussion in *Oral Instructions on Singing.*

the ear which, on hearing, excites an awareness of impermanence through sound.

Rangyoku means a superlative singing voice. It is the rank that one reaches after having thoroughly learned the way in every sort of performance, having raised oneself above it and mixed positive and negative in a single sound to create a voice that is "similar, yet never the same."[7] I wonder whether this rank might not compare with one they speak of among the ten styles in the vocation of poetry, the strong rank that "grapples with and subjugates a demon."[8] This is a musical rank at which, facing about and doubling back,[9] one sings with ever surpassing virtuosity. To attain this essential level, one must possess great finesse. This will be known to those to whom it is relevant.

• As discussed earlier, the previous articles should, in sum, be regarded as matters of virtuosity in singing.[2] Now, matters of vocal pattern are of crucial importance at points of vocal articulation. You could even say that they are the ultimate accomplishment in singing. "To be enlightened to enlightenment is tantamount to no enlightenment,"[10] as they say. In these articles, *shiugen*, *yūkyoku*, *renbo*, *aishyau*, and *rangyoku* are, every one of them, vocal styles in which melodies and embellishments are set to appropriate texts in accord with the rationale for these types of singing; to master the melodic form well and sing it with full competence measures up to the model set by the melodic structure. What I call expressiveness, then, is creating a pattern over and above this.[3] But even bringing such a rank to its fullest is still limited to resemblance in expression. Genuine virtuosity in singing can be found where excitement in sound is manifest beyond perception or cognition, after this rank has been long forgotten. Someone who has attained such a rank as this, I would call a master of expressiveness.

Articles in which the palpable qualities of singing are compared to several trees and its intent is illustrated using poetic styles (with attached comments):

7. See *Pick Up a Jewel and Take the Flower in Hand.*

8. *Oni wo torihishigu*, which gives a name to the *oni-hishigi-tei* or *rakkitei* (demon-quelling or demon-subjugating style). The word stems from a poetic style discussed in treatises such as *Sangoki*, spuriously attributed to the poet Fujiwara no Teika. For its use in poetics, see Robert H. Brower and Earl Miner, *Japanese Court Poetry* (Stanford, Calif.: Stanford University Press, 1961), pp. 247–48, and Paul Atkins, "The Demon-Quelling Style in Medieval Japanese Poetic and Dramatic Theory," *Monumenta Nipponica* 58, no. 3 (2003): 317–46. For Zeami, the "demon-quelling style" is related to the Demon of Violent Movement, a heterodox performance style. See *Figure Drawings of the Two Arts and the Three Modes.*

9. *Kōko kyakurai* (orth. *kauko kyakurai*). This single occurrence, apart from its appearance in a citation in *Five Sorts of Singing*, has been an important entrée into Zeami's late style. It seems to be an extension of the more common Zen term *kyakurai*. See *Nine Ranks* and the brief but important late text *The Flower in . . . Yet Doubling Back.*

10. See *Pick Up a Jewel and Take the Flower in Hand.*

• The Pine

Yorodzu yo wo matsu ni zo kimi wo iwaitsuru
Chitose no kage ni suman to womoeba [*sic*][11]
(the attitude of *shiugen*)

It's in the pine I magnify my lord,
for full ten thousand years,
For I think how I might shelter,
like a crane,
in his millennial shade.

Among the golden dicta of Prince Regent Shōtoku, it is recorded that "the age of the True Law comes to an end and cedes to Zen; the several trees wither in favor of the pine";[12] and so forth. From the outset, the pine is a magical tree and does not change color according to the season. It is the effect and attitude[13] of a thousand autumns and by itself presents the full display of all-encompassing verdant mountains. It is altogether fitting for the vocal music of *shiugen* and the musical excitement that comes of complete confidence in performance.

• The Cherry

Mata ya min Katano no mino no sakuragari
Hana no yuki chiru haru no akebono
(the attitude of *yūkyoku*)

Might I once again attend
the royal chase at Katano
hunting for the cherry trees?

11. *KKS* 356, with the headnote "Composed for the celebration of Yoshimine no Tsunenari's fortieth year on behalf of his daughter by the Monk Sosei."

12. The source of this quotation has not been identified, and the attribution to Prince Shōtoku is probably spurious, but Zeami's use of it seems to reflect a sense that the older forms of Buddhism would give way to Zen once the orthodox age of the True Law had passed, just as the pine alone would remain green after frost had withered the leaves of deciduous trees.

There are some ironies here, however, and it could be that the "True Law" referred to was not part of the cycle "True Law—Counterfeit Law—Latter Days of the Law" but that the "True Law" is to be contrasted with heresy and that the heresy in question is Zen. This is not how Zeami understood the question.

13. That is, *fūshi*, as in *Fūshi k(w)aden*—that is, *Transmitting the Flower Through Effects and Attitudes.*

A snow of blossoms falls:
the blushing dawn of spring.[14]

From the outset, of all trees, the cherry is a magic one and a central feature among the sights of spring in both China and Our Realm. That is why it serves to create musical excitement as the aura of melodious song, the sublime chanting of poetry, and the sights and sounds of flowers and birds themselves.[15]

• Colored Leaves

Shitamomiji katsu chiru yama no yūshigure
Nurete ya shika no hitori nakuran[16]
(the attitude of *renbo*)

The colored leaves are fallen
from the lower branches of the trees,
here and there, a passing shower in the hills at dusk.
Is it because he's wet
that the stag cries, all alone?

Colored leaves reveal the feeling inherent in the autumn dusk and carry over to thoughts of romantic longing and the complaints of lovers, dyed as they are with passion, a display of sorrow at the dewfall.[17, 4]

• Winter Trees

Ashikare to omohanu yama no mine ni dani
Wou naru mono wo hito no nageki ha[18]
(the attitude of *aishyau*)

14. *SKKS* 114, "Among five verses composed for the house of the Regent Chancellor," by Master in the Empress's Household Office, Shunzei.

15. The highly impressionistic (and somewhat purple) passage links, though not very specifically, the beauty of the cherry with the efficacy of *yūkyoku*.

16. *SKKS* 437, "At Royal Bureau of Poetry, when boys were composing poems, on the topic of a stag at dusk," by Hereditary Peer Fujiwara no Ietaka. The stag's erotic urges are decorous enough for treatment in poetry (and even music, for example, the *shakuhachi* classic, *Shika no tōne*), and the wetness here suggests sexual ardor as well as moisture from the rains, thus its appropriateness for *renbo* (romantic longing).

17. Dew was, as the poetic lore holds, what colored the leaves in the autumn.

18. *Shika wakashū* 333, "Composed out of resentment for a man," by Izumi Shikibu.

Try as I might to think no ill of him—
would that I could—
the very trees that cap the mountain peaks
bespeak resentment:
what of my regrets?

A stand of trees in winter, long past the spring with its blossoms and after the autumn's colored leaves when it has been assailed by frost, buried in the snow, its leaves fallen, its branches altered: just as it is, this reflects deeply the scene of *aishyau* and *bauwoku*.[19]

• The Cedar

Itsushika to kamisabinikeru Kaguyama no
Musugi ga moto ni koke no musumade ni
(the attitude of *rangyoku*)

When, I wonder, did it take on
such a sacred air, the spear-shaft cedar
on Mount Kagu
Moss has even grown there
among its roots.

The cedar makes a display even more surpassing, a sacred tree surrounding the august precincts of magic shrines; a perspective afforded by distance shows it to be "similar to other trees, yet never the same." For this reason, the resonance of a unique musical virtuosity, the peerlessly surpassing vocal impression is best figured in the cedar. You should make every effort to learn the way and bring this kind of virtuosity in singing into effect.

• The Fundamental Vocal Attitude, the Singing of *Shiugen*

For the vocal roots of this, I take a piece like the following:

Sore hisakata no kamiyo yori,
Ametsuchi hirakeshi kuni no hajime . . . [20]

19. *Bauwoku* is of uncertain meaning. See the introduction.
20. A brief passage from the opening of an independent congratulatory piece called "Fushimi." There is a longer citation of the piece in *Five Sorts of Singing*.

From the age of gods, immemorial,
from the genesis of land,
when earth was drawn apart from sky, . . .

• The Fundamental Vocal Attitude, the Singing of *Yūkyoku*

(*Yūkyoku* is a performance style common to all five classes of music.)

Yūkyoku is exemplified in the expressive manner of the following song:

Hiwori seshi
Ukon no baba no ko no ma yori,
Ukon no baba no ko no ma yori,
Kage mo niofu ya Asahidera no,
Haru no hikari mo ama miteru,
Kami no miyuki no ato furite,
Matsu mo kodakaki 'nmegae no,
Tachie mo miete kurenayi no,
Hatsu hanaguruma meguru hi no,
Nagae ya kita ni tsudzukuran,
Nagae ya kita ni tsudzukuran.[21]

From between the trees
by the feted archery grounds of the Guards of the Right:
by the feted archery grounds of the Guards of the Right:
the Dawn Sun Temple holds Her sacred aura,
Its spring light fills the skies.
The god's divine procession passes by as age-old pines
tower in the sky and branches of the plum
stand high, their crimson blossoms
circling 'round, first flowers, as one day turns into the next,
and to the north, the carriage shafts stretch on,
and to the north, the carriage shafts stretch on.

The songs and *kusemai* and such since the Ōei era (1394–1427) are all *yūkyoku*. There are far too many to list.

21. *Ageuta* from the *maejite*'s entry from the play *Ukon*. The play is about the appearance of a goddess at the archery grounds of the Guards of the Right (Ukon no baba), which had been the site of a royal archery fete on the fifth day of the fifth month. The play, however, is set under the blossoming plum, which would be near the beginning of the year. Zeami quotes only the first two lines, but I have taken the liberty of adding the remainder of the song, in italics, to give a better sense of context.

• The Fundamental Vocal Attitude for the Singing of *Renbo*

Renbo is exemplified in the fundamental vocal pattern of the following song:

Shinoburedo,
Iro ni 'denikeri waga kohi ha,
Mono ya omofu to
Hito no tofu made[22] *hadzukashi no*
Morikeru sode no namida ka na.
Ge ni ya kohi su te fu,
Waga na ha madaki tachikeri to,
Hito shirezarishi[23] *kokoro made,*
Omohishirarete natsukashi ya,
Omohishirarete natsukashi ya.[24]

Though I try to hold it back,
My passion has, I see, blushed forth,
So much so that someone asks,
Is something on your mind? What indiscretion!
Look, tears spilled out here upon my sleeve . . .
The word's already out that I'm in love,
How could they know when, in this bashful heart,
I'm only now aware myself,

22. *Shūi wakashū* 622, "From a poetry contest during the august Tenryaku era," by Taira no Kanemori (d. 990).

23. Partial quotation of *Shūi wakashū* 621, "From a poetry contest during the august Tenryaku era," by Mibu Tadami, which immediately precedes the poem just cited: *Kohi su te fu waga na ha madaki tachinikeri / Hito shirezu koso omohisomeshi ka* (The word's already out that I'm in love, no one's supposed to know—I've only now just fallen in love).

24. The two brief lines quoted by Zeami are augmented from a fuller citation of this song in Zenchiku's *Go ongyoku no shidai*, where the entire song appears, with basic musical notation, and is cited as an example of *renbo*. See Omote Akira and Itō Masayoshi, eds., *Konparu kodensho shūsei* (Tokyo: Wan'ya shoten, 1969), p. 112. I have italicized the augmented portions here as well. It is specified as an *ageuta* and further designated an *eikyoku*. The song is quoted in *Kanginshū* 265, in Shinma Shin'ichi, Shida Nobuyoshi, and Asano Kenji, *Chūsei kinsei kayōshū*, NKBT, vol. 44 (Tokyo: Iwanami shoten, 1959) (but with the final, repeated, line reading *hadzukashi ya* [how embarrassing] rather than *natsukashi ya*), and can be found in a manuscript of assorted songs formerly owned by the Uesugi, now in the Nō Research Institute of Hōsei University, as one of two *ageuta* from the play *Keburimi Senju* (*Lady Senju Watching the Smoke*). It is uncertain whether this play had been written by the time Zeami wrote *Articles on the Five Sorts of Singing*. Zenchiku's classification of the piece as an *eikyoku* suggests that it was an independent song in its own right before being incorporated into the play in question. I am grateful to Michael Watson for helping me identify this piece.

And stricken, for that, yet more tenderly
And stricken, for that, yet more tenderly.

The final sections of *Matsukaze Murasame*,[25] *Hanjo* (and *Misogigawa*)[26] are all primarily *renbo.*

• The Fundamental Vocal Attitude for the Singing of *Aishyau*

Aishyau is exemplified in the fundamental effect of the following song:

Isshyau ha kaze no mae no kumo,
Yume no aida ni sanjiyasuku,
Sangai ha midzu no ue no awa,
Hikari no mae ni kien to su,
Iranden no uchi ni ha uwi no kanashimi wo tsuge,
Hisuyi no chyau no uchi ni ha,
Muro no gwanriki ari to ka ya,
Eigwa ha kore haru no hana,
Kinofu ha sakan naredomo,
Kefu ha otorofu [g]wanriki no,
Aki no hikari,
Ashita ni zōji,
Iube ni genzu to ka,
Haru sari aki kitatte,
Hana sanji ha otsu,
Toki utsuri koto henjite,
Tanoshimi sude ni satte,
Kanashimi hayaku kitareri,
Asagao no,
Hana no ue naru tsuyu yori mo,
Hakanaki mono ha kagerofu no,
Aru ka naki ka no kokochi shite,
Yo wo aki kaze no uchinabiki,
Murewiru tadzu no ne wo nakite,
Shide no tawosa no hitokoe mo,

25. That is, *Matsukaze.*

26. *Misogigawa* (orth. *Misogigaha*) is probably an old name for the play known today as *Minasegawa.* This play is not listed in the primary manuscript used for *ZZ* (and here) but has been supplied from other manuscripts.

Taga yomiji wo ka shirasuran,
Ahare narikeru ningai wo,
Itsu ka ha hanarehatsu beki[27]

An entire lifetime, as clouds before the wind,
prone to scatter in the space of a dream.
The three worlds are froth on the water,
soon to vanish in the light.
Even in the Yilan Palace, the sadness inherent in being is declaimed
and even behind a screen of sumptuous jade, devotion holds its strength.
The glory of this world is a mere flower in spring:
though yesterday it prospered, in full sway,
today it withers away, and devotion
strengthens in the autumn morning light,
only then to fade with dusk.
Spring is gone, autumn comes,
flowers scatter, leaves fall, time passes, things change,
pleasures are gone, sadness comes on,
the blossoms of morning glories,
bedecked with dew
could hardly be more fragile
and fragile things impart a sense of gossamer––
now here now gone, 'til surfeited with the world,
the autumn sends its buffeting wind,
the crane cries out from its teeming flock,
the voice of a herald of the world below:
who will let us know the road to death?
See how sad it is, this human world,
When might I escape it, once and for all?[28]

27. Zeami quotes only the first two lines, but I have included the entire song, for context, as before, in italics. This song is now the *kuse* of the play *Shōki*, but in Zeami's time, it appears to have been an independent song. Zenchiku quotes from it and precedes it with a *sashi* that has not found its way into *Shōki*. See Omote, in *ZZ*, p. 481n.119, and Itō Masayoshi, "Go on, Aishō," *Kanze*, February 1964.

28. The Yilan Palace was the palace of the Han Emperor Jingdi (r. 156–140 B.C.E.) and the birthplace of his successor, the celebrated Emperor Wudi (r. 140–187 B.C.E.).

• The Fundamental Vocal Attitude for the Singing of *Rangyoku*

Rangyoku is exemplified in the fundamental effect of the following song:

> Sore ichidai no keubou ha
> Goji hakkeu wo kedzuri . . . [29]
>
> Verily, the Dharma teachings of the first generation
> specified Five Ages and Eight Doctrines, . . .

"The *kusemai* of Prince Regent of the Upper Palace"[30] and Shirahige[31] partake of this expressive manner. Passages in *kotoba* also are performed in *rangyoku.*

For the most part, there should be no choral accompaniment in unison to *rangyoku* singing. Self and other are different, to be sure, yet sometimes a musical rationale may yet be known to all parties. The reason, then, that there should be no choral unison to *rangyoku* singing resides in a crucial element in its musical rationale. That is, since this kind of singing proceeds from spontaneous response to the moment once you are firmly resident in a rank of full confidence, there can be no musical rationale in it for accompaniment by a chorus. Could there be, however, some possibility of mutual performance by one real master with another real master?[32] Even in a case like this, it should be the melody that is shared by the two, but in regard to the aural expressiveness, that should, in two different singers, be distinct. This aural expressiveness is an intuitive shift taking place beyond both perception and cognition. For that reason, it consists of the virtuoso vocal style of each particular person; there can be no common musical rationale shared between self and other. This should be clearly understood. To carefully discriminate the musical rationale and become a master of this kind of performance is the ultimate accomplishment in singing. It is a secret transmission. For the most

29. Originally from the play *Jinen koji,* though no longer included in the text. An extended passage can be found in *Five Sorts of Singing.*

30. An earlier version of a song known now as simply "Prince Regent of the Upper Palace," also known as simply "Prince Regent's *kusemai.*" An extended passage can be found in *Five Sorts of Singing.*

31. Originally an independent *kusemai,* later to become the *kuse* of a play of the same name. The piece is quoted extensively in *Five Sorts of Singing.*

32. There is a possible analogy in some of the virtuosic pieces (called *rangyoku,* related to but not identical with Zeami's *rangyoku* singing style) occasionally performed on the modern nō stage (usually for anniversaries and memorial performances). These are pieces for one master singer, but they sometimes are performed jointly with one drummer or flute player, a master in his own right.

part, the melodic frame in which any type of music up to the level of *rangyoku* may be set should be amenable to unison singing. (This is, I repeat, a deep secret.)

• The Mao preface to the *Classic of Songs* says,

> The music of an ordered world is pleasurable in its confidence. Its government is concordant.
> The music of a disordered world is irate in its rancor. Its government is alienating.
> The music of an ill-fated world is preoccupied in its despondency. Its people suffer.
> For this reason, there is nothing nearer to hand than poetry for authenticating loss and gain, moving heaven and earth and exciting gods and spirits.[33]

• "The will of Heaven is known as Nature, to follow Nature is known as the Way," and so on, as they say. Thus, Nature must be Heaven, the Way must be the earth. If you frame this in terms of singing, then *shiugen* must be Nature. The frame in which this Nature is made concordant with aural appeal is called *yūgen*. The rank that imparts a deepened melodic excitement to *yūgen* should be called *renbo*. When you augment the singing of *renbo* with a sensibility of ill fatedness, it is known as *aishyau*. If you study each of these to the fullest, arriving at a rank of perfect confidence, then that is what we call mastery in singing, the voice of *rangyoku*. This, in effect, is the Way. This is the measure by which the singing in this vocation attains its consummation.

• The *Great Learning* says, "When the roots are in disorder, there is no ordering of the branches."[34] What is meant by "the myriad" is "the power of the one."[35] The aforementioned *shiugen*, *yūkyoku*, *renbo*, and *aishyau* amount to the power of the confident plenitude of sound in *shiugen*. To sing in each of these styles perfectly is ease and confidence in the fullest degree. A vocal style of surpassing virtuosity is the level at which you are firmly resident in the rank of complete confidence. That all returns to that original sound of ease and confidence is the power of the one. This is because it is an unsurpassed accomplishment in learning the way. When the roots are not in disorder, there is order in the branches. That being the case, it is imperative that you consistently sustain the correct power in training.

33. This classic statement on the relation between poetry and ethics in traditional East Asia comes, as Zeami says, from the Mao preface to the *Classic of Songs*. See Omote, in *ZZ*, pp. 481–82n.120.

34. See *A Course to Attain the Flower*.

35. Literally "ten thousand is the power of one," based on the abbreviated Chinese graph 万 (ten thousand), which is written with the graphs 一 (one) and 力 (power).

• What I mean by the specifications for learning the Way of singing is that the foundation of the singing voice is the proper use of the voice. You are not likely to achieve the greatest outcome in terms of beautiful singing unless you put the voice to good use, gain the experience of a variety of styles of singing, and augment as necessary any deficiency in the voice so that you can attain whatever level of vocalization your mind may intend. That is why we consider the proper use of the voice as the foundation for singing. So you should learn the melody very carefully from your teacher and master it by entering into the model completely. This rank is still the measure of the beginner. After that you should gain an understanding of *wau* and *shu* in the voice, and depending on the word in question, attack those in the *wau* voice that should be attacked in *wau*, attack those in the *shu* voice that should be attacked in *shu*, and make the basis of your vocalization a Double Proficiency in the requisite passages; gradually you will ascend the ladder to achieve a full training as you learn the Way. "Learning the Way" means just this much. Beyond that is a measure of expressiveness that cannot be transmitted to you from some other person.

There is a rationale to explain why one cannot learn this expressiveness. The reason is that this expressiveness we refer to is something that we do not, in fact, have in hand. (This is to remain secret.) If you talk about what we do have in hand, it would be the melody. That being the case, there is no model for expressiveness that we might transmit. What I mean by expressiveness is something that comes into being by itself as the aural Instance of a process in which you have laid the foundation for the singing voice through the proper use of the voice, then thoroughly mastered the melodies, *wau* and *shu*, Double Proficiency, each and every one, finally to settle down firmly into the confidence in singing born of unsurpassed accomplishment in its mastery. This is an acquired virtuosity in singing that is gradually brought together through long training and experience. That is why we speak of melody as being and expressiveness as nothingness. It is in arriving at this rank, gaining fame, grasping the way, and obtaining certification[36] in the lineage of your master that you may at last call yourself a master as well. I'll say it again and again: you must know that expressiveness is not something that we have at hand in learning the Way.

Where, then, can we identify the residence of this expressiveness that is nothingness? Is it perhaps simply a matter of virtuosity in singing? It also can be said that there must be a place where in using the voice one is used by the voice. To use the voice is melody. To be used by the voice is expressiveness. Does the music of expressiveness found here, then, penetrate the mind's ear

36. Zeami uses the term *inka*, which is the formal Zen term for the certification of (lit., "the seal upon") enlightenment. The term is also found in *The Flower in . . . Yet Doubling Back* and twice in the 5:14 letter to Konparu Zenchiku.

in the audience? That audience, after all, may not be composed entirely of virtuoso listeners. It is in that excitement transmitted even to the mind's ear of the women and children in the audience that we actually find expressiveness, isn't it? I imagine we might also call this virtuosity in singing. This is the excitement in singing that comes about somehow beyond both perception and cognition, through the five sounds and the four types of accent.[5] There is much here I don't understand myself.

Notes

1. The word is usually written in *kana* or as 節訛り but here is written with a pun as 節鉛, the second graph meaning (the metal) "lead," lending weight to an untranslated metaphor ("deeply buried"), which in my rendering is "thoroughly integrated."

2. 此条々、已上、是ハ、タヾ詮ズル所、声懸ニアルベキ也. Omote breaks the sentence line after 已上, but I am not persuaded that this is the best parsing and follow Konishi Jin'ichi instead, reading a single sentence through 也 (*Nōgakuron kenkyū* [Tokyo: Hanawa shobō, 1961]). The word 声懸 can be pronounced either *kohagakari* (mod. J. *kowagakari*) or *seiken* and appears as early as *Technical Specifications for Setting a Melody* and *A Collection of Jewels in Effect* (in the former pronunciation) as my "vocal pattern." But there seems to be a qualitative recalibration in Zeami's usage, so that by the time the word appears in *Articles on the Five Sorts of Singing* and thereafter, it indicates not only the character of the voice or vocal pattern but also a high degree of virtuosity in vocal production. Thus near the end of this paragraph and later in this set of notes, I have translated the term as "virtuosity in singing."

3. サテ、其上ニ文ヲナスヲ、曲ト云。The vocabulary chosen by Zeami here complicates understanding. *Kyoku* (曲), in particular, has a range of uses that seem to vary greatly in valence, from a transient vocal embellishment to, as here, the difference between rote competence in rendering a melody and virtuosic expression that, while grounded in the melody, adds something entirely individual and inimitable. Kōsai Tsutomu articulates some of the complexity in *Zoku Zeami shinkō* (Tokyo: Wan'ya shoten, 1962), pp. 113–17. I have relied on his insights regarding Zeami's aural appropriation of Zen vocabulary in translating the previous sentence as well. See also Omote, in *ZZ*, p. 480n.115.

4. 露ヲカナシムヨソヲイ [*sic*], in another manuscript reads 露置キ並ブヨソヲイ (a display of the dew fallen over [the leaves]).

5. 五音四尚, apparently an allograph for 五音四声.

Five Sorts of Singing

五音

In some senses, *Five Sorts of Singing* is an undiscovered gem in the corpus of Zeami's writing. Although it has been treated by scholars as one of the *nōgakuron*, or "discourses on nō," it is actually an anthology of songs, chosen with care and with an eye to diversity and quality. The songs are wonderful. They exemplify the art of song in *sarugaku* typologically, of course, and provide models for the actor's training, in order from *shiugen*, through *yūkyoku*, *renbo*, and *aishyau*, to *rangyoku*. In this way, they supplement Zeami's definitions in *Articles on the Five Sorts of Song.*

The songs are exemplary in another way as well. With characteristic modesty, Zeami claims that he has delineated his "five sorts" only "provisionally" and that there are other types of song and other ways to cut the pie. He nevertheless collects here a group of fascinating and beautiful pieces of rich and sometimes startling diversity. Included are songs from many famous plays, which were as popular as *sarugaku* in Zeami's time as they are as nō today. What he chooses to cite from those plays also is interesting. Zeami seems particularly disposed toward the songs called *sashi* or *sashigoto*, musically straightforward pieces in noncongruent rhythm that often come shortly after the central character in a drama has appeared on stage.

Among these songs are also some truly unusual, even eccentric, pieces. The long quotation from *Arrowroot Trousers* (*Kuzu no hakama*), for example, shows us a piece that seems to be as much *kyōgen* as nō. (Perhaps this is what *sarugaku* was, a dramatic form in which those two arts had not yet separated.) In "Rokudai no utai" (The Song About Rokudai), we also find a piece consciously constructed to illustrate the structural principle *jo-ha-kyū*, yet it is also a fascinating reconsideration and restructuring of a more conventional narrative from *The Tales of the Heike.* There are pieces akin to Buddhist sermons, the substantial excerpts from *Jinen koji* and *Shunnei*, for example, as well as long independent songs that do not hold places in plays but exist more or less as "recital pieces." Two of these, "Going Down the Ocean Road" and "Going Down to the West Country," were written by Tamarin, a *renga* poet and intellectual with connections at the shogunal court. (These two are conspicuous in the collection as unusually long and particularly insistent in punning on place-names.) *Five Sorts of Singing* also contains extensive excerpts from plays that have not remained in the repertory. A couple of these have been lost altogether, except for the few words quoted here; others are extant in manuscript but have long since been abandoned for performance.

In earlier texts in the *Performance Notes*, Zeami had written out passages from some plays. In his texts *Oral Instructions on Singing* and *Articles on the Five Sorts of Song*, for example, he quotes several plays at length, among them, *Tōru* and *Sekidera Komachi*. Here, however, he goes to much greater lengths.

The complete text of *Five Sorts of Song* has been printed in full only twice, once in Nose Asaji's now outdated *Zeami jūrokubushū hyōshaku* in the 1940s and then in Omote Akira's landmark volume *Zeami, Zenchiku*. Even in the latter, though, the text is, sadly, truncated. When Omote found it, it was divided into two parts, the first covering *shiugen*, *yūkyoku*, *renbo*, and *aishyau* and the second part devoted to *rangyoku* and a number of extensive recital pieces. Each of the two parts is represented by three extant manuscripts of varying completeness. None of the extant manuscripts is in Zeami's hand; they all range from the late Muromachi period (early sixteenth century) through the early Edo/Tokugawa period (early seventeenth century). Part I is radically abbreviated in all extant manuscripts and includes only a few words from each of almost all the songs chosen by Zeami. It is clearly a quickly executed copy for an actor who knew the repertory well enough that all he needed for reference was a word or two to bring to memory the entire song—perhaps the entire play—from which it was derived.

The modern reader, however, needs more than this. Luckily, the manuscripts for the second part of *Five Sorts* provide a good model for reconstructing the entire text. In these manuscripts, we find full texts for several *shōdan* from each play listed, and most of these are relatively well annotated musically. Occasionally Zeami breaks the list of songs to explain his reasons for including particular groups of songs in the categories in which we find them. Many of the songs are *kusemai*, which is not surprising given their rhythmic interest and often engaging narrative content.

Both the highly abbreviated nature of the manuscripts of part I of *Five Sorts of Singing* and the existing musical notation, particularly in part II, create significant challenges to translating the text. But they also offer excellent opportunities. On the one hand, the highly abbreviated nature of part I as we have it leaves us with only the sketchiest idea of what *Five Sorts of Singing* really represents. The fact that it gives us, even in its abbreviated form, such a large number of songs grouped into generic categories means that it represents much more than what we actually see on the page. Almost all the songs mentioned in the text can be traced to other texts and filled out on that basis, so as modern readers, we can more fully appreciate Zeami's five genres than we would first believe when looking at part I of Omote's text. To that end, I have traced the texts for all the extant songs in *Five Sorts of Singing* and translated the entire *shōdan* for each. For part II, I have, of course, relied on the

Japanese text as redacted by Omote in *Zeami, Zenchiku*. For part I, I have taken as much text as possible from Omote's text and supplemented it when necessary from other sources. The quotations from *Zeami, Zenchiku* are in roman type, and my supplements are underlined in the original Japanese and italicized in the translation. First I looked at the texts in the two volumes entitled *Yōkyokushū*, edited by Omote Akira and Yokomichi Mario.[1] When I could not find the song in question there, I used *Yōkyoku nihyakugojūban shū*, edited by Nonomura Kaizō and Ōtani Tokuzō.[2] Occasionally I had to look farther afield, in which case I noted the source of my supplementary texts in the endnotes.

The Japanese text for each of the songs that Zeami quotes is on the facing page. For the Japanese, I mainly follow the practices used in *Yōkyokushū* and *Yōkyoku nihyakugojūban shū*. Other sources I cite individually, without trying to make them consistent. This means that some texts use *kyū kanji*, and others use *tōyō kanji*. Both the lineation and the punctuation vary somewhat. I punctuated the Japanese texts following Omote in *Zeami, Zenchiku* and Omote and Yokomichi in *Yōkyokushū*, which means that the punctuation marks in the Japanese text represent musical or prosodic, not necessarily grammatical, divisions. The orthography of the texts also follows the source from which I have taken them and is more or less standard historical orthography (*rekishiteki kanazukai*), although in the second part of *Five Sorts of Singing*, I followed the text in *Zeami, Zenchiku* very closely, so some of the orthography is not standard.[1]

Musical notation for singing in *sarugaku* is hard to find and, when it exists, is very sparse compared with modern nō libretti. But because *Five Sorts of Singing* is one of the most complete sources for such annotation still extant,[2] I have used the musical annotations from the *Five Sorts of Singing* text in *Zeami, Zenchiku* as much as possible. There is some ambiguity in their placement in the Japanese texts because of the horizontal format used here, but I have tried to make them as consistent as possible with their source. In the translations, this ambiguity is exacerbated because, of course, Japanese and English word orders are very different. This presents a problem in that some

1. Omote's text is printed vertically, whereas mine is printed horizontally, which accounts for the discrepancies between the two. The common device used in vertical texts to indicate the repetition of two or more graphs cannot be adequately adapted to horizontal texts, so I have chosen to copy out the repeated text in full. The device used in traditional texts to indicate singing or a change in speaker (〽) does not function quite as well in horizontal texts as vertical texts, but I have used it anyway where Omote uses it in *Zeami, Zenchiku*. Both *Zeami, Zenchiku* and *Yōkyokushū* contain many glosses (*furigana* and *okurigana*) to help reading the *kanji*. I have not included these in the Japanese texts reproduced here.

2. Zeami's holograph manuscripts of eleven plays (one of which is a later copy) also provide relatively extensive musical notation. See Omote Akira and Getsuyōkai, eds., *Zeami jihitsu nōhonshū* (Tokyo: Iwanami shoten, 1997).

of the musical annotations are clearly meant to come at the beginning of a *shōdan*, and others are bound to a specific word or phrase in the text. I have striven for as justifiable as possible a tie between the term in question and the text for which it is intended, but inevitably in some places this is possible only in a general way.

The text contains occasional marginal and interlinear notes, some in black, some in red. It is not clear whether Zeami added these or whether they came later in the textual history. Such notes are in parentheses in the translation, often with footnotes for further detail. Although Omote's text in *Zeami, Zenchiku* cites the original manuscripts, supplemented with *kanji* and *kana* glosses, I have omitted these in the Japanese texts here. I have also omitted Omote's notations regarding the precise manuscripts from which marginal notes and textual variants are taken.

Many of the titles given for these songs are either place-names or personal names, in which case, I usually leave them untranslated. In other cases, I cite the original title, romanized, and add a translation in parentheses.

I

On Singing in Our Vocation: in Yamato and Ōmi, and further, with the melodies of *dengaku*, this . . . should not proceed from. . . . [3] Now in Yamato, although there are many different *sarugaku* performers, it is the melodic style of my late father, Kwanze,[3] which has been taken as the standard for our troupe. In Ōmi, it is the expressiveness of Inuō.[4] As for *dengaku*, Kiami's is best. These great performers have passed away, and now their singing voices remain in the world as the old style, passed from generation to generation. After them, authentic mastery of the art was broken off, and the lineage was severed; in both Ōmi and *dengaku*, the writing of plays was abandoned, while among our troupe, I passed on the tradition, if only for form's sake,[5] by making a record of how it's done and transmitting the three elements of playwriting (Seed, Structure, and Writing), so as to preserve our vocation by training in performance; it is for that reason that our style of singing has spread, so that since the Ōei era, it has carried the day as the finest play in song.[6]

3. That is, Kannami.

4. Orth. Inuwau. See the note in *Three Courses*.

5. *Kata no gotoku*, apparently a remark intended to express Zeami's modesty.

6. Zeami refers to the dominance of Yamato *sarugaku* in the first three decades of the fifteenth century. This may at first seem an overstatement and also seems odd, following the excessive modesty of the previous lines, but it is true that *dengaku* performance had failed to produce heirs once Zōami of the New Troupe (Shinza) had died (his dates are unknown). The popularity of Ōmi *sarugaku* seems to have declined irreversibly after the Inuō Dōami's death in 1413.

In any case, most people have only the slightest knowledge of singing, and no one understands the basic difference between *kusemai* and *tadautai* singing, much less the distinction between the *shiugen* and *bauwoku* vocal styles; therefore I have provisionally divided the art of singing into five different classes: *shiugen*, *yūkyoku*, *renbo*, *aishyau*, and *rangyoku*; these I call the Five Sorts of Singing. You should study them carefully, concentrating intently on the flavor of each of these five sorts of singing as milestones in learning singing.

To that end, I have noted here a number of songs and *kusemai* that have grown familiar to the ear in recent years, including as well a few old pieces by past masters. You should make careful efforts to discriminate among them in training.

SHIUGEN

We call this the sound of complete confidence. Within this plenitude and confidence are songs of passion as well.[4]

Kasugano ni wakana tsumitsutsu yorodzu yo wo
Iwafu kokoro ha kami zo shiruran[7]

Out on the moor of Kasuga,
we pinch off newly sprouted shoots,
intent on celebrating countless happy years for you.
The gods themselves
will know what's in our minds!

Would this be an attitude of confidence and plenitude?

The "finest play in song" (遊曲) is discussed in appendix 3.

7. Priest Sosei, *KKS* 357: "A song written on a screen of the four seasons behind the guest of honor, on the occasion when Naishi-no-kami [i.e., principal lady-in-waiting], Manshi, feted her elder brother, General of the Right Fujiwara Sadakuni, on his fortieth birthday."

伏見

指声夫久方の神代より
天地ひらけし国のはじめ
天のにほこのすぐなれや[5]
名も二柱の神爰に
八島のくにを作をき
すべら世なれや大君の
御影のどけき時とかや、

あほによし、
ならの葉もりの神心、
ならの葉もりの神心、
末暗からぬ都路の、
直なるべきか菅原や、
伏見の里の宮造、
大内山の陰高き、
雲の上なる玉殿の、
月も光りや磨くらん、
月も光りや磨くらん。

FUSHIMI[8] My late father's composition

SASHIGOE From the age of gods, immemorial,
from the genesis of land,
when earth was drawn apart from sky,
—how straight the jeweled spear thrust down from up on high!—
the dual gods were brought to being
and set down here
upon this Country in Eight Islands
this land in the hand of Heaven's Sovereign,
and the Great Lord's august image presides upon our peaceful age,

Rich in blue earth:
Nara, under oak leaves, safe within the mind of god,
Nara, under oak leaves, safe within the mind of god,
the path to the capital, unshaded to its end,
straight on to Fushimi on Sugawara Moor, o, there to raise a palace,
where the silhouette of Mount Ōuchi rises high,
a palace with jeweled halls, nestled in the clouds,
and burnished by the very moonlight,
burnished by the very moonlight.

8. Although apparently originally an independent song, this sequence of *sashi* and *ageuta* is now incorporated into the play *Kinsatsu*.

足引山

指声足引の山下水も絶えず、
浜の真砂の数積もりぬれば、
今は飛鳥川瀬になる恨みも聞えず、
さざれ石の岩ほとなる悦のみぞあるべき、
然ば天に浮かめる浪の一滴の露より起り、
山河草木恵みに富みて、
国土安静の当代なり。

千代木の風も静かにて、
朝暮の雲も収まれり。

上いざここに、
わが代は経なん菅原や、
わが代は経なん菅原や、
伏見の里は久方の、
天照らす日も影広き、
瑞穂の国は豊かにて、
民の心も勇みある、
御代の治めはありがたや、
御代の治めはありがたや。[9]

9. Quoted as well in *Oral Instructions on Singing*, where somewhat more extensive musical notation is found.

Ashibikiyama

SASHIGOE Below the trudging mountains, water runs unendingly,
grains of sand upon the beach, their number piled so high, that
no complaint of shallows in the Asuka River is ever heard,
nothing indeed but the joy of pebbles swelling into boulders:[10]
Just as waves rise to the heavens swollen out of a single drop of dew,
mountains, rivers, grass, and trees are rich with blessings,
this age of ours brings peace and reassurance throughout the realm.

The wind in the millennial pine is calm,
clouds at dusk and dawn are quieted.

Here then,
Will I pass my days, O Sugawara Moor,
Will I pass my days, O Sugawara Moor!
The village of Fushimi lies beneath a wide expanse
of sky, filled with sunlight, under the sway of Amaterasu.
This land of ripened sheaves of grain is rich,
the people's hearts are valiant.
How propitiously peace spreads throughout the realm!
How propitiously peace spreads throughout the realm!

10. The conceit of "pebbles growing into boulders" is old in Japanese poetics, with a famous locus in *KKS* 7:343: *Waga kimi ha chiyo ni yachiyo ni sazareishi no ihaho to narite koke no musu made* (A thousand generations, no, eight thousand generations to you, My Lord, 'til pebbles should to boulders grow, and moss bedeck the top). It envisions the possibility that rocks might grow vegetatively over a very great length of time and thus turns up in wishes for enduring political stability and longevity.

松ガ崎

さし寂寞たる深谷、
重畳たる岩間づたひを . . .

上哥山陰の、
茂みを分る薮里に、
茂みを分る薮里に、
知られぬ梅の匂ひ来て、
あらしぞしるべ松ヶ崎、
千代の声のみのどかにて、
なを十返りの末遠き、
御代の春こそ久しけれ、
御代の春こそ久しけれ。

MATSUGASAKI[11] The composition of Jūrō Motomasa

SASHI[12]Treading a path between the layered crags, stack on stack,
in a gaunt and isolated gorge . . . [remainder abridged].

AGEUTAUnder mountain shadows,
cleaving the way through verdant growth, to a village in the woods,
cleaving the way through verdant growth, to a village in the woods,
I smell the fragrance of an unfamiliar plum.
SHIORU[13]The gale will be my signpost to Pine Point.
Alone at peace, the voice of a thousand ages,
here at last, the end of this tortuous road:
spring goes on and on in this great age,
spring goes on and on in this great age.

11. The play from which these songs are extracted is now lost but also is mentioned in *Conversations on Sarugaku*. See *ZZ*, p. 290.

12. An abbreviation for *sashigoe*, according to Omote, a term in use from the late Muromachi on.

13. *Shioru* (orth., inconsistently, as *shihoru* and *shiworu*). The term is Konparu terminology for a vocal embellishment at a high pitch, which is known in the Kanze line as *kuru*.

淡路

[上]それ[しほる]天地かいびゃくの初めといっぱ、
混沌未分やうやく分れて、
<u>清く明らかなるは天となり</u>、
<u>おもく濁れるは地となれり</u>。. . . [さし・くせ舞]

[上]天下を保ち給ふ事、
すべて[しほる]八十三万、
六千[しほる]七百余歳也、
かゝるめでたき王子たちに、
御代をゆづり[寄]葉の権現と、
あらはれおはしま す、
いざなぎいざなみの御代も、
ただ今の国土なるべし。

AWAJI My late father's composition (a *kusemai*)

[JŌ]Lo, [SHIORU]in the genesis of Heaven and Earth, when they came open
and apart,
the indiscriminate chaos at long last divided, so it is said:
what was clear and bright became Heaven
while Earth emerged from
what was ponderous and dark. . . .
[Remainder abridged, *sashi* and *kusemai*.]

[JŌ]The gods have sustained all under heaven
for some [SHIORU]eight hundred thirty-six thousand,
[SHIORU]seven hundred years, and more.
And in the grant of an auspicious reign
to each of these august Lords,
made manifest as gods on earth, under the daphne's gracious leaves,[14]
the sacred age of Izanami and Izanagi
is truly present here in our land this very day.

(This, even though it is *shiugen*, also has the flavor of both *rangyoku* and *yūkyoku*. Concentrate intently on it.)

14. Actually, *yuzuriha* (*Daphniphyllum macropodum*), an attractive tree whose leaves seem to relinquish places one after the other in an ordered transfer.

富士山

序上抑此富士山と申すは、
月氏七だう第三、
天竺より飛びきたる主声ゆへに、
すなはち新山と云と也。. . .

上御門そののちかぐや姫の、
教へにまかせつつ、
富士の嶺の上にして、
不死の薬を焼き給へば、
煙ははんしほるてんに立のぼりて、
主うんかしほるぎゃくふうに勲じつつ、
日月星宿もすなはち、
あらぬ光をなすとかや、
さて延こそもろこしの方士も、
この山に登り不死薬を、
求め得て帰るなれ、
しほるこれわが朝の名のみかは、
西天唐土扶桑にも、
並ぶ山なしと名を得たる、
富士山のよそおい、
まことに上なかりけり。

FUJISAN[15] ("Mount Fuji"), a *kusemai*

JO, JŌ Now, the mountain we call Fujisan is
a great peak that took flight
from the seven circuits of Gwasshi,
SHU NO KOE which is why it is called "New Mountain."
[Remainder abridged, *sashi* and *kusemai*.]

His Majesty then put his trust
in the instruction of Princess Kaguya
and burned the elixir of immortality
atop the peak of Mount Fuji;
the smoke rose up to the myriad SHIORU heavens,[6]
whence SHU clouds and mists SHIORU blew back to earth,
filled with a heavenly fragrance,
and the sun, moon, and starry constellations
shone, they say, with unexampled brilliance.
And NOBE[16] that is why even wizards of Cathay
climb this mountain in their search
for the elixir of immortality.
SHIORU The mountain itself is unrivaled, then,
not just in our realm
but in India, China, and Japan alike,
and the sight of Mount Fuji,
is a vision truly unsurpassed.

Although the melodic style of this piece is *rangyoku*, its singing shows an appropriate gentleness because the text is *shiugen*. It takes special training to imbue the sound of complete confidence with the savor of *rangyoku*.

In addition, there are the *shiugen* songs of the four seasons.[17]

15. *Fujisan* is a *waki* nō that still is in the repertory of the Konparu and Kongō schools. The parts quoted by Zeami are the *kuri* and the latter part of the *kuse* from the *kuri–sashi–kuse* sequence.

16. According to Omote, this is a "melodic notation relating to rhythm."

17. A collection of some sixteen pieces, arranged in seasonal categories and entitled "*Shiugen* Songs of the Four Seasons," is extant, in the possession of the head of the Kanze school. One of the summer songs in the collection seems to be the subject of a comment in *Conversations on Sarugaku* (*ZZ*, p. 279), and it is widely assumed that the songs Zeami mentions here refer to that collection. See Omote, in *ZZ*, pp. 467–68n.81.

Yūkyoku

This entails a softening of the sound of complete confidence for the sake of beauty, making expressiveness the focus of aural appeal and burying the melody within. It might be called "an expressiveness that cherishes the fragrance of the flower."

Mata ya min Katano no mino no sakuragari
Hana no yuki chiru haru no akebono[18]

Might I once again attend
the royal chase at Katano
hunting for the cherry trees?
A snow of blossoms falls:
the blushing dawn of spring.

This, perhaps, the attitude of *yūkyoku*?
There are to be degrees of depth in *yūkyoku*, too.[19]

18. *SKKS* 114: "Among five verses composed for the house of the Regent Chancellor," Master in the Empress's Household Office, Shunzei. Quoted earlier in *Articles on the Five Sorts of Singing*, also at the subhead for *yūkyoku*.

19. This passage is not included in all manuscripts. The placement of the subhead is based on Omote's restoration of the original order of pages in a secondary manuscript of excerpts from *Five Sorts of Singing*.

吉野山

指声いにしえのかしこき人の遊びけん

上雪とのみ、
誤たれゆく白雲の、
絶えだえかかる山の端の、
上に霞のひま見えて、
ほのぼのと明くる夜の、
金の御岳の春の空。
げにや時も春、
所も花の名にし負ふ、
吉野の山はたぐゐなや、
吉野の山はたぐゐなや。

YOSHINOYAMA[20] With a *kusemai* attached,[21] Motomasa's composition

Bygone majesty would make excursion here . . . [remainder abridged].

Mistaken for snow,
time and time again: white clouds,
time and time again, white clouds
hang here and there upon the mountains' rim,
and above, there, a gap in the haze, where
night is gently giving way to day:
the spring sky over Golden Peak.
The time is spring indeed,
the place is celebrated for cherry blossoms.
There is no peer for Yoshinoyama,
there is no peer for Yoshinoyama.

20. This play, known later as *Yoshinogoto*, is no longer in the repertory. The quotation includes the first line from the *sashi* of the *shite*'s entrance and the subsequent *ageuta*.

21. An interlinear note.

敷島

それ敷島の国つわざは
天の浮橋の下にして、
二柱の神代より、
起り伝はる道とかや。

須磨

[指]是は津の国すまの浦に釣りを垂れ、
焼かぬ間は鹽木を運び、
浮き世を渡る者にて候。
又この須磨の山陰に一木の花の候。
名に負ふ若木の櫻なるべし。
古光源氏の御旧跡も、
この所にてありげに候。

静

[次第]花の跡訪ふ松風は、
花の跡訪ふ松風は、
雪にや静かなるらん。

SHIKISHIMA[22]

Now then, the arts of the land of Shikishima
Find their beginning in the vocation handed down
From the two gods,
At the foot of the floating bridge of heaven . . .

SUMA[23] Note: Genji

SASHI I am *one who makes his weary way through the world*
dangling a fishing line off the coast of Suma in the province of Tsu,
carrying brine-soaked logs, if not burning them.
Now there is a tree in bloom here, sheltered by the Suma coastal range,
It appears to be a certain celebrated "sapling cherry."
This place, it seems, bears some ancient affinity
with Shining Genji of times long passed.

SHIZUKA[24] My late father's composition

SHIDAI The pine-blown wind trails on in the wake of blossoms,
The pine-blown wind trails on in the wake of blossoms,
but so quietly—perhaps due to the snow? . . .
[remainder abridged].

22. "Shikishima" was most likely first an independent song and only later was incorporated into a play originally entitled *Yoshino Saigyō* (orth. *Saigyau*), in which the *waki* was identified as the priest Saigyō. Already in the second half of the fifteenth century, however, Saigyō had been replaced in at least some performances by Ki no Tsurayuki. The play is thus more commonly known simply as *Yoshino*. *Yoshino* was performed into the early Edo/Tokugawa period by the Konparu troupe. See Omote, in *ZZ*, p. 484n.127, and his article on the play, "Zeami saku no *Shikishima* to *Yoshino Saigyō* no yukue," in *Nōgakushi shinkō* (Tokyo: Wan'ya shoten, 1979), vol. 1, pp. 45–73. The song quoted is the *kuri* from a somewhat unorthodox *kuri–sashi–kuse* sequence.

23. The line quoted is from the beginning of the *sashi* following the *shite*'s first entrance in *Suma Genji*. In modern versions of the text, the reference to the province of Tsu is missing.

24. Apart from these lines, the piece is apparently lost.

桜川

これに出でたる物狂の、
故郷は筑紫日向の者、
さも思子を失ひて、
思ひ乱るゝ心筑紫の、
海山越えて箱崎の、
波立ち出でて須磨の浦、
又は駿河の海過ぎて、
常陸とかやまで下り来ぬ、
実にや親子の道ならずは、
はるけき旅を、
如何にせん。

通小町

忝き御譬なれ共、
悉多太子は、
浄飯王の都を出で、檀特山のさがしき道、
菜摘み水汲み薪とりどり、
様々に御身をやつし、
仙人につかへ給ひしぞかし。
況やこれは賎の女の、
摘み慣ひたる根芹若菜、
わが身をだにも知らぬ程、
賎しくかろきこのみなれば、
おもしと持たぬ薪なり。

Sakuragawa[25]

The home of this madwoman come before you
is Hyūga in the Province of Tsukushi,
I've lost my dear baby, you see, and out of mad distraction have I come,
such a crushing sadness in my heart,
Traversing seas and mountain peaks from Hakozaki,
past the coast of Suma where the waves stand high,
and past the Bay of Suruga as well,
all the long way, to this place they call Hitachi,
and whyever—were it not in the search of a mother for her child—
would I embark upon
such a trip as this?

Kayoi Komachi[26]

SASHI The analogy is far too profligate for the likes of me,
but when Prince Siddhārtha
left the capital of King Śuddhodana
and climbed the steep road up Mount Daṇḍaloka,
He plucked wild herbs, drew water, and picked up firewood where he could,
and humbled himself in this way and that,
and gave himself over in service to the holy men there, so they say.
So how hard could it be for someone such as me,
a wench so little noticed she hardly has a name,
to bring along a bit of parsley and some wild herbs,
such as I am used to picking, together with
these few sticks of firewood?

25. The passage quoted is from the *nochijite*'s *sashi*, shortly after her entrance in the last act.

26. The passage quoted is a *sashi* sung by the *tsure* in the first half of the play, before the *rongi*, now performed only in the Konparu, Kongō, and Kita schools.

井筒

さなきだに
物の淋しき秋の夜の、
人目まれなる古寺の、
庭の松風更け過ぎて、
月も傾く軒端の草、
忘れて過ぎし古を、
忍ぶ顔にていつまでか、
待つ事なくてながらへん、
げに何事も思ひ出の、
人には残る世の中かな。

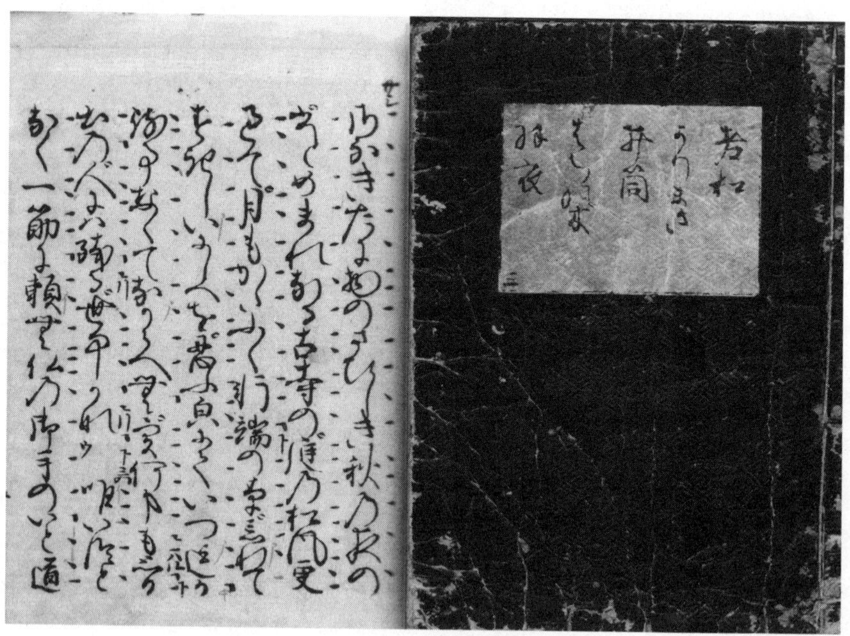

IZUTSU[27]

The autumn night is lonely as it is, *but more so here,*
For no one comes to this old temple garden
where the wind blows through the pines,
deepening the night, as the moon inclines toward slanted eaves
Covered with forgetful-grass: the now forgotten past
comes back in a thicket of recollection;
But how long will I live on in this tangle of longing, with nothing to look forward to?
All things lead to memories, and
memories alone remain to me in this world
lingering on after he is gone.

A Kanze school nō libretto (*utaibon*) for the plays *Oimatsu*, *Yorimasa*, *Izutsu*, *Hachinoki*, and *Hagoromo*. The cover is on the right, and a page from *Izutsu*, beginning with the passage quoted in *Five Sorts of Singing*, is on the left. The colophon mentions the date 1624, but it is printed in a different hand from that of the text itself and may be spurious. Inexpensive *utaibon* like this were printed in great numbers in the Edo/Tokugawa era, attesting to the popularity of nō chanting among a broad swath of Japanese society at the time. The play text and musical notation are printed in black, from woodblocks, but additional musical annotations are added by hand in red. (Photograph courtesy of the translator)

27. The passage quoted is a *sashi* sung by the *shite* shortly after her entrance in the second *dan* of the play.

松風

心づくしの秋風に、
海はすこし遠けれども、
かの行平の中納言、
関吹き越ゆるとながめたまふ、
浦曲の波の夜々は、
実に音近き海人の家、
里離れなる通路の、
月より外は友もなし。
実にや浮世の業ながら、
殊につたなき海人小舟の、
わたりかねたる夢の世に、
住むとや云はんうたかたの、
汐汲車よるべなき、
身は蜑人の袖ともに、
思ひを乾さぬ心かな。

融

陸奥はいづくはあれど塩釜の、
うらみて渡る老が身の、
よるべもいさや定なき、
心も澄める水の面に、
照る月並を数ふれば、
今宵ぞ秋の最中なる、
実にや移せば塩釜の、
月も都の最中かな。

MATSUKAZE[28] My late father's composition

Although, in the heartrending autumn wind
the sea is a little way off, the curve of the shore,
where Middle Counselor Yukihira intoned his verse,
"Blowing 'cross the barrier . . ."
that shore where the waves lap and lap again,
sounds so close from this fisher's hut.
Far from any village, on the path I ply, day by day,
there is no other friend for me but the moon.
Any work in this world is hard, it's true,
but this labor on a flimsy fishing skiff is
barely enough to make my way in this world of dreams.
Can you even call this living, this froth upon the waves,
dragging a salt cart aimlessly along,
No more than a brine-soaked drudge am I,
with no chance of dry-eyed resignation, in my sodden sleeves.

TŌRU[29]

"However it be elsewhere in The Hinterlands,
gazing out here at the coast of Shiogama,"
I am filled with chagrin to be so old.
Where am I to find cover, in this
uncertain state of mind? Yet all the same
that clarity on the face of the water,
where the moon shines, may yet clear my head.
To count from moon to moon, from month to month:
ah, this night is autumn's very heart,
and with the transfer of that place to this,
the moon of Shiogama shines right into the center of Miyako.

28. The passage quoted is a *sashi* sung by the *shite* shortly after her entrance in the second *dan* of the play.

29. The song is, as earlier, a *sashi* sung by the *shite* shortly after (in this case) his entrance in the second *dan* of the play. Both it and a substantial portion of the play following it are quoted in *Oral Instructions on Singing.*

葵の上

一声三の車に法の道、
火宅の門をや出でぬらん。
夕顔の宿の破れ車、
遣るかたなきこそ悲しけれ。

箱崎

箱崎の松の葉守の神風に、
月もさやけき夕かな、
浦波までもうち時雨、
秋ふかげなるけしきかな。[7]

汐汲

指われ汐を弄する身にあらずは

盛久

指なむや大慈大悲の観世音、
さしも草さしも畏き誓の末、
一称一念なほ頼あり、
ましてや多年知遇の御結縁空しからんや、
あら御名残惜しや。

AOI NO UE[30]

ISSEI Riding in three carriages down the road of the True Law,
who will, in the end, pass through the gateway of the burning house?[31]
Abandoned here beside these lodgings covered with moonflowers,
a broken carriage, nothing to be done, how wretched!

HAKOZAKI[32]

ISSEI At Hakozaki the sacred winds rise in the guardian spirit of the pine.
How clear the moon tonight!
The season's showers reach as far as the coastal waves,
the scene bespeaks the advent of late fall.

SHIWOKUMI [SIC] ("Dipping the Brine"), composed by Kia[mi][33]

ISSEI Were I not one who takes delight in the saltwater . . .

MORIHISA[34] Composed by Motomasa

SASHI Glory be to *Kanzeon*[35] of great love and compassion,
bounteous as the grass are the blessings of her holy vow
such that a single prayer, a lone appeal to her name, inspires confidence.
So how could the affinity of long devotion fail to prove true?
Yet all the same, how sad to think of parting!

30. The song is the *shite*'s entry piece.

31. The "burning house" is a celebrated metaphor for the world of delusion in which we live. The Lotus Sutra contains a famous parable about a father who offers his children a choice of three fine carriages, one drawn by a sheep, one by a deer, and one by an ox, in order to trick them into leaving their own burning house.

32. The play is a *waki* nō with a female *shite*. It fell out of the repertory in the early Edo/Tokugawa period. The passage quoted is the *shite*'s *issei* from the second *dan*.

33. This piece has been lost. Kiami was an important *dengaku* actor.

34. The passage quoted is a *sashi* following a brief dialogue at the opening of the play.

35. Kanzeon is another version of the more common Kannon, Japanese for the name of the bodhisattva Avalokisteśvara.

蘇武

それ遠く異朝を引いて見るに、
漢の御門の御時

宇治山

せうわうほうしふわうのせいとく

布留

初深雪布留の高橋見渡せば、
布留の高橋見渡せば、
誓かけてや神の名の、
布留野に立てる、
三輪の神杉と詠みしもその験見えて面白や。
か様にながめせば、
さなきだにさも暮れ易き冬の日の、
けふの細布にあらねども[ざれど]、
われも身のはたばりはなき、
麻衣の営を、
かけ副へて洗はん
営をかけて洗はん。

SOBU[36] ("Su Wu")

Now if we have reference to a faraway foreign court, during the time of the Emperor of Han . . .

UJIYAMA Composed by Kongō[37]

The power of Shōō Hōshūō . . .

FURU[38] ("Falling"), text composed by my late father

"The first deep snow falling more in Takahashi:
gaze out over the moor in Takahashi and there,
at Miwa, stands the sacred cedar of Falling Moor, a god we pledge on, a witness to our vows, how fine!"
That's how they praise it in song
and now, though the winter day, short as it is
is not so thin as the cloth of Kyō,
nor is my lot, quite so thin as that, and yet,
I work away at the hemp weave, stretching it to wash,
work away at my weaving, stretching it to wash.

36. An independent *kusemai* about the Chinese hero Su Wu, with a link to an episode from *The Tales of the Heike.* Both the episode in the *Heike* and the *kusemai* are known today as "Sotoba-nagashi." The passage quoted no longer appears in the text but perhaps is a *kuri* that was originally part of the piece. See Omote's detailed note in *ZZ*, p. 484n.128.

37. The piece has been lost. The composer is most likely Kongō (orth. Kongau) Gonnokami, an otherwise little-known contemporary of Kannami. The line quoted is obscure.

38. A *waki* nō with a female *shite* that was dropped from the repertory in the Muromachi period. The title refers to a place-name, the site of an important Shinto–Buddhist syncretic religious establishment on the Nara plain, where a martial deity with origins in ancient Japanese myth was worshipped. By the middle ages, there was a town nearby. The name Furu is homonymous with the word "to fall," as of rain or snow. The passage quoted is the first choral song, an *ageuta.*

恋の重荷

たれ踏み初めて恋の路、
巷に人の迷ふらん。
名も理や恋重荷、
げに持ちかぬるこの荷かな、
それ及びがたきは高き山、
思ひの深きはわたづみのごとし、
いづれもってたやすからんや、
げに心さへ軽き身の
塵の浮世に長らへて、
由なく物を思ふかな。

班女

げにや祈りつつ
御手洗川に恋せじと、
たれか言ひけん空言や、
されば人心　誠少なき濁り江の、
澄まで頼まば神とても、
受け給はぬは理や、
とにもかくにも人知れぬ、
思ひの露の
置き所、
いづくならまし　身の行くへ。

KOI NO OMONI[39] ("The Heavy Burden of Love")

Who walked first in the ways of love?
A person's prone to go astray at the crossroads there.
It's too true to its name, love. Such a heavy load!
It's really more than I can bear.
More hopeless and remote than a mountaintop,
deep, in its longing, as the blue unfathomable sea,
and what alternatives are left me?
I am a man of little sense and negligible quality,
living out my days in the dust of the world.
What's the point of being so completely lost to love like this?

HANJO[40] ("The Girl Han")

Who was it, after all, who prayed,
"nevermore to fall in love,"
and sealed the pledge at the Mitarashi River—what nonsense—
and with what little truth as there was in his polluted heart!
Put your faith in that silt-clouded pool
and even the gods
will turn your prayers away, and no wonder.
Whether you go this or that way,
there's only tears;
nowhere to settle
this unquiet love,
what's to become of one?

39. The passage follows an adjustment to the *shite*'s costume as he prepares for his futile attempt to hoist a weight, a test that would give him access to the woman he loves. Although no subtitle separates this piece from the previous songs, it does seem to be the first of the pieces in the category *renbo*, and, indeed, the first graph of *renbo* is the same as that pronounced *koi* (orth. *kohi*) in the title *Ko(h)i no omoni*.

40. The passage is from a *sashi* sung by the *shite* near the beginning of the last *dan*, shortly after a *kakeri* dance. The poems quoted in part here and in the passage from *Minazukibarae* later are *KKS* 501: *Kohi seji to / Mitarashigaha ni/ seshi misogi / kami ha ukezu zo / narinikerashi mo* ("Nevermore to fall in love," I swore, and sealed the pledge at the Mitarashi River. It seems the gods refused to hear my prayers).

六月祓

げにや数ならぬ身にもたとへは在原の、
跡は昔に業平の、
この川波に恋せじと、
かけし御祓も大幣の、
ひくてあまたの人心頼むかひなきかねことかな。
とは思へどもわれは又、
うきねに明かす水鳥の、
賀茂の河原に御祓して逢瀬をいざや祈らん。

MINAZUKIBARAE[41] ("Lustrations of the Sixth Month")

Me? I'm no one of account, after all, *and yet there is something*
to that way of putting it, a trace left behind by Narihira,
so pledging to these waves, "Nevermore to fall in love," reaching for and
pulling a hand back
from the streamers tossed onto the waters,—so many other hands were
there beside my own,
how could I expect to take his heart, no matter what he promised?—
I tell myself that much, and yet, let me arise from a fitful sleep
and go to the Kamo River, where the ducks flock on the bank,
and wash away my sins, and pray to meet him once again.

41. The *minazukibarae* (sixth-month lustrations) took place at the end of the sixth month of the lunar year and were intended to clean out the pollution that had accumulated during the first half of the year. Various ceremonies at shrines gave believers opportunities to separate themselves from this pollution, and the lustrations served also as a social event. In this case, a woman has gone mad out of longing for a man from whom she has been separated. At the Kamo River, where she has gone to perform the lustration, she encounters the man. In addition to the poem also quoted in part in *Hanjo*, mentioned in the preceding note, this song quotes, in part, a poem from episode 47 of *The Tales of Ise*: *Ohonusa no hikute amata ni narinureba / omohedo e koso tanomazarikere* (Pulling a hand back from the streamers tossed onto the waters—so many other hands were there beside my own; although I fell in love, how could I hope to take his heart?).

As with *Hanjo*, the passage quoted here is from a *sashi* sung by the *shite*, shortly after a *kakeri* dance in the first half of the play.

花形見

われ應神天皇の尊苗を継ぎながら、
帝位を踏む身にあらざれども、
天照大神の神孫なれば、
毎日に伊勢を拝し奉る、
その神感の至りにや、
群臣の選みに出だされて、
誘はれ行く雲の上、
巡り逢ふべき月影を、
秋の頼みに残すなり、
頼めただ、
袖觸れ馴れし月影の、
暫し雲居に隔てあれともと
書き置き給ふ水茎の、
跡に残るぞ悲しき。

松風

げにや思ひ内にあれば、
色ほかにあらはれさむらふぞや、
わくらはに問ふ人あらばのおん物語り、
あまりに懐かしうさむらひて、
なほ執心の闇浮の涙、
ふたゝび袖を濡らしさむらふ。

HANAGATAMI[42] ("The Flower Basket Keepsake")

"*Although I* stem from the august line *of Heavenly King Ōjin,*
I was not such a person as might expect to step into royal rank,
yet since I claim a lineage back to the Great Goddess Amaterasu,
I have made it my office to pay daily reverence to Ise,
and thus, perhaps, through the blessing of the goddess,
We have been singled out from among the members of the court,
and summoned to lofty eminence beyond the clouds.
The moon will, in its course, come 'round, returning once again
in autumn, shining down upon the ripened grain.
Simply keep your faith
that the moonlight you have come to expect upon your sleeve,
will shine there yet again, even though for a time it may be veiled by clouds."
SAGEUTA *How wretched to be left behind, empty handed,*
with only this, his letter penned with a stalk of wild-ginger!

MATSUKAZE (Final *dan*)[43]

Yes, of course it's true: when there's love within,
then passion finds its way without.
But the way you call that poem of his to mind:
"If one, by chance, should ask of me . . ."—brings memories too dear,
and once again this aching want, these benighted tears
soak through my sleeves.

42. The passage quoted, known as *fumi no dan* (the letter song), follows the brief dialogue that begins the second *dan* of the play. The speaker is the consort of a once-exiled prince who has been recalled to the capital to take the throne. Most of the song is a quotation of his letter to her.

43. The quoted passage has the formal characteristics of a short *sashi* but appears amid a dialogue between the *waki* and the *shite* and *tsure* in the long third *dan* of the play. The quotation is from *KKS* 962, by Ariwara no Narihira: *Wakuraba ni tofu hito araba Suma no Ura ni / moshiho taretsutsu wabu to kotaheyo* (If, by chance, anyone should ask of me, tell them that I languish on the coast of Suma, dripping tears, like salty brine off seaweed).

難波

或は男山の昔を思ひ出でて、
女郎花の一時をくねると言へども、
いひ慰むる言の葉の、
露もたわゝに秋萩の、
元の契りの消え返へり、
つれなかりける命かな、
さればかほどに衰へて、
身を羽束師の森なれども、
言葉の花こそたよりなれ。

錦木

陸奥の信夫もじずり誰ゆゑに、
亂れそめにしわれからと、
藻にすむ蟲の音に泣きて、
いつまで草のいつかさて、
思ひを乾さん衣手の、
森の下露起きもせず、
寐もせで夜半を明かしては
春のながめも如何ならん、
あさましやそも幾程の身にしあれば、
なほ待つ事の有り顔にて、
思はぬ人を思ひ寢の
夢か現か寢てか覚めてか、
是や戀慕の慣ひなる。

NANIWA[44]

Whether given to recall the past when one was, say, "a mountain of a man,"
or finding fault with the brevity of "the maidenflower's little time,"
we find our consolation in the words of poems,
which may bring love back once again,
vulnerable as dewdrops hanging heavy from bush clover:
what a slender and uncertain life I lead!
And here I am, reduced to this, and shamed by what I've come to,
but even in the tangles of Hazukashi Wood,
there's still the flower of words to count on.

NISHIKIGI[45] ("The Staff Wrapped in Brocade")

"Tangled in the fern-print patterns
of Shinobu in The Hinterlands,
my heart is tangled up in longing—who would be the cause?"
It's all down to me. Down in the seagrass, insects chip unceasingly:
so much the longer, then, before these sodden sleeves of mine come dry?
Here I lie, among the dewdrops laid upon the ground, I lay myself down,
can't get up, can't sleep, but lie awake the whole long night,
what of the silly sights of spring!
And what exasperation! How long can someone live with this!
What's the use of waiting as if something were to change?
Falling asleep with thoughts of someone who doesn't think of me,
is this a dream or some reality, am I asleep or wide-awake?
Can this be what it means to be in love?[46]

44. Not from the *waki* nō known by this title today, but from the play known today as *Ashikari*. The passage quoted is a *sashi* from the *kuri–sashi–kuse* sequence late in the play.

45. The song is, like that in the preceding note, a *sashi* sung by the *shite* shortly after his entrance in the second *dan* of the play. The song opens with a quotation of most of *KKS* 14:724: *Michinoku no Shinobu modjizuri tare yuye ni, Midaremu to omofu ware naranaku ni* (Tangled in the fern-print patterns of Shinobu in The Hinterlands, my heart is tangled up in longing—yet I'm not one to lose his/her heart so easily. Who would be the cause?).

46. The word in the text that I have translated here as "be in love" is *renbo*.

王昭君

これはもろこし合甫の里に住まひつかまつる者にて候。
さてもこの所にははくどう王母と申す夫婦の人、
一人の息女を持つ、
それを昭君と名付く、
されば並びなき美人にて候ふほどに、
帝に召されてご寵愛限りなかりしところに、
さる仔細ありて故国の夷におくられ給ひて候、
夫婦の嘆きただ世の常ならず、
近所のことにて候ふほどに立ち越え訪はばやと思ひ候。

盲打ち

くどき梓の弓の

松浦

生国は筑紫肥前の者、
在所は松浦わざと名字をば申さぬなり。
或人の妻にて候ひしが、
夫は讒臣の申し事により、
無實の科を蒙り、
都へ上り給ひしが、
かつて音信聞かざれば、
死生をだにも辨へず。[8]

Ōshōkun ("Wang Zhaojun"), composed by Konparu[47]

I before you *am a person who lives* in the village of Hefu in China.
Now in this place, live a man and wife, Baidao and Wangmu, by name.
They have a daughter.
They named her Zhaojun and
she is prettier than anyone else, and for that, she was summoned by the emperor,
and enjoyed his boundless favor, but because of certain circumstances,
she has been sent off to the barbarians in their alien land.
The grief that this has caused the man and wife is far beyond the usual,
so since I am a neighbor to them, I am going off to see them to offer my condolences.

Mekurauchi[48] ("Beating the Blind Man"), composed by my late father

KUDOKI The catalpa bow's . . .

Matsura[49] Composed by Fukurai[50]

By birth *I am* from Hizen in the province of Tsukushi,
now I live in Matsura. I have my reasons for not telling you my name.
I was the wife of a certain someone, but
because of the accusations of a slanderer, my husband
though innocent, was charged with a crime,
and he has gone up to the capital.
I haven't had a word about him ever since;
I don't even know if he's dead or alive.

47. *Ōshōkun* (orth. *Wauseukun)* is known in the modern repertory as *Shōkun*. The passage quoted is the *waki*'s self-introduction at the beginning of the play. "Konparu" is Konparu Gonnokami, Zenchiku's grandfather.

48. The play has been lost.

49. The piece is apparently the same as an independent *kusemai* today known as *Matsura monogurui*. The passage quoted is from the beginning of the piece. The text here is from Kanze Sakon, ed., *Kanzeryū yōkyoku zoku hyakubanshū*, Taiseiban ed. (Tokyo: Hinoki shoten, 1973), pp. 1248–49.

50. Apparently an actor of Echizen *sarugaku* but otherwise little known.

哀傷

一生は風の前の雲

江口遊女

それ十二因縁の流転は車の庭に廻るがごとく、
鳥の林に遊ぶに似たり、
前生また前生、
かつて生々の前を知らず、
来世なほ来世、
さらに世々の終りを辨ふることなし。

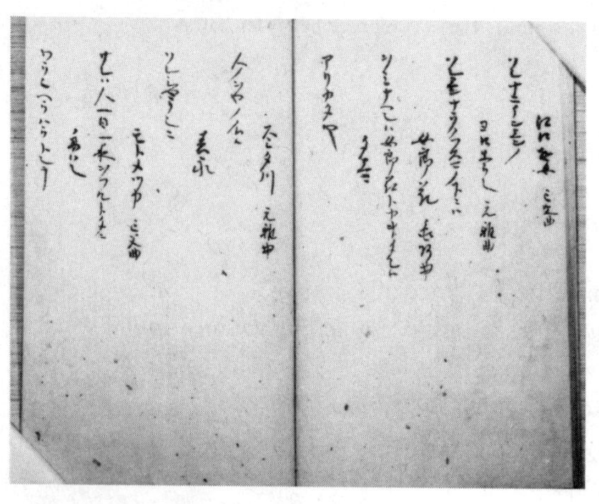

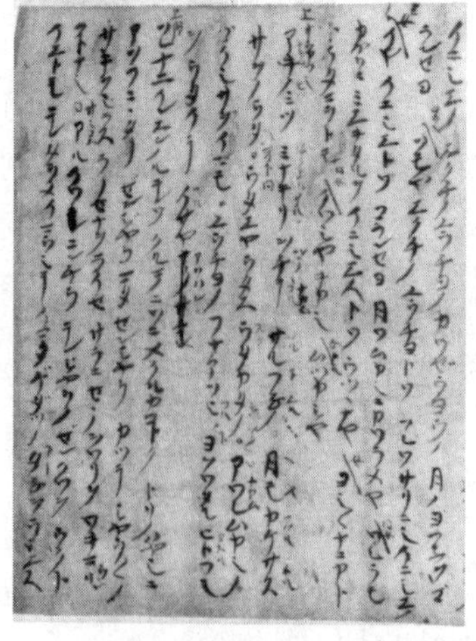

AISHYAU[51]

An entire lifetime, as clouds before the wind, . . .

EGUCHI NO YŪJO ("The Party Girl of Eguchi"), composed by my late father[52]

Turning, then, through twelve links of cause and consequence *is like*
a cartwheel revolving in the yard,
or the frolicking of birds in the woods.
Before your last life there were yet other earlier ones,
and you cannot know what came before these lives upon lives in your past;
and so too, after the next world there will be yet another as well,
there is no way to tell the end of worlds on worlds.

An early text of *Five Sorts of Singing*, part I. This manuscript shows the highly abbreviated form in which this text is typically transmitted. The plays it lists by category are identified only by title and a very brief passage from one of the songs in the play. Here is a listing of eight plays, beginning with *The Playgirl of Eguchi*, at the right, and extending through *Funabashi*, at the left. The passage from *Eguchi* reads *sore jūni in'yen no* (then, . . . twelve links of cause and consequence). The tags from the plays are written mostly in *katakana*. The text dates to the late Muromachi period and, although unsigned, has been determined to be in the hand of Kanze Sōsetsu, seventh head of the Kanze line and an important collator and forger of nō texts. (Photograph from the collection of Kanze Bunko Foundation)

The text of *Eguchi* in Zeami's autograph manuscript of 1424. The passage quoted briefly in the preceding figure appears here as well, beginning at the top of the fifth line from the left. The text is written almost entirely in *katakana*, apparently to prevent actors from using regional dialects. The musical notation in this manuscript, although hardly extensive, is the most detailed of all of Zeami's autograph play scripts. Some of this annotation can be seen, for example, among the small graphs in the top margin. Besides its quotation of a *kusemai* attributed to Kannami, the text reveals numerous corrections. (Photograph courtesy of Hōzanji temple, Ikoma, and the library of Nara joshi daigaku)

51. An independent song, apparently a *kusemai*, part of which was later incorporated into the play *Shōki* (orth. *Shyauki*). A second line was also quoted in *Articles on the Five Sorts of Singing*. The entire *shodan* is quoted there.

52. The play is now known simply as *Eguchi*, and a manuscript in Zeami's hand exists. The passage quoted is from the *kuri* preceding the *kuse*. As the text records, the *kusemai* sequence was presumably composed by Kannami, but it seems likely that Zeami wrote the rest of the play.

弱法師

それ鴛鴦の衾の下には、
立ち去る思を悲み、
比目の枕の上には、
波を隔つる愁あり、
いはんや心あり顔なる、
人間有為の身となりて、
憂き年月の流れては、
妹背の山の中に落つる、
吉野の川のよしや世とも
思ひも捨てぬ心かな。
恨めしや前世に誰をか厭ひけん、
今又人の讒言により、
不孝の罪に沈むゆゑ、
思の涙かき曇り、
盲目とさへなり果てゝ、
生をも変へぬこの世より、
中有の闇に迷ふなり。

YOROBŌSHI[53] ("The Tottering Priest"), composed by Motomasa

Now, if even mandarin ducks, sheltering under a coverlet,
hate the thought that they should ever part,
and flounders pillowed together
begrudge such waves as might wash in, between them,
how much more will a person,
cognizant of actions and consequences,
resent a separation dragging on through dreary months and years?
"In Yoshino, if the course of love
'twixt Maiden Hill and Lad's Hill
run with tears,
then let it be,
the world is as it is."[54]
Yet in my heart I cannot find such resignation,
—I hate it!—
Whom did I offend in a previous life
to deserve this now! Whose slander
now precipitates the sinful dispossession
I sink into, my vision so clouded with tears
that I have in fact, in the end, gone blind,
and while still alive, wander lost among the shades.

53. The title is now read *Yoroboshi*, without the macron on the "o." The passage quoted is from a *sashi* in the second *dan*. As is common in this section of *Five Sorts of Singing*, only the first line of the song is quoted. I have filled in the remainder of the *sashi* on the basis of Zeami's holograph manuscript of the play. See Omote Akira and Getsuyōkai, eds., *Zeami jihitsu nōhonshū* (Tokyo: Iwanami shoten, 1977), vol. 2 (*kōtei hen*), pp. 222–23. Zeami's orthography is nonstandard, differing from both modern Japanese spelling and traditional standard spelling (*teika kanazukai*). Another long quotation from *Yorobōshi* can be found in *Five Sorts of Singing*, part II.

54. *KKS* 828, The full poem contains a very slight difference in the last line (which can hardly be reflected in the translation): *Nagarete ha, Imose no yama no naka ni otsuru, / Yoshino no kaha no yoshi ya yononaka*. Part of the meaning of the poem depends on the homophones Yoshino (a placename), *yoshi ya* (let it be), and *yo no naka* (affairs of the world), which do not resonate in the translation.

女郎花

おみなへしは女郎花と書きたれば

当麻

ありがたや諸仏の誓様々なれども、
わきて超世の悲願とて、
迷の中にも殊になほ、
五つの雲は晴れやらぬ、
雨夜の月の影をだに、
知らぬ心の行方をや西へとばかり頼むらん、
実にや頼めば近き道を、
何遥々と、
思ふらん。

OMINAESHI[55] Composed by Kia

One writes the word for the flower pink with graphs reading "Lady Flower" . . .

TAEMA[56]

What a blessing! *Buddha's vows are of all sorts,*
but His pledge of compassion transcends all the rest—
especially for those whose hearts
cannot discern the moon through the rainy night and the stubborn fivefold clouds—
that pledge of compassion,
is it just a matter of relying on the West as destination?
Truly, if you have faith, the road is short,
why would someone consider the aim remote?

---

55. Orth. *Ominaheshi*. This apparently was an independent song to be distinguished from the play in the modern repertory entitled *Ominameshi*, whose title is written with the same graphs. The passage in question comes from a part of the piece that is no longer extant. "Kia" is the celebrated *dengaku* actor Kiami. "Lady" here may be a euphemism for "prostitute." The word in question, *djorau* (mod. J. *jorō*), earlier had been a term for a high-ranking lady, but by the Edo/Tokugawa period, it had become a synonym for *yūjo* (lit., "playgirl").

56. The passage intended is probably the *sashi* of the second *dan*, although the words quoted also occur in an *issei* in the last *dan*: ありがたや、尽虚空界の荘厳は、眼は雲路にかかやき、轉妙法輪の音聲は、聴寶刹の耳に充てり (What a blessing! *In the brilliance of the world of ultimate emptiness, sight is dazzled blind in its path through the clouds. Voices singing as the wondrous wheel of the Law is turned fill the ears throughout the cosmos*). Another extensive quotation from *Taema* can be found in *Five Sorts of Singing*, part II.

隅田川

げにや人の親の心は闇にあらねども、
子を思ふ道に迷ふとは、
今こそ思ひ白雪の、
道行き人に言傳てゝ、
行くへをなにと尋ぬらん。

SUMIDAGAWA[57] Composed by Motomasa

It's true: "a parent's heart *is no deep darkness, yet*
we go astray in love for children," *as they say;*
that, I've come to know all too well now,
can I get a message through somehow to someone on this snowy road,
so that, some way or other, I can find out what's happened to my boy?

57. The passage quoted is from the *sashi* of the second *dan*.

春栄

それ生死に流転して、
人間界に生るれば、
八つの苦み離れず、
過去因果経を惟んみよ、
殺の報殺の縁、
譬へば車輪のごとし、
われ人を失へば、
かれまたわれを害す、
世々生涯、
苦しみの海に浮き沈みて、
み法の舟橋を、
渡りもせぬぞ悲しき。
ことさらこの国は、
神国といひながら、
または仏法流布の時、
教の法も盛んなり、
ことに所は東方、
仏法東漸にあり、
有明の月の、
わづかなる人界、
急いで来迎の夜念仏、
聲清光に弥陀の国の、
涼しき道ならば、
唯心の浄土なるべし。
所を思ふも頼もしや、
こゝは東路の、
故郷を去つて伊豆の国府、
南無や三島の明神、
本地大通智勝仏、
過去塵點のごとくにて、
黄泉中有の旅の空、
長闇冥の巷までも、
われらを照し給へと、
深くぞ祈誓申しける、
雪の古枝の枯れてだに、
ふたたび花や咲きぬらん。

SHUNNEI[58]

When, *while circling* through life and death,
we are born into the human sphere,
there is no escaping eight forms of suffering—
behold the Sutra of Past Cause and Consequence:
retribution for killing is entanglement in killing,
the one entraining the other as the turning of a wheel.
When I bring loss upon someone,
that person returns the injury to me,
through generations, life to life,
tossed up and down in a sea of suffering;
what wretchedness in failing to cross over
the floating bridge of Dharma!
How much more so, given that this is both a sacred land
and a place where, once the Buddha's Law spread forth,
the teaching of Dharma grew and prospered.
For this is the East and
the Buddha's Law progresses eastward as it spreads.
Rather, then, than reckoning on the human sphere,
pale like the dawn moon's fading disk,
quickly turn your mind to Buddha's advent,
chanting through the night,
with voices clear and full, for the land of Amida;
since the path to the Pure Land Paradise is cool and refreshing
there within your heart.
This eastern land gives us hope,
we have left our homes behind
to travel eastward to the provincial center of Izu,
This is Mishima, sacred to the Shining God,[59] *praise be,*
avatar of the Buddha Mahābhijñānābhibhū,[60]
shine down your light upon us
from the past, unthinkably remote,
all the way to this station of our tribulations,
this infernal journey in limbo.
Humbly and deeply, we beseech You, so,
for even branches withered under frigid snow
may once again sprout blossoms in the spring.

58. The passage quoted is the *kuse*.

59. The deity's formal name is Kotoshironushi no kami.

60. Daitsūchishō (Victorious Through Great Penetrating Knowledge), from the Lotus Sutra, "Parable of the Conjured City." This also is mentioned in "Going Down the Ocean Road."

求塚

されば人、
一日一夜をふるとだに、
一日一夜をふるとだに、八億四千の思ひあり。
況んや我等は、
去りにし跡も久方の、
天の帝のおん代より、
今は後の堀川の、
御宇にあはゞわれらも、
二たび世にも帰れかし。
いつまで草の蔭、
苔の下には埋もれん、
さらば埋もれも果てずして、
苦しみは身をやく、
火宅の住みかご覧ぜよ、
火宅の住みかご覧ぜよ。

舟橋

往事渺 茫としてなに事も、
身残す夢の浮橋に、
猶数添へて舟競ふ、
堀江の川の水 際に、
寄るべ定めぬ徒波の、
憂き世に 帰る六つの道、
逃れかねたる心かな。

MOTOMEZUKA[61] Composed by my late father

. . . but be that as it may, a person
living through but one day and night,
living through but one day and night, *has some eighty million and four thousand errant thoughts.*
And how much more someone like me,
since that time long ago when I left the world—
as remote as the celestial emperor of that age,—
'til now, happening by chance into this latter age of Sovereign Horikawa,
how I wish to come back to the world once more!
How much longer must I stay buried beneath the moss,
and at that, but half buried . . .
the suffering scorches my very being,
Look: this is what it is to live in "the burning house,"
Look: this is what it is to live in "the burning house."[62]

FUNABASHI[63]

Affairs from the past are shrouded and remote,
all just a dream, spirited across over a floating bridge,
and yet, along the water's edge,
by the canal where they still run races, now more than ever,
back we come again, aimless as the lapping waves,
our minds unable in the end to spurn
the six benighted ways.[64]

61. Orth. *Motomedzuka.* The passage quoted is a choral *ageuta* from the last *dan.*

62. "The burning house" refers to a parable in Lotus Sutra, mentioned earlier.

63. The passage quoted is the *shite*'s *sashi* from the second *dan.*

64. There are at least three citations from earlier poetry. The first two lines come most proximately from Bo Jüyi, *Wakan rōeishū* 743, under the category "Remembering the Past." The next lines rely on Ōtomo Yakamochi, *MYS* 20:4462: *Funagihofu Horie no kaha no minagiha ni / kiwitsutsu naku ha miyakodori kamo* (Along the water's edge on the Horie River, where boats run races, birds alight and squawk. Are these, then, "capital birds"?). Finally, the mention of *yume no ukuhashi* alludes to Teika's celebrated poem from *SKKS* 1:38: *Haru no yo no yume no ukihashi todahe shite / Mine ni wakaruru yokogumo no sora* (The floating bridge of a spring night's dreams is snapped away, and there's the sky: a streak of cloud leaves the mountain peak behind).

The six benighted ways are the *rokudō*, the six realms of unenlightened existence: those of heavenly beings, asuras, humans, animals, hungry ghosts, and existence in hell.

禿高野

花は散って根にあれど、
また来む春も頼み有り、
月は出でて入るなれど、
夜つきせずは見るべし。
夫人間の別れはまたいつのよにか逢ふべき、
かかる憂き世に徒し身の、
なに中々に生まれ来て、
さのみにものや思ふらん。

橋立

それ親の子を思うこと、
人倫に限らず、
焼け野の雉夜の鶴、
梁の燕に至るまで、
子ゆゑ命を捨つるなり。

KABURO KŌYA[65] Composed by Kia

The blossoms have scattered and lie among the roots,
but spring will come again, we can count on that.
The moon may rise and set, but we go on admiring it,
as long as night falls at the close of day.
But when people are parted, then when are they to meet again?
Why are we, in this flimsy way,
born into a world of grief and weariness?—
that commands my thoughts.

HASHIDATE[66]

Now, the love of parents for their children
reaches beyond the limits of humankind.
The pheasant overtaken in a field by fire, the crane deep in the night,
even the swallow in the rafters, would each, so they say,
give up its life to save its brood.

65. Orth. *Kaburo Kauya*. It is also known as *Karukaya*, which is no longer performed. It recounts the tale of a child, Matsuwaka, and his mother, who set off from northern Kyushu to visit her husband and his father, Karukaya, who had earlier abandoned them and entered a monastery on Mount Kōya. Before they reunite, the mother becomes sick and dies. The boy eventually meets his father and takes orders himself, and the two of them pray for the repose of the spirit of the wife and mother. The passage quoted is the *sashi* preceding the *kuse*, uncharacteristically close to the end of the play. The full play can be found in Haga Yaichi and Sasaki Nobutsuna, eds., *Kōchū yōkyoku sōsho* (Tokyo: Hakubunkan, 1914), vol. 1, pp. 525–31.

66. Also known as *Tango monogurui*. The passage quoted is the *kuri* in the *kuse* section.

鵺

[指]悲しきかなや身は籠鳥、
心を知れば盲亀の浮木、
ただ闇中に埋もれ木の、
さらば埋もれも果てずして、
亡心なにに残るらん。

鵜飼

げにや世の中のうしと思はゞ捨つべきに、
その心さらにに夏川に、
鵜使ふことの面白さに、
殺生をするはかなさよ。
傳へ聞く遊子伯陽は、
月に誓つて契りをなし、
夫婦ふたつの星となる、
今の雲の上人も、
月なき夜半をこそ悲み給ふに、
われはそれには引きかへて、
月の夜頃を厭ひ、
闇になる夜を喜べば、
鵜舟にともす篝火の
消えて闇こそ悲しけれ。

Nue[67]

SASHI How utterly wretched, *I am a caged bird!*
Would you know my frame of mind? I am a tortoise,
blind, and groping for a foothold on any scrap of flotsam,
or I am bogwood buried in the dark, but only half-buried.[68]
Why is my ruined mind left behind?

Ukai[69]

Once one truly *apprehends the wearying vanity of* the things
of this world, *then will they be abandoned, . . .*
but for one who is not of that mind,
there's nothing like cormorant fishing from the riverside in summer.
But such a shabbiness in taking life like that . . .
As I am told, the lovers Youzi and Baiyang
made their pledge to the moon, and it came true,
So they were wedded together in the sky as double stars,
And that would be why courtiers, lofty as the clouds, begrudge a moonless night.
But for my part, I shun those very nights when the moon is shining
and take my pleasure in the darkest nights,
when I can fish from my cormorant boat to the firepot's blaze.
Only when that fire's gone out do I find myself wretched in the dark.

67. The passage quoted is the *sashi* from the *shite*'s first entrance.

68. The blind tortoise groping for a foothold on a scrap of flotsam is a metaphor for the remoteness of encountering a buddha, in various Buddhist texts, among them, the Nirvana Sutra and the Lotus Sutra 27: "The former affairs of the wonderfully appareled king."

69. The passage quoted is the *sashi* from the *shite*'s first entrance.

千寿

さても本三位の中将

忠度

はづかしや亡き跡に、
姿を返す夢のうち、
覚むる心はいにしへに、
迷ふ雨夜の物語り、
申さんために魂魄に、
移り変りて来たりたり。

高野

聞きしに越えて貴く有りがたかりし霊地かな。
真如平等の松風は、
八葉のみねに吹きわたり、
法性随縁の月の光は、
八つの谷に曇らず。[70]

70. A slightly different version of the song can be found in a manuscript signed by Yamashina Yauemon, in Tanaka Makoto, ed., *Mikan yōkyokushū* (Tokyo: Koten bunko, 1963–1980), vol. 5, p. 72.

SENJU[9]

Now then, the Middle Captain of full third rank . . .

TADANORI[71]

How it shames me
to return to this, my former shape,
now but in a dream:
My mind, aroused, errs, befuddled in the past.
I appear to tell a rainy night's tale,
taking on this ghostly form, I come.

KŌYA[72] Composed by my late father

This is a sacred place more *precious and blessed* than I had heard.
The wind in the pines
blows over Eight Peaks with the full equality of tathatā,[73]
the light of the moon
is cloudless over Eight Valleys,
Dharma nature's accord with each affinity of being.

71. The passage quoted is from the *shite*'s *sashi* as he enters in the latter half of the play.

72. An independent piece for singing consisting of a *sashi*, a *sageuta*, and an *ageuta*, no longer performed. It is now known as "Kōya no maki." I have supplemented the single phrase quoted in *ZZ* with the rest of the *sashi* from Tanaka, ed., *Mikan yōkyokushū*, vol. 5, p. 70. There are close similarities to part of the excerpt from *Kōya kusemai*, quoted later, but this is still a different piece from that. The Eight Peaks are eight prominent mountain peaks in the overall topography of Mount Kōya. In general, the site is spoken of as also having either nine or ten valleys, but in this case, and in the chapter of *The Tales of the Heike*, book 10, also known as "Kōya no maki," eight valleys are mentioned. It is unclear where this designation comes from, apart from the parallelism with the Eight Peaks.

73. Sanskrit for "thus-ness," a heuristic term for absolute reality.

II

• *Rangyoku*

In this, there is a special kind of melodic appeal. It entails an essential mastery on whose basis you can, because of your transcendent virtuosity, sing anything. Such voices as may accompany you should sing, for the most part, what's written. Truth be told, though, this is the singing of a soloist. That is because at such a level you might sing anything at all in accordance with your spontaneous response to the occasion. This is a performance rationale that departs from the other four sorts of singing, *shiugen*, *yūkyoku*, *renbo*, and *aishyau*, even as it comprehends them. There are oral instructions (a deep secret). This is already the rank of a master lineage. (The *Analects* says, "How masterful the practice of virtue in the Middle Way!")[10]

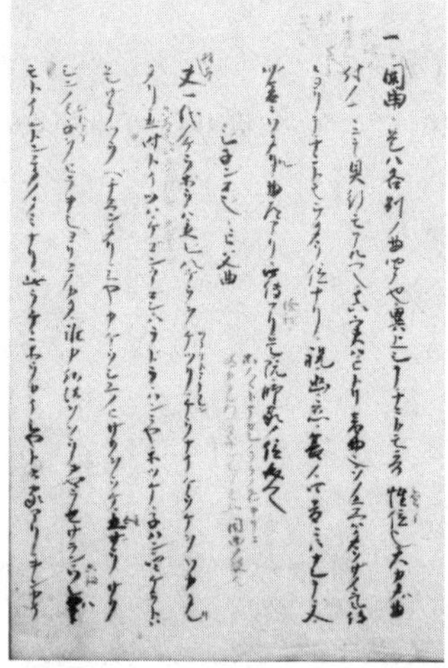

An early text of *Five Sorts of Singing*, part II. Unlike all other manuscripts of this text (and all the manuscripts of *Five Sorts of Singing*, part I), this manuscript includes full texts for most of the songs it quotes. It is of particular interest in that it contains Zeami's remarks on, and songs for, the important category *rangyoku*. The paragraph beginning on the right side of the leaf describes *rangyoku* and is followed by the first part of Zeami's quotation from a long passage from the play *Jinen koji*. Like Zeami's autograph play scripts, this text is written primarily in *katakana* and contains some musical notations. The text dates to the late Muromachi period and appears to be in the hand of Kanze Sōsetsu. (Photograph from the collection of Kanze Bunko Fondation)

Honobono to Akashi no ura no asagiri ni
shimagakureyuku fune wo shi zo omofu[74]

My longing trails
after a boat that hides,
fading away
behind the isles
in the morning mist on Akashi coast.

(This, perhaps, the attitude of *rangyoku*.)

74. *KKS* 9:409, probably anonymous, although sometimes attributed to Kakinomoto Hitomaro.

自然居士

指声夫一代の教法は、
五時八教をつくり、
教内教外を分かたれたり、
（只声也。此声位無上大事有）
五時といっぱ華厳阿含方等般若法華涅槃、
四教とは是蔵通別円たり、
釈迦教主の秘蔵を受け、
主五ざうさうじんのむねを開きし下よりこのかた、
誰か仏法を崇教せざらん。
只詞われはもと隠遁国の民なり、
此内に法界舎と云家あり、
禁戒を垣として悪しき友をば近づけず、
さればかく身を捨て果てば、
静なるを友とし、
貧を楽とすべき、
隠遁のすみか、
禅観の窓こそ望む所なれども。
下ただし山に入てもなを心の水のみなかみは求めがたう、
市にまじはりても、
をなじ流れの水ならば真如の月などか澄まざらん。

JINEN KOJI Composed by my late father[75]

SASHIGOE Lo, the Dharma teachings of the first generation
specified Five Ages and Eight Doctrines,
dividing Scriptures from Apocrypha.

(The next lines are spoken. Unsurpassed demands are made on the caliber of voice here.)

Those Five Ages are the Kegon, the Agon, the Hōdō, the Hannya, and the Hokke-Nehan.[76]
The Four Teachings are the Lesser Vehicle, the Common Teaching, the Discriminate Teaching, and the Well-Rounded Doctrine.
Ever since the Dharma Master Śākyamuni received the Secret Treasury,
SHU and made manifest the essence of the GE Five Repositories of the Sacred Canon[11]
who could fail to revere the Buddha-Dharma?

TADAKOKOBA As for me, I am one of the people of the Land of Renunciation.
In that land there is a house called Dharma-world Lodge.
The monastic code gives us our sanctuary there, and keeps bad friends away,
And once we have abandoned our positions in the world, we find a good friend in quietness.
Our sole desire was a hermitage where we could find the joy of poverty, a window onto meditation and insight,
but you cannot reach the headwaters of clarity of mind merely by GE withdrawing into the mountains, and even in commerce with the marketplace,
as long you draw on that same clarity in its source,
how could the moon of Genuine Reality fail to shine down clearly?

75. Although the play *Jinen koji* remains in the repertory, this passage is no longer performed. It apparently is from the beginning of the play, when the eponymous Jinen is delivering a sermon.

76. In Mahāyāna scholasticism, the five ages are divisions in the chronology of Śākyamuni's teachings that are believed also to reflect stages in sophistication and precision vis-à-vis Buddhist truth.

[只詞]かやうに思ひしより自然心得、
今は山深きすみかを出で、
かかる物狂となり。
[哥]花洛の塵にまじわり、
花洛の塵にまじわり、
[しをる]かくかの[寄]波に裳裾をぬらし、
万民にを[よする]をもてをさらすも恨みならず、
ほうのため[懸切]なれば身を捨つる。
[延]ふく風の寒き山とて入月に、
指を[しほる]さしてもとめ[よする]がたきは、
つながぬ月日なりけりや、
つながぬ月日なりけりや。

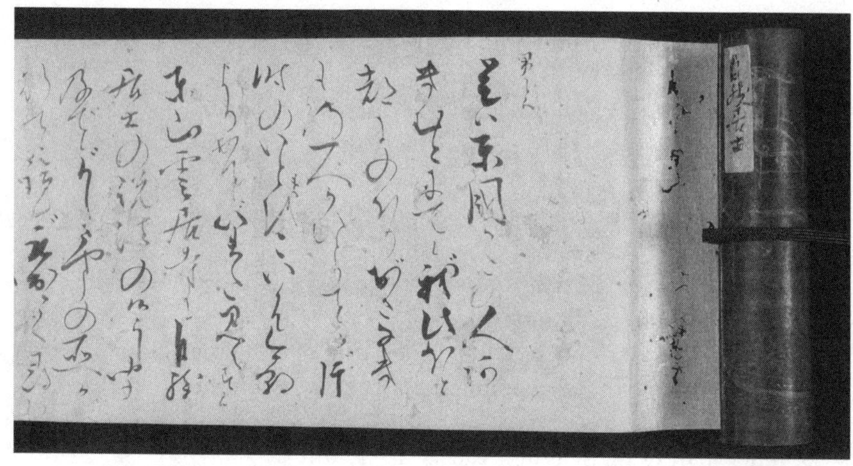

TADAKOKOBA Having come to consider matters thus, I determined of my own accord to leave behind my hermitage in the mountain fastness, and here I am before you, in all my madness.

UTA In mingling with the dust of the flowered capital,
In mingling with the dust of the flowered capital,
SHIORU see how my hem is wet with YOSURU waves like this.
I find no dislike in showing YOSURU my face to anyone and everyone,
and if it's KAKEKIRI for the Dharma, I will gladly sacrifice myself.
[NOBE] The wind's grown cold on the mountainside, time to go inside,
the moon itself takes refuge on the horizon—
SHIORU point at it all you like, YOSURU you cannot hold it back
nor can you tether the passing days and months,
nor can you tether the passing days and months.

A text for the play *Jinen koji* in hand-scroll format. With the large-scale development of woodblock printing in the seventeenth century, nō libretti were widely printed, in both large and inexpensive editions and beautiful, luxury versions such as this one. Earlier, they sometimes had been written in a scroll format like this, particularly for the Konparu troupe. This text is in the hand of Konparu Zenpō (1454–1532), Zenchiku's grandson. The portion in the photograph is delivered in recitative-like *kotoba* form and contains no musical notation. Later in the text, where the chant turns to song, musical annotation is included. (Photograph courtesy of the Noh Theater Research Institute, Hōsei University)

葛の袴

指声神勅にしたがいて知顕集を開けば、
なになにかの内大臣経信の卿、
過ぎにし九月十三日に、
住吉に詣で候。
下伊勢物語の不審を教えて賜べと志したまいしに、
今日は名におう秋の二夜なれば、
海の面漫々と明らかにして、
松の風磯辺の波を語らうなれば、
心空にあこがれて。

下哥四所明神を巡礼し、
釣殿に出て、
月を眺むる所に、
ここに怪しかる老翁、
忽然と出できたり。
その姿を見るに、
霜雪よするかしらに重なて、
鬢髪に黒き筋なし、
波浪額にたたんで、
面貌しきりに皺めり、
高眶とまかぶら高に、
醜陋にしてみにくく、

KUZU NO HAKAMA[77]

("Arrowroot Trousers"), composed by my late father; Sogan wrote the lyrics.[78]

SASHIGOE When, in accord with divine command, I opened *The Collection of Knowledge Manifest,*
I learned that Lord Tsunenobu, Palace Minister of Something or Other
had made a visit to the Sumiyoshi Shrine
on the thirteenth day of the ninth month, just passed,
hoping to have satisfied certain doubts he harbored
GE regarding *The Tales of Ise.*
Now today, as it happens, is the celebrated Second Night of Autumn,
the brilliant surface of the sea stretches off without end,
a wind in the pines converses with the waves at shore
and my mind goes wandering aloft.

SAGEUTA I had gone to pray at the Shrine of the Four Bright Gods,[79]
and I came to a pondside pavilion
and gazed out at the moon,
when all at once, a strange and ancient gentleman appeared.
To look at him,
one saw a YOSURU head piled with frost and snow,
not a single black hair to be seen,
his forehead was rippled with the waves of old age,
his visage wreathed in wrinkles,
he was alti-palpebraeceous (which is to say, with flaccid lids lying loose over his shrunken eyes),
he was impulchritudinous (in other words, homely and unbeautiful),[80]

77. Apart from the text quoted here, the play has been lost. It is probably the same play as that known by the title *Sumiyoshi no sengū no nō*, in *Conversations on Sarugaku*, where Kannami's unparalleled excellence in the central role is discussed. See *ZZ*, pp. 264–65

78. The last phrase is ambiguous but does appear to be the name of a person rather than a comment (as it has sometimes been read), meaning "only the part recorded here," or something similar. If it refers to a person, various individuals have been suggested. Takemoto Mikio suggested a known *renga* poet, Sōgan, and his conjecture is supported by Taguchi Kazuo's reconstruction of a possible textual slippage, which would have turned that name into Tangan. Another plausible suggestion is that by Okuno Jun'ichi, who reads the last two graphs as an abbreviation for Genna (or Gen'a) from Tajima. See Taguchi Kazuo, "*Kuzu no hakama* (*Sumiyoshi no sengū no nō*) nanku kō," *Geinōshi kenkyū*, October 1979, pp. 21–22.

79. *Shisho myōjin*, perhaps the same "Four Bright Gods" held in reverence there today: Sokotsutsuo no mikoto, Uwatsutsuo no mikoto, Nakatsutsuo no mikoto, and Empress Jingū.

80. According to the ancient reading strategy called *monzen-yomi*, the two phrases here are constructed with obscure Chinese compounds followed by native parsings. See Taguchi, "*Kuzu no hakama*," pp. 17–18. A modern example of the practice can be found in the exclamation "Oy vey!"

白き水干の、
古く赤み果てたるに、
(名風の見聞在レ之也)
葛の袴のここかしこ破れ損じたりけるに、
錆色の立烏帽子を耳の際に引き入、
うそぶき月に向かえば、
せいしつのゆうゆうたるをあけては、
きちべうにはれ、
[主]てうゐのかんかんたるをくだきて、
うんてんはんにをさまる。
尉に是を怪しめて、
この物語の不審を、
少々尋ぬれば、
此翁歯もなき口を広らかに打ち笑みて。
[上]い[延]さとよ対面のはじめに、
いせ[しほる]ものがたりの不審を、
くれぐれと語らんは、
[しほる]かつうはそら恐ろしや、
かつうは道の聊爾なりとて、
左右なくいわざりけりとや。
いざや伊勢の神垣、
越えけん跡を尋ねん。

[論義]秘する所の言の葉は、
秘する所の言の葉は、
数々なりと申とも、
ことに憚り多きは、
馴れにし人の名字なり、
〽そも名字のしみとは、
なに事を申たりけるぞ、
〽数々ありしその中に、
取り分き十二人なり、
〽十二人も三人も、
われは全く知らぬなり、
第一番はたれやらん、
〽あだなりと、
名にこそ立てれさくら花、
〽とし[延]にまれなる人も待ちけり、
〽此歌の主をば、

oy being a Hebrew word, glossed immediately by the Yiddish *vey* (cognate with German *weh* [woe]).

he wore an overrobe once white,
but muddied and threadbare of long usage,
his arrowroot trousers were torn and worn-through here and there,

(This is the place for which the piece is famous, both aurally and visually.)
his high-pitched court cap had faded to blue gray,
and he wore it perched just above his ears.
He directed his attention to the moon,
and as its bright radiance rose languidly in the vault of heaven,
SHU the air endowed the earth with fine clear skies,
and rained down, all around, a lambent shower.[12]
With my suspicions aroused,
I brought myself to question the old fellow with regard to the tales,
and he opened his toothless mouth in a broad grin.

JŌ "Were I, on NOBE first meeting,
to make a detailed response to your questions
about *The* SHIORU *Tales of Ise*,
I should both be SHIORU apprehensive of the consequences
and guilt-ridden out of disrespect for the way,
so I realize, I cannot respond casually.
But come along, let's see if we can find
a way over the sacred palisade surrounding Ise.

RONGI "There are, among the terms we keep secret,
There are, among the terms we keep secret,
many sorts of things,
but the ones requiring the most discretion
are the names of people with whom we have become familiar."

"What about these secrets in names?"[13]

"Among the many I could mention there are, in particular, twelve people's names . . ."

"I don't care whether it's twelve people or thirteen people, but let's get to the first of them."

"Ah yes,

'Cherry blossoms have a name for faithlessness, they scatter
fruitlessly, . . ."

"'. . . yet they have waited, as have I, for one who comes so rarely through the NOBE year.' People have written that the one who sang out this poem was called 'the SHIORU woman who awaits her lover,' but . . ."

人待つ女と書きたりしを、
〽紀のあ延りつねはむすめと(名論義)、
あらわすは尉が僻事。
〽さて其後は逢坂の、
関の関屋の真木柱、
〽立つ名もくやし、
思ひくちなんと、
恋死に死せしをば、
〽物病みのしをる女とかきたりしを
〽大納言、
長谷雄の卿のむすめと、
あらはす尉が僻事か。
同げにや住吉の、
松の老木の口がましや、
物言いしける翁なり、
しをるなおも長居せん、
筋なきことや夕暮の、
月もろともに住吉の、
松の葉杖にすがりて、
津守の浦に帰りけり、
津守の浦に帰りけり。

"if I were to give her away as Ki no A-NOBEritsune's daughter, NA-RONGI[81]oh! what a blunder!—well, I am an old man . . ."

"Aha! And then,

'At the barrier of Ausaka, the guards' hut is built of black pine posts, to last . . ."
"'But oh! how fast my name has come to gossip's tongues; now his love, exposed, will soon be gone.

'and with that she died of love.' That one was called 'the woman who was sick with love,' and were I to give her away as the daughter of Greater Counsel Lord Haseo, oh! what a blunder!—well, I am an old man . . ."

CHORUS"Truly, what a blabbermouth is the ancient pine of Sumiyoshi—
this old man has spilled the beans!"

SHIORUIt would be nice to linger longer, but
no useful end would be served by that, and the evening has grown late,
so like the clear moon overhead at Sumiyoshi,
back he goes to the coast of Tsumori, leaning on a staff of needled pine,
back he goes to the coast of Tsumori, leaning on a staff of needled pine.

81. 名論議. This note could signal another celebrated passage in the piece, a famous *rongi* or a *rongi* about names.

野守

指声是に出たる老人は、
この春日野に年を経て、
山にも通ひ里にも行、
野守の翁にて候也。
ありがたや慈悲万行の春の色、
三笠の山に長閑にて、
五重唯識の秋の風、
下春日の里にをとづれて、
まことに誓ひも直なるや、
神の主宮路に行き帰り、
運ぶ歩みも老の、
さかゆく御影頼むなり。
下哥唐土までも聞えある、
此宮寺の名ぞ高き。
上むかし仲丸が、
むかし仲丸が、
わが日の本を思ひやり、
天の原、
ふりさけ見ると詠めけん、
三笠の山かげの月かも。
それは明州の月なれや、
こゝは奈良の都の、
春日主のどけき気色哉、
春日のどけき気色哉。

NOMORI[82]

SASHIGOE The old man before you
has spent years on this Moor of Kasuga,
going back and forth to the hills and visiting the villages;
he is an ancient fellow, the Guardian of the Moor.
What a blessing: spring's colors are suffused with innumerable acts of
compassion,
It is peaceful on Mikasa Mountain,
GE the autumn wind blows through the village of Kasuga
with the Fivefold Doctrine of Pure Consciousness,[83]
how straight and true the vow of the god,
in the return on the SHU path to his shrine;
with each step, the old man trudges farther up a hill,
all the while with faith in the flourishing grace of god.

SAGEUTA Celebrated as far away as China,
What fame for the name of this temple-shrine![84]

Nakamaro, long ago,
Nakamaro, long ago
cast his thoughts back to this Land of the Rising Sun
and, so they say, recited, "I gaze off to
the high plain of heaven, . . . look, the moon over Mount Mikasa."[85]
But that was the moon of Mingzhou;
this is the Nara capital,
under the SHU gentle light of a springtime sun,
under the gentle light of a springtime sun.

82. The passage quoted consists of the *sashi*, *sageuta*, and *ageuta* of the second *dan*.

83. The Hossō school of Buddhism, with its head temple being Tōdaiji in Nara, where the play takes place, holds that reality is basically a matter of consciousness, which has five different levels.

84. The site intended is Kōfukuji, the tutelary temple of the Fujiwaras. The great Kasuga Shrine traditionally was under the administration of Kōfukuji, and Kōfukuji itself was thought to embody a harmonious blend of Buddhism and Shinto; thus, this is a *miyadera* (temple-shrine).

85. Abe no Nakamaro was an early emissary to China (698–770). He settled there for a number of years and composed a poem that is partially quoted, and more broadly evoked, here. Nakamaro's poem reads, *Ama no hara furisakemireba Kasuga naru / Mikasa no yama ni ideshi tsuki kamo* (I gaze off to the high plain of heaven, and look, / it's the moon arisen over Mount Mikasa in Kasuga).

弱法師節曲舞

上序　主夫しをる仏日西天の雲に隠れ、
慈尊の出世しをるまだはるか、
三会のあかつき未だなり。
指声然るにこの中間にをいて、
なにと心を延ばへまし。
こゝによつて上宮太子、
国家をあらため万民をしえて、
仏法流布の世となして、
あまねき恵みを弘め給う。
すなわち当寺を御建立あつて、
はじめて僧尼の姿をあらはし、
四天王寺と名付給ふ。
曲舞金堂の御本尊は、
如意輪の仏像、
救世観音とも申とか、
太子の御前生、
四だん国の思禅師にて、
わたらせ給ゆへ、
出仮の仏像に応じつゝ、
今日域に至るまで、
延仏法遣声さい初の御本尊と、
現はれ給ふ御威光の。
まことなるかな延や、
末世相応の御誓ひ、
然れば当寺の仏閣の、
御作の品々も、
赤栴檀の霊木にて、
塔婆の金宝に至るまで、
閻浮檀金なるとかや。

YOROBŌSHI KUSEMAI[86]

AGEUTA SHU Now SHIORU the Sun Buddha has hidden in the clouds on the western horizon, and the advent of the Lord Revered for Compassion is SHIORU still remote;
the dawn of the Three Great Assemblies is not yet on hand.[87]

SASHIGOE How, in such a middling state,
is the mind to find any solace?
It is in just this context that the Prince Regent of the Upper Palace
Has remade the state and educated the people,
made this a world for the Dharma,
and spread its blessings far and wide.
That is to say, he has established this temple,
and in giving us our first examples of monks and nuns,
bestowed upon it the name Shitennōji.
KUSEMAI The central focus of reverence in the Golden Hall
is the Buddhist image of Kannon, granter of wishes,
or Kannon who saves the world, so they say.
Since the Prince Regent himself in an earlier life was
the great Chinese dhyana master Huisi,
he arrived incarnate in this Realm of the Sun
as the image of Buddha in the world,
making himself manifest
NOBE as the first focus of reverence for the YARUKOE Buddha-Dharma.
So then, His majesty is YORU genuine:
a sacred vow, tailored to these Latter Days.
They say the articles with which he furnished this mansion of Buddha
are of sacred wood, red chinaberry,
and right as far as the finial on top, all Jambunada platinum.

86. The play is the same as that quoted earlier. Here the entire *kuri* and *sashi* and much of the *kuse* are quoted without reference to an author or a composer. In the earlier case, Motomasa was given credit for the play as a whole. Scholarly consensus holds that the *kusemai*, an account of the origins of the great Buddhist temple Shitennōji, was written by Zeami and inserted into Motomasa's play.

87. The "Sun Buddha" is Śākyamuni, the historical Buddha, and the "Lord Revered for Compassion" is Maitreya, the future Buddha. The "Three Great Assemblies" are three gatherings for the enlightenment of those beings left in delusion after the death of Śākyamuni, and they are to take place after the manifestation of Maitreya under the bodhi tree.

上万代に澄める亀井水までも、
水上清し西天の、
無熱の池水を受けつぎて、
しほるながれ久しき代々までも、
五濁の人間を導きて、
延さいどの舟をも寄するなる、
難波の寺の鐘の声、
異浦々に響き来て、
普き誓ひ満ち汐の、
をし照る海山も、
皆成仏の姿也。

JŌTurtlewell Spring, pristine for ten thousand generations,
is drawn from Anavatapta Lake,[88] in India
SHIORUage to age, on it flows.
NOBEThis is where the barque of salvation is brought to dock,
guiding humans liable as they are to the five pollutions.

The call of the bell at Naniwa Temple
echoes back from other shores,
the universal pledge fills the rising tide,
both the surface of the sea and the hills all around
glitter in the evening sun
the image of Buddhahood for all.

88. "The Lake of No Fever (and Suffering)," believed to be in the Himalayas and to be the source of India's four great rivers.

歌占

指声是は伊勢の国二見の浦の神子にて候。
それ歌は天地開け始まりしより、
陰陽の二神、
天の巷に行下合の、
小夜の手枕結び定めし、
世を守り国を治めて、
今も絶えせぬ妙文なり。
下歌占問はせ給へや、
上歌占問はせ給へや。
上神風や、
伊勢の浜荻名を変へて、
伊勢の浜荻名を変へて、
葦といふも芦と云も、
同じ草しほるなりと聞く物を、
所は伊勢の神子なりと、
懸切なにはのことも問ひ給へ。
人心、
引けば引かるゝ梓弓、
伊勢や日向の、
ことも問ひ給へ、
日向の事も問ひ給へ。

UTAURA[89] Composed by Motomasa

SASHIGOE Here before you, I am a shrine priest from the Twinsights
Coast[90] in the land of Ise.
Ever since the beginning, when earth was drawn apart from heaven,
ever since the gods of yin and yang came together in the celestial
realm,
song has sanctioned the choice of pillow partners,
preserved the world and brought the nation peace,
and to this day it is a wondrous form of writing.[91]
SAGEUTA Proceed with the divination,
JŌ Proceed with the poetic divination.
JŌ Sacred winds rise,
the beach reeds at Ise change their names,
the beach reeds at Ise change their names,
some call them *yoshi* reeds, some call them *ashi* rushes[92]
although they are the same SHIORU beach reeds, or so one hears.
Now I may be a priest from Ise, but don't peg me to that,
but ask me something about KAKEKIRI Naniwa as well.
It may be hard to draw from the heart
the secrets it holds, but draw the bowstring
of a catalpa bow, and draw it well
for secrets it can tell, whether at Ise or
at Hyūga, ask me something,
Ask me something about Hyūga as well.

89. The passage quoted is the *shite*'s *sashi*, *sageuta*, and *ageuta* from the second *dan*.

90. Futami no ura (Futami ga ura).

91. The slippage here from *uta* ("song" or "poetry") two lines earlier, to *myōmon* (orth. *meumon*) is noteworthy. *Myōmon* may refer not only to a "wondrous form of writing" but also to the Buddhist scriptures, especially the Lotus Sutra.

92. *Yoshi* and *ashi* are alternative names for apparently the same plant, a reed or rush. As it happens, the words are also antonyms for, respectively, "good" and "bad." This coincidence is used for puns throughout the tradition.

蟻通

[指声]瀟湘の夜の雨しきりに降つて、
遠寺の鐘の[横声懸]声もきこえず 、
なにとなく宮寺なんどは、
深夜の鐘の声、
御灯の光などに社、
（嵐吹遠山本のむらかしは誰が軒端より雪はらふやらん）
神さび心も澄みわたるに、
[主声]しやとうを見れば燈し火もなく、
すゞしめの声も聞えず、
神は宜禰が習はしとこそ申に、
宮守ひとりも見えぬことよ。
よしよし御 燈は暗くとも、
和光の影はよも曇らじ、
あら無沙汰の宮守どもや。

[下]雨雲の、
立ち重なれる夜半なれば、
ありとほしとも思ふべきかはと、
あら面白の御歌や。

Aritowoshi[93]

SASHIGOE The night rain falls ceaselessly over the Xiao and Xiang,
but the sound of the WAU NO KOWAGAKARI vespers bell, shrouded in the distance, cannot be heard.
(The gale blows / from far off by the stand of oaks / at the foot of the mountain, there. / Whose eaves will it clear / of snow?)[94]
Temples and shrines have a full air of holiness
and the mind is most able to achieve full clarity
in the sound of a bell, deep in the night,
and in the votive lantern light.[95]
SHU NO KOE Yet if you look at the shrine here, there are no lanterns,
there are no voices supplicating the gods,
and even though they say the majesty of gods depends on the habits of the priest[96]—what's this?—there isn't a single caretaker in sight.
Well, well, even if the sacred lanterns are unlit,
the softened brilliance of god's image will never be clouded,
but what negligence on the part of the caretaker! . . .

GE "On a night like this," you say,
"when rain clouds pile in layers through the sky,
How was I to know if there were stars?"[97]—what an interesting poem!

93. The passage quoted includes a *sashi* sung by the *shite* when he first comes on stage, as well as a *kakeai* sequence with the *waki* and a subsequent *sageuta*, *ageuta*, and *kuse*.

94. A poem by Fujiwara Ietaka (*Minishū*) has been inserted in an interlinear gloss in red. The poem is identical to no. 14470 in Zoku Kokka taikan, ed., *Matsushita Daizaburō* (Tokyo: Kadokawa shoten, 1968). But a version with the first phrase *udzumoruru* [*tohoyamamoto no . . .*] (The snow is piled high [in the far off stand of oaks . . .]) is preferred in the more recent edition: Taniyama Shigeru, ed., *Shinpen kokka taikan* (Tokyo: Kadokawa shoten, 1985), vol. 3, no. 2598.

95. At roughly this point in the manuscript, a marginal note in red has been added consisting of the following poem: *Arashifuku tohoyamamoto mo / mura-kashiha taga nokiba yori yuki harafuran* (At the base of the distant mountains, the gale blows through the groves of oak, / from who's eaves will it sweep away the snow?). The poem is identical to a poem in the personal poetry collection of Fujiwara Ietaka, *Minishū*, Winter 2598, apart from the first phrase, which there reads *udzumoruru*.

96. *Kami ha kine ga narahashi*, apparently a proverb.

97. The poem depends on a rather clunky pun in which the name of the shrine, Aritohoshi, is read to mean, rather eccentrically, "[how was I to know] if there were stars." The story that is taken as the source for the play (in *Tsurayukishū* 9) includes a poem similar to this one, but for unknown reasons, the form in which the poem is quoted here is somewhat different from the original version, which reads, *Kakikumori ayame mo shiranu ohozora ni / aritohoshi woba omofu beshi ya ha* (Clouds fill the air—on a night like this, when rain clouds pile in layers through the sky. / How were I to know if there be stars?). See Yokomichi Mario and Omote Akira, eds., *Yōkyokushū*, NKBT, vol. 40 (Tokyo: Iwanami shoten, 1960), vol. 1, p. 448n.166.

下哥をよそ歌には六義あり、
これ六道の、
巷に定め置いて、
六つの色を見するなり。
上されば和歌の事態は、
されば和歌の事態は、
神代しほるよりも始まり、
いましほる人倫にあまねし、
たれかこれを褒めざらん。
中にも貫之は、
御書所をうけたまはりて、
いにしへ今までの、
歌の品を撰びて、
喜びを延べし君が代の、
直なる道をあらはせり。
下およそ思つて見れば、
歌の心すなほなるは、
これ以て私なし、
人代に及んで、
はなはだ興る風俗の、
長歌短歌旋頭、
混本の類ひ是なり、
雑体一つにあらざれば、
げむ延りうやうやく茂る木の、
花のうちの鴬、
又秋の蝉の吟の声、
いづれか和歌の数ならぬ。
されば今の歌、
わが邪をなさゞれば、
などかは神も憐れみの、
心を受くる宮人は。

[SAGEUTA]Now, in general terms, there are six principles to poetry,
and these have been equated with the six benighted ways,
and shown to have six different styles.

[JŌ]Thus the practice of poetic composition
Thus the practice of poetic composition
began as early as the [SHIORU]age of gods
and now is spread throughout [SHIORU]humankind,
and who can fail to hold it in esteem?
From among all the others, it was the poet Tsurayuki
who assumed the role of head of the royal libraries,
and ever since, from a time long ago,
the joy we feel at the sovereign's reign
and his honest practice of the Way of the King,
has found expression in carefully selected forms of poetry.

And come to think of it,
when poetry finds its sense most directly,
it is not simply a personal matter.
In the age of humankind,
poetry has shown a remarkable popularity,
in genres such as *chōka*, *tanka*, *sedōka*, and mixed styles.
The original source of poetry has branched into
a [NOBE]lush and verdant tree,
with blossoms sheltering warblers,
and the insects' chirping voices in the fall—
with its many varied styles,
what, indeed, falls outside the realm of poetry?
And so, given this poem of mine just now,
how could the god fail to show compassion,[14]
since it reveals that my transgression was without ill intent?
You sir, who attend upon the god, will know His mind.
To have met with such a prodigy on Meeting Mountain,
where, in the clear stream by the barrier gate, you see the moon
reflected . . .

上かかる奇特に逢坂の、
関の清水に影見ゆる、
しほる月毛の此駒を、
引き立て見ればふしぎやな、
もとのごとくに歩みゆく、
ゑつ延てう南枝に巣をかけ、
胡馬北風に嘶へたり。
歌に和らぐ神心、
誰か神慮の、
まことを仰がざるべき。

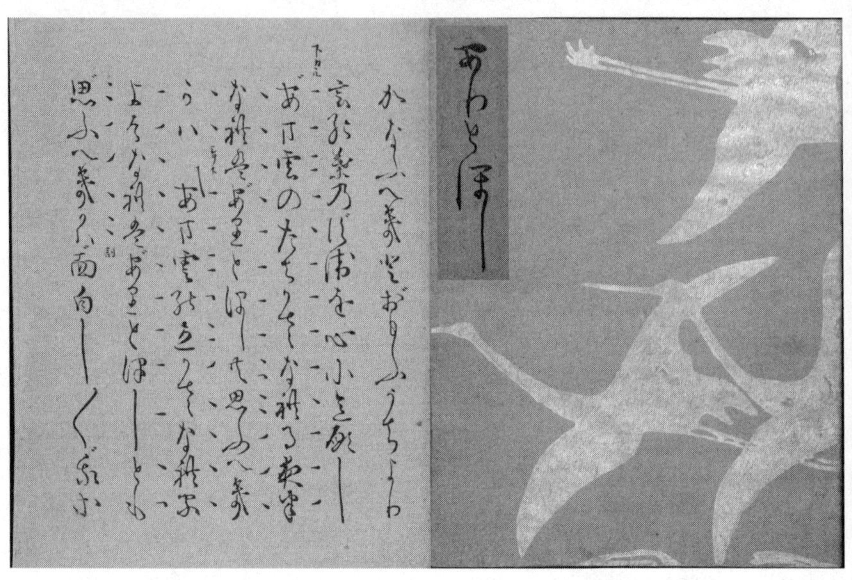

—what a surprise—my SHIORU moonlight-dappled pony stands up once again
and walks, just as before.
NOBE "A bird from tropic climes nests in the southern branches,
A horse from foreign steppes neighs in the northern wind."[98]
When the mind of god is mollified by poetry,
who can fail to revere the deep sincerity of
his divine consideration?

A nō libretto (*utaibon*) for the play *Aritohoshi*, *Kōetsu-bon*. The cover is on the right, and a page from the text is on the left. The poem that gives the play its name is quoted twice on this page, beginning in the third line from the right. The *Kōetsu-bon* editions of nō libretti are monuments in the history of art as well as the history of printing. The artist, Hon'ami Kōetsu (1558–1637), is one of Japan's most celebrated artists, and for these libretti, he used movable type, the technology for which had just been imported into Japan from Korea, in the aftermath of Toyotomi Hideyoshi's invasions in 1592 and 1596. (Photograph courtesy of the Noh Theater Research Institute, Hōsei University)

98. A quotation from *Wenxuan* 249, inverting the two lines.

実盛

指声笙歌はるかに聞ゆ孤雲の上、
聖衆来迎す落日の前、
あらありがたや今日もまた紫雲の立ぞや
只声鐘の音念仏の声聞え候、
さだめて聴聞の貴賎群集なるらん。
さなきだに立居くるしき老の波の、
寄りもつかずは聴衆の庭に、
よそながらもや聴聞せん。
主一念称名の下声の内には、
摂取の光明曇らねども、
老眼の通路なほ以て明かならず。
よしよしすこしは遅くとも、
こゝを去る事遠かるまじや、
南無阿弥陀仏。

〽いかに尉殿、
この程聴聞に参り候へども、
御身の姿を見る人なし、
誰に向かひて言葉を交はすぞと皆人申合えり、
いかなる人ぞ名乗給へ。

Sanemori[99]

SASHIGOE Music for pipes and voices sounds far off on high, beyond the clouds,
the sacred company descends before the setting sun.
Ah, what a blessing to see that purple clouds have arisen again today!
TADAGOE I hear the sound of bells and voices chanting the name of Buddha.
There must be an assembly of the faithful come to listen, high and low.
As it is, we elderly find it hard to get up and down—the waves of age overtake us—
and to make my way into that crowd, that would be too much,
so I'll listen here, from some ways off.
SHU Within a single call GE upon the name of Buddha
the light of guidance and welcome shines unclouded,
but in an old man's fading eyesight, the road is still uncertain.
And yet, if I simply take my time and put one foot after the other,
it can't be all that far away,
Namu Amida butsu.

"Excuse me, old gentleman,
I note you have been coming to listen to these services,
but no one else can see you.
They're all asking me who it is I'm talking with.
Make yourself known, who are you?"

99. The passages quoted include the *shite*'s *sashi* of the second *dan*, part of the subsequent *mondō* with the *waki*, and the *ageuta* that follows that *mondō*.

是は思ひもよらぬことを承候物かな、
もとより所は天離がる、
鄙人なれば人がましく、
名もあらばこそ名のりもせめ、
ただ聖人 の御下向、
すなはち弥陀の来迎なれば、
かしこうぞ長生して
此称名の時節に逢ふ事、
[下]盲亀の浮木優曇華の、
花待ち得たる心地して、
老いのさいはい身に越え、
喜びの涙袂に余る、
されば身ながら安楽国に生るゝかと、
無比の歓喜をなすところに、
輪廻妄執の閻浮の名を、
又あらためて名のらん事、
口惜しくこそ候へとよ。

[哥]篠原の、
草葉の霜の翁さび、
草葉の霜の翁さび、
人な咎めそかりそめに、
あら[延]はれ[しほる]いでたる実盛が、
名をよそに知らせんは、
亡き世語もはづかしとて、
御前を立ち去りて、
行くかと見れば篠原の、
池のほとりにて姿は、
幻となりて失せにけり、
幻となりて失せにけり。

"Well, this is unexpected, what you ask of me!
This is the back country,
almost as remote as the very sky,
and if I had a name, as other people do, then I might tell it to you,
but as it is, I simply attend upon your reverence's appearance here,
like as it is to the coming of Amida himself,
and think how clever am I to have lived so long,
to chance upon this occasion of sacred chanting,
I feel like a '[GE]blind tortoise that managed to find a foothold on a scrap of flotsam,'
or like someone who's 'waited out the blossoming of the uḍumbara flower,'[100]
Great good fortune like this is more than I deserve,
tears of joy drip from my sleeves—
that even one like me might find rebirth in the Paradise of Peace and Ease—on the occasion of such incomparable happiness
that I should once again announce that name
I was known by in the clinging cycle of worldly delusion,
that really seems so shameful . . .

[UTA]"At Shinowara,
see how old I am: the frost settles down on me as on the grasses,
see how old I am: the frost settles down on me as on the grasses.
But don't hold it against me, I come here
to [NOBE]appear [SHIORU]but briefly, Sanemori—
but don't give my name away—
a sorry tale is the story of my life gone by,"
said he, and left the scene,
no sooner did he seem to move away
than there, by the pond, his very figure
transformed into a phantom, and was gone,
transformed into a phantom, and was gone.

100. Both are metaphors for the wondrous unlikelihood that one should encounter a buddha. The first one appears also in the passage quoted from *Nue*, in which the unlikelihood is emphasized. Here, instead, it is the wonder that is foregrounded.

高野節曲舞

上序そもそも此しをるたかのさんと申は、
平城を去て二百里、
郷里を離れて無人声。
指声然ば末世の隠所として、
結界清浄の道場たり。
中にもこの三鈷の松は、
大同二年の御帰朝以前に、
わが法成就円満の地の、
印に残り留まれとて、
三鈷を投げさせ給ひしに、
光とともに飛来たり、
この松が枝の木末に留まる。
しかれば諸木の中にも分て、
松に留まるその例、
千代万代の末かけて、
久しかれとの御方便、
くはしく旧記にあらはれたり。
節曲舞されぱにや、
主しん如平等の松風は、
八葉の峰を、
静かに吹き渡り、
法性随縁の月の影は、
八つの谷に曇らずして、
まことに三会の、

KŌYA KUSEMAI[101] ("Mount Kōya"), composed by Motomasa

JŌ JO As we shall see, the aforementioned SHIORU Mount Takano is
some two hundred leagues remote from the Heijō Capital;
SASHIGOE distant from human settlement and devoid of a human voice.
It is, in other words, a pristine site
for spiritual offices in the Latter Days of the Law.
Of particular interest here is the Pine of the Three-Pronged *Vajra*,[102]
for in the second year of the Daidō era, before returning home to
Japan,
Kūkai[103] threw a three-pronged *vajra* into the air,
commanding that it come to rest, as a symbol,
in the place where his practice of Dharma
would come to fulfillment and plenitude,
whereupon in a flash of light the *vajra* flew right to the top of this tree.

When, of all trees,
it settled upon this pine, that illustrated the skill in means[104] whereby
the pine should serve as an example
for one thousand, nay, ten thousand generations.
It all appears in old records.
KUSEMAI And this must be the reason that the pine-blown wind
rustles softly over Eight Leaf Peak, SHU with the full equality of
tathatā,[105]
while the light of the moon,
shines unclouded above the Eight Valleys,
Dharma nature's accord with each affinity of being;

101. Originally an independent *kusemai*, this piece was eventually incorporated into a play entitled either *Kauya monogurui* or, simply, *Kauya*. The Hōshō text, lightly annotated, can be found in Nonomura Kaizō, ed., *Kaichū Yōkyoku zenshū* (Tokyo: Chūō koronsha, 1935), vol. 3, pp. 475–90.

102. A *vajra* is an implement used in esoteric Buddhist ritual, like that performed in the Shingon sect that Kūkai founded. *Vajra* represent various things, among them a thunderbolt. They are based on ancient Indian weapons and symbolize the power to destroy illusion. They most commonly come in single-prong, triple-prong, and five-prong versions.

103. Although his name is not mentioned explicitly in the original text, "he" refers to the founder of Japanese Shingon Buddhism, Kūkai or Kōbō Daishi (774–835), who established the religious complex on Mount "Takano"—that is, Mount Kōya.

104. *Hōben*, Sanskrit *upāya-kauśalya*.

105. Sanskrit for "thus-ness," a heuristic term for absolute reality. For Eight Peaks and Eight Valleys, see note 72.

[延]あかつきを待つ心也。
しかれば即身、
成仏の相をあらはし、
入定の地を示しつつ、
し[持切]んしんたる奥の院、
深山鳥の声寂びて、
飛花落葉の嵐風まで、
無常観念のよそほひ、
是とても又常住の、
[延]皆令仏道、
円覚の相をあらはせり。
[上遣声]しかれば、
時移り事去るや、
四季おりおりのをのづから、
光陰惜しむべし、
時[しほる]人を待たざるに、
貴[しほる]賤のくん[しほる]じゅの雲霞、
かかる高野の山深み、
谷峰の、
風常楽の夢さめ、
法の称名妙音の、
[しほる]心耳に残り満ち満ちて、
唱へ行ふ聞法の、
声は高野にて、
静かなる霊地なるべし。

this is the heart of our expectation
for the NOBE dawn of Maitreya's Three Great Assemblies.[106]

Thus, it reveals the vision of Buddhahood attained
and marks an entry into nirvana,
and in the MOCHIKIRI[107] inner depths of the Oku-no-in,[108]
in the remotest mountains, the raven's caw grows faint,
the howl of a gale, scattering blossoms and strewing the landscape
with leaves,
gives an insight into transience
even as it shows the eternal surety of NOBE universal Buddhahood
and full enlightenment.
JŌ[109] YARIKOE Be that as it may,
time moves on, our affairs come to an end,
the seasons in their cycle of change make apparent
to us that every moment is to be cherished.
Since time SHIORU waits on no one,
the clouds and haze of SHIORU human interaction,
of both the SHIORU high and low,
hang over the farthest recesses of Mount Takano and
the winds which blow from its peaks and valleys
waken us from dreams of endless bliss;
the wondrous sound of the chanting of Dharma
SHIORU fills our ears and fills our hearts,
voices making the Dharma heard in holy chanting,
fill the air over this quiet and sacred ground.

106. As in note 53, this refers to the three great assemblies under the bodhi tree for the benefit of the as yet unenlightened, once the future Buddha, Maitreya, is manifest in the world.

107. Unique here. The place is, as Omote points out, treated with special melodic figures in modern performance in each school.

108. Oku-no-in is a deeply revered mortuary temple on the site of the foremost Shingon temple complex in Japan on Mount Kōya.

109. The graph here could be read either *jō* or *age*. If the latter, it would indicate the *age*[*ha*], a solo for the *shite* at a particular point in a danced *kuse*. Zeami does not seem to have used the term himself, so I have retained the reading *jō*.

当麻

上序 そもそも此しほるたえまのまんだらと申すは、
仁王四十七代の御門、
はいしほるたい天皇の御宇かとよ、
横萩の右大臣豊成と申し人。
指声其御息女中将姫、
この山に籠り給ひつゝ、
称讃浄土経、
下毎日読誦し給ひしが、
心中に誓ひ給ふやう、
願はくは生身の弥陀来迎あて、
われに拝まれおはしませと、
一心不乱に観念し給ふ。
しからずは畢命を期として、
この草庵を出でじと誓つて、
一向に念仏三昧の定に入り給ふ。
節曲舞所は山陰の、
松吹く風も涼しくて、
さながら夏を忘れ水の、
音も絶々の、
心耳を澄ます夜もすがら、
主せう名、
観念の床の上、
坐禅、
円月の窓の内、
寥々とある折節に、

Taema[110]

JŌ JO Now then, with regard to the SHIORU Taema Mandala:
apparently in the reign of His Majesty, the deposed sovereign,[111]
the forty-seventh of the Benevolent Kings,
a certain person named Toyonari, Yokohagi Great Minister of the Right,[112]
SASHIGOE had a daughter known as Chūjō-Hime.
She took up a secluded residence on the mountain here
and spent each day reciting
GE the teachings of the Glorification of the Pure Land, and
within her heart, she made a solemn pledge
that she be granted the opportunity to make obeisance
to Amida Buddha, who should manifest himself to her personally,
setting her mind resolutely on this devout wish.
Should this be impossible, she determined to end her days here,
never to set foot outside this mountain hermitage,
and entered into a deep and single-minded meditation in praise of Buddha.
KUSEMAI The place is sheltered by the mountain,
the wind that blows through the pine is so cool
one could forget the summer heat;
throughout the night, the murmur of a secluded spring alone
may reach the recess of the mind's ear, from time to time—
SHU glorify the Name!—
there, upon the site of her determination,
as she was rapt in seated meditation,
into her window, lit by the full moon's disk,
in the solitude of night,

110. The passage quoted is the *kuri*, *sashi*, and *kuse*.

111. The text in *Five Sorts of Singing* reads *haitai tenwau no gyou ka to yo* here, whereas modern performance texts skip the line and go on directly to the mention of Yokohagi. *Haitai* means "deposed sovereign," referring to the sovereign Junnin (733–765, r. 758–764). He was forced out of his position and retired to Awaji, to become known as Awaji *haitai* (the deposed sovereign in Awaji). Perhaps this line has been removed from the text because of the inauspicious circumstances surrounding Junnin, which might be seen to contradict the characterization of him as one of the "benevolent kings."

112. Fujiwara Toyonari (704–765) was an important government minister during the Nara period who rose to the important position of great minister of the right (横萩佩). For a time, he was sidelined as *dazainosotsu* (governor-general in Kyushu), but returned to power later. His sobriquet, Yokohagi no udaijin (Great Minister of the Right with the Sidelong Banners), has been reinterpreted as the perhaps more poetical but less comprehensible "Great Minister of the Right with the Sidelong Bush Clover."

一人の老人の、
忽然と来り佇めり。
是はいかなる人やらんと、
尋ねさせ給ひしに、
老尼答へてのたまはく、
誰とはなどや愚か也、
呼べばこそ来りたれと、
仰せられけるほどに、
中将姫はあきれつゝ。
上遣声われはたれをか呼子鳥、
たづきも知らぬ山中延に、
声立つることとては、
なむしほる阿みだぶの称へならで、
又他事もなきものをと、
答へさせ給しに、
それこそ我が名なれ、
声をしるべに来れりと、
のたまへば姫君も、
さては此願成就して、
生身の弥陀如来、
しほるげにらいかうの時節よと、
感涙肝に銘じつゝ、
綺羅衣の御袖も、
しをるばかりに見え給ふ。

an aged nun
suddenly appeared and settled down.
When she asked
who this person might be,
the nun replied:
"Why, what did you expect!
I came only because you called,"
was her reply.
Chūjō-Hime was amazed.
JŌ YARUKOE "Who called? A calling-bird
would go astray in these deep mountains. NOBE
The only calling I have done
is SHIORU calling on the name of Amida,
and nothing more,"
she answered.
"And that precisely is my name,
I came because you called me,"
said the old one, and only then did Chūjō-Hime
realize her prayer was answered:
there, in the flesh, was Amida,
SHIORU this was the moment of his welcoming appearance.
Tears of excitement were graven on her heart,
her robes of gauze and damask silk
looked as though they'd wilted from the weeping.

熱田

指声抑当社と申は、
景行第三の王子、
御名は大和武の尊、
地神五代には、
天照太神の御弟、
下すさの男の尊、
出雲の国に跡を垂れ、
しばらく宮居し給へり。
さしこゝに簸の川上に、
てい[こ]くする 声あり、
下みこと至りて見給へば、
老人夫婦 が中に、
少女を抱きて泣き居たり、
是はいかにと尋ぬれば。
節曲舞老人答え申すやう、
我は手名椎足名椎、
女を稲田姫と，
云も寄のにて候が、
大蛇の生贄を、
悲しむ なりと申せば、
しからば其姫を我に得させよその難を、
逃すべしとのたまへば、
喜悦の心 妙にして、
尊に姫を奉る。
上や延がて大蛇 を従へ、
その尾にありし剣を、
叢雲のしほるけんと名寄付しこそ、
八剣の宮の御事よ。
されば 簸上の明神は、
源太夫の神と現れ、
東海道 の旅宿を、
守らんと誓ひ給へり。

ATSUTA[113] Composed by Kia

[SASHIGOE]Now then, what they say about this shrine:
is that the third son of the Sovereign Keikō—
Prince Yamato-dake by name—
was an earthly manifestation
of the [GE]august Susano-o,
younger brother of the Great Goddess Amaterasu,
who descended to the land of Izumo and
for some time resided in the palace there.
[SASHI]Now it came to pass that voices crying and wailing
could be heard from up the Hi River.
[GE]When the prince arrived there
to see what had happened
he found an old couple, weeping
as they held a young girl in their arms.
When he asked what was wrong,
[KUSEMAI]The old man re-[YOSURU]plied,
We two are Tenazuchi and Ashinazuchi,
and this is our daughter Inada-Hime.
We are miserable because of the living sacrifice
we are bound to make to a great serpent;
at that, the prince said, "Give me the hand of your daughter
and I will help you escape this danger."
Their hearts were filled with a wonderful elation,
and they offered their daughter to the prince.
[JŌ]Straight-[NOBE]away he subdued the great serpent;
the sword which he found in its tail
was none other than the one [YOSURU]named
[SHIORU]"Sword of the Huddled Clouds,"
which is now in the Palace of Eight Swords.
The Bright Deity of Hikami is, then,
[SHIORU]Inada-Hime from this occasion.
Her father, the old man, is Tenazuchi,
manifest as the god Gen Dayū,
who pledged to be a guardian
of stations along the Eastern Sea Road.

113. The play is either the modern *Gen Dayū*, in the repertory of the Konparu and Kita schools, or an earlier form of that play. The passage quoted is the *sashi* and *kuse* of the fourth *dan*. There are some slight differences from the modern performance text(s).

竹取り歌

次第あるに甲斐なき世中を、
あるに甲斐なき世中を、
古畑打つ「ぞ」悲しき。
哥ゑのこ草、
種まくほどもなかりしに、
種まくほどもなかりしに、
しほるあはのなるとの一あひを
よくよくこれを引き捨てて、
蒸せる粟に延にたるは、
女郎花と云草、
薄苅萱吾木香、
蓬をことに引き捨ててよ、
もとの古根や残るらん、
もとの古根や残るらん。

Taketori uta[114] ("The Bamboo Cutter's Song") by the same composer[115]

To live on in a world where living avails one nothing,
To live on in a world where living avails one nothing,
How sad to cut the same old fields again!
Foxtail thickets grow
without the need for planting seed,
without the need for planting seed.
Take special care to pull out all the bunches of foxtail millet
when they go to seed,[15]
and like that millet, which can be steamed,
pay heed to the maiden flowers, as they're called,
and the plume grass, lemongrass, and burnet,
and pull out the wormwood, in particular.
What if the old roots get left behind?
What if the old roots get left behind?

114. The title literally means "Bamboo Cutter's Song," but the piece seems actually to be about a grass cutter. One of the graphs for grass (艸) was perhaps mistaken for that for bamboo (竹) in copying an earlier manuscript. The piece seems to be a song from a lost play. The passage consists of a *shidai* and an *ageuta*, as Omote notes, an unusual succession of *shōdan*.

115. Dōkyokusha, apparently Kia[mi].

指声抑むかし曠劫よりこのかた、
五道六道に廻る事は、
下なにのゆへぞや、
由なき妄執に引かれ、
本来空道を忘れて、
生死の海に浮沈せり、
さていつまでの心ぞや。
下哥まだ夜を籠めて煩悩の、
離れ難き家を出で。
上菩提を誘ふ横雲の、
菩提を誘ふ横雲の、
引くより後の舟呼ばひ、
我が乗る舟は行共、
真の岸はとうせじ。[16]
げにや心から、
浮きたる舟に乗初めて、
一日も浪に濡れぬ日の、
なき世の旅はいつまでぞ、
なき世の旅はいつまでぞ。

[*NO TITLE*] By the same composer[116]

Now then, what might be the reason
we are bound to circulate in the Five Ways and the Six Paths,
ever since the remoteness of distant aeons past?—
Dragged on by pointless clinging,
forgetful of the fundamental emptiness of things,
we float up and down in the sea of life and death.
How long are we to maintain this state of mind?
Though it is deep in the night,
and we are locked into the house of our delusions,
streaks of cloud entreat us to set out toward awakening,
streaks of cloud entreat us to set out toward awakening,
and once they drift out of sight, I call to the boat, to go aboard,
but when the boat sets out, we must not lose sight of the true shore.
It's of my own will, yes,
that I've set out upon this boat, at the mercy of the current,
and there hasn't been a single day I wasn't splashed by the waves,
how long will this journey through the insubstantial world go on?
how long will this journey through the insubstantial world go on?

116. The entire passage is missing in the best extant manuscript, and even as supplemented here, from a secondary manuscript, the title is missing. Apparently, this is a passage from a complete play, now lost.

西行歌

指声それ春の花は上求本来の梢にあらはれ、
秋の月は下化冥暗の水に宿れり。
下たれか知る行く水に三伏の夏もなく、
澗底の松の風、
一声の秋を催すこと、
草木国土をのづから、
見仏聞法の結縁たり。
下哥教え置く、
その品々の法の門。
上哥開くる道はひとつぞと、
開くる道はひとつぞと、
知るや心の水清き、
御しをる法の舟なれば、
行ことやすき彼の岸に、
至り至りて暗からぬ、
二世安楽は有難や、
二世安楽は有難や。

Saigyō no utai[117] ("Saigyo's Song")

SASHIGOE Look, the spring blossoms appear in the treetops up above,
aspiring to the fundamental awakening of all,
the autumn moon has found lodging in the waters here below,
inspiring our transformation out of delusion.
GE Who really understands,
that the ever-flowing river takes no rest, even in the hottest weeks of summer,
that the pine-blown wind on the valley floor summons autumn's advent with a single murmur.
The grasses, the trees and the earth itself provide us impetus to see the Buddha and hear the Dharma.
SAGEUTA The teachings set before us
in this disparate array of phenomena
AGEUTA open Dharma's gate upon a single path,
open Dharma's gate upon a single path.
Do you know the clarity of the water of mind?
SHIORU The Dharma is a boat,
and you can easily push off for the other shore,
in peace and pleasure both here and there, what a blessing!
in peace and pleasure both here and there, what a blessing!

117. Orth. *Saigyau no utahi*. The passage quoted consists of a *sashi*, a *sageuta*, and an *ageuta*. Only the first of these continues to be performed and finds its place in the play *Saigyōzakura*, as the first song of the *waki*, Saigyō. Omote suggests that the *sageuta* and *ageuta* were dropped from the play. With its references to a boat and its metaphysical concerns, this song seems well paired with the previous one.

伏見の翁歌

上序抑しほる伏見の翁の事、
名も久方の天照らす、
神の代継ぎの末ひさに、
君道を守る誓ひあり。
さししかるに仁王代々を経て、
時雨降り置ける楢の葉の、
名に負ふ宮路正しくて、
下うつりつゞくや雲の上、
花の都の春の空、
平安城におさまれり。
中にも伏見の宮所、
国家を守る神心、
知るや阿古根の浦までも、
四海のはらは静か也。
節曲舞仁王五十代、
桓武天王の御宇かとよ、
当国伏し見ての、
里に移らせ給ひて、
大宮造り始めつつ、
皇居を定め給ひしに、
伏見の翁は現はれて、
いざこ延こに、
我が世は経なん菅原や、
伏見の里の、
荒れまくも惜しと、

FUSHIMI NO OKINA UTAI[118] ("The Song of the Old Man of Fushimi")

JŌ JONow, about the SHIORUold man of Fushimi:
his fame spreads abroad like the boundless light of heaven,
and reaches ahead like the perennial generations of the gods
in his pledge to preserve the Sovereign's Way.

SASHIAnd so, through generations of Benevolent Kings,
like the Nara oak leaves flushed with the season's showers,
the celebrated path of rule proceeds
in decorous succession, GEage on age,
and up beyond the clouds,
the spring sky of flowery Miyako
is clear and serene, above the City of Peace and Tranquillity.[119]
Within, in the palace of Fushimi,
the minds of those gods that sustain the nation
recognize that peace pervades the four broad seas,
even as far as the coast of Akone.

KUSEMAIIn the fiftieth generation of Benevolent Kings,
during the reign of His Majesty Kammu, so they say,
when in looking down upon this land
he deigned to move his home,
and began the building of a great palace
designating it the royal residence,
an old man appeared in Fushimi and recited a poem:
"Well then, NOBEhere it is:
among these sedge fields of Sugawara
will I pass my days.
What a shame, were the village of Fushimi
e'er to fall to ruin."[120]

118. Orth. *Fushimi no okina utahi*. The passage quoted consists of the *kuri*, *sashi*, and *kuse* of the old play *Fushimi*, which is no longer in the repertory. There are small differences between the passage here and other extant texts of the play. Omote suggests that the sequence quoted here may originally have been an independent song.

119. Heian jō—that is, Kyoto.

120. *KKS* 18:981. The poem originally referred to a village of Fushimi near Ikoma, west of Nara, but here has been reinterpreted to relate to the village of the same name on the southern edge of Kyoto.

詠めけるとかや。
其後、
巫に託しつつ、
なをかさねてのみことのり、
我は神風や、
伊勢の阿古根の浦の波、
治まる御代の例ならん、
伏見に見そなはして、
君辺に住むべしとの、
御神勅に任せつつ、
大宮造りし給へり。
[上延]抑ふしみといふことは、
まづ我朝の惣名にて、
伊弉諾伊弉冊の、
あまの[しほる]岩くらの苔筵に、
[しほる]ふして見てし国なれば、
[しほる]ふしみと名付給ふ也。
さればにや、
国富み民豊かにて、
たれも我が代に合竹の、
伏見の里を、
守らんの御誓ひ、
百王万歳に、
平の都なるべし。

This, they say, was his poem.
Thereafter yet again an august proclamation,
through the shrine priests:
in accord with the gods' proclamation that
they should reside near the sovereign,
I have built the palace [NOBE]here in Fushimi,
lying down to take the measure of the site:[121]
Let the waves at Ise,
settled by a sacred wind
on Akone coast
set a fit example for our well-ordered generation.
[JŌ NOBE]So then, when we say "Fushimi,"
that is a general term for our kingdom,
itself a land that was seen by
Izanagi and Izanami when they lay down
upon a mat of moss in a [SHIORU]cave on the high plain of heaven
and that was named [SHIORU]Fushimi, accordingly: [SHIORU]"lie down and see."
It must be for this very reason
that the land is rich
the people prosperous,
and that all who happen to live in this, Our generation,
benefit from the pledge to preserve the village of Fushimi,
in this our peaceful capital where a hundred kings rule for ten thousand years.

121. Literally, "lie down and see"; this word is a pun from the toponym Fushimi (伏し見). It occurs again a few lines later.

太子くせ舞

指声我朝にその威光をひろめ、
漢家にその名をあらはし下たまいしは、
上宮太子にてをはします。
彼欽明天王三十二、
一月一日の夜半に御夢想の告あり、
下金色の僧［童男］来り給いて、
后に告げてのたまはく、
われに久世の願あり、
すなわち后の御胎内に、
宿るべしとありしかば。
曲舞后答えてのたまはく、
妾が胎内は垢穢なり、
いかで尊き御体を、
宿し給わんとありしかば、
僧［童男］重ねてのたまはく、
我は垢穢を厭はず、
主ただ望むらくは人間に、
着到せんが為也、
后辞するに所なし、
ともかくもと有りしかば、
この僧大きに喜んで［后の玉殿に、
光御なると御覧じて］、
后の御口に、
飛入給うと御覧じて、
暁月軒にかたぶき［かかやき］、
松風夢をやぶり［おさめ］て、
五更の天も明けにけり。
御門この由聞こし召し、
悦の色をなし給う、

TAISHI KUSEMAI[122]

("The Prince Regent Shōtoku"), composed by my late father

The lyrics of this song were revised here and there after the birth of his young lordship, Eikyō 6 [1434]:2:9.[123] Long ago this was part of the *kusemai* of the legend of the prince regent.[124]

SASHIGOE It was the Prince Regent of the Upper Palace
who spread his glory throughout our kingdom
and GE gained fame among the Chinese.
The twenty-third Heavenly Sovereign, Kinmei,
was vouchsafed a prophecy within a dream,
deep in the night of the final day of the first month.
GE A golden ~~boy~~ priest[125] came to the queen and announced,
"I have taken a vow to save the world,
should I be able to lodge in Her Majesty's womb."

KUSEMAI Her Majesty responded,
"Our womb is unclean.
How is it that you should lodge your precious body herein?"
Thereupon the ~~boy~~ priest once again spoke, saying,
"I have no aversion to uncleanness.
SHU I simply desire to come into the presence of human beings."
Her Majesty was unable to refuse.
"If that is, in all events, what you desire, then let it be."
The priest rejoiced greatly ~~a great light was seen in Her Majesty's palace~~, and he leapt into her august mouth.
The full moon descended to ~~shone upon~~ the eaves,
the pine wind ~~brought to an end~~ ripped away the dream,
and the heavens brightened over the last vestiges of night.
Hearing an account of these events,
His Majesty showed a joyful countenance,

122. Orth. "Taishi kusemahi."

123. This note is written alongside the title in red. The song text contains similar revisions, some of them in red, which seem to be those made on the occasion of the birth of Ashikaga Yoshikatsu (1434–1443), the "young lord" mentioned in the note. Yoshikatsu was the son of Yoshinori and was designated as shogun in 1441 after the latter's assassination, but he himself died of dysentery within two years.

124. A second note, this one in black ink following the name of the composer.

125. The annotations are inconsistent from one manuscript to another. In some cases, the word "boy" (童男 or トウナン) has been crossed out; in others the word "priest" (僧 or ソウ) is crossed out. Because of a later reference in which the boy is not mentioned, I have translated them so that the mysterious apparition is understood to be a priest. I have, however, left the excised text in the translation with a strike-through. So also with the other strike-throughs in the text.

后かならずしやうらんを、
うけ給うべしとありしかば。
上隙行く駒をつながねば、
しをる大ばつ大河の池の水、
すしをるまでにごれる心地して、
十二月と申には、
同声南殿の御馬屋にて、
しをる御さんへいあん、
王子御誕生なる、
馬やどの王子と申も、
上宮太子の御事。

and asked for an audience with Her Majesty.
JŌ There's no tethering a pony as it speeds by a window slit,
and forever muddied is the water in the lake into which the SHIORU great
river Taibatsu flows,[17] likewise was her cast of mind troubled,[126]
but when the twelfth month came,
a royal prince SHIORU was born safe and secure
in the royal stables of the ONAJI KOE Southern Mansion.
The prince came to be called "Prince of the Royal Stables";
he was none other than Prince Regent of the Upper Palace.

126. The phrase may relate to a similar reference in the preface to *Hosshinshū* by Kamo no Chōmei, or it may relate to a Zen kōan in *Mumonkan* 38, but there the pony is replaced by a water buffalo: "Master Wuzu said, 'Consider, for example, when an old water buffalo passes along outside the window grate. The head, the horns, the four legs all pass by, so why doesn't the tail pass by as well?' "

飛火

只詞抑当社と申すは忝も、
神護景雲二年に、
河内国牧岡より、
此春日山本宮の峰に移らせ給ふ。
さればこの山、
もとは端山の陰浅く、
木陰一つもなかりしを、
陰頼まんと藤原や、
氏人寄りて植えし木の、
もとより恵み深ければ、
程なくかやうに深山となる。
されば当社の御誓にも、
人の参詣はかへすがへす嬉しけれども、
木葉の一葉も裳裾に付けてや去りぬべきと、
惜しみ給もなにゆへぞ、
人の煩い繁き木の、
陰深かれと今もみな、
諸願成就を植へ置くなり。

指声されば慈悲万行の日の影は、
三笠の山にのどかなり、
五重唯識の月の光は、
春日の里に隈もなし。
下哥陰頼みおはしませ、
ただかりそめに植ふるとも、
草木国土成仏の、
神木と思し召し、
あだにな思ひ給ひそ。

Tobuhi[127] ("Flying Fire")

TADAKOTOBA Now then, this particular shrine was, to our great benefit,
moved from Hiraoka in the province of Kawachi
to a peak within the precincts of the main shrine here at Kasuga.
The mountain was a small one affording little protection
for the growth of trees,
indeed, there was hardly a single tree under which to shelter,
but the clansmen of the Fujiwara,
under the shelter, instead, of their devotion,
planted trees and were so deeply favored
that before long this deep forest covered the slopes.
Now it is, of course, cause for happiness,
in accord with the vow made at the founding of the shrine,
that pilgrims should be plentiful,
but the loss of even a single leaf from these trees,
stuck to the hem of a robe on a passerby,
would be much regretted,
so the people who come here for relief
from the forest of troubles they endure in the world
plant seedlings to sustain this shelter for them,
and even unto this day, they find fulfillment of their many wishes.
SASHIGOE Thus the brilliance of the sun[128] in its myriad practices of compassion shines gently over Mount Mikasa, and the light of the moon
of Fivefold Doctrine of Pure Consciousness[129]
fills every corner of Kasuga Village.[130]
SAGEUTA Find shelter underneath these trees;
although they grow here only for a while,
regard them as divine, a testimony to
the buddhahood of plants and trees and all the nation's land—
don't take them lightly.

127. The quotation corresponds to the *katari*, *sashi*, *sageuta*, and *ageuta* sequence of the play *Uneme* in the modern repertory. There seems to be no reason to associate the title as Zeami cites it, as *Tobuhi*, with the play *Uneme*. Omote conjectures that the passage originally comes from a play no longer extant but now borrowed for use in *Uneme*.

128. In the original text, *kage*, the word I have translated as "brilliance," is identical to the frequently occurring word translated as "shelter" earlier and later in the text. I have been unable to find a single English rendering that captures both meanings.

129. See note 83.

130. The place-names relate to age-old and celebrated sites on the Yamato plain. Kasuga "village" is the site of the Fujiwara tutelary shrine.

上あらかねのそのはじめ、
あらかねのそのはじめ、
治まる国は久方の、
あめはしほるゝこぎの緑より、
しほる花ひらけ香残りて、
仏法流布の種久し。
昔は霊鷲山にして、
妙法華経を説き給ひ、
今は衆生を度せんとて、
大明神と現はれ、
この山に住み給へば、
鷲の高嶺とも、
三笠の山を御覧ぜよ。
さて菩提樹の木陰とも、
盛りなる藤咲きて、
松にも花を春日山、
しほるのどけき陰は霊山の、
浄土の春に劣らめや、
浄土の春に劣らめや。

JŌ Ever since the land, rich in raw ore,
Ever since the land, rich in raw ore,
was brought to order
under the broad expanse of heaven,
from among the SHIORU verdant green of the broom trees
SHIORU a flower opened, its scent remains,
and the seeds of the spread of Buddhism have long prospered.
In the distant past, the Miraculous Scripture of the Lotus Flower
was propounded on Vulture Peak,
And now, to save all sentient beings
the Great Bright God of Kasuga is made manifest
upon this very mountain, here, so
you may regard it as both Vulture Peak and Mount Mikasa.
For under the shelter of the bodhi tree
wisteria blossoms in profusion,
and lends its flowers to the pines of Mount Kasuga,
under such a gentle light
how could this spirit-mountain fail to match a spring in paradise,
how could this spirit-mountain fail to match a spring in paradise?

雪山

指声有難や位高う恵み厚うして、
降るや深雪の年を積む、
大内山の道直に、
越え来る年の下はるかけて、
寒風も残る雪のうちに、
越路を移す雲井の庭、
みな白妙の明けぼのゝ山、
あら面白の気色やな。

論義〽げにげにあまりに面白き、
折に引かれて我ながら、
われにもあらぬ心空に、
〽うそぶく月の影ともに、
〽積もる雪山
〽雲の御笠、
〽花の梅壷、
〽御河の波、
同音よるの気色の面白さよ、
古人の言葉こそ、
思ひ出でられて候へ。
下主あかつき梁王の苑に入て雪群山に満ち、
夜庾公が楼に登れば、
月千里に明らか也。
上哥曇りなやこの御代の、
曇りなやこの御代の、
豊の明かりの初めより、
千代木の風も収まり、
雪しほるほうねんに深かりき、
をもし下ろの雪山や。

Yukiyama[131]

SASHIGOE What a blessing! lofty of rank and richly endowed,
deep falls the snow and the passing years pile high,
straight along the path we go, across Mount Ōuchi,
and into spring at the turn of the year.
A chill wind may still blow over the blanketed snow
in a royal garden, mirroring the sights of Echigo.[132]
Everywhere it's white: the mountains spread out pristine white at dawn:
look, what interest the landscape holds!

RONGI Interest indeed . . . too much, in fact—
despite myself, the occasion draws me out
I'm hardly myself, my heart's as light as air.
In the moonlight
a mountain of snow,
drifting up against a hedge of clouds
a courtyard filled with plums in flower
wavelets rippling the river.
DŌ-ON How interesting, the nightscape here!
Why, it even calls the words of the ancients to mind:
GE SHU First light breaks into the garden of Liangwang,
snow fills the range of hills,
Night ascends the tower of Yaogong,
the moonlight spreads over a thousand leagues.

AGEUTA Not a cloud in sight in this august age,
Not a cloud in sight in this august age,
from the outset of the Flushed Faces Festival[133]
the wind falls still on the thousand-year-old trees,
the snow piles deep in a fertile year,
what GE interest there is in a mountain of snow!

131. Apparently a song rather than a play, this is all that remains of the piece.

132. Echigo was a province on the northwestern coast of the main island of Japan. The region continues to be famous for deep snow in the winter.

133. The "Flushed Faces Festival" was one of a series of harvest-related celebrations and rituals that took place at the end of the old year and beginning of the new year, with particular ceremony in a new reign. "Flushed Faces" itself occurs on the first day of the dragon after the Niinamesai, in which the sovereign drinks wine made from new grain and distributes it among the court. See Helen McCullough and William McCullough, trans., *A Tale of Flowering Fortunes: Annals of Japanese Aristocratic Life in the Heian Period* (Stanford, Calif.: Stanford University Press, 1980), vol. 1, pp. 375–78.

春ごとに、
君を祝いて若菜摘む、
わが衣手に降る雪は、
払はじ払はで、
そのままに受くる袖の雪、
しほるはこび重ね懸切ゆき山を、
千代に降れと作らん、
雪山を千代と作らん。

Each and every spring
we pluck young greens to celebrate our prince,
and with the same sleeve
I'll catch the SHIORU falling snow
and keep it, there, no I won't shake it away
but rather, SHIORU carry it off to pile up high, let it snow for a thousand
years,
I'll make a KAKEKIRI mountain of snow to last a thousand years.

李夫人

[指声]かたじけなき御たとえなれどもいかなれば漢王は、
李夫人の御別れを嘆き給て、
朝まつりごと神さびて、
夜の大殿もいたづらに、
ただ思ひの涙御衣の袂を濡らす。
又李夫人は好色の、
花のよそほひ衰えて、
しほるる露の床の上、
塵の鏡の影を恥ぢて、
つゐに御門に見え給はずして去り給。
[節曲舞]御門深く嘆きて、
其御かたちを、
甘泉殿の壁に写し、
われも画図に立添ひて、
明け暮れ嘆き給けり。
されどもなかなか、
御思ひはまされども、
物言ひ交はすことなきを、
深く嘆き給へば、
李少と申太子の、
いとけなくましますが、
武帝に奏し給やう。
[上]李夫人はもとはこれ、
[しほる]じゃう界の辟妾、
くわすい国の仙女也。
一旦人間に、
[しほる]むまるるとは申せども、
つゐにもとの、
仙宮に帰りぬ、
泰山府君に申さく、
[しほる]りふじんの面影を、
しばらくここに、

RI FUJIN ("Lady Li"), composed by my late father[134]

SASHIGOE The parallel may seem impertinent,
but as the story goes, the Royal Sovereign of Han
out of grief in being parted from Lady Li,
grew careless in his observance of duties at court by day
and neglectful alike of his role in the royal chambers at night,
relinquishing himself to tears of longing, moistening the sleeves of his august robes.
And Lady Li, for her part, once such a beauty,
faded away like a withering flower
and wilted upon her bed as if under a heavy dew;
embarrassed by her reflection in the now undusted mirror.
In time, she passed away, never again seen by His Majesty.

KUSEMAI His Majesty bewailed her loss profoundly,
and had her likeness transferred to
a wall in the Ganquan Hall,
where he could join her, standing there, by the picture
passing day and night in his grief, so they say.
With all that, though, his longing
merely grew more painful,
and since he regretted in particular that
he could not speak with her,
the crown prince, Li Shao, yet but a child,
came to the sovereign and announced,
JŌ "Lady Li was from the start
SHIORU a companion sent my lord from the world beyond,
an immortal from the Wonderland of Kwasui.[135]
Although she was SHIORU born into this world below for a time,
she was, in the end, bound to return to her palace there.
Let the Mount Tai Magistrate-in-Chief[136] release her SHIORU shade,
if only for a short while,

134. Although this piece was incorporated into the play *Hanagatami* as a *sashi–kuse* sequence, it appears originally to have been an independent *kusemai*. See Yokomichi and Omote, eds., *Yōkyokushū*, vol. 1, p. 453n.189.

135. Kwasuikoku, apparently a land of immortals. The general context and the word itself suggest a name in Chinese, but it is written entirely in *kana*, so it cannot be determined what Chinese word it would be.

136. Taisan Bukun or Taizan Fukun (or, as in *The Three Courses*, Taisan Moku), a Daoist divinity who supervises the longevity of human beings. There is a nō play in his name.

招くべしとて、
九華帳の内にして、
反魂香を焚き給。
下夜ふけ人静まり、
風すさまじく、
月秋なるに、
それと思ふ面影の、
あるかなきかにかげろへば、
なをいや増しの思ひ草、
葉末に結ぶ白露の、
手にも溜まらで程もなく、
ただいたづらに消えぬれば、
へうべう悠々としては、
又尋ぬべき方なし。
上悲しさのあまりに、
しほるりふじんの住み慣れし、
甘泉殿を立去らず、
空しき床を打払ひ、
故き衾旧き枕、
ひとり袂を片敷けり。

to be summoned here," said he
and lit the Incense-That-Calls-Spirits-Back
within the flowered curtains of the bedchamber.
[GE]Late into the night when people took their rest,
the wind wailed forlornly,
the autumn moon shone high, and
a shade that seemed to be the lady's
trembled in the air, now here now gone,
feeding the pain of his love all the more,
yet no more substantial than a drop of dew
teetering off a leaf tip and gone
before you can catch it in your hand—
just so, her image flew away, remote and indistinct,
leaving no hope that it might be summoned again.
[JŌ]In the extremity of his sadness,
he would not budge from
the Ganquan Hall where [SHIORU]Lady Li had lived,
he brushed off the sheets of the empty bed,
and spread his lonely sleeve out
by her vacant pillow, by her cast-off quilt.

The rationale for the Five Sorts of Singing is, for the most part, as just indicated. There are other types of singing, both old and new, but they need not each be accounted for in writing. All the same, because they approximate the styles mentioned here, you should take care to understand how they might best be categorized in this way.

• The sequence in which one learns the way to sing begins with reading through the text and getting the melody down just right, then polishing one's expression, then getting a good grasp on the stretching and condensation in the rhythm and bringing the singing voice to its fullest realization, then understanding the acoustic properties of the performance venue. Unless the voice is heard clearly, there can be no full realization of the performance. Virtuosity in singing is what we call the rank at which each of these articles is fully incorporated into the singing to create a completely confident plenitude of sound. (Again and again: unless the voice is clearly heard, it is likely to sound like just noise. It is as if the moon's reflection on the water were spoiled by clouds of silt.) All in all, during training in the vocation, the melody is the matter of concern, whereas the aural appeal becomes the matter of concern once the training is finished. (As for expressiveness, it is to be found here within.)

• In its tradition, *kusemai* has a different sort of sound from normal *tadautai* singing. *Kusemai* within the Five Sorts of Singing, though, is perhaps patterned vocally along the lines of normal *tadautai*. Ever since my late father long ago took the "Kusemai Shirahige" (White Beard) into the repertory of *sarugaku*, it has composed one type of singing in this vocation of ours. Now although "Shirahige," "Yura no minato" (The Port of Yura), and "Jigoku" (Hell)—all are performed in *sarugaku*, they are still like real professional *kusemai*. Then there are "Kaidōkudari" (Down the Sea Road) and "Saigokukudari" (Down to the West Country) composed from a text by Tamarin set to music by Naa and Kanze (my late father). These two *kusemai* have expressive elements that are gentler than real professional *kusemai*.

What I mean by real professional *kusemai* performers are troupes like the Kamidō, the Shimodō, the Nishi no take, the Tenjiku, and the Kagajo. (My late father was trained in the last of these by Otozuru.) They say that Kagajo was descended from the women's *kusemai* made famous by Hyakuman in the Southern Capital.[137] By now, all these *kusemai* dancers have, in themselves, perished, and were it not for the last remnants of Kagajo, there would be nothing left. The *kusemai* that appears on a float in the Gion Festival parades derives from this line.

137. Nara.

白鬚曲舞

上夫此国の起り家々に伝うる所、
おのおの別にして、
其説まちまちなりといへども、
しばらく記する所の一義によらば。

天地すでに分れて後、
第九の減劫、
人寿二万歳の時。
下かせう世尊西天に出世し給ふ時に、
大聖釈尊その授記を得て、
兜率天に住し給ひしが。
指声我八相成道の後、
遺教流布の地いづれの所にか有るべきとて、
この南瞻部州を普く飛行して御覧じけるに、
漫々とある大海の上に、
下一切衆、
生悉有仏性如来、
常住無有変易の浪の声、
一葉の芦に凝り固まつて、

SHIRAHIGE KUSEMAI[138]

("White Beard"), music composed by my late father; *rangyoku*, text written by my late father

Now then, the story of the genesis of this land has been transmitted in
various houses,
each with its own traditions,
and varying accounts, but all the same,
according to matters on which they agree, briefly stated,
once heaven and earth had separated, one from the other,
in the ninth lesser kalpa,[139] when human longevity was twenty thousand years,
the Buddha Kāśyapa[140] made himself manifest in Western India,
whereupon the prophecy[141] was proclaimed for the buddhahood of the
great saint, Śākyamuni,
and he ascended to reside in Tuṣita Heaven.

"Once I have manifested my eight Great Aspects,
where shall I bequeath my teachings?" he asked himself
and flew over all the great continent in the south to see what he could
see,
and there, far and wide across the open sea—
where the waves murmured that all sentient existence
partakes of Buddha Nature,
and the Tathāgata lives on eternally, unchanging—
there, he saw that the sea gave itself up
into a single reed and then from the reed

138. This *kusemai*, the first apparently to be performed by *sarugaku* actors rather than professional *kusemai* performers, was later made the center of a play by the same name. *Nōhon sakusha chūmon*, a late Muromachi attribution list, attributes the play to Zenchiku but notes that the *kuri–sashi–kuse* sequence had existed long before the play. See *ZS*, pp. 263–64.

"Shirahige kusemai" seems to preserve characteristics of a professional *kusemai* that do not take root in later *kusemai* when they were incorporated into nō plays. In particular, the two lines following the *kuri* in noncongruent rhythm at a lower pitch are apparently not found elsewhere. See Omote's detailed explanation, in *ZZ*, pp. 486–87n.135.

139. The existence of a cosmos is allotted twenty "lesser kalpas" (a kalpa being a Sanskrit term for an enormously long time). Of these twenty lesser kalpas, some are termed "diminishing kalpas" and others, "expanding kalpas." During a diminishing kalpa, humans begin with a life span of eighty thousand years. Every hundred years, their life span is reduced by one year until it reaches a mere ten years, at which point the process reverses and time enters an expanding kalpa, during which they gain a year in life span every hundred years.

140. Sixth of the seven buddhas of the past.

141. Sanskrit, *vyākaranṣa*. A prophecy to the effect that Śākyamuni would attain buddhahood.

一つの島となる、
今の大宮権現の波止土農也。
節曲舞其のち人寿、
百歳の時、
悉達と生れ給て、
八十年の春の比、
頭北面西右脇臥、
跋提の波と消え給。
されども仏は、
常住不滅法界の、
妙体なれば昔、
芦の葉の島となりし、
中つ国を御覧ずるに、
時はうがや、
ふきあはせずの、
尊の御代なれば、
仏法の名字を、
人知らず。
こゝに比叡山の麓、
さゝなみや、
志賀の浦のほとりに、
釣を垂るゝ老人あり、
尺尊かれに向つて、
翁もし、
此地の主たらば、
此山を我に与へよ、
仏法結界の、
地となすべしとのたまへば
延おきな答へて申やう、
我人寿、
六千歳のはじめより、
此山の主として、
この水海の七どまで、
芦原なりしをも、
まさに見たりし翁也、

came an island
upon which stood
the bridge-house of our own avatar Ōmiya.[142]

Then later, when human longevity
was one hundred years,
he was born as Siddhārtha
and in the spring of his eightieth year,
with head to the north, face to the west, lying on his right side,
he vanished with the waves of Hiraṇyavatī River.
All the same, since a Buddha,
is the wondrous matter
of a Dharma world, ever persisting, never to pass away,
he cast his gaze to this Central Land of the Reed Plains,[143]
that had clustered together as an island around a reed leaf.
This was the era of the god Ugaya-fukiawasezu (born in a half-
 thatched hut),[144]
when people didn't know the word "Buddha."
Now there was at this time
an old man who dangled his fishing line into the water,
at Shiga shore "of the rippling wavelets,"
there at the foot of Mount Hiei.
Śākyamuni addressed him, saying,
"You, old sir,
If you be the master of this land,
would you bestow this mountain upon me
so that I might make of it
a sacred precinct for the Buddhist Law?"
The old man replied,
"Ever since people had a life span of six thousand years,
I, as the master of this mountain, have overseen
the retreat and return of the sea on these reed plains a full seven times,
 in fact.[145]

142. Ōmiya (orth. Ohomiya) Gongen is one of the deities associated with Mount Hiei, and his shrine is located at the foot of the mountain. Here, the "bridge-house" is taken to be a place where he is made manifest.

143. Another name for Japan.

144. The son of Hiko-hohodemi-no-Mikoto and Toyotama-hime and the father of the mythical first sovereign of Japan, Jimmu tennō. His birth in a half-thatched hut is the subject of the nō play *Unoha*. See *ZS*, pp. 168–69.

145. The lore of Lake Biwa includes accounts of the waxing and waning of its waters to such a degree that parts of the lake bed turn to reed plains, only to be covered over again by the lake. The

ただしこの地、
結界となるならば、
釣する所失せぬべしと、
惜み申せば、
釈尊力なく、
今は寂光土に、
帰らんとし給へば。
時に東方より、
浄るり[しほる]せかいの主薬師、
[しほる]こつぜんと出で給ひて。
よきかなや、
釈尊この地に、
仏法をひろめ、
給はん事よ、
我人寿二万歳のはじめより、
此所の主たれど、
老翁いまだ我を知らず、
なんぞこの山を、
惜み申べきはや、
開闢し給へ、
我も此山の主となて、
ともに五々百歳の、
仏法を守るべしと
[延]かたく契約し給て、
二仏、
東西に去り給、
その時の翁も、
今の白鬚の神とかや。

---

old god claims to have seen this come and go some seven times. My thanks to Takahashi Yūsuke for his insights on this.

Should this become a sacred precinct for the Buddhist Law
I would surely lose my fishing spot," said he,
finding he couldn't bring himself to acquiesce to the request.
Powerless, Lord Śākyamuni
now turned to leave,
to go back to the Paradise of Tranquil Light when
then and there, from the east
the Master of the Pure Lapis Paradise, the Medicine Buddha
made a sudden appearance and spoke, "There, there, Lord Śākyamuni intends
to spread the Buddhist Law here.
Although I, for my part, have been
the real master of these lands, since the beginning,
when a human lifespan was twenty thousand years,
this old fellow still doesn't know about me.
How could we possibly begrudge Lord Śākyamuni this land!
No, open the way to Śākyamuni.
I too will join with him in mastery of this mountain
and together we will guard the Buddhist Law
in these Latter Days of a half millennium."
Thus, making a firm pledge
the two Buddhas went their separate ways, to the east and west.
The old man from that time is now
the god, White Beard, so they say.

由良湊節曲舞

上しをる凡人間の八苦の中に、
愛別離苦しほるぐふどつくといふことは、
さのみはよもと思しに、
わが身のしほるうえになりてこそ、
悲しきことは知られたれ。
指声いにしへ人にあひ慣れて、
偕老同穴浅からず、
同じ契りと思ひしに、
人の心の花かとよ、
葛城山の嶺の雲、
よそに通ふと聞きしかば、
ひとり心は住吉の、
ねたくも人に待つと言はれじと包みしに、
男山の女郎花の、
くねる心にあくがれ出でて、
涙の雨の古里を、
足にまかせて立出づる。
節曲舞由良の湊の泊り舟、
和泉の国に着きしかば、
信太の森の葛の葉の、
しばし待たんと思へども、

YURA NO MINATO NO KUSEMAI[146]

("The Port of Yura"), music, likewise, by my late father; *yūkyoku* (All in all, this was the first *kusemai* in the manner of *yūkyoku*. My late father also wrote the text.)

JŌ SHIORU Among the Eight Pains general to human life,
I had little fear of the pain of separation from those one loves
or the SHIORU pain of not getting what one wants,
but now that these have been visited upon me SHIORU in my own
experience
I have come to understand the grief they bear with them.

SASHIGOE Once I lived with someone a long time, accustomed to the
thought
that we should come, in time, to share a common grave—so strong, it
seemed, was the bond between us—
but then I learned that he'd begun to visit someone
off beyond the clouds that cover Katsuragi peak, leaving me alone
(some other flower must have come into bloom within his heart),
but I kept my resentment hidden away;
I was resolved in my own heart,
that no one should say I'd been left behind.
But eventually, like the maiden flower on Man Mountain,[147]
I was, in my jealousy, drawn away and I set off
wherever my feet would take me,
under the rain of tears blanketing my home.

KUSEMAI I set out on a boat from Yura Bay
and when we docked in Izumi Province,
I thought I would bide my time
among the arrowroot tangle in the Shinoda Forest,[148]

146. An independent *kusemai* that survives as a special recital piece, now known as "Yura monogurui." I have compared the text in *ZZ* with that in Sanari Kentarō, ed., *Yōkyoku taikan* (Tokyo: Meiji shoin, 1964), vol. 7, pp. 86–88.

147. Compare *KKS*, *Kana* preface: *Otokoyama no mukashi wo omihiidete, ominaheshi no hitotoki wo kuneru ni mo, uta wo ihite zo, nagusamekeru* (In recalling the past of "Otokoyama" or regretting the brief time of the Maidenflower, it is with poetry that we find consolation).

148. Shinoda Forest, by way of *SKKS* 1820, was associated with the reunion of lovers: *Utsurohade shibashi Shinoda no mori wo miyo / kaheri mo zo suru kudzu no urakaze* ([After Lady Izumi had been forgotten by her husband Michisada, Prince Atsumichi heard that he had begun a flirtation, so he sent this to Lady Izumi:] "Don't turn your affection away, but bide your time and watch the leaves in Shinoda Forest; the wind may yet blow him back to you as it blows over the arrowroot leaves").

我には人の帰らず、
訪はれし頃は待ち慣れし、
夕の境の鐘を聞く、
難波の寺に参れば、
かの国に、
生まるる心地して、
西を遥かに伏し拝み、
入江の芦の仮の世に、
いつまで物を思ふべき。
濃き墨染めに様変へて、
誠の道に入らばやと、
思ひ長柄の橋柱、
千度まで悔しきは、
捨てざりし身のいにしへ。
過ぎにし方の旅衣、
春も半ばになりしかば、
花の都に上りて、
清水寺に参れば、
上大慈大悲の日の光、
しほるえんえんとある地主の桜、
延まことに権現の誓ひかや、
しほる花のあたりは心して、
松には風の音羽山、
音に聞きしよりもなをまさり、
尊き面白さに、
下向の道も覚えず。
下かくて夜に入れば、
まどろむ隙もなくして、
御名を唱へてゐたりしに、
同じ様に通夜して、
近く寄り添ふ女あり。
語らい寄りて申やう、
痛はしやかたがたは、

yet he didn't come back to me,
and then I heard a temple bell, separating day from dusk,
like the one I used to hear while I waited for him before,
when he still used to come to call,
so I went to the Naniwa Temple
and felt as though I'd been reborn in Paradise,
so I made a bow to the far off west;
by the inlet there, where they cut the seaside reeds,
I stood in thought: how long, after all, should I put up with the fickleness of life?
I gave myself over to nun's black weeds,
but for all my longing to enter onto the True Path, even with the best intentions
I found what rankled, time and time again, was a resentment
deep as the pilings of Nagara Bridge,
that I could not shed my past.
I stretched the thread of my journey
farther and farther away from where I'd been
as the season turned to spring,
and I came up to the flowery capital,
to make a prayer at Kiyomizu Temple:
JŌ bathed in the sunlight of great compassion
among the SHIORU radiant blossoms of the *jishu* cherry[149]—
NOBE as in the promise of the sacred avatar—
I came to a better sense of things,
waiting there among the SHIORU flowers,
even more than I'd been told on the wings of hearsay,
there in the shade of Mount Sound-on-Wings.[150]
A blessed interest captivated me,
and all thought of leaving that spot vanished.
GE When then night fell,
I chanted the Holy Name
without dozing off for even a moment
and noticed a woman nearby,[151]
spending the whole night, same as me, in prayer.
What she said when she approached
gave me hope: "I'm so sorry.

149. A celebrated cherry tree, associated with Jishu (orth. Djishu), avatar in the precinct of Kiyomizu Temple, Kyoto.

150. Otohayama, a mountain to the east of Kyoto.

151. Sanari's version, based on a Kanze text, specifies a man, whereas a Kita version says "an older woman."

思ひありと見えたり、
思し召す事あらば、
心の内を語りて、
御慰みもあれかしと、
ねんごろに申せば、
頼もしく思ひて、
立寄る蔭もなき身也、
様変えたきと申せば、
痛はしき事かな、
わが住む里にしばらく、
足を休め給て、
まことに様を変へ給はば、
しかるべき尼寺に、
引きつけ奉るべし、
とくとくと誘はれて、
延身を浮き草の根を絶えて、
清水寺を立ち出て、
なをも思ひを志賀の浦、
大津とかやに下りぬ。
上矢橋の浦の渡し舟、
さしてそことも白波を、
しほるぬす人とは思はで、
東路さして売られ行、
過ぎにし方も覚えず、
行く末もなを遠江の、
掛川の宿に年たけて、
又越ゆべしと思ひきや、
命なりけり、
小夜の中山、
なかなかに残る身ぞつらき。

It seems there's something
troubling you,
If there's something on your mind
why don't you tell me about it.
Maybe I can offer some consolation."
So kind seemed her condolences that I let her know
I had no source of shelter in the world, and
had set my hopes on entering a religious life.
"How touching," she exclaimed,
"Won't you come home with me
and rest your legs a little while,
and if you still want to take holy orders,
then I can introduce you
to the right sort of nunnery."
She offered strong encouragement, and I,
myself no more than a waterweed uprooted, at the mercy of the
stream,[152]
left Kiyomizu Temple,
and came down to a place called Ōtsu
on the Shiga shoreline, with my thoughts unsettled still.
JŌThe ferry boat from Yabase shore,
sets out for an unknown destination,
over the white waves.
Little did I know that they were SHIORUthieves
taking me away to sell into slavery in the east country.
My memory of the past uprooted,
and still more remote, my destination, away in Tōtōmi,
in the way station at Kakekawa, "Did I ever think
I'd cross the pass again, at this great age?
What a life this is!
The Middle Mount of Sayo."[153]
Living on like this at odds and ends,
what an unbearable way to exist.

152. Ono no Komachi, *KKS* 938: *Wabinureba mi wo ukikusa no ne wo taete / sasofu midzu araba inamu to zo omofu* (So lost in want and loneliness am I that were there an inviting current I would, I tell you, cut my roots and drift, wherever the stream might take me).

153. Saigyō, *SKKS* 987: *Toshi takete mata koyubeshi to omohiki ya inochi narikeri Sayo no naka yama.*

地獄節曲舞

上しほる昨日もいたづらに過ぎ今日もむなしく暮れなんとす、
無常の虎 の声肝に銘じ、
しほるせっせんの鳥鳴いて、
思ひをいたましむ。
指声一生はただ夢のごとし。
たれか百 年の齢を期せむ、
下万事はみな空し、
いづれ か常住の思ひをなさん。
命は水上の 泡。
風にしたがつて廻ぐるがごとし、
魂は籠中の鳥の、
開くを待ちて去 るに同じ、
消ゆるものは二たび見えず、
去るものは重ねて来らず。
節曲舞須臾に 生滅し、
刹那に離散す、
恨めしきかなや、
釈迦大士の慇懃の教を忘れ、
悲しきかな や、
閻魔法王の、
苛責の言葉を聞く、
名利 身を助くれども、
いまだ北邙の、
煙をまぬかれず、
恩延ないに、
心を悩ませども、
たれか黄泉の、
責にしたがはざる。
これがために馳走す、
所得 いくばくの利ぞや、
これによて追求す、
しよしや多罪なり、
しばらく目をふさいで、

Jigoku no kusemai

("Hell"), music composed by Naami. This is in the *aishyau* vocal style. (The lyrics were written by Yamamoto,[154] from the play *Hyakuman*.)[155]

Yesterday passed vainly and today comes to an empty end,
Impermanence is as ferocious as a tiger's roar—that much is graven on my heart,
the cry of the Himalayan cuckoo torments my thoughts with uselessness.[156]

My entire life is like a dream.
Who can expect to live for a hundred years?
Since all is vanity,
who can aspire to immortality?
Life is the froth on the waters,
blown around in circles by the wind,
the soul is the same as a caged bird,
waiting, merely, for an open door in order to escape:
as the bird flies off, never to be seen again,
so the soul, once gone, will never again return.

Born one instant,
scattered away the next,
what hateful caprice!
Heedless of the tender creed of Noble Śākyamuni,
what sadness!
These the admonitions we hear in the words of Dharma King Yama.
Though fame and profit support your standing in life,
you still cannot evade the smoky crematoria on Mount Beimang,[157]
despite the cares of love and affection entangling the heart,
who, in the end, can escape the tortures of the Yellow Springs?
What does it profit you
to scramble after earthly gain
when the acts it provokes in you
are filled with sin?
Shut your eyes for a moment,

154. Unknown.

155. The *kusemai* on hell was earlier performed in the play *Hyakuman* but was later incorporated into *Utaura*.

156. Legend holds that the "cuckoo of India's snowy peaks" cries in a voice that reminds listeners that they have ignored the approach of death and failed to accumulate good works.

157. Mount Beimang, north of the Chinese capital Loyang, was the site of a royal graveyard.

往事を 思へば、
旧遊みな亡ず、
指を折て、
古人のかぞふれば、
親疎多くかくれぬ、
時移り事去つて、
今なんぞ、
渺茫たらんや、
人とどまりわれゆき、
たれか又常ならん。
上三界無安猶如火宅、
天仙なをし死苦の身なり、
いはんや下劣、
しほるひんせんの報においてをや、
などか其罪軽ろから寄ん、
死に苦しみを受け重ね 、
業に悲しみなほ添ふる。
下ざんすい地獄の苦しみは、
臼中にて身を斬る事、
せつたつして、
地らきた り、
一日の其うちに、
万死万生也、
剣樹地獄の苦しみは、
手に剣の樹をよづれば、
はくせきれいらくす、
足に刀山踏むときは、
剣樹ともに解すとかや、
石割地獄の苦しみは
りやうぐわいの、
大石もろもろの、
罪人を砕く、
つぎの火盆地獄は、
頭に火焔をいただけば、
はくせきの骨頭より、
炎々たる火を出す。
ある時は、
焦熱大焦熱の、
ほのほにむせびある時は、
紅蓮大紅蓮の、
氷に閉ぢられ、
鉄杖頭を砕き、
火燥足裏を焼く。

think upon the past:
all your old friends are dead;
count out your companions on your fingers
only to find that they are vanished, both intimate and mere
    acquaintance.
Time passes, things disappear,
how can you rest
obtusely unaware of this now?
Someone stays behind, you yourself pass on,
yet who in the end endures?

"The Three Worlds are filled with danger, like unto a house on fire,"
even angels and wizards are subject to death and pain,
so the threat can only be that much greater for us of lower being;
given our poverty and degradation,
how could the retribution meted unto us be anything but grave?
Beyond our death, wave on wave of suffering and anguish,
added to injury in consequence of our sins.

Agony in the Hell of Slicing and Crushing,
No sooner are our bodies smashed in a mortar,
our blood gushing forth in a flood,
than we are brought to life again.
In a single day ten thousand deaths, ten thousand resurrections.
Reach for a branch in the Hell of the Forest of Blades
and your misery will entail dismemberment of all the limbs,
and should you set foot on the Mountain of Swords,
it will sever each of your appendages.
In the Hell of Twin Crags,
every last sinner is squashed under massive boulders.
In the Hell of the Fiery Basin, a crown of fire is kindled on your head
while jets of flame burst from every joint.
Smothered on the one hand in the Hells of Blazes and Great
    Conflagrations,
jailed in ice on the other in the Hells of the Flayed Lotus and the
    Greater Flayed Lotus,
a club of iron crashing into your skull
even as a blaze incinerates the soles of your feet.

上飢ゑては鉄丸を呑み、
渇しては、
銅汁を飲むと かや、
地獄の苦しみは無量なり、
餓鬼の苦しみも無辺なり、
畜生修羅の悲しみは、
われらにいかで勝るべき、
身より出せる咎なれば、
心の鬼の身を責めて、
かように苦をば受くるなり、
月の夕の浮き雲は、
後の世の迷ひなるべし。

When you're hungry, gulp iron pellets,
when you're thirsty, molten copper cascades down your throat,
The agonies of hell are without bounds.
The agonies of hungry ghosts may be beyond all limitation, but
how, for all their horror, could the miseries of beasts and asuras
exceed our suffering?[158]
The guilt for this comes from our very selves,
the demon of our very own minds castigates our being;
we gather unto us, thus, this misery.
The floating clouds of a moonlit evening
may in the end lead us astray.

158. The references to hungry ghosts, asuras, and beasts relate to the six benighted ways into which unenlightened existence is traditionally categorized. The order varies according to the account, but in one influential version, they range from (at the top) heavenly beings, human beings, and asuras (warring titans), to animals, hungry ghosts, and the denizens of hell (at the bottom). See also note 64.

海道下

上抑甲しほる此もり久と申は、
平家譜代の侍、
武略のしほる達者なりしかば、
鎌倉殿まで知ろしめしたるつはものなり。
指声これにて計らひがたしとて、
関東にくだしつかわさる、
花の都を出でしより、
音に鳴きそめし賀茂河や、
下すへ白河をうち渡り、
粟田口にも着きしかば、
今はたれをか松坂や、
四の宮河原四つの辻。
節曲舞関の山路のむらしぐれ、
いとど袂や濡らすらん、
知るも知らぬも逢坂の、
嵐の風の音寒き、
松本の宿に打出の浜、

KAIDŌKUDARI[159]

("Going Down the Ocean Road"), music composed by Naa[mi]. (The vocal style of this *kusemai* is [. . .] *rangyoku*.[18] This, for its part, is in each case applicable as well to *yūkyoku*. Lyrics by Tamarin.)

JŌNow KAN SHIORUthen, this Morihisa, as he's called,
was in a line of samurai serving the Heike for several generations,
an SHIORUexpert in martial strategy, and for that,
a warrior well known to his lordship in Kamakura.

SASHIGOESince it was impossible to pass judgment on him locally,
he was sent down to the East.
Leaving the Flowered Capital,
he crosses the Kamo River in tears, there where the birds first sing in spring,
and then GEacross the Shirakawa, uncertain of what may lie ahead,
until he reaches the furthest limit of the city, at Awataguchi,
and then beyond, near Pine Hill—no one to pine for him—
he comes into the crossroads at Yotsunotsuji by the Shinomiya Riverbed.

KUSEMAIWinter showers come and go along the pass through the mountain barrier,
more sodden now his tear-soaked sleeves.
At Meeting-Pass Mountain, where both friends and strangers pass each other by,
a cold gale howls,
past Matsumoto Station to strike out on

159. Also called "Azumakudari" or "Tōgokukudari." The context of the song concerns Taira no Morihisa, who had been an officer in the royal police (*hangan*) as well as the chief of the crown prince's stables. As an enemy of the Genji, he was sentenced to execution, and this song tells the story of his gloomy journey to the site where that was supposed to take place.

As a song of journey, the piece is also a *monozukushi*, that is, a catalog of the many place-names he encounters on the route, often with puns and other wordplay integrated into the names. The song was apparently incorporated into the play *Ausaka monogurui*, a predecessor of the play *Semimaru* in the modern repertory. See Susan Matisoff, *The Legend of Semimaru, Blind Musician of Japan* (New York: Columbia University Press, 1978), pp. 103–6, and P. G. O'Neill, "The Structure of *Kusemai*," *Bulletin of the School of Oriental and African Studies* 21 (1958): 100–110. The piece has been translated by P. G. O'Neill as "The Journey Down to the Eastern Provinces," in *Early Nō Drama: Its Background, Character and Development, 1300–1450* (London: Lund Humphreys, 1958), pp. 153–60.

Morihisa became the subject of a play by the same name written by Zeami's son Motomasa, which describes the miraculous intercession of the bodhisattva Kwanzeon (mod. J. Kanzeon), who saved him.

湖水に月の影落ちて、
氷に波や立ぬらん、
越と辞せし范蠡が、
扁舟に棹を移す也、
五湖の煙の波の上、
かくやと思ひ知られたり。
昔ながらの山里も、
都の名をや残すらん、
石山寺を拝めば、
これまた久世の悲願の、
世に超え給御誓ひ、
頼もしくぞや覚ゆる、
瀬田の唐橋影見へて、
長虹波にただよへり、
憂き世の中を秋草の、
野路篠原の朝露、
をき別れゆく旅の空、
幾夜な夜なを重ぬべき。
上露も時雨も守山は、
下葉残らぬ初紅葉、
夕日に色や増さるらん、
いにしへ今を、
鏡山、
形をたれか忘るべき、
勇む心はなけれ共、
其名ばかりの武者の宿。
下まだ通ひ路も浅茅生の、
小野の宿より見渡せば、
斧斤を研ぎし磨針や、
番場と音の聞こえしは、

Uchide Shore, where the image of the moon falls on the lake—
could waves rise, in this ice?—
"Fanli must have felt something like this
when, in parting from Yue,
he set out over the waves
in the brume of Wu Lake,
pushing along his little skiff with a pole."[160]
Even this mountain village of Nagara,[161]
once the capital itself,
still has something of its ancient aura, doesn't it,
and prayers at Ishiyamadera
strengthen our faith in
Kannon's compassionate wish to save the world,
a vow transcending worlds.[162]
The Chinese bridge at Seta
is reflected in the water,
a rainbow floats above the waves.
He sets off again, surfeited on the world's grief
under a traveler's sky no more substantial
than the morning dew on Shinohara's autumn grass;
how many more nights, one after the other, to pass on the road?
JŌEvery last leaf on the maples of Mount Moruyama
has been colored by dew and drizzle,
and in the light of dusk they turn redder still.
Mirror Mountain
reflects today onto memories of the past,
and who can evade reflection on his own yesterdays?
No fierceness wells up in the mind now,
Even at the name, Warrior Way Station.
He gazes out from Ono Station, then,
GEwhere paths little trodden are overgrown with grass,
and hears a scraping sound at Banba,
like an ax head on a whetstone:

160. Fanli was a minister in the state of Yue during China's Spring and Autumn period, who came to the aid of his king, Juxian, to attack the king of Wu, and became a great general. Identical lines can be found in the play *Hakurakuten*, in the *shite*'s entry songs.

161. The former capital (667–672) of Emperor Tenji (626–671, r. 668–671), more commonly known as Ōtsu-no-miya.

162. There is a visual association between the name Kuse [Kannon], "Kannon who saves the world," and *yo ni koe* (transcending worlds), although it is hidden in aural terms because of the Sinicized reading of *se* for "world" in the first case, whereas in the second the reading is the native *yo*.

この山松の夕嵐、
旅の夢も醒井の、
みづから結ぶ草枕、
たれか宿をも柏原、
月も稀なる山中の、
不破の関屋の板庇、
久しくならぬ旅にだに、
都の方ぞ恋しき。
垂井の宿を過ぎ行けば、
青野が原は名のみして、
みな夕霜の白妙、
枯れ葉に洩るる草もなし、
かかる憂き世に青墓や、
捨てぬ心を杭瀬川、
墨俣足近の渡りして、
下津貝津打ち過ぎて、
熱田の宮に参れば。
[上]蓬莱宮は名のみして、
けい[しほる]りくに近き我身の、
不死の薬やなかるらむ、
[延]あし間の風の鳴海潟、
干汐につるる捨小船、
ささで沖にや出でぬらん。
[指声]ささがにの、
蜘蛛手にかかる八橋の、
沢辺に匂う杜若、
有原の中将の、
はるばる来ぬと詠ぜしも、
わが身の上に知られたり。
[節曲舞]なを行く末は白真弓、
矢矧の宿赤坂、
松に波立つ藤さはの、

that's the gale coming off Mount Surihari,
through the mountain pines at dusk;
the traveler awakens from his dream at Samé well,
—he wove himself a pillow of grass,
for where, after all, was lodging be found—
and Kashiwa Plain is so deep in the mountains
that even the moon is rarely to be seen from under the bare plank
eaves
of the guardhouse at Fuwa Barrier.
Even on a short journey,
one longs to be heading back toward the capital.
Once past Tarui Station,
Greenfield Plains are green in name alone,
and spread instead all white with evening frost, like hempen cloth;
not a leaf has escaped the withering winter blast.
In this wearying world, he comes to Green Grave, ho,
uneasy at the tenacity of his regrets at Kuize River,
then by Sunomata and Ajika Ford, where he makes a crossing,
right past Oritsu and Kaizu,
to make obeisance at Atsuta Shrine.
JŌ"The Palace of Penglai Paradise" in name alone,
I've come so close to a SHIORUcapital conviction,
surely there's no elixir of immortality for me.
The winds NOBEblow through the reeds at Narumi Bay,
An abandoned skiff, directionless,
is pulled out to sea at low tide.
SASHIGOEA bridge in eight sections stretches
as would a crablike spider's legs
through the marsh, fragrant with sweet flags;
it's easy to understand now
how Lieutenant Ariwara felt,
coming here, "far, so far, from home."[163]
KUSEMAIBut farther still from here, to Shiramayumi,
to Yahagi Station, then to Akasaka,
and Fujisawa where the pines are blown in waves,

163. Ariwara no Narihira, *KKS* 410: *Karakoromo kitsutsu narenishi tsuma shi areba / harubaru kinuru tabi wo shi zo omofu* (For a long time, lovingly I've worn, a robe of Chinese silk, gazing now upon the hem; far, so far this journey takes me from my love!). The poem is an acrostic that pulls the word *kakitsubata* ("[sweet] flags" or "Japanese iris") out of the first syllable of each line and puns the word *tsuma* (hem) on *tsuma* (wife).

木末の花を宮路山、
わたうど、
今橋打ち過ぎ、
雲と煙の二村、
山は高師の名のみして、
野里に道や続くらん。
上延浪の満ち干の潮見坂、
れうかしほるいてんに連なりて、
雲に漕ぎ入、
沖つ舟、
呉楚東南にしほるわかれて、
乾坤日夜浮かめり、
しほるかへらんことも白須賀に、
しばし下りゐる水鳥の、
下安からぬ心かな。
下夕汐のぼる橋本の、
浜松が枝の年々に、
行春秋を送りけん。
山は後の前沢、
夜は明け方の遠山に、
はや横雲の引馬より、
天竜川も見えたり。
衰え果つる姿の、
池田の宿鷺坂、
旅寝とだにも慣れぬれば、
夢も見付の国府とかや。
岸辺に波を掛河、
小夜の中山中寄々に、
命の内は、
しらく寄もの、
又越ゆべしと思ひきや、
憂き事のみを、
菊川や、
旅の疲れの駒場が原、
変る淵瀬の大井川、
川辺の松に言問わん。
上花紫の藤枝の、

and Miyaji Mountain, where you see the blossoms on the farthest twigs,
then Watōdo, and across Imabashi Bridge,
through low banks of cloud and smoke,
the mountain is named Lofty Mount in name alone,
the road leads on through a village on the moor.
[JŌ]Shiomi Hill, where you can see the waves rise and fall,
stretching off in the distance to the place where the sea meets the sky,
a boat in the offing
rows off into the clouds
between [SHIORU]Wu in the east and Chu in the south,
afloat night and day between the heavens and earth.
At Shirasuga, with [SHIORU]no prospects for a return to the capital,
his mind is flighty to its depths,
like a waterbird alighting for a little time here below.
How long have the pine boughs flourished
[GE]on the beach at Hashimoto where the evening tide comes in—
how many springs and autumns have they seen?
At Maesawa, where a marsh lies to the front and mountains behind,
the night has begun to brighten and on the far peaks,
long clouds spread like banners; from Hikima
the Tenryū River can be seen.
The sight of me has gone decrepit and
at Ikeda Station and Sagisaka
inured to sleep on the road,
is that the Kofu lookout I see in dreams?
Throwing in my lot with the waves that lap the shore at Kishibe,
I know nothing more substantial than the clouds:
"The Middle Mount of Sayo:
Living on like this [YOSURU]at odds and ends,
Did I ever think
[YOSURU]I'd cross this pass again?"[164]
At Listening River, with nothing
but weariness in what I hear,
exhausted by the pains of travel over Komaba Plains,
we must change our mounts again to cross
the Ōi River at Fuchise Shallows,
to make address to the pines on the riverbank:
[JŌ]how many [SHIORU]springs in fragrant blossom,

164. Saigyō, *SKKS* 10:987: *Toshi takete mata koyubeshi to omohiki ya inochi narikeri Sayo no naka yama*, as quoted earlier in *Yura no minato no kusemai*.

しほるいく春かけて匂ふらん、
慣れにししほる旅の友だにも、
心岡部の宿とかや。
蔦の細道分け過ぎて、
着慣れ衣を宇都の山、
現や夢と成りぬらん。
下みなとに近く引綱の、
手越の河の朝夕に、
思ひを駿河の国府を過ぎ、
清見が関の中々に、
戸ざさぬ旅や憂かるらん、
薩埵山より見渡せば、
遠く出たる三保が崎、
海岸そことも白波の、
松原越しに眺むれば、
梢に寄する海士小舟、
あまりに袖や濡らすらん、
由比蒲原をも過ぎしかば、
田子の浦回も近くなり。
上西天唐土扶桑国、
しほるならぶ山なき富士の嶺や、
延ばん天の雲を重ぬらん。
浮島が原を過ぎ行けば、
左は湖水波寄せて、
凌波潜水の浮鳥の、
上毛の霜を打払ふ。
右は蒼海かすかにて、
漁村の孤帆遥かなり、
頓教智解衆生の、
火宅の門を出で初めし、
羊車鹿車大牛の、
車返しはこれかとよ。
上伊豆の国府にも着きしかば、

branches of wisteria, flowered lavender?
Even a [SHIORU]well-worn traveler
and old companion on the road
cannot but have some anxiety
at Okabe Station here.
Threading a way along a narrow road through the ivy,
to arrive at Utsunoyama, where my well-worn clothes
are pounded on the fulling block, and
reality recedes into dreams.
[GE]Morning and evening at Tegoshi River,
near the bay where the nets are hauled in, hand over hand,
sunk in thought, I pass through the provincial seat in the land of Suruga,
no matter how clear the view from Kiyomi Barrier,
this unending journey were ever more wearying.
When I gaze out from Satta Mountain,
The spit of land at Miho Point reaches far away,
and there—is it the seacoast?—breakers, white,
beyond the field of pines, when I look through there,
fishing skiffs draw up, as if to treetops,
why are tears drawn down to wet my sleeves?
once we've passed by Kanbara Plain in Yuhi,
we've come well nigh upon the Coast of Tago.

[JŌ]The lofty peak of Mount Fuji,
[SHIORU]unparalleled in India and China, or elsewhere in Japan,
stands, strewing clouds [NOBE]throughout the heavens,
over the Plains of Ukishima, and once we've passed it by,
on the left the waves of the lake lap at the shore,
rugged breakers on the hidden pools
rinse frost away from the top feathers of water birds.
Off to the right the blue sea is shrouded in mist,
a solitary sail rises in the distance from a fishing boat.
Are these not the sheep and deer carts, and the great ox carts
on which we should begin to make our way
out of the gate of the burning house,[165]
an abrupt teaching to free the great host from delusion?
[JŌ]Once we've settled in the provincial seat in Izu,[166]

165. On the "burning house," see note 31.

166. The rest of the piece has been incorporated into Zeami's play *Shunnei*, in the end of the *kuse*.

南[しほる]無や三島の明神、
本地大[しほる]つうちせう仏、
過去塵点のごとくにて、
くわう[延]せん中有の旅の空、
ぢや[しほる]うあんみゃうの巷までも、
我らを照らし給へと、
[しほる]ふかくぞ祈誓申ける、
雪の古枝の枯れてだに、
二たび花や咲くらん。

let us raise our voices in SHIORU praise of the Shining God of Mishima,
Avatar of the SHIORU Buddha Mahābhijñānābhibhū![167]
"Shine your light on me,
from the incalculable past
as I wander NOBU beneath the sky of travel
whether to SHIORU Limbo or to the Yellow Springs,
or unto whatever land beyond, long locked in obscurity."
This my SHIORU heartfelt prayer.
For even as old branches wither under falling snow.
the blossoms will come sometime, once again, to bloom.

167. In Leon Hurvitz's translation, "Victorious through Great Penetrating Knowledge," a buddha of the Lotus Sutra, "Parable of the Conjured City" (*Scripture of the Lotus Blossom of the Fine Dharma* [New York: Columbia University Press, 1976]).

西国下り

指声寿永二年の秋の比、
平家西海におもむき給う、
西南の離宮に至り、
都を隔つる山崎や、
関戸院に玉の御輿をかき据へて、
八幡の方を、
下ふし拝み、
南無や八幡大菩薩、
指声人王はじまり給ひて、
十六代の尊主たり、
下みもすそ川の底澄みて、
末を受け汲む御流れ、
などか捨てさせ給ふべき、
節曲舞他の人よりはわが人と、
誓はせ給ふなる物を、
西海の波に立ちかへり、
二たび帝都の雲を踏み、
九重の月を眺めんと、
深く祈誓申せども、
悪逆無道のその積もり、
神明仏陀加護もなく、
貴賤上下に捨てられ、
帝城の外におもむく、

SAIGOKUKUDARI[168]

("Going Down to the West Country"), music composed by my late father. Tamarin's lyrics.

SASHIGOE In autumn of the second year of Juei
the Heike set out toward the Western Sea.
They made their way toward the southern palace, past Yamazaki,
parted from the capital by hills,[169]
and in the estate at Sekido, brought the bejeweled palanquin to rest,
GE to make obeisance
in the direction of Yawata Shrine:[170]
"Praise be to the Great Bodhisattva Hachiman![171]
SASHIGOE Sixteenth in the line of divine lords
that began with the first human Heavenly Sovereign.[172]
Surely Thou wilt never abandon
our august lineage, drawing as it does,
GE on the stream of Mimosuso River."[173]

KUSEMAI "Here we are, afloat on the Western Sea, even though
Thou hast pledged protection to our own kind before all others.
Sure as the waves turn back to the shore,
will we return to tread the ninefold cloudbanks
of the imperial city and see the moon again
from within the palace grounds,"
thus they prayed with deepest reverence;
but burdened with their high crimes and betrayals of the Way,
they had lost the protection of the gods and the Buddha,
they were forsaken by both high and low,
as they turned away from the capital city.

168. Like the preceding song, this is a *monozukushi* based on a journey, in this case, the journey of the Heike evacuating the capital after the Genji attacked. An annotated version of an only slightly different text can be found in Sanari, ed., *Yōkyoku taikan*, vol. 7, pp. 33–38.

169. These two lines are identical to the first lines of the *waki*'s *sashi* of the first *dan* of *Tadanori*.

170. Otokoyama Hachiman Shrine.

171. The Great Bodhisattva Hachiman was conceived to be an avatar of Amida Buddha, who appeared as the Heavenly Sovereign Ōjin.

172. Although a patron deity of the Minamoto, the Great Bodhisattva Hachiman was, from the mid-ninth century, believed to have been incarnate as the sovereign, Emperor Ōjin. Although Ōjin is generally regarded as the fifteenth, rather than sixteenth, emperor, in this case Empress Jingū has been counted as a predecessor, thus changing the count. Compare *The Tales of the Heike*, book 7.

173. Mimosuso River is another name for the Isuzu River, which flows through the sacred precinct of the shrine of Amaterasu in Ise and therefore is associated with her putative earthly lineage in the Japanese royal line.

なにと成行水無瀬河、
山本遠くめぐりきて、
昔男の音を泣きし、
鬼一口の芥川、
弓やなぐゐをたづさへて、
駒にまかせて打ち渡る。
馴れし都を立出て、
しほるいづくに猪名の小條原、
一夜仮寝の宿はなし、
芦の葉分の月の影、
隠れて澄める昆陽の池。
生田の小野のおのづから、
この河波に浮き寝せし、
鳥は射ねどもいかなれば、
身を限りとは嘆くらん、
千山の雨に水まさり、
濁れる時は名のみして、
さらすかひなき布引の、
滝津白波音立てて、
雲のいづくを流るらむ、
五手船の名残に、
五百の舟を作りて、
御調を絶えず運びしは、
武庫の浦こそ泊まりなれ。
福原の故郷に着きしかば、
人々の家々も、
年の三歳に荒れはてて、
上ふくろう松桂の枝に鳴き、
しほるきつね蘭菊の、
くさしほるむらに隠れ住む、
ありし名残も寄なみ風の、
荒磯館住み捨てて、

Without a notion of what was to come,
they passed the Minase River, wreathed in haze,
and trailed along the foothills
where "the man of old" once cried aloud with grief,
and came to the Akuta River,
where a demon once gobbled up a girl in a single bite,[174]
and with their bows and quivers in hand,
gave their ponies their head to surge across.
The beloved capital they had left behind––
what was to become of them?—
they spent the night in the open
in SHIORU the fields of bamboo grass at Ina,
and made their way through the reeds
at Koya Lake, while the moon now hid, now shone down bright upon them.
By Ono in Ikuta,
they rocked in their sleep on the river's waves, like birds,
and even though they were not targeted by rival archers,[175]
they were assailed all the same by premonitions of impending doom.
The waters rose under rain, blanketing a myriad peaks,
the river roiled with silt,
and only in name could Nunobiki Falls be thought
"a bleached ribbon of white"
as the rapids rushed, who knows where beyond the clouds.
They took their rest along the Muko Coast,
where once five hundred ships were fitted out to carry unceasing tribute.
When they arrived at their erstwhile Fukuhara home,
they found their estates of three years back in ruin.
JŌ Owls hooted from branches of pines and cinnamon trees,
SHIORU Foxes hid away
among the orchids and chrysanthemums,
the vestiges of their estates were all but gone
and YOSURU waves pounded the shore in a gale from off the sea:

174. According to a story in *The Tales of Ise*, 6, a "man of old" once eloped with a woman to the banks of the Akuta River, where, in seeking shelter from a storm, they took refuge in an old warehouse, unaware that it was the abode of a demon. While the man kept watch by the door, the demon gobbled down the woman in a single gulp. When the man figured this out, he wept and wailed and stomped his feet in grief.

175. Although they are reduced to floating, like birds, at the behest of the waves, they are not like the mandarin couple who were targeted by rival archers in the story providing the background for the play *Motomezuka*.

ただ海士の子の住み所、
宿も定めぬ旅寝かな。
下相国の作り置かれし、
所々もひきかへ、
故宮の軒端月洩り、
金玉を交へしよそほひ、
花の轅を集めしも、
只今のやうに思はれて、
昔ぞ恋しかりける。
上釈迦一代の蔵経、
しほる五千よ巻を石に書き、
蒼海の底に沈めて、
一居の島を築きしかば、
しほるすせんぞうの船を泊め、
風波の難を助けしは、
しほるありがたかりし形見なり、
世をうき波の夜の月、
沈みし影はかへらず。
指声かくてあるべきにあらねば、
主上を初めたてまつり、
みな御船に召されけり。
慣はぬ波の浮き枕、
思ひやるこそ悲しけれ、
南殿の池の竜頭鷁首の御船ぞと。
曲舞思ひなせども寒江に、
釣の翁の棹の歌、
まだ聞きなれぬ声々に、
沖なる鷗磯千鳥、
友呼び連れて立さはぐ、
風帆波に遡り、
艪声は月を動かす、
和田の御崎をめぐれば、
海岸遠き松原や、
海のみどりに続くらん。
須磨の浦にもなりしかば、
四方の嵐もはげしくて、

nothing there now but the huts of fishers,
unsettled refuge for the restless sleep of travel.
[GE]The city laid out there by the prime minister had reverted to vacant land;
palace eaves let moonlight leak through, unimpeded;
to recall anew how once the same site glittered with gold and jade,
how carriage moorings, now left idle and empty
only yesterday had flowered with life;
all this sharpened their yearning for the past.
[JŌ]Śākyamuni in his time had had the treasury of scriptures, [SHIORU]five thousand scrolls and more, carved in stone,[176]
and when they sank to the bottom of the azure sea
they formed the bed of an island
where [SHIORU]countless boats were moored
and rescued from the dangers of the wind and waves:
that was a [SHIORU]blessing born of the vestiges of time gone by.
In the present case, though, the moon's reflection rode the waves,
and the sunken remains of Fukuhara showed no reflection of the past.
[SASHIGOE]Nothing there was as it should have been,
so they all took to boats, beginning with the sovereign himself.
How sad, the very thought of them, trying to find rest
on unfamiliar pillows, tossed up and down by the waves!
They labored to imagine that their boats were festive barges
graced with dragons or *yi*-birds on the prow,[177]
[KUSEMAI]but what they heard was the clamor of alien sounds:
oarsmen's laments as they plied the frigid coast,
the strange cries of gulls in the offing,
and the plovers along the rocky coast,
calling back and forth with their companions as they fluttered into flight,
the rush of a billowing sail pushing its ship headlong into the waves,
the slap of an oar nudging the moon from wave to wave.
Once they rounded Wada Cape, there,
the pine field on the seacoast,
carried the green of the ocean onto the land.
When they came as far as the coast of Suma,
the four winds wailed, blowing over the pass,

176. Compare *The Tales of the Heike*: *Kyō no shima no koto*.

177. Festive boats that were used for parties in the capital. They came in pairs, one of which had the head of a dragon on the prow, and the other, a *geki* bird, a mythical bird with bluish white feathers, reminiscent of a cormorant or heron.

関吹き越ゆる音ながら、
後の山の夕煙、
柴と云物ふすぶるも、
見なれぬかたのあはれなり。
上琴の音に、
引き留めらるると詠じける、
ご延せつの君のこの浦に、
しほる心をとめて筑紫船、
昔はのぼり今くだる、
波路の末ぞ悲しき。
かたぶく月の明石潟、
しほる六十あまりの秋を経て、
問はず語りのいにしへを、
思ひやる社ゆかしけれ。
ふ延ねより車に乗り移り、
暫しここにと思へども、
須磨や明石の浦づたひ、
源延氏の通ひし道なれば、
平家のぢ延んにはいかがとて、
又この岸を押し出だす。
塩瀬は波も高砂や、
尾の上の松のはつ嵐、
舟をいづくにかよふらん、
室の泊の苫屋形、
影は隙洩る夕月夜、
遊女のうたふ歌の声、
憂きよを渡る一節も、
まことにあはれ成けり。
慣らはぬ旅は牛窓の、
瀬戸の落ち汐心せよ、
げに荒けなき武士の、
梓の弓の鞆の浦、
にきわふ民のかまどの関、
夢路を誘ふ波の音。
上月落ち烏啼き、
霜天にしほるみちてすさまじく、
江しほるそんの漁火もほのかに、
半夜の鐘のひびき延は、

but the smoke of evening fires still rose beyond the mountains:
an unfamiliar sight to them, and piteous for that,
as brushwood flooded the air with smoke, but little heat.
A NOBE *gosechi* dancer once SHIORU left her heart here on this coast,
JŌ "pulled back by a strain of koto music," sang she,
but the Kyushu ship she traveled on was headed to the capital
while they now plied the waves away
to such a distant destination, how sad![178]
The moon declined in the sky over Akashi Bay,
and in a tale unbidden they felt the pull of the past,
some SHIORU sixty autumns distant.
They were tempted to rest a while there,
to NOBE transfer from these boats to carriages
to trace the coast of Suma and Akashi,
following the path of NOBE Shining Genji in his day,
but how could that serve the YOSURU advantage of the Heike?
No, off they pushed from the coast into the open sea.
The salty spray rises at Takasago, ho!
The pine stands on a brow of land in a fresh gale,
where should they point the boats to make their way?
The silhouette of a hut at the mooring station of Muro
showed gaps where the moonlight would seep through.
The singing voice of a party girl,
a phrase lamenting passage through the faithless world,
struck home with a poignant ache.
Take heed of the low tide at Ushimado,
pressing on in this unwonted journey.
The sound of the waves
pulled them into the path of dreams
at Kamado Barrier with its raucous crowds,
and on the Tomo Coast,
true to its martial name:
archers snapped their catalpa bowstrings on their wristguards.
JŌ The moon fell, ravens cawed,
frost SHIORU enveloped the heavens with a chill.
Fishers' fires in the inlet SHIORU villages glowed faintly,
a bell resounded through the NOBE depths of night

178. Allusion to a poem composed by the *gosechi* dancer in the "Suma" chapter of *The Tale of Genji*: *Koto no ne ni hikitomeraruru tsunate naha, / tayutafu kokoro, kimi shirarume ya* (Pulled back to him, as if I were tied to a tow rope as he plucks and damps his koto strings—would that my lord knew how my heart goes slack with his hesitation, like that tow rope).

客の舟にや通ふらん、
ほうしをるそう雨しただりて、
知らぬ潮路の楫枕、
かたしほるしく袖や萎るらん、
荒磯波の夜の月、
沈みし影はかへらず。

to reach their boats offshore.
Drops of rain splashed off SHIORU the thatch outside the window,[19]
and sleeping by the rudder on a sea journey to who-knows-where,
they wilted their SHIORU rain-soaked robes again with tears.
The moon, deep in the night, sank
into the waves along the rocky coast, not to come again.

Kusemahi from the Ōan era (1368–1375) to the Shitoku era (1384–1387) are accounted for above. "Shirahige," "Yura no minato," and "Jigoku" *no kusemai* fall within the repertory of *sarugaku*. The lyrics to "Kaidōkudari" and "Saigokukudari" were written by Rinna, but the music is by Na'a and Kanze.[179] They have not, however, been taken over into *kusemahi* performance proper and are alike in style with the pieces in this fine play in performance.[180] In recent years, the *kusemai* of Zenkōji and Hyakuman have appeared in addition to these, and although you could call them "modern" *kusemai*, they are correct essentially with regard to the fundamentals of singing and simply exhibit a softening of the vocal pattern. I wrote the lyrics. (It goes without saying.)[20]

179. That is, Kannami.
180. That is, *yūgaku*. See the introduction and the glossary.

六代の歌

夫世間の無常は旅泊の夕べにあらはれ、
有為の転変は草露の風に滅するがごとし。
我一所不住の沙門として、
縁にまかせて諸国をめぐれば、
名所旧下跡おのづから、
捨ててまじわる世の中の、
夢も現もへだてなく、
向去きゃく来の境界に至る。
只詞爰に大和国救世の観世音、
霊験殊勝の御事なれば、
しばらく参籠し、
山寺の致景を見るに。
下哥山そびへ谷めぐりて、
人家雲につらなり、
晩鐘雨にひびき来ぬ。
上川隈も、
なを暮れかかる雲の波、
なを暮れかかる雲の波、
さながら海のごとくにて、
ふしほるだらくもかくらくの、
初瀬の寺はありがたや。
げにや海士小舟、
初瀬の山に降る雪と、

Rokudai no utai[181]

("The Song About Rokudai") (I was asked by an august person to take certain source materials, render them into *jo-ha-kyū* form, and offer them up; this is the resulting song.)

If in nightfall at a traveler's lodging,
the transience of this world is plain to see,
then in the vanishing of dewdrops on the wind,
we find the likeness of all things' mutability.

(In this case, from the *jo* here, we have the tone of *rangyoku.*)[182]

I am a humble priest with no fixed residence, wandering the provinces wherever my affinities may take me, and in a world where famous sites and ancient ruins present themselves, I can either pay heed or pass them by; there is no separation between dream and substance, and I arrive in the realm of facing about and doubling back.[183]

TADAKOTOBA Here in the land of Yamato, where the miraculous power of the Savior Kanzeon is particularly strong, I will go into retreat for a time and admire the landscape around this mountain temple:

SAGEUTA Mountain peaks stand tall,
valleys all around,
Houses vanish seamlessly into the clouds,
the vespers bell resounds through rain.

JŌ Dusk has begun to fall
at that bend in the river, clouds rise in waves,
at that bend in the river, clouds rise in waves,
and bring the sea to mind; Potalaka must be just like this:
Secluded Hatsuse Temple, how rich in blessings!
It's true, after all, as they say,
"with snow fallen on Hatsuse Mountain,

181. Hatsuse (or Hase) Rokudai was the son of the Koremori and great-grandson of the Heike dictator Kiyomori. As such, he was the focus of deep suspicion by the Genji, even though he was just a child. In the account of his life in the last chapters of *The Tales of the Heike*, book 12, he is hunted out of seclusion with his mother and sisters at about age twelve and captured. The priest Mongaku manages to procure a pardon for him from Yoritomo just as he is about to be executed, and he takes the tonsure, surviving until about age thirty when suspicions about him arise again and he is finally executed, the last of Kiyomori's direct line.

182. This is a note written in next to the line "then in the vanishing . . ." in one manuscript.

183. 向去却来. This unusual word also appears in *Articles on the Five Sorts of Singing*; apparently, it is an extension of the Zen term *kyakurai* (却来). See *Nine Ranks*.

詠みしもさぞなかく河の、
浦の名にある気色哉、
浦の名にある気色哉。

只詞爰にあはれなる事の候、
御堂の西の脇に局しつらひて、
女性の籠りて候が、
まことに身に思ひありと覚しくて、
忍びかねたる言の葉の、
下色に出で音に立てても、
ただ泣くのみなる有様也。
指ある時女局たちと覚しき人、
局を出で、
御堂の四面を廻り、
千度の歩みを運ぶかと見えし、
数も終わらざるに、
あはただしく局に走り帰り、
あさましき御事をこそ聞きてさぶらへ、
只今集まり上りたる旅人、
駿河の国千本の松原とかやにて、
平家の棟梁六代御前、
只今斬られさせ給とて、
人の集まるを見て候と申を聞きてさぶらふとて、
下なみだにむせび伏し転びたり。
主の女房、
さりともとこそ思ひつるに、
この子ははや斬られけるかと、
声も惜しまず伏し沈み給ふ。
さては六代の母にてましましけるよと、
その時こそ人も思ひたれ。
上伝へ聞くしほるこうしは鯉魚に別れて、
思ひの火を胸に焚き、
はつしほるきよゐは子を先立てて、
枕に残る薬を恨む。
下是みな仁義礼智信の祖師、
文道の大祖たり、
いはんや末世の衆生と云、

a fishing skiff shoves off from the shoals . . ."[184]
the view is justly famous, here at the Kaku River,[185]
the view is justly famous, here at the Kaku River.

TADAKOTOBA Something deeply affecting has happened here: a room has been partitioned off, back to the west side of the temple hall, and a lady has taken refuge there. There seems to be some grave apprehension pressing upon her; although the reason isn't clear, it's plain from her appearance, and in the words she cannot keep entirely secret, that there is some cause of grief that keeps her weeping and wailing on and on.

SASHI From time to time a person who appears to be her serving maid comes out of the room and circles the four sides of the temple hall. She seems to be performing the Thousand Paces,[186] but before she can finish all the steps, she hurries back into the room, and says, "I've heard terrible news. Travelers on their way back to the capital have come together here just now, and they say they saw a crowd assembled, talking about how His Lordship, the Heike chief Rokudai, has just been slain at a place called the Pine Grove of Senbon, or some such, in the province of Suruga. I heard the travelers talking about this," she says and collapses in tears. The lady, for her part, had reassured herself that no matter what, this would never happen, but now she raises her voice in an unstinting wail and falls to the floor weeping. So now, the rest of us all realize that the lady must be the mother of Rokudai.

(From this point, *aishyau*.)

JŌ As we've been told,
SHIORU Confucius felt a fire charring his heart
when he had to part from his child Liyü,
and SHIORU Bo Jüyi conceived a hatred for medicine,
left at the bedside when his child died before him.
GE The framer, on the one hand,
of "Benevolence, Integrity, Propriety, Wisdom, and Trust,"
a founding Master, on the other,
of the Way in writing;
If men like these were so stricken by grief,
how much more then, someone in these latter days,

184. *MYS* 2347: *Amawobune Hatsuse no yama ni furu yuki no kenagaku kohishi kimi ga ne zo suru* (How long I have languished in longing for you, long as the snow falling on Mount Hatsuse, where the fisher boats draw up; now I can hear you coming).

185. Perhaps the name of a stretch of the Hatsuse River but also a pun on *kaku* (thus).

186. A devotional practice performed in the hope that one's wishes will be fulfilled by supernatural intercession.

しかも女人の心として、
恩愛の別を悲しむ事、
げにもまことに理なれども、
その理を過ぐるばかり、
よその袂もうるほへり。
ややあて母御前、
涙を押さへてのたまふやう、
さるにてもこの子は、
上人の御助けをこそ頼みしに、
其御甲斐もなきやらん、
又はまことに斬られなば、
さい藤五斎藤六、
走りも来たり申べきが、
ただよそ人の伝にだに、
早くの聞ゆるほどなるに、
なにとて彼等は遅きやらんと、
申しもあへぬ言の葉の、
露も心も忘草、
なにをか種と思ひ子の、
なき世に残る身ぞつらき。
節曲舞初瀬の鐘の声、
つくづく思へ世の中は、
諸行無常の理、
かりに見えし親子の、
夢幻の時の間を、
かねてはかくと思へども、
まことの別れになる時は、
お延もひし心も打ち失せて、
ただくれぐれと絶へかぬる、
胸の火は焦がれて、
身は消ゆる心のみ也。
さるにても我が子の、
失はれんとしけるとは、
聞けどもなをやさりともの、

and a woman at that: in her mind
the grief at parting from someone so beloved
could only be expected,
but this sadness passed all reasonable bounds,
and moved the hearts of the bystanders too,
to soak their sleeves in tears.
After a while, the mother,
wiping away her tears said,
"All the same, my child put his trust in the succor of a holy saint—
how could that have been in vain!
What's more, if he were really slain, then Saitōgo and Saitōroku
should come running with the news;
and if we caught wind of it from strangers first, then how is it
that they haven't at least come along in the strangers' wake to confirm
 the story?"
Before she could even finish speaking, her words, like leaves,
were moistened with a dew of tears; however would her heart forget
 the slightest part of this?
how would she live on in the world
with this beloved boy of hers,
the seed of his line, already gone!
KUSEMAI"Strike the bell at Hatsuse,
and the sound will strike deep in my thoughts:
the world makes its sense in the impermanence
of each and every action, and the little time given over
to a mother for her child is but the trifle of a vision or a dream;
this, I thought I understood long ago, but now,
faced in earnest with this deprivation,
NOBEall my erstwhile resolution is vanished in an instant,
I am cast into darkness,
my heart is seared unbearably with longing,
I can think only that my being
is on the verge of disappearance.
But even so, even as I hear
my child is lost to me

頼みかけまくも、
かたじけなくも蔭頼む、
[延]南延無や大悲の観世音、
願はくはもとよりの、
御誓願にまかせつつ、
ね[延]び、
く[懸切]はん音力刀刃、
段々の功力げに、
偽らせ給はずは、
剣をも折らせて、
我が子を助け給へや。
[上]かかりける所に、
男一人来りつつ、
斎藤五参りたると、
[しほる]申せば御母も、
いかにいかにとのたまへば、
御喜びになりたり、
[寄]するがの千本にてすでに、
斬られさせ給しを、
上人其時に、
駒を早めて走り下り、
喜びの御教書にて、
助からせ給ふと、
申せば御母も、
あまりの事の心にや、
嬉しとだにもわきまへず、
ただ茫然とあきれつつ、
ありがたの事やとて、
[しほる]手をあはせ給ふ袂にも、
覚えず落つる涙の、
嬉しき袖をだに、
干さぬや心なるらん。

I cling to the hope,
the precious sanctuary of belief—
NOBE All praise to Kwanzeon, Great in Compassion!—
I put my faith in her originary vow, that's all I desire,
NOBE Rouse thy faith in KAKEKIRI[187] Kwannon's might,
'which sunders to pieces the slayer's blade . . .'[188]
Pray be true to that vow!
shatter the enemy's sword, and save my child!"
JŌ At just that moment
a man appeared and announced
that Saitōgo had arrived;
the mother called out,
what's happened, what's happened?
and his answer filled her with joy.
YORU "At Senbon in the province of Suruga,
after Rokudai had been cut down,
a holy man—at that very time—
raced his pony over, dismounted,
and saved his life
with felicitous orders from on high,"
said he, whereupon
the mother—her heart must have been overwhelmed—
was unable even to discern her own happiness,
and sat in a stupor of amazement.
"What a blessing," said she,
and put her hands together in prayer, her sleeves
were moistened with unconscious tears,
she must have felt her robes would never dry.

Keichō 3 [1598]:7:21
A copy, the same in every particular as [the text of] my aged father.
Myōan Gen'yu (seal)[189]

187. Omote notes the use of the same term in *Jinen koji*, *Utaura*, and *Yukiyama* but suggests that in contrast with its use in those pieces, here it is not an indication of a rhythmic pattern but is to be understood with the direction *nobe*.

188. Lotus Sutra 8:25, "The Universal Gateway": "If . . . a man who is about to be murdered calls on the name of the bodhisattva He Who Observes the Sounds of the World, then the knives and staves borne by the other fellow shall be broken in pieces, and the man shall gain deliverance" (Hurvitz, trans., *Scripture of the Lotus Blossom of the Fine Dharma*, p. 312).

189. Orth. "Meuan Gen'iū," the Buddhist name of Hosokawa Yukitaka, third son of the celebrated Hosokawa Yūsai (細川幽斎, 1534–1610). This colophon is found in one of the manuscripts of *Five Sorts of Singing*, part II. It is noteworthy because of the connection to the aforementioned Yūsai, who was not only a statesman and general in the turbulent last years of the sixteenth century but also a poet and figure of great cultural renown.

NOTES

1. Yokomichi Mario and Omote Akira, eds., *Yōkyokushū*, NKBT, vols. 40 and 41 (Tokyo: Iwanami shoten, 1960, 1963).

2. Nonomura Kaizō and Ōtani Tokuzō, eds., *Yōkyoku nihyakugojūban shū*, 2 vols. (Kyoto: Akao shōbundō, 1978).

3. Insect damage obstructs an understanding of the sentence.

4. (恋曲), possibly a mistranscription for 懸曲 (appealing songs) or 応曲 (corresponding songs).

5. The manuscripts read, incomprehensibly, *shihoko* in this line, rather than *nihoko* (瓊矛 [jeweled spear]). I follow Omote's emendation.

6. *Hanten*. Zeami's text is written phonetically, and the meaning is uncertain. Modern performance texts interpret it as *banten*—that is, 萬天, my "myriad heavens."

7. The text for *Hakozaki* is not easy to locate in printed form but is available online through the helpful Web site JALLC Tanomoshi No. 1 (http://www.kanazawa-bidai.ac.jp/~hangyo/utahi/text/yob01.txt).

8. Apart from the line quoted in the "short" manuscript of *Five Sorts of Singing*, the text here is taken from Kanze Sakon, ed., *Kanzeryū yōkyoku zoku hyakubanshū*, Taiseiban ed. (Tokyo: Hinoki shoten, 1973).

9. 千寿, apparently to be distinguished from the play *Senju* (written 千手) in the modern repertory. Although the graphs with which the title is written might be subject to variation like this, the line quoted is not found in the play called *Senju* in the modern repertory. Omote argues, moreover, that the *kuse* in the modern *Senju* is insufficiently syncopated to make a true *kuse* and that the use of the *kuri* pitch in the modern play does not accord with Zeami's instructions on how and where to use that pitch. He concludes that the play in the modern repertory known as *Senju* cannot be by Zeami and that the play referred to here is not that play.

10. *Analects* 6.27 (29 in some editions) reads 中庸之為徳也、其至矣乎、民鮮久矣 (How perfect is the practice of virtue in the Middle Way! It is a long time since it was vital among the people). Zeami quotes only the first two clauses, and the second is mistranscribed as 其主矣乎 in all extant manuscripts of *Five Sorts of Singing*, part II. It is not clear whether this is merely an error in transcription or an outright mistake in understanding.

11. 五ザウサウジン: It is impossible to tell precisely what is intended here. The word sounds like something from the vocabulary of scholastic Buddhism, but given only a *katakana* rendering such as we have, the translation must remain tentative.

12. The passage, which is written almost exclusively in *katakana*, has long been obscure, but after some ingenious detective work, Taguchi Kazuo has clarified most of its difficulties in "*Kuzu no hakama* (*Sumiyoshi no sengū no nō*) nanku kō," *Geinōshi kenkyū*, October 1979, pp. 21–22. He shows that the passage is based on a *fu*, or rhapsody, on the moon by Xie Xiyi in *Wenxuan* 13 and parses it as 嘯き月に向かえば、西日の悠々たるを擧げては、吉飆に晴れ、凋萎ノカンカンタルヲ砕きて、雲天ハンニ治まる. The relevant excerpt from the *fu* reads:

> Once the air with fine clear skies the ground endows
> and clouds, upon the horizont, settle far away,
> Then at last do wavelets on Lake Dongting rise
> and leaves, about to fall, twitter in the air;
> Chrysanthemums scatter their scent among the mountain pepper,
> Geese pour out their sadness to the shoals,
> Languidly bright radiance ascends the vault
> to rain down, all around, a lambent shower.

David Knechtges translated the entire *fu* in *Wen xuan, or Selections of Refined Literature* (Princeton, N.J.: Princeton University Press, 1996), vol. 3, pp. 31–39. His version of the passage is on p. 37.

13. The line is obscure: 名字のしみとは.

14. *Nado ka ha kami mo aharemi no kokoro wo* . . . This is a difficult spot in the text. *Nado ka ha* suggests a rhetorical question, brought to closure with a negative verb later in the sentence, but there is no negative verb there. Some modern performance texts of *Aritohoshi* read *Nado ka ha kami mo nōjiu no, kokoro ni kanō* . . . and are only slightly less problematic, pulling *kokoro nakaran* out of *kokoro n*[*i*] *kan*[*ō* . . .]. All the same, the context suggests the sort of sense into which the text has been translated.

15. あはのなるとの一あひを: The passage is difficult to pin down. One reading seems likely to mean 粟の成ると[き] . . . (when foxtail millet goes to seed . . . [make sure to pull it up . . .]) but remains to be explained. There is also a pun on the whirlpool at the straits of Naruto in the province of Awa (阿波の鳴門).

16. まことのきしはとうせじ: The manuscript reads きこと, but I follow Omote's amendment to まこと. The end of the sentence is obscure.

17. The passage is obscure: 隙ユクコマヲツナガネバ、大バツ大ガノ池ノ水スマデニゴレル心地シテ. Nose Asaji reads the middle phrase as 大跋提河ノ池ノ水, apparently assuming the Sinicization of a river with a Sanskrit name, but he does not elaborate (*Zeami jūrokubu shū hyōshaku* [Tokyo: Iwanami shoten, 1944], vol. 2, pp. 226–27).

18. 此クセ舞ノ幽ハ者ハ闌曲: The passage seems to have been mistranscribed, and even an old annotation reads "obscure." Nonetheless, it is tantalizing in suggesting a typological linkage between *yūkyoku* and *rangyoku*, as also suggested by the subsequent passage.

19. Reading ほうそう as 蓬窗.

20. Omote reads the original 為云不及, which exists only in the *Kōhon* text, as a mistake for 為書不及 (It doesn't really amount to writing), apparently understanding it as an expression of modesty by Zeami. The graphs in question are, it is true, very similar in a cursive hand, but the emendation doesn't seem any more convincing than simply reading the phrase as written, as I have done.

Learning the Profession

習道書, 1430:3

The only text in *Performance Notes* that is addressed to the entire troupe rather than to a single individual or two, *Learning the Profession*, deals with each of the major roles in a typical play, outlining the actors' or musicians' particular responsibilities.

The text provides a fascinating insight into the division of roles in *sarugaku* performance and is particularly valuable for its account of the flute's and the *kyōgen* actor's roles. Despite occasional discrepancies between the procedures discussed here and those of modern nō performance, the text shows the unequivocal centrality of the *shite* role in *sarugaku*, providing a clear link to nō and its uniqueness as a theatrical experience.

❁

Specifications in Learning the Profession for the Performers of a *Sarugaku* Troupe, Role by Role

There is good reason why the performers responsible for a *sarugaku* performance, each of whom brings his own particular skills to the enterprise, should carefully consider the occasion. The excitement that brings the troupe's efforts to consummation will not be created unless the members of the troupe use their talents cooperatively. The singing and dancing overall will not come to consummation unless the troupe works together, no matter how effective each member may be at his own particular skills. Since that is the case, the performers should maintain a frame of mind in which the dancing and singing can be performed through an effective fusion of self and other. None should imagine that he can carry it off on his own power alone. Each person should take the troupe leader's mastery of the profession as his model and perform his part as the troupe leader indicates. Specific comments follow.

• The role of the troupe leader and primary actor is to come out of the green room on the occasion of performance, to take his place on the *hashigakari*, to deliver the lines of his *issei*, then to move onto the stage proper and sing the music from the *sashigoto* to the end of that section, by himself. If his

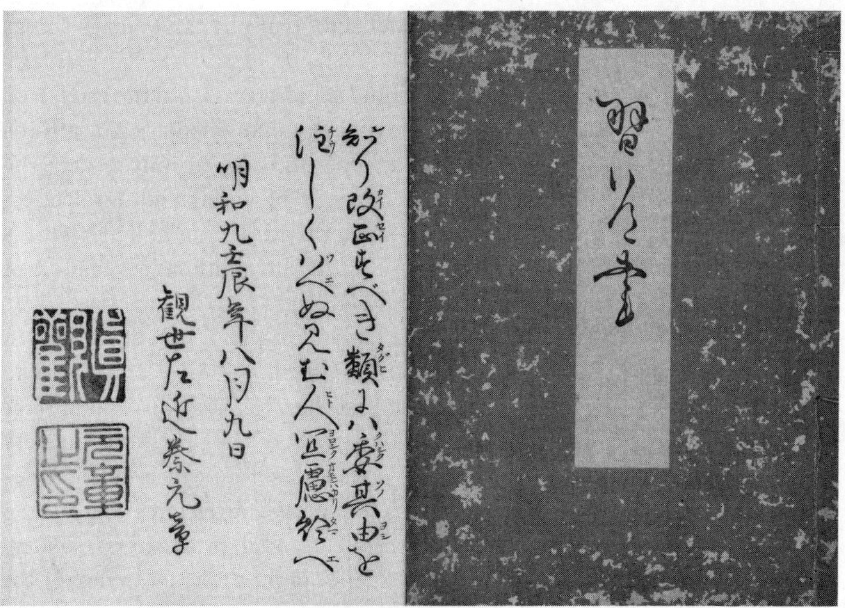

The cover and final page of *Learning the Profession* in the printed edition of 1772. This text was the only one among Zeami's *Performance Notes* intended for transmission to his entire troupe, rather than to just one or two individuals in a direct artistic and family lineage. In keeping with that intention, the fifteenth head of the Kanze troupe, Kanze Motoakira (1722–1774), had a small edition of the text printed for distribution among members of the troupe. He apparently also had plans to print *Transmitting the Flower Through Effects and Attitudes*, but those plans did not, in the end, come to fruition. (Photograph courtesy of the Noh Theater Research Institute, Hōsei University)

voice is inadequate to the task and he cannot manage this section beginning with the *issei*, then he should not be the primary actor. In accordance with the subject of the play, if more than one person comes onto the stage at that time to perform, an old man and old woman, say, as husband and wife or the like, then that's as it should be. It is not acceptable professionally if when a single person is meant to appear, the primary actor instead does something amateurish like bringing someone else with him, extraneous to the play, on the ground that he himself isn't up to it or can't manage the singing. It is entirely unprofessional when the primary actor relinquishes the opportune effect to be created by his own particular solo performance to several subordinates—or even worse, to the chorus and such, seated to the side—on the grounds that he can't do it himself. In all the arts, being the troupe leader and primary actor means that you have already attained an expert level of performance. You cannot be considered expert if you don't have enough power to hold the attention of the audience, even if your singing voice isn't completely sufficient; that's what it means to be an expert. To be expert requires being so accomplished in the profession of actor that you can manage things even when you aren't entirely up to it.

After that, then, the primary actor should stand across from the *waki*, take advantage of the dialogue with him and the vocal augmentation it affords along with the cooperation of the full troupe, and sing in unison with the others, setting his mind on attaining a fusion of visual and aural effect throughout the performance, by means of all the attractions at hand. This is what we consider the profession of troupe leader. In addition, it is the role of the primary actor to set the pitch in vocal exchanges with other actors.

• Matters the *waki* should be aware of: The sole responsibility of the *waki* in performance, to which he must devote his full intent, is this: it is up to him to bring the occasion together by being the first character to come out on stage and by clearly articulating the thematic material of the play from the very first lines uttered. These opening lines are the verses from which the full day's performance makes its departure, and they express *shiugen* in calling all eyes to focus and all ears to attend; as such, they require full professional mastery. From that point on, he should make the fluency of the collective endeavor the foundation of his effort, exhibit a complete command of rhythm, and perform in a vocal style that harmonizes with the troupe as a whole.

Now, there are certain principles that a *waki* should particularly take to heart. The *waki* actor is called *waki* [i.e., "collateral"] because he follows the directions of the troupe leader. If the troupe leader is deficient in some way, even then—especially then—given that he is, like it or not, the leader of the troupe with responsibility for the troupe as a whole, the *waki* should follow his directions. Should the *waki*, using his expertise, perform in a vein different in intent from the leader's on the ground that the leader is deficient, then the entire troupe will be in disarray and the play will not take its proper course. It is by following the troupe leader, for better or worse, that the *waki* is who he is. This is the agreement from the beginning. Without this agreement, the very character of the performance is put at risk. Understanding the rationale here and bringing the troupe together on account of it is what the vocation of the *waki* actor entails.

Also, any other subordinate actors should gain a professional mastery of the rhythmic patterns characteristic of the troupe's performance style, establish a common intent, and achieve consistency in expression. This is the way the various subordinate actors should perform.

Overall, the number of actors who should appear in a given play should not exceed four or five. So, in the old days, even though there were many actors, they would perform a play with one or two parts using one or two actors.[1] Just because there are plenty of actors available, that doesn't mean they

1. Omote says that "many actors" (*shite amata arishikadomo*) refers to nō actors specifically and does not include *kyōgen* actors or musicians.

should appear on stage to sing together in their street clothes, with *eboshi* and *suō*;[2] that is entirely unprofessional. It shows great carelessness. It's only recently that this form of expression has come into vogue. I find it impossible to comprehend.

• Matters that the *tsuzumi* drummer(s) should be aware of: After you get up the beat[3] but before the *shite* has come on stage for the *issei* and *sashigoto*, you should set your mind to playing at your very best because this part is entirely up to you; play it up using all the drum patterns in your repertory to the greatest musical effect.[1] Then as the play develops into the Two Arts of dance and singing and on to dramatic imitation, here you should not be obtrusive. Follow along with the intent of the *shite* and perform using the Two Arts as your guide. This is the professional way for a *sarugaku tsuzumi* drummer to perform.

Taiko drummers should have the same intent. In general, no matter which *taiko* part we're talking about, when you get the beat up,[4] it should be a *ranjō*.[5]

• Matters for the flute player: The musical function of the flute player is of great difficulty in that it is his responsibility to maintain an exciting sonority from the *jo* through the *ha* and the *kyū* for the entire enterprise of the performance. It is his role to blow the flute for a while before the performance begins, in order to settle the audience and to touch them with a palpable sense of excitement at the very beginning of the performance proper. Once the play has progressed into its dancing and singing, he should listen carefully to the *shite*'s singing voice, create an exciting sonority, and tint it with color.

There is a matter of professional importance here that the flute player must understand above all else. Since the flute is the instrument responsible

2. The *suō* (Zeami writes *suwau*, but more conventional spellings are *suhau* and *suawo*) is an unlined hemp garment that tucks into matching long trousers and is marked with a family crest (*mon*) at the chest and upper back. It was the everyday dress of samurai in the Muromachi period and, as such, is excluded from Zeami's conventions for *sarugaku* costume. The *suō* is used on the modern nō stage, however, and is used yet more widely for *kyōgen* performance.

3. *Sude ni uchitatete* suggests that the drumming has gone on long enough to build to a certain level of excitement. Omote parses the word in modern Japanese as *zensō no hayashi wo tsuzumi ga sakan ni uchihayashite*.

4. *Uchitateba*: As immediately preceding, this could mean something broad like "play energetically" or "quickly," or perhaps it could refer more specifically to the particular techniques in *taiko* drumming when the drumsticks are held aloft before striking the drum, to allow for more volume, resonance, and dramatic effect. Zeami's remarks are, unfortunately, too brief to give much indication of what he intends here.

5. Orth. *ranjyau* (乱声). Omote says this corresponds to today's *raijo* (来序). *Raijo* is used in some *waki* nō, demon plays, and *tengū* plays for the *shite* or occasionally the *tsure*, to leave the stage before the *ai* intermission. A more formally replete version, the *shin-no-raijo* is used exclusively in certain *waki* plays for the entrance of a character playing the Chinese emperor. It is exceedingly solemn and slow.

for pitch, it has an indisputably fundamental role to play in that regard, but in ensuring the consummation of the entire enterprise, there is yet another, separate responsibility. There is a fine point in the way the nō flute differs from the flute used by court musicians. What is that fine point? It amounts to this: occasionally the singing of the *shite* may be somewhat sharp or flat in relation to a fixed pitch. If the flute player is insensible to this and simply continues to play at the pitch established from the beginning, there will be a discrepancy between the *shite*'s pitch and the flute's pitch. In such a case, the potential for excitement in the music for that performance will probably be lost. Thus, if the flute player responds to the particularities of the *shite*'s voice by taking stock of these variations in a subtle way, in order to stimulate excitement in the sonority, it will not sound out of tune to the house. It should create excitement in the music without any sour notes.

Also: the fact that the *shite*'s pitch might be somewhat sharp or flat is not in itself considered a serious deficiency. Sometimes the pitch in song both sacred and secular[6] also is somewhat sharp or flat in relation to a fixed pitch. In the case of *sarugaku*, since the singing voices associated with its many types of dramatic imitation—with *shiugen*, or *bauwoku*, *renbo* or *aishyau*, Hatred or Anger, Dance or Sparring—are so diverse, the pitch may sometimes be sharp or flat without one's being aware of it. For his part, the flute player should be aware of the reason for this and use his ingenuity to follow the singing voice of the *shite*, searching out the appropriate pitch, and then, in a break in the dancing and singing, he should take the opportunity to return to the pitch established at the beginning, making the change in such a way that no one takes notice of it and the excitement in the sonority continues uninterrupted; this is the professional way for a *sarugaku* flute player to perform. (It's for the sake of the *sarugaku*, after all, that the flutist is playing.)

• In *sarugaku*, the *shite* is not deficient if his pitch is somewhat sharp or flat: his singing voice may, after all, change on a moment's notice to a myriad different sounds in response to the demands of dramatic imitation.

In old Yamato *sarugaku*, there was an expert flute player by the name of Meishō. He was a performer of such expertise that lay priest Lord Kyōgoku no Dōyo (known as the Sado Judge)[7] was moved to say of him, "It's no good

6. "Song both sacred and secular" is used to translate specific references to two traditional genres of vocal music: *shōmyō* (orth. *seumyau*) and *sōga* (orth. *sauga*). *Shōmyō* is the music of Buddhist chant and ritual, which is still performed, particularly in the Tendai and Shingon sects. *Sōga* is a lost medieval form of singing. Some *sōga* texts remain, but the way they were sung is no longer well understood.

7. Sasaki Takauji (1306–1373) is better known by his Buddhist name, Dōyo (orth. Dauyo). He hailed from the branch of the Sasaki who were given the surname Kyōgoku (orth. Kyaugoku) as a result of military accomplishments during the Kamakura period (1185–1333). Dōyo himself was a

when the pauses in a *sarugaku* performance stretch out too much, but you know, when I hear Meishō's flute, I forget altogether about the passage of time."

On one occasion at a *sarugaku* performance dedicated to a shrine, the *shite* was singing a *rongi* duet with a boy actor in the mode *rankei*.[8] The boy's voice hadn't yet changed, and he tended to slide up to *banshiki* mode. The *shite*'s voice remained in *rankei*. As their exchange of lines proceeded, the discrepancy in mode threatened to ruin the performance, but Meishō, all the while continuing to play in *rankei*, took account of the boy's singing and adjusted his mode accordingly, giving it something of the feel of *banshiki* even while playing with the *shite* in the original *rankei*, so that the discrepancy in pitch didn't seem out of place and the performance was quite interesting. During the performance, then, no one seemed to be aware of what the flute player had accomplished, but the *shite* later complimented Meishō, saying, "Your flute today was really and truly divinely inspired," whereupon Meishō replied, "Since you have been so kind as to take notice of it, I will admit, that fine point in playing a *rongi* between an adult and a child really does require a good deal of effort."

It was entirely because he played like this, changing the mode for adult and child, that continuity between the two modes was achieved and the performance succeeded with no sense of discord. I wonder whether this in fact corresponds to that "voice in a well-ordered age," the voice that "expresses joy in that it is confident." In the old days, expert musicians in this way made the focus of their efforts the excitement produced by their troupe's actors, so they were able to bring about a consummation in the performance then and there; shouldn't this, then, be the model even today? The preface to the *Classic of Songs* says, "The music of an ordered world is pleasurable in its confidence."

• Matters for the *kyōgen* actor. The comic actor's performance strategy takes as his material either verbal wit or the telling of stories for which some sort of enthusiasm can be achieved; that's how it is to be. There shouldn't probably be much consideration given to making the audience

major player in the emergence of Ashikaga power in the mid-fourteenth century and controlled vast estates throughout Honshū and beyond. He was a poet of some distinction and an early patron of *dengaku* and *sarugaku*. There are numerous legends about his life.

8. The incident is mentioned in *Conversations on Sarugaku*, identifying the *shite* in question as Kannami and the child as Zeami. See *ZZ*, p. 297, and Erika de Poorter, *Zeami's Talks on Sarugaku: An Annotated Translation of the Sarugaku Dangi, with an Introduction on Zeami Motokiyo* (Amsterdam: Gieben, 1986), p. 119, sec. 157. The modal systems referred to here do not map clearly into modern nō performance. In effect, though, a *rongi* is a sung dialogue between two characters or one character and the chorus. In modern performance, the two parts often intentionally vary their pitches, but apparently in Zeami's day it was common practice to maintain a single set of pitches for the piece. *Rankei* would base the pitches on roughly B-flat, whereas *banshiki* would center on B. For individual terms, see also appendix 1 and the glossary.

laugh at the explanations the *kyōgen* actor offers during a nō play proper.[9] The professional objective in this case is simply to lay out the rationale for the play and give the audience a dignified account of it.

Now then, it is surely a vulgar form of understanding that comedy should necessarily produce guffaws in the crowd. Pleasure, they say, is contained in a smile.[10] This is excitement in intent based on interest and happiness. A comic actor who can produce a smile in his audience and incite their enthusiasm by attuning them to such intent should be considered a comic with the best sort of *yūgen* and interest. This is expertise in a comic actor. *Kyōgen* by Tsuchi Dayū in the old days was of this caliber.

In this connection, it occurs to me what a great blessing it is for a performer if he, by nature, has the adoration of the public. Then he can devote himself to wit and pleasantry such as will gain him the ear of the exalted and the highborn without doing anything vulgar, whether in speech or expressive manner. I'll say it over and over again: you shouldn't even dream of using crude language or expression on the pretext that it's comical. Be aware of this.

• The matter of the number of plays in a program of *sarugaku*. In the old days, there were no more than four or five. Likewise, for a shrine performance or a subscription performance now, there should be five plays, three nō plays and two *kyōgen* plays. In recent years at His Excellency's palace, in exceptional circumstances, seven or eight, even ten, plays were performed, a great number, at His Excellency's command, not by my personal choice. Be that as it may, in performance, the matter of *jo-ha-kyū* means that the *waki* play[11] comprises the *jo*. The second, third, and fourth play are the *ha*, and to bring things to conclusion, the fifth play fulfills the role of *kyū*; the requirements of *jo-ha-kyū* are thus fulfilled and that should bring about a consummation for all the fine play of performance. When, however, the number of plays is increased, contrary to our expectations, *jo-ha-kyū* comes around again, through its full cycle, and the expression is turned topsy-turvy in musical terms. I'll say it over again and again; this is of the greatest difficulty for the performers. All the same, when it's a command performance, one is powerless to change the situation.

9. This seems to refer to the ancestor of the *ai-kyōgen* parts performed between the major parts of a typical nō play. In modern performance, these *ai-kyōgen* can be fairly long and usually include an interchange between the *waki* and the *kyōgen* actor as well as a narrative by the *kyōgen* actor. Sometimes music is performed as well. All of this, however, seems to be an elaboration created in the late Muromachi period (1392–1573). Zeami's reference seems to be to much briefer and simpler interaction between the *kyōgen* actor and the *waki*. See Omote, in *ZZ*, p. 492n.146.

10. *Yemi no uchi ni tanoshimi wo fukumu* sounds like an old proverb but has not yet been identified more specifically.

11. See *Three Courses*.

Even so, the troupe all should understand that they need to hold themselves back at the transition between the *ha* and *kyū*, restrain their technique, keep their expressiveness in check, and have confidence that the best strategy is to hold something back and not exhaust the play completely. This might be just the time when the power of a truly accomplished master is shown. If you stretch out the cycle of *jo-ha-kyū* in performance, it should be in accord with the advance preparations you have made regarding this problem.

This is how the whole troupe is to master the profession of *sarugaku*.

Eikyō 2 [1430], a day of the third month. Written for the benefit of the members of the troupe.

Note

1. せいひょうおんりきの手かずをつくして、はやしたつべし. *Seihyō* is unknown. Omote suggests 精妙, and I have followed his lead in the translation.

Traces of a Dream on a Single Sheet
夢跡一紙, 1432:9

This brief text records the death of Zeami's eldest son, Motomasa. In addition to its personal poignancy, it underlines the importance of artistic transmission in the traditions of *sarugaku*.

❁

Ne ni kaheri furusu wo isogu hanatori no
onaji michi ni ya haru mo yukuran[1]

Blossoms to their roots return,
while birds betake themselves in haste
to ancient nests.
And spring? Does it go off
along that same path too?

A composition of fine and serious feeling, to be sure, with its love for the blossoms and envy of the birds.[2] That a parent—how true it is—should resent the senseless birds and blossoms because of an unshakable excess of grief in longing for a lost child and find that even in his distraction at the sights and sounds they incite, he goes "off along that same path too."

You see, my son Zenshun[3] passed away on the first day of this eighth month past in Anonotsu in the province of Ise. It may seem strange that someone should be so taken aback by the common fact of uncertainty in life for both the young and the old, but in my bewilderment at the shock of this,

1. Nijō Tamesada, *Shin Senzaishū* 185, with an allusion (i.e., *honka*) to Sutoku-In, *Senzaishū* 122: *Hana ha ne ni, tori ha furusu ni kaheru nari / haru no tomari wo shiru hito zo naki* (They say that blossoms to their roots, and birds to ancient nests, return, but there's no one who can tell where spring, in parting, goes to rest).

2. Zeami alludes to a passage in the preface to *Kokin wakashū* describing some of the foci of poetic sensibility in the natural world: "In this way, their sensibilities are diverse, loving the blossoms, envying of the birds, being moved by the mist and regretful of the dew, and they are cast in many different kinds of language."

3. Apparently, the posthumous Buddhist name of Zeami's eldest son, Jūrō (orth. Jifurau) Motomasa.

my old mind imposes a crushing burden on this body of mine, and my sleeves are rotten with weeping. But for all that, there are some seventy years between the time long ago when my late father gained a name for the family in this vocation of ours, and now, when I, Shiō,[4] have passed the art on—and Zenshun, though my own son, was a master of unparalleled accomplishment. . . .[5] Because Zenshun seemed to overtake even the mastery of his grandfather Kannami, I passed on to him in written form the secret transmissions and ultimate achievements of our vocation, each and every last one, in accord with the dictum "When someone is to be spoken to, and you fail to speak to him, you waste a person";[6] but now all that is nothing more than the sort of dream you might have in the time it takes to cook a pot of rice.[7] I see that I am to accomplish nothing more than to turn it all into dust and smoke, unmastered and profitless. And supposing I were to make such a transmission at this late date—what good would it do, for whom? There's a poem that captures the frame of mind just right: "If not to you, then to whom shall I show the plum blossoms?"[8]! In any case, our vocation approaches the verge of destruction, and my old life drags on pointlessly. In times like these, such a world before my very eyes is unbearably sad. It breaks my heart! When Confucius was parted from his Liyü, they say, the fire of love charred his heart, and when Bo Jüyi was left bereft of his boy, he conceived a hatred for the medicine remaining by his child's pillow.[9] Zenshun comes back to me as a phantom. I think of how the link between us is now broken forever, and I am given to attach this trivial ink-scrawl to all those thoughts; it must be, truly, from an excess of love.

> Omohiki ya mi ha mumoregi no nokoru yo ni
> sakari no hana no ato wo min to ha
>
> Did ever I think that in this world
> where I live on as but a block of wood

4. Zeami continued to use the name Zea[midabutsu] even late in his life, but he also used the religious names Shiō (orth. Shiwou) and Zenpō (orth. Zenpau).

5. *Ko nagara mo taguwi naki tatsujin to shite.* The clause is unmoored grammatically in the original text.

6. Confucius, *Analects* 15 (Wei Ling Gong), 7; previously quoted in *A Course to Attain the Flower.*

7. *Issui no yume*, from the Chinese tale of Handan, who had a dream of great glory while resting at an inn as his supper was being cooked. The tale is the original basis for the play *Kantan.*

8. Ki no Tomonori, *KKS* 38: *Kimi narade tare ni ka misemu ume no hana iro wo mo ka wo mo shiru hito zo shiru* (If not to you, then to whom shall I show plum blossoms? Of both their beauty and their fragrance, only the one who knows, really knows).

9. Zeami evokes the same parallels when writing the song "Rokudai no uta(h)i." See *Five Sorts of Singing.*

buried in the mire,
I would see the end
of that glorious bounty of flowers?

Eikyō 2+2 [1432], a day of the ninth month, written by Shiō[10]

Ikuhodo to omohazari seba oi no mi no
namida no hate wo ikade shiramashi

I cannot think
there is much time left
for this elderly body of mine.
How ever am I to know
an end of tears?

10. Shiō, again, is Zeami's Buddhist name. See the note on Zeami's names in appendix 3.

The Flower in . . . Yet Doubling Back
却来花, 1433:3

Like *Traces of a Dream on a Single Sheet*, this is a very short text. It opens again with laments over the death of Motomasa but then goes on to discuss what Zeami purports to be a highly secret performance technique called "doubling back," in which the supremely accomplished performer acquires a perfect freedom of action in performance.

Next Zeami discusses those elements of dancing unique to the Dance of the Heavenly Maiden. Although it is not possible to gain much sense of what that dance was like, this reference has been important to establishing its central role in the development of Dance (i.e., *mai*) in the modern nō repertory.

With Motomasa dead, it is not entirely clear for whom Zeami wrote this text, but Zenchiku refers to a dance performed in the "right–left–right" sequence mentioned here, and on that basis, it is assumed that he saw at least that portion of *The Flower in . . . Yet Doubling Back*. Indeed, considering his relation to Zeami after Motomasa's death, it seems likely that the text was addressed to him.

Of the many elements of our artistic legacy received from my father, learned throughout my own life unto this extremity of age and on from there to my son Motomasa—every last one of these, omitting not one of the ultimate accomplishments of our vocation, was transmitted in full, and I, Zea[mi], was just waiting for the final great event of my life; but now, without warning, Motomasa has met an early death; the lifeline of our vocation has snapped; and our troupe is on the verge of destruction. In the midst of all this, our heir is but an infant. So bound am I in aged attachment to this orphaned vocation of my father's and mine that my greatest spiritual aspirations are endangered. Were there anyone, even a stranger, to whom I might entrust my legacy, I would do just that, but no such artist exists.

But here, now, is Konparu Dayū,[1] brought up in his artistic capacities correctly, a person who will watch out for the vocation, too, although he doesn't

1. Konparu Ujinobu—that is, Zenchiku, Zeami's son-in-law, although it is not known whether he married Zeami's daughter before or after this document was written.

yet appear to be a great master. With time, though, if his experience in the art grows deep and he comes into his prime, he could well become a uniquely gifted person. It is unlikely that I, Zea, will live that long, so who, then, in this vocation of ours is likely to be able to witness and set a seal on his accomplishment?[2] Motomasa, they say, allowed Konparu to see a scroll of very great moment from among our secret transmissions, so he must, for his part, have believed that there was no one to whom we might entrust the name of our line in this vocation if not this Konparu.[3]

Now then, although as I said, Motomasa had fully persevered into the ultimate accomplishments of our vocation, there is one particular secret of performance,[4] a secret technique that is not to be revealed to anyone under forty, which he never actually demonstrated, even though I had told him about it.[5] It is called "the effect of doubling back" and is an effect in performance that one uses once in a lifetime. Although Motomasa had already persevered fully into our vocation in his essential artistic capacity, this particular effect is necessarily a secret transmission and a technique that is not to be performed before one is fifty,[6] so he knew of it only because of what I had told him. Just before his death, I explained to him how once you are truly enlightened,[7] you don't do things that are unnecessary. Knowing in your mind that you don't do things that are unnecessary is none other than enlightenment in performance.

2. Zeami uses explicitly Zen terminology for the transmission and certification of attainment, with words like *inka*, my "seal," and *shōken*, my "witness." This follows other Zen vocabulary in the previous sentence: *ichū no i*, my "uniquely"; *kōjō* (orth. *kaujyau*), my "surpassing greatness"; not to mention the word *kyakurai* (doubling back) in the title and *tokuhō* (attain enlightenment) later.

3. Possibly *A Mirror to the Flower*. See appendix 2, note 11.

4. *Hikyoku*. Although the word is used today in reference to particular plays, from the context here in which Zeami speaks of it, it refers instead to a performance technique or accomplishment rather than a specific play. Note his previous reference, *hikyoku ikkajō* (orth. *ikkadeu*), in which the last three graphs indicate an item or an article.

5. Nose Asaji (*Zeami jūrokubushū hyōshaku* [Tokyo: Iwanami shoten, 1944)] and Konishi Jin'ichi (*Zeami shū*, Nihon no shisō, vol. 8 [Tokyo: Chikuma shobō, 1970], p. 360) read this passage as "there is one particular secret of performance, a secret technique that is not to be revealed to anyone under forty. I had not yet actually demonstrated it for him, even though I had told him about it." That is a possible reading of the text, but Omote argues that given the contention that the technique in question was not to be performed by an actor before the age of fifty, it is more likely that Zeami means that Motomasa had not yet reached the time when he could perform it, even though he had been told about it. My translation follows Omote's interpretation.

6. The mention of fifty here contradicts the earlier mention of forty, although it may be that the technique can be taught to the actor before he is fifty (but after he is forty), even though he is not to use it until after he is fifty.

7. *Tokuhō* ("get the Dharma" or "attain enlightenment"), a Zen term that is used repeatedly in the last things Zeami wrote—for example, *Nine Ranks*; this text; and his final collection of songs, *Kintōsho* (*Notes from the Isles of Gold*), as well as the first of the two letters he wrote to Zenchiku. There also is a single appearance early in *Transmitting the Flower*.

Now what we call expressiveness in the effect of doubling back is a supreme secret transmission of a wondrous style. They say, "On the verge of doubling back, the doubling back is not to be hurried."[1] This is a secret form of musical expression that is not to be spoken of, and it is for transmission to Motomasa alone, but since he has died early, there may never be anyone who even knows the name of this kind of expression in the future, so the fact that I am committing it to ink and paper must be kept a deep, deep secret.

• In dance there is a figure in which you move left–right–left, left–right–left.[8] There also should be places where this is performed right–left–right, right–left–right. This requires a secret transmission. (It dates from an occasion during the reign of the sovereign Kiyomibara when a divine maiden descended from heaven and danced at Yoshino, flipping her sleeves five times.) In our fine play in performance, it's left–right–left, beginning with the Two Arts and the Three Modes and all the characters that have a role to play on stage, and the same with the carriage of the body, with expressive gestures, and with even the intentional structures formed in the mind; that's how we are to think of them. This is a wondrous effect in which all the thousands of performance styles and roles are brought to consummation and linked affectively. There is an oral transmission on this.

The Dance of the Heavenly Maiden then must be the basis for the Dance performance. We have adopted it into this vocation of ours, and we dance it exclusively. Inuō of Ōmi was particularly adept at it. For this reason, there are some who say the Dance of the Heavenly Maiden has its origin in Ōmi *sarugaku*. Do they say this simply because Inuō was adept at it? That doesn't mean it originated there. We should assign the authentic effect to reside only where there has been an oral transmission through a proper lineage. I have not heard anything to the effect that Inuō actually passed on the tradition of this secret of performance, this Dance of the Heavenly Maiden. What's more, unless some form of witness and seal is manifest stating that so-and-so has transmitted a given troupe's ultimate achievements and so on, it is impossible to determine that it is authentic. In a general way, I explained the essential points in the Dance of the Heavenly Maiden in *Figure Drawings*. You should have a good look at that for your instruction.

8. *Mahi ni sa-iu-sa, sa-iu-sa ari*. The original is more succinct than my translation. It seems to refer to a fixed pattern of movement, "left–right–left, left–right–left," and may well correspond to the modern nō *kata* called a *sayū*, a very common pattern in both instrumentally accompanied dances and the dancing to the text that typically occurs in the last section of a play. Despite the visions of a military march that "left–right–left" conjures up in English, in nō this movement is far less prominent in the feet and legs than in the arms and the carriage of the torso.

Also, the Suruga Dances stem from the lineage of heavenly maidens who were manifest at Udo Beach in Suruga.[9] I have not heard that this secret of performance was ever transmitted in *sarugaku*. (It is said that a sleeve of the heavenly feather cloak from that occasion was left with the Kiyomidera temple in Suruga and is still there.)

• On the matter of the *shirabyōshi*. These dances originated in the Ennen performances at the Vimalakīrti Congregation[10] in the Southern Capital.[11] This you can see right before your own eyes every year, so you should seek it out and learn from it. It is the proper transmission of vocational lineages like this that you should consider authentic.

All the same, since the dances of *sarugaku* depend on all the many characters open to dramatic imitation, how can we say that any particular one is the authentic model for our dances? Shouldn't the Okina Dance then be the authentic dance in *sarugaku*? There is a separate oral instruction on this. It's no small matter. It's a deep, deep secret.

• This scroll is a secret transmission intended for Motomasa's oral instruction. Since he, however, came to an early death, I commit it herewith to ink and paper because otherwise no one in the future would even know the name Doubling Back for the Flower. If only the proper person should come to my attention, I would give him this as Zea[mi]'s legacy for future generations. It is a deep, deep secret.

Eikyō 5 [1433], a day of the third month. Zea (signature)

Note

1. 望却来々々不急: a puzzling expression that looks very much like some sort of Zen dictum (in which case, perhaps the puzzlement is not to be overcome rationally). Omote reads the Chinese as きゃくらいをのぞみて、きゃくらいをいそがず, with *kyakurai* as the object of both verbs, *nozomu* and *isogazu*, which might result in a translation like "desiring to double back, one does not hasten doubling back," certainly possible given the inconsistencies in Zeami's use of Chinese. But all the same, there seems to be some justification to making the second *kyakurai* the subject of *isogazu*. It also is conceivable that the first *kyakurai* is not the object of *nozomu* but the indirect object and that *nozomu* is not "desire" but "be on the verge, look out over."

9. The Suruga *mai* (Suruga Dances) are part of the ancient court repertory of *Azuma asobi*. See *A Mirror to the Flower*.

10. Yuima-e. A gathering held in Nara at Kōfukuji temple that lasts for a week during the tenth lunar month, the focus of which is a series of lectures on the Vimalakīrti nirdeśa Sutra.

11. Nara.

Two Letters to Master Konparu

金春大夫宛書状

Only two of Zeami's letters survive, both addressed to Konparu dayū, "Master [of an artistic troupe] Konparu," in this case, Konparu Zenchiku, Zeami's son-in-law. The letters establish Zenchiku's material relationship to Zeami in the latter's final years, one of them explicitly during Zeami's exile on Sado Island.

The letter dated "fifth month, fourteenth day" was written in response to a query from Zenchiku that must have reflected a concern about his capabilities on stage. Zeami replies, twice citing Zenchiku's "certification," using the Zen term *inka*, and suggesting some kind of formal transmission of artistic technique (although the technique in question is, frustratingly, never mentioned.) Since Zeami used the same term in *The Flower in . . . Yet Doubling Back*, which refers to Zenchiku, some scholars have assumed a specific relation between that text and the certification mentioned here, and a *terminus post quem* for this letter. Zeami's attitude toward Zenchiku in *The Flower in . . . Yet Doubling Back*, however, is notably ambivalent, and it may well be that the "certification" is not intended in such a formal way.

The second letter (which does not necessarily antedate the first) was written from Sado Island, where, for reasons unknown, Zeami had been exiled by the shogun, Yoshinori, in 1434. Zeami specifically refers to the financial support that Zenchiku has made available to his family, mentioning Juchin, presumably his wife. (The same name has been found in a memorial register with Zeami's Buddhist names at Fuganji temple, where Zeami's ashes seem to have been interred at one time.)

The letter is more than merely a greeting and an expression of gratitude. It also addresses questions of performance regarding demons and is important to ascertaining the change in Zeami's attitude toward this role, which had been a staple of Yamato *sarugaku*, Zeami's own tradition.

❀

[The 5:14 Letter]

To be delivered to Master Kon[paru]
From Zea[mi], Kiya[machi, Kyoto][1]

Oroka naru kokoro yo to miru kokoro yori
Yoso ni ha nani no tama wo mimashi ya

Beyond the very frame of mind
that looks upon this mind of mine
in all its foolishness,
what else have I to look to
as the jewel of my awareness?[2]

I am most grateful for your letter; I have read it carefully. I understand you are to make a trip to the north country. What good fortune for you! But how sad I find myself to learn that you are going far away.

Now, to turn to the matter of performance you inquired about: as I said recently, you already have been fully certified[3] to take a leading role. On this basis, further considerations will depend on your individual disposition. Lord Mimura saw your performance in Ōmi. He reported that the performance came off very well. He is a man of fine discrimination, so there should be no doubt about this; put your mind at ease. Of course, since one picture is worth a thousand words,[4] I would very much like to see a performance of yours and put the matter entirely to rest. As for those plays I have already found satisfactory, you are already fully certified for those. In Buddhist practice as well, as the second chief priest of Fuganji temple has said, the master puts his greatest effort into study after the attainment of Dharma. In that context, then, your performance is undoubtedly the proof of your attainment of Dharma.

As for the techniques you ask about, maintain a grand and expansive view of the visual and aural attractions of the Two Arts and the Three Modes. Polish and refine the effects of your attainment of Dharma, ever and always to the

1. This is the address of the letter, written in such a way as to be visible after the letter itself has been folded.

2. The poem is an *otte-gaki*, a kind of postscript, even though it is written to the far right of the sheet on which the letter is written. It is indented below the level of the letter's prose text and may well have been written after the prose was completed, just before the address to Zenchiku, which is at the left of the letter, at the end.

3. Zeami uses the technical term *inka*, which expresses the certification of a Zen master for his disciple's enlightenment. The term also is found in *The Flower in . . . Yet Doubling Back* and *Articles on the Five Sorts of Singing.*

4. *Senmon mo ikken ni ha shikazu* (lit., "a thousand hearings are not as good as one seeing"), apparently a proverb. Zeami repeats it verbatim near the end of the letter.

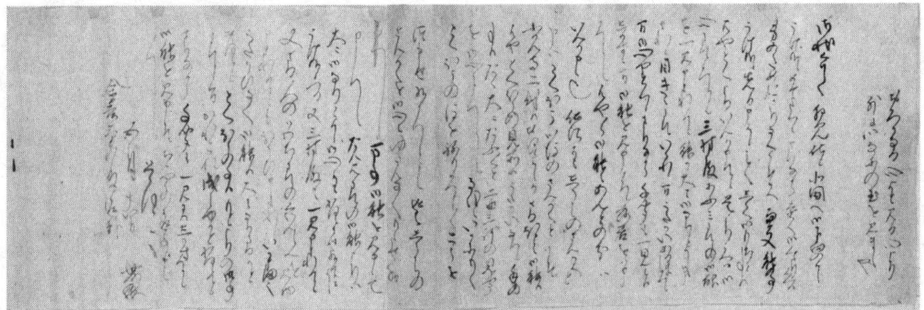

Letter to Master Konparu, 5:14. Neither of the two surviving letters in Zeami's hand cites the year in which it was written, even though the month and day are clearly noted. In its written form, the letter shows a mix of Chinese graphs and *hiragana* in the middle ground between the almost exclusively phonetic writing of the autograph nō play texts and the extremely Sinicized writing of *Performance Notes*, such as that of *Figure Drawings of the Two Arts and the Three Modes*. (Photograph courtesy of Hōzanji temple, Ikoma, and the library of Nara joshi daigaku)

greatest degree possible, and continue to accumulate experience. You must maintain and make the greatest effort not to neglect in your awareness what you have studied under your master. In all myriad matters, one is to speak only on the basis of observing performance. I have heard how you yourself have experienced how much better your performances have come off since that performance of yours in Tanba. And again, Lord Mimura was able to see it. Moreover, a certain person of consequence saw you perform at a subscription performance in Kawachi and spoke highly of it. I have the sense that your performance must have come off very well in every respect, no doubt. Given that the attainment of Dharma is the foundation of all else, I have the sense that in this respect you must have attained your artistic consummation. All the same, it is the case that one picture is worth a thousand words. Once I've seen your performance, I will be able to give you a definite response.

With great respect,
this fourteenth day of the fifth month
Zea[mi] (*kao* signature)
To the Head of the Konparu Troupe, in response.

[The 6:8 Letter]

To the Head of the Konparu Troupe
From Zea[mi]
To the Head of the Konparu Troupe,

Thank you for your letter; I have read it carefully. Let me take this opportunity to express my gratitude for your recent generosity to Juchin and to add that thanks to your personal consideration, I am managing to keep up appearances here in the provinces. I gratefully acknowledge the receipt of ten *mon*. How I would like to tell you in person, and more specifically, how thankful I am, if I should, by some chance, be able to return home.

Now, in your letter you asked about the performance of demons. This is something we do not acknowledge in our troupe. As a rule, we go beyond the Three Modes only as far as the Style of Intricate Movement. The Style of Violent Movement and the like are the concern of other troupes. My late father, however, occasionally would portray a demon and would only go as far as to express that kind of force in his singing voice, so we follow his lead. Even at that, I took on such a role only after I had taken the tonsure. The best way for you to think about this would be that one should perform the role of the demon only after having mastered the vocation of performance, in old age, having had long years of experience.

Those things we talked about earlier I will set down on paper in general terms and send them on. You should pay close attention to them. This place is so far out in the country you can hardly believe it, and it's difficult to find decent paper; you must wonder what's come over me, writing it out in such a way. All the same, even the Wondrous Dharma in scripture diverse can be written with a brush of straw, so if the content concerns the wondrous text of our vocation, then you should regard this paper as if it were finely gilt. May you continue to preserve the Dharma well.

Letter to Master Konparu, 6:8. Although both of Zeami's surviving letters are of great biographical interest, they also touch on concerns relating to performance. This letter is important for its equivocations regarding demonic roles and particularly for its bald rejection of the Style of Violent Movement. Zenchiku had apparently inquired about this style of performance, which was traditionally, no doubt, of great significance to his troupe. Zeami's response to him in this letter, although brief, is an important piece of the puzzle in understanding demonic roles in *sarugaku* and nō. (Photograph courtesy of Hōzanji temple, Ikoma, and the library of Nara joshi daigaku)

With great respect,
this eighth day of the sixth month
Shiō (*kaō* signature)

P.S. I cannot thank you enough for your generosity and consideration to me and, in my absence, to my family.[5]

5. Again, an *otte-gaki*, or postscript. In the original letter, this appears to the far right of the sheet on which the letter is written, indented below the level of the prose text. Because of the content, it seems appropriate in the translation to put it here.

APPENDIX 1

Music, Dance, and Performance in *Sarugaku*

Many of the texts in the *Performance Notes* concern questions of music and dance in general terms, but at least eight or nine of them are more specifically and technically related to these central features of *sarugaku* performance. For music, five texts are especially noteworthy: *Oral Instructions on Singing, A Collection of Jewels in Effect, Technical Specifications for Setting a Melody, Articles on the Five Sorts of Singing,* and *Five Sorts of Singing.*

We are both tantalized and frustrated by much of what appears in these texts. First, they attest to the presence of magnificent actors on the late-fourteenth- and fifteenth-century stage. Zeami's passing remarks in the *Performance Notes* about Kiami and Inuō Dōami, not to mention his father, Kannami, offer hints about this (and those hints are elaborated in *Conversations on Sarugaku*, in which the great *dengaku* actor Zōami also comes in for high praise). But all we really know about Kiami, Dōami, and Zōami are comments like these. There are no extant plays in their hand, as far as we know.[1] And even if we did have plays by them, that still would give us only a vague idea of what they must have been able to do as actors. But then, that was the case for all actors anywhere until the development of recording technologies that could give us a more detailed picture of what the greats of the past did on stage.

It is not merely for the evocation of past masters that we turn to these texts. We also can see in them, remarkably clearly, how closely the contours of the typical nō play conform to Zeami's prescriptions for *sarugaku*. We find here, as well, some of the most important evidence to consider when trying to evaluate for ourselves the importance of "tradition." Tradition is everywhere trumpeted as a reason to value forms like nō, bunraku, kabuki, *kathakali*, or even the religious plays of Oberammergau, but all too often, the tradition in question is not really that old, not plausibly "authentic," and maybe not very edifying. In the case of *sarugaku* and its descendant nō, we have enough good information to give us a strong basis for reconsidering questions about the integrity of tradition, and we also have the clear testimony, especially in Zeami's own words, about the unparalleled importance of the here and now for performance.

If all the texts are technically daunting, given the removal of Zeami's performance from what it is possible for us to know in the twenty-first century, they nonetheless deserve close attention because they show the paradox of form in Zeami's thought, and despite their (often baffling) technical specificity, they do provide an unsurpassed view of what fifteenth-century performance of *sarugaku* must have been like. Many of nō's most salient features are apparent in *sarugaku*, and Zeami clearly promotes the centrality of the *shite*, both artistically and aesthetically. His assertions about the *shite*'s primary role in performance are numerous and persuasive, especially from the perspective of modern nō performance. Perhaps the most typical feature of nō, which distinguishes it from many other kinds of theater in the world today, is its focus on a central subject. It is interesting to read between the lines in texts such as *Learning the Profession*, which mentions the failure to recognize the centrality of the *shite* as hurting the troupe's success.

We also learn from *Learning the Profession* and the other five texts just mentioned that singing is the central musical feature of *sarugaku*, yet we discern particular places where instrumentalists play an important role as well. We find generally less information about dance. Although *Figure Drawings of the Two Arts and the Three Modes* discusses dance in detail, apart from its bewildering comments at the end of the text about varieties of stomping, it doesn't specify what happens but instead opts for a more abstract and philosophical ground from which to discuss dance. Remarks like "Substance is intent, and force is to be cast aside" (in the passages on the Woman's Mode) are typical.

Zeami's detailed discussions of musical performance in the *Notes* make generous use of terminology from Sino-Japanese music theory. This was the theory underlying *gagaku*, the instrumental ensemble music played at the ancient Japanese court, which was first introduced into the country perhaps as early as the sixth (or even fifth)[2] century and increasing in importance as part of the vast importation of continental culture through the late ninth century. The musics that became *gagaku* have roots in many parts of Asia, including Central Asia and the coast of Annam as well as, of course, China and the Korean Peninsula. *Gagaku* continues to be performed even today, although it has been vastly altered in transmission.

Sarugaku is very different from *gagaku*, but most of the formal theory of music available to Zeami was what was used to discuss *gagaku*, so however great the discrepancy between *gagaku* theory and *sarugaku* practice might have been, we must deal with some of the terminology and conceptual assumptions of this theory in order to understand Zeami's detailed comments about music.

The most common references relate broadly to pitches and pitch structures, which might loosely be called *scales* or *modes*. These scales or modes are created by combining a system of degrees (i.e., positions that individual notes hold vis-à-vis other notes within the same system, like do, re, mi, fa, etc.) with a system of fixed pitches. The Chinese systems that had been imported into Japan divided the octave into twelve named pitches and then identified certain groups of pitches with fixed relationships that could be transposed into different keys. Of the twenty-eight theoretical groupings they produced, thirteen were popularly used in China at the time. Six of these "modes" were used in the species of *gagaku* most closely associated with Chinese antecedents (Tōgaku [Tang music]).

In China, the modes were divided into two scale types: *ryo* (呂, in Mandarin *lü*, third tone) and *ritsu* (律, in Mandarin *lü*, fourth tone). When the system was adapted to the Japanese practice in *gagaku* performance itself, it underwent numerous alterations. Accordingly, its application to other types of music in Japan has "rarely provided insight,"[3] but the terminology nonetheless is found in Zeami's discussion.

Zeami refers (though only rarely) to the degree names of the Chinese system, 宮商角徵羽, using Japanese pronunciation, *kiu* (mod. J. *kyū*), *shyau* (mod. J. *shō*), *kaku, chi*, and *u*, respectively. He refers more frequently to pitch or modal names, especially *waushiki* (黄鐘, mod. J. *ōshiki*) and *banshiki* (盤涉).

In modern *gagaku* performance, *ōshiki* corresponds generally to A and *banshiki* to B, but there is no absolute pitch in modern nō performance, so the significance of these pitch terms itself wavers. Modern nō actors are not concerned with absolute pitch in their singing and generally do not use these technical terms with reference to singing.[4] In the repertory of the nō flute, however, the old pitch and mode names do retain some significance, particularly the distinction between *ōshiki* and *banshiki*. In this case, though, the terms do not refer to an absolute pitch but to the specific fingerings of the principal tones in a given piece.

Moreover, the construction of the modern nō flute actually makes impossible the identification of any absolute pitch with reference to *ōshiki* and *banshiki*, because flutes are not made to particular pitch specifications. Furthermore, one of its physical features (the so-called *nodo* [throat]) distorts the relation between a particular note in one octave and its counterparts in the octaves above, so that even if, say, *ōshiki* were A 440 in the lowest octave of a nō flute, it would not produce an exact octave when played in the register above that lowest octave.

It would be easy enough simply to relinquish notions of absolute pitch altogether when discussing *sarugaku*, if in the *Performance Notes*, Zeami did not make several references suggesting that in his time, pitch relations between singing and the flute were more exact than they are today. In *A Mirror to the Flower* and *Oral Instructions on Singing*, for instance, he seems to suggest that the *shite* should take his pitch from the pitch of the flute:

> It is the *ki* that sustains the pitch. If you focus on the pitch of the flute first and use this occasion to match the *ki* with it, then close your eyes, draw in a breath, and only after that produce the voice, your voice will come forth from within the pitch from the start.[5]

It is not impossible that the word I've translated as "pitch" (*teushi*, mod. J. *chōshi*) should be understood in a more emotional way as, say, a general aesthetic or emotional tenor. But this is unlikely, given other places where it is difficult to interpret *teushi* as meaning anything other than pitch or a system of pitches (roughly analogous to a musical mode or scale). Consider, for example, this anecdote from *Learning the Profession*:

> On one occasion at a *sarugaku* performance dedicated to a shrine, the *shite* was singing a *rongi* duet with a boy actor in the mode *rankei*. The boy's voice hadn't yet changed, and he tended to slide up to *banshiki* mode. The *shite*'s voice remained in *rankei*. As their exchange of lines proceeded, the discrepancy in mode threatened to ruin the performance, but Meishō, all the while continuing to play in *rankei*, took account of the boy's singing and adjusted his mode accordingly, giving it something of the feel of *banshiki*, even while playing with the *shite* in the original *rankei*, so that the discrepancy in pitch didn't seem out of place, and the performance was quite interesting.[6]

Rankei should be the note B-flat / A-sharp, whereas *banshiki*, as we saw, is B, but the passage seems to suggest more than the mere transposition of one note to another, a half step higher. Instead, it seems to suggest a system of notes based on B-flat, something like a key, which the flautist Meishō had to transpose into a system of notes based on B.[7] The problem has not been resolved, but even if the *shite* and the flute were to sing at the same pitch at some point in a play in *sarugaku*, that does not guarantee that the pitch in question was an absolute one.

These Sino-Japanese pitch systems are not exclusively a matter of the physics of sound but were more broadly implicated in a cosmological system of "Five Phases." In this system, various phenomena in the material world were understood to be naturally linked to emotional states, ideological predispositions, and aesthetic experiences.[8] The Five Vital Organs (liver, lungs, heart, kidneys, and spleen, in one influential version) could be coordinated with the Five Directions (the four cardinal directions plus the middle), Five Phases (wood, fire, earth, metal, and water), Five Colors (green, red, yellow, white, and black), Five Flavors (sour, bitter, sweet, acrid, and salty), and so forth. The Five Notes of the Chinese system of musical degrees were readily adapted to this scheme, on which Zeami's theoretical matrix for singing and flute music has a certain grounding. Despite its ubiquity, however, Five Phases theory is constantly undermined by groupings of more or fewer than five elements, such as the *six* senses of scholastic Buddhism (the usual five plus consciousness) and the *four* seasons.

Consider briefly this specific musical example: the pitch *banshiki* was associated with water and waves, and as such was de rigueur for groundbreaking ceremonies because the association with water was thought to ward off the danger of fire. *Banshiki* also was the proper key for funerals and mourning, so the inherent celebratory character of a groundbreaking was marked as well by the funereal character of the *banshiki* pitch system. As we see in nō performance, a further complication comes, for instance, when a Dance in *ōshiki* is transposed to *banshiki* for a particularly festive performance of the so-called Banshiki Haya-mai, "a *mai* that is danced in a carefree and joyful way by the spirit of a courtier or a woman who has attained Buddhahood."[9]

Zeami seems to have accepted the basic premises of the system of Five Phases and added to them in his own way. He chose a five-part typology to classify singing and made it correspond to, for example, five types of trees to characterize the emotional tenor of different types of plays.[10] The trees give him a metaphorical vehicle with which to comment on certain plays and, as such, are relatively unproblematic, but as we saw in the introduction, the classification of five types of singing turns back on itself and is deconstructed in revealing ways.

In contrast to the highly articulated theoretical system underlying questions of pitch and mode in *sarugaku*, there seems to be very little explicit theory to explain rhythm. But clearly, rhythm is an important practical concern for Zeami. In *Technical Specifications for Setting a Melody*, he states, "[Rhythm] is the life of musical expression."

In *Mirror to the Flower*, he provides a similar assertion with related statements about the importance of other aspects of musical performance:

> Also, about the order in studying singing: First memorize the words, and after that, master the song; after that, create distinction in the melody; after that, discern the proper accent for the words; after that, grasp the intent. The rhythm must be understood throughout, at the beginning, in the middle, and at the end.

We can, moreover, discern several important aspects of rhythmic practice that shed light on *sarugaku* performance and even allow some correlation with modern nō performance. The connection, for instance, between rhythm and the performing art *kusemai* (曲舞, orth. *kusemahi*) is of particular interest. In Kannami's time and before, *kusemai* was a separate performing art danced and sung by female itinerants. Kannami is known to have adopted it into nō to great effect. The original form of *kusemai* is not clear, but even in modern-day nō performance, the *kuse* has a distinct and discernible rhythmic character that allows for extensive syncopation.

Before Kannami brought elements of *kusemai* performance into *sarugaku*, the primary rhythmic configurations in the art were limited to what is called *tadautai* (orth. *tadautahi* [regular singing]). In modern nō performance, *tadautai* usually consists of alternating lines of five and seven syllables. They are sung in a relatively predictable relationship to the beats of the drums and offer little rhythmic variation from song to song. *Kusemai*, in contrast, though also usually written in five- and seven-syllable lines, have a greater proportion of metrically irregular lines and, even with regular metrical lines, tend to introduce vocal embellishments and metrical extensions that necessitate greater rhythmic flexibility and variety.

We cannot confidently and specifically correlate *kusemai* singing from Zeami's day with the modern practice, but Zeami does make telling comments to demonstrate the importance of rhythm in *kusemai* in his day, and they provide a plausible antecedent to modern practice. From *A Collection of Jewels in Effect*, for instance, consider the following:

> Also, you should make allowance for expanding or contracting in singing in the transitions between 7–5 verses, in accordance with the rhythm beat out by the drum(s). The matter of expanding or contracting the rhythm depending on a verse or a word is for learning by transmission from your teacher. Beginners should pay great attention to this transmission.

In *Technical Specifications for Setting a Melody*, he says, similarly,

> *Kusemai.* This line of singing is different from the typical sort. First and foremost, it takes rhythm as its Substance and should proceed expeditiously, relying on rhythm. The melody should be set in such a way that it passes across beats in the rhythm, shrinking and opening up to the movement through the 7–5 verses as it is counted out in the mind, and adjusting this way and that.

In a broader sense, rhythm is, of course, closely correlated with the overall structure of performance. This is Zeami's concern in parts of *Transmitting the Flower*, in the short text called *An Extract from Learning the Flower*, and most extensively in *Three Courses*. Unlike his discussion of pitch systems that we have reviewed, the treatment of the overall structure of *sarugaku* plays is for the most part clear and concise. In some cases, Zeami even goes so far as to specify the number of verses that should be allotted to a given song. The individual song types require some special annotation, which I have relegated to the glossary. Otherwise, Zeami's remarks about the construction of individual plays are, I think, clear enough to be read without special annotation here.[11]

Beyond the limits of a single play, Zeami expresses fairly clear ideas about the preferred sequence of plays in a full day's performance outside, or in shorter performances indoors, usually at night. His overall principle *jo-ha-kyū* was mentioned in the introduction and is laid out in detail in *A Mirror to the Flower*, *Three Courses*, and *Oral Instructions on Singing*, but Zeami devotes much attention to linking structural features with emotional characterizations to inform the flow of performance in major competitions and, eventually, to shape the individual actor's entire career. This linking was discussed in the introduction.

In addition to extensive discussion of the music in *sarugaku*, three of the texts in the *Performance Notes—Oral Instructions on Singing*, *Articles on the Five Sorts of Singing*, and *Five Sorts of Singing*—also contain quotations from plays and songs illustrating the generic categories that Zeami was formulating. *Five Sorts of Singing* is particularly generous in providing examples, listing seventy-one individual pieces. Many of these are plays that continue to be performed in the modern repertory, as well as numerous excerpts from individual songs that may never have been fixed in a specific play. A number of the citations are from *kusemai*, whether or not adapted to the conventions of *sarugaku*. Some musical notation is included among these citations, although it is, by modern standards, very limited, and some of the terminology is difficult to understand. Zeami's primary aim seems to have been to offer his audience familiar examples of singing to exemplify the generic categories he had formulated, but for modern readers, a different purpose is served. In many cases, we can see how thematic content correlates with genre, how the performative context of stories known from other sources is shaped for presentation on the stage, and, to some degree, how texts are set musically (although there has not yet been very much research in this area).[12]

Text setting is an important concern to Zeami. In addition to the examples he cites in *Five Sorts of Singing* and elsewhere, he also speaks at length about the close relation between text and song in *sarugaku*. His discussion of these matters is commonsensical and accessible in, for example, *Three Courses*, in which he talks about establishing a lyrical ground for the articulation of identity in warriors, say, or he emphasizes intelligibility in the choice of subjects and their treatment in a five-part dramatic structure. In focusing more tightly on the relation between text and song at the level of individual words and phrases, however, his remarks are among the most technical and bewildering of all the writing in *Performance Notes*. In some cases, we really have little idea of what he intends. Perhaps most puzzling of all is a distinction he makes (first in *Oral Instructions on Singing*) between two varieties of vocalization, *wau no koye* ("*wau* voice," mod. J. *ō no koe*) and *shu no koye* ("*shu* voice," mod. J. *shu no koe*) These words usually are written in *kana*, but sometimes he uses the graphs 横 (sidelong) for *wau* and 主 (primary) for *shu*. The latter seems to be a borrowing for the more unusual graph 竪, also pronounced "shu" or "ju," meaning "upright," which forms a more comprehensible pair with "sidelong." The felicitous combination of the two voices is termed *ahiwon* (mod. J. *aion* [lit., "biphonic," or my "Doubly Proficient"]),[13] and it is used to refer to both musical passages in which such an effect is desirable and actors who are naturally capable of such singing.

Although such "Doubly Proficient" actors were known to Zeami, most actors are perceived to sing in either a *wau* voice or a *shu* voice, so they must be trained and encouraged to develop their ability to use both types of singing. In writing *kusemai* songs, the composer is encouraged to usually keep the two types of voice separate but to compose *tadautai* songs with the voice types in combination, says a passage in *Conversations on Sarugaku*. It is disappointing to find that the terms *wau* and *shu* do not occur at all in the extant play texts in Zeami's hand, and even the extensive quotations of song in *Five Sorts of Singing*, *Oral Instructions on Singing*, and *Articles on the Five Sorts of Singing* have few annotations specifying *wau* and *shu* voicings.[14]

Zeami correlates *wau* voice with the *ryo*-scale type and *shu* with the *ritsu*, but modern scholarship has as yet found no practical way to understand this apart from Omote's conjecture that the *wau* voice, with its *ryo* connections, represents a "thick, strong, masculine voice," whereas the *shu*, with its *ritsu* connections, represents a "thin, weak, feminine voice." In a very general way, this suggests a difference in modern performance practice between *tsuyogin* and *yowagin* chant structures, but Omote states definitively, "It is not possible to recognize any direct connection between modern *tsuyogin* and *yowagin*, on the one hand, and *wau* and *shu*, on the other."[15]

Nomura Shirō, an actor of the Kanze school, however, suggests that *wau* voice may be the voice typically associated with the primary pitches in nō music, and the *shu* voice, with the transitional pitches between.[16] In nō, these *wau* voices would then be associated with *jō*, *chū*, and *ge* pitches, whereas the *shu* voice would be associated with *chū-uki, ge-no-chū, kuri,* and other such subsidiary pitches. The suggestion is intriguing and may, in the future, lead to a better understanding of *sarugaku* practice, although it will be necessary to bear in mind that the relation among *jō*, *chū*, and *ge* itself was different in *sarugaku* than in nō.

When we turn from vocal types to the elocution of individual words in *sarugaku* texts, we find a clear distinction in Zeami's understanding of two types of "mispronunciation."[17] This mispronunciation can occur when the natural accents of individual words are disrupted by melodic inflections. In Zeami's view, it is acceptable to mispronounce grammatical particles (he refers to these in shorthand as *te*, *ni*, and *ha*) when it serves the performer's musical purposes but is unacceptable when the mispronunciation distorts the "word" itself. (For "word," Zeami uses *moji*, which means a written word and probably refers to those words habitually written in Chinese graphs: mostly nouns, verbs, and adjectives. Most grammatical particles cannot be written with Chinese graphs, and even those that can usually appear only in *kanbun*, Chinese, or Sino-Japanese texts.)

So far, Zeami's point is relatively easy to understand but becomes more complicated when he begins to describe a mispronunciation and why it is undesirable. He refers to systems of "Five Sounds and Four Accents," and the principal difficulty here is that the systems he uses apparently are Chinese. In particular, the "Four Accents" come from Chinese prosody and indicate linguistic tones. The system is crucial to Chinese verse and reflects the tonal variation that is a feature of Chinese languages. But it is not relevant to Japanese, which is not a tonal language, and thus provides little useful information about the specifics of text setting.

Omote notes how such a forced theoretical model could be attractive as an exclusive oral transmission, despite fundamental errors in identifying the four tones of Chinese prosody with Japanese accent and mistaking differences in tone as reflecting differences in pitch that could be identified with degrees of the scale. In medieval Japan, great industry was devoted to secret transmissions. (They even are thematized in *sarugaku*, and one particularly intriguing example is quoted at length in *Five Sorts of Singing.*)[18]

Whatever the biographical circumstances in which Zeami received his transmission in Sino-Japanese music theory, his understanding of it and its relation to elocution seems to be based on the Kamakura-period text *Goin han'on seu*, although he was mistaken in some of his understanding of even this text. The prestige of *gagaku* and *shōmyō* probably led him to believe that such a theoretical underpinning was desirable, although tellingly Zeami remarks near the beginning of *Technical Specifications for Setting a Melody*,

> [W]hat I mean by a person truly accomplished in elocution and the Six Modes and what I mean by someone who is expert at singing are two different things. Some people understand elocution but don't know about singing. Some experts in singing are not accomplished in elocution. That said, though, once they have risen to a rank of true expertise, some people are, as a matter of course, fully competent with regard to elocution, even without receiving a formal transmission in the subject. Someone once said, "Neither the teacher nor the student really knows the way elocution and musical modality work. They exist, rather, of their own accord in the hands of a truly accomplished master."

If some of the frustration one feels in reading Zeami on music theory comes from the opacity of his technical explanations, the case is different with Dance. He does not try to fit his practice into a technical framework, and such theory of dance as we find in the *Performance Notes* is more abstract and philosophical or cosmological.

Dance was clearly of great importance to *sarugaku*. Zeami ranks it, along with singing, as one of the Two Arts central to the aesthetic effects to which he was aiming. Throughout the *Performance Notes*, a vigorous type of movement that Zeami terms *hataraki* (my "Sparring") is distinguished from a more graceful kind of dance movement termed *mahi* (mod. J. *mai*, my "Dance"). The former was native to Zeami's home tradition of Yamato *sarugaku*, whereas the latter seems to have derived from the rival tradition of Ōmi *sarugaku*.

In modern nō performance, the distinction between Dance and Sparring remains clear, even though we acknowledge that the modern descendants of these two basic dance categories are probably significantly different from their antecedents in *sarugaku*. Modern Dances are themselves divisible into two broad categories, those based on a cyclical musical structure cumbersomely named *ryo-chū-kan*-style *mai* and non-*ryo-chū-kan*-style *mai*. (*Ryo*, *chū*, and *kan* are names of melodic figures repeated in sequence with, actually, a fourth, *kan-no-chū*.)[19]

For Zeami, Sparring usually meant activity with some mimetic basis, a fight between a warrior and a demon, for example, whereas Dances are more formal and abstract. This distinction holds up quite well with modern nō performance, too. Sparring entails stage exercises in which supernatural characters "demonstrate their power and authority, moving around violently,"[20] and it often shows a strong mimetic basis in depicting fights or battles, hot pursuit, or other kinds of struggles. In the related *kakeri* and *iroe* forms, the battles are psychological, or interior, but no less intense.

The Dances in modern nō seem very likely to have derived from a particular and rather uncharacteristic dance called the Tennyo no mai (Heavenly Maiden's Dance) in Zeami's day,[21] which leaves unanswered the question of what a more typical dance in *sarugaku* might have looked like. Complicating this is the fact that the separate performing art, the *kusemai*, was brought into *sarugaku* performance by Zeami's father, Kannami, and this no doubt had some effect on the development of dance in *sarugaku* and subsequently nō as well.

A central problem in *sarugaku* dance seems to have been how to make the most of the positive elements of Sparring, on the one hand, and Dance, on the other, without suffering their negative characteristics. For all its vigor and excitement, Sparring could degenerate into coarseness and crudity, whereas in the wrong dancer, the elegance and grace of Dance could seem like nothing more than weakness. The problem is not exclusive to dance—it has its counterparts in singing and acting in general—but it seems particularly clear in dance, and Zeami discusses it at some length in "Written Preparations for the Flower," in *Transmitting the Flower*.

Although there is activity on the nō stage throughout any given performance that today we might in general terms call "dance," because of its formality and artistry, the dancing in nō, in a more precise sense, generally takes place near the end of a play. This was true as well of *sarugaku*. Zeami notes matter-of-factly in *Three Courses* that the last section of a play contains a dance, "whether a Dance or Sparring, or *hayabushi* or *kiribyōshi*, or the like."[22]

Instrumental music is essential to nō drama and is used in many ways, always in dances, frequently for characters' entrances, less often for their exits, and in other places, such as for on stage costume changes. The flute and the two hourglass drums also accompany much of the text delivered by the *shite* and other actors and the chorus. In *sarugaku*, though, the use of musical instruments is difficult to gauge. It is certain that a flute, at least one hourglass drum (*tsuzumi*), and the stick drum (*taiko*) were used, but when they were used or what sort of music they played is not completely clear.

Zeami's most detailed remarks about the use of instruments on the *sarugaku* stage are in the sole text he wrote for the troupe as a whole (rather than for transmission to a select individual or two). The text, *Learning the Profession,* begins with a brief encouragement to all the participants in the drama to cooperate and then talks about the prerogatives and obligations of each role. Zeami outlines the *shite*'s manifold responsibilities, acknowledges the *waki*'s importance at the beginning of a particular play, and also reminds us that he and other actors in the troupe are to remain subordinate to the *shite.*

The remarks directed at the drummers are brief and surprising: they are encouraged to show off at the beginning of a play and afterward to restrain themselves. Although the restraint is consistent with remarks elsewhere in the text, which leave no doubt that the *shite* is the center of the production, the encouragement to flashy playing at the beginning is not characteristic of modern nō performance and seems at odds with the overall tenor of Zeami's remarks about the development of *jo-ha-kyū* in dramatic structure.[23]

The two varieties of drums mentioned by Zeami, the *tsuzumi* and the *taiko,* are still in use today in nō and elsewhere, and both have early ancestors in Japanese music.

The *taiko* (more precisely, *shime-daiko*) is a shallow, barrel-shaped drum with horsehide or cowhide heads stretched over a ring frame. The heads are tied together with ropes, holding the barrel tightly between them. The drum is held with one head facing up on a wooden frame and is played by striking the upward-facing head with two thick drumsticks, one for each hand. Drum strokes are aimed at the center of the upper head, where, on modern drums, one finds an extra circular piece of leather.

The *tsuzumi* is often called an hourglass drum because of the shape of its wooden body. It, too, has two circular heads, made of horsehide or cowhide stretched over ring frames. As with the *taiko,* the heads are tied together with ropes, enclosing the wooden body of the drum. The distance between the heads is greater for the *tsuzumi* than for the *taiko.* The performer's left hand grasps the ropes, and he strikes one of the drum heads with the right hand. In certain cases, to produce a desired sound, the ropes on the smaller of the two drums used in modern performances are tightened by hand when the drum is struck.

In modern nō, two *tsuzumi* are played in every performance.[24] One, the *kotsuzumi,* the smaller of the two, is held in front of the right shoulder. Its heads are relatively thin and are partly lacquered. It is capable of a wide variety of sounds and, in the hands of a master performer, is subtle and sensitive. The other, the *ōtsuzumi* (or *ōkawa*), is held horizontally on the knees of the seated performer and, when struck, can produce a loud, dry wooden crack. In nō, the two drums play interlacing patterns of great variety and ingenuity, almost always playing as a pair.

In *sarugaku,* however, it is uncertain whether two *tsuzumi* were used at all. Zeami mentions only the *tsudzumi,* not distinguishing between *kotsuzumi* and *ōtsuzumi*, so we have no way of knowing whether the interlocking patterns characteristic of the *tsuzumi* players in nō have their ancestor in the fifteenth century, or only later. Zeami does speak of *tekazu* (手かず), however, which suggests the kind of drum patterns used in nō, although we find no mention of specific patterns apart from one possible exception, the *kashira*. Zeami does mention the word *kashira* in reference to drumming. In nō, *kashira* are a genre of conspicuous cadential patterns. The mention of both *tekazu* and *kashira* points to the presence of drum patterns in *sarugaku*, as we have them in nō, but we don't have any indication of specific patterns used in any given play. Zeami also mentions what seem to be drum calls,[25] suggesting that the vocalizations so indispensable to modern nō drumming may have been a part of *sarugaku* drumming as well.[26]

The most extensive remarks in *Learning the Profession* are directed at the flute player, suggesting that the flute played an important role in *sarugaku*. Zeami calls the instrument simply *fue* (flute), giving us little lexical indication whether or not it had the unique structural features of the modern nō flute, the *nōkan*. The *nōkan* is a lacquered bamboo transverse flute with seven finger holes. An extra bamboo tube (called the *nodo* [throat]) is inserted into the flute bore between the first finger hole and the mouth hole, giving the *nōkan* a unique timbre and pitch structure. In its overblown (or second) octave, the lower notes are somewhat sharp, whereas the higher notes are somewhat flat.[27] The *nōkan* also is capable of producing a certain number of piercing shrieks called *hishigi*, useful for cueing actors backstage (and waking dozing members of the audience). There is no precise standard length or bore size for the *nōkan*, so each flute plays its own pitch, and there is no expectation that two *nōkan* should be in tune with each other.

In appearance, the *nōkan* is very much like the *ryūteki*, an older transverse flute used in *gagaku*. This suggests a common lineage for the two flutes. It is interesting to note, though, that Zeami distinguishes between the "flute used by court musicians" (likely the *ryūteki*) and the flute used in *sarugaku*:

> There is a fine point in the way the nō flute differs from the flute used by court musicians. What is that fine point? It amounts to this: occasionally the singing of the *shite* may be somewhat sharp or flat in relation to a fixed pitch. If the flute player is insensible to this and simply continues to play at the pitch established from the beginning, there will be a discrepancy between the *shite*'s pitch and the flute's pitch.

The *ryūteki* is made to play exact pitches, and a competent *ryūteki* performer should be able to stay in tune with a competent singer without much effort. Zeami's remarks suggest that is not the case for the *sarugaku* flute player, which may indicate that the flute used in *sarugaku* already had some of the pitch anomalies characteristic of the *nōkan*.

NOTES

1. There is a beautiful form of women's mask, *zō-onna*, which Zōami is supposed to have invented.

2. The *Nihon shoki* records the appearance of *gagaku* musicians from the kingdom of Silla (on the Korean Peninsula) at the funeral obsequies for Sovereign Wingyō (mod. J. Ingyō *tennō*) in 453, but his very existence is deeply enshrouded in legend, so we cannot be sure this date is accurate. By the late sixth century, however, it becomes much more plausible that *gagaku* had been introduced into Japan.

3. The differences between *ryo* and *ritsu* are summarized in *Grove Music Online* as follows:

> Prior to the late 19th century the only extensive modal theory was that for gagaku (court music); early theorizing did not extend to detailed analysis of tonal function or melodic patterns, and the focus was mainly on scales (tonal material), tunings and modal classification of pieces. It was recognized, however, that court music modes fell into two groups, *ritsu* and *ryo*, each with an anhemitonic pentatonic core with two "exchange tones" (*hennon*, from Chinese *bianyin*) that could replace two of the core degrees (in ascending melodic passages in the case of *ritsu*, in descent for *ryo*). The modal terminology of gagaku was sometimes applied to other genres but rarely provided insight. (Japan, §I: General 4. Scales and modes)

4. Special variant performances of the plays *Eguchi* and *Yoroboshi* use the names *hyōjō-gaeshi* and *sōjō-no-mai*, respectively. The lower pitch name *sōjō* (originally, the pitch G) seems to appear in *Yoroboshi*, although again, this is not an absolute pitch designation but, in effect, a flute fingering. The use of *hyōjō* in *Eguchi* is more puzzling. Neither the pitch *hyōjō* (equal to E) nor the fingering analogous to it seems to prevail in the relevant section of the play. See Yokomichi Mario, "*Eguchi* no hyōjō-gaeshi," in *Nōgeki shōyō* (Tokyo: Chikuma shobō, 1984), pp. 3–44.

5. This example is from *A Mirror to the Flower*, but the text is nearly identical in *Oral Instructions on Singing.*

6. *Learning the Profession.*

7. It is likely, moreover, that the transposition would be still more complicated than the transposition of the key of B-flat to the key of B. At least if we are to judge by the case of *gagaku*, the transposition of one *teushi* to another also requires changes in the pitch relations between degrees within the pitch system as well as differences in the way certain notes are approached. Perhaps a better analogy would be the transposition of one *raga* to another, or of, say, the Phrygian mode into the Mixolydian.

8. A helpful sketch of this system can be found in "The Five Phases," in Wm. Theodore de Bary and Irene Bloom, eds., *Sources of Chinese Tradition*, 2d ed. (New York: Columbia University Press, 1999), vol. 1, pp. 347–49.

9. Tōyō ongaku gakkai [The Society for Research in Asiatic Music], ed., *Nō no hayashigoto* (Tokyo: Ongaku no tomo sha, 1990), p. 300.

10. See his treatment in *Articles on the Five Sorts of Singing.*

11. For a study of the relation between play construction and typical plays in the modern repertory, see *ZS*.

12. These citations are, moreover, often attributed to particular authors and composers and serve as the most important source for early authorship of nō plays. See *ZS*, esp. pp. 42–48.

13. The distinction between *wau* and *shu* seems to come from *shōmyō* (Buddhist liturgical chant). Omote cites two sources to back this up in *ZZ*, p. 444n.32. *Ahiwon* seems to be Zeami's coinage.

14. Omote identifies only one annotation for the *wau* voice but thirteen for the *shu* voice. For a detailed account of the problems inherent in identifying these voice types and the texts that offer evidence about them, see *ZZ*, pp. 443–44n.32.

15. Omote, in *ZZ*, p. 444n.32. For an account of modern *yowagin* and *tsuyogin*, see *ZS*, pp. 59–60.

16. Personal communication, December 18, 2006.

17. I translate Zeami's word *namari* as "mispronunciation" here. The word also means "dialect" or "regional accent." Zeami was concerned that his actors use a pronunciation acceptable to his elite audiences, and that may have been a matter requiring careful monitoring on his part. All the extant play texts in his hand are written in *katakana*, presumably to reflect a precise pronunciation of the texts in question (*hiragana* or *kana-majiri bun* would have been more typical of written texts at the time) and to prevent regionalisms from creeping in.

In the case of these references to text setting, however, the concern is not for dialect or regional variation but for the potential for mispronunciation because of melodic inflection clashing with the normal accentuation of given words. "Mispronunciation" therefore is what is intended here, not "dialect."

18. It is entitled *Kuzu no hakama* (*Arrowroot Trousers*).

19. The actual sequence is *chū–kan–kan-no-chū–ryo*. This unit of four melodic figures is called *ji* (ground), and it serves as a common element to all *ryo-chū-kan*-style *mai* (the individual *mai* being distinguished on the basis of unique melodic figures played between sequences of *ji*). Non-*ryo-chū-kan*-style *mai* are structured on longer and more internally varying sequences of melodic figures. Typical *ryo-chū-kan*-style *mai* in nō are the *chū no mai*, the *kami mai*, and the *jo no mai*. Typical non-*ryo-chū-kan*-style *mai* are the *kagura* and *gaku*.

20. Tōyō ongaku gakkai, ed., *Nō no hayashigoto*, p. 416.

21. Not to be confused with the simplified version of the *chū no mai* called *tennyo no mai* in the nō repertory. See Takemoto Mikio's important and influential article, "*Tennyo no mai* no kenkyū," *Nōgaku kenkyū* (Nōgaku kenkyūjo kiyō) 4 (1978): 93–158.

22. *Three Courses*.

23. Although the flashy performance and the "getting up the beat" (*uchitatsu* is the word he uses) to which he refers may be ancestors of the music used for *waki* and especially *shite* entrances, pieces such as the *shidai*, *issei*, and *deha*.

24. In the ritually important play *Shikisanban* (or *Okina*), three *kotsuzumi* are played during parts of the performance.

25. *Conversations on Sarugaku*, in *ZZ*, p. 261: "*Tsudzumi wo mo 'ya, tei tei' to uchite.*"

26. Roughly three generations after Zeami, at the time of Konparu Zenpō (1454–1532), there was clearly a distinction between *kotsuzumi* and *ōtsuzumi*.

27. Hugh de Ferranti, *Japanese Musical Instruments* (Oxford: Oxford University Press, 2000), p. 68.

APPENDIX 2

On the Manuscripts

The reflection of Zeami in written texts since the fifteenth century shows a significant imbalance that was corrected only gradually in the twentieth century. On the one hand, his name was legendary as a writer of nō plays, and in some compilations of authorship dating from the early sixteenth century, he was credited, erroneously, with 150 or more plays. On the other hand, his reputation as a writer of other kinds of texts, such as those in *Performance Notes* or his extensive memoir, *Conversations on Sarugaku*, was hidden. With the exception of some sections of *Transmitting the Flower Through Effects and Attitudes* and *Learning the Profession*, this material existed only in manuscript copies of very limited circulation. That changed in 1908, when Yoshida Tōgo discovered a large collection of texts by Zeami that had recently come into the possession of the Matsunoya Library (松迺舎文庫) from the estate of important vassals of the Tokugawa, the Hori family. After publishing *Conversations on Sarugaku*, Yoshida turned his attention in 1909 to a large body of the *Notes*, which he published as *A Collection of Sixteen Pieces by Zeami* (世阿弥十六部集). Although the texts on which he based his printed editions were destroyed in the Great Kantō Earthquake of 1923, they had already been published in a photographic facsimile that has since served as an invaluable record of these briefly found, now forever lost, manuscripts. In the following discussion, this photographic facsimile is counted as an "extant text."

Numerous other manuscripts of the *Performance Notes* have been released to public examination since Yoshida's epoch-making discovery. The most authoritative edition is found in the Nihon shisō taikei series under the title *Zeami, Zenchiku*, meticulously edited by Omote Akira with an essay by Kato Shūichi and voluminous notes by Omote.[1] In addition are many other valuable editions of some of these texts, among them those edited by Nose Asaji, Konishi Jin'ichi, and Yamazaki Masakazu and, in English, a volume of collected texts edited by Thomas Rimer and Yamazaki Masakazu, as well as a series of carefully annotated individual translations by Mark Nearman.[2] In addition, there are fine studies of some of the individual texts, such as that by Shelley Fenno Quinn on *Three Courses*.[3]

With the exception of *Learning the Profession*, which was written for the members of his troupe as a whole, Zeami wrote all the texts translated here for either his direct descendants and blood relations or his son-in-law Konparu

Zenchiku. After his death, these texts seem to have been dispersed among three different lines. Some went to the Kyoto Kanze line (perhaps through Zeami's brother Shirō), but most of them seem to have been transmitted through the Ochi Kanze, through Zeami's sons Motomasa and Motoyoshi rather than through the Kyoto Kanze, until Jūrō Dayū of Kyoto Kanze lineage revived the moribund Ochi line and gained access to the texts.[4] (Jūrō Dayū was the eldest son of Kanze Motohiro, the sixth head of the Kyoto Kanze line.)[5] These texts were copied and added to the Kyoto Kanze line's collection. A third group seems to have been given to Konparu Zenchiku. These were eventually given to the Hōzanji temple in Ikoma, between modern-day Osaka and Nara, and through the temple's generous offices, they have come to public attention.

Here I present some basic textual information about each of the texts in the *Performance Notes.*[6] *Transmitting the Flower Through Effects and Attitudes* (*Fūshikwaden* [風姿花伝 or 風姿華伝], mod. J. *Fūshikaden*) has the most complicated textual history of all the *Performance Notes* because it came together over more than two decades, was not originally conceived to be a single unified book, and was more broadly disseminated than most of the rest of the *Notes.* The name of the text, clearly indicated by Zeami in extant manuscripts, was given to it after major sections had already been written. This title appears at the head of the whole text in the primary manuscript used for this translation, but within the text, Zeami more often refers to the text as simply *Kwaden* (花伝, mod. J. *Kaden*), *Transmitting the Flower.* The full title, *Transmitting the Flower Through Effects and Attitudes*, may not have been created until the first five books were brought together in 1402, as indicated in the colophon to "Ultimate Achievements."

The text is commonly known as *Kadensho* (花伝書) in both Japan and the West because when Yoshida Tōgo published the first modern edition of some of the *Performance Notes* in 1909, that is the title he gave it. That this name has stuck is widely lamented by nō scholars, primarily because it is leads to confusion with several other texts or bodies of texts. For instance, the generic term *kwadensho* (花伝書) has been used to refer to a number of medieval and early modern texts on nō performance, and it can also be applied to texts on flower arrangement as "a text regarding transmissions about flowers." The partial homophone *kadensho* (家伝書, in modern Japanese, a perfect homophone) has an even broader application, meaning "a text transmitted within a given house." There is, moreover, a particular variety of texts entitled *Hachijō k(w)adensho* (八帖花伝書), or *Hachijōbon k(w)adensho* (八帖本花伝書), published in several editions throughout the seventeenth century, which include extracts from both *Transmitting the Flower* and many other later texts on nō.

The textual history of *Transmitting the Flower Through Effects and Attitudes* has been studied in detail,[7] and the argument that it should not be called *K(w)adensho* but *Fūshik(w)aden* is persuasive. It is surprising, then, that little attention has been paid to what the title means and how it fits into the broader intellectual currents of medieval Japan.

The title is a four-graph Chinese compound to which Zeami often refers by the last two graphs, *Kwaden.* The first two graphs, *Fūshi*, can be read as a single word relating to notions of appearance or shape, but the graphs' individual components are widely used in *Performance Notes*, either independently or in combination with other graphs. Here they suggest discernible aspects of performance, so I have translated them independently as "effects" and "attitudes."[8]

Kwaden seems to have escaped analysis, apart from the constellation of homonyms mentioned earlier, even though it has been naturalized in modern Japanese with explicit reference to Zeami. Reading from the text itself back to the title, it seems quite natural that a text in which aesthetic attraction is figured through the image of a flower should use the term "flower" in its title. Likewise, the idea that this text should be a "transmission" is made explicit in many places and clearly was intended to be transmitted within a strictly limited artistic lineage.

But the "transmission of a flower" did not begin with Zeami, and given the *Notes*' widespread use of terminology from Zen and other forms of Buddhism, it is likely that Zeami had in mind a celebrated and eloquent kōan from *Mumonkan* when he selected the title.[9] This kōan, "The All-Revered Holds Up a Flower," reads as follows:

> Long ago, from amid His congregation on Mount Gṛdhrakūṭa, the All-Revered One [Buddha] took up a flower between his fingers and showed it to the crowd. At that time, the crowd all stayed silent. Worthy Kāśyapa alone broke into a smile. The All-Revered said, "The treasure eye of the true dharma is with me, the wondrous mind of nirvāna, the formlessness of true form, the gate of intricate wonder. I vouchsafe to thee, Great Kāśyapa, outside the teachings, a separate transmission in which language has no standing. (*Mumonkan* 6)[10]

Zeami seems to have used this kōan for his own ends in a relatively straightforward way. Figured as a flower, aesthetic achievement has the potential to provoke a smile (a smile of pleasure, a knowing smile, a smile of acknowledgment or collusion), although it is not clear whether the "transmission of the flower" is to be understood as the handing over of a flower or a transmission of something that in turn produces a flower. The difference between the two may be significant when considering the content of Zeami's transmissions.[11] Although manuscripts from *Transmitting the Flower* are relatively numerous, we have no single manuscript containing all of its seven books. Books 6 and 7 were separated from the other five books in transmission and were passed down independently. A fine manuscript of book 6 in Zeami's hand is extant, as is an incomplete manuscript of book 7.

Although the text entitled *Learning the Flower* is no longer extant in its full form, it was originally written after *Transmitting the Flower.* "An Extract from *Learning the Flower*" (*Kwashiu no uchi, nukigaki* [花習内抜書], mod. J. *Kashu . . .*) does survive, however, in Zeami's autograph (no signature is attached to the manuscript, but particular details of the *katakana* used to write it testify to Zeami's own hand). The text may have been transmitted to Zeami's younger brother Shirō.

Manuscripts of *Oral Instructions on Singing* (*Ongyoku kuden* [音曲口伝]) do not have a title as such, but they do have a subtitle, though applicable to only the first article in the text: *Ongyoku kowadashi kuden* (音曲声出口伝), *Oral Instructions for Vocal Delivery in Song.* Omote names the text *Ongyoku kuden* on the basis of a reference in the colophon to one of the manuscripts, asserting that this is a more appropriate title for it. I have followed his lead. Indeed, the specificity of this text seems to have been much appreciated, and some thirty manuscripts are extant. Of these, three have been in possession of the Kanze house since the Muromachi period and have served as the basis for Omote's text in *Zeami, Zenchiku.* Some of the material from *Oral Instructions on Singing* is presented again in *A Mirror to the Flower* in a somewhat more polished form. We thus have the advantage of the polish of *A Mirror to the Flower* but can refer back to *Oral Instructions* to uncover detail that was polished away in the later treatise. The fact that no manuscripts for this text were transmitted through the Ochi Kanze line or the Konparu line suggests that it may have been transmitted to Zeami's younger brother Shirō and from him to his son Kanze Motoshige, also known as Onnami.

A Mirror to the Flower (*Kwakyau* [花鏡], mod. J. *Kakyō*) is signed with the date 1426:6, but as we have seen, it duplicates very closely material from *Learning the Flower* and *Oral Instructions on Singing.* For this reason, Omote believes that the date 1426 represents only a final compilation of the text and that, like *Transmitting the Flower,* the bulk of the text developed over several years. He therefore situates the text before *A Course to Attain the Flower* and *Figure Drawings of the Two Arts and the Three Modes,* even though those two texts are dated earlier than 1426. I have followed Omote in this.

The note accompanying Zeami's signature at the end of *A Mirror to the Flower* indicates that he considered this text to be his own contribution to the study of performance, whereas in large part, *Transmitting the Flower* was a rehearsal of what his father taught him. The fact that Zeami's note is followed by a colophon signed by "Tsurauji" points to this text's intriguing transmission history. Another text transmitted in the Kanze line, *Shiki shūgen* (*Auspicious Songs for the Four Seasons*), contains a final note reading:

> *A Mirror to the Flower* was transmitted to Motomasa (Jūrō). The *Three Courses* was transmitted to yours truly, (Shichirō) Motoyoshi. We were told that these two texts were not to be copied. I, however, because I took

the tonsure, entrusted mine to the Konparu. Later, because of the estrangement, they probably have it, too.

The last line of this brief note is anything but clear. "Because of the estrangement" (*naka wo tagau aida*) remains a mystery. It may refer to an estrangement between Zeami's descendants through his daughter and son-in-law Zenchiku, on the one hand, and his nephew Onnami (the son of his younger brother, Shirō), on the other, although this cannot be determined with certainty.[12] Shichirō Motoyoshi was one of Zeami's sons, to be sure, and apparently was younger than Motomasa, Zeami's designated heir. (Motoyoshi was Zeami's amanuensis for his memoir, *Conversations on Sarugaku*.)

In any case, according to this testimony, the texts of *A Mirror to the Flower* and *Three Courses* were intended to remain unique manuscripts, but in the course of events, a copy was made and held by the Konparu line. This is the copy that "Tsurauji" (probably Zenchiku) rejoices in having, based on the colophon to *A Mirror*. In *The Flower in . . . Yet Doubling Back*, Zeami says that Motomasa let Zenchiku see an important text of the Kanze line, which may have been *A Mirror to the Flower*.

In most manuscripts, *A Course to Attain the Flower* (*Shikwadau* [至花道], mod. J. *Shikadō*) sets out five topics at the beginning, almost like a table of contents. These topics are followed by a final note regarding audiences' increasing critical acuity and Zeami's apprehensions that actors had generally not kept up with it. In a manuscript transmitted through the Konparu line, however, this final note is omitted, replaced by the text of the *Five Ranks*, which otherwise is considered to be a separate text and is treated as such in this translation. The oldest manuscript of *Figure Drawings of the Two Arts and the Three Modes* (*Nikyoku santai ningyauzu* [二曲三体人形図], mod. J. *Nikyoku santai ningyōzu*) is in Zenchiku's hand and includes simple drawings, also assumed to be in his hand and similar to drawings from Zeami's original, which is no longer extant. Parts of the text are written in a highly artificial and complex pseudo-Chinese, reflecting Zeami's increased consciousness of his intellectual position in the early fifteenth century.[13] Seven manuscripts of the text or parts of it are extant, some of which contain valuable phonetic glosses (in *katakana*) for the obscure collocations of the original. Much of the Zenchiku manuscript is reproduced in photographs along with the translation of the text.

Four manuscripts of *Three Courses* (*Sandau* [三道], mod. J. *Sandō*) are extant. Three seem to be descendants of the other one. Yoshida erroneously entitled the text *Nōsakusho*, but in *Conversations on Sarugaku* and the text *Shiki shūgen*, Zeami refers to it as *Sandō*. The recent discovery of a traced copy of the *Matsunoya-bon* text (the manuscript of which had been lost to fire) has excited interest in the information that the copy reveals about the textual history of *Three Courses* and about graphic idiosyncrasies elsewhere in the *Performance Notes*. Few of the variants in this new traced copy have influenced this translation, and I have not otherwise commented on the traced copy apart from the endnotes to *Three Courses*. Interested readers can find details in articles by Takemoto Mikio and in Quinn's book.[14]

The title of the text *Technical Specifications for Setting a Melody* (*Fushidzuke shidai* [曲付次第], mod. J. *Fushizuke shidai*) is recorded in both extant manuscripts, but those manuscripts are Edo/Tokugawa-period copies of earlier manuscripts that are no longer extant and originally may not have had this particular title. With neither date nor colophon to rely on, we cannot precisely situate this text in the history of the *Performance Notes*. Omote suggests, however, that *Specifications* was written before *A Mirror to the Flower* and *The Three Courses*. He points to the increasing use of Chinese graphs in Zeami's orthography at the end of this text and compares it with the creation of a quasi-Chinese style at the beginning of *Figure Drawings of the Two Arts and Three Modes*. Yoshida named the text as *Fushi(d)zuke sho*.

As mentioned earlier, *A Collection of Jewels in Effect* (*Fūgyokushiu* [曲付次第], mod. J. *Fūgyokushū*) apparently received its title from Retired Emperor Gokomatsu. It is well known that Gokomatsu took pleasure in *sarugaku* performances, although his preference seems to have been for the Tanba actor Umewaka. He was to have seen Zeami and Motomasa's performance in 1429 at the Sentō palace, but Shogun Ashikaga Yoshinori forbade them from appearing before him.[15] All the same, Omote thinks it likely that he did "bestow" the title *Fūgyokushiu* on this text, either creating the title itself or else writing it out in his calligraphy for Zeami to attach to the text. (In this case, the term *gedai*, 外題, "title," can be used to indicate either the creation of the title proper or the writing down of such a title.)[16] Disagreeing with Omote's view, Itō Masayoshi suggested that Gokomatsu was unlikely to have had any interest in a text like this and that the "Retired Emperor" to which the text refers must have been a later one who bestowed the title in some other connection at the request of a Kanze descendant.[17] But Omote countered that this is even less likely than the scenario he proposed.[18]

Of five extant manuscripts of *An Effective Vision of Learning the Vocation of Fine Play in Performance* (*Iugaku shudau fūken* [遊楽習道風見], mod. J. *Yūgaku shudō fūken*), only one is complete, but some of the others, bound together with *Nine Ranks*, give us a picture of the fluidity of the concept of a text in this tradition. Moreover, it is noteworthy that one of the incomplete texts of *Effective Vision* was transmitted within the Kongō school, in that it points to the broadening of Zeami's stature as a theorist outside the strict bloodlines within which most of his texts were transmitted. Yoshida calls this text *Iugaku shudau kenpūsho*.

Five Ranks (*Gowi* [五位], mod. J. *Goi*) is extant in three different manuscripts, one of them being the Konparu-line manuscript, which is appended to a manuscript composed of the five main articles of *A Course to Attain the Flower*. Four manuscripts of *Nine Ranks* (*Kiuwi* [九位], mod. J. *Kyūi*) are extant, some of which are bound together with partial texts of *Effective Vision*. Two manuscripts of *The Six Models* (*Rikugi* [六義]) are extant, one a copy of the other. The older manuscript bears Zeami's signature and is considered by some to be an autograph text. But the body of the text itself is not in Zeami's hand, and the paper on which this manuscript is written is itself atypical, suggesting an unusual context for the composition of the text. Apparently, Zeami had the text copied by someone else and only added his signature to the end.

Pick Up a Jewel and Take the Flower in Hand (*Shifugyoku tokukwa* [拾玉得花], mod. J. *Shūgyoku tokka*) exists in a single manuscript which was "discovered" and made public only in 1955. The text had been thought to be in the hands of the Konparu line because of references to it in Zenchiku's work, but until then it was unknown. Once it was made public, it seems to have stimulated broader study of Zeami's theoretical and pedagogical writing. The text itself contains a large number of *katakana* glosses and some eccentric readings for *kanji*.

Three manuscripts of *Articles on the Five Sorts of Singing* (*Go ongyoku* [*no*] *deudeu* [五音曲条々], mod. J. *Go ongyoku* [*no*] *jōjō*) are extant, and one of them, to judge from the calligraphy, is in the hand of the seventh head of the Kanze line, Kanze Mototada, better known as Sōsetsu. Sōsetsu was an important collator of nō manuscripts and produced the oldest remaining book of stage directions for nō, the *Sōsetsu shimaizuke*.

Five Sorts of Singing ([五音] *Go on*) is undated but, like the previously cited text, seems to have been compiled late in Zeami's life. Nonetheless, it was probably compiled before Motomasa's death in 1432 and certainly before 1434 because of the mention of that date for the revision of the *Kusemai on the Prince Regent Shōtoku*, in a note attached to the quotation of that piece. As we have it today, the text is divided into two parts. In the former, only very brief tags and titles are used to identify the songs, and in the latter (describing *rangyoku*) more complete quotations are cited, culminating in extended quotation of six little known songs in *kusemai* style. No single complete manuscript of *Five Sorts of Singing* is extant, but a study of the text reveals that all six of the extant portions are derived from a single manuscript. The original seems to have been divided into two books, the former comprising *shiugen*, *yūkyoku*, *renbo*, and *aishyau*, and the latter, *rangyoku* and *kusemai*. Many of the texts quoted more extensively in *Five Sorts* contain some musical notation, but curiously, they use the term *shihoru* or *shihori*, a Konparu-school term for a vocal technique known in Zeami's Kanze line as *kuru* or *kuri*. This suggests that the original manuscript of the text was transmitted to Zenchiku and that this terminology entered the text on that account.[19]

The only text in *Performance Notes* intended for dissemination to more than one or two of Zeami's immediate family members is *Learning the Profession* (*Shudausho* [習道書], mod. J. *Shudōsho*). The text has come down to us in two manuscripts and one printed edition. The printed edition was completed in

1772, commissioned by the head of the Kanze troupe, Kanze Motoakira. Even given the text's broader intended audience, it was nonetheless meant for the eyes of only important members of the troupe, and the printed edition was small. Motoakira added notes reflecting performance practice in his day.

Traces of a Dream on a Single Sheet (*Museki isshi* [夢跡一紙]) is a brief text recording the death of Zeami's eldest son, Motomasa. In addition to its personal poignancy, it underlines the importance of artistic transmission in the traditions of *sarugaku*. Two manuscripts are extant. Similarly, *The Flower in . . . Yet Doubling Back* (*Kyakuraikwa* [却来花], mod. J. *Kyakuraika*) begins with a deep lament about Motomasa's death and then discusses certain extremely specialized techniques in *sarugaku* performance. It is no longer extant except in the photographic reproduction from Yoshida's text that survived the Kantō earthquake. Yoshida calls it *An Oral Transmission After Seventy* (七十以後口伝), but collateral references to the text from the Edo/Tokugawa period lead us to believe it was originally entitled *Kyakuraikwa*.

The two letters to Master Konparu included here were found among a body of texts transmitted through the Konparu line and eventually deposited at Hōzanji temple in Ikoma. Until the mid-Tokugawa period, the Konparu line had had possession of yet a third letter, but it has since disappeared.

Notes

1. Omote Akira and Katō Shūichi, eds., *Zeami, Zenchiku*, Nihon shisō taikei, vol. 24 (Tokyo: Iwanami shoten, 1974).

2. Nose Asaji, *Zeami jūrokubushū hyōshaku* (Tokyo: Iwanami shoten, 1944); Konishi Jin'ichi, *Zeami shū*, Nihon no shisō, vol. 8 (Tokyo: Chikuma shobō, 1970); Yamazaki Masakazu, *Zeami*, Nihon no meicho, vol. 10 (Tokyo: Chūō kōronsha, 1969); J. Thomas Rimer and Yamzaki Masakazu, trans., *On the Art of the Nō Drama: The Major Treatises of Zeami* (Princeton, N.J.: Princeton University Press, 1984); Mark Nearman, trans. and ed., "*Kakyō*: Zeami's Fundamental Principles of Acting," *Monumenta Nipponica* 37, no. 3 (1982): 333–74; 37, no. 4 (1982): 461–96; 38, no. 1 (1983): 51–71; "*Kyakuraika*: Zeami's Final Legacy for the Master Actor," *Monumenta Nipponica* 35, no. 2 (1980): 153–97; and "Zeami's *Kyūi*: A Pedagogical Guide for Teachers of Acing," *Monumenta Nipponica* 33, no. 3 (1978): 299–332.

3. Shelley Fenno Quinn, *Developing Zeami: The Noh Actor's Attunement in Practice* (Honolulu: University of Hawai'i Press, 2005).

4. Jūrō Dayū, fleeing the capital in a time of war, went to the province of Suruga and there became acquainted with the future shogun, Tokugawa Ieyasu, who was, at the time, being held as a hostage by the Imagawa clan. Jūrō seems to have given some of the texts in his possession to Ieyasu, but they later were copied by Jūrō's younger brother, Mototada (Sōsetsu) and his adopted son, Motonao.

5. In the official Kanze genealogy, Motomasa is excluded from the line, which moves from Kannami to Zeami and then to Zeami's nephew Onnami. See *ZS*, pp. 35–36, 262n. 84.

6. For more detailed information, the reader might wish to consult the extensive notes at the back of *ZZ* (pp. 542–73) or Omote Akira's even more detailed studies in *Nōgakushi shinkō*, vol. 1 (Tokyo: Wan'ya shoten, 1979).

7. As usual, Omote's work is exemplary. Briefer accounts can be found in *ZZ*, pp. 551–53, but full-length studies of various manuscripts are collected in *Nōgakushi shinkō*, vol. 1.

8. More detailed discussion of these and other appearance words in *Performance Notes* can be found in appendix 3.

9. Kōans (Ch. *gong'an* [public cases]) are cryptic or paradoxical dialogues between a master and one or more disciples, traditionally and especially used in Rinzai Zen, in order to jar aspirants out of the logical constraints of language so that they may better grasp nonduality. *Mumonkwan* (Ch. *Wumenguan*, mod. J. *Mumonkan*) is one of the foremost collections of kōans, compiled in 1229 by the Chinese monk Wumen Huikai.

Zeami uses the word *kōan* frequently in *Transmitting the Flower*, not primarily in the technical Zen sense, but to mean "problem" or "challenge."

10. I have referred to the text minutely analyzed in Akizuki Ryōmin and Akizuki Mahito, eds., *Zenshū goroku kanbun no yomikata* (Tokyo: Shunjūsha, 1993), pp. 91–96. The text consists of the kōan just quoted; a commentary by the Chinese master Wumen, who compiled it; and a poem or hymn (*ju*). Wumen's commentary on the kōan is highly critical of Śākyamuni, but that doesn't seem to concern Zeami. There is no reason, indeed, to think that he knew of either the commentary or the *ju*, and his knowledge of the kōan itself may well have come from conversations or other "unwritten transmissions."

11. This seems particularly relevant to his attempt to commodify the flower as a transmission within a particular family line. See Zeami's discussion of transmitting initial intent to descendants in *A Mirror to the Flower*; and Thomas Hare, "Nō Changes," in James Brandon, ed., *Nō and Kyōgen in the Contemporary World* (Honolulu: University of Hawai'i Press, 1997), pp. 137–39.

12. See *ZS*, pp. 32–36.

13. I discuss the pseudo-Chinese in appendix 3.

14. Takemoto Mikio, "Yoshida bunko zō shinshutsu-bon Sandō ni tsuite" (Engeki kenkyū sentā kiyō: Waseda daigaku 21-seki DOE Puroguramu, 2004), pp. 1–7, and "Yoshida bunko Zeami nōgakuron shiryō shōkai," *Bungaku* 4, no. 4 (2003): 199–206; Quinn, *Developing Zeami*, pp. 291, 380–92, 398–401, passim.

15. See *ZS*, pp. 35–36.

16. Omote, in *ZZ*, pp. 469–70n.86.

17. Itō Masayoshi, *Konparu Zenchiku no kenkyū* (Tokyo: Akao shōbundō, 1970), pp. 234–35.

18. Omote, in *ZZ*, pp. 469–70n.86.

19. For details, see Omote, in *ZZ*, pp. 566-67n.16.

APPENDIX 3

Zeami's Languages

The perspective we gain on medieval Japanese by comparing Zeami's plays with the *Performance Notes* is detailed and rich, perhaps uniquely so in the four centuries of "middle ages" from 1200 to 1600. There were, of course, many other important writers in those times, and some of them bequeathed to us not only a variety of texts but also texts in a variety of written styles. Nonetheless, the densely compact lyrical style typical of certain song forms in Zeami's plays shows only one aspect of his use of language, which is supplemented by a more matter-of-fact narrative style elsewhere in the plays. The prose of his earlier *Performance Notes,* especially *Transmitting the Flower Through Effects and Attitudes*, brings other voices to light, expository and dialogic. Some of the *Notes* of the early 1420s betray a writer struggling to Sinicize his Japanese to an extreme degree, whereas the last of the *Notes* reveal a rigorous but well-integrated prose style that has been transformed by Chinese but is reconciled once more to intelligibility after the murky gestures of the early 1420s.

In general terms, medieval Japanese had achieved a relatively stable orthography for the notation of its compromises between the purportedly native Japanese of court romance and *waka* poetry, on the one hand, and the Chinese or Sino-Japanese of official discourse, on the other hand. The result has been dubbed *wakan konkōtai* (Sino-Japanese mixed literary style). Although it is routinely characterized as cumbersome and complicated, it is culturally and lexically rich, enabling a wide variety of voices in writing and a broad reach across different linguistic registers. Its combination of graphs representing sound alone (*kana*) and graphs with a built-in semantic content (*kanji*) clearly shows its lineage in modern Japanese.

Although the struggle to create written Japanese was long and arduous, by the last decades of the fourteenth century, increasing numbers of people were literate, with great facility in the use of the *kana* syllabaries, especially *hiragana*, the more "cursivized" form. A large number of Chinese loanwords, especially from Buddhist sources, had been adopted into Japanese, and some of the aesthetic aims typical of earlier *hiragana* writing had given way to a more pragmatic approach in written expression. The more angular *katakana* syllabary was employed primarily in technical and scholarly contexts (originally for pointing Chinese texts) and signaled different discursive intentions, which Zeami used for the precise notation of pronunciation on stage.

In belles lettres, the monumental hypotactic architecture of Heian Japanese—with its long periods and fluid shifts among dialogue, description, narrative, and verse—had given way to more parataxis, pivoting, and other strategies of echoing and association. The highly ramified Heian systems of honorific and humilific language had been simplified, and a new style (which came to be called *sōrōbun*) had been created.

Choices in how to write have an obvious basis in education, and the deployment of numerous Chinese graphs to write Japanese demands a considerable educational investment. For Zeami, this came well into his middle age, but even before that he was clearly able to write *kana* in a fine fluent hand.[1] In *Transmitting the Flower*, he writes a grammatically fairly orthodox and orthographically fairly well informed variety of medieval Japanese. In his plays, the degree of his linguistic artistry is breathtaking, but it is not conspicuously *written* artistry. Instead, it represents the subtle control of a large body of poetic discourse, an ability to tell stories, a fine attentiveness to dramatic structure, and a clear and sensitive awareness of how a story can be dismembered and told more effectively because of the dismemberment.[2]

The aural artistry of Zeami's plays is complemented by a conscious articulation of concern for elocution in, for example, *Oral Instructions on Singing.* Zeami's interest in "correct" diction is further evidenced in his autograph texts of ten nō plays (each of them written out in *katakana* to ensure precision in pronunciation).[3] Highly figured songs in the plays show an archaizing tendency, which followed readily from Zeami's emphasis on training in the conservative poetics of *waka*,[4] but they also exhibit the fluid syntax and lithe conceptual associativeness of *renga* (linked verse), the prime poetic form of his day.[5]

Some evidence of Zeami's training in the belletristic tradition is extant in a couple of early *renga* links he composed with the renowned poet and statesman Nijō Yoshimoto.[6] But it is difficult to discern how Zeami learned his everyday written style of the language of *Transmitting the Flower*. This style is marked by various formal rhetorical devices (such as the use of *sore*, *somosomo*, and *mazu* at the beginnings of sentences), and it sometimes takes question-and-answer form, literally marking the questions and responses with the graphs 問 (ask) and 答 (answer). Zeami seems to like lists and typologies, and he sometimes lines up different observations by beginning a new addition with the graph "one" rather than with a more logically connected transition. (This strategy for presenting information is like the use of bullets in English administrative documents, and consequently I have opted to translate "one" with a bullet •.)

Zeami takes pride in quoting earlier authorities, and although he is not always correct in doing so, his misprisions and misquotations are sometimes more apposite to the situation he is discussing than a more orthodox and bookish reading would have been.[7] In the introduction, I mentioned Zeami's acknowledgment of ambiguity and uncertainty. In technical terms, this entails the relatively frequent use of the Japanese auxiliary adjective *beshi* and its inflections. This is a common element in Zeami's written style in the *Notes*, but since it may indicate obligation as well as conjecture, his stance vis-à-vis a particular statement is sometimes unclear. (Usually the context provides supplementary aid in reconstructing his intent.) Only rarely is honorific language found in *Transmitting the Flower* (or in the other *Performance Notes*, for that matter), and when it is found, it almost always refers to the actions of a third person, usually someone of high social status. (The exceptions that prove the rule here are in the light honorific usages found in the sixth book of *Transmitting the Flower*). Verbal terminations and other words in which status can be marked in Japanese remain plain (that is, unmarked) throughout the *Performance Notes*, and pronouns are uncommon as well. This indicates that the texts were written to be read by Zeami's social equals or subordinates, which accords with the colophons of many of the texts, which usually designate them for a specific person, one of Zeami's sons or his son-in-law Zenchiku.[8]

Transmitting the Flower and other early texts in the *Notes* show a degree of eloquence and wide-ranging knowledge and sensibility but not so a strong sense of familiarity with East Asian classics. The *Oral Instructions on Singing* of 1419 shows an awareness of the technical vocabulary of Chinese music theory. But because we lack more concrete detail on how it informed performance in Zeami's day, we cannot be certain that Zeami understood the vocabulary according to its original context. In the early 1420s, however, Zeami tried something new.

Both *A Course to Attain the Flower*, dated to the sixth month of 1420, and *A Mirror to the Flower,* to the sixth month of 1424, exhibit many more conspicuous references to Chinese classics as well as Zeami's numerous attempts to use Chinese, The latter text, for instance, opens with six articles with Chinese or Sino-Japanese aphoristic titles.[9] The most extreme example of this tendency to Sinicisms may be found in *Figure Drawings of the Two Arts and the Three Modes* of the seventh month of 1421. The oldest manuscript of this text, in the hand of none other than Zenchiku, contains extensive passages in eccentric Sino-Japanese. It opens, for instance, as follows:

> 二曲三体之次第、至花道加式誌云共、見体目前不㆑有、其風難㆓証見㆒
> 依、人形之絵図移、髄体露也。
> 三体之風姿、意中之従㆑景見風所㆑作、各々風名付。能々見得〆、分明有
> 主風之芸体可㆑至物也。

As an illustration, we might translate this passage as follows:

> It can be said concerning the disposition of Two-Turns-and-Three-Bodies that in *A Course to Attain the Flower, de singulis agens* I recorded [it], but since before the eyes is$_{2}$ there$_{1}$ no visual body, is$_{2}$ its effect$_{1}$ difficult to

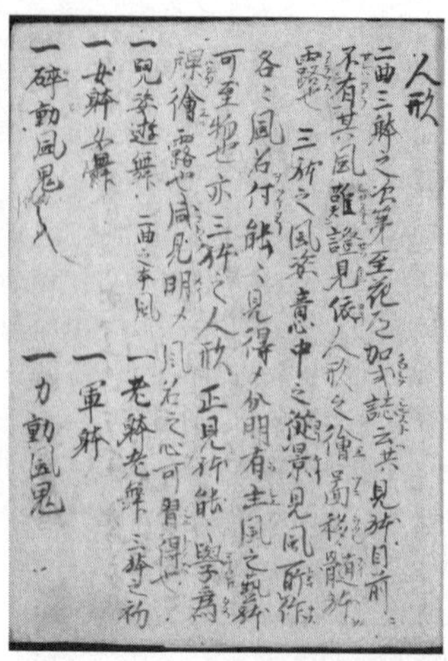
人形
二曲三躰之次第至花道ニ加テ誌云共見躰目前ニ
不有其風難證見依人形之繪圖移顯所
露也 三躰之風於意中之景見風所作
各々風名付能々見得分明有主風之藝躰
可至物也亦三躰之人形正見所能學爲
一 兒姿遊舞 二曲之本風
一 老躰老舞 三躰之初
一 女躰女舞
一 軍躰
一 砕動風鬼
一 力動風鬼

The opening of *Figure Drawings of the Two Arts and the Three Modes*, showing Zeami's pseudo-Chinese, with some Japanese glosses in *katakana*. This text shows Zeami writing in his most drastically Sinicized form. Although he stepped back from this extreme graphemic experiment in his last decades, he continued to write with a large number of Chinese words and Chinese-style neologisms. The last three columns are the first part of a sort of table of contents for the text. (Photograph courtesy of the Noh Theater Research Institute, Hōsei University)

prove to sight, thus to human figure's drawings have I moved [them], that being essential, the body to denude.

As for the Three Bodies' Windshapes, are made˪ their *effets visuels*, from the scene within intent, and effect names have I attached thereto. They are things that, having acquired them in vision, clearly, attain˪ they-may to a proprietary effect's artistic body!

A translation that makes better sense of this passage by obscuring its stylistic presumptions and depending on the interlinear gloss in an old manuscript and the best modern Japanese scholarship on the *Notes*—what we might call a "rationalized" translation—might read as follows:

> Although I gave a detailed account of the disposition of the Two Arts and Three Modes in *A Course to Attain the Flower*, there is no visual representation of them to be seen there, so it is difficult to gain a full apprehension of their appearance. I therefore have transferred them into figure drawings to display their material essence.
>
> Epigraphs have I attached to each of the forms of the Three Modes, in that they take their visual effect from a scene within the mind. The point here is to gain a careful visual impression so that one attain a clear and precise subjective effect in the corpus of performance.

I have taken some pains to produce the earlier translation, even though it can reflect in only the most impressionistic way the texture of the original writing.[10] Part of the problem is lexical. The literal rendering of some of these words doesn't come near the *mot juste*, and even if there usually isn't a *mot juste*, there is plenty of room for improvement in some of these cases. "The Two Turns and

Three Bodies" is excessively literal. In the most general sense, *nikyoku* (二曲) might, I suppose, mean something like "Two Turns," but here the term is actually an abbreviation of *kabu nikyoku* (歌舞二曲 [the Two Arts of Singing and Dancing]). This is technical vocabulary that has grown out of the pedagogy of acting as Zeami understood it. Any adequate translation of it must be coordinated with other references in the *Performance Notes*, which are, mercifully, less obtrusively Sinicizing and pedantic.[11]

Although the difficulties presented by technical vocabulary are ubiquitous in the *Notes*, this text is even more troubled by a different sort of syntactic and structural problems, which exemplify one of Zeami's preoccupations in the early 1420s. The translation I produced for the preceding awkward passage is, of course, unfair in its procedure, because some of what I have did there was to carry over the syntactic structure of Japanese directly into English, which can only create an entirely backward sense of the original. Some of the central problems in this text, though, are not a matter of the disjunction of English and Japanese syntax or the opacities of specialized technical vocabulary. Chinese is a party to the problem, too, particularly because the text Zeami wrote aspires to a kind of Chineseness, although it is faithful to neither the subject-object-verb syntax of Japanese nor the subject-verb-object syntax of Chinese. Instead, it is a written pidgin, the attempt of a nonnative writer to re-create the structures of a foreign language on the basis of a sketchy and ad hoc awareness of how that foreign language actually works.

For example, the clause 其風難$_{\text{二}}$証見$_{\text{一}}$依 comes out "since . . . is$_2$ its effect$_1$ difficult to prove to sight" and aspires to a topic-comment structure along the lines of Chinese. But this is a dependent clause, requiring an indication of its relation to the previous and subsequent clauses. There are, of course, numerous ways in which this might have been accomplished in Chinese. Most probably, some sort of marker, like *yin* (因) would have signaled the dependent character of the clause at its head, but following his Japanese instincts, Zeami appended a conjunctive phrase (*ni yorite*) to the *end* of the clause. This, however, requires the indication of where a certain Japanese particle falls in order to lead into the conjunctive phrase, which in turn uncovers the necessity of transposing three of the Chinese graphs in the original into a different, Japanese, order. This has been indicated in the original by marking the text with the small numerals "one" and "two," an effect I have tried to mimic in the translation with subscripts 1 and 2. Similarly, the sign レ in the translation is borrowed from the original, where it indicates the transposition of two graphs to create Japanese word order out of the Chinese.

The overall effect of this written pidgin is a heavy burden to understanding. As I pointed out, the oldest extant manuscript of the text, in the hand of Zeami's son-in-law Zenchiku (1405–1468), betrays an attempt, with extensive pointing and interlinear glosses, to get around the difficulties presented by the form of the text.[12] Even so, it continues to challenge understanding. When creating a translation, one of the prime considerations must be how much of this difficulty may be legitimately reproduced or simulated in the translation, and how much of it should be swept under a kind of philological rug.

Why did Zeami set off into these brambles of pseudo-Chinese when a practicable Sino-Japanese had already been available for more than two centuries? And how should his ill-considered foray into this pseudo-Chinese be reflected in a translation of his work?

Fortunately, the dimensions of the problem are not overwhelming. The most extreme examples of his pidgin Sino-Japanese are limited to certain texts of Zeami's sixth decade, and some of these texts are closely related to other texts in his *Performance Notes* that are written in a more conventional form. Omote Akira, the foremost textual scholar of the *Notes*, explains that this is

> a special sort of text, written almost exclusively in *kanji* lined up one after the other, with almost no *kana*, showing readings by means of a *katakana* interlinear gloss. . . . This phenomenon speaks to the fact that Zeami increased his familiarity with *kanji* from around [1421] . . . and took every opportunity to put them to use. It's reasonable to conclude that the notes at the end of *A Course to Attain the Flower* and the text of *Five Ranks* [as well as the *Figure Drawings of the Two Arts and the Three Modes*, which occasioned these remarks in the first place] were written about the same time, given their stylistic similarity. It is clear as well, however, from the abandonment of this plan in the middle of [*Figure Drawings of the Two Arts and the Three Modes*], that using a style like this in the prose sections of the manuscript proved impracticable. Zeami did not take this approach in later texts. All the same, even in his last works, he tended to use lots of *kanji* and to make up neologisms extravagantly. I believe this is worthy of note because it serves as an indication from which we may approximate the level of Zeami's general education.[13]

The contention that we might gauge the approximate "level of Zeami's general education" from this kind of prose seems at once both reasonable and ambivalent. The picture we get is not complimentary given the many solecisms and missteps the text reveals. But the attempt in itself may show in a trenchant, concrete way how highly esteemed in medieval Japan was the ability to write bureaucratic Chinese (for all its absurdity). How many aristocrats' sons were trained in these conventions and produced *conventionally* bad Chinese, in contrast with Zeami's *idiosyncratically* bad Chinese? From that perspective, Zeami's attempts are endearing, perhaps even admirable, albeit wrongheaded.

The greater use of Chinese vocabulary and, to some extent, Chinese syntax is not usually so problematic in the *Notes*. In fact, in many cases, the increased awareness of Zen and other types of Chinese scholasticism raise the philosophical tenor of Zeami's discussions and sharpen his intellectual and psychological focus.

There are, of course, many other kinds of problems attached to this translation. Although translating Zeami's *Performance Notes* into English has been a great pleasure for me, I remain frustrated by my inability to find a fully satisfying rendering of many of his terms and to reproduce his Japanese with a comparable economy of phrasing in English. I won't continue too long about specific problems in this regard—some are addressed directly in the notes—but there are a few loose ends I'd like to tie up here.

One of them concerns the word I have most often translated as "mind" or "intent." This is a challenging term in a vast range of East Asian writing because the concept it conveys is both extremely common and extremely important. In Japanese the word is *kokoro*, generally written with the graph 心, although occasionally it can be written more precisely with 意 or 憶. Frequently the term is translated as "heart," and sometimes entirely appropriately, but I usually found that word too sentimental and romantic for *kokoro. Kokoro* (or *shin*, its Sino-Japanese pronunciation in compounds) is the seat of cognition, perception, and emotion in the body. And it also is the internal organ that pumps blood. In Japanese *kokoro* may also mean "meaning" or "essence" or the disposition of intent. The general challenge of translating this word is familiar to anyone working in Chinese, Korean, or Japanese, which I will illustrate with a particular case from Zeami's texts.

One of the most famous of Zeami's dicta to the Japanese is *shoshin wo wasuru bekarazu*, from the last section of *A Mirror to the Flower*. I have translated this as "Don't forget your initial intent." My rationale is that intent is the object of one's mind in attempting to do something, a goal or aim but blurred from objectification in that you hold this intent in your own mind, it is how your mind is directed in certain circumstances, and how you understand the relation between yourself and the goal. That is, I believe, the better part of the meaning of *-shin* in Zeami's challenging formulation, and it is of course related to the particular map of *kokoro*, which is so extensive in traditional Japan, so mental, so engaged with the subject in, to be sure, an intellectual way, but also as a mark of the subject's integrity, that is, in its integratedness and subjective unity, despite its social ambition to savoir faire, deep understanding, essence, meaning, the content of mind. All these interconnections make "mind" (and certainly "heart") an inadequate map of the territory.

Another problem I have encountered has a more palpable, especially visual, nature. Zeami's success, especially early in his career, seems to have relied heavily on creating a beautiful and believable visual impression. He comments at length, for example, on how important it is to move according to the conventions of the class to which a given character belongs, especially if that character is of a high class. (Shakespeare had similar concerns.) To

Zeami, appearance was the most direct and reliable tool with which to captivate an audience, so appearance is a common concern in the *Notes*. One of the terms relating to appearance that has been particularly challenging is *fū* (風). The word appears countless times in the *Notes*, but rarely with its most common meaning in modern Japanese, "wind." It appears in the title of the first and most famous of the *Performance Notes*, the *Fūshik(w)aden* (風姿花伝),[14] my *Transmitting the Flower Through Effects and Attitudes*, there in the company of another appearance word, *shi* (姿). *Shi* is, plausibly and less problematically, "shape."

Fū is a term that in both Chinese and Japanese has blown far afield from its putative ideographic origins as a wind-filled sail to mean such things as

- go into a rut
- teaching
- custom
- principle
- energy
- appearance
- gesture
- *feng* (sometimes translated "air" and, in the Mao preface to the *Shijing*, indicating a type of poetic composition intended to tactfully criticize government or society in order to effect political change)
- song
- hint at

It also plays a part in compounds for

- shape
- scenery
- sicknesses ranging from a common cold to madness, malaria, and leprosy

Zeami constantly uses the term in *Performance Notes*, both singly and in some hundred-odd compounds. We can discern in some of these cases a type of artistic or dramatic effect such as *kank(w)afū* (閑花風), the Effect of the Tranquil Flower, or *senmonfū* (浅文風), the Effect of Shallow Patterns. But *fūshi*, like the majority of these *fū* words, is less specific than that. It indicates something about appearance but not something specific. *Fū* and its cousins in compounds with other graphs are, moreover, just one subset of a large crowd of appearance words populating the *Performance Notes*, words such as *sugata* (姿), *sama* (様), *yosohoi* (装い), *ken* (見), *kenshi* (見姿), and *tai* (体).

Despite the *Performance Notes*' fascination with nonvisual experiences of aesthetic pleasure, and achievement, which are an important part of Zeami's aesthetic, most of his descriptions of acting techniques relate in some way to visual appearance and visual effects. So how do we convey these in English? I find this to be a great frustration. Some of these words, like *kankwafū* (閑花風), seem to be specifically technical terms. These are the easiest to deal with, because once I have settled on a rendering, I can use it every time that particular term appears. (I believe that when the term is technical, it should be rendered into something identifiable as *that* particular technical term each time it appears.)[15] The other words, though, are difficult to translate. Context does provide certain clues, but the context is not always clear and straightforward. "Context," says Mieke Bal, "is a text and thus presents the same difficulty of interpretation as any other text." Paraphrasing her, we might then observe, "Context cannot define the [word]'s meaning because context itself defies unambiguous interpretation as much as the [word]."[16]

This suggests to me that the translator is working simultaneously on multiple levels of calibration and adjustment but that at any given moment, a movement at one of those levels may precipitate unpredictable shifts at the other levels. Sometimes I feel like Professor Heisenberg, aware that I cannot know precisely the value and the trajectory of a (verbal) particle at the same moment. There is, truly, no reliable general solution to this problem, but I suppose that when a term must be translated differently in different contexts, we can at least assume that it is not (merely) a technical term. Technical terms are relatively inert and reliable, no matter what the context is, whereas words in more general and colloquial usage are protean and unpredictable.

Finally, I would like to mention another word in the *Notes* that has been frustrating but, I think, very important. It is the word *iugaku* (遊楽, mod. J. *yūgaku*). The second graph in this compound can mean "music," "pleasure," or "ease" (or their synonyms), but with the pronunciation *gaku* rather than *raku*, it usually means "music," so it is less difficult to work with than the first graph is. In modern Japanese, that character is usually read *asobu*, meaning "(to) play" or its substantive partner, *asobi*, or "play." Zeami's usage has an element of "play," too, but he also draws on other traditional meanings of this graph. In Chinese, although it may mean "play," it once had the meaning of "travel" or "move about," particularly to "move about unfettered," to go on pleasure excursions or to visit, especially, the mountains with the aim or spiritual solace or cultivation (most famous in this context would, I suppose, be the title of a chapter of the *Zhuangzi*, "Xiaoyao you" [逍遥遊, "free and easy wandering" or something similar]). That meaning, too, is present in Zeami's usage. But *asobu/asobi* is also the old word for "(play) music," particularly the music of the ancient court, *gagaku*, so in Zeami's formulation, we find a supplementary meaning of *gaku* as "music" with this sense of *asobi*.

Zeami first introduces *iugaku* as a synonym for *sarugaku*, as Omote notes, but already the difference in nuance is destined to grow into something more important. If *sarugaku* is the traditional name for Zeami's performing art (a name also with unfortunate ambiguities, as we saw earlier),[17] *iugaku* has a more individualistic sense. It is not just a performing art but also a way to experience freedom on the basis of long training and mastery, as I explained in the introduction. That is why I have settled on "fine play in performance," despite its awkwardness. Related words, such as 遊曲, 遊舞, 遊道, and 遊風, appear less frequently in the *Notes*, with a similar range of nuance. I have made it my policy to comment on these words in the notes when they first appear.

A Note on Zeami's Names

In many modern contexts, including the Library of Congress, Zeami is called Zeami Motokiyo, but this name is a modern invention, and there is no reference to it contemporary with Zeami himself. There is, indeed, no reference to "Zeami" in any of his own writings, although *Hitorigoto*, by the younger contemporary Shinkei, does mention him specifically as "Zeami."[18] Zeami signed several of the individual manuscripts in *Performance Notes* with the name Zea, an abbreviation of Zeamidabutsu (世阿弥陀仏), his full formal artistic name, which is mentioned only once, in the address to a letter to him quoted in *Conversations on Sarugaku*. This full name has obvious Buddhist overtones and stems from *ami-gō, or* "*-ami* name," appellations of the Ji sect. In the fifteenth century, legions of artists took *-ami* names, raising questions about whether they had Ji-sect affiliations. There is no evidence for such an affiliation for Zeami, although his play *Sanemori* takes a sympathetic view of a Ji-sect preacher. In his play *Taema*, Zeami inserts a pun on his name, much as he does with the name of the *shite* in other plays.[19]

Zeami is called Zeshi (世子), or "Master Ze," throughout *Conversations on Sarugaku* and in a colophon to *A Mirror to the Flower*, apparently written by Zenchiku, following the hoary Chinese tradition that inserts *-shi* (Ch. *zi*) after the names of philosophers, as in Kongzi (mod. J. Kōshi [Confucius]) and Mengzi (mod. J. Mōshi [Mencius]).

Shiwou (至翁, mod. J. Shiō) is the Buddhist name Zeami uses to sign *Traces of a Dream* and one of two surviving letters. It also is the name that appears in the record of a memorial endowment for Zeami at the temple where his bones and ashes were interred, Fuganji (補巌寺) in Yamato. His wife apparently also was interred there, as Juchin (寿椿).

Zeami also used another Buddhist name, Zenpau (善芳, mod. J. Zenpō) to sign his final collection of songs, *Kintōsho*.[20] Technically speaking, Zenpau is a *hōki* (法諱), a "Dharma name," such as one typically receives when entering Buddhist orders. Shiwou is a *daugau* (道号, mod. J. *dōgō*), an "appellation in the Way," which typically comes from one's Buddhist master or fellows to mark the attainment of a certain rank. Zen priests typically used both names, but in Zeami's case, the two names do not appear together in any document.

As a child, Zeami was known as Oniyasha (鬼夜叉), and later as Fujiwaka (藤若), the latter a special nickname associated with his participation in a *renga* poetry sequence he composed with Nijō Yoshimoto.

Zeami's most formal secular name, Hada no Motokiyo (秦元清), appears only once in the *Performance Notes*, along with an ersatz court rank and position at the end of "Notes in Question and Answer Form," in *Transmitting the Flower Through Effects and Attitudes.*

Notes

1. See, for example, his autograph manuscript of "Written Preparations for the Flower," part 6 of *The Transmission of the Flower*, in Omote Akira and Itō Masayoshi, eds., *Fūshi kwaden, eiin sanshu* (Tokyō: Izumi shoin, 1978).

2. See, for example, his masterful manipulation of time with language in the play *Izutsu*, discussed in detail in *ZS*, pp. 154–57.

3. In addition to these ten, there is also a text of *Tomoakira*, which seems to belong to the same sheaf of texts. The *Tomoakira* text, however, is signed by Hisatsugu rather than Zeami; the hand is different; and it is written almost entirely in *katakana*. For more information about these texts, see *ZS*, p. 55.

4. See, for example, the opening of *The Transmission of the Flower*, where he encourages his descendants to "engage in the vocation of poetry . . . because it is an ornament to graceful performance and an inducement to long life."

5. For the intersection of *sarugaku* and *renga*, see Janet Goff, *Noh Drama and The Tale of Genji* (Princeton, N.J.: Princeton University Press, 1991).

6. These are translated and discussed in *ZS*, pp. 17–18.

7. He draws on, among others, Confucius, Mencius, *The Classic of Songs*, Heart Sutra, Platform Sutra, *Kokin wakashū*, *The Tales of Ise*, texts relating to the medieval hagiography of Prince Regent Shōtoku, and narratives of the miraculous origins of temples, particularly in the Nara area.

8. *Conversations on Sarugaku*, though, shows the use of mild honorific language, in accordance with the facts of its transcription as a memoir of Zeami written down by his son Motoyoshi.

9. I make an (admittedly awkward) distinction here between those "Chinese" epigraphs that seem to use Chinese syntax successfully and those "Sino-Japanese" epigraphs that show evidence of an attempt to write Chinese but that nonetheless retain Japanese word order or other eccentricities. An example of the former is "First hear, then see" (先聞後見), and, of the latter, "The dance has its root in the voice" (舞聲為根). The latter phrase could be read as Chinese but would then mean something like "The dancing voice makes the root," whereas the meaning here, as is clear from the first sentence of the article ("Unless the dance emerges from the singing voice, there is unlikely to be any excitement") makes more sense as translated here. (Omote marks the text with *furigana* as まひはこゑをねとなす. This apparently is his own editorial addition, but the *Yasuda-bon* manuscript has the aphoristic title 舞者為根聲, the second graph making explicit that the word "dance" should, be the subject of the line, which would be impossible if the line were read in orthodox Chinese.)

10. There is, of course, no way to express the graphemic eccentricities of this, or any, Japanese text using the roman alphabet. These are sometimes clever, sometimes comical, and almost always interesting.

11. These "Two Arts" are the abstract artistic basis on which performance is grounded, and they are to be inculcated into the child from the beginning of his training. The "Three Bodies," more appropriately "Three Modes" (of imitation), are the most basic, partially mimetic, conventions through which the actor creates characters. "Turning" certainly has a figural relation to both singing and dancing. Melodies turn up and down within the matrix of a scale or musical mode, and dancing involves a good deal of turning this way and that, but it's easy to see that "Two Turnings and Three Bodies" will never convey the sense of the phrase in question. This lexical problem is an elementary sort of misconstrual.

12. We have no way of knowing whether Zeami himself realized the difficulty and added such glosses himself or whether this was Zenchiku's supplement.

13. See *ZZ*, p. 558. Omote uses the traditional era (*nengō*) date, Ōei 28, rather than the Western equivalent.

14. Zeami does gloss the easier part of the title, -*kaden*, near the beginning of the fifth section of the text, saying that "it is a matter of the flower transmitted from mind to mind by the acquisition of its usages." The more difficult *fūshi*, though, he leaves unexplained.

15. This is probably the right place to inoculate myself by mentioning that reputedly most difficult of technical terms in medieval Japanese aesthetics, *yūgen*. First of all, let me say that I don't think this poses such a great problem to translators because it cannot be translated. It has been profitably described in various places as "mystery and depth" and as "'what lies beneath the surface'; the subtle, as opposed to the obvious; the hint, as opposed to the statement." In the *Notes*, Zeami gives his own examples, some more helpful than others, and taken together with the way he exemplifies the word in his discussions, his brief descriptions seem to provide an adequate pointer toward the experience he intends by that word.

There is, of course, a historical dimension to be accounted for, in that the term originated in Song China in a religious or philosophical context. There it means something somewhat different from what it came to mean in twelfth- and thirteenth-century Japanese poetics, and, in turn, that is different from what it means in the context of nō performance.

I think *yūgen* has passed that nebulous threshold of awareness where those who are interested in these matters will probably have heard of the term and be relatively willing to naturalize it into English. Those who haven't may, moreover, be enticed into discovering for themselves what it means to them by not having it defined in advance. This sort of purposeful mystification cannot be used often in translation, but if there's any word in the *Notes* that is appropriate to such treatment, it is the word *yūgen*.

16. Mieke Bal, *Reading Rembrandt: Beyond the Word Image Opposition* (Cambridge: Cambridge University Press, 1991), p. 6. Bal herself is directed to this observation on the basis of Jonathan Culler:

> The notion of context frequently oversimplifies rather than enriches discussion, since the opposition between an act and its context seems to presume that the context is given and determines the meaning of the act. We know, of course, that things are not so simple: context is not fundamentally different from what it contextualizes; context is not given but produced; what belongs to a context is determined by interpretive strategies; contexts are just as much in need of elucidation as events. Yet when we use the term context we slip back into the simple model it proposes (*Framing the Sign: Criticism and Its Institutions* [Norman: University of Oklahoma Press, 1988], p. xiv).

17. *Sarugaku* as "monkey music."

18. 猿楽にも、世阿弥といへる者、世に無双ふしぎの事にて、色々さまざまの能共、作りをき侍り (In *sarugaku*, also, the person called Zeami created for us a great variety of plays, unparalleled in the world and prodigious). Note the reference to *nō* as plays, not as the art form, which is called

sarugaku, though not with the graphs Zeami preferred. See *Hitorigoto*, in Hayashiya Tatsusaburō, ed., *Kodai chūsei geijutsuron*, Nihon shisō taikei, vol. 23 (Tokyo: Iwanami shoten, 1973), p. 474, lower block of text.

19. See *ZS*, pp. 161–64.

20. Translated by Susan Matisoff in "Images of Exile and Pilgrimage: Zeami's *Kintōsho*," *Monumenta Nipponica* 34, no. 4 (1979): 449–65.

GLOSSARY

This glossary offers brief definitions of specialized vocabulary from Zeami's *Performance Notes*. Some of the terms are English words used as standard translations for certain Japanese technical terms or terms of art in Zeami's discussions. I have tried to use such words consistently and sometimes have capitalized them to indicate their special status in the *Notes*. Other terms are romanized versions of Japanese terms retained in the translation because they were not amenable to precise and economical translation into English. Many of these words, song names or other musicological terms, relate to the structure of *sarugaku* or nō plays or to medieval Japanese ideas about music. Some of these words, such as the famous term *yūgen*, are aesthetic concepts unique to the culture. Others are the proper names of performing arts in traditional Japan. In addition, I have identified certain Japanese terms with particularly rich associations, even though these words sometimes do not appear as romanized Japanese in the translation. Such terms form the nexus for various English terms used in the translation, but I believed that it might be helpful to focus on some of them and their range of meanings in English.

The terms in the glossary cite the original Japanese (*kanji/kana*) renderings whenever practicable. As I explained in the introduction, some of these terms have been retained in the orthography that Zeami used, whereas others have been rewritten in modern Japanese orthography. When deemed relevant, both here and in the footnotes and endnotes, I have cited the alternative form, using "orth." to indicate Zeami's original orthography and "mod. J." to indicate modern Japanese orthography. I have relied on my glossary in *Zeami's Style* for some of these definitions, particularly for song names and musicological terms, and I have tried to maintain a historical distinction, when relevant, between *sarugaku* and nō.

Ageuta (上哥; in nō, 上歌) *Ageuta* is a *tada-utai shōdan* that begins in the upper register and ends in the lower, generally written in two sections. Most typically, the *ageuta* is written in verse in the syllabic pattern 5, 7–5, 7–5, . . . , 7–5. The last line and the first full 7–5 line are often repeated. *Ageuta* are among the most common songs in *sarugaku* and nō and fulfill a variety of functions. The only place where the term *ageuta* appears in Zeami's *Performance Notes* is in the musical notation in some of the passages quoted in *Five Sorts of Singing.* Since the extant manuscripts for that text are not contemporary with Zeami, it is quite possible that the musical notations use later terminology and that Zeami himself did not use the term *ageuta*. The *shōdan* in question, however, is common in Zeami's plays, and he refers to it in the *Notes* as a *hito-utai.*

Ai-kyōgen (間狂言) An *ai-kyōgen* is an actor or, alternatively, a part of a nō performance performed by that actor. If the latter, *ai-kyōgen* refers to the text and performance during the interval between the first and second acts of a typical nō play. During that interval, the *shite* leaves the stage and goes back to the green room, usually to change his costume and mask. The *ai-kyōgen* actor then comes on stage and, usually in dialogue with the *waki*, explains the circumstances leading to the appearance of the *shite* in the first act of the play. The *ai-kyōgen* actor sometimes recounts the events of the first act of the play and sometimes delivers a narrative explaining why the *shite* has appeared. He delivers his lines in a variety of medieval Japanese that is more colloquial than the language typically used by the *shite* and *waki*. In some cases, the *ai-kyōgen* consists of a play within a play, which may be comical. *Ai-kyōgen* actors perform in both nō plays and separate plays (*kyōgen* plays) between individual nō plays in full, multiplay performances. The role of the *ai-kyōgen* in *sarugaku* is not entirely clear, but it is apparent (from, for instance, Zeami's holograph manuscripts of certain plays) that an *ai-kyōgen* role did exist at the time. Zeami calls the *ai-kyōgen* an *okashi* (comic).

Aishyau (哀傷, mod. J. a*ishō*) *Aishyau* is the fourth of the "Five Sorts of Singing," entails "grief and suffering," and is said to augment the third class, *renbo*, by deepening its emotional tenor to include dejection or even tragedy. Although *Five Sorts of Singing* does not contain a subtitle identifying the pieces that specifically exemplify *aishyau* in extant texts, it seems likely that the category begins with the line mentioned from a piece entitled "Aishyau." *Aishyau* is discussed further in *Articles on the Five Sorts of Singing* and the introduction. Examples of songs in the class *aishyau* can be found in *Five Sorts of Singing.*

Banshiki (盤渉) Originally a term taken from ancient Chinese musicology, *banshiki* can mean either a specific pitch or a musical mode or scale based on that pitch. In modern *gagaku* performance practice, *banshiki* corresponds to B, but in nō performance, pitch is not absolute, and *banshiki* refers most concretely to the fingerings used in certain types of flute performance. The most representative of these performances is in the Dance called the *(Banshiki) haya-mai.*

In *sarugaku*, the significance of *banshiki* is somewhat more nebulous. Zeami may have intended to designate a specific pitch (in either voice or flute) in his references to *ōshiki*, *banshiki*, *sōjō*, *ichikotsuchō*, and the like.

Bauwoku/bouwoku (mod. J. *bōoku*) The term *bauwoku* seems to change before our eyes in *Performance Notes.* In his earliest references to it, in *Oral Instruc-*

tions on Singing, Zeami seems to characterize *bauwoku* as the catchall term for all alternative types of singing apart from *shiugen*. He associates it with the *ritsu* voice and thus with sadness. But four years later, by the time of *Three Courses*, *bauwoku* seems to be more specifically identified as the last of a five-part typology of poetry: *shiugen*, *yūgen*, love, complaint, and *bauwoku*. In Zeami's usage, *bauwoku* is usually written in *kana*, but scholars have conjectured about the ideas behind the sounds of the word by assigning various *kanji* to it. Among the much disputed alternatives are the graphs 亡臆 (devastated heart), 望憶 (longing thoughts), 亡憶 (devastated thoughts), as well as 茅屋, which means "a sedge-thatched hut" and seems to imply a life of lonely poverty such as might give birth to the emotion in question. By the time of *Five Sorts of Singing*, probably the early 1430s, Zeami seems to have abandoned the term *bauwoku*, saying that no one properly understood the distinction between *shiugen* and *bauwoku*, and to have reconstituted his typology as *shiugen*, *yūkyoku*, *renbo*, *aishyau*, and *rangyoku*. See *Five Sorts of Singing* and the introduction.

Chūnori (中ノリ). See *Hayabushi*.

Congruent rhythm (拍子合う, *hyōshi au*) Congruent rhythm is one of the major divisions of rhythmic structure in nō singing. Songs sung to congruent rhythm have a beat; that is, they assume a particular relationship between the beats of the eight-beat measure and the metrics of the text. Nō has three types of congruent rhythm: *hiranori*, *chūnori*, and *ōnori*. *Hiranori*, the most typical configuration, matches twelve-syllable verses with eight beats in such a way that four caesuras are inserted in the line (in predictable ways that have shifted over the centuries). *Chūnori* matches two syllables to each beat, and *ōnori* matches one syllable to a beat. All three types of congruent rhythm make allowance for syncopation and vocal embellishments that stretch the typical configuration in various ways. Although Zeami doesn't use the terms *hiranori*, *chūnori*, and *ōnori*, the rhythmic configurations they represent do appear in his plays. He calls *chūnori hayabushi*; he calls *ōnori kiribyōshi* (orth. *kiribyaushi*). He divides *hiranori* into two categories: *tadautai* (orth. *tadautahi*) is the more regular of the two, and *kusemai* (orth. *kusemahi*) represents the more artful and complex form (although *kusemai* can be understood in other ways, too). See also *Hayabushi*, *Kiribyōshi*, *Kusemai*, and *Tadautai*.

Dan (段) *Dan* is a term common in traditional Japanese music, drama, and certain types of literature. Generally, it means something like "section." In *kabuki* and *jōruri*, the term can be used to designate an act of a play; in *jiuta* and *sōkyoku* (koto music), it indicates a section within the formal structure of a composition, as in the celebrated piece *Rokudan*.

The word *dan* has several applications in nō. It can refer to a section of an instrumental dance or the particular musical patterns marking the beginning of such a section. Certain celebrated songs also are known as "the such-and-such *dan*"—for example, *Tama no dan* (the jewel *dan*) in the play *Ama*, *Kasa no dan* (the sedge-hat *dan*) in *Ashikari*, and *Makura no dan* (the pillow *dan*) in *Aoi no ue*.

Most relevant to Zeami's use is the application of *dan* to the major sections of a typical play. The most orthodox form, that of a play in the Aged Mode about a male god, has five *dan*. In the first, the *waki* comes on stage and introduces himself. In the second, the *shite* appears and sings songs hinting at her identity. In the third, the *shite* and *waki* engage in a dialogue. In the fourth, the *shite* delivers a narrative (often centered on a *kuse*). Finally in the fifth, the *shite* does a dance. Zeami explains this form in detail in *The Three Courses*. The *dan* forms the basic unit of formal analysis in studies of nō, such as that by Yokomichi Mario and Omote Akira in their edition of *Yōkyokushū*, and is the ground from which Yokomichi creates the term *shōdan* (little *dan*), indicating the individual songs that provide the building blocks for full *dan*.

Dance (舞, *mai*, orth. *mahi*) Dance, capitalized, refers either to my translation of the technical term *mai*, as in *ryo-chū-kan no mai* or, lowercased, to a more general term for dancing of a variety of types including, but not limited to, the *ryo-chū-kan no mai*.

Demons (鬼, *oni*) Zeami's home tradition of performance, Yamato *sarugaku*, was famed for the dramatic imitation of demons, among other things. But during his career, Zeami came to reject demons "of violent movement" (力動 [*rikidō*]) because, as he says, if you imitate them properly, they evoke only fear, not pleasure or admiration. He does not, however, reject demons "with a human mind" but sets them apart as demons of "intricate movement" (砕動 [*saidō*]). See *Figure Drawings of the Two Arts and the Three Modes* and *The Three Courses*.

Dengaku (田楽) *Dengaku* is a performing art, often characterized as a sister art of *sarugaku*, which was influential in the development of nō. Originally, *dengaku* included dance and music associated with planting; *dengaku* literally means "field music." By the late fourteenth century, however, it seems to have been professionalized and to have come to share many of the aesthetic aims of *sarugaku*. *Sarugaku* and *dengaku* were rivals for patronage, and in *Conversations on Sarugaku*, Zeami speaks admiringly of certain *dengaku* actors, especially the celebrated Zōami.

Doubling back (却来, *kyakurai*) "Doubling back" refers to the ability of a true virtuoso to reach down into otherwise unacceptable forms of action on stage to produce something of striking novelty and interest. The practice of "doubling back" is available to only the utmost masters of the art, and it is to be used very rarely. The term stems from Zen apparently and certainly entails a transcendence of dualism.

Doubly proficient (相音, *aion*) As early as his text *Oral Instructions on Singing*, Zeami identifies two types of vocalization: the *wau* voice and the *shu* voice. These vocal types represent the natural propensities of different individuals.

Each is connected to various types of vocalization in singing for *sarugaku* performance, and each has its strengths and weaknesses. To be "doubly proficient" is to be ambidextrous with regard to the *wau* and the *shu* voice, and for individuals so endowed, it is a great virtue. For others, Zeami stresses the importance of developing a capacity in the vocal styles to which one is not naturally inclined and to be, therefore, "doubly proficient" by training.

Dramatic imitation (物まね, *monomane*) The imitation of various types of characters on stage is a mainstay of drama and holds great importance for *sarugaku* and, later, nō. Zeami's own tradition of Yamato *sarugaku* was known particularly for its skillful imitation of certain types of characters, especially madwomen and demons. In Zeami's earlier notes, notably in "Notes on Dramatic Imitation," the second section of *Transmitting the Flower Through Effects and Attitudes*, he catalogs various character types of particular importance in *sarugaku*. Zeami also is concerned about limiting the degree to which certain kinds of characters can be depicted, and as his career develops, he shows an increasing interest in other performance values, especially *yūgen*.

Effect (風, *fū*) Zeami is fond of creating words ending with the graph *fū*, and a number of important technical terms in the *Notes* also begin with the same graph. The word is discussed in more detail in appendix 3. In short, however, it usually refers to something visible that has an effect on the way the audience perceives a character, an actor, a type of dance, and so on. For example, *fūkyoku* (風曲) means something like "artistic appeal" or "the attractions of performance."

Fūshi (風姿), as in the title *Fūshi k(w)aden*, my *Transmitting the Flower Through Effects and Attitudes*, has a strong visual sense but is not static. The "attitudes" in question (postures, conventions of movement, and the like) are to be considered pragmatically for their effects on the audience.

Fūtei (風体) is a compound linking the abstraction of *fu* with the concrete sense of *tei*. *Fūtei* can mean "body." The compound seems to relate to the actor's expressive capacity, and means something like "manner of expression" or "expressive effect."

Fuzei (風情) is another word in this general semantic field. It comes from poetics and criticism, first in China and then from *waka* criticism, in which it seems to means something like "poetic conceit" or "aesthetic exaggeration." In that context, it can have a negative connotation. But in the *Performance Notes*, the word does not seem to carry a negative sense and instead ranges from a neutral reference to stage business to something more positive, like attractive and eye-catching movement. *Fuzei* is related to *kakari* in both poetics and *sarugaku*, although the latter word is far more common.

In several cases, *-fū* is a suffix meaning "style" or "manner." Used in this way, the word signals the typology of effects in performance that Zeami discusses in *Nine Ranks*, but it also appears in the term *mushufū* (無主風) to designate the failure of an actor to establish his own personal style or presence in performance. I have translated this as "[an actor] without an effective subject."

Enken (遠見) *Enken*, which means "remote view" or "distant sight," is used by Zeami from the time of *Mirror to the Flower* and afterward, although he gradually changes its meaning. Early in its usage, he departs from the word's literal meaning, using it for the artistic basis on which a performer draws from his past training and experience. *Enken* also means a "perspective at some remove" or a "vision afforded by distance." The word also is related to the even more important terms *riken* and *riken no ken*.

Excitement (感, *kan*) Zeami terms as *kan* the actor's success in creating a sense of excitement and pleasure in the audience, particularly through the felicitous combination of what is seen and heard. *Kan* implies great enthusiasm and engagement with the performance, but Zeami prefers to see these emotional responses as preceding and, at least in some degree, distinguishable from the conscious awareness that a performer is succeeding in his performance. In *A Mirror to the Flower* and later in *Pick Up a Jewel and Take the Flower in Hand*, he emphasizes this in a discussion of *kan* and the Chinese graphs with which it is written.

Flower (*hana*, 花 or 華, or, in compounds, *kwa*, mod. J. *ka*) Zeami uses a flower, or blossom, as a metaphor for successful performance in a broad range of circumstances. Early in the *Notes*, the word tends to relate to concrete visual beauty, but later in the *Notes*, it encompasses a wider field of aesthetic achievement. Many of the titles of individual *Notes* contain the graph for flower, which is pronounced *kwa*. *Hana* has an obvious relation to the interest in blossoms, especially cherry blossoms, in Japanese poetry, and blossoms appear in the extant illustrations of *Figure Drawings of the Two Arts and the Three Modes.* For further discussion, see the introduction.

Fū- and *-fū* (風). *See* Effect.

Genzai (現在) *Genzai* refers to nō plays in which the *shite* portrays a living human being.

Although Zeami did not use the term, he apparently did write a few plays that are so categorized by today's standards, such as *Shunnei* and *Hanagatami*. His preference was clearly for *mugen* plays. See *Mugen*.

Hashigakari (橋がかり) The nō stage and most of the stages used for *sarugaku* have a performance space extending from the back left of the stage to the green room backstage. This space takes the form of a bridge (*hashi*). The *hashigakari* is used for entrances and exits by important characters, and it also provides extra space for the enactment of battles and journeys by land and water. See also the illustrations in *A Mirror to the Flower.*

Hayabushi (はや曲) *Hayabushi* is a rhythmic configuration used characteristically in *shura* plays that typically allocates two syllables of text to each beat in the eight-beat "measure," with allowance for various types of syncopation. In nō, this rhythmic configuration is known as *chūnori*.

Hiranori (平ノリ). See *Kusemai* and *Tadautai*.

Hito-utai (一歌, 一歌い, 一うたひ, orth. sometimes *hito-utahi*) *Hito-utai* means "a song" or "a little singing" but refers technically to the most typical sort of rhythmically congruent type of song in *sarugaku*, which in nō is called an *ageuta*. Zeami also occasionally uses the term *ageuta*, but only in the actual notation of songs, as in *Five Sorts of Singing*.

Instance. See *Tai-yū*.

Intricate movement (砕動 *saidō*). *See* Demons.

Issei (一声) *Issei* is a melismatic *shōdan* often sung by the *shite* shortly after coming on stage, set in the higher register with a substantial amount of ornamentation. The typical *issei* is set to the metrical pattern 5–7–5/7–5 with, in some cases, a second verse, called *ninoku*, of 5–7/5–7 meter.

Jo-ha-kyū (序破急, orth. *jo-ha-kiu*) Zeami used *jo-ha-kyū* to describe the primary structural principles underlying performance. They are borrowed from *gagaku* (court music), where they apply to specific movements in a given piece. In *sarugaku* and subsequently in nō, they take on a more comprehensive meaning, indicating the full course of a play or a full day's performance. *Jo*, literally "preface," refers to the opening of the play and is generally characterized as smooth and even. *Ha* means "break" and indicates a change in tone from the *jo* as well as the main body of development of the play's theme. *Kyū* means "fast" and is the play's finale or climax. Zeami came to see *jo-ha-kyū* as a universal organizational principle for all things existing in time and applied the term not only to the play as a whole but also to individual *shōdan* and even to the enunciation of individual syllables of a given text. His discussions of *jo-ha-kyū* can be found in "An Extract from *Learning the Flower*," and, with slight emendations, *A Mirror to the Flower.*

Kagura (神楽) *Kagura* originally was the music and dance performed in Shinto shrines to placate the deities of Japan's indigenous religion. By Zeami's time, *kagura* had long been in contact with Buddhist ritual and musical performance but still retained a close connection to the worship of nature gods. In fact, it was closely related to early *sarugaku*, which Zeami explicitly acknowledges in his discussion of the word *sarugaku* in *Transmitting the Flower.* The kind of dance and singing he associates with *kagura* is difficult to pin down. There is a class of *kagura-mai* in nō today (*kagura* and *sō-kagura* and their variant forms), but their relation to a dance called *kagura* in Zeami's day is unclear. The name *kagura* in the specific context of a dance performed as part of a nō play first appeared in 1520. *Sō-kagura* as such did not appear until the late Edo/Tokugawa period, but since this piece is not so much a distinct piece as it is a fully elaborated version of *kagura*, *sō-kagura* performance may have antedated its textual mention by a long time.

Kakari (かかり, 懸) *Kakari* is a notoriously difficult word because of its abstraction. It is related to the Sinicism *fuzei* but does not have as long a heritage in Sino-Japanese poetics as *fuzei* does. *Kakari* may be applied to visual appearance but also is used in reference to pleasing vocal delivery, which is dependent on elocution and transition from syllable to syllable, word to word, and phrase to phrase. The word is far more common than *fuzei* in *Performance Notes*, largely because of its sonic significance, but it also forms a part of many other compounds such as *kusemai-gakari* and *koutai-gakari*, in which case it means something like "[in the] style of ——."

Ki (Chinese *qi*, 気) *Ki*, the East Asian characterization of vital energy or material force, is not easily translated. *Ki* relates to breath and has metaphysical connotations in some cases, but it is an impersonal quality in living or dynamic things and has never been conceptualized as a deity. Zeami's most important use of the word comes in the sequence "first pitch, second *ki*, third voice" in *Oral Instructions on Singing* and *A Mirror to the Flower*. Zeami writes the word with an unexpected graph, which may relate the notion of "vital energy" to time through the idea of the opportunity (at which one sings).

Kiribyōshi (きりびやうし, orth. *kiribyaushi*) *Kiribyōshi* is a rhythmic configuration usually used near the end of a play that allocates one syllable of text to each beat in the eight-beat "measure," with allowance for various types of syncopation. In nō this rhythmic configuration is known as *ōnori*.

Kōnomono (甲の物, orth. *kafunomono* or *kaunomono*) In general terms, *kōnomono* is a song in the upper register (compare the use of *kan*, written with the same graph, in *shakuhachi* and *ryūteki* flute music, or the same word, usually written with the graph 干, in music for the nō flute). In many cases, the *kōnomono* is an *ageuta*, but it may also refer to the latter half of a *kuse*, beginning with the *shite*'s solo line, the *ageha*. See *Kusemai*.

Kotoba (詞) In nō, *kotoba* is a form of declamation or stylized speech, with neither a fixed rhythm nor a recognizable melody but only a general pattern of inflection, in which the first part of a phrase is delivered more or less in a level pitch and the second half in a swelling phrase with a sharp jump at the beginning and a return to the original level at the end. In *sarugaku*, *sashigoe* was considered a type of *kotoba*, but nō clearly distinguishes between the two. The term *tadakotoba* is a synonym.

Koutabushi (こうたぶし, こうた節, こ歌ぶし) *Koutabushi* is a form of popular song termed *kouta* (小歌) from the mid-fourteenth century. A strong melody, rather than rhythm, provides the primary melodic basis for the vocal music of *sarugaku*. Zeami refers to this style of singing as *koutabushi*. It also laid the foundation for much of the vocal music in congruent rhythm in nō. *Koutabushi* is contrasted with *kusemai* vocal music, in which the rhythm assumes a more conspicuous role. In *Five Sorts of Singing* and *A Collection of Jewels in Effect*, Zeami refers as well to *koutabushi-kusemai* (小歌節曲舞),

showing the amalgamation of the two types of singing, which was important to Zeami's transformation of *sarugaku*.

Kudoki (くどき, クドキ) *Kudoki* is a *shōdan* in the lower register in *sashinori*.

Kuri (クリ) *Kuri* is a short melismatic *sashinori shōdan* focusing on the upper register and rising to *kuri* pitch, the highest standard pitch level in nō. In *Conversations on Sarugaku*, Zeami does not use the noun *kuri* but does use the verb *kuru* (繰る [rise to high pitch]) as well as the term *kuru fushi* (繰る節 [a melody that rises to high pitch]). The *kuri* also is an important part of a full *kusemai* sequence.

Kusemai (節曲舞, 曲舞, or くせ舞, *kusemahi*) *Kusemai* is one of the most important musical terms in the vocabulary of *sarugaku* and nō, with several different, interrelated meanings. First, *kusemai* was an independent performing art performed by itinerant women in the fourteenth century. The art's attractions apparently centered on its highly rhythmic singing and a dance form (of the same name) using a fan. Kannami admired a particular *kusemai* performer, Otozuru (orth. Otodzuru) and adapted her style of performance for inclusion in *sarugaku*. See *Five Sorts of Singing*.

The song form that emerged in Kannami's adaptation of *kusemai* for *sarugaku* also is called *kusemai* and occupies the central aural position in a typical *sarugaku* or nō play, usually in the fourth *dan*. This is the section in which the *shite* relates a narrative. The heart of this narrative is a *shōdan*, which in nō is known as the *kuse*. The full sequence begins with a *shidai*; proceeds to an *issei*, a *kuri*, and a *sashi*; continues with the *kuse*; and concludes with a *shidai*. The *kuse* itself usually consists of three sections, the third of which begins with a solo line for the *shite*, which in nō is called the *ageha*.

Songs like these were widely appreciated in Zeami's day and were apparently sung sometimes independently of the plays with which they were identified. In several cases, plays seem to have been created around preexisting *kusemai*.

The *kusemai* is also, of course, a dance in nō and apparently in *sarugaku*. Unlike many of the other dances in both genres, this dance is always accompanied by a sung text as well as a complement of instruments from the ensemble. In a nō performance, the *kusemai* takes a relatively conventionalized form and is danced to the accompaniment of a *kuse*. Not all *kuse*, however, are danced. In some, the *shite* remains seated. These are called *iguse* (seated *kuse*), and the danced *kuse* is called a *maiguse* (danced *kuse*). It is not clear to what degree this reflects the practice in *sarugaku*.

As Zeami explains in *The Three Courses*, the *kusemai* consists of two parts, the initial part of twelve to thirteen verses and then a *kōnomono* (orth. *kafunomono*) of twelve to thirteen verses. The *kōnomono* (higher part) does indeed begin in the higher pitch register and in modern practice corresponds to a section of the *kuse* known as the *ageha*, consisting of a line sung solo by the *shite* in a higher pitch, marking the final section of the *kuse*. For the way the word *kusemai* is written in various manuscripts of the *Performance Notes*, see Omote, in *ZZ*, pp. 447–49n.38. For several examples of *kusemai*, see also the last section of *Five Sorts of Singing*.

Kyoku (曲) The Chinese graph *kyoku* appears frequently and, in some cases, ambiguously in *Performance Notes*. In literal terms, the word means "curved," "twisted," or "bent." In some cases, it is intended to be read *fushi* and is then synonymous and homophonous with a word more typically written with the graph 節.

Fushi means, most simply, "melody," in contrast to *hyōshi* (rhythm). In *Oral Instructions on Singing* and *Mirror to the Flower*, however, Zeami distinguishes between *fushi* and *kyoku*, stating: "The *fushi* provides the outline; vocal style relates to movement from word to word; and *kyoku* is a matter of the mind" (節はかた木、かかりは文字うつり、曲は、心なり). In this context, I have distinguished between *fushi* and *kyoku* by calling the former "melody" and the latter "expression." Elsewhere as well, *kyoku* appears to refer to the particular expression of a given melody in the style of a particular performer on a particular occasion. It may be that *fushi* is to be understood as Substance, whereas *kyoku* is Instance.

The graph *kyoku* was also read *kuse*, as in the word *kusemai*. Particularly in classical and medieval Japanese, *kyoku* may mean "unconventional," "eccentric," or "interesting" and in this way seems to relate to a performer's unique characteristics, his particular manner of expression.

Maejite (前仕手、前為手) The *maejite* (or *maeshite*) is the *shite* in the first "act" of a two-act nō play. In *mugen* plays, the *maejite* usually appears in disguise as a living human being.

Mode I have used the word "mode" with the specific technical sense in which Zeami uses *-tai* (体) in his terms *rōtai* (Aged Mode), *nyotai* (Women's Mode), and *guntai* (Martial Mode). His most extensive treatment of these modes is found in *The Three Courses*. In each case, the mode is more than a dramatic imitation of a particular character type. It also has formal, musical, and dance-related implications, as well as related forms of performance that in themselves do not focus specifically on the aged, women, or warriors.

Mondō (問答, orth. *mondau*) *Mondō* is a common word, literally "question and answer," with a technical musical meaning as well. In common usage, it refers to a dialogue. Zeami, in fact, uses this dialogue form himself in various places in the *Performance Notes*—for example, in the third chapter of *Transmitting the Flower Through Effects and Attitudes*. More technically, the *mondō* is a *shōdan* within a *sarugaku* or nō play in which two characters (typically the *waki* and the *shite*) engage in a dialogue in *kotoba*—that is, stylized speech—with perhaps an occasional line in *sashinori*.

Mugen (夢幻) *Mugen* is "phantasmal nō" or "nō of dreams and apparitions," plays in which the *shite* is a being from another dimension of existence, whether a god, a demon, a plant or an animal spirit, or, most typically, the ghost of a human being. In many *mugen* plays, the *waki* is explicitly said to have gone to sleep, and the second act is a representation of his dream—thus the term "dreams and apparitions." This thematic element had an indelible influence on play structure in that the revelation of identity became the pivot for many plays and included a character who appears in one act in disguise, only to come back in the second as in true form. *Mugen* even influenced the structure of plays that are, technically speaking, *genzai* plays (because their *shite* are living human beings), of which *Hanjo* is a good example. It appears that Zeami invented the form, although he did so by building on antecedents in which a god or ghost miraculously appeared to the *waki*.

Nochijite (後仕手, 後為手) The *maejite* (or *maeshite*) is the *shite* in the first "act" of a two-act nō play. In *mugen* plays, the *maejite* usually appears in disguise as a living human being.

Noncongruent rhythm (拍子不合, 不合, [*hyōshi*] *awazu*) Noncongruent rhythm is one of the major divisions of rhythmic structure in nō singing. Songs sung to noncongruent rhythm have no regular beat and assume no specific relationship between the syllables of a text and the beats of a measure. Such songs may be relatively simple melodically (e.g., the *sashigoto* or *sashi*), or they may use considerable ornamentation and melismatic singing (e.g., the *issei*). See also *Issei* and *Sashi*.

Ōnori (大ノリ). See *Kiribyōshi*.

Ōshiki (黄鐘, orth. *waushiki*) Originally a term taken from ancient Chinese musicology, *ōshiki* can mean either a specific pitch or a musical mode or scale based on that pitch. In modern *gagaku* performance practice, *ōshiki* corresponds to A, but in nō performance, pitch is not absolute, and *ōshiki* refers most concretely to the fingerings used in certain types of flute performance. *Ōshiki* is the default case for most of the instrumental music in nō, so it generally is not mentioned except when it is unusual (e.g., *Ōshiki haya-mai*).

In *sarugaku*, the significance of *ōshiki* is somewhat more nebulous. Zeami may have intended to designate a specific pitch (in voice or flute) in his references to *ōshiki*, *banshiki*, *sōjō*, *ichikotsuchō*, and so forth.

Play (遊, *yū*, orth. *iu*) "Play" is a provisional translation for a lexical element used in several Sino-Japanese compounds in *Performance Notes*. In a general sense in modern Japanese, the graph means "play" or "have fun" and is typically pronounced in its native Japanese reading, *asobu*. This sense is not irrelevant to the meaning in which Zeami uses the word, but the kind of "play" to which he refers is not the unself-conscious play of a child but the fruit of experience and talent in performance that enables a consummate actor a high degree of expressive freedom within the performance conventions of *sarugaku*. The most important word in this group is *yūgaku* (遊楽). Although it changed its meaning in the course of Zeami's thought, it came to represent a kind of synonym for *sarugaku*, implying complete virtuosity and freedom in performance. Accordingly, I have translated it as "fine play in performance." Related words include *yūkyoku* (遊曲 [fine play in musical expressiveness]) and *yūbū* (遊風 [fine play in expression]). These terms also are discussed in the introduction and appendix 3.

Rangyoku (闌曲) In developing a heuristic typology of types or sorts of singing, Zeami eventually identified *rangyoku* as a class that thematically includes his other five sorts (*shiugen*, *yūkyoku*, *renbo*, and *aishyau*), even as it transcends them artistically through the unparalleled virtuosity it requires. The other four sorts are defined by where they lie on a thematic and emotional register ranging from the celebratory and auspicious character of *shiugen* to the grief of *aishyau*. *Rangyoku*, for its part, may partake of a wide variety of themes (and their concomitant emotional states) but can be performed only by actors who have mastered the repertory and achieved complete confidence in their performance. The *ran-* in *rangyoku* occasionally is found in other compounds, also with the sense of "virtuosic," and it can be used in its native Japanese pronunciation of *take*(*taru*) (virtuosic).

It is probably not coincidental that many of the specific *rangyoku* pieces to which Zeami refers in *Five Sorts of Singing* are *kusemai*, given those pieces' rhythmic demands on the performer. *Rangyoku* is discussed further in *Articles on the Five Sorts of Singing* and the introduction. Examples of songs in the class *rangyoku* can be found in *Five Sorts of Singing.*

Rank (位, *kurai*, orth. *kurawi*) Throughout the *Performance Notes*, Zeami is concerned with the performer's rank—that is, his level of artistic attainment. In large measure, rank is a matter of careful training and experience brought to fruition in performance, but there is an intangible and likely innate element in the high rank to which some performers attain, and occasionally such a rank can be discerned in even young actors without the benefits of long experience and training. Zeami's earliest discussion of rank comes in *Transmitting the Flower*, where he contrasts it with the synonyms *take* (stature) and *kasa* (grandeur). The emphasis on rank in *Performance Notes* may seem somewhat disconcerting and obscure, and it does link Zeami's thought to the strictly hierarchical social theory of traditional Japan. For Zeami, though, rank is not primarily a matter of social class or birth, and it is amenable to improvement through hard work in training.

In discussing rank, Zeami sometimes singles out particular types for a detailed examination, for example, his rank of utter confidence (安位), and the "rank of great virtuosity" (闌位, *ran'i*, also *taketaru kurai*) is given its own section in *A Course to Attain the Flower.*

Renbo (恋慕) "Love and longing" is a straightforward rendering of the Japanese word *renbo*, and Zeami's use of the word as one of his five classes of singing seems little removed from such an understanding. Although *Five Sorts of Singing* does not contain a subtitle identifying the pieces that specifically exemplify *renbo* in extant texts, the category probably begins with the line mentioned from *Kohi no omoni*, *kohi* (mod. J. *koi*) being the native reading of the graph read *ren* in *renbo*. All the pieces following that are concerned with romantic love and longing in some degree, until the mention of the piece "Aishyau," which seems to inaugurate the listing of pieces in the class *aishyau*. *Renbo* is discussed further in *Articles on the Five Sorts of Singing* and the introduction. Examples of songs in the class *renbo* can be found in *Five Sorts of Singing*.

Riken (離見) and *riken no ken* (離見の見). *See* Vantage from a Vision Apart.

Ritsu (律) Zeami's somewhat eccentric musicology of *sarugaku* employs various technical terms borrowed from other forms of East Asian music and, in a broader sense, philosophy. In most cases, he reinterprets the terms, often with great insight and to the great benefit of *sarugaku* (as with *shiugen* and *jo-ha-kyū*, among others). In some cases, however, the terms in question seem to add little to our understanding either because Zeami himself misapplied them or because we do not have sufficient understanding of what he intended by them. *Ritsu* is one of those terms. Earlier, the word was native to court music (*gagaku*), in which it referred to one of two scale or modal types, the other being *ryo*. Both terms came from Chinese musicology, but even the Japanese *gagaku* derived from Chinese ensemble music altered the system and its terminology. In applying the term *ritsu* to *sarugaku*, Zeami links it with a particular style of vocalization, the *shu* voice. Apart from this particular association, little else is certain with regard to Zeami's use of the word *ritsu*. For further discussion, see appendix 1.

Rongi (論義) *Rongi* is a *tadautai shōdan* much like an *ageuta*, except that it is written as a dialogue between two characters or between a character and the chorus. The last part is sung by the chorus. Zeami singles out four different specialized types of *rongi* in addition to his mention of the term generically. These are the *seme-rongi* (責め論義), *utai-rongi* (謡論義, orth. *utahi-rongi*), *kotoba-rongi* (詞論義), and *na-rongi* (名論儀, also *mei-rongi*). The *utai-rongi* does not seem to differ from the generic *rongi*, and this term appears to have been used merely to distinguish it from the *kotoba-rongi*, apparently that form of dialogue in *sashinori* and *kotoba* known more commonly in nō as a *kakeai*. *Seme-rongi* has not been clearly differentiated from *utai-rongi* and *kotoba-rongi*, although Nose Asaji, in *Zeami jūrokubushū hyōshaku*, conjectured that it meant a *rongi* performed more quickly than other types of *rongi*. Omote asks whether *seme-rongi* might instead relate to the thematic content of the song, suggesting that a *seme-rongi* might press the logic of a case. *Na-rongi* occurs only once, in *Five*

Sorts of Singing in the interlinear notes to the unusual piece *Arrowroot Trousers*, next to the line, "If I gave her away as Ki no Aritsune's daughter." According to this, a *na-rongi* might be a *rongi* that mentions a name. But Kannami was famed for his performance of this *rongi*, so perhaps the term means "a well-known *rongi*."

Ryo (呂) Along with *ritsu*, *ryo* is a term that Zeami borrows from the musicology of *gagaku* (court music), derived from Chinese musicology imported into Japan beginning in the seventh century. In its original context, *ryo* referred to one of two scale or modal types, the other being *ritsu*. In applying the term *ryo* to *sarugaku*, Zeami links it with the *wau* voice, itself not well understood. Apart from this particular association, little else is certain with regard to Zeami's use of the term *ryo*. For further discussion, see appendix 1.

Ryo-chū-kan no mai (呂中干の舞) In nō, the most typical and frequently deployed instrumental genre and the dance it accompanies are termed *ryo-chū-kan no mai*. All the pieces in this genre are structured around a series of *dan* (sections,) that occupy the greater part of the piece, but many are opened with a brief introduction (generally termed a *kakari*) or a longer introductory "preface" (*jo*). Moreover, the sections are usually separated by brief passages in a more flexible rhythm with unique melodies (*oroshi*). The melodies of the *dan* of all *ryo-chū-kan no mai* are closely related and based on four phrases—individually called *ryo*, *chū*, *kan*, and *kan-no-chū*—that are repeated in cycles. Typical *ryo-chū-kan no mai* are the *Chū-no-mai*, *Otoko-mai*, *Haya-mai*, and *Jo-no-mai*.

Although Zeami does not use the term *ryo-chū-kan no mai*, the ancestor of all the modern dances so named is likely the *tennyo no mai* (Dance of the Heavenly Maiden), which he discusses in *Figure Drawings of the Two Arts and the Three Modes*. For further discussion, see appendix 1 and Takemoto Mikio, "Tennyo no mai no kenkyū."

Sashi (指、サシ) *Sashi* is a common *shōdan* in nō, often sung as part of a character's entry on stage, but also elsewhere in nō, as in the *kuri-sashi-kuse* sequence in the last section of a typical play's first act. The *shōdan* is sung in *sashinori* (サシノリ) style; that is, it is a noncongruent song with relatively little melodic inflection. With neither strong rhythmic marking nor a complicated melody, it is reminiscent of recitative in opera and often is used to deliver lines the audience should hear clearly. Both *sashigoe* (指声, さし声, orth. *sashigoye*) and *sashigoto* (指事、さし事、サシゴト) are related to the *sashi*, although in some cases, *sashigoe* seems to refer to the *waki*'s self-introduction, which in nō is delivered in *kotoba* and termed a *nanori*. The *nanori* sometimes may have been sung in *sarugaku* (see Omote, in *ZZ*, pp. 462–63n.69). The term *sashi* appears in *Five Sorts of Singing*, but the extant manuscripts for that text are not contemporary with Zeami, and copyists may have used the term as an abbreviation for one Zeami would have written out as *sashigoe* or *sashigoto*.

Shidai (次第) The *shidai* is a short rhythmically congruent *shōdan* in *tadautai*. It often is used at the beginning of a play and also appears as the first *shōdan* in a full *kusemai* sequence. It typically consists of a 7–5 line that is repeated and followed by a 7–4 line. The term is current in nō, but Zeami also used it in writing about *sarugaku*.

Shiore (しほれ, orth. *shihore*) An important element in Zeami's figuration of interest as a "flower" is that flowers are subject to wilting and decay. He implies in a passage from *Transmitting the Flower Through Effects and Attitudes* that bringing this "flower" into existence is only part of the actor's task. To exploit its potential most fully, the accomplished actor carries the interest out of its flowering into this state of *shiore*. The classical Japanese word Zeami writes most readily connects with modern *shioreru* (萎れる), meaning "wilt," "languish," or "to be depressed," but technically, that word should be spelled *shiworu* rather than *shihoru*, as he sometimes writes it. There is, however, a word correctly spelled *shihoru* (霑る), which means "to be drenched" or "to be wet." Zeami occasionally uses unconventional spellings, and he never writes the word in question with a Chinese graph, so it is difficult to tell what his precise intention may have been. He does provide two *waka* poems to illustrate the effect he is talking about, but whereas one seems to suggest the latter meaning, the other suggests the former.

In both cases, however, Zeami is referring to the impermanence of the effect produced on stage and to the way that a master actor can use that impermanence to his advantage. In that the associations of *shiore* are, in both cases, redolent of passing away and fading, Zeami establishes here an important precedent for the muted, wistful, and melancholy aesthetics of the late fifteenth century.

The technical term *shiori*—used in nō and *kyōgen* for a movement in which the actor lowers his head and brings his hand, palm upward, toward his face—may be related to *shiore*. This gesture indicates weeping or the suppression of tears.

Shirabyōshi (白拍子, orth. *shirabyaushi*) Like *kusemai*, *shirabyōshi* was an independent performing art of the late Heian and Kamakura periods. It was performed by women (also called *shirabyōshi*) who often doubled as prostitutes and danced in male clothing, sometimes wearing swords. By Zeami's time, *shirabyōshi* performers seem to have disappeared, but they lived on in legend and became a character type for imitation in *sarugaku*. See *Transmitting the Flower Through Effects and Attitudes*.

Shite (仕手 or 為手) *Shite*, which means "doer" or "performer," is often used by Zeami to mean "actor." In nō, it has come to mean the central actor in a play, and Zeami sometimes intends it in that latter meaning as well.

Shiugen (祝言, mod. J. *shūgen*) *Shiugen* is the term Zeami uses to exemplify the aesthetic and ritual characteristics of plays opening a proper performance of *sarugaku*. Such plays are supposed to be straightforward and auspicious and neither too difficult nor too interesting. The plays in the Aged Mode (see *Three Courses*) typically express this aesthetic character. In Zeami's day, they had an ideological link to performance and patronage in that they expressed gratitude for benevolent rule. Early in *Performance Notes*, Zeami tends to see *shiugen* as the foundation for all performance, but this suggestion seems to belie the character of many of the best plays in his repertory. As his theory of genre develops, *shiugen*'s place is gradually diminished, partly replaced by the idea of *yūgaku*, the fine play in performance that places more emphasis on the individual actor's attainment than on the play's thematic and formal character. For further discussion, see the introduction.

Shōdan (小段) *Shōdan* means a "little *dan*," a term coined by Yokomichi Mario for the individual songs and spoken passages of which a nō (or *sarugaku*) play is composed (*Yōkyokushū*, NKBT, vol. 40, pp. 13–28). Although Zeami does not use the term *shōdan*, he clearly was familiar with the concept and does mention several individual *shōdan* in *Performance Notes*, such as *ageuta*, *sashi*, and *rongi*.

Shu voice (主の声, *shu no koye*, mod. J. *shu no koe*) The binarism *wau/shu* is one of the most puzzling aspects of Zeami's discussion of singing. These terms are used to indicate two different styles of vocalization, but neither survives in modern performance practice. Furthermore, Zeami's descriptions, such as they are, provide few clues to how the styles differed practically. The *shu* voice apparently is a more slender, weaker, "feminine" sort of voice (see Omote, in *ZZ*, pp. 443–44n.32). It is paired with music in the *ritsu* modes. A performer who is proficient in both types of vocalization is termed "doubly proficient." See also the introduction to *Oral Instructions on Singing*.

Shura (修羅) *Shura* is the name used in nō for a particular type of play, the second full play in a full day's performance. For that reason, the *shura* play may also be called a *nibanme-mono* (second-category play). *Shura* plays are generally *mugen* nō and always have a warrior or the ghost of a warrior as the *shite*, often reenacting an important battle scene from his life or giving an account of his sufferings in hell. Many other (living) warriors appear in nō, but they are not termed *shura*. In *sarugaku*, *shura* seems to mean much the same thing as in nō. The term is derived from the Sanskrit *asura*, meaning a "warring titan" or "demigod."

Sparring (はたらき, *hataraki*) Zeami identifies two broad types of formal, extended action on stage as the centerpiece of the final act of a *sarugaku* play. One he terms *mai* (*see* Dance) and the other *hataraki*, my "Sparring." Sparring generally entails an imitation of a fight between two samurai or between a samurai and a demon and often includes parrying with swords or other weapons. In nō, the term *hataraki* is used to indicate a genre of dance-like activity, composed of several different specific performances, including, for example, the *mai-bataraki* and *kirikumi,* which enact physical conflicts between adversaries, either human or supernatural, and other kinds of activities such as the *kakeri* or *iroe*, expressing psychological conflicts.

Substance. See *Tai-yū*.

Tadakotoba (只言葉, 只詞, ただ言葉). See *Kotoba.*

Tadautai (只歌, 只謡, orth. *tadautahi*) *Tadautai* means "standard singing," a synonym for *koutabushi.*

Tai-yū (体用, also *tai-yō*) Zeami uses the pair *tai* and *yū* to explain the relationship between training and the performance conventions of *sarugaku*, as well as their specific and unique manifestations in any performance. *Tai* is translated here as "Substance" and *yū* as "Instance." The pair has roots as far back as the third-century commentary on Laozi by Wang Bi (226–249) but was perhaps most influential for Zeami in its reuse in Chinese translations of *The Awakening of Faith in the Mahāyāna* (*Dacheng qixinlun*, J. *Daijō kishinron*, a text attributed to Aśvaghoṣa but no longer extant in the putatively original Sanskrit). Zeami's discussion is found in *A Course to Attain the Flower.* See also Konishi Jin'ichi, *Nōgakuron kenkyū,* pp. 186–88.

Three Modes (三体, *santai*). *See* Mode.

Vantage from a Vision Apart (離見の見, *riken no ken*), Vision Apart (離見, *riken*) Zeami places great emphasis on the master actor's ability to put himself in the place of the spectators and to understand how they perceive his presence on stage. In particularly visual terms, this awareness is called *riken no ken*, my "Vantage from a Vision Apart." This vantage gives the actor an advantage in his performance and may be read as both concrete and abstract, concrete referring to the actor's body as perceived from front, sides, and back, and abstract as a vision transcending consciousness, linking the actor and the audience in a state of wonder. See, for example, *Mirror to the Flower* and *An Effective Vision of Learning the Vocation of Fine Play in Performance.* When Vision Apart first appears, it refers to simply the perspective of the audience on the actor's performance, especially in visual terms. It appears later, however, in the description of the top of the Nine Ranks, in a somewhat puzzling way linked with an aesthetic wonder transcending not only vision but also consciousness itself.

Violent movement (力動, *rikidō*). *See* Demons.

Waka (和歌, 和詞) *Waka* can mean "Japanese poetry" in a broad sense, but more often, it refers to the classic form in thirty-one syllables, arranged 5, 7, 5, 7, 7. Zeami deems the study of *waka* poetry and poetics as essential to a playwright. In such a context, however, he usually refers to *waka* simply as *uta* ("songs" or "poems"). When he uses the term *waka*, he means a particular *shōdan* (in nō, known as *waka* [ワカ]), sung in a melismatic style in noncongruent rhythm, often opening and/or closing an instrumental dance. The text for such *waka* often consists of a *waka* poem.

Waki (脇) As Zeami uses the term most commonly, *waki* is the name for the secondary role in a play. This role is generally that of a priest, wandering through the country to see what he can see. The *waki* comes on stage at the beginning of a typical play to announce who he is and to set the scene for the appearance of the main character, the *shite*. The *waki*'s interaction with the *shite* is essential to the play and usually reaches a high point in a dialogue in the third *dan* and in further interaction in the final *dan*.

Wau voice (横の声, *wau no koye*, mod. J. *ō no koe*) The binarism *wau/shu* is one of the most puzzling aspects of Zeami's discussion of singing. These terms are used to indicate two different styles of vocalization, but neither survives in modern performance practice. Furthermore, Zeami's descriptions, such as they are, provide few clues to how the styles differed practically. The *wau* voice apparently is a broad, strong, and "masculine" sort of voice (see Omote, in *ZZ*, pp. 443–44n.32). It is paired with music in the *ryo* modes. A performer who is proficient in both types of vocalization is termed "doubly proficient." See also the introduction to *Oral Instructions on Singing.*

Yūgaku (遊楽). *See* Play.

Yūgen (幽玄) The word *yūgen* has a long history in Japanese aesthetics, with antecedents in both Chinese philosophy and religion. In the late twelfth century, *yūgen* became a central term in poetics, designating a mysterious and dark profundity not apparent on the surface of a poem but crucial to its understanding. Zeami adopts the term first to characterize the aesthetic attractions of rival troupes from Ōmi and seems to use it for an elegant, romantic, formal, and largely visual beauty. He lays a claim on *yūgen* for his own troupe, and much of his success might have been a result of the successful incorporation of *yūgen* into the style of his and related Yamato troupes, which had been known primarily for dramatic imitation (*monomane*) rather than *yūgen*. See also the more detailed discussion in the introduction.

Yūkyoku (幽曲) *Yūkyoku* is one of Zeami's five classes of singing and represents a more intricately detailed and sensitive expression than *shiugen* does, even though it preserves most of its auspicious and celebratory character. *Yūkyoku* is discussed further in *Articles on the Five Sorts of Singing* and the introduction. Examples of songs in the class *yūkyoku* can be found in *Five Sorts of Singing.*

BIBLIOGRAPHY

Akizuki Ryōmin and Akizuki Mahito, eds. *Zenshū goroku kanbun no yomikata.* Tokyo: Shunjūsha, 1993.

Atkins, Paul. *Revealed Identity: The Noh Plays of Komparu Zenchiku.* Ann Arbor: Center for Japanese Studies, University of Michigan, 2006.

Bal, Mieke. *Reading Rembrandt: Beyond the Word Image Opposition.* Cambridge: Cambridge University Press, 1991.

Bialock, David. "Voice, Text, and Poetic Borrowing." *Harvard Journal of Asiatic Studies* 54, no. 1 (1994): 212–13.

Brandon, James, ed. *Nō and Kyōgen in the Contemporary World.* Honolulu: University of Hawaiʻi Press, 1997.

Brown, Steven T. *Theatricalities of Power: The Cultural Politics of Noh.* Stanford, Calif.: Stanford University Press, 2002.

Culler, Jonathan. *Framing the Sign: Criticism and Its Institutions.* Norman: University of Oklahoma Press, 1988.

de Ferranti, Hugh. *Japanese Musical Instruments.* Oxford: Oxford University Press, 2000.

Dumoulin, Heinrich. *Zen Buddhism: A History, Japan.* Bloomington, Ind.: World Wisdom, 2005.

Goff, Janet. *Noh Drama and The Tale of Genji.* Princeton, N.J.: Princeton University Press, 1991.

Haga Yaichi and Sasaki Nobutsuna, eds. *Kōchū yōkyoku sōsho.* Tokyo: Hakubunkan, 1914.

Hakeda, Yoshito, trans. *The Awakening of Faith, Attributed to Aśvaghosha.* New York: Columbia University Press, 1967.

Hayashiya Tatsusaburō, ed. *Hitorigoto.* In *Kodai chūsei geijutsuron.* Nihon shisō taikei, vol. 23. Tokyo: Iwanami shoten, 1973.

Hisamatsu Sen'ichi and Nishio Minoru, eds. *Karonshū nōgakuronshū.* Vol. 1, *Chūsei no bungaku.* NKBT, vol. 65 Tokyo: Iwanami shoten, 1965.

Hōsei daigaku nōgaku kenkyūjo, ed. *Kōzan bunkozō nōgaku shiryō kaidai.* 3 vols. Tokyo: Hōsei daigaku nōgaku kenkyūjo, 1998.

Hurvitz, Leon, trans. *Scripture of the Lotus Blossom of the Fine Dharma.* New York: Columbia University Press, 1976.

Itō, Masayoshi. "Go on, Aishō." *Kanze*, February 1964, pp. 3–5.

Kanze Sakon, ed. *Kanzeryū yōkyoku zoku hyakubanshū*. Taiseiban ed. Tokyo: Hinoki shoten, 1973.

Kikkawa Eishi. *Hōgaku hyakka jiten: Gagaku kara min'yō made*. Tokyo: Ongaku no tomo sha, 1984.

Knechtges, David, trans. *Wen xuan, or Selections of Refined Literature*. Princeton, N.J.: Princeton University Press, 1996.

Knoblock, John. *Xunzi, a Translation and Study of the Complete Works*. 3 vols. Stanford, Calif.: Stanford University Press, 1988–1994.

Kobayashi Shizuo. *Zeami*. 2d ed., rev. Tokyo: Hinoki shoten, 1963.

Konishi Jin'ichi. *Nōgakuron kenkyū*. Tokyo: Hanawa shobō, 1961.

———. "Shihori no setsu." In *Bashō*, pp. 241–49. Nihon bungaku kenkyū shiryō sōsho, vol. 32. Tokyo: Yūseidō, 1969.

———. *Zeami shū*. Nihon no shisō, vol. 8. Tokyo: Chikuma shobō, 1970.

Kōsai Tsutomu. *Nōyō shinkō*. Tokyo: Wan'ya shoten, 1972.

———. *Zeami shinkō*. Tokyo: Wan'ya shoten, 1962.

———. *Zoku Zeami shinkō*. Tokyo: Wan'ya shoten, 1970.

Koyama Hiroshi, Satō Kikuo, and Satō Ken'ichirō, eds. *Yōkyokushū*. 2 vols. Nihon koten bungaku zenshū, vols. 33 and 34. Tokyo: Shōgakukan, 1973, 1975.

Maruoka Akira. *Kokin yōkyoku kaidai*. Tokyo: Kokin yōkyoku kaidai kankōkai, 1984.

Matisoff, Susan. "Images of Exile and Pilgrimage: Zeami's *Kintōsho*." *Monumenta Nipponica* 34, no. 4 (1979): 449–65.

———. *The Legend of Semimaru, Blind Musician of Japan*. New York: Columbia University Press, 1978.

McCullough, Helen. *Brocade by Night: "Kokin wakashū" and the Court Style in Japanese Classical Poetry*. Stanford, Calif.: Stanford University Press, 1985.

McCullough, Helen, and William McCullough, trans. *A Tale of Flowering Fortunes: Annals of Japanese Aristocratic Life in the Heian Period*. 2 vols. Stanford, Calif.: Stanford University Press, 1980.

Nakamura Itaru. *Zeami densho yōgo sakuin*. Tokyo: Kasama shoin, 1985.

Nearman, Mark, trans. and ed. "*Kakyō*: Zeami's Fundamental Principles of Acting." *Monumenta Nipponica* 37, no. 3 (1982): 333–74.

———. "*Kakyō*: Zeami's Fundamental Principles of Acting." *Monumenta Nipponica* 37, no. 4 (1982): 461–96.

———. "*Kakyō*: Zeami's Fundamental Principles of Acting." *Monumenta Nipponica* 38, no. 1 (1983): 51–71.

———. "*Kyakuraika*: Zeami's Final Legacy for the Master Actor." *Monumenta Nipponica* 35, no. 2 (1980): 153–97.

———. "Zeami's *Kyūi*: A Pedagogical Guide for Teachers of Acting." *Monumenta Nipponica* 33, no. 3 (1978): 299–332.

Nishino Haruo and Haneda Akira. *Nō kyōgen jiten*. Tokyo: Heibonsha, 1987.

Nonomura Kaizō and Ōtani Tokuzō, eds. *Yōkyoku nihyakugojūban shū*. 2 vols. Kyoto: Akao shōbundō, 1978.

Nose Asaji. *Zeami jūrokubushū hyōshaku*. Tokyo: Iwanami shoten, 1944.

Omote Akira, ed. *Nō*. Bessatsu Taiyō books, no. 25. Tokyo: Heibonsha, 1978.

Omote Akira. *Nōgakushi shinkō*. Vol. 1. Tokyo: Wan'ya shoten, 1979.

Omote Akira and Getsuyōkai, eds. *Zeami jihitsu nōhonshū*. Tokyo: Iwanami shoten, 1997.

Omote Akira, Ijichi Tetsuo, and Kuriyama Riichi, eds. *Rengaronshū, nōgakuronshū, haironshū*. Nihon koten bungaku zenshū, vol. 51. Tokyo: Shōgakukan, 1973.

Omote Akira and Itō Masayoshi, eds. *Konparu kodensho shūsei*. Tokyo: Wan'ya shoten, 1969.

Omote Akira and Takemoto Mikio. *Nōgaku no densho to geiron*. Iwanami kōza, Nō to kyōgen, vol. 2. Tokyo: Iwanami shoten, 1988.

O'Neill, P. G. *Early Nō Drama: Its Background, Character and Development, 1300–1450*. London: Lund Humphreys, 1958.

———. "The Letters of Zeami: One Received from Jūni Gon-no-kami and Two Sent to Zenchiku." *Nōgaku kenkyū* 5 (1979–1980): 134–50.

———. "The Structure of *Kusemai*." *Bulletin of the School of Oriental and African Studies* 21 (1958): 100–110.

Poorter, Erika de. *Zeami's Talks on Sarugaku: An Annotated Translation of the Sarugaku Dangi, with an Introduction on Zeami Motokiyo*. Amsterdam: Gieben, 1986.

Quinn, Shelley Fenno. *Developing Zeami: The Noh Actor's Attunement in Practice*. Honolulu: University of Hawai'i Press, 2005.

Rath, Eric. *The Ethos of Noh: Actors and Their Art*. Cambridge, Mass.: Harvard University Asia Center, 2004.

Rimer, J. Thomas, and Yamzaki Masakazu, trans. *On the Art of the Nō Drama: The Major Treatises of Zeami*. Princeton, N.J.: Princeton University Press, 1984.

Sanari Kentarō, ed. *Yōkyoku taikan*. 7 vols. Tokyo: Meiji shoin, 1931–1939.

Shinma Shin'ichi, Shida Nobuyoshi, and Asano Kenji, eds. *Kanginshū*. In *Chūsei kinsei kayōshū*, NKBT, vol. 44. Tokyo: Iwanami shoten, 1959.

Smethurst, Mae, and Christina Laffin. *The Noh Ominameshi: A Flower Viewed from Many Directions*. Ithaca, N.Y.: East Asia Program, Cornell University, 2003.

Taguchi Kazuo. "*Kuzu no hakama* (*Sumiyoshi no sengū no nō*) nanku kō." *Geinōshi kenkyū* 67 (1979): 21–22.

Takeda, Sharon, in collaboration with Monica Bethe. *Miracles and Mischief: Noh and Kyōgen Theater in Japan*. Los Angeles: Los Angeles County Museum of Art and Agency for Cultural Affairs, Government of Japan, 2002.

Takemoto Mikio. "Tennyo no mai no kenkyū." *Nōgaku kenkyū* (Nōgaku kenkyūjo kiyō) 4 (1978): 93–158.

———. "Yoshida bunko Zeami nōgakuron shiryō shōkai." *Bungaku* 4, no. 4 (2003): 199–206.

———. "Yoshida bunko zō shinshutsu-bon Sandō ni tsuite," pp. 1–7. Engeki kenkyū sentā kiyō: Waseda daigaku 21-seki DOE Puroguramu, 2004.

Takemoto Mikio and Hashimoto Asō. *Nō kyōgen hittaku*. Bessatsu kokubungaku, vol. 48. Tokyo: Gakutōsha, 1995.

Tanaka Makoto, ed. *Mikan yōkyokushū*. 31 vols. Tokyo: Koten bunko, 1963–1980.

Tanaka Yutaka, ed. *Zeami geijutsuron shū*. Shinchōsha koten shūsei, vol. 35. Tokyo: Shinchōsha, 1976.

Taniyama Shigeru, ed. *Shinpen kokka taikan*. Vol. 1, *Chokusenshūhen*. Tokyo: Kadokawa shoten, 1983.

Thurman, Robert, trans. *The Holy Teaching of Vimalakīrti*. University Park: Pennsylvania State University Press, 1981.

Tōyō ongaku gakkai [Society for Research in Asiatic Music], ed. *Nō no hayashigoto*. Tokyo: Ongaku no tomo sha, 1990.

Yamanaka Reiko. *Nō no enshutsu: Sono keisei to hen'yō*. Tokyo: Wakakusa shobō, 1998.

Yamazaki Masakazu. *Zeami*. Nihon no meicho, vol. 10. Tokyo: Chūō kōronsha, 1969.

Yampolsky, Philip, trans. *The Platform Sutra of the Sixth Patriarch*. New York: Columbia University Press, 1967.

Yanase Kazuo, ed. *Kamo no Chōmei zenshū*. Tokyo: Kazama shobō, 1980.

Yokomichi Mario. *Nōgeki shōyō*. Tokyo: Chikuma shobō, 1984.

Yokomichi Mario and Omote Akira, eds. *Yōkyokushū*. NKBT, vols. 40 and 41. Tokyo: Iwanami shoten, 1960, 1963.

INDEX

Nō plays are listed according to the modern spelling.

TRANSLATIONS FROM THE ASIAN CLASSICS SERIES

Major Plays of Chikamatsu, tr. Donald Keene 1961

Four Major Plays of Chikamatsu, tr. Donald Keene. Paperback ed. only. 1961; rev. ed. 1997

Records of the Grand Historian of China, translated from the Shih chi of Ssu-ma Ch'ien, tr. Burton Watson, 2 vols. 1961

Instructions for Practical Living and Other Neo-Confucian Writings by Wang Yang-ming, tr. Wing-tsit Chan 1963

Hsün Tzu: Basic Writings, tr. Burton Watson, paperback ed. only. 1963; rev. ed. 1996

Chuang Tzu: Basic Writings, tr. Burton Watson, paperback ed. only. 1964; rev. ed. 1996

The Mahābhārata, tr. Chakravarthi V. Narasimhan. Also in paperback ed. 1965; rev. ed. 1997

The Manyōshū, Nippon Gakujutsu Shinkōkai edition 1965

Su Tung-p'o: Selections from a Sung Dynasty Poet, tr. Burton Watson. Also in paperback ed. 1965

Bhartrihari: Poems, tr. Barbara Stoler Miller. Also in paperback ed. 1967

Basic Writings of Mo Tzu, Hsün Tzu, and Han Fei Tzu, tr. Burton Watson. Also in separate paperback eds. 1967

The Awakening of Faith, Attributed to Aśvaghosha, tr. Yoshito S. Hakeda. Also in paperback ed. 1967

Reflections on Things at Hand: The Neo-Confucian Anthology, comp. Chu Hsi and Lü Tsu-ch'ien, tr. Wing-tsit Chan 1967

The Platform Sutra of the Sixth Patriarch, tr. Philip B. Yampolsky. Also in paperback ed. 1967

Essays in Idleness: The Tsurezuregusa of Kenkō, tr. Donald Keene. Also in paperback ed. 1967

The Pillow Book of Sei Shōnagon, tr. Ivan Morris, 2 vols. 1967

Two Plays of Ancient India: The Little Clay Cart and the Minister's Seal, tr. J. A. B. van Buitenen 1968

The Complete Works of Chuang Tzu, tr. Burton Watson 1968

The Romance of the Western Chamber (Hsi Hsiang chi), tr. S. I. Hsiung. Also in paperback ed. 1968

The Manyōshū, Nippon Gakujutsu Shinkōkai edition. Paperback ed. only. 1969

Records of the Historian: Chapters from the Shih chi of Ssu-ma Ch'ien, tr. Burton Watson. Paperback ed. only. 1969

Cold Mountain: 100 Poems by the T'ang Poet Han-shan, tr. Burton Watson. Also in paperback ed. 1970

Twenty Plays of the Nō Theatre, ed. Donald Keene. Also in paperback ed. 1970

Chūshingura: The Treasury of Loyal Retainers, tr. Donald Keene. Also in paperback ed. 1971; rev. ed. 1997

The Zen Master Hakuin: Selected Writings, tr. Philip B. Yampolsky 1971

Chinese Rhyme-Prose: Poems in the Fu Form from the Han and Six Dynasties Periods, tr. Burton Watson. Also in paperback ed. 1971

Kūkai: Major Works, tr. Yoshito S. Hakeda. Also in paperback ed. 1972

The Old Man Who Does as He Pleases: Selections from the Poetry and Prose of Lu Yu, tr. Burton Watson 1973

The Lion's Roar of Queen Śrīmālā, tr. Alex and Hideko Wayman 1974

Courtier and Commoner in Ancient China: Selections from the History of the Former Han by Pan Ku, tr. Burton Watson. Also in paperback ed. 1974

Japanese Literature in Chinese, vol. 1: *Poetry and Prose in Chinese by Japanese Writers of the Early Period*, tr. Burton Watson 1975

Japanese Literature in Chinese, vol. 2: *Poetry and Prose in Chinese by Japanese Writers of the Later Period*, tr. Burton Watson 1976

Scripture of the Lotus Blossom of the Fine Dharma, tr. Leon Hurvitz. Also in paperback ed. 1976

Love Song of the Dark Lord: Jayadeva's Gītagovinda, tr. Barbara Stoler Miller. Also in paperback ed. Cloth ed. includes critical text of the Sanskrit. 1977; rev. ed. 1997

Ryōkan: Zen Monk-Poet of Japan, tr. Burton Watson 1977

Calming the Mind and Discerning the Real: From the Lam rim chen mo of Tsoṇ-kha-pa, tr. Alex Wayman 1978

The Hermit and the Love-Thief: Sanskrit Poems of Bhartrihari and Bilhaṇa, tr. Barbara Stoler Miller 1978

The Lute: Kao Ming's P'i-p'a chi, tr. Jean Mulligan. Also in paperback ed. 1980

A Chronicle of Gods and Sovereigns: Jinnō Shōtōki of Kitabatake Chikafusa, tr. H. Paul Varley 1980

Among the Flowers: The Hua-chien chi, tr. Lois Fusek 1982

Grass Hill: Poems and Prose by the Japanese Monk Gensei, tr. Burton Watson 1983

Doctors, Diviners, and Magicians of Ancient China: Biographies of Fang-shih, tr. Kenneth J. DeWoskin. Also in paperback ed. 1983

Theater of Memory: The Plays of Kālidāsa, ed. Barbara Stoler Miller. Also in paperback ed. 1984

The Columbia Book of Chinese Poetry: From Early Times to the Thirteenth Century, ed. and tr. Burton Watson. Also in paperback ed. 1984

Poems of Love and War: From the Eight Anthologies and the Ten Long Poems of Classical Tamil, tr. A.K. Ramanujan. Also in paperback ed. 1985

The Bhagavad Gita: Krishna's Counsel in Time of War, tr. Barbara Stoler Miller 1986

The Columbia Book of Later Chinese Poetry, ed. and tr. Jonathan Chaves. Also in paperback ed. 1986

The Tso Chuan: Selections from China's Oldest Narrative History, tr. Burton Watson 1989

Waiting for the Wind: Thirty-six Poets of Japan's Late Medieval Age, tr. Steven Carter 1989

Selected Writings of Nichiren, ed. Philip B. Yampolsky 1990

Saigyō, Poems of a Mountain Home, tr. Burton Watson 1990

The Book of Lieh Tzu: A Classic of the Tao, tr. A.C. Graham. Morningside ed. 1990

The Tale of an Anklet: An Epic of South India—The Cilappatikāram of Iḷaṅkō Aṭikaḷ, tr. R. Parthasarathy 1993

Waiting for the Dawn: A Plan for the Prince, tr. with introduction by Wm. Theodore de Bary 1993

Yoshitsune and the Thousand Cherry Trees: A Masterpiece of the Eighteenth-Century Japanese Puppet Theater, tr., annotated, and with introduction by Stanleigh H. Jones, Jr. 1993

The Lotus Sutra, tr. Burton Watson. Also in paperback ed. 1993

The Classic of Changes: A New Translation of the I Ching *as Interpreted by Wang Bi*, tr. Richard John Lynn 1994

Beyond Spring: Tz'u Poems of the Sung Dynasty, tr. Julie Landau 1994

The Columbia Anthology of Traditional Chinese Literature, ed. Victor H. Mair 1994

Scenes for Mandarins: The Elite Theater of the Ming, tr. Cyril Birch 1995

Letters of Nichiren, ed. Philip B. Yampolsky; tr. Burton Watson et al. 1996

Unforgotten Dreams: Poems by the Zen Monk Shōtetsu, tr. Steven D. Carter 1997

The Vimalakirti Sutra, tr. Burton Watson 1997

Japanese and Chinese Poems to Sing: The Wakan rōei shū, tr. J. Thomas Rimer and Jonathan Chaves 1997

Breeze Through Bamboo: Kanshi of Ema Saikō, tr. Hiroaki Sato 1998

A Tower for the Summer Heat, by Li Yu, tr. Patrick Hanan 1998

Traditional Japanese Theater: An Anthology of Plays, by Karen Brazell 1998

The Original Analects: Sayings of Confucius and His Successors (0479–0249), by E. Bruce Brooks and A. Taeko Brooks 1998

The Classic of the Way and Virtue: A New Translation of the Tao-te ching *of Laozi as Interpreted by Wang Bi*, tr. Richard John Lynn 1999

The Four Hundred Songs of War and Wisdom: An Anthology of Poems from Classical Tamil, The Puṛanāṉūṛu, ed. and tr. George L. Hart and Hank Heifetz 1999

Original Tao: Inward Training (Nei-yeh) *and the Foundations of Taoist Mysticism*, by Harold D. Roth 1999

Lao Tzu's Tao Te Ching*: A Translation of the Startling New Documents Found at Guodian*, by Robert G. Henricks 2000

The Shorter Columbia Anthology of Traditional Chinese Literature, ed. Victor H. Mair 2000

Mistress and Maid (Jiaohongji), by Meng Chengshun, tr. Cyril Birch 2001

Chikamatsu: Five Late Plays, tr. and ed. C. Andrew Gerstle 2001

The Essential Lotus: Selections from the Lotus Sutra, tr. Burton Watson 2002

Early Modern Japanese Literature: An Anthology, 1600–1900, ed. Haruo Shirane 2002

The Columbia Anthology of Traditional Korean Poetry, ed. Peter H. Lee 2002

The Sound of the Kiss, or The Story That Must Never Be Told: Pingali Suranna's Kalapurnodayamu, tr. Vecheru Narayana Rao and David Shulman 2003

The Selected Poems of Du Fu, tr. Burton Watson 2003

Far Beyond the Field: Haiku by Japanese Women, tr. Makoto Ueda 2003

Just Living: Poems and Prose by the Japanese Monk Tonna, ed. and tr. Steven D. Carter 2003

Han Feizi: Basic Writings, tr. Burton Watson 2003

Mozi: Basic Writings, tr. Burton Watson 2003
Xunzi: Basic Writings, tr. Burton Watson 2003
Zhuangzi: Basic Writings, tr. Burton Watson 2003
The Awakening of Faith, Attributed to Aśvaghosha, tr. Yoshito S. Hakeda, introduction by Ryuichi Abe 2005
The Tales of the Heike, tr. Burton Watson, ed. Haruo Shirane 2006
Tales of Moonlight and Rain, by Ueda Akinari, tr. with introduction by Anthony H. Chambers 2007
Traditional Japanese Literature: An Anthology, Beginnings to 1600, ed. Haruo Shirane 2007
The Philosophy of Qi, by Kaibara Ekken, tr. Mary Evelyn Tucker 2007
The Analects of Confucius, tr. Burton Watson 2007
The Art of War: Sun Zi's Military Methods, tr. Victor Mair 2007